EARLY INTERVENTION FOR HANDICAPPED AND AT-RISK CHILDREN

An Introduction to Early Childhood-Special Education

Nancy L. Peterson
University of Kansas

LOVE PUBLISHING COMPANY
Denver · London

To my mentor and colleague, *Dr. Robert L. Egbert*

former Chairman of Graduate Education, Brigham Young Univeristy
National Director of Project Follow-Through, U.S. Department of Education
Dean of Teachers College, University of Nebraska

and to

P. Potte

whose encouragement played a significant part in finally bringing this book to press.

Photo Credits

Cathy Callen: pp. xi, 7, 55, 78, 94, 132, 135, 137, 154, 158, 214, 222, 225, 249, 273, 275, 281, 293, 325, 327, 331, 362, 389, 407, 409, 432, 440, 470, 473
Nancy Peterson: pp. 1, 21, 87, 100, 134, 166, 185, 201, 270, 319, 354, 373, 405, 447, 461, 493, 496
Jerry Harkness: pp. 369, 415, 467, 489, 558
Dave Lutz: p. 42
Robbin Loomas-Kern: 418
The Capper Foundation: p. 184

Cover painting of his son and cover design: Walden Swank

Library of Congress Catalog Card Number 86-81467

Copyright © 1987 Love Publishing Company
Printed in the U.S.A.
ISBN 0-89108-129-1

Contents

III DELIVERING SERVICES TO YOUNG CHILDREN WITH SPECIAL NEEDS

Figures

Tables

Preface

This book is based on the premise that the field of early childhood-special education is unique and that early intervention for infants and preschoolers with handicaps and at-risk conditions calls for new, innovative approaches. These approaches cannot be a mere downward extension of special education as traditionally applied with school-aged students, or of practices in regular early childhood education as traditionally applied to normally developing children. Early childhood-special education inherits a rich set of traditions and accomplishments from these fields and from compensatory education (including intervention programs such as Head Start and Follow-Through), which paved the way for its birth. Yet the development of this new field calls for the evolution of its own philosophy, its own intervention strategies, and its own service delivery approaches that address the unique characteristics and needs of handicapped infants and preschoolers.

Professionals in this new, evolving field, I hope, can capitalize upon the lessons we have learned in developing appropriate and effective educational programs for handicapped school-aged students and can avoid the pitfalls of counter-productive practices such as premature, inaccurate labeling, inappropriate and biased testing and diagnosis, and unnecessary segregation. Ideally, we can capitalize upon the achievements of regular early childhood education by integrating the best that field offers into practices that will help professionals intervene effectively in the lives of young children who have handicapping/at-risk conditions. I believe that professionals in the field of early childhood-special education have a different kind of mission—that of providing an effective and timely intervention in the lives of young handicapped children *before* a handicap or at-risk condition alters and perhaps undermines their development and future capabilities.

This text is intended for students and professionals in special education, regular early childhood education, and related disciplines who are interested in working with young children who have handicapping or at-risk conditions before they reach school age. The purpose is to provide a comprehensive overview of the field, its mission, and the unique approaches for helping this young clientele.

Section I of this book gives an overview of early childhood-special education beginning with the rationale for early intervention in Chapter 1, addressing the foremost question: *Why should we intervene in the lives of handicapped/at-risk young children?* Chapter 2 describes recent achievements that established the field as a bona fide professional and service area. It further offers a description of what is unique about the field, including the features that distinguish it from its "parent" fields and call for new policies and new service delivery strategies. Chapter 3 gives a historical review of the achievements in special education, regular early childhood education, and compensatory education that paved the way for the birth of the new field of early childhood-special education.

Section II of the text turns to the question: *Who are the young children who need early intervention?* What is the impact of their disabilities or at-risk conditions upon early development and learning? Chapter 4 reviews conditions that render a child at-risk for developmental disabilities, and chapters 5 and 6 address the types of disabilities found among children. The purpose of these chapters is not merely to provide a traditional review of types of handicapping conditions but, instead, to examine how these disabilities are manifest in young children.

The applicability of various disability labels for describing irregular development or handicaps in young children is discussed, along with the unique impacts of various handicapping conditions upon the development and learning of infants and preschoolers. Given this discussion, it is hoped that practitioners will be more sensitive to the problems and issues of early diagnosis and the need for alternative criteria to establish the eligibility of young children for early intervention services. We must recognize and avoid the pitfalls of premature diagnosis and labeling when the intent is to intervene early in the lives of young children to minimize or prevent handicapping conditions or reduce their impacts upon development and learning.

Section III deals with the actual *delivery of services to young children with special needs and their parents.* Key topics related to early intervention services include: assessment, service delivery strategies and planning considerations, alternative models for early intervention, the components of a well defined program model, teaching and interdisciplinary considerations, and other information a well prepared interventionist or student needs to know.

Finally, Chapter 12 offers some useful professional information to the prospective teacher, therapist, or practitioner in the field, with the important message: *Know your resources!* Resources in the form of printed information, instructional materials, special information retrieval services, and other tools of the profession are growing at an astronomical rate. But if all these resources are to be of value, students and professionals must know about them and how to use them. This chapter offers a helpful, practical guide to using resources related to the field of early childhood-special education.

In sum, this book offers a vision and a philosophy of what early childhood-special education is and what it can be. It gives perspective to what the notion of early intervention actually entails, with the hope that those who read it will more fully understand the challenge ahead if practices and policies that are appropriate to the needs of handicapped and at-risk infants and preschoolers are to evolve.

Acknowledgments

To the many handicapped young children, their parents and families, and to the teachers and interdisciplinary staff in my Preschool Intervention Program at the University of Kansas, I am eternally grateful. My work with them and with other community agencies as director of that program for the past 18 years has taught me a great deal personally and professionally of what early intervention is all about. My experiences as a national consultant with Head Start and Project Follow-Through and my associations with colleagues in other programs have helped shape my philosophy and my visions of what this new field of early childhood-special education is and can become.

Appreciation is expressed to the KU students in my early childhood-special education courses who read volumes of typed manuscript instead of a nicely bound text. Their praise and candid criticisms have greatly enhanced the quality of this book.

I am indebted to the many who gave their support, encouragement, and assistance over the years of writing and bringing this book to press. Special thanks to Pat Barber, Barbara Bartz, Barbara Brackman, Michelle Cleveland, Carolyn Cooper, Ed Gibbons, Dorothy Johanning, Judy Mantle, Jane McNally, Elaine Nelson, Ray Rackley, Caryn Robbins, Sherry Saathoff, Lynda Schoonmaker, Judy Tate, Lisa Wilshire, Lina Zeine, Sally Ahl, and Toni Adams. Special recognition and appreciation are extended to Cathy Callen for her outstanding photography included in this book and to Dave Lutz and Jerry Harkness, who also provided their assistance on the photo work. Gratitude is expressed to Bob Hoyt and to Carolyn Acheson for their editing of the manuscript. My appreciation also goes to Stan Love, whose belief in this book, its message, and even its length brought it to publication.

And to my family—who read the manuscript and became excited about this new field, too—thank you.

I
AN OVERVIEW OF A
GROWING NEW FIELD

1
The Rationale
For Early Intervention

W̲hy is early education so important for young children who are handicapped or at-risk for becoming handicapped? Does early intervention really make a difference with young children whose development is delayed or abnormal? Consider for a moment how you would respond if you were in the shoes of the parents described in the following vignettes. What kind of urgency would you feel if your child obviously needed help or if you had that disconcerting feeling that "something is wrong—"

When Jan Markison gave birth to her first child, her joy was short lived when she saw the grave look in her doctor's face. The words—"I'm sorry, but your baby has Down syndrome"—still sting. The later news that her new son had a heart defect along with other physical deformities made that awesome day even more difficult. Jan and her husband, Jerry, knew little about the genetic abnormality that suddenly had become a reality in their lives.

Now, 6 months later, they are still trying to adjust to the painful diagnosis that their son, Keith, is handicapped and will be mentally retarded. To Jan and Jerry, their son's future is a big question mark, varying according to what book they read or to whom they talk. Some relatives avoid them and hardly mention their new son. Jerry's parents ignore the diagnosis and deny the fact that their grandson is different.

Luckily, a few friends have been encouraging and understanding, but Jan and Jerry have lots of fears conjured up by old pictures they have seen of institutionalized mongoloids. They don't want their son to be known as the "retarded kid on the block." They have many questions and worries; yet, underneath it all is a firm conviction that they want to help their young son live a happy, useful life. This is mixed with a helpless feeling about what they should do for this special child. How different will he be from others? If his development will be slow, how can they help him? Will he learn to walk, talk, or read like other kids? Where can they get help?

Jessica was 2 years old when her mother had those first haunting feelings that something was not quite right. The little girl learned to say "mama" and "dada" long after other children. She was sluggish and slow to respond even in simple games like patty-cake and peek-a-boo. Yet there was no reason to expect her development to be different from that of her older brother. There were no complications during pregnancy, no birth irregularities, no catastrophic diseases.

Now Jessica is 3½, but she behaves like a much younger child. Those old fears have become a serious concern for both Jessica's mother and her pediatrician. Jessica's development is unquestionably delayed—significantly so. She still shows little responsiveness to toilet training. What speech she has is garbled. She does not label familiar objects accurately—a behavior her mother has attributed for perhaps too long to mere stubbornness. Jessica, too, seems frustrated and fretful. She is becoming more difficult to handle. Temper tantrums are frequent.

Mrs. Jameson works with her daughter as much as she can, but it obviously is not enough. But what can she do? Her local community offers no services for handicapped preschoolers. Lakeville, some 35 miles away, has a special program. Despite the cost and hours of travel required, Mrs. Jameson is willing to drive Jessica there daily if it will help. "Something has got to happen," she says, "if Jessica is going to be ready to start kindergarten."

Matthew is a bright, curious, brown-eyed little boy who is always into everything. When he failed to babble and respond readily when others talked to him, his parents wondered if he had a hearing loss as a result of some severe infections he had contracted during his first year. Tests by an audiologist confirmed their fears. Matt did have a severe hearing loss in both ears. The audiologist and speech pathologist from the clinic explained to Matt's parents that a severe hearing loss would affect his ability to acquire speech and language. They stressed the importance of extra kinds of stimulation to help Matt learn.

Since Matt may possibly hear only very loud noises, he definitely will require special help to develop the communication skills that most normally hearing children pick up spontaneously. He also will need help in learning through channels of communication other than just auditory ones if he is to learn concepts about his environment and keep up with his peers intellectually.

Matt's mother is concerned about providing the special help Matt requires, because she works full time. Can the sitter give Matt the attention he needs? Will she understand his special needs and be willing to put out that extra effort? Does she even have the know-how to teach him the special skills he must learn? Matt's mother believes that he needs much more. After all, Matt is a smart little boy who is just as capable as his friends! The urgency of finding special help for him is so real. What will happen if Matt does not learn to talk until he is 5 or 6?

The premise of this book is that early childhood-special education programs can make a difference for Keith, Jessica, Matt, and other young children like them. But people who are unfamiliar with the notion of early intervention for handicapped and at-risk young children still raise questions. They ask: What is the impact of special programs upon the growth and development of these children? Won't most youngsters simply outgrow many of the development problems they exhibit during their early years? Can't public school programs take care of the special education needs of these children when they enter kindergarten or first grade? Isn't a loving, nurturing home enough for a handicapped infant or preschooler?

Questions like these may seem pointless. Every child—particularly a handicapped child—could surely benefit from early education. Yet to agree that something can be beneficial does not guarantee that public action will be taken to establish early intervention programs. These questions must be answered convincingly to taxpayers, legislators, and educators so that special education programs will be provided at public expense to handicapped preschoolers and infants.

Those of us who recognize the importance of early education for handicapped children like Matt, Jessica, and Keith face a major challenge in this decade. We must educate the general public, including our friends, neighbors, and legislators, that early intervention programs for children with special needs are not only beneficial, but are in fact *essential*. Because preschoolers and infants are cared for at home by their parents or by caregivers in day-care centers until they reach school age, their special needs may not be visible to the general public. Thus, while professional and lay citizens may accept the value of special education for school-aged youngsters, they must be convinced that (a) handicapped infants and preschoolers need help—and so do their parents, (b) early intervention programs are effective; they do facilitate development and learning in young children whose futures are uncertain because of a disability, and (c) communities have to assume responsibility for making special services available to these children.

All too often, parents like Matt's, Jessica's, or Keith's are without services. They have no choice but to keep their handicapped youngster at home, doing the best they can with limited resources, until the time comes for kindergarten. When their children finally start school, we so often hear their teachers say, "If only we could have worked with these children earlier!"

The following pages examine several key premises that collectively build a strong argument for early intervention, along with some evidence from which it is derived. Also, some typical arguments by those opposing early education for the handicapped will be reviewed.

> The provisions of Public Law 94-142, The Education for All Handicapped Children Act of 1975, should not be misunderstood here. Although the law does require a free and appropriate education for all handicapped children from age 3 to 21, the mandate for children under school age depends upon laws in the individual states. Under PL 94-142, provision of services to handicapped infants and preschoolers is required *unless it is incompatible with state law*. This means the actual decision as to whether early childhood programs are created is left to each state legislature.

VIEWPOINTS ON WHICH A RATIONALE FOR EARLY INTERVENTION IS BASED

The rationale for early education of the handicapped rests upon a number of different arguments derived from theory, empirical research, expert opinion, and our societal values. *Theories* about learning and about the importance of the early developmental years offer one source of support for early intervention. Various theories help us understand what factors facilitate or impair growth and development in young children. For example, Piaget's theory of cognitive development emphasizes the importance of the early years as a foundation for subsequent learning. We will examine this theory in more detail later as one example of theoretical viewpoints that support the early intervention notion.

A second source of support is *empirical research* on human development and on factors that facilitate or impair cognitive functioning in children. Research findings provide both *direct* and *inferential support* for early intervention. For example, research literature describes the direct benefits of early intervention programs with institutionalized mentally retarded children, disadvantaged children, and handicapped young children. Other research on characteristics of children with developmental disabilities shows how handicaps can interfere with a youngster's ability to engage in and profit from experience. Research on the effects of early stimulus deprivation shows that children whose disabilities restrict their physical/social environment need additional stimulation in order to learn. Some of this empirical evidence will be explored later in the chapter.

Expert opinion concerning social and educational problems and the means for their resolution provides a third source of support for early intervention. Positions taken by recognized authorities usually are based upon theoretical or empirical evidence. Sometimes they reflect logical analyses of societal issues or needs and of alternative strategies for resolving them. The simple logic used by knowledgeable and respected professionals can provide some convincing arguments that appeal to the social, political, and economic concerns of a community and its citizens. For instance, positions may be taken stressing the need to prepare handicapped youngsters for successful entry into public school to avoid later problems. Experts may point out the economic benefits to taxpayers in preparing handicapped children from their early years to live independent, productive lives.

Values held by society at large or by an influential subgroup concerning our nation's obligations to the educational welfare of its children are a final source of support for early intervention. Values are a powerful force in decision-making processes within our nation's court system, in state and federal legislative bodies, and in local governing councils. Values also help shape the educational systems we create. For example, look at how our values about human rights have influenced Americans. As a result of the democratic value that every citizen has an equal right to freedom, employment, and pursuit of happiness, tremendous change has occurred during the past 20 years in regard to the rights of minority groups.

Other values, concerning the handicapped as a minority just as racial-ethnic groups and the poor are, also have made a significant impact upon current educational practices. These values include:

— that handicapped individuals should not be discriminated against because of their disability by being denied the right to a free public education;
— that providing handicapped individuals with the same educational experiences given to nonhandicapped students is not necessarily equal treatment.

Through the influence of articulate leaders and their lobbying efforts, these values have greatly altered educational practices today in both regular and special education.

Educational or societal values do not always have a factual or empirical basis per se. They often are rooted in a set of ethics and ideals not shared by everyone. Arguments based upon values often are emotional ones, inciting public interest because of their appeal to human concerns and feelings. Although numerous arguments of this type can be made for early intervention with handicapped children, they seldom are sufficient in themselves to convince decision makers to finance and initiate the necessary programs.

MAJOR PREMISES OF EARLY INTERVENTION

The rationale for early education of handicapped and at-risk children can be built on eight major premises. Collectively these premises produce a cohesive argument as to why early intervention programs are needed to help handicapped children develop as normally as possible in spite of their limitations. When a young child is found to have a handicap or to be at-risk for developmental disabilities, intervention should be initiated as early as possible because:

1. During the early years the initial patterns of learning and behavior that set the pace for and influence the nature of all subsequent development are established.
2. Research suggests the presence of certain critical periods, particularly during the early

years, when a child is most susceptible and responsive to learning experiences.

3. Intelligence and other human capacities are not fixed at birth but, rather, are shaped to some extent by environmental influences and through learning.

4. Handicapping conditions and other factors that render a child at-risk for developmental disabilities can interfere with development and learning so that the original disabilities become more severe and secondary handicaps will appear.

5. A child's environment and early experiences, particularly the degree to which these are nurturing or depriving, have a major effect upon development and learning; both greatly influence the degree to which a child reaches his or her full potential.

6. Early intervention programs can make a significant difference in the developmental status of young children and can do so more rapidly than later remedial efforts after a child has entered elementary school.

7. Parents need special assistance in establishing constructive patterns of parenting with a young handicapped or at-risk child and in providing adequate care, stimulation, and training for their child during the critical early years when basic developmental skills should be acquired.

8. Early intervention implies some economic-social benefits in that prevention or early treatment of developmental problems in young children may reduce more serious, burdensome problems for society to cope with later, including their accompanying costs.

These premises do not include all those we could use to argue in behalf of early intervention, but they do represent the major points of view from which other arguments can be derived. Each premise is discussed in detail next, and supportive research, theory, expert opinion, or educational-social values are cited.

The importance of the early years

> ★ *In early years the initial patterns of learning and behavior that set the pace for and influence the nature of all subsequent development are established. The time from birth until a child enters school is a particularly significant period in the continuum of human development inasmuch as (a) growth is extraordinarily rapid, and (b) basic traits in the areas of motor, sensory, social-emotional, cognitive, and physical development, which provide a foundation for all subsequent learning, are formed.*

By the time they enter kindergarten, young children have mastered thousands of new skills. Consider what dramatic growth these five years represent physically, intellectually, sensorially, socially, and emotionally. Even basic personality characteristics are evident at just 2 or 3 years of age. One needs only to observe these processes during the early years to realize that this period is one of unprecedented growth, second only to the prenatal period, when physical development is most rapid of all. Logically, then, this seems an ideal time to facilitate development and to capitalize upon a child's readiness for learning.

Experts look at infancy and early childhood   Over the past 25 years many experts have emphasized the importance of the early years as a time of crucial developmental

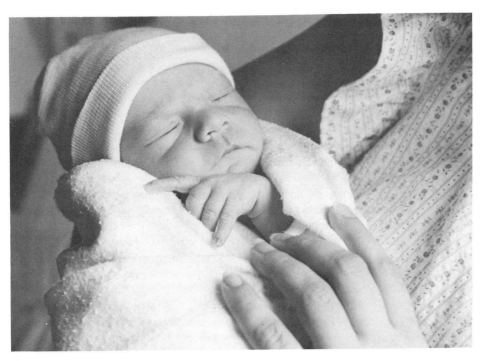

Learning begins at birth—not at age 5 when a child enters kindergarten.

milestones. Thus, it can be argued that actions adults take to facilitate development in young children through early educational programs can be beneficial. This would seem particularly true for handicapped or at-risk youngsters whose development is not likely to proceed as smoothly as that of children who are not handicapped. Here is what just a few experts say about the importance of the early years.

J. McVicker Hunt (1961) made an extensive review of research on intellectual development and environmental influences in his historic book, *Intelligence and Experience*. He concluded that society should pay greater attention to what takes place in the lives of young children and should stop leaving things to chance during this important period. Hunt suggested, "The counsel from experts on child rearing during the third and much of the fourth decades of the twentieth century to let children be while they grow and to avoid excessive stimulation was highly unfortunate . . . . The problem . . . is to find out how to govern the encounters that children have with their environments to foster both an optimally rapid rate of intellectual development and a satisfying life" (pp. 362-363). Hunt proposed that procedures could be developed to optimize children's interactions with their environment, particularly during the early years, to help them achieve a substantially faster rate of intellectual development and higher adult level of intellectual capacity.

Arnold Gesell, a well known developmentalist whose systematic observations of infants at the Yale Clinic of Child Development resulted in the largest body of normative data in the literature on human development, regarded the early years as most critical. In his historic book *The Preschool Child,* Gesell (1923) noted that the preschool period is ". . . biologically the most important period in the development of an individual for the simple but sufficient reason that it comes first in a dynamic sequence; it inevitably influences all subsequent development" (p. 2).

Benjamin Bloom (1964), in his now classic book *Stability and Change in Human Characteristics*, stressed the importance of early environment and experience in a child's life. After reviewing a number of longitudinal studies on human development, he explained—through three basic premises—the critical nature of the first few years in relation to children's later developmental accomplishments. First, variations in early environment are important because they shape human characteristics during the periods of most rapid formation. Second, environment and early experience are especially significant because of the sequential nature of human development. Each human characteristic develops cumulatively on top of earlier, more incomplete stages of that characteristic. Third, learning something new is easier than stamping out old, inappropriate, behaviors and replacing them with new behaviors.

Burton White, a noted author and researcher in child development, stated in a *Report to Congress* (1979) on early childhood and family development programs that a child's experiences between 8 and 36 months have more influence on future success and well-being than any other set of experiences for a similar time period in life. White (1975) earlier had suggested that children begin to reveal discernible trends in their development by 1½ years of age. Foundations for development in language, social competence, curiosity, and intellectual performance are well established during the first three years of life. For instance, White suggested that from 7 or 9 months to about 36 months, most young children acquire the ability to understand most of the language they will ultimately use in ordinary conversation throughout their lives. Language, of course, is fundamental to many other activities and particularly affects a child's capability for learning. It also affects subsequent interactions with the environment. Personality traits also are stabilized by age 2. White argued that social patterns probably will not change significantly after age 2 without rather drastic changes in the environment.

Milton Akers (1972), at one time the Executive Director of the National Association for the Education of Young Children, noted the rapid physical and mental growth that characterizes the child's earliest years, stating, "At no other period in life is he so susceptible and responsive to positive environmental influences which enhance and expand his development. Environmental influences, if of a sterile or destructive nature, may have negative effects on his intelligence, his motivation and ability to learn, his concept of himself, his relationship with others, and on his later health" (p. 3). Akers concluded, "There is little doubt that the optimal fulfillment of potentials that are uniquely his [the child's] and his emergence into greatest effectiveness as a socially competent adult are critically affected by what happens to him in infancy and childhood" (p. 3).

Other experts have stressed the heightened responsiveness of young children to initial learning experiences during their early years and, hence, the importance of intervention with children who show signs of abnormal development. Fowler (1975), in a report on the outcomes of an infant stimulation program at the Ontario Institute for Studies in Education, stated, "Infancy is the most malleable, rapidly changing and least organized period of human development. Never again will there be the same potential for establishing the basic forms of understanding, style, and feeling in all domains of experience. Early experience is the primary matrix from which all of later development is generated" (p. 341).

Early learning as a foundation for subsequent learning   Many of us have had the dismaying experience of watching a child fall further behind peers as problems have compounded into deficits across many developmental areas. Disadvantaged children are prone to these compounding performance deficits because they often enter kindergarten lacking basic skills that most middle-class children have already mastered. With less knowledge, a different backgound of experience, and a lack of prerequisite skills, deficiencies increase even more because these children are then unable to tackle new academic tasks successfully at school (Ramey & MacPhee, 1985). Handicapped children face an even greater risk of compounding performance deficits. Their disabilities often interfere not only with learning itself but also with their ability to engage in activities through which learning occurs.

Jensen (1966) used the term *progressive achievement decrement* to describe these decelerating growth curves we see in some children as they fall farther and farther behind expected norms of achievement for their age levels. This means their developmental status becomes increasingly worse as they grow older. As Jensen described it:

> When the habits, skills, or cognitive structures that are prerequisite for some new learning have not been fully acquired, the capability for new learning will be impaired. Learning will be retarded, inefficient, incomplete, or even impossible, depending upon the degree of inadequacy of prerequisite skills. Since learning builds on learning, weakness at any stage creates still greater weakness at later stages. Because subsequent learning depends upon transfer from prior learning, learning deficits are cumulative. (pp. 40-41)

Many other educators have expressed the same grave concern about the multiplying effects of early developmental and learning problems and their implications for disadvantaged, handicapped, and at-risk children (Bereiter & Engelmann, 1966; Bricker & Iacino, 1977; Hayden & McGinness, 1977; Palmer & Siegel, 1977; Ramey & Baker-Ward, 1982; Sameroff, 1975).

Bereiter and Engelmann's description of *cumulative achievement decrements* in disadvantaged children explains the implications of a child's continued failure to achieve major developmental milestones or to master expected intellectual skills. When children fall significantly behind their agemates in certain areas, one simple reality becomes evident: *If they are ever to catch up, learning must be accelerated to a faster than normal rate.*

Although Bereiter and Engelmann's work deals largely with educational problems among disadvantaged children, their point of view applies equally to young children with handicaps. They have suggested that if educators are to deal realistically with educational problems of children who have learning deficits, they must eliminate the magical thinking that children can suddenly "blossom forth intellectually in the same way they occasionally blossom forth emotionally when exposed to a highly favorable, stimulating environment." Experts know what a slow, continuous process is involved in intellectual development and what enormous amounts of learning, practice, and simple trial-and-error learning go into each new intellectual achievement. Thus, when genuine learning occurs in a child, educators and parents realistically cannot expect sudden, gigantic leaps. Nor will leaps ever occur without sufficient cause, such as a change in the environment, in child-rearing practices, in the learning opportunities made available, or in the child's own physical and emotional state.

If intervention is to be considered, two implications are evident. *First,* the challenge of achieving a faster-than-normal rate of progress involves identifying ways to produce accelerated learning in children. *Second*, the chances of ever catching up are directly related to how quickly intervention begins after deficits are identified and how great the discrepancy has become between a child's real and expected levels of performance.

Children with physical, sensory, or mental disabilities are prime candidates for this kind of cumulative achievement decrement. Although an initial handicapping condition may not in itself produce a learning deficit, a handicapping condition can interfere with normal learning processes. Blindness or a vision loss that prevents a small child from exploring the environment and manipulating objects will thwart ordinary avenues for learning. A child with neurological impairments resulting in immobility will be less able to explore the environment and participate in age-appropriate learning experiences. As experiences are curtailed, so is the learning of new skills. As the gap between the development of this child and that of normally developing peers widens, the greater is the probability that it will become of sufficient magnitude to be designated as a case of abnormal, retarded development. Early intervention is critically important if we are to prevent cumulative developmental deficits from becoming so large that they cannot be overcome.

The premise that the early years provide a foundation for all subsequent learning and, hence, represent a time when intervention can be most influential is supported by White's (1975) research on early patterns of development. In his book *The First Three Years of Life*, he asserted that children begin to manifest their own unique growth patterns between 1 and 3 years of age. During these early years foundations of learning are established in four key areas of development: language, social development, curiosity, and intellectual performance. Based upon his extensive data on rates of growth in young children, White noted that:

— most children around age 2½ to 3 years begin to perform on achievement measures in ways that are increasingly reflective of the levels of achievement they will attain in years to follow.
— the rate at which children acquire visual-motor skills and other intellectual skills can be modified rather dramatically by manipulating environmental and child-rearing conditions.
— poor development is often not apparent during the first year or more of life in children who perform poorly later on because they have not yet actually developed the *deficits—* at least to a degree that they are clearly measurable on standardized tests or observable by parents and professionals. Typically, deficits begin to appear at the end of the second year, with more clear patterns of inadequate learning by the time they are 3 years old.

Figure 1.1 summarizes White's view by showing the variance among children whose early development creates a pattern of learning and a rate of development that is likely to perpetuate itself unless dramatic environmental changes occur. Curve A depicts development for most children—those whose development progresses within a normal range beginning at birth to about age 5½ years. (This depicts overall development—not just intellectual, but social and language skills as well.) Curve B represents approximately 5% of the population of young children whose development is irregular for one reason

Figure 1.1
Developmental Variance Among Young Children

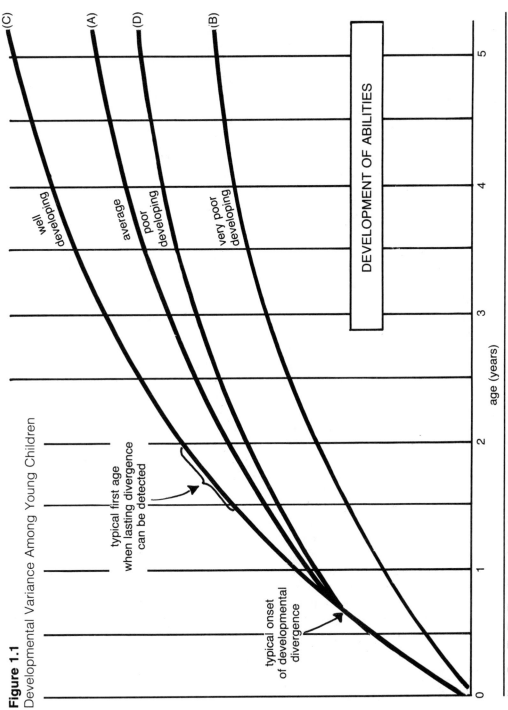

or another right from birth or shortly thereafter. That group, says White, "stays in large trouble."

In light of Bereiter and Engelmann's (1966) point that learning must be accelerated if a delayed child will ever catch up, major and intensive intervention is needed to make a meaningful impact on the children whom White depicts by the developmental curve marked B. Divergence in the developmental progress of young children begins at about 8 months of age. It is here that individual differences become more apparent (see curves C and D).

Theories emphasizing importance of early years Most theories on human development recognize the relationship between the early years of life and later growth and learning. Implications can be drawn from nearly every developmental theory, suggesting that if difficulties are exhibited in a child's early development, the time to intervene is *now*, not later. Otherwise, continued disruption of growth processes will have far-reaching effects at the time and in later years. Since we cannot discuss all of those theories here, we will review just one that is cited frequently as support for the value of early intervention for the handicapped.

Piaget's theory of cognitive development * has influenced our thinking about intellectual development in young children perhaps more than any other single theoretical perspective. Piaget's conceptualization of cognitive development and the growth of intelligence clearly emphasizes the critical nature of the early years. Early learning is an irreplaceable and prerequisite step for more complex and abstract forms of thinking and cognitive operations.

To understand Piaget's views of the early years, one must understand his explanation of two entities: the cognitive *operations* that comprise intelligent behavior and the *stages of development* through which cognitive competence is achieved (Piaget, 1960, 1963, 1970). First, Piaget depicted intelligence as a *developmental phenomenon*—something that evolves through experience and interaction with one's environment. It is not a fixed, unchangeable entity present from the time a child is born. Cognitive operations, comprising what we term *intelligence*, change both qualitatively and quantitatively over time.

Second, Piaget described intellectual development as a natural process between a child and his or her environment. In essence, intelligence in itself can be characterized as *an adaptive process*. As an individual interacts with the environment, acquiring new skills to maintain some state of equilibrium, Piaget visualized the central nervous system as progressively improving in its capacity to handle more complex tasks. This increased ability to adapt to the environment is reflected *qualitatively* (that is, in terms of the cognitive sophistication used in mental operations) and *quantitatively* (that is, in terms of the amount and complexity of stimuli that can be processed and responded to appropriately). Every interaction with the environment is an adaptive process involving two types of actions. An individual must adjust to the external realities of the environment or situation (*accommodation*) while modifying the environment to the extent possible to meet his or her own requirements (*assimilation*). The adaptive process, or what we view as intelligence, involves the continuous use of these two processes to maintain some *equilibrium* and, hence, to bring about continuous development.

---

*Several excellent sources have been used in this discussion of Piaget's theory: Flavell (1963); Hunt (1961); Ginsburg and Oper (1969); Robinson and Robinson (1976).

Third, Piaget suggested that behavior patterns or *schemas* are the basic structures of an individual's mental equipment. A schema is an organized response sequence. Schemas tend to be repeated when an individual encounters certain situations in the environment or receives certain types of stimuli. When a child repeats schemas again and again, they become increasingly stable and integrated within that person's performance repertoire. As more schemas are acquired, they combine to form more complex response patterns. Thus, as a child is given opportunities to acquire and practice these schemas, he or she progresses to higher levels of cognitive proficiency. This developmental process is dependent upon a stimulating, nurturing environment.

Finally, Piaget outlined a set of developmental stages through which all individuals pass in the same order, albeit at different rates. Since intelligence is a developmental process, cognition becomes increasingly more sophisticated in each successive phase. Each stage is prerequisite to the next one. Each builds upon the intellectual achievements of its precursor. Gradual changes in a child's schemas are achieved at each stage as new thought processes emerge. The four major stages of development identified by Piaget are summarized in Table 1.1, along with the approximate age ranges for each, as described for normally developing children. The table gives a broad overview of the unique accomplishments and stereotypic ways in which children think and interact with the environment at each stage.

In looking at early development from a Piagetian point of view, several important implications are evident:

1. Experience is the vehicle through which an individual builds the capacity to engage in increasingly complex forms of cognitive activity. Conditions (including handicaps) that limit a child's opportunity to interact with the environment or to develop schemas along with internalized representations of things in the environment can restrict progress onto higher levels of intellectual functioning.
2. A child's readiness to learn and perform certain mental functions is dependent upon mastery of cognitive processes in the previous developmental stages. Failure to achieve the cognitive milestones of a particular stage will interfere with movement to more advanced forms of cognitive thinking.
3. When a child reaches a particular developmental-intellectual stage, he or she needs an environment that provides appropriate experiences and materials through which the necessary schemas can be practiced and mastered. Failure of the environment to be responsive to a child's needs makes it difficult, if not impossible, to acquire the necessary cognitive operations. Cognitive development is an outcome of the interactions that take place between a child and the environment. Thus, depriving environments (including those created by a handicap) are not particularly conducive to acquiring schemas or learning more sophisticated cognitive processes.

The notion of critical periods

★ *Research suggests the presence of certain critical or sensitive periods, particularly during the early years, when a child is most susceptible and responsive to learning experiences. During these times, environmental stimuli may be more powerful in eliciting certain responses or in producing certain types of learning. In these periods, development also is occurring most rapidly and, hence, are*

Table 1.1
Summary of Piaget's Developmental Stages

Stage	Primary Characteristics of Period	Major Developmental Achievements
Period of Sensorimotor Intelligence 0-2 years	Intellectual functioning is characterized by overt acts and "knowing by doing." Intelligence is in no way reflective; child deals only with the most concrete aspects of the real world.	Piaget subdivides this period into six stages through which the child performs the following: • Child practices reflex schemas that become more stable and efficient. • Schemas begin to form as a result of learning as opposed to the result of neurologically "wired-in" response patterns. Infants begin to discover relationships between a behavior and the observed result. • Child becomes more oriented to outside world, showing beginning recognition of familiar objects; also becomes more concerned with effects of own actions upon the environment. • Child shows increasing interest in pursuing new experiences by seeking to sustain or recapture experiences or to seek out novel ones by experimentation. • First indicators are manifest of foresight and ability to plan.
Period of Preoperational Thought 2-7 years	Thinking becomes representational and internalized, allowing child to talk and think about objects and things not present physically.	Child becomes capable of internalized, symbolic manipulations of reality as he or she achieves the following: • A system of internalized symbols representing real objects and things is developed. These are in the form of *signifers* (words, symbols, or abstract ideas standing for some aspect of reality) and *significates* (the child's understanding of the aspect of reality). • Thought processes reflect basic egocentricity; that is, everything is viewed from the child's perspective with no need to define his or her views or justify the logic behind them. Children at this stage are rarely aware of their own thought processes.

| Period of Concrete Operations 7-11 years | Child forms complex and well organized cognitive systems, thus making it possible to deal with a wide range of problems. An emerging form of logic is manifest; the starting point for which is, however, the real as opposed to the possible. | • Well organized cognitive systems are established, enabling child to mediate cognitive actions and to deal more effectively with the environment.
 • Child shows capacity to think about the past, present, and future and about the real, unreal, or fantasized.

 Child begins to show more stable equilibrated kinds of thinking, as manifested by the following:

 • Cognitive systems are formed, allowing child to analyze a concept, reverse operations by mentally putting something together, or by shifting between his or her point of view and that of others.
 • Thinking is less egocentric and more socialized.
 • Problems can be solved if they are presented either verbally or in some abstract manner.
 • Child can make hierarchical classifications of concepts and reflect understanding of the relationships between parts of the classification system.
 • Child recognizes that some features or qualities of objects can change while still remaining the same object. |
| Period of Formal Operations 11 years on | Thinking becomes characterized as primarily hypothetical, deductive, and theoretical. Child becomes capable of beginning with what is possible as opposed to what is real. | • Child becomes freed from the limitations of concrete thinking as he or she becomes capable of operating purely upon verbal statements and logic, as manifest in the following:

 • Logic can be built by relating one element to another, by experimentation, or by dealing with propositions and analogy.
 • Thinking and mental operations can be performed on verbal data only, even when they have no concrete referent in reality. |

times when a child is especially vulnerable to the effects of depriving or optimal environments. This seems to be a prime time for providing enrichment and special education for children whose development and learning are not progressing as expected.

What is a critical period? Horowitz and Paden (1973) have described it as a time when certain stimuli must be presented or special experiences must occur for a particular pattern of responses to develop. Infants may have a critical time in which to learn to discriminate visual and auditory stimuli, a time to establish attachments and early social behavior, a time for babbling, a time for learning to crawl and to walk. Critical periods also are described as times of lowered psychological or neurological thresholds for certain experiences that produce growth. These optimal periods for learning a new behavior can be brief or prolonged. The threshold is at its lowest—and hence optimal—time for learning. As a result, a young child will be most responsive and alert to selected kinds of stimuli that need not be of necessarily high intensity or frequency (Bee, 1985; Spreen, Tupper, Risser, Tuokko, & Edgell, 1984). Perhaps this explains why young children may seem to suddenly master skills after only limited opportunity to practice or observe the behavior in others. Many parents have reacted with amazement to their child's latest accomplishment: "When did our son learn to do that?" Children seem so ready and eager to learn that acquiring some skills seems almost spontaneous.

Under the most rigorous application of the concept of critical periods, the absence of appropriate experience or stimulation during the important growth periods (for whatever the reason) could result in: (a) failure of a response to be learned and the possible loss of the capacity for acquiring it, or (b) delay in acquisition of the response until later, when the skill may still be acquired but perhaps with less efficiency and spontaneity (Caldwell, 1962; Denenberg, 1964; Mussen, Conger, Kagan, & Huston, 1984).

Although some learning can occur after the optimal period for acquisition, Spreen et al. (1984) have suggested that the stimulation needed to achieve the same developmental outcome may have to be of much greater intensity and duration. The question is: What are the probabilities that a child's environment will provide such intensive stimulation to a child who seems now too old for that activity? In some instances, the threshold may rise to a level at which stimulation normally available to a child to elicit the desired behavior will not be sufficient to produce learning.

Animal research on critical periods   The concept of critical periods came initially from animal studies. Lorenz (1937) popularized the concept when he described *imprinting*, a phenomenon he observed in young birds. Lorenz noted that newly hatched birds became attached to a moving object (ordinarily the mother bird) as soon as they acquired locomotion. Thus, a young bird naturally follows the response patterns of its own species.

After exposing some young birds to members of other species, including a human being and some mechanical toys, Lorenz found that birds attached themselves to whatever animal (or moving object) they encountered during the critical period after hatching. Once the bird was imprinted to an adopted species, it became impervious to its own species. Ducks became imprinted even to mechanical trains, cats, dogs, and wooden decoys. Later in adulthood the birds would attempt to mate with the adopted group and showed no inclination to respond sexually to their own species.

Other evidence of critical periods has been described (Lipton, 1976). Newborn chickens, if prevented from pecking for some 48 hours after hatching, will fail to exhibit that behavior later and starve to death even in the midst of a pile of grain. Kittens whose eyes are sewed shut for several months from birth will remain functionally blind when their eyes are opened, even though their eyes are physiologically normal. In his classic studies of mothering and social isolation in young rhesus monkeys, Harlow (1958, 1961) concluded that adequate infant-mother contact and interaction are prerequisite to later social adjustment with peers. Infant monkeys who were isolated and denied usual contacts with either their mothers or their peers during the first year of life were seriously affected in their social, sexual, and aggressive forms of behavior later on.

This initial animal research on imprinting and critical periods led to later application of the concept to human beings. Experts since have stressed the critical nature of the first three to four years of human life in regard to development of intelligence, personality, language, and a sense of self (Ainsworth, 1969; Bloom, 1964; Bowlby, 1969; Erickson, 1963; Freud, 1933; Hunt, 1961; Klaus et al., 1972; Piaget, 1960, 1963; White, 1975). Thus, the notion of critical periods can be related to the development of young children in two ways:

1. The early years as a whole, from birth to ages 4-5, may be viewed as a critical period inasmuch as this is a time of unprecedented growth, development, and learning. What occurs during this early time in a child's life continually affects all subsequent development and learning.
2. Certain skills can best be acquired during a number of critical periods in the early life of a child. For example, certain speech and language skills, emotional responses and attachments, and motor skills generally are acquired at predictable ages. If this learning is missed, later learning may be slower and more difficult. A handicap may prevent some children from having experiences or receiving stimuli that are needed to learn skills at times when they normally would be acquired.

The notion of critical periods gives strength to the argument that education during the early years should be especially powerful. Hayden and McGinness (1977) have suggested that educators should utilize these times with children when they are most likely to be responsive. Any effort to make the environment more responsive and stimulating for a child during these times enhances the probability that major developmental milestones will be achieved. Extra support or intervention is especially necessary in the case of handicapped children whose normal learning processes may be obstructed by disability, a depriving environment, or simply by illness. Early intervention could not be more timely than when initial learning should be taking place.

Importance of continuity in experience   Some professionals argue that the early childhood years are not disproportionately more influential in determining development than are later childhood years. Proponents of this point of view, called the *life span position*, see early experience as an essential and highly important link in the developmental chain. But they argue that early experience is not, in and of itself, more important than experiences in later childhood years (Goldhaber, 1979). This position is outlined in detail by Clarke and Clarke (1977), in their book *Early Experience: Myth and Evidence*, and advocated by others who emphasize the continuum of development across the entire life span (Baltes & Reese, 1984; Horowitz, 1980; Kagan, 1976; Kagan & Klein, 1973; Zigler,

1977). They maintain that the quality of environment in which a child is reared after age 5 is a continuing important variable.

In examining the concept of critical periods, Clarke and Clarke (1977) have offered some cautions:

1. Educators should avoid concluding that if critical periods are missed, learning is lost forever. There are continued chances for intervening in a child's life and teaching developmental skills.
2. Though early learning is important because of the foundation it provides for later learning, adequate stimulation, learning, and educational opportunities remain continually and equally important throughout later developmental stages.

That continuous learning is important, and that all human capacities do not rest totally on the first four years of life, is indeed an appropriate reminder. Development does continue throughout life. We cannot become so absorbed in early childhood that we forget the child once he or she exits from early intervention programs. Research findings from Head Start emphasize the importance of continuity of educational opportunity and enrichment if gains from preschool intervention are to be maintained throughout the elementary school years (Westinghouse Learning Corp., 1969; Smith & Bissell, 1970). The Follow-Through program, initiated when Head Start gains were lost as children entered the elementary grades, demonstrated that intervention must be continuous if the performance of disadvantaged students is to be maintained at levels commensurate with their middle-class peers. (See chapter 3 for more information on Head Start and Follow-Through projects.)

As advocates of the life-span position, however, Clarke and Clarke go to another extreme. Their position suggests that early intervention programs are not necessarily so important as to be the most weighty influence on a child's future developmental status.

In considering the Clarkes' point of view, we could easily back ourselves into the age-old controversy concerning what influences development most or which period is most critical. To engage in this fruitless debate, for which there is no clear empirical answer, is to evade the real issue. It only fuels the fire for more rhetoric while children wait at the sidelines until professionals decide if the early childhood years are of sufficient importance to warrant early education programs. I believe that the question is not what period of life is most important. We have sufficient evidence to show that handicapped children do not necessarily keep up with expected developmental norms during their early years and do have developmental or intellect deficits when they enter school. We know by simple observation and experience that handicapped children have difficulty learning many of the things normal children achieve more spontaneously. We know that early educational programs can promote skill learning in young handicapped and at-risk children. For them, the early years are truly a critical time, and so are the years that follow.

The plasticity of intelligence and other human traits

★ *Intelligence and other human capacities are not fixed at birth but, rather, are shaped to some extent by environmental influences and through learning. Environmental factors can be potent forces in shaping the nature of every human being. These include physical care and nutrition, child-rearing practices, the*

quality and amount of stimulation available, emotional-motivational tempera-
ment of the home, parental values, and educational-learning opportunities.

At the heart of every intervention effort is the basic premise that human traits are malleable and that early education and environmental enrichment help shape the destiny of a handicapped child. If we believe that intelligence is unalterable and human traits are forever fixed at birth, early intervention programs are useless. But considerable evidence has accumulated to refute the notion of fixed intelligence (Ramey, Yeates, & Short, 1984). Two sources of such evidence will be reviewed here. First, studies on the consistency of IQ and other human traits over time and on the variables associated with gains or losses in these traits document the plasticity of human abilities. Second, studies on the effects of depriving and enriching environments on development attest to the strength of environmental influences in determining a person's ultimate functional abilities. This includes research on the effects of early education and training on intellectual development.

Research on the consistency of IQ and other human traits   Studies in which children have been tested repeatedly on standardized IQ measures over time document the potential IQ changes that can occur for individuals. Although the mean IQ may remain relatively consistent for a total group of individuals tested at two points in time, extreme variations are evident when individual scores are examined. During the 1940s and 1950s, when intelligence testing was at its height of popularity, several major studies were conducted on the issue of IQ consistency. Most noteworthy were the *Berkeley Studies* at the University of California, which involved 40 children who were tested repeatedly over several years (Honzik, MacFarlane, & Allen, 1948). Results showed that IQ scores for some children varied as much as 50 points over a period of years. About 9% of the subjects showed IQ changes of 30 or more points, and 58% changed 15 or more points. Only 15% of the children showed changes in IQ scores of fewer than 10 points.

This finding is of particular interest inasmuch as a 15-point change in IQ can significantly alter the interpretation of an IQ score. Since the standard deviation of most individual IQ tests is 15 or 16 points, a change of this magnitude could make the difference between designating a person mildly retarded or of normal intelligence, or labeling a person as mildly versus moderately retarded. Although variations in IQ may be partially due to testing error and may not represent true shifts in IQ, this study emphasizes that changes in measured IQ scores are possible.

What factors are associated with children who show significant gains or losses in measured IQ? Children of highly educated parents are likely to show increases in IQ. Those showing decreases are most likely to come from families with a lower level of education. Further, parents of IQ gainers have been found to be more encouraging of academic achievement in their children and to provide more educational experiences (McCall, Appelbaum, & Hogarty, 1973). Children from intellectually impoverished home environments are more likely to show IQ declines with age (Roberts, Crump, Dickerson, & Horton, 1965). Often, extreme variations in IQ are highly correlated with concurrent changes in children's environments. This gives weight to our premise that changes brought about in a child's life through some form of educational intervention may produce concomitant changes in measured mental ability.

Changes in IQ also have been correlated with some personality/motivational characteristics of children who are *gainers* or *decliners*. Those personality traits clearly are influenced by environmental and experiential factors. Children whose IQs seem most likely to increase appear to be more intellectually curious, more achievement-oriented and competitive, and more independent and self-initiating (Kagan, Sontag, Baker, & Nelson, 1955, 1958; McCall, Appelbaum, & Hogarty, 1973). Gainers also are more friendly, more cooperative, and more attentive than children whose IQs are less likely to increase (Bayley & Schaefer, 1964).

The extent to which early scores of mental ability predict later scores suggests that the constancy of IQ scores is influenced by consistency, or lack of it, in a person's environment. If human abilities are not fixed, experience along the developmental continuum potentially could produce variations in children's performance on tests of mental ability. This would seem to be most likely if environmental changes are particularly dramatic, highly potent, or maintained for an extended time. Studies of the predictive capabilities of IQ tests give further evidence that human abilities are not fixed entities.

★ *Assessments of very young children during the first 1-1½ years are almost useless in predicting mental ability at later ages. Tests on infants 3-6 months of age are particularly weak predictors* (Bayley, 1949, 1958, 1970; Honzik, 1976; Honzik, MacFarlane, & Allen, 1948; Knobloch & Pasamanick, 1960, 1967; Lewis & McGurk, 1972, 1973).

★ *Stability of children's IQ test scores increases as they grow older. Thus, the correlation between test-retest scores is higher if youngsters are older at the time of the original testing. Consistency also is increased when the interval between testing is shorter. This minimizes the chance for changes to occur in children's experience and environments that would produce variance in scores* (Bayley, 1970; Erickson, 1968; Fishler, Graliker, & Koch, 1964; McCall, 1976; McCall, Hogarty, & Hurlburt, 1972).

★ *Stability of IQ scores with retarded children is fairly high if they are tested after the preschool years and if no dramatic changes occur in their environment or educational training between testing. The more severely handicapped the child is, the more stable abilities appear to be* (Goodman & Cameron, 1978; Alper & Horne, 1959; Collmann & Newlyn, 1958; Ross & Boroskin, 1972). *Caution must be exercised, however, even with children who obtain very low scores. Several studies have shown that one child in four or five who are diagnosed as definitely retarded, even up to ages 2-3, will not be judged as retarded later on* (Holden, 1972; Koch, 1963).

Research on IQ changes as a result of environmental factors The alterability of intelligence as a result of environmental influences has been demonstrated in many studies. This research usually takes one of two forms: (a) children have been removed from nonstimulating, sterile environments (e.g., some of the early institutions for the retarded) and placed in more stimulating care settings, (b) environmental conditions have been improved by the addition of infant stimulation or preschool education programs (Ramey, Bryant, & Suarez, 1985; Ramey & Haskins, 1981). Research in the latter area is examined in more depth in other sections of this chapter (see Effects of Environment and Early Experience on Development, and Outcomes of Early Intervention Programs).

We will look at just a few studies here, to give support to the thesis that intelligence is pliable and alterable to some degree by environmental forces. One should note that not all research involving some manipulation of children's early environments has shown concurrent IQ changes. This is partially because of the vast number of intervening variables that affect child outcomes, including: (a) the nature, intensity, and duration of early interventions with children, (b) differences in the degree of deprivation and lack of appropriate care imposed on children and age at the time intervention was initiated, and (c) differences in research methodology. Furthermore, some interventions have not been designed to change IQ but, rather, have focused upon other child behaviors such as language, mother-child interactions, or play and social behavior. Yet, many investigators have tested IQ to see if IQ changes would be a byproduct of such programs. In many cases, expectations that such limited intervention approaches could produce major changes in overall intellectual capacity are unrealistic.

An early *study by Skeels and Dye* (1939) was one of the first to show changes in IQ as a result of children's removal from a sterile, unstimulating environment to a more enriched, nurturing one. Thirteen children under 3 years of age were removed from an orphanage and placed on a ward with institutionalized mentally retarded women. There they received considerably greater amounts of stimulation as they were cared for and played with by the female residents. Toys and other educational materials were made available. In the children's previous environment, few materials were available, little

Research shows that stimulating, interesting, and engaging environments do facilitate more intellectual, social, and language development in young children.

contact with adults occurred, and stimulation was minimal. IQ data were collected on the experimental children (who were moved to the new environment), as well as on a control group that remained in the sterile environment of the orphanage. Experimental children showed a mean gain of 27.5 IQ points, but controls showed a loss of 26.2. Every experimental child individually showed IQ gains; one subject even showed a 58-point gain. In contrast, all except one control subject lost IQ points. Five subjects dropped more than 35 points; 10 children showed losses between 18 and 45 points.

The *Milwaukee Early Intervention Project* produced dramatic IQ changes in young children who were subjected to more stimulating, enriching environments from very early infancy (Heber & Dever, 1970; Heber, Dever, & Conry, 1972; Garber & Heber, 1977). Children whose mothers had measured IQs below 80 and were from low sociocultural and economic backgrounds were divided into experimental and control groups. Those who were subjected to a high intensity intervention program as compared to a control group made significant IQ gains over time. When the study began, the two groups appeared relatively similar, but when the children were 5½ years old, mean IQ for the experimental group was 124 compared to a mean of 94 for the controls.

Results from the *Carolina Abecedarian Project*, initiated in 1972 as a longitudinal early intervention program, also attest to the plasticity of intelligence as a result of environmental forces (Ramey & Campbell, 1977, 1984; Ramey, McGinness, Cross, Collier, & Barrie-Blackley, 1982). The target population and intervention strategies employed in the Carolina Project are similar to those used in the Milwaukee Project. Upon birth of the target children, qualifying families were matched in pairs on the basis of maternal IQ, number of siblings, and total high-risk scores. Assignments then were made to experimental and control groups. Experimental subjects participated in a day-care program, which provided curriculum in language development, social development, perceptual and cognitive development, physical and motor development. Results were similar to those of other studies. First, control and experimental children showed no initial disadvantage on standardized infant tests during their first 12 months despite their impoverished background. Second, a performance decline began to appear at about 12 months in test scores of the control subjects on the Bayley Scales of Infant Development and on the Stanford Binet Intelligence Test. This was not shown for the experimental subjects who were participating in the early intervention program. Third, at 24 months, differences were apparent in IQ scores—a mean score of 97 for the experimental children and 81 months for the controls (Ramey & Bryant, 1982; Ramey & Smith, 1977).

In summary, research suggests that IQ is not a fixed, unchanging human characteristic. Though the IQ does appear to become more stable over time, it can vary, and especially so during the early years. After conducting an extensive analysis of the stability and change in human characteristics from some longitudinal data, Bloom (1964) concluded that intelligence is a developing function for which stability increases as a child grows older. He noted that the pliability of intelligence is greatest when a child is young and that intellectual functions develop most rapidly during the early years. Environmental influences, therefore, would have their greatest impact, either positively or negatively, during that time. Bloom's opinion was that by age 8 exposure to dramatically different environments would have relatively little effect on a child's measured IQ. (Also see Ramey & Haskins, 1981; Ramey, Bryant, & Suarez, 1985.)

Effects of handicapping and at-risk conditions on children

★ *Handicapping conditions and other factors that render a child at-risk can interfere with development and learning to the point that original disabilities become more severe or secondary handicaps appear. Disabilities can hamper normal learning processes by blocking some of the usual avenues for interacting with the environment. Left to educational opportunities typically available to normally developing infants and preschoolers, handicapped children are likely to be less efficient learners on their own. They may be less adept at engaging their environment in ways that are growth-producing. If young handicapped children are to participate in and benefit from experiences that they need to acquire major developmental skills, some form of special help and intervention is required.*

The effects of specific types of handicaps on development and learning in young children are reviewed in chapters 5 and 6. Here we will highlight some arguments for early intervention that become apparent when examining the broader kinds of impacts that at-risk or handicapping conditions can have on a person's life. First, it is helpful to distinguish between the *effects of diagnosed, primary handicapping conditions* and the *effects of conditions that simply place a child at-risk* for potential disabilities.

For children with a diagnosable, primary handicap (such as cerebral palsy, visual impairment, or physical deformities), the impairment is a clear reality. Certain effects of these handicapping conditions are inevitable. For example, a hearing impairment will reduce a child's ability to learn through that sensory modality, which will hamper speech and possibly language development—especially if the loss is severe. Other effects of a diagnosed primary handicap depend upon the extent to which medical, educational, and therapeutic intervention is possible. In any case, *identifiable handicaps create an immediate urgency for intervention.* Effects of the impairment upon behavior and learning are observable. The risks for normal intellectual development, if special help is not given to the child, are known.

In contrast, children *at-risk for developmental disabilities* usually show no initial handicap per se. At least no significant abnormalities in learning and performance are evident early in life. For this type of child, there is no immediate impact of a handicapping condition to be described—only a *projected impact*. Knowing that certain environmental and developmental factors are correlated with later performance difficulties, we predict an increased probability that the child will manifest developmental problems as he or she grows older. But because there is often no diagnosed handicap per se, and no developmental irregularity of sufficient magnitude to be labeled abnormal during infancy or the preschool years, parents and some professionals can easily assume the wait-and-see attitude.

Small growth deficits are of dubious concern. Sometimes it is not even clear whether the slowness in development suggests an emerging problem or if it is simply a part of a child's unique but normal growth pattern. The predicament with the wait-and-see approach, however, is that the effects of small deficits can compound and accumulate into significant developmental disabilities including mental retardation. Concern may be brushed aside because no *one* problem represents a significant deviancy. Unfortunately, by the time problems become severe enough to be labeled and to warrant educational intervention, the child will already have felt the impact. The question is: Can we afford to risk a child's developmental well-being while we wait to see if a serious problem materializes? Or should we intervene to prevent these occurrences as much as possible?

Another helpful distinction to discuss as we examine the impact of handicaps upon young children is the difference between handicapping conditions *within a child* and at-risk conditions *external to the child*. Diagnosable impairments *within* a child have the most direct effects. The child's own physical body or mental mechanisms are deformed or malfunctioning. Fortunately, medical advances today allow many of these conditions to be corrected. A cleft palate can be closed, and deformed limbs and other body parts can be restructured through surgery. Drugs can control many metabolic and neurological disorders to the extent that they are no longer handicapping.

But for children whose abnormalities are not subject to medical or therapeutic correction, the disability is an ever present reality. It will be carried wherever its bearer goes. A crippled 4-year-old boy will bear the inconvenience of his own physical immobility in any environment—at home, in a preschool classroom, or on a playground with his friends. Although he can dream at night of growing up to be a football player with the Kansas City Chiefs or fantasize about running faster than his friends in a game of tag, he will wake up each morning to the realitites of his physical deformity. The point to be emphasized is: *The extent to which these internal disabilities interfere with learning activities available to other children is influenced by the intervention provided by others.*

When handicapping conditions exist within the individual, intervention programs are needed to focus upon some rather specific kinds of goals:

- To provide an educational environment or to adapt existing ones so they are responsive in ways that do not penalize a child for a handicap. Experiences must be brought *to* the child rather than waiting for the handicapped child to seek out and create his or her own learning opportunities. This strategy compensates partially for learning experiences otherwise lost because of a child's handicap.
- To teach the child special skills that help compensate for his or her disability and overcome some of the limitations imposed upon learning and upon normal everyday activities experienced by most other children.
- To create alternative avenues for learning or performing that circumvent limitations imposed by a handicapping condition by using special materials, adaptive equipment, prosthetic devices, and teaching techniques.
- To teach the child developmental skills that should be acquired but which may or may not emerge through the normal course of events in the young handicapped child's life because of the disability.
- To help the child acquire adaptive skills leading to greater independence and competence so that he or she can (a) function within the mainstream of our society alongside normal peers, (b) achieve a sense of self-mastery, and (c) develop a positive self-image.

Conditions *external to the child* that threaten normal developmental processes are typically those used to designate one as "at-risk." Although a child is intact physically and mentally, certain conditions place his or her future growth in question. This condition is not necessarily one that follows the child wherever he or she goes—at least not initially. If a child is at-risk because of poor sociocultural and economic conditions in the home, the condition characterizes only the home setting. It does not necessarily exist at school or in the immediate community. Only as the impact of that environment produces deficits in the child's performance does it become a limitation that he or she then imposes upon his or her own experiences.

Early intervention programs with children whose well-being is threatened by external forces are slightly different in focus than are programs for children with specific handicapping conditions. The focus or the goals of programs for children from impoverished environments are:

- To improve upon and enrich the child's learning environment so that sufficient stimulation, learning opportunities, and physical care are provided.
- To remediate any skills or learning deficits that may have resulted from the conditions, such as an impoverished home environment, that place a child at-risk for developmental abnormalities.
- To help children broaden their range of experience and achieve successes that build positive self-concepts and help them gain skills for interacting with and acting upon their own environment.

Most often, conditions that cause a child to be considered at-risk are environmental in nature. Intervention, then, is primarily one of *environmental change* or *remediation of learning deficits* in the child. This is the task Head Start focused upon in its attempt to break the cycle of poverty. By supplementing the early learning experiences of children from disadvantaged homes, the intent was to remediate early learning deficits and thereby prevent failure in the elementary school.

In developing a rationale for special education-early childhood programs, we can draw from the arguments traditionally used to justify programs for disadvantaged and at-risk populations of preschool youngsters. But early intervention is important to young handicapped children for other, even stronger reasons. These children clearly have disabilities that will affect their ability to seek out new experiences and to learn. Because all areas of development are so highly interrelated in children during the early years, disabilities in one area can disrupt development in other performance domains. Failure to remediate one handicap can result in "spillover" of difficulties into the learning of other skills. Children are vulnerable to these impacts because they are in no position to alter their environment. A child can live in an environment that lacks stimulation and educational opportunity and will accept it as reality. Children know nothing different and are in no position to change their depriving circumstances.

Handicapping conditions impose further limitations that make early educational intervention crucial. These are described briefly.

Limitations in quality of the environment   As Caldwell (1973) put it, "The environment of a young handicapped child is by definition depriving" (p. 4). Many disabilities restrict the sensory, motor, or cognitive processes required for a child to attend to, intake, or assimilate stimuli from the environment. The visually impaired child's experiences, for example, may be restricted to objects and things within only a few feet. Thus, a blind child's world can be described as "limited to the length of the child's arms."

Deprivation also occurs when a handicapped child is less able to engage the environment in interactive processes that foster learning and generate additional experiences. By being less responsive to opportunities in the environment (for whatever the reason), by being less energetic and independent, or by lacking skills that make new learning possible, the handicapped child's behavior thwarts his or her own growth process. Compared to normal children of the same age, handicapped children miss out on many important experiences.

Limitations in child's ability to intake information from environment   Every human being is dependent upon sensory processes for learning to occur. We see, we hear, we touch and feel, and we smell the odors around us. We also learn by doing, engaging in motor responses as we explore and manipulate the environment and master the movement capabilities of our own bodies. Our cognitive apparatus allows us to attend to and gain meaning from those experiences. But certain handicaps disrupt this intake process. A retarded child, for instance, is less able to understand the meaning of stimuli. Too many stimuli can produce confusion, causing the child difficulty in sorting out the most important from the unimportant (Zeamon & House, 1963). Youngsters with motor impairments are less able than those without motor impairments to explore their surroundings. Hearing and visually impaired children have limited stimulation through those sensory modes.

Limited ability to receive sensory stimuli is not as debilitating if many basic skills have been mastered first. Adults who lose a sensory function such as hearing have alternative ways to cope. But a very young child who has not yet acquired basic developmental skills is highly vulnerable to the effects of a sensory disability.

Limitations imposed on new learning by delayed prerequisite skills   In a sense, handicapped children are placed in double jeopardy by their condition. Not only does the impairment itself restrict learning, but it also can interfere with development in other areas that could be normal. When basic perceptual, motor, language, attentional, and discrimination skills are missing—many of which are prerequisite to other skills— further delays are almost inevitable. For example, Horton (1976) noted that hearing impaired youngsters show .5 to 2 years educational retardation on the average during their first years of elementary school. Deaf children tend to be about 4 years educationally retarded. The longer the amount of time that passes before they receive language stimulation and training, the less efficient later language facilities will be (Tervoort, 1964). Jensen (1966) argued that the primary hope for combating the cumulative deficits we see in children is to deal with problems as close to their sources as possible . . . in the preschool years.

Limitations in child's responsiveness to learning opportunities   A handicapping condition can significantly reduce a child's motivation and curiosity because of the tremendous effort required to tackle even a most simple task. How tiring heavy braces can be when trying to move around, or holding and manipulating a toy can be when a child has excessively poor coordination! Children have trouble paying attention to a task when one sensory mode is not operating. Even adults tire greatly when they forget their glasses and try to read for several hours. Children have to have tremendous perseverance and patience to put up with the frustrations that handicaps cause. They become discouraged as they watch others run and play or go places that are impossible for handicapped children to go without help. They become frustrated and even frightened when they hear sounds and do not know where they come from or what they mean. Even more frustrating is when children want to, but cannot, communicate their needs or express their ideas to others.

Young children react in various ways to these types of frustration. Some express their anger through temper tantrums or behaviors that make learning even more difficult. Others withdraw and simply stop trying. We often observe listless, unresponsive behavior in young handicapped children. Their lack of curiosity shows how quickly interest can be extinguished if attempts to satisfy it require more effort than the pleasure derived from learning. All too often we interpret lack of interest as another symptom of the disability, and possibly of mental retardation. Perhaps we should wonder how much it is a sign of a turned-off child whose natural curiosity and energy for learning have no means for expression.

Limitations in mental ability and cognitive functions   All handicapping conditions, if unchecked and of sufficient severity, can disrupt cognitive functions and result in a diagnosis of mental retardation. This is a major reason to minimize the debilitating effects of physical, sensory, and motor disabilities so that learning and skill acquisition can proceed as normally as possible. To allow minor disabilities to interfere with cognitive functions is to incapacitate a child even more. Mental retardation is not ordinarily something that suddenly happens, except in cases in which physical injury or genetic factors damage the brain. More often, mental retardation develops over time as growth curves decelerate and deficits cumulate to widen the discrepancy between a child and his or her peers.

We do not know the degree to which secondary disabilities can be prevented, but we do know that some of them can be minimized through early education. As Karnes (1973) pointed out, "One of the best arguments for early education for the handicapped is that it can eliminate many problems that may become entrenched if they persist into later years—thus reducing the necessity for placement in special classes or special services" (p. 49).

Effects of environment and early experience on development

★ *A child's environment and early experience, particularly the degree to which these are nurturing or depriving, have a major effect upon development and learning. Both greatly influence the degree to which a child reaches his or her full potential. The continuity of experience into later childhood years also is crucial. It determines whether positive, stimulating experiences or early trauma and deprivation have a lasting impact.*

The quality of environment is particularly significant with handicapped children because it helps determine the extent to which a disability actually becomes handicapping. Environmental variables influence to some degree how much a disability interferes with normal developmental processes and the extent to which handicapped young children gain access to learning activities ordinarily available to their nonhandicapped peers.

When children are at-risk for developmental abnormalities or when early problems are manifest, the environments in which they live will either help maintain their status quo or foster change. That is, some environments are of sufficient neutrality that they do nothing more than sustain whatever pattern of development is spontaneously manifest in a child. If a child's early development is delayed, some environments can be so unresponsive that they fail to provide the kinds of stimulation needed to produce more rapid rates of learning.

Qualities of stimulating environments for young children

What are the environmental antecedents for some of the variations we see in children's early intellectual development? After analyzing research on growth patterns and change in human characteristics, Bloom (1964) derived a list of critical environmental influences. He suggested that differences among children in *general intelligence* are related to the extent the environment provides: (a) stimulation that fosters verbal development, (b) pleasurable consequences for verbal-reasoning accomplishments, (c) encouragement for problem solving, exploration, and skill learning.

Yarrow (1970) suggested that an optimal environment must include three classes of stimulation: *sensory*, *affective*, and *social*. By examining each of these modes of stimulation, we can see what experiences children need and how handicapping conditions can interfere with the quality of stimulation a child gets. *Sensory stimulation* is important in that it arouses, directs, and focuses a child's attention on his or her external environment. It elicits responses that bring a child into interaction with people and things in the environment, which produces learning and adaptation. If stimulation is to be sufficient to elicit responses and maintain behavior once it is learned, it must be of appropriate intensity. It must be above a child's threshold of awareness, yet not of such intensity that the stimulation becomes overwhelming, physiologically disruptive, or painful. Yarrow explained that certain qualities of sensory stimulation are necessary for an environment to be responsive to the needs of the individuals therein.

- *Several modalities of sensory stimulation are essential, including visual, auditory, tactile, vestibular, and motoric inputs.* Deprivation may have differential effects in particular sensory modalities at different developmental periods. For example, a baby's tactile contact with the mother is important during the early months of life, but the same stimulation is less critical later on.
- *Variety in stimulation is important from both a neurophysiological view and a psychological-behavioral perspective.* Monotonous and unvaried stimulation does not maintain attention and likely decreases curiosity, interest, and motivation. A lack of stimulus variety leads to habituation so that a particular type and intensity of stimulation loses its evocative power with a child or adult.
- *The quantity and quality of sensory stimulation are keys to nurturing, supportive environments.* How much stimulation is necessary and what constitutes quality stimulation in a good environment are not clear. Quite likely, individual children require differing amounts of stimulation depending upon their own unique temperaments, special needs, and behavioral patterns. The key is a responsive caregiver who is sensitive to what a child needs and can deliver appropriate levels of stimulation.

Affective stimulation involves the interactions between a child and other persons communicating messages that contribute to, or interfere with, the child's feelings of competence, security, trust, self-worth, and belonging. At a very young age, children acquire a passive or assertive approach to their environment. They soon reflect an attitude of either "I can do it" or "I can't do it." Studies document abnormalities in social affect and personality characteristics among children reared in highly depriving circumstances, particularly those lacking in opportunities for physical contact, mothering, or development of attachments to other significant persons (Egeland & Sroufe, 1981; Provence & Lipton, 1962; Rubenstein, 1967; Yarrow, Goodwin, Manheimer, & Milowe, 1973).

Characteristics of these individuals as they grow older often include generalized lack of responsiveness to other people, a lack of social initiative, generalized blandness or nondiscriminative emotional approaches to others, and limited manifestations of customary playful activities. Most significant of all in young children deprived of affectional stimulation is the lack of basic rudimentary imitative skills for playing simple games such as peek-a-boo. As these youngsters grow older, they often lack social sensitivity and the ability to respond discriminately to emotional expressions from others.

Social stimulation plays a central function in that a caregiver or peer usually is the person who brings a young child into contact with the other types of stimulation described here. Social stimulation includes several variables:

1. The frequency and quality of social interaction between a child and caregiver or peers.
2. The affective and affectional underpinnings of those exchanges.
3. The depth of relationship with caretakers or significant others reflected in interactions that facilitate or interfere with the development of trust, a positive self-image, and feelings of safety and security.
4. The responsiveness of caregivers to a child's needs and developmental stages. This includes the behavioral/personal characteristics of caregivers and peers that provide models with which a child can identify and imitate.
5. The consistency and predictability of caregivers in their behavior and the continuity of significant people in a child's life.

Young children are dependent upon others to provide contact with appropriate learning materials and play objects, to manipulate environmental conditions for their protection, and to create experiences that bring intellectual and personal-social growth. Because of this dependency relationship, children—especially children with handicapping or at-risk conditions—are easily victimized by a socially depriving environment. They have no other alternatives; they are not able to seek other stimulation if caregivers fail to provide for them. A parent or caregiver thus serves an important mediational function for a young child by buffering events or stimuli that the youngster is not ready or able to handle. If parents are sensitive to a child's needs and abilities, they can regulate activities to fit the child's level in ways that will be most beneficial.

Another important feature of the social environment is its capability for what Yarrow (1963, 1965, 1970) termed *contingent responsiveness*. This is crucial if learning is to take place. If smiling, vocalizing, and attempts at social contact are reinforced, they are strengthened and become a part of a child's learned repertoire. If behaviors are not solicited by parents and are not regarded as important enough to warrant reciprocal attention, a child will probably stop exhibiting them. According to Piaget's theory, discussed earlier, this reciprocal interactive process with people or things is the basis for the development of cognitive competence and intelligence.

Effects of depriving environments: Animal research Stimulus deprivation can have devastating effects on both children and animals if it occurs for an extended time during early development. Most research on deprivation has involved animals, since humans cannot deliberately be subjected to extreme experimental conditions.

Research during the 1950s and 1960s documented a variety of developmental abnormalities and behavioral deficits in animals resulting from environmental deprivation. The most devastating impacts occur when deprivation is more enduring, when it is imposed during particularly critical periods of development, or when growth is most rapid. The famous studies of Clarke, Heron, Fetherstonaugh, Forgays, and Hebb (1951) compared dogs reared in isolated lab conditions where stimulation was minimal with litter-mates raised as pets either in the same labs or in homes. Deprived dogs became deficient in intelligence, emotionality, motivation, and social behavior. Dramatic differences between animals were apparent when they were played with, talked to, and allowed to roam about freely.

Similar experiments documented other deficiencies in deprived animals, such as reduced social competency (Melzack & Thompson, 1956), tendencies for epilepsy (Thompson, Melzack, & Scott, 1956), and general impairments across several areas of development (Melzack, 1962; Melzack & Burns, 1965; Fuller & Clark, 1966). In summarizing these results, Thompson et al. (1956) pointed out that deprived dogs presented a clear picture of retarded psychological development. When grown, their behavior resembled that of puppies rather than mature dogs. Menzel (1964) and his colleagues (Menzel, Davenport, & Rogers, 1963) compared the learning and behavior patterns of chimpanzees reared in normal laboratory conditions, restricted environments, and the wild natural environment. Results showed that animals reared in the restricted environments were timid, dull, stereotypic in their behavior, and less willing to approach novel objects in their environment, as compared to control animals.

The best known research on the effects of social isolation with primates and the lack of physical, tactile stimulation with a mother figure was conducted by Harry Harlow and his associates at the University of Wisconsin. Over many years, Harlow reported a series of experiments with young monkeys who were separated from their mothers or peers and reared under a variety of social-environmental conditions (Harlow & Mears, 1979; Harlow, 1958, 1961, 1965; Harlow, Harlow, & Hansen, 1963).

Harlow reported that early deprivation produced significant changes in the social and adaptive behavior of monkeys. How lasting the effects were depended upon the length of time deprivation was imposed, when it occurred, and what kinds of subsequent experiences occurred when the deprivation treatment was terminated. Briefly, these findings can be summarized as follows: (a) Extreme isolation in which monkeys were removed from any contact with another living thing for 3, 6, or 12 months produced severe effects, and the longer the isolation, the more dramatic and lasting were the deficiencies; (b) the most prominent effect of extreme isolation was fear, and simple play activity never appeared; (c) monkeys who had been subjected to extreme social isolation for 6 or more months tended to engage in uncontrolled aggression as adults; (d) female monkeys subjected to social isolation became inadequate mothers and had disturbed mating behavior; and (e) monkeys raised with peers but separated from their mothers did not show the deficiencies of those separated from both mothers and peers, and monkeys likewise seemed to surmount a lack of socialization with peers if the mother provided affection and stimulation.

Other animal experiments have shown that specific types of sensory deprivation can impair development in particular domains. Riesen and Aarons (1959) and Baxter (1966) found that animals reared in darkness from infancy showed impaired visual functions later. Cats deprived of patterned stimulation during the first 8 weeks of life were unable to later discriminate between a moving and a stationary visual stimulus (Riesen, 1965). In another classic experiment, Riesen (1961) found notable physiological and morphological growth changes in animals reared in darkness; catastrophic effects occurred within the retina, which markedly altered the capacity of the eyes.

Effects of depriving environments: Human research   This research has primarily involved children reared in poor, unstimulating, institutional type environments or children who experienced some form of maternal deprivation (Casler, 1968; Caster, 1971). One of the first and most quoted large-scale studies of infants in institutional-type settings was reported by Spitz (1945, 1946, 1947), who studied infants from two different institutional environments. One group of infants was reared in a foundling home where stimulation and social attention were minimal. The other group of infants lived in a nursery attached to a penal institution for delinquent girls. There, the mothers continued to care for and play with their babies daily. Babies in the foundling home were those of mothers considered socially well-adjusted but simply unable economically to support themselves and their children. Mothers in the penal nursery were largely delinquent minors described as socially maladjusted, mentally retarded, physically handicapped, psychopathic, or criminal.

Developmental assessments on infants in the foundling home, where stimulation was minimal, showed progressive declines during the first year. Their mean developmental quotient (DQ) was 131 at 2-3 months but fell to 72 around 10-12 months. Spitz pointed out that while the nursery babies' DQ scores were maintained at the approximate same level, their maternal backgrounds were not the most desirable. Yet babies with the more desirable maternal background who were reared in the depriving environment of the foundling home showed developmental losses resulting in a difference of almost 28 points from that of infants in the comparison group. Babies in the depriving environment manifested additional symptoms such as weepiness, oversusceptibility to infection, weight loss, and withdrawal.

Spitz concluded that the developmental losses were a result of lack of mothering, although he noted they could be attributed to other inadequacies in the environment. His study has been criticized for some major methodological flaws (Pinneau, 1955a, 1955b). Nonetheless, as Hunt (1961) pointed out in his review of the Spitz study, it still suggests that depriving or nurturing environments can alter children's intelligence.

Goldfarb (1945, 1949, 1955) conducted another series of early historical studies comparing the development of two groups of institutionalized children. One group spent the first years of life in an institution before placement in foster homes. Children in a second group were placed in foster homes before age 1, and thus spent only a short time in the institution. All children had been separated from their natural mothers before 9 months of age. Institutional conditions were similar to those reported in Spitz's study—sterile, nonstimulating, and lacking opportunities for child-adult contact.

At the time Goldfarb conducted his follow-up study, all subjects were between 10 and 14 years old. Children who had spent their first 3 years in the institution were found to be deficient in intellectual development, speech, and ability to conceptualize. They were hyperactive, less able to concentrate, and performed poorly in school. Socially, they were described as immature, unpopular, and insatiable for affection although simultaneously unable to form genuine attachments. In contrast, the youngsters who had spent only their first 6 months in the institution showed no ill effects. As older children, their development appeared to be normal. Goldfarb blamed the emotional and cognitive deficits of the one group on lack of mothering during the first 3 years.

Since that time, Goldfarb's studies also have been criticized. Questions have been raised about the probability that the institutionalized children were abnormal in the first place. Though such dramatic conclusions may not be warranted and the exact variables responsible for the negative cognitive and social outcomes cannot be isolated, studies consistently have verified that maternal separation early in life can have lasting negative social-emotional effects.

Other studies of depriving environments have shown what effects can be wrought on young children. Case studies have been presented of children reared in emotionally depriving environments in which the children manifested physical, endocrinal disorders resulting in a condition termed *deprivation dwarfism* (Gardner, 1972; Harris, 1982). Symptoms included notable weight loss, retarded bone growth, inhibition in the secretion of hormones from the pituitary gland, and thus a stunting of physical growth. Children also exhibited listless, unresponsive behavior and sleeplessness.

Provence and Lipton (1962) studied children in a nursery where minimal contact occurred between caregivers and the children. Substantial impairments were noted in their social responsiveness, body awareness, language development, and pain avoidance. The research findings particularly pointed to the interdependence of early stimulation with emergence of language functions and personal-social development in children. Differences as early as 2 months were found between home-reared and institutionalized infants in the frequency, type, and quality of their vocalization. Retardation in the development of functional language was apparent by the end of the first year. The repertoire of sounds that normal infants use to express reactions such as pleasure, displeasure, anger, eagerness, anticipation, and excitement was virtually nonexistent in the institutionalized children. They clearly were delayed in development of differential vocal signals to communicate their needs. In fact, none had mastered specific words by age 1.

Though research clearly shows that sterile, depriving environments can produce abnormal behaviors and developmental delays in children, the specific variables most responsible for mental retardation are not always clear. Probably no single variable is responsible. Instead, the complex interactions of several forms of deprivation most likely combine to produce mild to severe outcomes in children. Also, an institutional setting per se does not necessarily interfere with development in young children. The quality of care, the stimulation (or lack of it), and the opportunities provided for learning within that environment are the primary influences. Many early institutions were characterized by only custodial forms of care, where children were simply fed, diapered, and left in cribs. But not all institutions have been operated this way. This could account for the few studies in which children developed normally in institutional environments. In addition, evidence (Clarke & Clarke, 1974) shows that early and intensified stimulation can help reverse abnormal developmental patterns. To what extent early damage can be undone, however, is not clear.

What are the effects of enriching, stimulating environments upon young children? Research has documented notable changes in children who are removed from nonstimulating, depriving environments and given increased sensory, cognitive, and social stimulation. This has implications for handicapped children inasmuch as their impairments can reduce stimulation in ways that cause their environment to be more restrictive and depriving. Adults, therefore, must intervene to counteract those losses by giving extra stimulation or training.

Outcomes of early intervention programs

> ★ *Early intervention programs can make a significant difference in the developmental status of young children and can do so more rapidly than later remedial efforts after a child has entered elementary school. Results from early childhood programs for disadvantaged children and a growing body of literature on programs for handicapped infants and preschoolers document the benefits of early childhood special education programs. Intervention can reduce the limitations a handicapping condition imposes upon a child's ability to learn from and interact with the environment. Early education and training also can minimize possibilities that a child will develop secondary disabilities and can increase the chances that developmental skills will be acquired when they otherwise might be delayed or simply not learned.*

Perhaps the most powerful of all arguments in behalf of early intervention stems from data documenting the positive, long-term effects upon children. Although the ultimate question we are concerned with here is whether early intevention with the *handicapped* makes a difference, intervention research with a variety of other populations has relevance. The largest collection of research literature deals with children described as impoverished, disadvantaged, or at-risk because of socioeconomic or environmental factors.

To determine the outcomes of early intervention upon young children, research can be drawn from several sources: (a) early historical studies in which children who were mentally retarded or developmentally delayed were removed from depriving to more stimulating environments or were given supplementary forms of stimulation to foster growth; (b) studies on early enrichment or intervention programs with children from low income and disadvantaged homes; and (c) studies on the outcomes of intervention programs for handicapped infants and preschoolers.

Effects of enriched environments and increased stimulation on children

Several historical studies are cited frequently to show that significant developmental gains can occur in children after being moved from inadequate, unstimulating environments to more nurturing ones. The study by Skeels and Dye (1939), described earlier, involved the transfer of 13 children under age 3 from a sterile, overcrowded orphanage into an institution for the retarded. The youngsters were placed on a ward with retarded women, where they received a great deal of attention and stimulation. Results were dramatic in that those children showed a mean IQ gain of 27.5 points, compared to a mean loss of 26.2 IQ points among those who remained in the nonstimulating orphanage environment.

The most significant results of the Skeels and Dye study came 25 years later when Skeels (1966) followed up on his original experimental and control subjects to determine their status as adults. As adults, the differences continued to be dramatic. Experimental subjects had completed a median grade level of 12 years of school, whereas controls had completed a median grade level of only 3 years. All control children remained in the orphanage or later were placed in state institutions for the retarded. Occupational achievements of the two groups were notably different, as shown in the following list of their vocational activities:

Experimental Subjects	*Control Subjects*
1 elementary school teacher	4 residents of institutions
1 registered nurse	3 dishwashers
1 licensed practical nurse	1 unskilled laborer
1 beautician	1 cafeteria worker
1 clerk	1 worked for institution where he
1 airline stewardess	had been a resident
2 domestics in a private home	1 typesetter for a newspaper
1 vocational counselor	1 had been in and out of institution;
1 sales manager for estate agent	during out times lived with
1 staff sergeant—air force	grandmother doing odd jobs for her
	1 died in adolescence

Samuel Kirk conducted other early landmark intervention studies. In a project started in 1949, Kirk placed 15 mentally retarded children 3 to 5 years old from an institution (with tested IQs between 40 and 60) in a preschool training program for two years. A control group of 15 children with the same ages and IQs was tested periodically but given no intervention. Results later reported by Kirk (1973, 1977) showed that children who attended the preschool program had a mean gain of 10.2 IQ points while the control group showed a loss of 6.5 IQ points. Those attending preschool showed a total average gain of 10.5 points on the Vineland Social Maturity Scale whereas controls lost 12.0 points. In fact, control subjects dropped on all measures of performance. None ever left the institution. At age 8 they were described as more retarded on measured IQ than they had been at age 6. Kirk considered the most significant outcome to be that seven of the 15 experimental children increased in IQ and improved in behavior sufficiently to be "paroled" from the institution and placed in foster homes. Four years later, six of the seven were still in community placements.

In 1958 Kirk reported a second study with retarded children ages 3-6 and IQs between 45 and 80 who were assigned either to early intervention preschool groups or to control groups who received no nursery school. Both control and experimental groups contained children who resided either at home or in an institutional setting. Results showed IQ gains between 10 and 30 points among the children who received the special preschool programs, despite the fact that half of them were diagnosed as having organic impairments. IQs of the control subjects declined. Follow-up results some years later showed that the experimental children maintained their gains, some for as long as 5 years. After a year of school, however, many control subjects living within the community tended to catch up. This was not true of community children from very deprived homes or of the institutionalized control group (the other control group was not institutionalized).

Numerous studies, both historical and more contemporary research, have demonstrated the benefits of extra forms of stimulation for young children. Dennis (1960) compared retarded children in three Iranian institutions, one of which provided more optimal care than the others. Staff members handled the children frequently, played with them, and provided varied kinds of stimulation. The other two institutions had sterile, depriving environments. Comparisons of the children across the three settings revealed that although all were retarded, those in the enriched environment resembled home-reared infants in their motor development. Children in the other two institutions showed serious motor delay.

Caster (1965) provided eight institutionalized babies with tactile stimulation beyond that normally available from the staff that cared for them. Pre-posttest comparisons on the Gesell Developmental Scales were made with a control group that received the same general care but not the extra stimulation. Overall developmental declines were found for both groups, but the experimental children showed a rate of decline only *half* that of the control group infants. Tactile stimulation for the experimental group appeared to improve functioning in areas of sensorimotor adjustment, language development, feeding ability, and capability for responding to problem situations. Caster attributed the general declines of both groups to the absence of other important kinds of stimulation.

Early stimulation has been shown to benefit young handicapped infants, as well as those considered at-risk because of prematurity. Planned intervention programs during the first few weeks of life have shown measurable effects on development by the end of the first year of life. Solkoff, Yaffe, Weintraub, and Blase (1969) reported that premature infants who had the benefit of 10 days of extra stroking from their nurses gained weight faster, cried less, and also were more active than a control group. Bayley Motor Scale scores at 8 months of age were higher for the stimulated group than for the control group. Freedman and Boverman (1966) found temporary weight gains and a noticeable increase in relaxation in premature infants who were rocked 1 hour daily using an inanimate rocking device.

Scarr-Salapatek and Williams (1973) conducted a study in which inanimate visual stimulation (mobiles) and animate auditory and tactile/kinesthetic stimulation (4 hours daily of rocking, patting, talking face to face) were given to low birth weight babies. Follow-up home visits and parent education continued during the infants' first year. At 1 month of age, the low birth weight infants who received intervention scored better on the Brazelton Neonatal Scales than did the control group. At 1 year of age, the experimental group again performed better on the Cattell Infant Intelligence Scale than did the control group.

Fraiberg, Smith, and Adelson (1969) reported notable benefits of early stimulation, particularly tactile stimulation, for premature blind babies. Because visual input is not a possible avenue for learning for these children, tactile stimulation is enormously important, but early care of premature babies in isolettes often minimized that contact. Initial observations of 10 blind babies found them resistive to cuddling after just 3 weeks in an isolette. After placement in a 3-year home intervention program in which parents were trained in teaching and management procedures, all 10 children showed marked improvements in behavior. Appropriate attachments were manifest, and differential smiling and vocalizing appeared.

Scarr-Salapatek and Williams (1972) documented the effects of early stimulation upon premature infants of impoverished mothers. The stimulation program included eight half-hour feeding sessions in which the caregiver provided the infants with visual and social stimulation such as rocking, fondling, and talking-to. Not only were significant results shown within a month, but at the end of one year, experimental infants were at normal or near-normal levels of development.

Effects of early intervention programs for the disadvantaged   Research on the efficacy of early stimulation with disadvantaged children is abundant—much too voluminous to summarize here. Only a few studies that have carefully documented child outcomes will be examined briefly.

The Milwaukee Early Intervention Project (Heber, Garber, Harrington, Hoffman, & Galender, 1972; Heber & Garber, 1973, 1975) was designed to reduce the incidence of mental retardation in families at high risk for producing such offspring. Findings from earlier research by Heber and his associates (Heber, Dever, & Conry, 1968; Garber & Heber, 1977) provided the basis for initiating the Milwaukee program.

1. Although a higher incidence of mental retardation is typically found among low socioeconomic groups, certain families among those groups were found to have a disproportionately larger number of retarded children. Data from a high-risk area of Milwaukee, because of its poorest housing conditions and lowest family income in the city, indicated that over one-third of the city's population of EMR children came from that area. Only 2½% of the city's population, however, resided within the same geographical boundaries. Other data revealed that 45% of the mothers were responsible for nearly 80% of the children who tested below 80 on standardized IQ measures.
2. Families at-risk could be identified primarily by one major variable—the mother's IQ, and, specifically, mothers with IQs below 80. Mothers with measured IQs below 80 tended to produce offspring who evidenced intellectual growth curves distinctly different from children of mothers with similar sociocultural and economic background and with higher IQs. Data indicated that children from seriously disadvantaged mothers with IQs below 80 declined significantly in IQ level between infancy and adulthood.

On the basis of these early findings, the Milwaukee Project was initiated to determine if the high rates of mental retardation could be curtailed through early identification and an intensive, comprehensive family rehabilitation program. Forty mothers (all with IQs below 75) who had a child between 3 and 6 months of age and who lived within the economically depressed, high-risk area of Milwaukee were selected. Although the children had no significant birth abnormalities, the risk for retardation within this population was 16 times greater than usual (a prediction based upon the earlier findings). The 40 selected families were assigned to either an experimental or a control group, and experimental families entered into a 6-year intervention program involving job training and a remedial education program for the mothers, an early educational program for the children, parent counseling, and family crisis intervention. (For a more thorough description of the intervention program, see Heber and Garber, 1975; Bronfenbrenner, 1974).

Results revealed impressive outcomes in view of the fact that the two groups appeared relatively similar when the study began. First, the experimental group showed a mean IQ of approximately 120 at 2 years of age compared to a mean IQ of 95 for the control group. By age 5½, the mean IQ for the experimentals was 124 and 94 for the controls—a difference of some 30 IQ points (Heber et al., 1972). Second, experimental mothers showed more positive self-concepts and more self-confidence than their control group counterparts. Experimental mothers were more responsive to their children's needs and were more verbal in their interactions. In contrast, control mothers continued to reflect a low level of confidence and to show a lack of responsiveness to their children. They tended to express the attitude that children were just one more problem in their lives. Third, the experimental group showed much more accelerated language on measures of language development, including tests of grammatical comprehension, sentence repetition, and morphology, compared to the control children (Garber & Heber, 1977). Those differences were magnified as the project progressed.

National reviews of early intervention research have reported on child outcomes across many independent early education programs for disadvantaged children. Two of these are of particular interest here. One, by Urie Bronfenbrenner (1974), is summarized in a document entitled *A Report of Longitudinal Evaluations of Preschool Programs, Volume II: Is Early Intervention Effective?** The second is by a group of researchers who formed the Consortium on Developmental Continuity and whose work resulted in two major reports, *The Persistence of Preschool Effects* (Lazar, Hubbell, Murray, Rosche, & Royce, 1977) and *Lasting Effects After Preschool* (Lazar & Darlington, 1979, 1982). All of the programs mentioned were initiated during the 1960s. None focused specifically upon handicapped children, although a few used IQ (between 50 and 85) as a basis for selecting enrollees. Although the intervention programs were precursors to or parallel to Head Start programs in some communities, none was actually a part of Head Start. All programs were independent of each other, utilized different intervention strategies, and applied their own methods for evaluating program outcomes. The results provide some insights into the effectiveness of programs of this nature and into the variables that influenced their success.

Bronfenbrenner's (1974) report entitled *Is Early Intervention Effective?* summarized research findings from two types of early intervention programs: (a) those conducted in group preschool settings outside the home, and (b) those conducted in the home with regularly scheduled visits by a trained person who worked with the child or parents, or both. Major conclusions from Bronfenbrenner's report are highlighted in Table 1.2.

Bronfenbrenner made some particularly notable conclusions in regard to interventions with parents. First, parent intervention appeared to serve as a "catalyst" inasmuch as it seemed to enhance the impact of other intervention activities concurrent with, or subsequent to, the parent program. Parent intervention also seemed to act as a "fixative" in stabilizing the effects of other intervention processes by placing parents in a better position to reinforce learning and continue stimulating activities at home. Second, Bronfenbrenner

---

*Volume I, by Sally Ryan, contains reports on individual intervention programs.

Table 1.2
Summary of Bronfenbrenner's Report
On the Effectiveness of Early Intervention

Effectiveness of preschool interventions in group settings

- All preschool programs resulted in substantial gains in children's IQ scores and other cognitive measures during the first year. Gains maintained as long as programs lasted. Upon termination of programs with no follow-through of services, gains tended to "wash out."
- Cognitively oriented, structured preschool curriculums produced more significant gains than play oriented programs.
- The greatest loss of children's gains from preschool intervention occurred after their entry into regular school. This suggests the need for follow-up and continuity in the intervention if lasting results are to be realized.
- Children who gained the least from intervention programs and evidenced the earliest declines were from the most deprived socioeconomic backgrounds. Specific variables most associated with this phenomenon were parental education, one-parent families, number of siblings, and employment status of the primary breadwinner.
- Home factors had an impact upon children's ability to benefit from group intervention programs at both the preschool and elementary school levels. Greatest losses in cognitive gains occurred during summer months for children from unfavorable home situations. In contrast, children from more favorable economic circumstances not only maintained their status, but actually made substantial gains during the same summer months.

Effects of home-based tutoring programs

- Home-based programs showed outcomes similar to group preschool interventions. Dramatic gains were shown by the children while the programs were in operation, but declines were evidenced once home visits were terminated.

Effects of parent-child interventions

- Children in parent-child interventions (in contrast to group-center-based programs) showed gains that maintained longer—some 3-4 years after termination of the program. Some erosion of gains did occur, but losses were small compared to those of children in center-based programs only.
- Effects of parent-child interventions were cumulative from year to year both during the intervention and, in some cases, after the intervention. Development of positive reciprocal interactions between mother and infant facilitated subsequent interactions; the mother trained the child and the child also trained the mother. Parent-child interventions typically were designed to enhance this relationship.
- IQ gains made by children in parent-child interventions were greatest in those enrolled early during their first or second year of life (IQ gains were inversely related to the age at which the intervention was initiated).
- Interventions including parents benefited not only the target child, but younger siblings as well. Greatest variance was found in young siblings closest in age to the target children. Such side benefits of early intervention were called the "vertical diffusion" of results. Just how far down the line this diffusion extends to even younger children is not clear.
- Parent intervention had differential effects upon children depending upon when it occurred. First, early parent involvement seemed to enhance the maintenance of early intervention gains over a longer time. Children who participated in early, intensive programs of parent intervention prior to preschool attained greater and more lasting gains in a subsequent group intervention. Second, parent interventions in isolation of other intervention approaches had limitations for helping children learn skills and specific content required in school. Yet, preschool interventions alone also had limited capacities for effecting change that would endure after intervention was discontinued. At the same time, combination parent and center-based preschool interventions seemed, at certain points in time, to interfere with program effectiveness.

Table 1.2 (continued)

Bronfenbrenner (1972) concluded that a "phased sequence" approach might be most profitable. He proposed:
(1) starting parent/family-centered intervention as early as possible and as the major focus in the early years.
(2) introducing preschool intervention later, with increasing emphasis as a child grows older.
(3) using parent involvement programs to complement and maintain gains as a child completes preschool and moves into the elementary school.

concluded that although parent involvement seemed to be a critical factor relating to the success of early programs, it appeared to have some limitations with families of extremely low socioeconomic status. Parents most willing to be involved in the programs tended to be from the upper levels of the disadvantaged groups. He suggested that parents from the more deprived homes were simply so overburdened with the task of survival that they lacked the time or energy to participate fully in intervention programs.

The second national review of research on intervention with disadvantaged children was conducted by a group of independent researchers, each of whom was operating early intervention programs around the country. These individuals followed up on graduates from their 12 early intervention programs to ascertain success in the elementary grades. Five major kinds of outcomes were reported (Lazar & Darlington, 1979, 1982; Lazar et al. 1977):

1. *Results on assignment to special classes.* Control children who received no intervention were placed more frequently in special education classes than were preschool graduates. There was strong, robust evidence that early education significantly reduced the number of low-income children assigned to special education classrooms.

2. *Results on retention in grade.* Control children tended to be retained at least once in the same grade more often than those who had received early intervention, although results in only one program were statistically significant.

3. *Results on underachievement.* Underachievement was defined as a dual variable—students who were assigned to special education and/or retained in grade and/or dropped out of school. Highly significant results were found across most of the programs. Low-income children who attended early intervention programs were significantly less likely to be classified as underachievers in their later school careers as compared to children in control groups.

4. *Results on what kinds of children benefited most from early intervention programs.* Findings supported the conclusion that preschool intervention makes a positive contribution to late school achievement of low-income children. No evidence showed that the programs helped brighter or less bright children more or less so than others, as determined by tests given before they entered into the programs. Results also suggested that the preschool experience was helpful to children regardless of their sex, ethnic, or family background.

5. *Additional findings.* Preschool also showed effects upon children's specific academic-cognitive skills, self-esteem, and intervention attitudes and values:

a. Experimental children scored significantly higher than controls on mathematics achievement tests, with a suggestive trend toward increased scores on fourth grade reading tests.

b. IQ score increases of preschool graduates at age 6 were attributable to the preschool experience and were independent of the effects of sex, initial IQ, and various measures of family background.

c. Preschool graduates were more likely than controls to give achievement-related reasons for being proud of themselves. Mothers of experimental children tended to articulate high vocational aspirations for their offspring, which were higher than what the children described for themselves. This parent-child discrepancy was not present in the control groups.

Effects of intervention programs on young handicapped children   Research literature on the efficacy of educational intervention with handicapped preschoolers and infants is expanding rapidly. Results reported to date, some of which are described here, suggest that programs are making an impact on the lives of young children. Continuing research is needed, however, to document the exact nature of these benefits, including long-term outcomes.

Results reported on the University of Washington Early Intervention Program for Down's Syndrome Children and its outreach programs (Hayden & Dmitriev, 1975; Hayden & Haring, 1976, 1977; Oelwein, Fewell, & Pruess, 1985), for example, show that early education is successful in generating and maintaining high rates of developmental progress in these children. In previous studies, Down syndrome youngsters who were reared at home with no early education programs showed progressive declines in performance compared to normal peers (Cornwell & Birch, 1969; Smith & Wilson, 1973; Dicks-Mireaux, 1972; Carr, 1975). Down syndrome subjects in the Washington intervention program showed much more positive developmental patterns as a result of their participation. Although they initially were able to perform only 62% of the tasks expected of their normal peers, those who had participated in the program and were between 3 and 4 years of age typically performed approximately 95% of those tasks. Other findings reported were:

- With increasing age, the children did not exhibit the performance declines observed in previous studies of Down syndrome children. At 8 years of age, their performance was still improving.

- Graduates of the preschool at around age 8 were still showing a positive relationship between age and developmental level, whereas the contrast group of children who did not participate in the experimental program seemed to manifest the predicted decline shown in earlier studies.

Outcomes of another intervention program with 33 Down syndrome infants and preschoolers (Clunies-Ross, 1979) had results comparable to those of the Washington Project. All 33 children showed accelerated development after intervention involving a

---

Variously printed as Down's Syndrome, Down's syndrome, and Down syndrome, we have chosen to use the latter except in reference to historical groups, official usages, and in material quoted directly from other sources.

combination of parent training, home-based instruction, and center-based instruction. They demonstrated achievements at above normal levels, and showed decelerating developmental profiles by age 3 or 4.

Numerous other reports attest to the positive outcomes of early intervention for young children with Down syndrome. Infants in a parent/infant program at Boston Children's Hospital attained developmental milestones earlier than a comparison group that had no early intervention (Zausman, Peuschel, & Shea, 1972). Moores (1973) reported that Down syndrome infants who received early tutoring programs from their mothers surpassed controls in both communication and cognitive skills. Another group of infants with Down syndrome, in a home-based program operated by the University of Oregon Center on Human Development, evidenced accelerated development exceeding that typically expected from youngsters with this genetic abnormality (Hanson, 1977).

Benefits of early intervention for young children with other specific types of disabilities have been documented. In a longitudinal study of 749 infants, Hockleiter (1977) reported that of the infants with delays in neurological development who received no intervention in their early lives, 64% later showed moderate to severe motor impairment; but of those who had neurodevelopmental treatment in their early years, 87% were able to achieve a normal lifestyle. Severely hearing impaired children studied by Horton (1976) made significant gains as a result of early training at the Bill Wilkerson Center in Nashville, Tennessee. Those who had intervention before age 3 attained significantly higher levels of achievement on tests of language complexity and academic achievement than did severely hearing impaired children who had no intervention until after age 3. Those who received the earliest intervention and stimulation were more similar to their normal hearing peers on both language and achievement measures. Ramey, Stedman, Borders-Patterson, and Mengal (1978) and Ramey, Yeates, and Short (1984) reported the effects of early intervention with mildly retarded preschoolers. Based on their review of reports from a number of early intervention programs, Ramey et al. concluded that systematic early education programs can produce superior intellectual performance in mildly retarded children over similar groups who do not receive such intervention.

Follow-up data reported by Hayden, Morris, and Bailey (1977) on other handicapped children enrolled in preschool intervention classes in the Washington Model Program also revealed positive outcomes. Their data indicated that:

- Children who participated in the intervention program were placed in special education programs less often than control children who received no preschool intervention.
- Graduates of the preschool program maintained their cognitive gains after they exited from the program. In fact, graduates placed in special education classes were found to score as high on IQ tests as did many children in regular education.
- Preschool graduates who were placed in regular classes did not repeat grades. Their performance records suggested that they were keeping up relatively well with classmates.

Other studies have documented positive outcomes from intervention programs with hearing impaired/deaf infants and preschoolers (Simmons-Martin, 1981), with mildly, moderately, and severely handicapped preschoolers (Bricker & Sheehan, 1981; Karnes, Schwedel, Lewis, Ratts, & Esry, 1981; Moore, Fredericks, & Baldwin, 1981; Schweinhart & Weikart, 1981; Zeitlin, 1981), and with handicapped or at-risk infants (Badger, Burns,

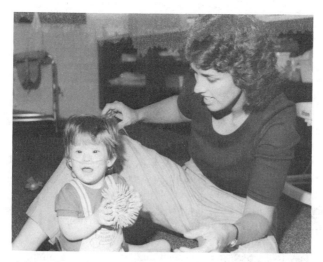

Jeff has been in an early intervention program since birth, when his parents were told he had Down syndrome. This early training is making a difference!

& DeBoer, 1982; Hanson, 1985b; Ramey & Bryant, 1982; Trohanis, Cox, & Meyer, 1982; Dunst & Rheingrover, 1981a).

A report compiled by the Colorado State Department of Education on the effectiveness of preschool special education (see McNulty, Smith, & Soper, 1983) documented positive outcomes and cost benefits from intervention programs for that state's handicapped preschoolers. Results from four Colorado school districts indicated that handicapped children who received preschool intervention compared to handicapped peers who did not (a) did significantly better in school over an extended time period, (b) scored significantly higher on assessments of their developmental achievements, and (c) needed less special education services later on. Nearly 33% of the intervention group entered the elementary grades with no special education services; another 37% entered regular classes with only special education support services.

The *Battelle Institute Evaluation* was a study of national scope on the outcomes of 32 HCEEP* Model Intervention Programs for handicapped young children (Stock et al., 1976). All programs were in their third year of operation. From these 32 programs approximately 18% of the children were pre- and posttested on the Children's Early Education Developmental Inventory. The instrument was developed by the Battelle Institute to test children from birth through age 8 across five developmental domains: motor skills, cognition, communication, personal-social, and adaptive behavior. Assessments were achieved through (a) structured one-to-one testing, (b) observation of the children's teacher, and (c) parent reporting of behavior. A parent survey also was used to measure parent perceptions of program effects, parent-family involvement in program operations, and parental satisfaction with the intervention. Results reported by the Battelle team (Stock et al., 1976) included:

1. *Overall program impact.* Programs had a beneficial impact upon children in four of

*Handicapped Children's Early Education Program.

the five growth areas, with the greatest impact in the personal-social domain and in the motor skills area. In the personal-social domain, pre- to posttest gains of children were 2.3 times greater than what would be expected by maturation alone. Average gain in adaptive, cognitive, and communication domains was 1.1 times greater than expected on the basis of maturation and 1.3 times greater than expected in motor skills.

2. *Impact of program type*. Both home- and center-based programs showed positive impacts upon children. Outcomes across the five growth domains suggested that the home-based programs produced greater impacts than did center-based programs. Center-based programs revealed only one statistically significant impact (in personal-social development), although gains were shown in all areas. Home-based programs, in contrast, showed statistically significant impacts in personal-social, adaptive, cognitive, and communication areas. Programs with structured curriculums appeared to have a greater benefit than programs not using a structured curriculum.

3. *Other findings*. Children who had parents of a higher educational level demonstrated greater gains than those who had parents of a lower educational level, although differences were not statistically significant. Children whose parents carried out daily activities with them at home as prescribed by the project made more gains than those whose parents carried out fewer daily program activities at home (i.e., one per week). Parent satisfaction/support for the programs was high. Benefits parents cited most frequently for themselves included knowledge on how to work with their children and staff assistance in helping them formulate realistic expectations for their child's future.

One of the most recent studies of national scope on the efficacy of early intervention with the handicapped was conducted by Roy Littlejohn Associates (Reaves & Burns, 1982). Outcomes of 280 demonstration projects under the Handicapped Children's Early Education Program (HCEEP), funded prior to 1981, were examined. Notable findings were:

1. The economy of early intervention was suggested in that 55% of children served by the HCEEP programs were later placed in integrated education settings with nonhandicapped children—which were less costly forms of education than specialized placements.

2. Positive developmental outcomes were suggested in that 67% of the children leaving the HCEEP programs performed in the average or above average ranges in relation to their peers, according to reports by staff in the regular or special education programs into which the children moved.

3. A significant return on the dollar invested was suggested; for every HCEEP federal dollar spent, some $18.37 was generated in programming for the children and their families. That is, the federal dollars served as "seed money" to generate additional resources that multiplied the initial investment significantly.

Other notable research of national scope was begun in 1982 by the Early Childhood Research Institute at Utah State University as part of a 5-year program to study the overall efficacy and cost effectiveness of early intervention with the handicapped. Reports on the Institute's research emphasized several findings:

1. Analyses of efficacy studies reported to date on intervention with disadvantaged and at-risk populations document substantial benefits for these children in spite of many

methodological flaws in the research designs (White & Casto, 1984; Casto, White, & Taylor, 1983; Casto & White, 1984).

2. Meta-analyses (or statistical integration) of results across more than 74 early intervention studies indicate that (a) early intervention with handicapped young children produces a positive and sizeable effect, and (b) longer, more intensive programs show the greatest efficacy (Casto & Mastropieri, 1985).

3. Research literature documents many positive outcomes of early intervention, and analyses of the early childhood special demonstration projects approved by the Joint Dissemination Review Panel indicate that programs have demonstrated effective methods of intervention and useful instructional/assessment tools. Continued research is needed, however, which is better designed and better controlled to document outcomes (Casto, White, & Taylor, 1983; White, Bush, & Casto, 1985; White, Mastropieri, & Casto, 1984).

Special needs of families to provide adequate care and stimulation for a handicapped child

★ *Parents need special assistance in establishing constructive patterns of parenting with a young handicapped or an at-risk child and in providing adequate care, stimulation, and training for their child during the critical early years when basic developmental skills should be acquired. Parents are faced with increased and perhaps taxing demands upon their personal, family, and economic resources if they are to meet the caregiving/learning needs of a special child. Because parents' capabilities for singlehandedly meeting these needs 24 hours a day are obviously limited, even for the most conscientious family, early intervention programs provide an invaluable source of support. These programs help the child directly; they help reduce family stress, and they enhance parents' abilities to provide a nurturing environment for the handicapped child.*

Early intervention is equally as important to parents and to the welfare of the total family as it is to the handicapped member. The entire family stands to profit many ways because of the circular relationship between a young child's behavior and that of a parent or other important caregivers. As a child becomes more responsive and manageable, the caregiving role becomes more rewarding, less burdensome, and less demanding. As the caregiver becomes a more responsive, skillful teacher and nurturer, the more likely the child will acquire needed developmental, social, and adaptive skills. A youngster, no matter how handicapped, who becomes increasingly more competent is more likely to be responsive and manageable at home or at school. When both parent and child are engaged in constructive, educationally oriented activities, both experience some sense of progress. In the end, a more supportive environment is created to meet everyone's need in the family.

To care for any young child can be taxing, both physically and emotionally. An infant is totally dependent upon the caregiver for food, stimulation, a change of wet diaper, warmth, and supervision. Daily routines usually have to be arranged to fit the infant's needs. Toddlers are demanding in a different way. Once they are mobile, their incredible curiosity gets them into everything—drawers, cupboards, everyone's personal belongings, and any other interesting object in sight. Because children's rapt curiosity motivates their exploration at this age, they have little understanding of the dangers involved. They reach for everything they see, and their mouths are the means for exploring new objects. This adds up to a caregiver who must be constantly alert to what the child is doing.

Expectedly, a parent feels much responsibility and protectiveness. This is not unwarranted. Young children between 10 months and about 3 years are prime candidates for accidents. Some 80% of all reported accidental poisonings take place within this age group (White, 1975). The predictable negativism of 2-year-olds can be a particular test of parental diplomacy. How does one direct a child's behavior and teach obedience, yet at the same time allow sufficient freedom and independence so the child can learn to be assertive and meet his or her own needs? Mothers learn many lessons about patience and perseverance when their 2-year-old child exerts that independence and exhibits how well he or she understands the meaning of "No!" with its implied "I can do it myself." Preschoolers also demand much attention and require much more structured teaching-learning activities from their parents. An active preschooler whose mobility, curiosity, and growing competence maintains activity that seems to persist 24 hours a day requires tremendous time and energy from parents. To provide a proper balance of structure, freedom, and emotional support is especially challenging to one's parenting skills.

Imagine how all of these demands involved in caring for a young child are multiplied when a youngster is ill—particularly if the illness persists for some time. Dependency is heightened. The child probably is fretful, often is difficult to manage, and may retreat to more immature forms of behavior. Caregiving demands are increased significantly. Care must be more continuous, with less time for a parent's own interests and needs. A similar situation is created with a handicapped child. Physical or cognitive impairments produce greater dependency, special requirements for daily care and supervision, and probably prolonged dependency. For children with moderate to severe disabilities, the most burdensome reality is that the condition will not likely go away in a week, a month, or even a year.

Parenthood is no easy task for anyone, but it can be even more awesome when abnormal physical or cognitive conditions in the child impose greater responsibility upon parents. Yet, families are central to the learning process that occurs in children during their first years. White (1975) suggested that, "The formal education families provide for their children makes more of an impact on a child's total educational development than the formal education system" (p. 4). If a family fails to meet the needs of a young member, that child will face a much less than optimal future.

How do early intervention programs help parents and families and support them in their rearing of a handicapped young child? We have already reviewed Bronfenbrenner's conclusions about the outcomes of early intervention programs for parents. Chapter 10 discusses in further detail the topic of parenting the handicapped child. For purposes of our rationale here, parents can best speak for themselves:

Mrs. Joan P.—mother of a 3-year-old girl with spina bifida and associated disorders:

> Sarah's special preschool was our lifesaver! With the help of her teachers and therapists, she's progressed more this past year than we ever believed she would. It's changed my attitude about her future a lot. That's probably why I'm much more at ease with her. I relate to her better now. For a long time, I didn't expect her to do anything. I vacillated between expecting her to be

normal—which she couldn't be—and not expecting her to do anything. Sometimes I treated her like a helpless infant. I was scared and naive. She seemed so fragile that I hardly dared touch her. I see what a mistake that was now. No wonder she was so frustrated! The program has done so much for Sarah. And it has helped me to be a more realistic parent.

Cheryl D.—single parent of a severely handicapped 4-year-old boy:

I never could leave John alone. He had to be constantly supervised for his own safety and, heaven knows, to keep our own household and personal belongings from being destroyed. It put a lot of stress on our family . . . on me, and on my other kids to be constantly watching, helping, babysitting. John's little sister suffered most. I never had time to do special things with her. I'm usually patient with my children, but it's hard to be patient with this one. I get so tired; sometimes I'd just like a break. It's hard to admit, but sometimes it's so easy to resent John and to be overly punishing with him.

That program [the preschool for handicapped children] was the best thing that could have happened. John is learning how to feed and help dress himself. He's so much more independent and manageable. You can't imagine what that's done for me! It's given me the first free time away from him since he was born. I'm spending a little time alone with his younger sister now. She's really blossomed with the extra attention. I think I'm a better mother for John now—more responsive and certainly more patient. Those parent-home teachers have really helped me solve a lot of problems here at home.

Bill G.—father of a 2½-year-old Down syndrome child:

I felt devastated when the doctor told us Jeff had Down syndrome. One part of me was saying, "He's still your son." Another part of me wanted to walk away and forget him. I resented what had happened to my wife and me. It was hard to even look at our friends' little kids. Fortunately, people from the local Association for Retarded Citizens who had a child like Jeff came to talk with us. They told us about the program for handicapped infants and preschoolers here in town. The first ray of hope we felt came from them. They helped us through some pretty tough times. It took getting involved in really working with Jeff and seeing his progress to help me begin to take pride in him. Now things don't seem all so bad. Jeff's a real person like anyone else. We've learned to love him.

Mrs. Robert K.—parent of a 3-year-old girl with cerebral palsy:

Being a parent seems so easy until you become one. We were just beginning to feel confident as parents with our other two children when Marcia came along. She abruptly changed all that. How do you teach a cerebral palsied infant to roll over or sit up? Things that came so easily for our other kids were things Marcia literally had to be taught how to do. But doing what comes naturally when it comes to being a parent simply hasn't worked with this one. Where are we supposed to learn to be a sort of physical therapist in order to teach her to walk, or hold a spoon and feed herself, or play with a toy? You don't learn those things by reading a book at the public library, and who's ever seen an adult education class on "How to Rear Your Handicapped Preschooler." When it comes to being a parent of a kid like Marcia, it's so exasperating to not know what to do. If there's any time we need help, it's now!

Joyce B.—mother of a moderately hearing impaired and developmentally delayed pre-schooler:

When a doctor tells you your child has a severe hearing loss, you know you've got to do something. But how do you know what to do? Teachers have years of college training to learn how to work with children with these problems. Are parents supposed to acquire all this know-how by osmosis? We really needed help, but there was nothing for us in the city where we used to live. We literally moved to another state, where my husband changed jobs so we could get Melissa into a special program. She deserves a chance like other kids. But it's meant major sacrifices for our family fo find services for her. It's been very hard for us.

Parents of handicapped young children have many needs that can be addressed by early childhood-handicapped programs. *First,* early intervention programs can provide support to parents through a period of time when their own emotions, conflicts, and grief about their child's disability are probably most intense. During this initial period parents establish their pattern of interaction with the child and their attitudes toward the child and toward their parenting role.

Bricker and Iacino (1977) have pointed out that the potentially disruptive effect of a developmentally disabled child on a family argues strongly for the value of early intervention programs. They contend that expecting families and parents to cope singlehandedly with the demands imposed upon them by a handicapped child, especially one who is severely or profoundly impaired, is both unreasonable and unfair. To expect parents to cope with and meet the extra child-rearing responsibilities without the help of trained professionals until the child is of age to attend public school is disheartening. It is to invite the development of parental attitudes that may not be positive toward the child or his or her future in that home. Excessive parental and family stress often is what leads to removal of a child from the home and possibly institutionalization when other actions could have been taken.

Second, early intervention programs can help to foster healthy interaction patterns and appropriate support systems with a handicapped young child. Hayden and McGinness (1977) noted that educators often encounter parents of handicapped children who, after a few years of helplessness and frustration ". . . are so worn down by shock, grief, and sheer physical fatigue thay they have become passive 'do-littles,' defeated at the threshold" (p. 163). One antidote for this situation is early intervention programming for both parent and child. It can support parents at their time of emotional adjustment and stress, reduce their feelings of helplessness, and model a positive interventionist role for them in working with their child. If a parent can assume a change-agent role from the very beginning, during the infant's first few months of life, defeat and passivity may never develop.

Third, early intervention programs assist parents by helping them acquire skills to manage normally expected caregiving needs of their child, as well as the special needs created by their child's handicap. White (1975) observed that parents may be unable to do an adequate or appropriate job of child rearing (a) because of ignorance, (b) because they are under excessive stress as a result of the many burdens of child rearing, or (c) because the necessary support systems and assistance are lacking. The special needs of a handicapped young child may demand new skills on the part of parents. The increased dependency and caregiving demands can add a new kind of stress. Often, parents must become their own experts in nursing, physical therapy, education, and psychology—to name but a few of the skills they need (Hayden & McGinness, 1977).

Economic-social benefits of early intervention

★ *Early intervention implies some economic-social benefits in that prevention or early treatment of developmental problems in young children may reduce cost and prevent more serious, burdensome problems for society later. If children's developmental problems are not addressed until they have obviously interfered significantly with learning, the probability that educational programs can re-mediate them is lessened. Under these circumstances, a handicapped individual becomes only* more *dependent, rather than* less *dependent, upon services and the protection of society. The burden upon the taxpayper thus becomes heavier and more enduring.*

The old adage "An ounce of prevention is worth a pound of cure" is convincing when we look at the cost incurred if a person requires special education services throughout the elementary and secondary school years. Even more costly is institutional or residential care for a mentally retarded or mentally ill person. We can project the economic benefits of early intervention by simply examining annual expenditures in the United States for support of special education, rehabilitation programs, and custodial care of the handicapped.

Costs of special education in the public schools   Exact costs of special services for the handicapped vary depending upon geographical region, grade or age of individuals served, types of services provided, and types or levels of disability represented among the persons served. Budget figures, therefore, must be interpreted with care. They should be viewed as merely suggestive of a range of cost that varies from state to state or program to program. Nonetheless, billions of dollars are spent annually to provide services for the handicapped. In reviewing these cost figures, we cannot avoid asking: Would these costs be reduced if the disabilities that interfered with these people's ability to remain in the mainstream of education and society were identifed and treated earlier?

Results of a major finance study on special education services by Rand Corporation (1981) indicated that excess costs* for direct instructional services were directly proportionate to the severity level of the handicapped youngsters served. According to the Rand Report, average excess costs each year were $2,516 for a blind student, $2,336 for a deaf student, $897 for an educable mentally retarded (EMR) student, and $813 for a learning disabled student. Furthermore, the less restrictive education placement for a handicapped student was less costly than more restrictive placements. Placement in a self-contained special class was an average of $1,578 in excess costs per student, whereas regular class placement with only part-time special class instruction cost $794 per student.

We can illustrate the impact of these costs by describing a hypothetical school district and its special services for mentally retarded pupils. Suppose an EMR student required special education from kindergarten throughout the high school years. Based upon the Rand Corporation figures ($1,578 per student in a self-contained special class per year), this student costs a minimum of $18,936 in excess of the regular educational costs. Now, suppose our hypothetical school district serves 40 EMR students per year in special classes. This represents an estimated cost of $63,120 per year. If these students remain in special education for the 12 years of their school careers, costs compound to some $757,440—nearly three quarters of a million dollars. This does not even take into account increases in cost arising from inflation!**

Considering that nearly 4⅓ million handicapped students in the U.S. received special education and related services in 1983-84 (figures reported in the *Seventh Annual Report to Congress on Implementation of Public Law 94-142*, U.S. Department of Education, 1985), the magnitude of the expense for society to serve the needs of school-aged hand-

---

*Excess costs refer to expenses above and beyond the base cost for regular education provided to all students.

**Caution should be used in interpreting the meaning of these figures in a literal sense. These figures are *average* costs per child. Actual costs may vary from child to child depending upon the programs that are presented individually in the IEP.

icapped children is clearly apparent. If early intervention can reduce the number of children needing special education in the schools or at least reduce the intensity of services required by individual children, significant savings are possible.

Costs of institutional and residential care   The dollars spent annually for institutional or residential care of handicapped persons show that important preventive measures must be considered. Costs would be cut significantly if we could reduce the number of persons requiring total care by teaching them functional living skills, increasing their basic developmental status, and thereby reducing their level of dependency. Early education, coupled with continued quality special education as needed during the school years, can potentially produce significant savings.

The cost of institutional care is exorbitant. Although expenses vary greatly from state to state, average costs range from approximately $38,000 to as high as $70,000 per person per year. In comparison, costs for a person who is cared for in a community group home vary from a low of $9,000 to a high of $19,000 per year (Blatt, Bogdan, Biklen, & Taylor, 1977; Fitzgerald, 1983; Wieck & Bruininks, 1980). Calculated at the lowest costs per year of $38,000 per resident, the yearly cost (for an estimated 1,200 institutionalized mentally retarded persons in one state) amounts to over $45.5 million! Yet, consider the savings if just 600 of the 1,200 persons were able to function adequately in community group homes and to receive care there. With reduced costs of approximately $9,000 per person per year, taxpayers would realize a savings of more than $17.5 million each year. Early intervention is just one step by which the numbers of persons who end up in our state institutions might be reduced so that less costly forms of support will be required later on.

Cost analysis of the benefits of preschool intervention   Direct evidence on the cost benefits of early intervention is now appearing, as follow-up data on graduates of early childhood programs are becoming available. One of the most thorough analyses of the economic benefits and educational/social benefits of early intervention preschool programs is reported on the Ypsilanti Perry Preschool Project (Berrueta-Clement, Schweinhart, Barnett, Epstein, & Weikart, 1984; Schweinhart, Berrueta-Clement, Barnett, Epstein, & Weikart, 1985; Weber, Foster, & Weikart, 1978). The Perry Preschool Project (also called the High Scope Program) served children who were drawn from the population of economically disadvantaged 3- and 4-year-old children in Ypsilanti, Michigan, who tested in the educable mentally retarded range (IQ of 50 to 85).

Cost analyses on the Perry Preschool Program have been based on actual dollar costs required to operate the preschool, in addition to child performance records in the public school following the early intervention experience and released parental time while children were attending the preschool. Other data, from U.S. Census and Employment reports, also helped in making projections on the earning power for experimental and control subjects. Cost data on special education services were obtained from the public schools in Ypsilanti, Michigan. Findings of the cost analysis for the Perry Preschool Project are summarized as follows:

- *Requirements for later special education services.* A substantial proportion of the costs required to operate the Perry Preschool Program was recovered from savings that accrued when graduates required less costly forms of extra educational support as they moved on through elementary and secondary schools. Graduates of the preschool intervention programs required less special education and none were placed into institutional types of care, as compared to children in the control group, who required more service and, hence, more costly forms of special education or institutional care. Thus, the expenditures for initial preventive programs appeared to increase the chance that costs would be lessened later when the children entered public school programs.

- *Projected lifetime earnings of experimental and control groups.* Using previous census data on employment of similar populations, along with records of the children's education progress in elementary and secondary school, their IQ scores, and family background, projections were made on the children's earning power. Perry Preschool graduates showed higher projected lifetime earnings than did children in the control group who had received no preschool training.
- *Value of parents' released time.* Parents' released time, resulting from the enrollment of their children in the preschool intervention program, was considered an economic benefit that amounted to approximately 4% of the undiscounted costs of operating the Perry Preschool. Time can be viewed as money in the sense that if parents are not occupied in one task, such as child care, they can be gainfully employed or engaged in activities that are of some benefit to the home or the community.

Taking into account the data reported above, Weber, Foster, and Weikart (1978) concluded that early intervention offered significant long-term savings. Savings per child for those who participated in the High Scope program were calculated to be $14,819. This amounted to a 243% return on the original dollar investment to operate the program.

Wood (1981) made an extensive analysis of the potential economic benefits of early intervention based upon data collected from studies of various infant and preschool intervention programs. Cumulative costs for special education to age 18 were calculated for a child who would receive services beginning at (a) birth, (b) 2 years of age, (c) 6 years of age with attrition back into regular education, and (d) 6 years of age with no eventual return into regular classes. Her cost analysis was then based upon data indicating that the cost of special education escalates at higher levels. That is, yearly median costs for special education (excess costs) are $2,021 for infants, $2,310 for preschoolers, and $4,445 for elementary or secondary students. Thus, special services begun at birth and ended at age 18 cost a total of $37,273. But if services begin at age 6, costs amount to $46,816 per student if there is attrition back into regular classes, or $53,340 if the student remains in special education until age 18.

Wood calculated that early intervention services begun during the preschool years or before could produce a savings of over $16,000 per handicapped student over his or her total years in school. Furthermore, she noted that the number of children who leave special education to reenter regular education is higher among those who received preschool intervention. To delay early intervention appears only to intensify the need for more special education services later on, which are of greater cost to taxpayers.

Antley and DuBose (1981) reported on the cost benefits for children who attended the Model Preschool Program at the University of Washington. The yearly costs for serving one child in the center were $3,432. They reported that if a child spent 3 years in their program (a cost of $10,296) but was then able to enter into and continue in regular education in the public schools, savings to the school district would equal $29,608 over 12 years. The cost of special education, if required, for one child would equal about

$58,104. If institutionalization were required, it would be even more costly ($38,000 per year in the state of Washington). A child receiving 3 years of early intervention and even 12 years of special education in the public schools would cost $68,400. But if the same child were to require institutionalization for the same period of time, costs would soar to $570,000. Thus, if institutionalization is averted in preference to education in special classes in the home school district, savings would be $501,600.

In summary, these cost figures for special education services have several implications. First, early intervention could help allay many of the problems some children exhibit that lead to their eventual placement in special education programs, institutions, or other, more costly forms of educational and life assistance. Second, the intent of special education is not necessarily to provide an educational system parallel or alternative to that typically available for normal students. The purpose is to prepare students to function as skillfully as possible in the mainstream of education and society.

If we agree with this basic premise, the question becomes one of where we can make our most promising investments with special education dollars? To suggest that all of our dollars should be placed in one type of program would be impractical. No one program, even an early intervention program, will be a cure-all for everything. At the same time, we must face the question of priorities and the issue of where society can gain the greatest return on its investment with children. Prevention or early treatment *before* problems become full blown seems the most practical strategy, whether it be undertaken by medicine, business, or education. Unfortunately, society all too often reacts to a problem *after* it has become a serious one rather than applying a few more powerful preventive efforts.

History in regard to treatment of handicapped persons clearly has shown that the learning problems of handicapped children rarely correct themselves or suddenly disappear. Learning problems continue, and so do the financial burdens they impose upon society. With inflation and rising costs, these burdens can only become greater. This does not mean that all early disabilities can be totally alleviated, but evidence has been cited suggesting that early intervention can reduce the impact of a handicapping condition. It also can reduce the number of children requiring intensive and costly forms of special education and home-care services.*

ARGUMENTS AGAINST EARLY INTERVENTION PROGRAMS

Although the benefits of special services for young handicapped or at-risk children and their parents seem self-evident, some individuals oppose public support of these programs. A few of the more common arguments against early intervention are summarized by Hayden and Pious (1979):

- Costs are too high for services that serve only a small minority.
- Educational needs for other populations of school-aged children place early intervention programs for handicapped children at lower priority.
- Intervention programs have not proven their effectiveness and should not be supported on a wide-scale basis until data are more conclusive.

*For an excellent discussion of the funding of special education programs, see "Financing and Education of Exceptional Children," in F. Weintraub, et al, *Public Policy and the Education of Exceptional Children,* 1976, Reston, VA: Council for Exceptional Children.

- There is not sufficient evidence to suggest a period of life when intervention is more critical than another; intervention at any time other than early childhood may be just as valuable.
- Early intervention programs are primarily babysitting, and what things of value could be taught to a child at such a young age are questionable.

Sometimes those who oppose early intervention programs for the handicapped point out that public support is not given to early education programs for all other normally developing children of the same age. Thus, they argue that public funds should not be spent on a small segment of that age group who are handicapped or at-risk. Their parents should pay for services along with parents of normal children. Peterson (1982a) also noted that opposition is occasionally raised by parents who do not have a clear understanding of parental rights and due process procedures for initiating special services as defined under PL 94-142. Parents of nonhandicapped children sometimes express opposition because they fear their child will be tested and placed in a program without their consent. Concerns of this nature are unfounded. These persons need information about their rights and about due process, which requires parental permission before any child can be enrolled in an early intervention program.

A myriad of other intervention literature could be cited in this chapter. For other comprehensive reviews, the reader is referred to the entire 1985 issue (Vol. 5, No. 2) of *Topics in Early Childhood Special Education*, which covered efficacy studies, and to the following publications: Bailey and Trohanis (1984); Brickman and Weatherford (1986); Dunst (1986); Halpern (1984); Garland, Stone, Swanson, and Woodruff (1981); Meisels (1985); Meisels, Jones, and Stiefel (1983); Simeonsson, Cooper, and Scheiner (1982); and Strain (1984).

SUMMARY

Young children need not be destined to restrictive, subnormal lives because of some initial physical or environmental assault to their well-being. Many developmental impairments are preventable. The impact of other disabilities can be diminished if proper and timely attention is given to help a child adapt and overcome the limitations imposed by the condition. Physical handicaps, sensory impairments, and cognitive disorders do restrict some areas of personal functioning, but their impact need not destroy the potential of every human being to progress normally in other areas of development. Hereditary factors do indeed play an important part in determining human potential, and they are not alterable by educators, but the environment—which plays an equally important role—can be influenced. In essence, it is the only tool we have to improve the lives of children who suffer from limitations imposed upon them by accident, by their genetic inheritance, or by their living circumstances.

Perhaps the oldest and most persistent scourge of mankind that affects children most and destroys their life opportunities is the failure of society to look beyond the handicap and to recognize the potential present in every human being. And a young handicapped child needs help to realize that potential. If any of us as adults were to be blinded tomorrow by some accident, to lose our hearing or our limbs and, thus, our mobility, we would undoubtedly wish to achieve the same self-fulfillment in life that we sought before our catastrophe. We would see ourselves as the same person with the same needs and rights for success, self-worth, acceptance, and personal growth. As adults, we probably would be quite vocal in asserting those rights and in communicating to our friends and family that we are no less a person after our accident than we were before.

Handicapped children who have impairments that interfere with their ability to perform or to benefit from experience are clearly at a disadvantage. Unlike the injured adult who already has had an opportunity to demonstrate his or her potential to others, a child's potential is yet to be seen. In addition, children are unable to be their own advocates and cannot even argue with society to give them a chance to try. They are at the mercy of their environment, and of those upon whom they are dependent for care and nurturance. But children, too, deserve an opportunity to achieve their life potential. After all, they are first children, first human beings, and only secondly persons with some malfunctioning part of their physical self. In some cases, it is not even the child that is irregular. It is an environment that is inadequate and unsupportive to the needs of a growing organism.

In this chapter, information from many different sources has been presented to help explain why early intervention programs are of value. Empirical evidence, theoretical viewpoints, expert opinion, societal values, and simply good argumentative logic support the position presented. To summarize, five significant benefits that come from early education programs for handicapped and at-risk young children are:

1. *Benefits to children* from early intervention come in numerous ways. Remember the three children you met at the beginning of the chapter: Keith, the Down syndrome child; Jessica, the 3-year-old whose development was delayed but for whom no clear etiology could be found; and Matt, the child who suffered from an early and severe hearing impairment. These children and others like them profit greatly from early intervention. They will have help in developing the skills they need as tools for future learning. They will have help before difficulties produce serious problems that will have to be remediated later. They will receive help when they need it, not later, when society may decide it is ready to help but after these children have already suffered their losses. These children will have an opportunity from the beginning to remain with their families and to have the best of all possible chances to achieve their greatest potential.

2. *Benefits to parents* are realized through early intervention. Parents of children like Matt, Jessica, and Keith can be helped to accept their child's limitations, yet to recognize the inherent capabilities that remain. Early intervention programs provide an avenue for parents to learn effective parenting skills that will help them teach and stimulate their special child in ways that can minimize the debilitating effects of a handicapping condition. They can receive support as they work through the initial stages of grief, confusion, and frustration that come with parenting a handicapped child. Early assistance can minimize further disruption in the family unit and establish positive patterns of interaction between parent and child. These benefits can have many desirable side effects as well: an opportunity for increased family solidarity, a possible lessening of the stresses placed on families by the presence of a handicapped child, and a greater probability that parents can find pleasure in the accomplishments of their special child, no matter how large or how small.

3. *Benefits to siblings* are as real to them as they are to parents and the handicapped young child. First, parents can be more responsive to the needs of other family members as they are helped to deal more effectively with the handicapped member. Second, feelings of self-worth can be enhanced when siblings are helped to understand the handicap of a brother or sister and are allowed to be a part of constructive family efforts to help that member. Feelings of frustration and of being left on the outside can be reduced when positive actions are being taken within the family unit. Finally, in families where a child's handicap possibly may be due to environmental limitations resulting from socioeconomic disadvantage, there appears to be a *vertical diffusion* or *spin-off effect* upon siblings. Gains shown by children after participating in an early intervention program often are mirrored in the growth patterns of younger brothers and sisters.

4. *Benefits to educators and professionals* who work with handicapped children occur as a result of early intervention. Special and regular elementary teachers in public schools find it easier to work with children who have already mastered some basic skills necessary for more formalized classroom learning. Otherwise they must spend valuable time correcting inappropriate behaviors, teaching a child to function in a classroom setting, and teaching other basic skills *before* other important kinds of cognitive and developmental learning can begin. So often, teachers say: "If only someone had started working with Johnny earlier, these problems wouldn't be so severe today." "We should be moving onto other important skills, but we had to go back and teach John basic skills he should have mastered long ago."

Professionals are likely to be more motivated and energetic in their own work when they think they have a chance to have a meaningful impact on a child. It is discouraging when one's teaching seems to be too much an after-the-fact attempt to teach skills that should have been addressed and could have been learned more easily years before. For educators who work with children, *time* is an ever-pressing reality. When the discrepancy between a child and his or her peers in developmental status and academic achievement is so wide that there is little probability of ever catching up, teachers also feel the hopelessness and discouragement that parents of a handicapped child face.

5. *Benefits to society* from early intervention are most real when we think of the contributions that individuals like Keith, Matt, and Jessica will make—or fail to make—to the society in which they live. When we multiply these three special children by several thousands and consider the many individuals whose future dependence or independence is determined in part by the educational preparation they receive, we can see the potential economic returns of early intervention. Society benefits as a whole when its members are not overburdened with taxes to support segments of its population who are returning little to the economy. Society benefits when the majority of its citizens are leading happy, fulfilling, and productive lives.

Early intervention will not cure everyone, but it will give children a greater opportunity to realize what potential they have. Blind children will still be blind, but their minds and other tactile and auditory senses need not be "blind" also. Physically disabled children will still be disabled, but they can learn to walk and be independent. *Yes, early intervention can make a difference!*

2
Perspectives on Early Childhood-Special Education

Chapter 1 dealt with the question: Why is early intervention important in the lives of young infants and preschoolers with handicapping and at-risk conditions? Given this background, the next questions are logical: Are programs available to provide the intervention we have argued is so important to their future? What is being done today to meet the special needs of these young children? This chapter addresses these questions. As legislators and the public at large began to recognize the special needs of young children and the value of providing assistance during the early years, the movement for early intervention began. This movement has given rise to a new professional field within education—*early childhood-special education (EC-SPED)*, sometimes called *early childhood education for the handicapped (ECEH)*.

First we will look at the changing values about young children that provided the impetus for this new movement, including the basic premises upon which early childhood-special education is built. Second, we will review the events that launched the movement for early intervention and officially established early childhood-special education as a bona fide area of study and human services. Finally, we will look at the unique features that define the character of EC-SPED as a field. As you read about each of these unique features, you will see how this new field differs from special education as it has been traditionally practiced with school-aged students, and from regular early childhood education as it has traditionally operated for normally developing young children. Some of the emerging issues that the leaders of this young field must begin to address will also become apparent.

A CHANGING PERSPECTIVE

Public and professional attitudes toward the early lives of children who are physically, sensorially, cognitively, emotionally-behaviorally handicapped, and those who are at-risk are much different today from attitudes prior to the mid-1960s. Tremendous change has occurred during the past three decades in how those children are viewed and in what services are available to them. Now we believe that handicapped children can learn and that important learning takes place long before kindergarten. We better understand the value of children's early experiences and recognize adults' responsibilities for providing the stimulation and preparation for schooling that will come later. We now recognize the dangers of concluding too early what a child's future capabilities are or are not. Today, we believe that the quality of living for young children with developmental disabilities can be greatly enhanced through education, training, and acceptance into the mainstream of life that other young children enjoy.

A look at where we were

Had an educator from a foreign country visited the United States in the 1950s to see educational services for young children with handicaps, the tour would have been a short one. As DeWeerd (1981) described conditions that existed then, the visitor would have discovered only a few small, isolated services. The tour might have included a visit to a program for children with cerebral palsy or for blind children operated within a clinic or private residential school. A few private agencies or mental health clinics serving young children with severe emotional disorders might have been included in the tour. A visit might have been planned to a public school where a relatively new program for hearing impaired kindergarteners or preschoolers might be operating. The visitor might have learned that many parents of the children being served had moved to a new location simply to get help.

Our visitor would likely have made other observations, too. First, of the programs that did exist, most served children with one specific handicap—usually a sensory disability such as deafness or a physical impairment such as cerebral palsy. Second, university training programs for preparing teachers of handicapped preschoolers or infants were nonexistent. What training was done was largely in conjunction with private agencies where training focused upon children with one type of handicap. Third, no real services were available for serving infants or children under age 2½ or 3.

The lack of services in the 1950s and before reflected public attitudes about education for the handicapped, particularly those under school age. They were not very optimistic. Children under age 5 with disabilities were a sort of "hidden population." Kept at home, they were not visible. Few opportunities existed for parents of handicapped preschoolers or infants to interact with parents of nonhandicapped children in ways that brought attention to their children's special needs. Furthermore, no publicly supported system of education existed for normally developing preschoolers. Without any precedent for widescale services to this age group, there was no catalyst to stimulate the idea that handicapped children needed something extra during their early years.

This lack of services meant that preschoolers and infants with developmental or physical abnormalities were generally dealt with by their families or by professionals in one of two ways. First, if their impairments were severe and apparent at birth or shortly thereafter, many were placed in institutions or simply kept at home, where they were cared for as well as parents could manage. Efforts to teach these children were regarded as questionable and possibly a waste of time that could be spent more profitably on more capable youngsters. The tactic was to let time pass and wait for the child to master basic developmental skills so he or she could move on to school. Handicapped preschoolers or infants thus received little educational training or special stimulation other than what their caregivers could provide. In some instances, children whose disabilities involved serious medical problems were allowed to die from natural causes by withholding medical treatment. Some people viewed that solution as more humane and realistic for a child whose future seemed so limited.

Second, children with more mild, subtle disabilities typically were handled a little differently. For small children who appeared normal initially, but whose development did not progress as expected, the "wait and see" approach was commonly applied. When parents expressed concern, they often were advised to be patient, give their child more time, and simply wait and see if the problem persisted to warrant treatment. Professionals tended to work under the *medical model*: Treatment was not given without a clear diagnosis of the problem; because developmental delay was not regarded as a serious problem and did not allow a definite diagnosis, treatment was considered unnecessary.

Given those attitudes, little help was available for parents or their children. Special programs for handicapped or developmentally delayed children under school age were almost nonexistent except in a few progressive communities. Even more frustration came when parents discovered that regular nursery or preschool centers were hesitant to take children with special problems who did not fit easily into regular routines. Most preschools had admission criteria that kept handicapped children out: Enrollees had to be toilet trained, able to follow instructions, and capable of functioning within a group. That eliminated most children with handicaps or developmental problems. And if children who were enrolled experienced difficulties or failed to "fit in," they were generally terminated from preschool. Regular programs were not considered responsible for serving that population of children.

The ironic and disheartening result of those practices was that when the excluded children reached school age, many lacked the skills needed to function successfully in kindergarten or first-grade classrooms. The old strategy for dealing with this was to hold children back another year—waiting for them to become "ready" for formal learning. This tactic only ignored their obvious and desperate need for help, but the strategy was justified on the premise that another year of maturation would help. The possibility that training and education would help them acquire skills that would make them "ready for school" was for the most part ignored.

An action-oriented view toward early development

The 1960s brought a whole new perspective about the early lives of children, particularly those who were disadvantaged, at-risk, or handicapped. The importance of the environment and of early stimulation took on new meaning. Researchers, educators, and parents all began to reject the passive "wait and see" approach and to press for more societal responsibility in the lives of children. These adults began to reject the notion that time alone will produce a competent child out of one who is delayed and unskilled in the basic developmental tasks of early childhood. Instead of waiting for a child to *become ready for school*, discussion turned to what parents and educators could do to *get children ready* for formal education.

A search began for better ways to teach basic skills when children were not making progress on their own. This was an important transition. Professionals and society began to take notice of the problems of young children. People began to ask questions: Can something be done? Can the failure of children in public schools be prevented by giving them a "head start" on their education through early enrichment and stimulation programs? Would early education help children be more successful once they started school?

A new set of values about disadvantaged, handicapped, and other young children at-risk gradually began to evolve. Some of these values and their implications are as follows:

1. If medical technology is going to save many children who otherwise might have died, society has a continuing responsibility for them. Obviously, a number of high-risk babies who are being saved are still left with possible physical, sensory, or developmental impairments. If we choose to save their lives by applying new methods of medical treatment, they should not be saved only to then be abandoned and not given the continuing special care they need.
2. Young children, regardless of a disability or condition that restricts their ability to learn, *can* learn. Their ultimate capabilities should no more be prejudged on the basis of some initial impairment than should a normal child's capabilities be prejudged on the basis of race or other physical traits—at least not before educational opportunity and training have been rendered and the child has built up some history of performance.
3. All children have potential that can best be nurtured and developed through education, training, and experience within a rich, supportive environment. A child's potential is most likely to be realized with a supportive-responsive environment and a sensitive caregiver who arranges opportunities that are conducive to learning.
4. Children with handicaps or conditions that interfere with and perhaps delay their developmental progress have the same right to education and to the care they need as do children who are developing normally.

5. Children with physical, neurological, sensory, or other impairments that interfere with normal activities of early childhood need special help. They have to depend on their caregivers and on society to recognize and respond to what they cannot do for themselves. Society and its systems of human services cannot shirk that responsibility.

Given these new values and a growing awareness of the special needs of the handicapped during their formative years, it was time for action.

EARLY INTERVENTION FOR THE HANDICAPPED COMES OF AGE

Public Law 90-538: The launching of a new movement

The early intervention movement for the handicapped began in 1968 with passage of Public Law 90-538, the *Handicapped Children's Early Education Assistance Act (HCEEAA)*. Congressional leaders had taken note of the plight of handicapped preschoolers and infants, and the lack of services for them. They recognized that the paucity of services was attributable, in part, to the absence of any exemplary models for delivering services to this special population of children and their parents. Up to that point the federal government or national leadership had offered little financial support to spearhead action on the problem. In response to those needs, both the House of Representatives and the Senate took action by passing PL 90-538.

The Handicapped Children's Early Education Assistance Act was significant in several ways:

1. It was a landmark piece of legislation in that it was the first in history to deal exclusively with education of handicapped children without being attached to another legislative bill.
2. It provided funds to stimulate and improve upon programs for young handicapped children and their parents.
3. It initiated the development of exemplary model programs for early intervention with handicapped preschoolers, infants, or their parents.

It also initiated other related demonstration, training, and dissemination activities nationwide. The intent of the new law was not to establish widescale service programs such as Head Start. The purpose was to experiment with procedures for working with young handicapped children, to identify the most effective procedures, and then to devise innovative program models that could be replicated in other communities. Thus, under the HCEEAA provisions, 3-year grants were awarded to projects across the country to develop what became known as *First Chance* or *HCEEP Demonstration Programs*.

The sequence of events leading to Public Law 90-538 is described in detail by LaVor and Krivit (1969) and by Harvey (1977). Those events reflect the spirit with which the new movement was launched and the concerns that Congress wanted to address. The action began on May 7, 1968, when Congressman Hugh Carey (New York) and Albert Quie (Minnesota) introduced their bill (HR 17090) to the House of Representatives. Some of Quie's remarks, as co-sponsor of the bill in the House, described its purpose and the motivation behind the proposed law:

Although the need for early educational development is recognized, educators do not have a fixed, positive approach as to how they can solve these problems. . . . We must seek to set up model, pilot programs on an experimental basis and to attempt thereby to determine the best means for helping our handicapped children. (p. H 3439 and as quoted by Harvey, 1977)

On the same day, May 7, 1968, a companion bill to that presented in the House was introduced in the Senate by four senators—Winston Prouty (Vermont), Jacob Javits (New York), Wayne Morse (Oregon), and Ralph Yarborough (Texas). In presenting the companion bill (S 3446), Senator Prouty remarked:

I am convinced that of the several tools we have provided for the children in the past two years, none will have more promise for affecting their lives than this new program. For a parent who discovers in the first day or weeks of the new baby's life that his child is handicapped, it is too much to ask that he wait until that child is 6 before he begins to get special education and training. (p. S 5045 and as quoted by Harvey, 1977)

The Senate bill eventually was included as part of the 1968 Amendments to the Vocational Education Act and was passed on July 11, 1968. In the months that followed, a new version of the original House bill was created. The testimony and remarks made by those supporting HR 18763, the final House bill, described their views about the needs of young handicapped and at-risk children. John Kidd, then president of the National Council for Exceptional Children, commented in his testimony:

We have paid lip service to education. . . . It is truly man's hope for coping . . . but as we are now operating education, it is much too little and far too late for many. (p. 5 and as quoted by Harvey, 1977)

Congressman Dominick V. Daniels of New Jersey, chairperson of the Select Subcommittee on Education, which expedited the bill through Congress, remarked on the significance of the bill for parents:

Few parents are prepared to take care of a child who looks different, behaves in grossly unacceptable ways or fails to respond even to the sound of a mother's voice. Parents of handicapped children may have fears and are often frustrated and bewildered. They need help in understanding their child's disability. They need help in working with their handicapped child. This bill will lead us into a new era of educating handicapped children. In addition, it is anticipated that this legislation will enlist the help of the parents as allies and associates of educators to provide a total program. (as quoted by LaVor & Krivit, 1969, p. 381)

Congressman William A. Steiger (Wisconsin), one of the 25 who acted as co-sponsors of the final House bill, gave the following statement to summarize the rationale behind the proposed legislation:

It has been said that a handicapped child produced a handicapped family and even a handicapped community. Indeed, the magnitude of the effect on the family is difficult to understand. Not so many years ago parents, out of ignorance and futility, often locked their handicapped children in the closets of their homes. While in most cases the physical closets are gone, the closets of the mind still handicap children in regard to their families and communities. H.R. 18763 not only seeks solutions to the educational problems of the handicapped child, but also focuses on the problems of his family and community by encouraging parental participation in the development and operation of preschool experimental centers and efforts to acquaint the community with the problems and potentialities of such children. For it is only through such a coordinated attack that we can begin to open the closets of the mind in which we have all locked the handicapped.

For years we have bowed to the magic age of six as the time for all children to begin their education. This belief has been based on the premise that children before reaching this age will learn naturally from their environment the skills they will need to succeed in formal education. Educators all over the world have proved conclusively that this contention is invalid and this bill also recognizes it by encouraging the establishment of experimental programs for handicapped children from birth to six. (pp. 382-383 and as quoted by LaVor & Krivit, 1969)

On September 16, 1969, the new version of the law was passed by the House, and then by the Senate. Finally, on September 30, 1968, President Lyndon B. Johnson signed HR 18763—to become known as the Handicapped Children's Early Education Assistance Act, PL 90-538 (see Johnson, 1968). That day marks the official beginning of the new field of early childhood-special education.

Developmental milestones for an evolving new field

Once a new movement is launched and a new professional field is created, other achievements are necessary before it can become firmly rooted and established as a bona fide field of study. Following enactment of PL 90-538, several subsequent events helped the new field of early childhood-special education grow and gain a stronger foothold within education and other disciplinary circles. Some of those major milestones are described in the following pages.

The Head Start-handicapped mandate   Any new field first must gain visibility if it is to receive recognition and status as an official field of interest. Broad involvement of citizens and professionals at all levels and in every community across the country is necessary to bring attention to a field. Financial backing is important, too. Project Head Start, a national preschool intervention program for disadvantaged children from low-income homes, brought together each of those three ingredients when it became involved in services for young handicapped preschoolers (see chapter 3 for a more detailed description of Head Start).

In 1972 Public Law 92-424 (The Economic Opportunity Amendments) mandated that Head Start services be extended to handicapped children from low-income families. This mandate required Head Start centers to reserve no less than 10% of their enrollments for handicapped children. Prior to this, handicapped children had generally been excluded from Head Start programs. At least, they were not sought out for participation. The 1972 mandate changed all this by opening the doors of Head Start centers to handicapped preschoolers.

The Head Start-handicapped mandate gave a tremendous boost to the growth of EC-SPED. First, Head Start's national scope brought immediate visibility to the needs of young handicapped children. Second, the Head Start philosophy of comprehensive services brought professionals from every discipline including parents into the effort to serve the needs of this special group of children. Third, Head Start became a well recognized and visible advocate for early intervention with the handicapped. Fourth, Head Start deployed a sizeable portion of its financial resources into its handicapped program component. This fact, and the mere reality that the growth of any field is dependent upon its financial resources and its visibility to the public, suggests that Head Start's investment in services for the handicapped contributed greatly to the growth of early childhood-special education.

University personnel training programs in EC-SPED   If a movement is to grow and establish new programs for its target population, it must have trained personnel. Recognizing this need, the federal Bureau of Education for the Handicapped provided the leadership and financial resources to initiate appropriate personnel training programs in universities throughout the nation. Beginning in the late 1960s and early 1970s, formal university programs for training personnel to work with handicapped preschoolers and infants began to appear.

Simultaneously, State Departments of Education began to define certification guidelines for teachers of young handicapped children (Hirshoren & Umansky, 1977; O'Connell, 1983; Stile, Abernathy, Pettibone, & Wachtel, 1984). This milestone gave the field a much needed identity in professional circles. As undergraduate and graduate training programs were created, interest in the education needs of this young population heightened among university faculty and researchers. As interest grew, a new advocacy group emerged to address the issues and challenges of the new movement. The growth of personnel training programs in EC-SPED was stimulated primarily through two major sources:

1. Federal funds were allocated to universities around the country in the 1960s to build special training and service centers relating to the handicapped. These *University Affiliated Facilities,* or *UAF Centers*, played an important role in spearheading the movement toward interdisciplinary team involvement in special education. UAF Centers were designed for two major purposes:

    a. To bring together the expertise and resources of a number of interrelated disciplines within universities to create innovative, exemplary service programs for handicapped individuals.
    b. To provide a setting wherein university students could receive interdisciplinary training to prepare them for professional roles in working with the handicapped.

    Because UAF Centers primarily addressed unserved or underserved handicapped populations, it is no surprise that many of them created special programs for children under age 6 and for the severely handicapped. Consequently, UAF Centers initiated much of the early personnel training relating to the education of handicapped infants and preschoolers. They also succeeded in bringing about the interest and involvement of *many disciplines* in clinical, educational, and social services.

2. Around 1968 the Bureau of Education for the Handicapped (BEH) began awarding grants to university departments of special education to support teacher training programs in early childhood-special education. In 1974 EC-SPED became one of BEH's top funding priorities to encourage special education departments to create formal personnel training programs. Although special education teacher training programs were well established within universities prior to that time across the more traditional categorical areas (mental retardation, deaf education, learning disabilities, etc.), emphasis had been placed upon training personnel who would serve *school-aged students.* The federal funds made it possible to create separate training programs focusing specifically upon education of handicapped children in their infancy and preschool years.

The founding of a professional organization for EC-SPED   Every growing movement soon requires a forum for its followers to share ideas, and to deal collectively with issues concerning its practices, values, and policies. Without a common meeting ground, a movement lacks cohesiveness and direction. In 1973 representatives within the Council for Exceptional Children (CEC), the professional organization representing special educators in the country, established a new division within its ranks—*the Division for Early Childhood (DEC)*. It was the first formal organization to provide that meeting ground and forum for those concerned with early education of handicapped children. In 1977 the new Division began publication of the *Journal of the Division for Early Childhood*. It was the first journal of its kind to devote exclusive attention to topics relating to the new field. The Division also began distributing its own newsletter, the *DEC Communicator*.

Organization of this new Division within the Council for Exceptional Children was an important milestone for the field of EC-SPED. It marked the passing of an era when early education for the handicapped was viewed as only a topic of academic interest and heralded its coming of age as a field and discipline in its own right. In the same way a person builds a new store front and hoists a sign to announce the opening of a new business in town, so did creation of the Division for Early Childhood serve to announce the birth of an important new field. This milestone gave EC-SPED its formal status as a peer among older, more established members of the education family. In 1978 a second organization emerged, called INTERACT (The National Committee for Very Young Children with Special Needs and Their Families). This organization represents a membership and some purposes similar to that of DEC.

State planning projects   Funding of State Implementation Grants (referred to as SIG Projects) by the federal government provided the impetus for state and local community officials to become involved in the new movement. *SIG Projects* provided incentives for state officials to begin systematic planning and program development in early childhood-special education. Education of handicapped children under the age of school admission had not been considered the responsibility of either State Departments of Education or local public school districts. In fact, it has sometimes been unclear as to where responsibility should lie.

Beginning in 1974 SIG Projects provided a vehicle for states to assess local needs, plan needed service programs, deal with issues of teacher certification, and review state legislative provisions related to funding and delivery of services for handicapped preschoolers and infants. Today, similar federal grants, called *State Planning–Development–Implementation Grants*, continue to provide the vehicle for state departments to develop EC-SPED services.

Public Law 94-142 endorsement of early intervention   Another important boost to education for handicapped children under school age came when Public Law 94-142, the Education for All Handicapped Children Act, was passed in 1975. That law gave formal endorsement to early education programs for children under age 5. It also provided incentive funds to encourage states and local education agencies to serve children from 3-5 years of age. This law is heralded as the single most important piece of legislation passed in behalf of the handicapped. It established that all children and youth between ages 3 and 21 are entitled to a free and appropriate education.

Although the law requires that special education be available to all students of school age, application of the law to children *under* school age is dependent upon state law. States are not required to serve preschoolers or infants if state law prohibits or does not authorize local education agencies to use public funds for handicapped children in this age group (Cohen, Semmes, & Guralnick, 1979). Nonetheless, inclusion of the 3- to 5-year-old population in the law represented an important achievement inasmuch as the legislation:

— formally recognized the importance of preschool education for the handicapped.
— established the public schools as the authorized agency for serving preschool and infant populations.
— paved the way for local education agencies to receive and expend federal special education reimbursement funds for preschool education if state law does not prohibit such action.
— encouraged states and local school districts to provide services to young handicapped children by offering incentive monies for those who elect to do so.

The Amendments to PL 94-142, passed in 1983 under PL 98-199, further supported the development of EC-SPED services down to birth by two notable additions. First, the Amendments provided grants (called State Planning Grants) to states to develop and implement comprehensive plans for EC-SPED services for all handicapped children from birth through age 5. Second, funds received by states under the preschool incentive grant program were opened up for use in services for children from birth to age 3 (Weintraub & Ramirez, 1985).

State legislative mandates for EC-SPED   Some states have responded to the intent of PL 94-142 by passing their own legislative mandates requiring local education agencies to provide special services for handicapped children prior to their entry into elementary schools at age 5 or 6 (e.g., Iowa, Massachusetts, Wisconsin, New Jersey, Nebraska, Maryland). States that have done this have provided a precedent for other states to follow and have added stability to a field in which many states without supportive legislation are still struggling. A few states still have prohibitive legislation that does not allow local school districts the use of certain state or federal funds on programs for children of certain age groups under school age.

New research in EC-SPED   Recognizing the need for research on early education for the handicapped, the U.S. Bureau of Education for the Handicapped began funding several *Early Childhood Research Institutes* at selected university or research sites around the country in 1977. The purpose of the institutes was to promote innovative research on early identification and intervention with young handicapped children. This was another significant milestone for the growing field, because research is an important ingredient in building any new discipline. It is an invaluable source of information for defining policy, building a theoretical base and rationale for its practices, and creating effective methodologies for its practitioners. Without it, a field cannot build credibility or establish its academic and professional footings. The Research Institutes represent a major financial investment that continues today.

The first set of institutes operated from 1977 to 1982 and included: the Carolina

Institute for Research on Early Education for the Handicapped, University of North Carolina-Chapel Hill; Kansas Early Childhood Research Institute, University of Kansas at Lawrence; Institute for the Study of Exceptional Children-Educational Testing Service, with research sites in Princeton, New Jersey and New York City; and the UCLA Research on Early Abilities of Children with Handicaps, University of California at Los Angeles. A second set of institutes was funded in 1982: the Early Intervention Research Institute at Utah State University (emphasis on cost analysis of early intervention); the Carolina Institute for Research on Early Education for the Handicapped, University of North Carolina-Chapel Hill (emphasis on families); and the Early Childhood Research Institute at the Western Psychiatric Institute and Clinic, University of Pittsburgh (emphasis on social development and interaction). (For summaries of the latest EC Research Institutes, see the June, 1983 (Vol. 7) issue of the *Journal of the Division for Early Childhood.*)

Current status of early childhood-special education

If you compare the status of services for handicapped infants and preschool children in the 1950s with where we are today in the 1980s, you will certainly come to one conclusion: "We've come a long way!" You can see evidence all around of the developmental milestones just described, which helped EC-SPED gain identity and recognition as a new field. Other, more specific signs of progress are (Allen, 1984; Beckman & Burke, 1984; Black, 1982; DeWeerd, 1981; Peterson, 1982a, 1982b; Spence & Trohanis, 1985; U.S. Department of Education, 1985):

1. Expanded numbers of agencies are now working in a variety of roles to bring services to young handicapped children and their parents. These agencies include:

   - Some public school districts in communities are now operating programs for 3- to 5-year-olds—and in some sites for infants as well.
   - The Administration for Children, Youth and Families (a federal agency) provides the funding to support Head Start and Home Start programs, which now serve a minimum of 10% handicapped children.
   - Maternal and Child Health or National Institutes of Health are funding states for Crippled Children's Services.
   - State Departments of Education (Special Education Divisions) are providing state-level leadership in planning and developing state and community services for handicapped children under 5.
   - The federal Office for Special Education Programs (formerly the Bureau of Education for the Handicapped) funds preschool demonstration projects, provides preschool incentive monies (under Public Law 94-142) to the states, funds and disseminates research relating to education of and intervention with handicapped young children, and provides financial support for universities to train personnel.
   - The Council for Exceptional Children now encompasses this new interest area and acts as a lobbyist and advocate for programs to serve this young population.

2. Increasing numbers of states are mandating services for handicapped children from birth to age 5 or a part of that age group. A summary of state legislation on mandated education services, given in the 1985 Report to Congress on the Implementation of Public Law 94-142, is shown in Table 2.1. According to that report:

Table 2.1

Summary of State Mandates for Handicapped Children
Aged 6 and Under

Age Range					
0-5	**2-5**	**3-5**	**4-5**	**5**	**6**
Iowa	Virginia	Alaska	Minnesota	Alabama	Indiana
Maryland		District of Columbia	--------	Colorado	Montana
Michigan		Hawaii	Delaware[5]	Florida	Oregon
Nebraska		Illinois	Oklahoma[6]	Georgia	Pennsylvania
New Jersey		Massachusetts	Tennessee[7]	Idaho	Vermont
South Dakota		New Hampshire	Washington[8]	Kansas	--------
--------		Rhode Island		Kentucky	Arizona[11]
Texas[1]		Wisconsin		Maine	Arkansas[12]
		--------		Missouri	Mississippi[13]
		California[2]		New Mexico	North Dakota[14]
		Connecticut[3]		New York	
		Louisiana[4]		North Carolina	
				Ohio	
				Utah	
				West Virginia	
				Wyoming	

				Nevada[9]	
				South Carolina[10]	

Note: States with different mandated ages for particular handicapping conditions and states with scheduled changes in mandated age are shown below the dashed line (--------).

Numbered Notes

Legend of State Terms

A	Autistic
AH	Aurally Handicapped
D	Deaf
DB	Deaf-Blind
HI	Hearing Impaired
MH	Mentally Handicapped
PI	Physically Impaired
SH	Severely Handicapped
SMH	Severely Mentally Handicapped
TMH	Trainable Mentally Handicapped
VI	Visually Impaired

1. Texas   3 —All handicapping conditions
    0 —(VI, HI, DB)

2. California   3 —All handicapping conditions

3. Connecticut   2.8—All handicapping conditions

4. Louisiana   3 —All handicapping conditions
    0 —Children with serious handicapping conditions that, without intervention, will become progressively more difficult for successful intervention by school age

5. Delaware   4 —All handicapping conditions
    3 —(TMH, SMH, PI)
    0 —(HI, VI, DB, A)

6. Oklahoma   4 —All handicapping conditions
    0 —(VI, HI, SH)

Table 2.1 (continued)

7. Tennessee	4	—All handicapping conditions	11. Arizona	6	—All handicapping conditions
	3	—(D)		5	—If LEA offers kindergarten
8. Washington	4	—All handicapping conditions	12. Arkansas	6	—All handicapping conditions
	3	—All handicapping conditions as of 1985-86 school year		5	—If LEA offers kindergarten
			13. Mississippi	6	—All handicapping conditions
9. Nevada	5	—All handicapping conditions		5	—All handicapping conditions as of 1985-86 school year
	3	—(MH)			
	0	—(AH, VI)			
10. South Carolina	5	—All handicapping conditions	14. North Dakota	6	—All handicapping conditions
	4	—(VI, HI, D)		5	—All handicapping conditions as of July 1985

Note. From *Seventh Annual Report to Congress on Implementation of the Education of the Handicapped Act* (U.S. Department of Education, 1985).

- 42 states mandate services to some portion of the preschool handicapped population from birth through age 5.
- Of these 42 states, 19 mandate services for all 3- to 5-year-old handicapped children, and 23 states mandate services for children of certain ages and handicapping conditions within this age range.

3. The number of handicapped children being served before age 5 is increasing steadily. In 1983-84 some 243,087 3- to 5-year-olds were reportedly served under Public Law 94-142. This amounts to an average of about 3% of the U.S. population of children in this age group. The percentage is small compared to an estimated 10%-15% needing services, but this figure still represents a .4% increase over the previous year.

In addition, Head Start serves over 41,000 handicapped children. This, too, represents tremendous progress. An estimated 190,00 handicapped children of preschool age are eligible for Head Start in the U.S. Although all those children are not being served, nor are enough facilities available to do so, the number of handicapped low-income children in Head Start has climbed steadily since the Head Start mandate was passed in 1972. (See Sixth and Seventh Annual Reports to Congress on the Implementation of Public Law 94-142, U.S. Department of Education, 1984, 1985.)

4. Professional involvement in the field has grown by leaps and bounds. For example:
- The Division for Early Childhood within the national Council for Exceptional Children has over 2,500 members, even though the organization is just over 13 years old as of this writing.
- Professional literature concerning EC-SPED, handicapping conditions in young children, and other related topics has mushroomed in the past 10 years. In the 1980

Catalog of Educational Products for the Exceptional Child, which summarizes commercial items being produced for special education students, over one-fifth, or 20%, are being classified under the area of early childhood. New books and other publications are appearing in the professional market at an increasing rate.

These achievements reflect the commitment and vigor with which parents and professionals have worked to establish this new field during the past decade. Strides are being made! But comparing the percentage of preschoolers and infants served with those who remain unserved, the clear message is that we still have a long way to go. The field of early childhood-special education is still very young, and important milestones for the field are yet to be achieved. Some of the major challenges that lie ahead are discussed at the end of this chapter.

PORTRAIT OF A NEW FIELD: ITS UNIQUE FEATURES

Whenever a new field of study or service program is launched, it is greeted with interest and curiosity. What is it about? What are its purposes? How will it bear upon and fit in with the related activities and services of existing fields? By now, you may be asking what early childhood-special education is actually all about and what it really entails. You also may be wondering how the new field resembles or differs from its forerunners— special education for school-aged students, regular preschool/day-care programs for normally developing youngsters, and compensatory education programs (such as Head Start) for disadvantaged students.

Before we describe some features that define the unique character of the field of early childhood-special education and its programs, we will point out what factors influence how a field is defined and how others view it. A new professional field is much like a new baby. A newborn does not have much of a defined personality—not yet. So people describe the baby in several other ways: "Look at all that hair!" "She's such a chubby little thing." Sometimes people avert to describing the new baby in terms of the parents' traits: "He has his dad's blue eyes"; "She's going to have her mother's good looks"; "He looks like his father's side of the family." Sometimes we describe this yet undefined person by projecting parental characteristics onto the child. We might even project a few of our expectations and dreams onto the baby: "I'll bet he's going to be a smart kid"; "He's so big, he'll probably grow up to be a football player like his Uncle Bill."

These descriptions may or may not reflect who this new human being really is or will become. But during the years when a child is just developing, adults are prone to define for them who they are and what they should do. Until children can define their own values and assert their own individuality, others define it for them. Unique styles of behavior, personal traits, and qualities that make up what we call "personality" take time to evolve.

Like a baby, a new professional field is a somewhat undefined entity when it first is launched. Lacking a clear definition of what it is about and what its policies will be, it, too, is easily defined by the characteristics of other fields from which it has evolved. If you ask someone to define a new field, it probably will be defined primarily in terms of *why* it exists. Much of the early discussion about an emerging field centers on why it is important, the needs to which it must respond, and what reasons justify its existence. Or, like the young child who—everyone says—is like Uncle Bill, a new field can be described as a mere extension of the characteristics and practices of its parent fields.

Special educators sometimes describe early childhood-special education as if it were largely a downward extension of special education and its values/traditions/practices as applied to elementary and secondary school students. On the other hand, another group of professionals—regular early childhood educators—commonly describe EC-SPED as an extension of their field. They may describe the new field as an expansion and adaptation of what they traditionally practice in early education and day-care services for normally developing children. Those working in early compensatory education programs such as Head Start may assume that services to all handicapped children can be simply an expansion of their practices and traditions to a larger, broader group of children. The point is that the image you gain of what the new field of early childhood-special education entails may depend upon whom you interview. Because EC-SPED is such a young field, its professional constituency has not yet established nationally recognized policies concerning the practices and values that define appropriate services for preschoolers and infants.

Understandably, one may easily assume that a new field is an extension of its parent fields. Each contributed in significant ways to its birth. Each has relevance to the goals and activities of professionals in the new field. Furthermore, founders of the new field likely come from the parent fields, where they received their training and original experience. To find professionals assuming that the policies, procedures, and features of the new field are or should be extensions of the other areas, then, is no surprise. And, since the new field is yet undefined, it must rely for a time upon the traditions and practices of other fields. Years and even decades must pass for a new field to reach its own clearly defined set of values, philosophies, methodologies, and policies. But given time, a new field, like a young child, will progress through its own developmental stages, evolving into an entity with its own unique character and individuality.

The premise of this text is that EC-SPED is in its own childhood. It inherits a rich set of traditions that led to its birth and that have some applicability to its evolving practices. The contributions from traditional special education (for school-aged students), from regular early childhood education, and from compensatory education are exceedingly important. They cannot be ignored and should be capitalized upon. But EC-SPED is a unique field in its own right. We cannot assume that practices in any one of its parent fields encompass all of what this new field is about. Neither can we assume that practices in any one of its parent fields should automatically be applied to the education of handicapped and at-risk children under age 5. We cannot assume that the policies and practices of any one parent field define what EC-SPED is—or should become.

Instead, the field must develop its own set of practices, drawing from that of its forebears when appropriate, and creating new ones to best address the issues concerning early intervention. Edwin Martin (1970), former Commissioner of the U.S. Office of Education's Bureau of Education for the Handicapped, stressed this unique character of EC-SPED when he stated:

> Early education for handicapped children is not just an extension of elementary education downward to children in their earlier years. It is a field of study in itself, with its own values and goals, and reasons for being, outside of preparation for education programs that will come later in a child's educational career. (p. 7)

What are the unique features that describe the evolving character of early childhood-special education as a field and distinguish it from its forerunners? In the pages that follow, nine features are presented to describe its evolving practices, philosophy, and character. Each feature defines what the field and its services for young children are about and reflects some of the emerging issues that must be confronted as the field continues to grow.

A blend of practices and values from three parent fields

★ *Early childhood-special education is a field that represents a blend of the practices, teaching methodologies, service delivery methods, and values that come from the three parent fields from which it has grown.*

Three primary fields within education—*special education, early childhood education,* and *compensatory education*—comprise the major roots from which early education for the handicapped has evolved. Were it not for accomplishments in each of these "parent" fields over several decades, EC-SPED would not exist today. (Those historical achievements and a description of how each field helped pave the way for the birth of the field of EC-SPED are described in chapter 3.) Even now, as this new field continues to grow and develop its own identity, the contributions and inputs of all three parent fields continue to shape its character. For example, though regular early childhood education has dealt primarily with the needs of normally developing preschoolers, its teaching methodologies and concepts about child development influence the planning of programs for handicapped children as well. Out of that field have come specifications for enriching children's environments and early experience and for providing the kinds of stimulation that foster normal development in young children. These can be of tremendous help to teachers in planning programs for handicapped children.

Similarly, though the field of special education evolved in response to the educational needs of handicapped students in our elementary and secondary schools, some practices have application to a younger clientele. Methods for prescribing individualized education and treatment programs, strategies for adapting educational materials, and methods of teaching by small increments are applicable to any handicapped learner, including the very young. Finally, although early intervention programs created as a part of the compensatory education movement focused primarily upon disadvantaged children, the intervention approaches have applicability to the handicapped. Significant research findings and principles about what constitutes effective intervention have come from programs such as Head Start and Follow-Through. As a result, this field offers a rich background of experience and know-how about effectively intervening in the lives of young children.

In summary, each of the three parent fields forms an important part of what early childhood-special education is as a field. No one parent field, by itself, however, can provide the methodology or the complete perspective of what is required to meet all the needs of handicapped young children and their parents. If one accepts the premise that EC-SPED represents a *blend* of the principles and practices of special education, early childhood education, and compensatory education, several implications can be derived. *Professionals from all three groups must work together, share responsibilities, and cooperate in developing the new field and its unique service delivery systems.* This is a significant point because, traditionally, these three fields have functioned separately from each other; each has operated programs for children under distinctly different administrative systems. But each field cannot view EC-SPED as a division falling solely under its own administrative and programmatic umbrella. Otherwise, that same separatism is easily perpetuated now when the question arises: Who should be involved in the development and administration of services for young handicapped preschoolers and infants in our community? Through cooperative planning and involvement of all three fields, the resources, expertise, and service delivery systems of each can be shared to build functional systems of services for children with handicapping and at-risk conditions.

A cross-categorical field

★ *Early childhood-special education is a cross-categorical field in that it addresses children with all types of disabilities, all levels of impairment, and ranging in age from birth to age 5 or 6 (depending on when they begin school).*

The field of early childhood-special education is unique in that its professionals deal with services for an unusually broad array of children with special needs. EC-SPED encompasses children with cognitive, physical, and neurological disorders, hearing impairments, vision impairments, severe health or behavior disorders, and multiple handicaps. It even includes children whose development is delayed or deviant in some way but who do not yet have a clearly diagnosable disorder. The field includes children with mild, moderate, and severe kinds of developmental difficulties. It encompasses children during rather different phases of their growth—infancy, the toddler stage, preschool and kindergarten years. Such a diverse population of children adds greatly to the complexity of early intervention programs. It also dramatically expands the potential roles and competencies needed by professionals who work in EC-SPED programs.

Because of the diverse population of children under the EC-SPED umbrella, personnel in this area must be versatile. One EC-SPED teacher may operate a cross-categorical preschool classroom containing children from 2½ to 5 years old with mild to severe handicaps of all types. Another teacher in a large city program may be assigned to teach a classroom of 3- to 4-year-olds with more narrowly defined needs. Children may be clustered into groups such as those with speech/language delays, physical/motor impairments, or general developmental delays and mild handicaps. Another EC-SPED teacher may work with infants and their parents in a home-based program. Still another person may act as a consultant to early childhood personnel in regular centers who are mainstreaming children with a variety of mild types of handicapping conditions. Consider the flexibility and the variety of skills one would need to be prepared to work in just one of these professional roles!

The significance of this diversity among the children served by single EC-SPED programs is more apparent if we contrast the field with special education for school-age children. Special education in our public schools encompasses a diverse population, too, but there is a major difference in how they are served and the roles that personnel assume. Special education teachers in elementary and secondary schools do not work with the entire spectrum of special education students. Instead, they are highly specialized and work with only a narrowly defined group of students. Teachers are trained and certified in categorical areas (mental retardation, behavior disorders or emotional disturbance, hearing impairments, visual impairments, learning disabilities). In some instances, personnel are further specialized to work only with students who have handicaps at one level of severity (e.g., mildly retarded only or moderately retarded only).

Personnel in early intervention programs do not work with such predictable groupings of children or in such precisely defined roles. Because children ages 0-5 with handicapping conditions are a low-incidence population, their numbers are small compared to the numbers of nonhandicapped children in regular preschools. Consequently, personnel serving preschoolers and infants with special needs must be prepared to serve a small and diverse population whose characteristics vary from year to year and from community to community.

The cross-categorical nature of early childhood-special education programs has major implications that affect both the training of personnel and the design of early intervention programs, as follows:

1. Early childhood-special educators must be prepared to function within a variety of roles. Because they may be employed to work with different combinations or groups of children, trainees need skills for working with children (a) at different age levels, (b) with different handicaps and disability levels, (c) with different functioning levels, (d) with different types of groupings, which may include integrated groups of handicapped and nonhandicapped youngsters or totally segregated special groups, and (e) in different types of service settings (e.g., home-based, center-based, hospital- or clinic-based). This can be a big order for both the trainee and the training institution!
2. The diversity of children to be served within EC-SPED programs demands that services and the systems for delivering them be flexible. Characteristics of children to be served and their breakdown in regard to things such as numbers at each age level, handicapping condition, and severity of disabilities will differ from program to program. It will also vary from year to year within the same program. This means that service needs will change if programs are to be matched to clientele needs.
3. The cross-categorical nature of the field and its services makes individualized planning of services for each child especially important. Given the potential diversity of children who may be enrolled in one program, services cannot be planned to aim at the middle of the group. Neither can they be planned on the basis of what a theoretical group of 3- to 5-year-olds might be like. Given the lack of predictability about what the composition of special children will be in neighborhoods, individualized planning to match the program with the unique population of children served becomes especially important.

A field with a purpose of intervention

★ *Early childhood-special education is first and foremost an intervention program for young children with handicapping and at-risk conditions.*

As an intervention program, the purpose of services for this population of children is to:

— minimize the effects of a handicapping condition upon a child's growth and development and maximize opportunities to engage in the normal activities of early childhood;
— prevent, if possible, at-risk conditions or early developmental irregularities from developing into more serious problems that become deviant to the extent that they

are labled as handicapping.

— prevent the development of secondary handicaps as a result of interference from a primary disability, which may alter a child's ability to seek out or receive certain types of stimulation, to profit from experience, to learn, or to progress through expected developmental sequences.

This intent distinguishes EC-SPED in significant ways from traditional special education for school-aged handicapped students and from regular early childhood education. For example, the intent of *special education in public schools* has been to serve students with existing, diagnosed disabilities by offering remedial, corrective, or supplemental instruction. The goal is to provide extra or special supplementary help so a student can function within regular education settings, if at all possible, or eventually return to that setting. Or the intent is to offer alternative educational opportunities for students who cannot function within the regular educational mainstream because of their disabilities (as in the case of students sometimes referred to as educable, trainable, or severely multiply handicapped).

Regular early childhood programs, on the other hand, typically have focused on another set of purposes. They center primarily upon *educational enrichment*. Parents' reasons for enrolling their normally developing children in a preschool and the preschool's objectives with those children may be social exposure and experience, preparation for kindergarten, day care while parents work, or simply enrichment to enlarge a child's experiences in ways that enhance development.

EC-SPED is more than an enrichment program and more than a remedial one, although it does encompass both of these dimensions to some degree. The purpose of EC-SPED intervention programs goes beyond enrichment in that the intent is to specifically teach children the developmental skills they need that may not evolve normally as a result of the experiences most children have. Likewise, the purpose of EC-SPED goes beyond remediation. Remedial education implies that a child already has failed to develop age-appropriate skills. The intent of early intervention programs is to take action *before* problems become full blown and provide help *before* children fall far behind their peers. The goal is to facilitate developmental processes through therapy, extra stimulation, and direct teaching.

Because the major purpose of EC-SPED is that of intervention, not merely enrichment or remediation, significant implications follow. These affect the nature of services and the way in which they are delivered. Ask yourself: If the goal is intervention, what must a program offer if it is to truly intervene in the lives of young children in an effective and timely manner? Does an effective intervention have elements that go beyond what would be considered a good educational program whose purpose is one of enrichment?

When the intent of a service program is that of intervention, time becomes a critical element. A sense of urgency pervades the planning and delivery of services. Lost time or programs that do not identify and address a child's special needs will not likely provide a true intervention. As Zigler (1978) pointed out, this spirit of urgency presses for application of the most efficient methods of intervention during a limited time period. This concept of attempting to reach intervention goals within the specific restricted time frames of the preschool child has not been common in special education for older students, nor has it characterized regular preschool services.

Research and the experiences of professionals in early intervention programs clearly have suggested that effective intervention requires at least four major ingredients. Services must be *intensive, comprehensive, continuous,* and *focused upon the individual needs of each child* (Moore, Anderson, Fredericks, Baldwin, & Moore, 1979; Westinghouse Learning Corporation, 1969; Bronfenbrenner, 1974; Datta, 1979). To achieve these ends requires service systems that are unique to EC-SPED and a blend of practices drawn from traditional approaches within each of the various parent fields.

First, if EC-SPED programs are to be a true intervention, services must be *intensive.* A preschooler or infant who is not developing normally and who will not learn normally without help requires daily educational intervention if at all possible. Special training with an infant or preschooler just 1 or 2 days a week for 20-30 minutes without follow-up is not a realistic approach if the goal is one of intervention. Traditional weekly schedules of regular preschool programs allow a normal child to attend 3 or 2 days a week (Monday-Wednesday-Friday, or Tuesday-Thursday) for 2-3 hours each time. Program schedules like these, if applied to handicapped children, reduce the intensity of the services. This in turn may reduce the chances for accelerating development so that the child can catch up or develop skills that are not emerging at the expected rate. The greatest chances for effecting change come when help is given more frequently. Effective EC-SPED training programs offer a good return for the investment of tax money if they do the job they are intended to do. This means that EC-SPED programs must include service delivery approaches that allow staff, parents, or both to work intensively with a young child.

Second, effective early intervention services must be *comprehensive* in that they must address the needs of the whole child. Development across all skill areas and a child's well-being physically, cognitively and experientially, and nutritionally is so intertwined that difficulties or disruptions in one area can affect progress in others. To treat just the problem area when dealing with a young child only puts a band-aid on the problem. There is a good chance that difficulties will appear in other areas of the child's development. This knowledge was well recognized in the design of comprehensive intervention programs such as Head Start. Thus, in designing effective EC-SPED programs, program content should be planned to deal with *all* areas of a child's needs and to coordinate the activities of all professionals who treat the child so that a coordinated, effective intervention can be rendered.

Third, effective intervention implies that if learning is to be accelerated to help a child avoid falling further behind peers, services should be offered *continuously.* This means that the traditional 9-month school year used in public schools with elementary-secondary students, followed by a 2½-month summer vacation, is not the best approach for effectively intervening in the lives of young children. Research and the experience of practitioners in the field tell us the greatest gains are made and then maintained when programs are longer and when children and their parents are not left several months without services (Palmer & Andersen, 1979; Datta, 1979). If we intend to intervene, we must provide assistance continuously—year round and, if possible, 4-5 days a week. Once intervention is begun with a child, services should continue until the time comes to enter public school. To provide continuous early education is obviously a costly proposition. This is another reason why new methods of service delivery have to be created for EC-SPED programs and why interagency cooperation and collaboration may provide a means for more economical and effective services.

A field with its own service delivery approaches

★ *Early childhood-special education employs a broad range of alternative ap-proaches for delivering early intervention services to infants, preschoolers, and their parents. These extend beyond approaches traditionally used in any one of its parent fields of special education for school-aged students, regular early childhood education, and compensatory education such as Head Start.*

One of the distinguishing characteristics of EC-SPED programs relates to the tremen-dous flexibility and creativity shown in delivery of services for this young population. Given the conditions under which services are created in each community—which are unique to every community—variability has been inevitable. As a result, the absence of a standardized system of service delivery from state to state or even within individual states is no surprise.

Administrative and program arrangements for delivering special education to school-aged students follow rather predictable, standardized formats, as you will see in chapter 8, Service Delivery Approaches. No matter where you live, special education students in elementary or secondary schools are likely being served through special classes, resource rooms, special schools, or itinerant consultants who help regular classroom teachers deal with the special needs of handicapped students. Furthermore, elementary and secondary schools operate under rather standardized administrative organizations. Regular preschool and day-care services for children under school age follow somewhat predictable patterns. Head Start programs, too, are organized around a service delivery system that is consistent with programs everywhere. The field of EC-SPED, however, is characterized by highly varied systems of service delivery that differ from state to state and even from program to program.

The variability in service delivery approaches within EC-SPED programs has occurred for several reasons. *First*, programs across the country are not operated by parallel organizations or agencies or under similar administrative structures. They are operated by public schools, private groups, citizens' advocacy organizations, universities, profit-making agencies, churches, and a number of other entities. Each has its own administrative organization and financial resources. This fact alone produces considerable variability in how services are delivered. *Second*, the age group served in any particular state, commu-nity, or even within an individual program may vary. What makes for an appropriate service delivery approach at one site may be quite inapplicable at another. *Third*, the number of children served and their geographical dispersion vary. *Fourth*, local resources for creating and supporting programs financially differ because funding sources are not standardized. *Fifth*, the handicapping conditions, the level of severity among the children served, and the total number of children needing services may differ greatly. The geog-raphical dispersion of children also will affect what service delivery approaches are most feasible. *Sixth*, the fact that some states have mandates (requiring school districts to provide services for a defined age group under kindergarten age) and that some states have no mandates produces considerable variability in services across the country.

Given these diverse conditions under which services currently are rendered to young children around the country, differences can be found on several dimensions: (a) the age of children to whom services are offered, (b) the primary target of those services, whether it be the child, the parents, or both, (c) the types of specific services included in the program, (d) the types of professional or paraprofessional staff employed to deliver the services, and (e) where the services are delivered, whether in an early childhood center, a clinic, at home, or some combination. (These are discussed in detail in chapter 8.)

A field with its own curricular priorities

> ★ *Early childhood-special education is a field in which curriculum and learning activities for the young handicapped child in early intervention programs reflect unique priorities that differ somewhat from those of traditional special education for school-aged students or regular early childhood education for normally developing preschoolers.*

The argument that public funds should be expended to support special programs for a select group of handicapped young children implies that they need something beyond what is offered in regular early childhood programs where any parent theoretically could enroll a child. It implies that those children need something extra or different to help them develop the skills their nonhandicapped peers acquire on their own through the normal course of events. For the handicapped child, time is especially important in the design of an early intervention program. The point is to capitalize on the formative years of a child's life by directly teaching the skills needed rather than waiting for them to emerge. For these reasons, greater emphasis is placed in early intervention programs upon *goal-directed training* and *more structured, individual activities*, designed to teach specific skills.

This difference in curriculum priorities is apparent if we contrast what parents of normally developing preschoolers typically want in a preschool with what parents of handicapped children want. Ask parents of handicapped or at-risk children why they enroll their child in a program and what they want for their child. Their answers usually include the following:

- To teach the child specific skills (how to walk, talk, feed himself or herself; how to play with other children, etc.).
- To help the child in areas in which he or she is not progressing as expected.
- To keep the child from falling too far behind other kids of that age because of a special problem or handicap.
- To help the child deal with some behaviors he or she has not been able to manage yet (such as being nonresponsive, noncompliant, or difficult to handle).
- To provide special therapy for the child in speech and language, motor development, or other specific areas.

Then ask parents of normally developing preschoolers why they enroll their child in a preschool or nursery school program. They likely will give one or more of these reasons:

- Social experience and the opportunity for the child to play with other children of the same age.
- Preparation for kindergarten, including familiarity with group situations and some basic skills that will make the transition into kindergarten easier.

- Extra exposure and learning experiences beyond what are available at home or in the immediate neighborhood.
- Good quality child care during the times parents are working, and a place to leave their child where his or her time will be constructively engaged in meaningful activities.

Regular early childhood programs generally are designed to respond to this latter list of needs. Programs are arranged to offer a rich variety of experiences and opportunities that facilitate normal developmental processes in young children. Activities are planned to give children choices, to entice interest and curiosity, and to enlist involvement in activities from which they will learn and discover new things in their environment. Thus, the curriculum typically is organized around activities such as story time, free play, snack time, outdoor play, field trips, group discussion time, art and music activities, and daily living activities such as cooking or making products. Highly specific objectives or individualized training programs for individual children are not typical or even necessary. More broadly defined goals that define the kinds of experiences all children need are usually adequate and work well for the enrichment purposes under which those programs operate.

Curriculum for school-age handicapped students reflects another kind of emphasis. Priority is placed on individualized planning of learning objectives and activities for each student, based on assessment of the student's strengths and weaknesses. An individual prescription based on that assessment defines the special curriculum he or she receives. Curriculum content for school-age students focuses primarily upon academic subjects— reading, spelling, arithmetic, writing, and subject areas such as science, language arts, and social studies. With more severely handicapped students, the curriculum focuses less on academic skills and more upon developmental skills such as motor development and cognitive skills.

EC-SPED reflects some of the same curricular emphases and learning activities found in both of these parent fields—the objective-based curriculum and individually prescribed programs typical of special education in the public schools and many of the curricular/learning activities found within regular preschool settings. But EC-SPED has some unique curricular priorities, too. Instead of defining curriculum primarily in terms of activities that are desirable for all young children, curriculum typically is defined in terms of developmental training areas that comprise the focus of a handicapped child's prescribed treatment program. Thus, curriculum in EC-SPED programs is more likely to be described in terms of language/speech training, fine and gross motor training, self-help skills, preacademic and cognitive learning, social and play skills, and special therapy. Specific, individually planned activities may be set for each child in these areas with short- and long-term goals written in a formal education plan or IEP.

If curriculum and learning activities place greater emphasis upon the mastery of specific developmental skills, this has implications for the nature of the resulting EC-SPED programs. First, when curriculum priorities and goals are so specific, teachers are more likely to define daily activities for each child. The teacher determines what the child will do rather than giving the child freedom to pick and choose activities. Second, daily activites are likely to be more structured to assure that each child works through a planned sequence of training/learning activities. Third, with specifically planned goals and objectives, more staff involvement in individual planning is necessary to define how each child

An appropriate early intervention curriculum for this 4-year-old girl is much different from the kind of education we provide to school-aged special education students.

will be helped to achieve these. This necessitates specific planning and curriculum design for every child, which in turn demands greater staff teamwork and planning. Less emphasis usually is placed upon group activities and free play, and more emphasis upon small-group and perhaps one-to-one instruction or therapy for each child. (Teaching and curricular considerations are discussed further in chapter 11.)

A field with its own assessment procedures

★ *Early childhood-special education is a field in which assessment procedures and their content differ somewhat from those typically practiced either with school-age handicapped students or with normally developing preschool-age children.*

The types of assessment applied with small children and their uses represent another dimension on which early childhood-special education differs to some extent from each of its forebears. Assessment procedures are commonly used in programs serving handicapped preschoolers and infants for five major purposes: (a) for casefinding and screening to identify children with developmental irregularities that warrant follow-up and possible intervention, (b) for diagnostic purposes to identify the nature of specific problems in areas of physical, sensory, motor, cognitive, and social development, (c) for developmental assessment to identify a child's functional skills and skill deficits so that an individualized intervention program with specific goals and treatment objectives can be outlined, (d) for monitoring each child's daily progress in the skills targeted for specific training, and (e) for assessing the overall outcomes of the intervention program.

Although these evaluation purposes are familiar to special educators who work with older students in public schools, such involved assessment procedures typically have not been used by personnel in regular early childhood programs serving nonhandicapped children. Extensive assessment procedures usually are not necessary given the clientele being served or the purpose of regular early childhood programs.

Assessment procedures with young children involve a determination of their developmental status across skill areas that differ from those assessed with elementary school students. Assessment with young children generally concerns skill areas such as gross and fine motor development, physical growth and development, self-care skills, cognitive development, speech and language skills, and so on. In contrast, assessments with school-aged students typically focus on academic performance as in achievement testing, or diagnostic evaluations for determining the nature of a child's learning problems. The latter involve intelligence tests, tests of mental ability, personality tests, or some combination of these. Also included are tests on specific performance areas such as language, perceptual motor behavior, and achievement tests in reading, math, and spelling.

Assessment with young children presents a unique set of challenges. How can meaningful evaluations be done with children so young? Compared to assessments with school-aged students, obtaining valid and reliable assessments with preschoolers and infants is much more difficult. The testing process itself presents serious problems. For example, diagnostic or academic achievement testing of elementary students usually involves a battery of tests administered in a few 1- to 2-hour-long testing sessions. Each test is administered just once. What the student does in the testing situation is assumed to be representative of his or her abilities. Standardized tests presume students are motivated to do their best. These assumptions cannot be made with an infant or preschooler. Furthermore, one-time assessments to evaluate the developmental or mental status of very young children are not practical for three reasons:

1. The behavior of young children varies considerably from day to day depending upon their physical and emotional status or conditions within the environment. One-time assessments may not accurately reflect a child's true abilities or developmental status.
2. Young children are in a period of rapid growth and development; thus, they do change quickly and learn new behaviors over just a few weeks or months. Skills that were not in place one month may be mastered in a short time.
3. Early signs of abnormal or delayed development or a poor test score may not necessarily be predictive of the same difficulties at a later stage or point of time.

In summary, the assessment of preschoolers and infants focuses on a different set of skills than those assessed in school-aged students. How assessments can best be conducted represents another dimension in which practices with young children differ from those with older students. When small children are involved, more frequent reevaluation and monitoring of behavior changes are necessary to keep up with their constant change in behavior. Early test scores are not good predictors of future intellectual or academic status. Interpretations placed upon test results, therefore, must be made with caution. (Special problems and considerations in evaluating children under age 5 are discussed in detail in chapter 7.)

A field requiring its own system of identification and labeling

★ *Early childhood-special education is a field in which the identification and labeling of young children who need services calls for a different kind of procedure than that traditionally used in regular early childhood education programs, in Head Start, or in special education for school-age students.*

The field of early childhood-special education faces a unique task in identifying candidates for early intervention and in establishing appropriate criteria for determining their eligibility for services. This raises a number of issues—ones that have not yet been resolved. Traditional methods of diagnosis used to identify and then label disabilities of school-aged students needing special eduation are not particularly appropriate for preschoolers and infants. As for identification practices in regular early childhood education, assessment of children for purposes of separating out a particular subgroup of children simply has not been a part of that field. Similarly, though Head Start might be termed an intervention program, identification of its clientele has involved only the use of data on parental income. Child assessment and diagnosis have not been a traditional part of Head Start's recruitment procedure.

As a field, EC-SPED faces some major issues in terms of the use of traditional diagnostic labels as a means for identifying children needing early intervention. Special education in the public schools has a well established tradition—now set by law in Public Law 94-142—that students shall not be given special education until a clear diagnosis of disability has been made. The student's handicap must be classified under one of the standard categories and must meet the diagnostic criteria (e.g., mentally retarded, sensorially impaired, emotionally disturbed, learning disabled) before he or she is eligible for special education services. This follows in line with the traditional medical model. Before special education can be initiated, the problem must exist and be of sufficient severity that it can be diagnosed. Although this procedure is practiced with school-aged students, much debate continues about the use of labels and their stigmatizing effect.

Using labels for preschoolers and infants who need intervention is highly questionable. The intent is to intervene in the lives of young children *before* problems have compounded into diagnosable abnormalities or before physical disabilities have interfered with development in other areas. To require diagnosis using traditional diagnostic criteria thwarts the very purpose of early childhood-special education programs. Also, categorical labels of disability are difficult to apply to young children because diagnostic criteria are often inappropriate for young children, and are nonfunctional for purposes of recruitment.

Physical disabilities, brain damage, or diseases that cause impairments can be diagnosed medically. Thus, they present fewer problems as diagnostic criteria. But disabilities involving disorders that are inferred indirectly from assessments of cognitive skills and behavior present serious problems in regard to the young child. The definitions for mental retardation, behavior disorders, and learning disabilities described in chapter 6 contain diagnostic criteria written largely for older children. How then does one make a fair, reliable, and definitive diagnosis of mental retardation in a preschooler or infant? What is a learning disability in a preschooler or an infant, and how would it be manifest? What is emotional disturbance, and how can it be diagnosed with confidence? Must one wait until a definitive diagnosis can be made while the child also waits for the early education that might prevent that diagnosis from being made later?

In short, early childhood-special education requires a new and fresh approach to the task of identifying and labeling early problems in young children. Application of traditional disability categories to infants and preschoolers, when the purpose of early childhood intervention is to minimize and possibly prevent the eventual diagnosis of "handicapped," suggests that applying labels before beginning intervention is inappropriate (and perhaps unfortunate).

The state of Washington is exemplary in the steps it has taken to define a "handicap" in a preschooler or infant in a more functional, appropriate way; eligibility guidelines for children under age 5 who can be served in early intervention programs avoid using the old categorical labels for diagnosis. This is an excellent case in point that categorical diagnoses do not have to be used to identify infants and preschoolers who need help, and to get services to them. The Washington eligibility criteria are contained in Table 2.2. This is a good example of how the pitfalls of inappropriate labels and the dangers of premature labeling can be avoided.

A field representing multidisciplinary involvement

★ *Early childhood-special education is multidisciplinary, involving services that overlap several professional fields. Effective intervention requires the input and cooperative teamwork of many professional disciplines and agencies who serve young handicapped and at-risk children and their families.*

The professional skills of persons from a variety of disciplines have always been an important part of the education and habilitation of the handicapped. A particularly important feature of early childhood-special education, however, is its heightened need for multidisciplinary input and its actual use of interdisciplinary or transdisciplinary teams to deliver services to children. Why such multidisciplinary inputs and teamwork are so valued is apparent if we consider:

— What are the special needs of young handicapped and at-risk children?

When a special problem or condition interferes with development, the impact is likely to be seen across all aspects of a child's development. Thus, if intervention efforts are to be effective, attention must be given to a child's total well-being, including physical, sensory, motor, linguistic, cognitive, and social development. Developmental progress across all these areas is highly intertwined. Delay in one area may interfere with development in another. Progress in one area facilitates gains in another. Intervention approaches must address a child's needs in every developmental domain. No one discipline alone has the capabilities or know-how for serving all those needs.

— What special services are necessary to meet the multiple needs of handicapped and at-risk children?

Comprehensive service programs are necessary if the multiple needs represented within a single handicapped child or in a group of children with different types of disabilities and severity levels are to be met. Child assessment, educational programs, special therapy, parent counseling and training, medical and nutritional intervention, and social services to the family are just a few of the possible components of an early intervention program. But how can these multiple service programs be rendered? What

Table 2.2
Eligibility Criteria for Handicapped Children, State of Washington

___

Definition of and Eligibility Criteria
For Developmentally Handicapped Preschool Students

A preschool student from birth until of chronological age to be eligible for first grade shall be considered to have a significant delay and to be developmentally handicapped if the student is functioning at 75% or less of his or her chronological age in two or more of the following developmental areas: fine motor, gross motor, expressive language, receptive language, social, self-help, cognitive, or sensory development.

All students considered for initial placement in special education as preschool developmentally handicapped shall be assessed and determined eligible for special education and related services according to the following:

(1) An annual multidisciplinary assessment of developmental level obtained from a functional profile that addresses performance in the following areas:

(a) fine motor, (b) gross motor, (c) expressive language, (d) receptive language, (e) social, (f) self-help, (g) cognitive, and (h) sensory.

(2) The assessment team shall include an individual trained in early childhood education or an individual with knowledge in the area of the student's suspected disability and two or more of the following as appropriate:

(a) psychologist, (b) physician or other qualified medical practitioner, (c) audiologist, (d) occupational or physical therapist, (e) school or public health nurse, (f) communications disorders specialist, (g) social worker, or (h) teacher.

(3) The functional profile shall be derived from individually administered, standardized, or professionally recognized developmental scales that result in chronological age equivalents. Observations and interviews shall be administered by the assessment team. Information obtained from the tests, observations, and interviews shall be compiled by the multidisciplinary team leader and . . . summarized according to the procedures . . . . A student shall be considered as having a significant developmental delay if he or she exhibits a deficit of 25% or more in any two of the areas listed above.

Provided. That in cases where the multidisciplinary team assessment of the student's developmental level has been concluded and where the results do not document a 25% deficit in two of the eight developmental areas provided for in the eligibility criteria, and a qualified medical practitioner has documented that the student has a high predictability of future developmental delays and is in need of special education and related services, the assessment may recommend placement in a special education program. The student who becomes eligible for first grade, based on chronological age, during the school year may remain eligible as a preschool student for the remainder of the year.

___

Note. From *State of Washington Rules and Regulations for Programs Providing Services to Children with Handicapping Conditions,* Chapter 392-171 of the Washington Administrative Code (amended and adopted August 19, 1980)(p. 16), Olympia, Washington: Office of the Superintendent of Public Instruction.

single discipline, or its representative, is in a position to deliver services of such a comprehensive nature? The combined effects of many professional disciplines are needed to create comprehensive services.

— What single discipline can administratively act as the sole agent to render a full range of services?

Current systems of educational, social , health, and family services that relate to the needs of children who are either handicapped or under school age are spread across several different agencies. Educators typically work under their own administrative systems and service networks. Health professionals work privately or are part of public health and welfare service systems. Social and family service professionals are usually part of social welfare service agencies. Yet all these services, operated under the auspices of different administrative systems, comprise part of the total service package for children and their families.

To complicate matters, individual agencies and their respective disciplines are usually charged with responsibilities and given funds to support only one type of service. Typically, education agencies are funded to provide education to children but not to parents and families. Social service agencies have funding for social services to families but not for educational services. Health agencies have funds for only health services, not for educational needs. Interdisciplinary and interagency cooperation is required to bring these service systems together into a combined effort that addresses the total needs of their common clientele (Peterson & Mantle, 1983).

Each of the above considerations points to some realities that have shaped the character of early childhood-special education as a field. The most obvious reality is that no one discipline has claim on all the expertise or know-how for building programs that can meet the total needs of these young children and their parents. A second reality is that EC-SPED, by its nature, is not anchored within any single professional area. Early intervention with handicapped young children is not the sole interest of special educators, of child development specialists, or of specialists in speech and language pathology. It is not the sole interest of social workers who work with families, or of health professionals who are concerned with the health and development of young children.

Because numerous disciplines have a vested interest in young children, the handicapped, and the welfare of families with special needs, several human service agencies hold partial responsibility for serving the same population. Often, professionals representing the various disciplines relating to handicapped preschoolers and infants are scattered across several different service systems. Seldom do they all fall under the jurisdiction of just one agency and one service system. This has important implications for the field of early childhood-special education. That is, though multiple agencies and disciplines have interest in young handicapped children and their needs, their efforts usually are not coordinated in a meaningful way. Thus, if effective, comprehensive, interdisciplinary programs are to be designed for young handicapped children, disciplinary expertise has to be drawn from more than one service agency. (Chapter 11 describes in more detail the interdisciplinary aspect of early intervention programs.)

A field involving parents as team members

★ *Early childhood-special education involves programs in which parental inclusion as team members and as participants in the actual intervention process is crucial if the intervention is to be successful.*

The heightened importance of parent involvement in the intervention process is another distinguishing characteristic of early childhood-special education. Effective intervention requires teamwork between parents (or the primary caregiver) and professionals if the best interests of young children are to be served. In fact, research on early intervention programs (discussed in chapters 1 and 10) tells us that children make the greatest and most lasting gains when their parents are a part of the intervention process.

Parent involvement is not an unfamiliar concept in any of the related fields from which EC-SPED has developed (Mallory, 1981). What is unique is that, in regard to parent involvement, EC-SPED calls for a combination of the traditions practiced by all three "parent" fields in order to achieve its own goals of intervention. Traditional forms of parent involvement in special education within elementary and secondary schools primarily have related to parent participation in planning the individualized education program (IEP) with school staff. Parent participation also has occurred through parent-teacher conferences and occasional school or classroom activities. Parents have not been involved much in day-to-day instructional activities of school-aged students. Teachers and school staff have assumed primary responsibilities for ongoing learning activities. Further, because students typically spend most of their day at school, less importance has been placed upon continued instructional activities when students go home. Parents may assist with homework or reinforce their children's efforts at school. These styles of parent involvement have applicability to early education programs for younger children and represent meaningful ways in which parents can provide support.

If we look at styles of parent involvement in regular early childhood education, another set of traditions becomes apparent. Because the use of IEPs is unique to special education, parent involvement of this nature generally has not occurred. Parent involvement in regular early childhood education takes on a different kind of emphasis. For example, because they usually provide their child's transportation to the early childhood center, parents frequently observe their child's activities in a preschool or day-care center. Consequently, they tend to be more aware of daily routines in the preschool classroom and interact more with center staff. This, in turn, means that they can assume more interest in a child's daily activities, accomplishments, state of well-being each day, and other events in their child's life.

Early childhood staff and parents typically develop a much more active line of communication because of this frequent contact. Parents are involved in class activities such as field trips, birthdays, special events at Christmas and other special occasions. They also may be involved in making materials or equipment for the classroom. In programs serving very young children, parent involvement and staff-parent contacts are encouraged. It is a time when parents are highly interested in (and also feel responsibility for) their child's activities. These practices certainly are applicable to programs or centers serving young children who are handicapped or at-risk.

Parent involvement in compensatory education programs such as Head Start offers some additional avenues for including parents in significant ways—as advocates, fund raisers, community liaisons, recruiters of other parents whose children need services, and participants in parent support groups. These forms of parent involvement, too, serve a useful and important function in EC-SPED programs.

Early childhood-special education thus offers almost unlimited options for including parents, stemming from not one, but all three of the "parent" fields. Other types of parent involvement, unique to EC-SPED, also are being used. For example, parents play invaluable roles as a source of evaluative information about their child. In fact, they may serve as a part of the evaluation team to assess their child's developmental status and to monitor progress. Parents may be more actively involved in the actual educational and therapeutic interventions with their handicapped child in EC-SPED programs. At times, they act as the key interventionist in working with their own child at the center or at home under the guidance and consultation of professionals. EC-SPED is unique in its extensive options and alternative ways for assuring parental involvement in the child's intervention program. Of course, programs differ considerably from site to site as to the type and extent of parent involvement they feature.

THE CHALLENGE AHEAD

What lies ahead? The greatest challenge for the new field of early childhood-special education in the future is an obvious one. Many needy infants and preschoolers with handicapping or at-risk conditions still remain unserved or underserved. As Dr. Edwin Martin (1979) suggested, "We need to set a goal for the '80's to serve every handicapped child from birth on." If services are to expand, the field of early childhood-special education, with its pioneers, practitioners, and advocates, must address several pressing needs (Anastasiow, 1981; DeWeerd, 1981; Greenberg & Calderon, 1984; Hanson, 1985a; Peterson, 1982b; Smith, 1984; Swan, 1981; Zigler & Berman, 1983):

- The need to designate clearer agency responsibilities for service to this young population of children and their parents. The responsibilities and jurisdictions of several educational, social service, and health agencies overlap considerably.
- The need for better coordination and collaboration among agencies that have interest in the handicapped, in young children, and in family services. Collaboration is needed at all levels—local, state, regional, and national. This should allow more sharing of resources, as well as reducing costs and avoiding duplicated services.
- The need to develop a new definition of "handicapped" or "at-risk" as it applies to children in their infancy and preschool years. This should be a definition recognized by all disciplines and agencies serving this population. It is difficult to provide services, identify eligible children, and achieve the purposes of intervention when there is no appropriate or commonly accepted definition.
- The need to build greater public awareness of the importance of early intervention for handicapped and at-risk children under age 5 or 6. Greater awareness among public leaders whose decisions affect early education programs (such as state legislators and congressmen, local city and county commissioners, and state and local education boards) will help initiate programs and gain financial support for them.
- The need for greater awareness and education of professionals from various disciplines who are serving or will be called upon to serve handicapped preschoolers and infants,

including physicians and other members of the health profession, educators, specialized therapists, social service personnel, and administrators of service agencies.

- The need to develop effective strategies or methods that apply to this young population in regard to (a) service delivery, (b) methods of teaching or training young children, (c) parent training, (d) interdisciplinary teamwork, and (e) interagency coordination. This includes demonstrating the efficacy of early intervention programs and strategies.
- The need to create new programs or to expand existing ones to assure that each offers a sufficient array of services to meet the comprehensive needs of handicapped/at-risk children and their parents. EC-SPED programs must be designed in ways that offer effective intervention as contrasted with those that merely offer enrichment activities or day care.
- The need for training practitioners from many disciplines to apply their expertise to preschoolers and infants and to the handicapped or at-risk. An associated need is to train professionals to work not in isolation but, rather, as effective members of interdisciplinary or transdisciplinary teams.

As EC-SPED continues to expand its services and grow as a professional field, a myriad of issues must be confronted. The degree of individuality and maturity reflected by a new field relates partially to the extent its members have addressed the issues relating to its practices. Through clarification of values underlying the field and its practices and resolution of those issues, policies governing a field evolve. Each of the 10 features of EC-SPED that you have read about not only describes evolving characteristics of the field, but each also raises a number of issues—most of which have not been resolved. Some of those issues that professionals in the field will be addressing in the years to come are reflected in the following questions:

- Can professionals bring together the best elements of special education, regular early education, and compensatory education to build a system of early educational intervention that effectively addresses the special needs of young handicapped/at-risk children? How?
- Can we create ways of locating and identifying children who need help *before* their developmental problems have progressed to become serious or before one disability has compounded into other developmental problems? Can we devise effective statewide systems for identifying children early enough so that *intervention* can truly be offered? How?
- Can we apply the lessons we have learned about the ills and stigmatizing effects of labeling school-aged students as we now attempt to identify and recruit preschoolers and infants needing help? Can we avoid the pitfalls of premature and inappropriate labeling? How?
- Can we devise ways of delivering services to children and their parents, in both urban and rural areas, that are both cost effective and comprise effective, appropriate intervention? How?
- Can we design programs to address the special needs of a diverse population of children so that each child receives individualized and appropriate intervention? How?
- Can we design early intervention programs that avoid unnecessary segregation of children from their normally developing peers, who provide helpful models of developmentally appropriate behavior? Can we do this and still be able to provide the intensive,

comprehensive, and continuous services needed if an effective and timely intervention is to be rendered? How?

● Can we devise ways of involving parents in their child's intervention in ways that benefit both but that do not place unfair expectations or excessive pressures on parents? How?

Section III (Delivering Services to Young Children with Special Needs) gives information related to planning appropriate assessments, service delivery approaches, teaching approaches, and overall intervention programs for special children. As you read the chapters in that section, you will gain some perspective on how some of these issues and questions can be addressed.

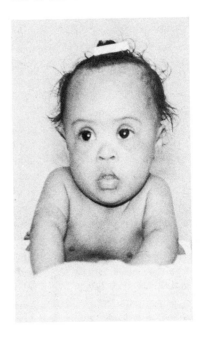

Shelby has Down syndrome. Will the state and community where she lives provide the services she needs? If it were your choice, could you refuse her special help?

Passage of PL 99-457 in October of 1986, which amended and reauthorized the Education for All Handicapped Children Act (PL 94-142), represents another major achievement for the field of EC-SPED. Under those Amendments, Congress appropriated significantly more incentive monies for preschool intervention services with the expectation that all states will have established services for all eligible 3- to 5-year-old handicapped children by the 1990-91 school year. Congress also provided specific guidelines and new funds directed at services for handicapped infants/toddlers from birth through age 2 and their families, encouraging states to establish a system of *coordinated, comprehensive, multidisciplinary, interagency programs*. Infant services are to be based upon an *Individualized Family Service Plan*, which includes case management.

SUMMARY

Early childhood-special education is a relatively new field, formally launched in 1968 with passage of the Handicapped Children's Early Education Assistance Act (PL 90-538) to address the special needs of young children with handicapping and at-risk conditions. EC-SPED emerged as a result of achievements in three related or parent fields (special education as practiced with school-aged handicapped students, regular early childhood education with normally developing children, and compensatory education including Head Start), which paved the way for its birth.

Though EC-SPED is a field in its own infancy, it is growing rapidly and has established its roots as a bona fide field of study through events such as: (a) the Head Start mandate for services to the handicapped, (b) establishment of university personnel training programs in EC-SPED, (c) funding of its professional organization (Division for Early Childhood under the Council for Exceptional Children), (d) funding of model intervention programs throughout the country, including state-level projects (SIGs) to promote state planning with funds from PL 90-538 and the current State Planning–Development-Implementation grants under PL 94-142, (e) passage of legislative mandates in several states, requiring services for handicapped preschoolers and infants, and (f) the launching of research on EC-SPED through funding of several institutes by the federal government beginning in 1977.

EC-SPED is a unique new field with its own identity and purposes for being that set it apart from its forerunners. Though it inherits a rich legacy of educational philosophy and practices from its parent fields, new policies and service delivery approaches are needed to fit the unique population of young children whom the field addresses. This means professionals cannot and should not automatically assume that practices characterizing the parent fields are appropriate to handicapped/at-risk preschoolers and infants or to the circumstances under which effective intervention programs must be implemented.

Nine key features describe the unique qualities of this new field. EC-SPED is: (a) a unique blend of practices and values from its parent fields, (b) a cross-categorical field serving children with all types of handicaps and all severity levels, (c) a field in which the program emphasis is on *intervention*—not just enrichment or remediation, (d) a field with its own unique service delivery approaches and needs, (e) a field with its own curriculum and educational priorities, (f) a field with its own assessment needs, procedures, and issues, (g) a field requiring its own system for identifying and classifying children who need services, (h) a field involving the inputs of many disciplines with expertise and responsibility for the same population of young children, and (i) a field involving parents as partners in the intervention process.

Professionals face a number of challenges in the years ahead as EC-SPED continues to grow as a field. For example, how can professionals from the three parent fields merge their interest and work together in ways that benefit young handicapped children? What policies will be established to define the services that EC-SPED should encompass, and what procedures are to be used to deliver them? What definitions of handicapping conditions should be used with infants and preschoolers, and how should eligibility for services be determined? What roles and responsibilities should various agencies assume in cases where their activities overlap? What service approaches offer the most effective and cost-efficient means for intervening in the lives of these young children? What strategies can be used to build better public support for programs to serve the large percentage of handicapped infants and preschoolers who still are unserved or underserved?

3
Historical Roots of Early Childhood-Special Education

Have you wondered why the notion of early intervention did not become popular until the 1960s and 1970s? Why did early intervention programs for disadvantaged, handicapped, or at-risk preschoolers and infants take so long to evolve? Were their special needs not apparent decades ago?

The notion of early education for preschool-aged children is not new. Centuries ago, early philosophers such as Comenius (1592-1670), Rousseau (1712-1778), and Pestalozzi

(1747-1827) stressed the importance of early childhood as a time of learning and planted seeds of thought about the education of young children. Some of the first nursery schools appeared in the late 1800s in Germany, England, and Italy. The concept of special education for the handicapped is not new. Special education programs began to appear in the 1800s, slowly increasing in number until the late 1940s, when the special education movement began to gain momentum. Those special programs, however, focused upon school-aged children until the late 1960s. Even the concept of early intervention is not new among educators. As far back as 1769, Jean Frederick Oberlin attempted to establish educational programs for impoverished children in Germany to improve the quality of their care. Nursery schools operated by the MacMillan sisters in England and by Maria Montessori in Italy in the early 1900s were created to reduce the deplorable neglect suffered by poor children. What is new is the merging of these three concepts—*early childhood education, special education,* and *early intervention*—into a single educational movement focused upon handicapped children from birth to school age. As you learned in chapter 2, this merger has occurred in just the past two decades.

One might ask: If the reasons for early intervention are so strong and the benefits so clear, why did it take so long for programs to be created? What events brought parents and professionals into action to provide early education not only for normally developing young children but also for those with developmental disabilities? As you will see in this chapter, the catalyst that brought about the birth of EC-SPED as a field through a synthesis of these three areas into one came only as other related social, political, and philosophical issues were addressed over many decades.

HISTORY AND ROLE OF THE ZEITGEIST

Historians speak of the *zeitgeist* to explain why certain historical events or discoveries fail to occur in one decade, yet occur readily in another. The zeitgeist is the spirit of the age, the trend of thought and feeling during a particular time. The zeitgeist serves as the catalyst for new ideas, inventions, or practices to be discovered and then to take hold in a society. If the spirit of the times is not ready for a new idea—even if some foresighted person conceives of it—its discovery will go unnoticed. Its significance will neither be recognized nor accepted. Many significant discoveries and ideas have been greeted initially by society as the preposterous fantasies of a mad scientist or of a "radical" because the zeitgeist was not ready for such thinking. Thus many ideas are born. But if the spirit and trend of thought of the times do not provide fertile ground in which a new idea can flourish, it will simply be lost. Later, when society becomes more accepting of such innovative thinking, the idea may be unearthed by another pioneer who will build and elaborate upon it.

History is filled with examples in which new ideas were born but the zeitgeist was not prepared for them. For instance, Copernicus (1473-1543) defied religious thinking of his day (that man and earth are the center of the universe) when he conceived his geocentric theory of the universe. Knowing the Church would be against him, he dared to present his ideas only as mere speculation. Not until after his death was his theory published suggesting the earth was simply one of many planets circling the sun. Versalius, who lived in the mid-1500s, is considered the father of modern anatomy. Yet, in his time authoritative traditions set by a previous scholar dictated the principles of anatomy. There was no room for a contradictory view. Versalius' ideas were not recognized or given credibility until almost a century later even though they were far more accurate than the ideas of his predecessor.

In more modern times reformers have advocated equal rights for all U.S. citizens and pointed to the inequities suffered by minority groups. Yet, until the 1960s, such blatant inequities in America were not seriously considered to be problems. The zeitgeist and the civil rights movement of the 1960s finally caused Americans to address the gap between our creeds and our social practices with Black Americans and other minority citizens such as the handicapped.

The influence of the zeitgeist is demonstrated repeatedly in the events preceding the birth of early childhood education for the handicapped. One of the best examples is shown in the events surrounding the appearance of the first pioneering studies on the effects on early intervention with young handicapped children. In the late 1930s Harold Skeels and Howard Dye conducted a study of 13 retarded children under age 3 after they were removed from a sterile, depriving environment and placed in a more stimulating, nurturing one. You will recall from an earlier description of this study (chapter 1) that Skeels and Dye reported startling findings. The children showed marked IQ gains while a comparison group of children who remained in the original substandard environment showed significant IQ losses over time. Today, those findings would be greeted with enthusiasm. Improvement of cognitive functioning in young children is believed to be plausible because we now recognize the impact of environmental factors upon development. But at the time of the Skeels and Dye experiment, the thinking of the times was much different. Human traits were considered to be an unchangeable entity fixed by heredity and dependent upon maturation. To challenge that notion or to present evidence to the contrary was unthinkable.

Public reaction was indignant when Skeels and Dye reported their findings. As Kirk (1977) described it: "The wrath of God fell upon Skeels." Professional colleagues responded with disbelief and ridicule. Accusations were even made that the data were fake. Had the times been right, Skeels' study could have launched early education for the handicapped back in the 1930s. But it did not. Despite the fact that researchers and educators were beginning to herald the importance of the early childhood years, and despite the popularity of nursery schools for "normal" children, the concept of early intervention with the handicapped did not take hold.

UNDERSTANDING OUR HISTORICAL ROOTS

Why is the history underlying a professional field so important? Edwin Boring (1950), author of a noted history book on the field of psychology, explained why history is so crucial to psychologists. The same reasoning applies to those in special education and related professions. According to Boring, every professional (and student) needs historical sophistication within his (or her) own sphere of expertise. He explained it this way:

> Without such knowledge he sees the present in distorted perspective, he mistakes old facts and old views for new, and he remains unable to evaluate the significance of new movements and methods. A psychological sophistication that contains no component of historical orientation seems to me to be no sophistication at all. (p. ix)

The historical beginnings of early childhood-special education hold special significance because events and traditions of the past continue to affect its development. Although EC-SPED has only a short history of its own, it inherits a rich legacy of values and educational practices established within the professional fields that preceded it and paved the way for its birth.

Three separate fields of education form the roots from which EC-SPED has emerged: (a) special education, (b) early childhood education, and (c) compensatory education (from which has come the early intervention movement). Achievements in each of these three parent fields paved the way for professionals to begin addressing the educational needs of handicapped preschoolers and infants. Special education first had to establish programs for handicapped students in our public schools, where attendance was mandatory, before it could give attention to exceptional children under school age. Regular early childhood education had to be established firmly as worthwhile and beneficial for young children in general. Had this not been achieved first, early education probably would not have been regarded as a useful or therapeutic experience for handicapped children. Educators also had to first accept the notion that early intervention could be an effective means of improving the educational performance of children, especially those from impoverished homes, who were simply lacking some readiness skills. Only then did educators begin to view early intervention as a means for minimizing the impact of handicapping conditions in young children.

EC-SPED, one must remember, is still in its own infant stages of development, and its own traditions are just now being formed. The field is still vulnerable to the social and economic ravages that thwarted the growth of its predecessors and delayed its own emergence until recent years.

HISTORICAL PERSPECTIVES ON SPECIAL EDUCATION

Special education as we know it today evolved primarily in response to the needs of school-aged handicapped students. Because of mandatory school attendance laws, special education logically would focus first upon youngsters in this age group. Hence, special education philosophy and service delivery practices have been built largely around the educational delivery systems in place within our elementary and secondary schools.

As a field, special education is relatively new. But its development into the discipline it represents today is the outcome of a long, colorful drama covering many decades. Its history encompasses many interrelated but separate events spanning the social, political, scientific, and educational arenas of our society. In a sense, the history of special education is an *account of change in societal attitudes* toward handicapped and deviant persons. It is the story of growing awareness and concern for the welfare of oppressed minorities who were not, until the past few decades, in a position to speak for themselves and be heard.

The history of special education also is an *account of continual educational experiments*, conducted by educators who demonstrated the benefits of training and educating handicapped persons. Their experiments, the educational "miracles" of their time, have shown that handicapped persons can learn, too. The deaf have learned to communicate. The blind have learned to read and to achieve academic feats not believed possible. The retarded have learned functional skills demonstrating that they, too, are capable of learning if given the opportunity.

Finally, the history of special education is a *story of change in societal values and policy* concerning the rights of its citizens, including the handicapped, and of change in educational principles and practices. Special education has been and continues to be an important catalyst for change in the broader system of American education.

Societal attitudes toward the handicapped

Looking back into history, attitudes toward the handicapped can be described in regard to four broad periods. In earliest times, handicapped persons were subjected to inhumane treatment and persecution. Ancient Greeks and Romans saw the disabled as bad omens, cursed by the gods, and unworthy of human rights. Deviant and malformed children often were killed or taken into the wilderness and left to die. A few more fortunate ones were chosen for the high position of fools or court jesters; they were cared for in their master's castle in return for entertainment they provided. Despite their coveted position as court jesters, they were laughed at and subjected to demeaning treatment. The Renaissance and the Reformation are considered as times of enlightenment; yet these movements brought continued persecution for the handicapped. People whose behavior was strange or unexplainable (this included many retarded, mentally ill, or disabled persons) were believed to be possessed by the devil. They were put in chains, thrown in dungeons, or subjected to cruel treatment by those who sought to exorcise evil spirits from them. Scholars such as John Locke began to suggest new ideas about the nature of man and about education, but these innovative thinkers were too few to bring about immediate change against a greater wave of traditional thinking.

The spread of Christianity marks a second period in history, when handicapped persons were protected and pitied. This was reflected in early European history and later repeated in early America. Protective homes and residential institutions were established by a few who stood as advocates and protectors of the handicapped. In the early 1800s *Johann Guggenbuhl* established his famous institution in Germany, where he hoped to cure cretinism through systematic treatment and good health care. In his time the medical cause of cretinism was unknown, but his leadership and worldwide travels provided the impetus for building institutions for the mentally retarded and other handicapped persons throughout the world.

In America one of the first residential institutions was built for the deaf in Hartford, Connecticut, in 1817. A school for the blind was established in Watertown, Massachusetts. Perkins Institute for the Blind in Boston was founded by *Samuel Gridley Howe* around 1832. Initially, these institutions were built to offer training and education, but over time, when funds became limited and interest lagged, many institutions (particularly those for the mentally retarded) deteriorated into places of custodial care. This imposed another form of neglect and deprivation upon the handicapped persons confined there.

A third period encompassed the development and expansion of educational programs for the handicapped. Beginning in the early 1900s and continuing until the late 1950s, special education services expanded gradually, but growth was characterized by spurts of interest followed by times of stagnation and disinterest. Economic depression in America, coupled with intermittent dissatisfaction with poorly planned programs and inadequately trained teachers, contributed to the vacillating support given to special

The special education movement resulted in the recognition that handicapped children have a right to education and that youngsters like this child can learn and profit from special training.

education for the handicapped during this time. Although care facilities and educational programs did increase in numbers, the approach was largely one of segregating and isolating the handicapped from the rest of society. The attitude was still one of "identify-hide-and-forget."

A fourth and final stage is reflected in our current society, where legal and legislative actions have established that all handicapped youngsters of legal school age are entitled to a free and appropriate public education. Prior to 1975 school districts were not obligated to serve handicapped children considered too difficult to teach. They could refuse admission with the justification that a child was unmanageable, unfit for traditional forms of education, nontoilet trained, uncooperative, or simply too retarded to be teachable. As a result, many handicapped students simply stayed at home. With the passage of Public Law 94-142 in 1975, exclusion of handicapped students is unlawful. Integration of the handicapped into the educational and social mainstream of society also has been a significant trend during this fourth period. Segregated special education classes were once the means for educating these children. Now a range of alternatives is offered to allow the best possible placement for meeting the individual needs of every handicapped individual.

These new practices represent a major change in public attitudes and policies concerning the education and treatment of this population. Even the terminology used today to refer to the handicapped attests to the radical change in society's view of those who are different. Today we talk about *exceptional children* or the *developmentally disabled*, for example. In earlier times the same individuals were called deaf mutes, deaf and dumb, mental defectives, idiots, morons, imbeciles, mental degenerates, and feeble-minded. Although these labels were accepted professional terms, they were laden with negative connotations as to the capabilities and value of those human beings.

While we take pride in the accomplishments that have come over the decades in behalf of handicapped persons, we continue to see vestiges of the old negative, fearful attitudes about those who are different in appearance or intellect. We still observe people staring at those with deformities that cause them to be irregular in appearance. We still see parents shriveling at the thought of their child associating with a handicapped peer. We still hear degrading remarks—by both children and adults—about handicapped people. The attitude that the handicapped should not be entitled to an equal education still confronts us when we see special educators and parents continuing to struggle with Congress and American taxpayers over the funding of special education programs. Some people continue to challenge the necessity of federal support to defray the costs of providing appropriate educational programs for the handicapped. In fact, some persons are once more asking whether severely/profoundly handicapped individuals are sufficiently "educable" to justify their participation in public education. Many states are still debating whether early education programs for handicapped infants, preschoolers, and their parents should be provided as a part of public special education services. Our society has not yet dealt sufficiently with the problems of adult retarded and handicapped persons. After leaving secondary school programs, these individuals may have no place to go, no useful or productive role in a community, and no sources of assistance to assure that they do not end up spending their remaining lives in a nursing home.

The early pioneers—advocates for the handicapped

Foresighted persons who believe in new ideas and are persistent in their beliefs are needed to provide the leadership that instigates change in our society. Yet change is often slow. Those who step forward with new visions and ideas are met, more often than not, with opposition. Some face contempt and ridicule for daring to challenge commonly accepted truths or values of their times. But their contributions pave the way for others to further the work. Every professional field—and each of us as professionals— is dependent upon the past contributions of pioneers. Many ideas, practices, and principles we accept in our professions today as common sense are actually the product of innovative thinking from earlier pioneers in our field.

So it is within the field of special education. Those who advocated for the handicapped, who worked with them and created special education programs, were catalysts who helped change the tide of persecution and neglect imposed upon disabled people. The contributions of a few early pioneers who were particularly significant are summarized in Table 3.1.

For more in-depth information on the colorful histories of these and other early leaders, see: Doll (1972); Scheerenberger (1983); Hewett and Forness (1977); Itard (1962); Rosen, Clark, and Kivitz (1976); Kanner (1964); and Jordan (1976).

Table 3.1

Pioneers in Special Education

Pioneer	Contribution
Jacob Rodriguez Pereire (1715-1760)	Introduced and demonstrated notion that a deaf person could be taught to communicate with others. Pereire simplified sign language and invented an arithmetical machine to teach a student how to calculate. He inspired Itard and Seguin's work with the handicapped.
Jean Marc Gaspard Itard (1775-1838)	Made one of first documented efforts to teach a mentally subnormal child. Through his work with Victor (a boy found running naked and wild in the woods of Aveyron, France, who was purported to have lived with a pack of wolves), Itard demonstrated that such a child could learn through systematic teaching and stimulation.
Thomas Gallaudet (1787-1851)	Known for founding the first American residential school for the deaf at Hartford, Connecticut in 1817. Taught deaf to communicate using a system of manual signs.
Samuel Gridley Howe (1801-1876)	An American physician and educator who demonstrated the feasibility of educating deaf persons. Known for his successful efforts to educate a deaf-blind child, Laura Bridgman. Founded the Perkins Institute for the Blind in Boston, Massachusetts, in 1832.
Dorothea Dix (1802-1887)	An American educator who advocated for and succeeded in getting reforms in U.S. mental hospitals and institutions. She argued for making such places treatment centers for the "sick" rather than prisons that were punishment-oriented and merely custodial.
Louis Braille (1809-1852)	A French educator who developed a revolutionary system of reading and writing for the blind that came to bear his name. Based upon an arrangement of raised dots in a six-dot cell that provides for 63 braille characters. Known as the Standard English Braille System.
Edward Seguin (1812-1880)	A protege of Itard who developed teaching methods for retarded persons, including special materials that were further developed and perfected later by Maria Montessori. Emphasized sensory-motor exercises as a means for training retarded children. Established the first school for the retarded in Paris in 1837.
Francis Galton (1822-1911)	Known for his work on individual differences in human abilities. Introduced concept of eugenics (a term he coined) as the science dealing with influences that improve the inborn qualities of a race. Published *Hereditary Genius* in 1869, which prompted notion that genius tends to run in families.
Alfred Binet (1857-1911)	Developed the Binet-Simon intelligence test—the first scales for measuring intelligence and for determining mental age.
Lewis Terman (1877-1956)	Revised the Binet-Simon intelligence test for use with English-speaking children, which became known as the Stanford-Binet Intelligence Scale. Also known for his longitudinal study of gifted children.
Anna Freud (1895-1982)	Used psychoanalysis to treat children's mental illnesses. Her work was based on methods developed by her father, Sigmund Freud.
Alfred Strauss (1897-1957)	Recognized for his description of a learning disabled child, which was termed the "Strauss syndrome." This marked the beginning of the field of learning disabilities.
Samuel Kirk (1904-)	Has had a major influence on the field of learning disabilities by translating language development theory into classroom practices. Developed Illinois Test of Psycholinguistic Abilities (ITPA) to isolate children's abilities and disabilities from which prescriptions for remediation could be drawn.

The special education movement in public schools

Special education services in public schools have a long history showing slow, gradual expansion of services until the post-World War II years. During the 1800s and until World War II, residential schools and institutions provided the few educational opportunities available to the handicapped. During those years a residential or training school was regarded as "the place" where handicapped children should go. By 1900 over 30 states had built this type of school for the deaf, the blind, and the retarded. Virtually every state eventually established facilities of this type.

Early beginnings of special education classes   The first special education class was established for the deaf in Boston in 1869. Nearly 30 years later, in 1896, the first special education class for the mentally retarded was organized in Providence, Rhode Island, followed by classes in Chicago and Boston in 1899, and New York City in 1900. A class for crippled children was started in Chicago in 1899 (Wallin, 1924). By 1911 over 100 large city school systems had special day schools and special education classes and by the 1920s over two-thirds of the large cities in the U.S. had special class programs, but they served only a small number of children who needed help. Most moderately to severely handicapped children were either sent to institutions and residential schools or simply kept at home. Mildly handicapped youngsters were left to fare on their own in regular classes if they could. If not, they became school dropouts. One of the most significant milestones achieved during this time was the founding of the *National Council for Exceptional Children* (CEC) in 1922 under the leadership of Elizabeth Farrell, who became its first president (Aiello, 1976).

Special education programs continued to expand until 1930, but then the impetus died. During the 1930s and 1940s special public school classes gave way to large-scale institutionalization and segregation of the handicapped. Residential schools and institutions became grossly overcrowded and understaffed, and the training purposes for which they originally were created were lost. Institutions became primarily custodial, and the deplorable conditions that came to characterize them imposed a new form of neglect and deprivation upon children placed there. Few residents ever left. If they did, they lacked the training and functional skills to survive in the outside world. This setback in special education resulted primarily from economic depression during the 1930s and widespread dissatisfaction with poorly developed programs staffed by inadequately trained personnel. The eugenics movement, also in vogue at that time, promoted the view that intelligence was fixed by heredity and thus was unchangeable. Given this philosophy, education for the handicapped (particularly the retarded) was considered of little value. Then came World War II. Americans turned to more urgent problems as financial and manpower resources were called elsewhere to cope with demands of the war.

The effects of World War II set the stage for the next phase of special education history in the public schools and for a significant shift in attitude. As a result of the massive screening and testing of young men and women for military service, large numbers of Americans were found to be physically, mentally, or behaviorally handicapped. This alarming reality prompted immediate concern among governmental leaders and the general public. The proportion of American citizens with disabilities was far beyond that imagined. Then World War II left tens of thousands of young men and women disabled. Many normal young adults who had left their homes to join the military forces returned as disabled persons. (The Korean and Vietnam wars also had the same effect.) When Americans welcomed their heroes and loved ones home, they had to confront their old biases and attitudes about the handicapped.

Expectedly, people became more accepting of handicapped persons and more sensitive to their plight. Parents became less likely to hide the fact that they had a handicapped child. They began to take their handicapped children out into public and away from institutions where they had been hidden from public view. Being a parent, sibling, or relative of a handicapped person was no longer considered so disgraceful.

Post-World War II thrust in special education   When the nation recovered from World War II, it was ready for a major thrust to improve care and education for its handicapped. Between 1947 and 1980, and when Public Law 94-142 went into full effect, a virtual explosion of services took place. State and federal legislation, litigation in the courts, investment of federal monies in special education, and federal leadership fueled the new movement. In just the years from 1947 to 1972, for example, the number of handicapped students in public school special education programs increased over 700% (Dunn, 1973)! Seven major factors helped revitalize special education:

1. *Achievements in research, technology, and general knowledge relating to the handicapped.*

A tremendous surge in research and technological development came in a number of fields relating to care and treatment of the handicapped (e.g., medicine, psychology, sociology, education). The mental measurements movement, which began with Alfred Binet's work on intelligence testing in 1901, gained more momentum during World War II, when massive testing was done to screen and place military personnel. The intelligence, personality, and other ability tests that were developed were used later to screen and identify handicapped persons for educational placement. Medical research resulted in discoveries about the causes of handicapping conditions and documented the effects of environmental variables upon learning and development. New medical technology made it possible to treat and, in some cases, prevent certain disabling conditions. As medical sophistication increased, more and more children who otherwise would not have survived were saved. Psychological research resulted in theories explaining human learning, memory functions, and developmental processes, which had subsequent applications in educational practices.

Following the War—especially in the 1960s and thereafter—significant developments in educational technology occurred. For example, behavioral technology revolutionized the field of special education by providing effective new tools for teaching mentally and emotionally handicapped children who previously had been viewed as uneducable.

2. *Parent activism.*

Following the War, parents became vocal about the needs of their handicapped children. They began to ask, "Why can schools serve other students but refuse admission to some children because of a handicapping condition?" National parent organizations appeared as parents united to press state and local education agencies to respond to the needs of their handicapped children. They included the National Association for Retarded Children (later changed to National Association for Retarded Citizens), United Cerebral

Palsy Association, American Foundation for the Blind, and Association for Children with Learning Disabilities. These parent organizations played a key role in revitalizing special education. They organized sheltered workshops and early intervention programs for infants and preschoolers, initiated community programs for unserved groups of moderately and severely impaired students, and worked to upgrade substandard conditions in state institutions.

Parent advocacy brought increased visibility to exceptional children, and parents also became an influential lobbying group with Congress and state legislatures. Parent organizations have been responsible for much of the political pressure that resulted in a redefinition of the rights and privileges of handicapped children through litigation and legislation (Melcher, 1976; Reynolds & Birch, 1977).

3. *Social and political advocacy.*

Prominent citizens began to give visibility to the needs of handicapped children and youth through their social advocacy and political endorsement of special education. Writers such as Pearl S. Buck, politicians such as John F. Kennedy, and performers such as Beverly Sills (the opera star) made the presence of a handicapped child in each of their families known to the public. Their acknowledgments helped remove the stigma that families felt in having a handicapped member. More important, individuals such as these became strong social and political advocates for educational and other services for the handicapped. Many personally donated money to those ends. For example, the private foundation of Joseph P. Kennedy, Jr. helped initiate new research in mental retardation and other areas of special education.

As prominent and visible figures across the country took up the banner for the handicapped, the subject of developmental disabilities and special education became an area of social concern and also a topic of popular interest. Popular interest was further promoted in movies, plays, and paperback books about the lives of handicapped children.

4. *Spillover of the civil rights movement to the handicapped.*

The civil rights movement during the 1960s and 1970s benefited not only Black Americans but handicapped persons as well by achieving two important outcomes: (a) It brought attention to the discrepancy between our principles and practices in American society with regard to the exercise of rights and privileges under the law by various subgroups; and (b) it brought other minority groups, such as the handicapped, into action to assume their equal rights and to bring unfair practices into review by federal and state courts. Armed with the legal precedents established by the civil rights movements, parents of the handicapped also turned to the courts. Early demands of the Blacks for equality in the public schools and nondiscrimination in their access to public places had notable parallels to the unfair practices imposed on the handicapped. Thus, the handicapped pressed also for equal educational opportunities and equal access to public buildings by removal of architectural barriers. It resulted in the demand that handicapped persons not be segregated and denied equal treatment on the basis of disability.

Given this background, it is easy to see why special education has become so intertwined with our country's legal and legislative system. Unlike some areas of education in which practices are dictated largely by professional opinion and group consensus at a local level, many special education practices have been established through legal and legislative actions at state and federal levels.

5. *Federal leadership.*

To be officially represented within the ranks of the federal government is a boon to any professional field or movement. Federal involvement in special education did not really begin until the 1950s. In 1946 a *Section for Exceptional Children* was established within the U.S. Office of Education, with Elsie Martens as Chief. In 1964 Congress elevated this Section to the status of a *Division* within the U.S. Office of Education. Samuel Kirk, a well known special educator, served as its first director. Then, through Public Law 89-750 in 1966, the *Bureau of Education for the Handicapped (BEH)* was created, with subdivisions for personnel training, research, and services. James Gallagher served as its first Director, followed by Edwin Martin, Jr., in 1970. With another reorganization in 1980, BEH was elevated to the *Office of Special Education*. In 1981, as part of a major revamping of federal offices in Washington, the Office of Special Education was reorganized and given the title of *Special Education Programs* (SEP).

Whatever the official title, important federal leadership has come from these offices. The federal office has gathered and dispersed important information on the status of handicapped children. It has played a central role in defining policy and dispensing federal funds to state and local projects for research and demonstration activities relating to the handicapped, personnel training of teachers and administrators in colleges and universities, and direct service programs for handicapped children and youth. Initial programs supported by the federal office addressed only selected categorical areas of disability (e.g., mental

Society had to be convinced first that normally developing children could benefit from preschool before we could consider that handicapped preschoolers could profit from early educational intervention.

retardation or deaf and hearing impaired). Gradually this expanded to all areas of exceptionality including the gifted. The federal office became increasingly powerful and administered growing sums of money. As federal leadership grew, states followed suit, and special education divisions were created within State Departments of Education and again in local school district administrative offices. This investment of millions of federal/state dollars and the growth of programs for the handicapped reflects the strength of the special education movement as it gained momentum in the 1960s, 1970s, and early 1980s.

6. *Court actions.*

Because advocates for the handicapped turned to the courts to bring about change, much of the re-analysis of educational practices with handicapped persons has come from court cases brought against institutions and school districts by handicapped persons or their parents. Issues such as testing, labeling, placement, rights to education or treatment, and the role of parents in the educational decision-making process have been the primary focus of these court cases. A myriad of cases is on record in state courts and in the U.S. Supreme Court concerning issues that impact upon handicapped individuals. Today, those cases affect practices and procedures used in schools to provide services to exceptional children. A few landmark court cases are summarized in Table 3.2.

7. *Legislation relating to the handicapped.*

Legislation dealing specifically with the handicapped did not appear until the 1960s. Although state legislatures throughout the nation had passed laws for either mandatory or permissive operation of special education programs, federal aid to special education prior to 1958 was minimal. Beginning in the mid-to-late 1950s special education was revitalized by several legislative acts at both state and federal levels. One of the first federal laws relating to education was the Cooperative Research Act (1954). It initiated cooperative research between the federal government and universities through funding of studies in critical issues of education. This served to alert professionals to the need for experimentation and careful study of practices that were being propagated as "the way" to educate handicapped students. During the late 1960s and 1970s attention to the handicapped by Congress escalated, resulting in more legislation supporting research, demonstration programs, personnel training, media development, and direct public school services for handicapped students (Martin, 1974; LaVor, 1976).

Federal legislation has been and continues to be a boon to the field of special education because it established policy and allocated funds for programs that states might never have initiated. Special educators and other professionals working with the handicapped have increasing needs to be informed about legislative regulations because (a) they affect the sources and amount of funds available to operate special education programs at the local level, and (b) they govern many of the practices professionals follow in serving handicapped persons. Table 3.3 lists some key federal acts that have had a significant impact on educational practices.

The most significant and far-reaching legislation passed by Congress is PL 94-142 (1975), sometimes known as the *Bill of Rights for the Handicapped* (Goodman, 1976). This landmark legislation was designed to achieve four major purposes: (a) to correct inequities in the education of handicapped individuals, (b) to assure the right of every handicapped child to a free, appropriate public education, (c) to specify fair and appropriate

Table 3.2

Summary of Selected Court Cases
Affecting Special Education Practices

Case	Judicial Decision
Brown v. Board of Education Kansas - 1954	Established the right of all children for an equal opportunity to education. Decision became cornerstone for application of the least restrictive alternative to the education of handicapped children. The Court established that the concept and practice of segregation has no place in public education; segregation is inherently unequal.
Hobson v. Hansen Washington, DC - 1967	Established that the placement of children into educational "tracks" on the basis of test performance was a violation of the equal protection clause of the U.S. Constitution. Court ordered the tracing system to be abolished. Tests used for placement were considered biased because they resulted in segregation of pupils by race and socioeconomic class.
Diana v. California Board of Education California - 1970	Established that children cannot be placed in special education on the basis of culturally biased tests or tests given in other than the child's native language. Children whose primary language is other than English shall be tested in both their primary language and English.
Wyatt v. Stickney/Wyatt v. Aderholt Alabama - 1971	Declared that individuals in state institutions have the right to appropriate treatment in those institutions.
Pennsylvania Association for Retarded Citizens (PARC) v. Commonwealth of Pennsylvania Pennsylvania - 1971	Established the right of parents to participate in major decisions affecting their children. The Court decision helped establish the principle that every child, no matter how variant from others, has the right to education. Public schools have obligation to provide appropriate education for literally all children, in their own facilities or by arrangement with other agencies.
Mills v. Board of Education of the District of Columbia District of Columbia - 1972	Established right of every child to an equal opportunity for education. Court declared that lack of funds was not an acceptable excuse for lack of educational opportunity. Court also ruled that no child can be excluded from a regular public school unless the district finances the child's education within special classes, private schools, or with tutors. Prior hearings and periodic assessments of both child status and educational program are a necessary part of the school's responsibilities toward such children. No matter how severely handicapped the child, the public school system must provide educational services and must demonstrate their adequacy.
Armstrong v. Kline Pennsylvania - 1980	Established that some severely handicapped children have right to schooling for 12 months instead of only for 9-month school year if proof can be given that they will regress during the summer recess. Court ruled that a state law requiring a 9-month school year violates PL 94-142 and Section 504.

Table 3.3
Selected Legislative Milestones
Relating to the Handicapped

1958 PL 85-926 National Defense Act	Provided grants to colleges/universities and state education agencies for training leadership personnel in education of the mentally retarded.
1961 PL 87-276 Special Education Act	Authorized funds for training professionals to train teachers of the deaf.
1965 PL 89-10 Elementary and Secondary Education Act (ESEA)	Provided funds to state agencies and local school districts for developing programs to serve economically disadvantaged and handicapped students.
PL 89-313 Amendment to Title I of the Elementary and Secondary Education Act	Provided funds for programs serving handicapped children in state-operated schools and institutions.
PL 89-750 Amendments to the Elementary and Secondary Education Act	Created the Bureau of Education for the Handicapped.
1973 PL 93-112 Vocational Rehabilitation Act Section 504	The first federal civil rights law that specifically protected the rights of handicapped individuals. The original law dealt primarily with employment. It was amended in 1974, however, under PL 93-516, to cover a broader array of services for the handicapped. The law established rights of handicapped for nondiscrimination in employment, admission into institutions of higher learning, and access to public facilities.
1974 PL 93-380 Education of Handicapped Amendments	Extended the Elementary and Secondary Education Act of 1965 to provide funds for state and local school districts to create programs serving the gifted. More important, the law provided a policy statement concerning the treatment of handicapped students in regard to due process procedures underlying placement, nondiscriminatory testing, and confidentiality of school records. Policy defined under 93-380 served as a basis for provisions that came later in PL 94-142.
1975 PL 94-142 Education for All Handicapped Children Act	Mandated a free, appropriate public education for all handicapped children without regard to the type or severity of handicap. Also outlined rights of handicapped children and their parents including procedures for due process, nondiscriminatory testing, program placement, use of records, etc.

procedures relating to testing, placement, and service delivery for handicapped students, and (d) to define the rights and privileges for due process to which parents and the handicapped child are entitled. Some major provisions of that law are reviewed next.

Special education today: Changing concepts

The rapid proliferation of special services for exceptional children between 1947 and 1975 brought some major transitions in values and practices of the field. If you were to have visited a typical school district in the 1950s and toured the programs and facilities for handicapped children, you would have found special education to be much different than it is today. Here are just a few examples of practices you likely would have observed in the early 1950s:

1. Special programs in the schools, though they were expanding, primarily served the educable (or mildly) mentally retarded and emotionally disturbed. Services were not extended to children with all types of handicapping conditions or to those with all levels of disability. Many parents had no option other than placing their handicapped child in a residential school.
2. Schools could and did deny admission to many handicapped children on the basis that they were too impaired, too disruptive and unmanageable, or that an appropriate classroom was not available.
3. Most special education services were delivered in separate, segregated special education classrooms. The resource rooms, consulting or itinerant teacher, and related interdisciplinary services used today were not among the options available. Children placed in special classes often retained their labels as "mentally retarded," "emotionally disturbed," and so forth, and remained in special education for the duration of their school career.
4. Placement of children with special problems was a decision handled primarily by the school psychologist. Input from other specialists or from parents was not a standard part of the review process unless the psychologist personally elected to follow that procedure. Parent involvement in placement decisions was minimal or nonexistent.

   In the 1960s special educators began to look critically at these practices and at the widespread use of special classes as the means for educating exceptional children. Lloyd Dunn's (1968) monumental article "Special Education for the Mildly Retarded—Is Much of It Justifiable?" provided the catalyst to bring about a major renovation in actual school practices. Dunn admonished special educators to "stop being pressured into a continuing and expanding special education program (special classes) that we know to be undesirable for so many children we are dedicated to serve." Since that time, special education has undergone a major transition. For example, the concept of what special education is and what it encompasses has been reexamined. Alternative models for service delivery have been initiated. Procedures for planning and delivering special instructional services have been revamped. Much of this change was brought about through the courts and in the legislation described earlier. Public Law 94-142, the Education for All Handicapped Children Act, provided the final means for putting these changes into practice across all states and with all handicapped children.

Changing perspectives of education and its purposes   The following list contrasts some of the recent conceptual shifts in special education, as well as in our society's values and philosophy about education and human rights.

Old Concepts	*New and Emerging Concepts*
Education is a privilege for those who can profit from it.	Education is a right for *all* children and is a means for preparing them to meet the demands of their environment, to learn,

Education consists of academic instruction in reading, writing, arithmetic, and in topic areas relating to the arts and sciences.

Children must be "ready" to begin formal education and should wait to enter public school programs if basic social, self-help, cognitive, and language skills have not been mastered.

If children do not fit into the curricular offerings or respond readily to the teaching methods used in the regular classroom, they should be removed and placed elsewhere. (Underlying this concept is the notion that children should be expected to fit the educational system rather than that the system should be created to fit the child.)

Handicapped children should be placed in special classrooms, where they will not disrupt the learning of normal children and can be together with others of their own kind.

A child's failure to learn is attributable to that individual's disabilities and incapacities or limitations. Schools do not fail—only students fail.

and to live as fulfilling, productive lives as possible.

Education encompasses whatever skills a child needs to allow optimal functioning in our society and environment. For some children, this may mean instruction in skills as basic as walking, eating, talking, and attention, or in motor functions hampered by a disability.

Children become "ready" through learning, experience, and training. The lack of prerequisite skills signals even more clearly a child's need for education and training and not the need to wait longer.

Educators fit curriculum and instructional methods to the needs of their students. Teachers and specialists should make the necessary instructional and environmental adaptations (within reason) to help a child learn before considering removal from the regular classroom.

Handicapped children should remain with their peers in the educational mainstream whenever possible unless their best interests clearly are better served elsewhere. If removed from the regular educational setting, it should be only for the time needed to deliver the special services. These children should not be isolated from normal peers or the mainstream of society in which we ultimately want them to be participating, functional members.

All children are capable of learning. A child's failure to learn reflects the failure of teachers and specialists to select appropriate learning activities, to break down instructional tasks into small, sequential steps that facilitate learning, and to monitor the child's progress in ways that allow unsuccessful learning strategies to be identified and revised.

Changing definitions of special education　During the 1950s and 1960s special education was almost synonymous with the segregated special classroom. As additional service delivery alternatives (e.g. resource rooms, itinerant teachers, and part-time special education classrooms) were created, many educators tended to view special education as the setting where handicapped students were placed for instructional purposes. Thus, special education continued to be defined in terms of administrative arrangements through which services were provided rather than in terms of the actual instructional assistance provided to students.

Recently, the concept of special education has become more instructionally oriented. It emphasizes the special kinds of instructional assistance and equipment/materials handicapped individuals need in order to learn and perform optimally within their environment. Kirk and Gallagher (1979) defined special education as:

> . . . those aspects of education that are applied to handicapped and gifted children but are not usually used with the majority of average children. . . . Special education . . . consists of the modifications of, or additions to, school practices intended for the ordinary child—practices that are unique, uncommon, of unusual quality, and in particular in addition to the organization and instructional procedures used with the majority of children. (p. 12)

Most definitions of special education are oriented toward the population of youngsters with whom the field has been primarily concerned—*school-aged students*. Service delivery approaches thus are conceptualized around the administrative systems and instructional approaches common to elementary, intermediate, and secondary schools. But as special education has expanded to include infants and preschoolers under school age and adults beyond the age of 17 or 18, new kinds of care and educational stimulation quite unlike that provided to students in traditional public school settings have been required. Unfortunately, most commonly cited definitions of special education do not reflect the expansion of the field to include these new populations or the unique kinds of services and service delivery mechanisms they require. For purposes of this book, an expanded definition is offered to capture the total scope of special education as it exists today. The following definitions describe special education first as a discipline and then in terms of its actual practices.

Special education as a discipline: Special education is a professional field or discipline with its own philosophy, methodology, research, and communication network created by its own journals, professional organizations, and advocacy groups. As a discipline, the field deals with individuals who have all types and degrees of exceptionality and are at all age levels. This includes infants and preschoolers from birth to the age of school admission, elementary and secondary school-aged youngsters, and adults who have completed secondary school programs but who require vocational habilitation and training in independent community living.

Professional activities of specialists within the discipline are primarily concerned with (a) direct services to handicapped and gifted persons, including the development of specialized materials and instructional methods, (b) training of staff to administer services or prepare personnel for job roles in the field through graduate and undergraduate training programs in colleges and universities, (c) research relating to special education, the nature of developmental disabilities, and the status of exceptional persons in our society, and (d) policy making and program planning relative to the rights, privileges, and service provisions for this group of citizens.

Special education as a service and instructional process: In practice, special education encompasses an array of services, instructional methodologies, materials, and equipment provided as alternative or supplementary forms of educational support for exceptional learners. The intent is to facilitate optimal development, learning, and life adjustment in exceptional individuals, which may not occur through the regular educational experiences available to normal persons. Special education is characterized by considerable complexity and diversity in its content and service delivery approaches for the following reasons:

- The purpose of special education varies across age groups of handicapped and exceptional persons. For children from birth to age 5 or 6, its purpose is that of *intervention* and *prevention* of secondary disabilities. With elementary and secondary school-aged students, special education generally is provided for *remedial* or *corrective* purposes with the handicapped and for *enrichment* purposes with gifted and talented students. The purpose of special education for older handicapped students also may become one of *adaptation*, to help a student develop adaptive skills that will compensate for disabilities that may be unalterable or to cope with skill deficits that may be viewed as no longer remediable. The purpose of special education with postsecondary or handicapped adult populations is primarily that of *vocational* or *social habilitation* to prepare them for successful integration in our communities and for independent or semi-independent living.

- Special education services are delivered across a variety of settings that include regular and special classes in public schools, and other educational and training centers such as community centers providing day care, preschools, sheltered workshop and vocational training programs. Services also are extended through special schools, clinics, and a child's own home setting.

- Special education is uniquely applied to each exceptional person in regard to its purpose, content, delivery mode, intensity and duration of service, and the service delivery agent(s). Services are prescribed on an individual basis and are determined primarily by four key variables: (a) the age group of the individual and the services normally available to members of that group, (b) the handicapping condition(s) characterizing each individual in need of special assistance, (c) the severity of those handicapping conditions and the extent to which they interfere with learning and with the ability of the person to profit from regular forms of educational experience, and (d) the educational needs of each person.

Expanding concepts and strategies in service delivery   Major changes in special education practices are now evident as a result of passage of PL 94-142. The law not only mandated a free and appropriate education for all handicapped children but also specified the processes by which this goal is to be achieved. The major provisions of PL 94-142 are summarized in Table 3.4. (Some of the specific regulations of the law that affect teachers and administrators in their direct practices with children and parents are discussed in chapter 11.)

Specific regulations under PL 94-142 have brought significant changes in educational procedures used with handicapped students. The provision of a free and appropriate education assures that no child shall be denied the *right to education* or to an "appropriate" education. Schools, therefore, must use a variety of service delivery strategies because no one approach can adequately meet the special needs of every child. The provision for *nondiscriminatory assessment* has forced educators to seek out new and more varied methods for evaluating student performance.

Criterion-referenced tests are coming into greater use along with standardized tests. Norms for norm-referenced tests are being revised using more representative populations including minority children and those performing at the lower end of the scale. Greater care also is being exercised in the use and interpretation of test scores. Arbitrary diagnoses based primarily on standardized, norm-referenced test scores are giving way to diagnoses based upon numerous forms of evaluation including adaptive and functional performance assessment on students across both academic and social environments.

Mandatory use of *individualized education programs* (IEPs) as a blueprint for planning and delivering services has brought considerable change within special education. IEPs require careful planning of what special assistance will be delivered to each handicapped child and what exactly is to be achieved by those services. In essence, special education must indeed be special or extra. Also, IEPs provide a means for ensuring more parent involvement in constructive and meaningful educational planning for their child. Further, IEPs provide a new means for accountability. They provide a permanent record of what services are to be provided and what outcomes are to be achieved. IEPs also provide a record of who is responsible for service delivery and how long services are to be rendered.

IEPs must be reviewed at least annually to assess the program's success. If a student is not making progress, the mechanism is in place for bringing problems to the forefront and for taking action to alleviate them. Previously, special education programs for handicapped students continued regardless of whether they were successful.

Principles of *due process* prevent isolated decisions in regard to a child's educational program and placement. Appropriate assessments and other information must be used as the basis for decision making. A child cannot be removed from the regular class simply because of inconvenient or troublesome behavior. Rights of the child and parents cannot be ignored and circumvented for the convenience of school personnel.

The concept of *least restrictive environment* has encouraged the mainstreaming of mildly handicapped individuals in regular classes. Part of the deinstitutionalization movement we see today is an attempt to move retarded individuals to less restrictive and more normalizing environments and to stop the unnecessary isolation of these persons from the mainstream of society. The concept of least restrictive environment also has caused educators to carefully consider all possible placement alternatives for each handicapped child, including the benefits and liabilities of each, before making a final placement. Under previous practices, certain types of children were automatically placed in certain types of educational settings.

Table 3.4

Major Regulations Under Public Law 94-142

Free and Appropriate Public Education (FAPE)

Every handicapped child, ages 3-21, must be provided an appropriate education regardless of the nature and severity of the handicap. This includes special education and related services (such as speech therapy, psychological services, physical and occupational therapy, transportation, and other support services). It is to be delivered at no expense to parents. This applies to *all* school-aged children in both private and public settings.

Nondiscriminatory Assessment

Individuals are protected against unfair testing and diagnostic procedures by the following procedures: (1) Evaluations must be conducted in the language primarily used by the child; (2) tests used as a basis for diagnosis and for determining eligibility for special education must not be culturally or racially biased; and (3) educational decisions concerning a child cannot be made on the basis of a single test score but, rather, must result from a number of assessment procedures.

Individualized Education Program (IEP)

An individualized eduation program, outlined in writing, must be provided to each handicapped child. The written plan (IEP) is to be developed by a team consisting of the child's teacher, a member of the evaluation team if the child is being evaluated for the first time, a school representative who is qualified to supervise the delivery of special education services, one or both of the child's parents, and the child, when appropriate. The IEP should be based on assessment information and input from the child's parents. It must be reviewed and updated annually. The written IEP must include:

— a description of the child's present levels of performance.
— a statement of annual goals for the child, including short-term instructional objectives.
— a statement of services needed by the child (without regard to availability).
— a listing of services to be rendered to the child.
— projected dates concerning when services will begin and the anticipated duration.
— objective criteria and evaluation procedures for determining whether short-term instructional objectives are being achieved.

Due Process

School districts and their staffs must follow specific procedures to assure the rights of handicapped children and their parents. These regulations are designed to protect the individual from improper classification, unnecessary labeling, and placement without fair and impartial consideration of the child's needs or informed consent by the parents or legal representative. Due process procedures require that:

— parents may examine all records pertaining to their child.
— parents have the right to obtain an independent evaluation of their child in addition to that provided by the school district and its staff.
— parents must be consulted about their child's education program prior to its implementation. They must be informed of the IEP conference and encouraged to participate. Meetings must be scheduled at times convenient for parents to attend, and appropriate communications must be maintained with them.
— parents or guardians must receive written notice if a change is proposed in their child's classification, evaluation, or educational placement.
— parents or guardians have the right to present complaints on matters concerning the identification, evaluation, or program placement of their child. If disagreements occur between parents and the school, parents have a right to an impartial due process hearing conducted by a hearing officer. Parents have the right to be represented by a lawyer, to give evidence, and to cross examine.

Table 3.4 (continued)

Hearings may be requested by the parent or by the school district.
— surrogate parents must be appointed to provide representation and informed consent for children whose parents (or guardians) are not known or are not available.

Least Restrictive Environment (LRE)

Handicapped children, including those in both public and private facilities, should be educated with children who are not handicapped to the maximum extent possible. Placement in special classes, separate schools, or any other form of removal from regular classes should be exercised only when a child's disability is such that education in a regular class environment cannot be achieved satisfactorily.

HISTORICAL PERSPECTIVES ON REGULAR EARLY CHILDHOOD EDUCATION

Our previous societal value that children should be kept at home during their preschool years has changed dramatically. Preschool experience for youngsters between 3 and 5 years of age is common today. Parents now are seeking out more educational and socializing experiences for their children outside of the home. In addition, more women are pursuing careers so the need for day-care services is accelerating. Acceptance of early childhood education as a valued part of our child-rearing practices, however, has not come about overnight. It is the outcome of a long struggle to establish preschools and day-care centers and to have them regarded as a necessary part of modern family life. The events that led to regular early childhood education programs provide an important foundation for the new field of early childhood-special education. Had we not believed that young children could profit from preschool programs and had we not first established them for nonhandicapped children, our society probably would not have considered preschool education as important for the handicapped.

One word describes early education programs for young children under school age as they exist today—*diversity*. Differences in programs stem from the unique traditions and historical roots from which each has grown. Early childhood as a field encompasses several separate but parallel movements that gave rise to the separate institutions of *kindergarten, nursery or preschool, day-care services,* and *compensatory education programs* such as Head Start and Follow-Through. Each of these entities stemmed from the ideas and contributions of different sets of educators and philosophers. Their points of view have left distinct marks upon each type of program, although changes have occurred over the years as their philosophies have been molded and reshaped by new ideas and changing cultural values. As we trace the historical underpinnings of early childhood education, the three separate movements are: the *kindergarten movement,* the *nursery or preschool movement*, and the *day-care movement*. Compensatory education programs are discussed in a separate section since they encompass not only preschool, but primary-elementary education as well.

The kindergarten movement

Its beginnings   The roots of today's early education programs can be traced back to early European philosophers who advocated for the rights of young children and emphasized the importance of childhood as a time for learning. *Comenius* (1592-1670) introduced the notion of unfoldment—a concept that dominated the philosophy of those who stressed maturation and heredity as the major determinants of a child's basic nature. He believed that what each child becomes is inherent within himself or herself. Thus, Comenius believed the teacher's role was to cultivate but not transform or force something that is not the child's natural disposition.

Although Comenius stressed the innate qualities of the child (a philosophy characteristic of his time), he also emphasized the malleability of human behavior. He likened the unfolding of a child's mind during the first six years of life to that of soft wax that will take any impression during the time it remains soft and malleable. Comenius went on to outline methods parents and educators should use to cultivate and guide children during their early years. Now, three centuries later, we know that a child's future social, emotional, physical, and mental growth is built upon a foundation set during the early formative years (Bee, 1985; Peters, Neisworth, & Yawkey, 1985).

John Locke (1632-1704) introduced the notion that human minds are not stocked with a reservoir of innate ideas, but that ideas come from sensation, activity, and practice. Therefore, children must be educated and trained for their place in society.

Rousseau (1712-1778) made his contributions to early thinking about education through his emphasis upon concepts such as: "Let nature take its course," and "Teach children by experience." In his famous book, *Emile*, Rousseau outlined one of the early explanations on stages of development from infancy to adulthood. These stages, he suggested, are *en*folded within the child at birth and destined to *un*fold in the stage-order predestined at birth. He viewed education as not so much what a teacher should do but, more important, what teachers should refrain from doing to not interfere with the natural unfolding of the child.

Pestalozzi (1746-1827) was not an "armchair philosopher," but one who actually taught young children and applied the ideas of earlier educational theorists to the classroom. He attacked longstanding educational practices of his day and was successful in changing some of them. He particularly rebelled against exclusion of the poor from early schooling, over-use of rote learning in schools (which he labeled "superficial verbosity"), and cruel punishments with children. He advocated love and kindness as the means for helping children develop their physical and intellectual abilities. Pestalozzi also originated the concept of "readiness." This notion later dictated many educational practices in America during the mid-1900s, when educators became concerned about not pushing a child into subjects such as reading and math until a point of readiness was attained.

Froebel's kindergarten   The first truly solidified approach to the direct instruction of young children came from Frederick Froebel (1772-1852). After teaching in his own private school and tutoring individual students, he developed his own philosophy of early childhood education and teaching. Froebel's contributions have been of lasting importance, because his notions stood as the "gospel" that initiated the kindergarten movement in both Europe and the United States. People who were converted to Froebel's ideas during the early days of the kindergarten in American preached his ideas with serious, almost religious dedication (Weber, 1969).

Froebel established his kindergarten (meaning a garden for children) in Germany during the early 1800s. Its philosophy emphasized several basic principles: (a) Education should be passive in the sense that it is primarily protecting and nurturing the child, but not prescriptive or controlling; (b) play is natural to children and should constitute the heart of curriculum; (c) play is the means by which children gain insights, and it is the means for mental development; and (d) play should be free play, not something to be interfered with by adult supervision.

On this latter point Froebel's practices were not particularly consistent with the permissive philosophy he articulated. Although he believed teachers should not intervene in the child's natural activities, he still outlined what children should do and learn. According to Froebel, the kindergarten's purpose should be to train children in habits of cleanliness, neatness, punctuality, courtesy, and deference toward others. Language, numbers, forms, and eye-hand coordination also were emphasized.

Froebel's kindergarten was built around a series of activities for children 3-6 years of age encompassed in what he called *The Gifts, The Occupations,* and *The Mother's Plays. The Gifts* focused upon objects. *The Occupations* presented activities children should experience and also provided an avenue for artistic expression. *The Mother's Plays* consisted of a number of songs and games. The small manipulative objects comprising Froebel's *Gifts* were to be used by children in specific ways. Each gift related back to certain spiritual-religious feelings to be cultivated. For example, the first gift consisted of a series of yarn balls of different colors symbolizing unity and wholeness of the universe. These were to create ideas in the child about form, motion, color, and direction, as well as to promote muscular development and coordination. A second gift consisted of a wooden sphere, a cube, and a cylinder, representing unity and diversity. These materials were to teach the child about properties and characteristics of objects. Froebel's curriculum had a total of 10 gifts. The *Occupations* consisted of selected activities children were to perform with certain kinds of materials: drawing, paper folding, sewing, painting, clay molding, cutting, and weaving.

As Froebel's ideas proliferated in Germany, the need for trained teachers increased, and he became involved in teacher training. Several of his trainees, who became known as *kindergarteners*, came to the U.S. during German migrations in the mid-19th century. They spread the gospel of Froebel's education system across America and established numerous kindergartens. Froebel's ideas soon saturated the early childhood field and became the backbone of early childhood practices in America. Primarily Froebelian educators established the early professional organizations relating to early childhood education. Even today, many of Froebel's ideas can be seen in early education practices.

Early kindergartens in America

Early kindergartens in America   Several individuals were particularly instrumental in the growth of Froebel's kindergarten in the U.S. *Margarethe Schurz,* one of his former students in Germany, migrated to Watertown, Wisconsin, and there established the first kindergarten in America for German-speaking children, in 1856. *Elizabeth Peabody* met Schurz on one of her lecture tours and became so enthusiastic about what she heard that she founded the first English-speaking kindergarten in Boston, in 1860. She traveled to Germany to see Froebel's schools in person and returned to America as an even more zealous advocate. She began a lecture tour around the country to spread the kindergarten cause. Some of her contacts also took up the banner for the Froebelian kindergarten. Milton Bradley, founder of the publishing company of the same name, heard one of Peabody's lectures and was inspired by her description of children's activities within the kindergarten. A short time later Milton Bradley Publishers produced the first illustrated guide for kindergarten in English, entitled *Paradise of Childhood, A Practical Guide for Kindergarten*.

Peabody also was instrumental in convincing school superintendent William Harris to begin an experimental kindergarten in the public schools of St. Louis, Missouri. It was the first program to be operated within a public school system. The results were so successful that Harris expanded it to other elementary schools in St. Louis. Elizabeth Peabody also wrote, with co-author Mary Mann, the first American textbook on kindergarten, in 1863, called *The Moral Culture of Infancy and Kindergarten*.

The momentum of any new movement depends upon strong leaders. As the baton of leadership transfers from one person to another, each carries the cause forward through his or her unique contributions. Schurz and Peabody set the stage for proliferation of the kindergarten concept in America and sowed the seeds of Froebelian doctrine across the American scene. *Susan Blow* put it all into action to become the leading proponent of Froebel's ideas in America. As director of the first public school kindergarten in St. Louis (which William Harris created in 1872), Blow formalized the concept of the kindergarten as a part of the public school system. A prolific writer and speaker, she wrote five books, presented innumerable papers in professional meetings, and lectured throughout the country.

Blow became the champion of Froebelism during a period when other voices within psychology and education were demanding change. Progressive education, as advocated by G. Stanley Hall, John Dewey, and others, presented ideas that were different from Froebel's concept of education. Blow's response was to defend Froebelian concepts more adamantly and to continue explaining their meaning and applications in even greater detail. She insisted on rigid adherence to the ideal applications of kindergarten practices and the use of Froebel's Gifts and Occupations, which she tried valiantly to protect from encroachment by those revolutionary ideas emerging from the new scientific thought and child development research.

After the experimental kindergarten was established in St. Louis by Harris and Blow, a Department of Kindergarten was created by the National Educational Association (NEA) in 1874. Harris' leadership in initiating kindergarten within public schools was recognized, and he became its first president. Not long after, NEA made an official recommendation that kindergartens should be a regular part of public school programs. Many more decades went by, however, before kindergarten became a common educational practice.

Programs were promoted under the sponsorship of various private agencies, mothers' clubs and philanthropic groups. Even in those early days, kindergarten was considered to be of particular benefit to poor children, especially those in large city slums and those who were recent immigrants to the U.S. Interestingly, many contemporary arguments used to justify early education programs for disadvantaged children today sound similar to those used by Susan Blow to promote the kindergarten notion. Yet, even now in the 1980s, some school districts do not offer kindergarten programs (Spodek, 1978; Weber, 1969; Osborn, 1975; Leeper, Witherspoon, & Day, 1984).

Reform in the kindergarten movement   Sooner or later in the course of any major movement, the initial enthusiasm that gave it birth and nurtured it during those early developmental stages gives way to more serious and rigorous refinement. No longer is the mere discovery of new, innovative ideas sufficient to maintain the earlier momentum. Eventually someone stops and questions what previously has been accepted as truth. What exactly are the tenets of this philosophy? How are they interpreted in actual practice with children? What variations are acceptable? As movements grow and recruit more and more individuals who speak in its behalf, the purism of its founder's ideas inevitably becomes subject to interpretation and reinterpretation. Questions arise and solutions are presented by those who consider themselves disciples. People vie for power, and the debates and conflicts begin.

So it was with Froebelism. Its growth in fertile American soil, where early educators were hungry for leadership, resulted in a strong foothold for Froebel's ideas. An army of advocates was formed, and the forum for discussion (a very biased one) was created within the organization of the NEA section on Kindergarten and the International Kindergarten Union (IKU). The latter was created in 1892 by a group concerned with the promotion of kindergartens. The movement grew to sufficient size that unity in the ranks could not be maintained indefinitely. The stage was set for the next phase of development in the American kindergarten.

Anna Bryan was among the first dissenters to question rigid adherence to Froebelian principles. She argued against slavishly following his methodology and suggested that some of his formalized teaching sequences produced mechanical, uneducative play (Weber, 1969). By the early 1900s a major split had occurred among proponents of kindergarten education. The traditionalists viewed Froebel as having defined the most important and universal elements of education for all young children; they adhered to Froebel's principles religiously. The liberal camp viewed Froebel's philosophy as an important contribution and a step in the right direction but believed that inappropriate methods in teaching young children should be discarded as more effective ones were developed. These people regarded Froebel's ideas more empirically and objectively as something to be modified, improved, and changed.

Patty Smith Hill, Anna Bryan's first student, carried the reform movement forward and became known as the innovator in kindergarten education. She stated most clearly the emerging philosophy of the kindergarten reform movement in her 1913 *Report for the Committee of Twelve* from the International Kindergarten Union. In that report she presented several key arguments:

1. Kindergarten curriculum should be related to the child's present circumstances rather than to the needs of children from another culture and another generation.
2. Children's personal experiences should be used as the vehicle for helping children gain insight and knowledge about their world.
3. Children should be allowed the freedom to engage in concrete, child-oriented play experiences based upon the natural activities of childhood.

In essense, the liberal reform was a simple attempt to retain Froebel's general philosophy, but to do away with unnecessary formalism that had so dominated the curriculum and teaching methodology (Spodek, 1978).

Two individuals, *G. Stanley Hall* and *John Dewey*, contributed significantly to the progressivism of the kindergarten reform movement. They were instrumental in linking research and scientific thinking in psychology with education, including early education. Prior to that, most educational practices with very young children were based upon religious and social values and "armchair" or intuitive philosophy. Little scientific research or theory had leaked into actual practices within the classroom.

G. Stanley Hall, credited with being the "father of child psychology," led the liberal kindergarten group into a new, progressive methodology. He introduced techniques of data collection, anecdotal records, and the analysis of children's products. He promoted the thesis: *Ontogeny (individual development) recapitulates phylogeny (development of the race)*. By this, he envisioned an evolutionary developmental sequence through which all children proceeded both biologically and behaviorally, which was reflective of the evolution of the species. A child has to progress through each stage for healthy development. To do this, youngsters need freedom and rich cultural material for normal growth to occur and to master each developmental stage before moving to the next. He believed that the characteristics of each stage (as defined by research) should determine early childhood curriculum.

An important difference in G. Stanley Hall's view of curriculum and what had been practiced previously was that he believed kindergarten practices should evolve from empirical, objective observations of the child. This was radically different from the traditional view that had relied primarily upon introspection, religious values, and intuitive knowledge as a basis for defining the nature of childhood and the purposes of early childhood education. Patty Smith Hill and her teacher, Anna Bryan, crossed paths with G. Stanley Hall and became aligned with him and his scientific study of children. Hall taught a seminar in the summer of 1895 for a number of teachers with whom he attempted to share his developmental research. His criticisms of Froebel and the approaches Hall advocated were so infuriating to the teachers that most left his seminar—all except Anna Bryan and Patty Smith Hill. They went on to study with him, learning his experimental methods and psychological orientation toward child development and early education.

John Dewey, one of G. Stanley Hall's students, carried progressivism on to its many practical applications in American education and the kindergarten. To test his educational theories, he established a laboratory school including a classroom for 4- to 5-year-olds at the University of Chicago. Anna Bryan became the director of his kindergarten. Dewey's ideas and pragmatism had a tremendous influence on American education and philosophy. He emphasized the functional purposes of education and argued that education should be integrated with life and socially practical for the child, rather than preparation for some abstract, remote future. He believed that education should involve active learning and problem solving, social interaction, and learning by doing things of interest to the child (Braun & Edwards, 1972; Weber, 1969).

The kindergarten reform continued into the 1920s and 1930s. It was fueled by a growing body of research from child research centers and laboratory schools across the country and the continuing debates between the traditionalists and the progressive educators. Over time, kindergartens did change, evolving into the modern early childhood programs of today.

Several key events since the 1930s added to the metamorphosis of the kindergarten into its modern-day character. First, economic conditions of the 1930s and 1940s, described earlier, resulted in a decrease of public school-supported kindergartens. Second, the mental health movement generated new awareness of social and emotional development, leading to a decline of the rigid formalism of education and of "habit training" that had been stressed earlier. Third, the "Sputnik shock," when the Russians put the first satellite into space, caused Americans to look more critically at school curricula and the academic preparation given to our future scientists and citizens. Reemphasis upon intellectual development in children led to a reemphasis upon kindergarten programs and other educational reforms in the elementary school during the 1950s and 1960s (Spodek, 1978). Fourth, research and experimental early childhood programs produced evidence supporting the importance of early education and early experience in young children. Theory and empirical data also pointed to the effects of early stimulation deprivation upon children. The result was, and has continued to be, an increase in public support for the kindergarten. Today it is viewed as a standard part of most public school systems.

The nursery school movement

Nursery schools evolved from a cultural context and a sequence of events different from the kindergarten movement. That history is much more recent, both in America and in England. In tracing the historical roots of the nursery school, British nursery schools of the early 1900s typically are given front stage. But a lesser recognized institution parallel to that initiated in England also was developing in Italy. At the same time that the MacMillan sisters were rejecting the formalism of British primary schools and attempting to deal with social problems of the London slums by creating new nursery schools, Maria Montessori was dealing with similar problems in Italy. She, too, was trying to break the traditional practices in Italian education by organizing early childhood programs for retarded children in institutions, and then for normal children from the slums of Rome.

The target population and the social concerns of the British Nursery School and the Montessori School were essentially the same. Both focused upon children of the poor. Both were influenced by Sequin's philosophy and methodologies, and both emphasized sensory education as a means for facilitating children's development. But the British nursery school was broadly conceived and delivered a comprehensive type of program, including work with parents; Montessori's system was more narrowly defined. The Montessori curriculum was more precisely developed—including its philosophy, teaching methodology, and materials. Montessori schools developed separately from nursery and kindergarten programs in America. Nonetheless, her methods strongly influenced the content and methodology of nursery schools as they evolved. To trace the birth and early development of nursery schools in America, the nursery school movement and the Montessori school movement are best dealt with separately.

The MacMillan sisters' early nursery schools in England   Rachel and Margaret MacMillan established the first nursery school in London, England. Concerned about health problems plaguing British slum children, the MacMillans initiated a health clinic in 1910 called the Deptford Schools Treatment Center (Whitbread, 1972). The clinic later evolved into an open-air school for which the sisters coined the term "nursery school." Their school was an attempt at early *prevention* of children's illnesses, both mental and physical. Their philosophy was one of nurturance and concern for the whole child, thus emphasizing social, physical, emotional, and intellectual aspects of children's well-being. The school was viewed as responsible not only for the education of young children, but also for "bathing them, clothing them, resting them, and seeing that they received plenty of fresh air and physical exercise."

Curriculum and teaching methodologies were inspired more by Sequin, the French educator who worked with retarded children, than by Froebel. Curriculum was based upon social concerns and values as opposed to the religious values that were basic to Froebel's approach. Children's activities focused on a different set of priorities: skills for self-care (such as shoe-tying and washing), learning responsibility (such as care of animals, cleaning the school rooms, caring for plants), and sensory education through music and rhythm activities, language education, and activities to teach form and color. Pre-reading, writing, math, and science also were emphasized.

The MacMillan sisters were highly successful in selling their nursery school concept in England. Their endorsement came in a sense through passage of the Fisher Act of 1918, allowing the organization of programs like theirs in British school systems. Monies to finance the effort, however, were never forthcoming, so the system didn't evolve as it was intended. This occurrence has repeated itself many times since then in the history of early childhood education.

Beginnings of the nursery school in America   The nursery school movement began slowly in the U.S., with much less active proselyting and fervent salesmanship than was associated with the kindergarten movement. Yet, several key events launched the nursery school on American shores. First, two women—each of whom had become acquainted with the MacMillan sisters—independently initiated nursery schools. *Abigail Eliot* brought the nursery school movement from England to the U.S. by establishing the Ruggles Street Nursery in Boston in 1922.* Eliot's school was consistent with the philosophy and methodology established by the MacMillan sisters. *Edna Noble White* also established a nursery program at the Merrill-Palmer School in 1922.

Both Eliot and White added some new dimensions to the nursery school philosophy as it was translated into the American version of nursery school education. Dr. Eliot was a social worker by training. Her concerns went beyond children to include their parents. Dr. White was a home economist whose background and professional training also produced an orientation toward the training of mothers and a concern for the total family. Both added this unique element to their early education programs—conferring an importance on parent involvement within the nursery school. This orientation has continued in nursery schools ever since, albeit to varying degrees and through different means for eliciting parental involvement. Eliot and White also injected a new interdisciplinary flavor to the field by initiating the involvement of professionals from fields other than education.

Other distinct differences between the nursery school and the early kindergarten were apparent. In kindergarten considerable attention was given to children's *readiness* for school. In contrast, nursery school goals were oriented toward "nurturance" and "satisfaction of exploration" of young children at 2, 3, and 4 years of age (Osborn, 1975).

In addition to the early influences of Eliot and White, a second happening helped establish the nursery school as an American institution. Several University Centers for Child Study established model programs. These were the beginnings of the university

---

*Osborn (1975) indicated that a cooperative nursery was established previously in Chicago, in 1916.

child development laboratories found in departments of home economics or departments of human development and family life. The Gesell Child Guidance Nursery at Yale University, the Merrill-Palmer Institute in Detroit, Teachers College at Columbia University, and the Iowa Child Welfare Research Station at the University of Iowa are examples. These laboratories served three important functions: (a) teacher training, (b) research, and (c) services to children. Important research came from these early child study centers (e.g., Gesell's normative, longitudinal studies on developmental sequences, Goodenough's IQ studies at Minnesota, Skeels' and his colleagues' studies on IQ at Iowa, and Parten's well known work that gave rise to the description of children's play as solitary, parallel, and cooperative). Other agencies followed the demonstration efforts of these child study centers and established nursery schools (Osborn, 1975). By the early 1930s approximately 200 were in existence, about half associated with colleges and universities, a third under privately owned schools, and another fifth operated by child welfare agencies. This unusual variety of sponsors has continued to characterize the operation of nursery schools in the United States (Spodek, 1978).

During the mid-1920s and early 1930s other significant events gave deeper roots to the nursery school movement. In 1925, under the leadership of Patty Smith Hill, a group of early educators established the forerunner of what is now the major national professional organization concerned with early childhood education. The group became the National Committee on Nursery Schools and changed its name a few years later to the National Association for Nursery Education (NANE). In 1964 that name was changed again, to the National Association for the Education of Young Children (NAEYC).

Impact of the Depression and World War II   The Depression of the 1930s and World War II had a significant impact on the development of nursery school programs. Teachers were left unemployed when previously thriving centers could no longer pay their salaries. The federal government took action in 1933 by funding nursery schools via the Federal Emergency Relief Act (FERA) and later under the Works Projects Administration (WPA), to provide jobs for teachers and other workers. These nursery schools were operated through the public schools. They provided educational services for young children and stimulated teacher training programs to help teachers acquire the skills needed to operate the programs. These federally sponsored nursery schools added up to several thousand—far more than had been in existence prior to the Depression.

WPA nursery schools came to an end as the Depression finally passed and World War II brought new social priorities. No longer was the problem one of unemployment for teachers. It was the opposite. Labor forces were needed for the war industry and for vacancies left by men who were called into the armed forces. Nearly one-third of the female population began working in defense plants and factories (Osborn, 1975; Spodek, 1978). Again, the need for education and care facilities for children of working mothers brought the federal government into the nursery school and day-care business. Through the Lanham Act of 1940, funds were allocated to establish care and educational centers for young children.

During this period the division between day-care and nursery schools at times became a bit fuzzy. Some programs provided only care and general supervision; others were concerned about the educational experiences available to children (Spodek, 1978). But then the war ended, and federal support for the programs was again withdrawn. Some programs were terminated. Day-care programs that survived continued to operate under the sponsorship of local governmental agencies and philanthropic organizations.

Post-War and contemporary nursery school trends   The nursery school movement continued to develop slowly and proceeded through its own organizational metamorphosis until the mid 1960s. Nursery education, however, did not experience the turmoil and national fanfare that characterized the kindergarten movement. Spodek (1978) pointed out that although changes took place over the years, the original eclectic philosophy upon which nursery programs were based allowed for considerable fluctuation and diversity in the approaches used without serious conflict among its leaders. This was not so with advocates of the kindergarten, who became involved in bitter debates about the purpose and methodology of the kindergarten. Some important changes that did occur in nursery or preschool programs included:

1. Nursery school education gradually moved away from its origins as a program for the poor to one for the affluent. Part of this transition is attributable to the continual problems in financing nursery education. When government support was absent, most schools survived on the basis of tuition payments from parents. As a result, many poor families could not participate.
2. Health aspects of the nursery school were deemphasized. Improved conditions in the U.S. resulted in a move away from schools' assuming responsibility for nutrition, health, and personal hygiene. Programs were shortened to half days and often 2- to 3-day-per-week schedules. With Head Start came a revival of these prior concerns and a reinstatement of health and nutrition as part of early education programs.
3. Curricular emphases expanded from a primary concern with "training the senses" to a broader educational program. Conditions that gave rise to reforms within the kindergarten movement also provided the impetus for change in the nursery education curriculum, including more attention to emotional development and social learning. More recently, however, the pendulum again has swung back to greater concern about cognitive and language development, although not to the extent that the emphasis upon a broad curriculum orientation has been lost.

Maria Montessori's nursery school in Italy   Parallel to the work of the MacMillan sisters in England, Maria Montessori (1870-1952) opened the first nursery school in the slums of Rome in 1907. A new housing development in the most poverty- and crime-stricken area of the city had been created as a private philanthropy. Its owners, hoping to minimize vandalism from children in the area, offered Montessori space for her school. Thus evolved Montessori's *casa dei bambini* (home of children), which accepted children from 3 years of age and older for care from 6 to 8 hours a day. There Montessori continued to refine the ideas and methodologies she had developed earlier in her work with mentally retarded children. Her successes far surpassed expectations of her sponsors and attracted worldwide attention. Not only was vandalism prevented, but many children learned basic academic skills such as counting, reading, and writing before they were 5 years old (Frost & Kissinger, 1976; Weber, 1969).

Montessori's background and her work are of special interest as we trace the threads of history underlying early childhood education for the handicapped. Maria Montessori was a physician, the first woman in Italy to receive the doctor of medicine and a Ph.D. degree in anthropology. Though her work is associated primarily with nursery and pre-school education for normal children, her early activities as a physician began with mentally retarded children. She drew upon the work of Itard and Sequin, modifying and elaborating their materials and methodology.

In 1898 Montessori became director of Rome's Orthophrenic School, an institution for retarded children. There she personally trained teachers to carry out her carefully designed education program. Her successes with the children were notable and largely attributed to her special materials and methods. If retarded children could progress to academic levels somewhat comparable to that of normal children in ordinary settings, what could normal children achieve if they were given well designed educational environments? The opportunity for Montessori to answer this question came when she established her *casa dei bambini* in Rome. She applied the methods she had used with retarded children to normal and disadvantaged children from the slums to create an ideal learning environment. She was convinced that the first six years of life were the most critical period in a child's development.

Maria Montessori wrote volumes describing her philosophy of early childhood education and what a nursery school environment should be. Her many books include *The Absorbent Mind, The Montessori Method,* and *The Advanced Montessori Method.* She prescribed the learning materials for children and the sequence in which they should be used. She also outlined the procedures teachers should follow. Montessori's method broke completely with the traditions of her time by organizing activities for the individual child rather than the group. Discarded was the formal classroom structure, including desks, benches, and stationary chairs. In their place came movable chairs, tables, and cupboards of child size so that they were indeed accessible. Learning was organized around "autoeducative" materials—that is, the child could use materials of his or her own choosing and engage in activities that were self-teaching.

Most central to the Montessori method is her *prepared environment,* which includes an array of organized and coordinated materials that promote certain kinds of learning. She advocated that a nursery school be scaled physically and conceptually to the needs of children—not adults. Thus, child-size furniture, eating utensils, work and play items are used.

The Montessori curriculum encompasses four primary areas of learning: motor, sensory, language, and academic education. Several key instructional and learning principles central to the Montessori method are (Evans, 1975):

— heterogeneous grouping of children by age.
— learning through involvement by children.
— self-selection of materials by child, and self-pacing.
— use of materials that are self-correctional.
— arrangement of learning activities in graded sequences.
— emphasis of learning activities on one sensory modality at a time.

The movement of Montessori education to America in the early 1900s was affected by the turmoil at that time among American educators over Froebelian doctrine. At the height of this controversy, Montessori education (which Froebelian advocates considered a rival) gained national attention. American kindergarten educators made a brief attempt to investigate Montessori's system. Some traveled to Italy to observe her school, but many went along with preestablished biases in favor of Froebelian philosophy, making it difficult to view the Montessori system openly. One influential visitor who traveled to Italy was William Kilpatrick, a highly respected member of the educational elite in America. Upon his return he wrote an extensive and critical analysis of the Montessori method, which had a deadly impact upon American interest in Montessori education. His report, *The Montessori System Examined* (Kilpatrick, 1914), delivered initially in a keynote address before the International Kindergarten Union in 1913, followed by a flurry of articles in the *Kindergarten Review* and a series of meetings of the Kindergarten Department within the National Education Association, exhausted all interest in the Montessori system.

By 1916 interest in Montessori had died. No further mention was made of it in meetings of the various organizations. Attention turned to more heated controversies among American educators over Froebelian philosophy and the new progressive, liberal education advocated by John Dewey and his followers. Looking at the philosophical controversy at that time, it is easy to see why Montessori notions did not gain popularity. The inflexibility of American educators was intensified by their own battles in which their own philosophical positions had to be solidified and sometimes exaggerated. Controversy was so hot that those involved formally declared their standing within one of three distinct camps: the conservative camp (which contained the traditional Froebelian educators), the liberal-progressive camp (which consisted of followers of John Dewey's progressive educational concepts), and the liberal-conservative compromise camp (which included those who wanted to integrate the best from both philosophical points of view). To bring another theoretical position into the midst of their heated debates would have been even more troublesome.

Montessori's ideas did gain the attention of some lay citizens, who established a few schools in the 1920s, but most disappeared during the 1930s and 1940s. Then in the 1960s interest in Montessori education revived. Private schools again began to appear, and the American Montessori movement was reestablished. Today, Montessori programs are growing in number—although with great variability in their adherence to the original system created by their leader. Some Montessori schools adhere strictly to the original methods; others use a modified approach; and still others use only her materials without particular attention to the methodology or philosophy.

Additional changes have taken place in Montessori education. Programs have moved away from an emphasis upon the poor to primary application with children from more affluent families. Original applications of the Montessori system with retarded and handicapped children tended to be forgotten, as most Montessori schools primarily serve normally developing children. Recently, however, some attention has been given again to applications of Montessori methods with disadvantaged children and young handicapped preschoolers (Orem, 1969). The impact of Montessori's ideas, and particularly her didactic materials, upon early childhood education in general is significant. Montessori materials or adaptations of them are found in most early childhood classrooms today.

The day-care movement

Child-care centers, sometimes called day-care programs or day nurseries, originally were designed to serve a caretaking rather than an educational function. They were an outgrowth of the Industrial Revolution, when the establishment of factory systems brought many women and children into the labor force.

The history of the day-care movement in America can be divided into three major periods (Steinfels, 1973). The *first period,* prior to the 1920s, was a time of rapid industrial growth. Just as day nurseries became common in Europe during its Industrial Revolution, so did they appear rapidly on the American scene. Child-care centers were viewed as essential services to allow women to assume jobs outside the home. The *second period,* from about 1920 through the 1940s, was a time when child-care services were limited primarily to cases of special need. As described earlier, the Depression and World War II had a major impact upon both child-care programs and the nursery school movement. Child-care centers increased dramatically then to free women for jobs in the war industry. The end of the war also brought an end, however, to federal support for child services. Programs that continued were more limited in scope and tended to be viewed as child welfare services to families in difficulty who were unable to assume traditional child-rearing responsibilities. This became a stigma that continued for many years in regard to day-care services (Hymes, 1972; Leeper, Witherspoon, & Day, 1984).

Some significant changes began to occur in the character of day-care centers during this second period. This can be attributed, in part, to the influence of the nursery school movement upon the day-care movement during the time of the Depression and World War II. Mixing of the two movements was inevitable, simply because both were concerned with the same age group of children. Some day-care centers began to incorporate more educationally oriented activities into their care procedures, although not to the extent they could be called educational programs. They also began to limit care to children of certain ages who could meet certain entry requirements (e.g., they were toilet trained, could feed themselves, and were sufficiently manageable to function in a group setting). This, of course, closed the doors of the centers to children who were unable to meet the prerequisites because of handicapping conditions and helps explain why handicapped children were consistently excluded from many of these programs. In addition, the continuing trend to institutionalize handicapped children, coupled with the skepticism about their ability to profit from education, contributed to their exclusion.

The *third period* in the history of the day-care movement came in the 1960s, when child care became a more standard and accepted part of the American way of life. Day-care, as well as nursery school programs, had fallen to a low ebb during post-World War II years. A revival began when the federal government again became involved in early childhood services through the Economic Opportunity Act and the Elementary and Secondary Education Act. Both laws focused upon the special needs of disadvantaged children. The civil rights movement also resulted in new services to minority groups. Day-care and nursery school programs once again began to flourish.

The 1970s brought new social forces into play that greatly affected children's programs. Inflation and economic growth sent increasing numbers of women back to work and into universities for higher education. Day care again became an important and acceptable institution for the average American working family—not just a service used by the poor. Attitudes about the care of children outside the home changed dramatically. Several factors made these attitudinal changes almost inevitable: the women's movement and the changing status of women in our society, increased urbanization and shifts from the nuclear family, new knowledge about child development, and research suggesting that quality child care and early education do not have a negative effect on children as had been believed previously.

In looking at the history of child care, government involvement has been a major force. Much of the federal government's involvement in child care and early childhood education since the 1960s has focused upon *compensatory education programs* (e.g., Head Start). These programs, by themselves, constitute a major movement in the U.S. and exert a major influence on early childhood education today. In the following section we shall take a look at the significant historical events surrounding development of compensatory education programs.

In reviewing the day-care movement, we find that no significant leaders became identified with the growth of day-care services. Programs resulted largely from important economic needs and emergency political conditions, not from the efforts of visible advocates parallel to those who took up the banners for kindergarten and nursery school education. Perhaps this explains why day-care programs have been less definitive about their purpose (other than that of general care), their philosophy about what constitutes quality child care, and their curriculum and caretaking procedures. Only as more educationally oriented figures crossed the lines into day care, and as the line between nursery school and day care became more unclear, have professionals from both fields worked together to address the programmatic and curricular issues of day care. For many years there was a major split between day-care and nursery school personnel, each looking disparagingly at the other and its practices.

An analysis of the early childhood education movement

Spodek (1978) characterized the spirit of the American early childhood education movement as one of *eclecticism*. The genius of the American approach, he suggested, has been in its eclectic nature, in that Americans were willing to accept new and foreign methods and theories—albeit with much debate. New ideas were not rejected but, rather, were absorbed in pieces or parts into American thought and educational practices. In fact, seldom did any pure form of any particular philosophy remain uncontaminated for long once it came upon American soil. America's pragmatism and dogged functionalism, which so characterized both psychology and education, constantly forced change. Debate or philosophical warfare was always going on between psychologists and educators. As a result of the interactions among the opposing ideologies, an American version of early childhood education emerged with its own unique flavor. As Spodek described it, American early childhood education was consistently yet flexibly developed. The best from Froebel, the MacMillan sisters, Montessori, and other European theorists was taken and incorporated into the philosophy of American educators such as John Dewey and Patty Hill and psychologists such as G. Stanley Hall, E. L. Thorndike, J. B. Watson, and William James.

Kindergarten and nursery schools have continued to be an important part of American education, but kindergarten has been supported largely by the public school system and nursery schools have remained the responsibility of a variety of agencies, including state and local governmental departments, private profit and nonprofit concerns, religious groups, universities and research centers, and philanthropic groups. Because of this diversity in sponsorship, nursery schools have not had the continuity that allows for systematic development of their methodology and philosophy. Nursery schools have been subject to the ups and downs of our economy and to the social-political influences that increase or depress the need for early childhood services. Current social trends have increased the demands for a more expertly blended combination of quality day-care and early education programs.

The increasing popularity of early childhood education and day-care programs is clearly shown in a recent federal report on *The Condition of Education* from the National Center for Educational Statistics (Dearman & Plisko, 1980). Results from a comprehensive study of children enrolled in kindergarten, nurseries, preschools, and day-care programs throughout the United States indicated the following:

1. The number of children who participate in preprimary programs prior to their entry into public school at age 5 or 6 is increasing rapidly. Over 50% of children 3-5 years of age participated in preprimary programs in 1978, whereas less than 30% attended such programs in 1966. At the end of 1980, enrollment of this age group in preprimary programs was estimated to be near 7 million.
2. Use of day services by families for care of children ages 3-5 years is increasing significantly. In 1976-1977 an estimated 18,300 day-care centers were serving over 900,000 children. Currently, the largest users of day-care services are single-parent families and low-income families.
3. Increasing numbers of children from low-income families are participating in preprimary programs. Over 400,000 preschoolers from low-income families are being served each year through Head Start programs. Although this number has increased significantly since Head Start began in 1965, it still represents only a small proportion (approximately 20%) of all preschool children living in poverty.
4. Interest among educated, middle-class parents in exposing their children to early educational experiences is accelerating. Almost two-thirds of 3- to 5-year-olds from homes in which the head of household has completed college degrees are participating in preschool or preprimary programs.
5. The rise in number of women reentering the work force and pursuing careers accounts for the growing popularity of nursery and preschool programs. Enrollment of 3-year-olds in programs appears to be clearly associated with employment status of mothers—that is, 30% of 3-year-olds with working mothers attend preschools, compared to 19% of those with mothers who are at home.

Conclusions from this nationwide study suggested that with the anticipated rise in births during the 1980s and the continued participation of women in the labor force, preprimary education will continue to grow in size as well as importance.

THE COMPENSATORY EDUCATION MOVEMENT

This movement is an important precursor to early childhood-special education in the sense that it was instrumental in establishing the notion of *early intervention*. Application of this concept came to the forefront primarily through poverty programs such as Project Head Start and Follow-Through.

Compensatory education programs, as the name implies, were created to compensate for real or perceived deficits in the early experience and education of disadvantaged children. The target of these programs was not the handicapped per se but, rather, children from low socioeconomic, poverty stricken homes. A large number of these children came from racial-ethnic minority groups. Research indicates that, as a group, these children showed performance deficits in mental ability (Scholnick, Olser, & Katzenellenboger, 1968), linguistic performance (Deutch, 1965), and other academic areas (Jensen, 1969; Findlay & McGuire, 1957). They also showed higher rates of failure in the public schools and more frequent placement in special education classes for the mentally retarded (Dunn, 1968; Mercer, 1973). A variety of compensatory education programs therefore was created to intervene in their lives and prevent the school failure for which they seemed so destined. Head Start and Follow-Through were two of the larger, most visible of these early intervention programs, although a myriad of smaller-scale programs also was created. As shown repeatedly in the early history of the nursery school and kindergarten movements, federal government involvement typically has been the catalyst for growth and innovation in early childhood education. Once again this was demonstrated with the compensatory education movement.

Project Head Start

Early history   Project Head Start was an outgrowth of the War on Poverty and the political climate of the 1960s that gave rise to the civil rights movement. The Kennedy and Johnson administrations and Americans at large rediscovered at that time what has been labeled the "other America" (Harrington, 1962). Some 35 million citizens were estimated to be living in poverty in the midst of what seemed to be an affluent American society. Reports to the Kennedy administration in 1963 revealed that over 9 million families existed on annual incomes of under $3,000. The family head in over 60% of those families had only a grade-school education (Johnson, 1965). The impoverished families lacked adequate food, housing, and health care. At the same time, growing unrest of the Black minority in America called attention to inequities in housing, living conditions, employment, and educational opportunities. These inequities and social discrimination placed a high proportion of minority groups among the ranks of the poor.

Rising crime rates and declines in qualified manpower for military services and private industry further pointed to social problems of the time. According to a report of the President's Task Force on Manpower Conservation (1964), of the men drafted for military service, over half of that group was physically or mentally unfit for service because of deficiencies arising from poor health and inadequate nutrition. Of those rejected, 40% were high school dropouts and another 40% had not progressed past the eighth grade. The Task Force suggested that the inferior living conditions and social behaviors characterizing the poor were passed on from generation to generation in a "cycle of poverty" (Moynihan, 1964). The Kennedy, and later the Johnson, administration viewed the problems and conditions of poverty as being so widespread that they threatened the nation's social and economic well-being, and called for immediate and widescale action. The federal government's War on Poverty and its social action programs sought to break this vicious cycle.

The War on Poverty embodied a basic belief that education would help children break out of the cycle of poverty (Zigler & Valentine, 1979). Head Start was conceived as one means for achieving this. In 1965 Project Head Start was initiated as an 8-week pilot program for children in over 2,600 communities through the auspices of the Office of Economic Opportunity (OEO). It was hoped that participation in Head Start would prepare children for more successful entry into the public school system. Soon after Head Start began, though, the need for a longer program became apparent. Consequently, Head Start was extended to a full year program.

Head Start was controversial from its outset. Events surrounding the program's initial planning and its initial years of implementation were colorful and filled with excitement. The tremendous deployment of resources and involvement of a wide cross-section of parents, professionals, community leaders, and all ethnic groups across the country to develop this early intervention program were impressive. A vivid, detailed account of the early history of Head Start is given in an excellent book, edited by Zigler and Valentine (1979), entitled *Project Head Start: A Legacy of the War on Poverty*. Head Start constituted the first comprehensive approach to early childhood intervention on a nationwide basis. It brought immediate national awareness to the concept of early intervention and generated tremendous enthusiasm about the promise it held for young children. It was also the first federal program designed to "strike at the very roots of poverty" by bringing about change not only in young children, but also in their homes, families, and community (Zigler & Anderson, 1979).

The plan behind Head Start   Project Head Start was built on three major premises (Evans, 1975; Zigler & Valentine, 1979): (a) Prekindergarten or pre-first grade education would facilitate successful entry of disadvantaged children into regular school programs, (b) the quality of intellectual development in young children is dependent upon their early experience and quality of care, and (c) impoverished environments contain elements (such as poor nutrition and health care, lack of educational opportunity, lack of stimulation, and an atmosphere of defeatism) that can impede achievement and intellectual growth in young children.

Head Start planners designed it to be something more than just a preschool readiness program. It was to be a comprehensive intervention into all aspects of children's early development—physical and mental health, social and emotional development, cognitive development, self-confidence and motivation, family relations and attitudes toward society and its institutions (Brain, 1979; Grotberg, 1969). The idea of a comprehensive preschool program for children of any socioeconomic group was new. Its planners urged the Office of Economic Opportunity to create programs aimed at the *whole child* and to "avoid financing programs which do not have at least a minimal level and quality of activities from each of the three fields of effort [health, social services, and education]" (President's Panel on Mental Retardation, 1963).

Head Start was intended to bring change at the very grass roots of American society—in children, their families, and their communities. Though the program had much in common with the kindergarten and nursery school movements, it embodied several unique dimensions. *First,* it was not viewed simply as an education or day-care program. Instead, it comprised a multi-component, comprehensive, multidisciplinary intervention approach encompassing the educational and preschool classroom program, medical-dental services, nutrition program, social services, psychological services, parent involvement and education, and a volunteer program. It also included staff training to prepare low-income parents for job roles within centers and to help low-income adults progress upward on a career ladder to carry them out of their poverty status.

Second, Head Start was not administered through traditional public school administrative structures. Programs were established under separate Community Action Agencies (or CAP Agencies, as they are called). CAPs directly operated Head Start centers or contracted with other community organizations (called "delegate agencies") to operate programs. Occasionally public schools serve as delegate agencies. This seems to be the exception, however, rather than the rule.

Third, Head Start emphasized parent involvement much beyond that practiced traditionally in elementary schools or nurseries and preschools. The intent was to bring parents into full partnership in the intervention with their child and in the operation of a social action program in their own community. Among the several unique avenues for parent involvement created within Head Start are: (a) involvement in decision making for the program through participation as members of Parent Advisory Committees (PACs), which were organized for each community, (b) involvement as volunteers for various program functions, (c) employment as paraprofessionals with subsequent training to allow a means for upward mobility along a career ladder (Valentine & Stark, 1979).

A *fourth* unique feature of Head Start was the involvement of professionals from many disciplines in its service program, because of the comprehensive approach to intervention. This contributed much to the beginning of the now more common team approach to early intervention.

Head Start initiated its handicapped services component in 1972 in response to a federal mandate that no less than 10% of its enrollment be reserved for handicapped children. This brought increased visibility to the special needs of this young population.

The effects of Head Start   Considerable attention has been given to the question: Is Head Start effective? Reports on the successes and failures of Head Start are conflicting. Heated debates have raged over interpretations of Head Start research data and conclusions to be drawn. In a historical overview of research on the outcomes of Head Start, Datta (1979) noted that interpretations of Head Start's effectiveness have shifted three times since 1965. From 1965 to 1968 Head Start was considered a tremendous success. This was the golden era, fueled by the enthusiasm of the "great society" and the idealized hopes that Head Start and other federal social action programs could marshal the forces of American society to attack the very roots of poverty. Research data were interpreted as evidence that the program had immediate and possibly durable benefits for young children. From 1969 to 1974 came the "winter of disillusionment," and with it much skepticism about the power of Head Start to produce the outcomes it had promised. The dampening of hopes for the program's success came from publication of the highly publicized 1969 Westinghouse Research Report. It represented one of the first comprehensive studies of Head Start outcomes from June, 1968, through May, 1969. From that study came four major conclusions (Westinghouse Learning Corp., 1969):

1. Summer programs appeared to be relatively ineffective in producing gains in cognitive and affective development that persisted on into the early primary grades.
2. Full-year programs appeared marginally effective in producing gains in cognitive development that could be detected in grades 1, 2, or 3 when viewed from an overall group analysis. Programs appeared to be of greater effectiveness for certain subgroups of centers.
3. Head Start children, whether from summer or full-year programs, still appeared to be

in a disadvantageous position in regard to national norms of standardized tests of language and scholastic achievement.

4. Head Start appeared to have a positive effect on parents. They voiced strong approval of the program and its influence on their children.

The Westinghouse report made several recommendations that provided the rationale for intervention strategies that were later initiated. In general, the report suggested that: (a) Programs should be year long if intervention is to be most effective; (b) if possible, intervention should begin in infancy and continue into the primary grades, (c) more refined and intensive intervention strategies should be applied with a curriculum focused specifically upon the areas of greatest deficiency in the children (such as in language, auditory association, and math concepts) and upon concepts and skills needed in the primary grades; and (d) parents should be trained to help their own children by becoming more effective teachers of their children at home (Westinghouse Learning Corp., 1969).

Although the Westinghouse study reported a number of significant and lasting benefits for some children (particularly Black urban children), the most publicized finding was that cognitive gains made by Head Start graduates faded away as they moved through the elementary grades. As a result, much of the Westinghouse Report was interpreted as evidence that the program had failed its mission. The debate that followed resulted in arguments that expectations placed upon Head Start were unrealistic and that it was not a cure-all. Some suggested that intervention strategies used in Head Start classrooms were not specific enough to address the performance deficits of disadvantaged children. Consequently, the intervention was not sufficient to produce notable and enduring changes on test scores for IQ, cognitive development, and academic achievement.

In essence, the criteria used to assess Head Start's effectiveness were not appropriate. Datta (1979) pointed out that the overly publicized findings of the Westinghouse Report brought a disproportionate emphasis upon its pessimistic conclusions to the neglect of many other parallel studies that showed positive outcomes. For some time, Head Start's future looked dismal.

A third shift in the outlook upon Project Head Start occurred around 1975 as the dark clouds of pessimism began to disperse. The climate of opinion changed to a more favorable, perhaps more realistic outlook on the outcomes of early childhood intervention programs. Although not all Head Start children maintained the cognitive gains they achieved, several studies showed that many children continued to show cognitive superiority over non-Head Start peers well into the elementary grades (Richmond, Stipek, & Zigler, 1979). New longitudinal studies from Yale University (Zigler & Yale Research Group, 1976) suggested a possible "sleeper effect" as Head Start youngsters proceed through school. For example, one group of Head Starters evidenced no greater gains than a control group at third grade. Yet, by the end of the fifth grade, the Head Start graduates demonstrated significant superiority in three of five measures of academic achievement. Palmer and Anderson (1979) reported a similar delayed effect resulting from preschool intervention programs. A summary of the findings and interpretations of Head Start effectiveness reported by Datta (1979) follows.

Community impact   Head Start was intended to provide a vehicle for effecting change in communities. Research findings suggest that it has successfully facilitated this process by (a) bringing greater education emphasis upon the needs of poor and minority groups, (b) modifying health services and practices to bring more attention and sensitivity to the needs of low-income children and their families, (c) increasing the participation of low-income parents at decision-making levels and in decision-making capacities, and (d) creating greater employment of local citizens in paraprofessional work (Kirschner Associates, 1970; Greenburg, 1969; MIDCO, 1972; O'Keefe, 1979).

Impact on children's personal-social development   A goal of Head Start has been to encourage children's self-confidence, including a motivation to perform well in school, and a capacity to relate positively to their families and peers. Studies on this outcome have examined a myriad of personal-social variables and employed many different measurement strategies. Positive outcomes have been found, including: (a) Head Start graduates showed short-term gains in task orientation, social adjustment, achievement orientation, and ability to form close friendships with other children (Dunteman, 1972; Coulson, 1972; Emmerich, 1971); (b) Head Start graduates were rated higher by their elementary school teachers in leadership, self-confidence, persistence, and emotional maturity, and in ability to create their own solutions to problems, as compared to non-Head Start graduates (Abelson, Zigler, & DeBlasi, 1974; Beller, 1974).

School readiness and achievement after Head Start   Although Head Start did not stress specific skills training in academic areas per se, one of its long-range goals has been to enhance the chances for children to succeed in the public schools. Several studies document significant gains in school readiness and a modest effect upon IQ test performance (Dunteman, 1972; Coulson, 1972; Stanford Research Institute, 1971a, 1971b, 1971c). Smith (1973) found accelerated rates of growth in children during the time they were in Head Start. The conclusions were that Head Start not only improved IQ scores for some children, but perhaps arrested an imminent decline in IQ performance that otherwise would be expected for disadvantaged children who received no intervention.

Impact of school achievement after Head Start   Studies have indicated that Head Start graduates, as a group, enter public school close to or at national norms on tests of school readiness. This advantage appeared to be maintained for the first year. It tended to wash out in regard to academic performance, however, as the children proceeded on into the higher elementary grades. Continued intervention through programs such as Follow-Through help prevent losses. Other research data on Head Start suggest that over the long haul, Head Start graduates are more likely to keep pace with classmates, to be placed less frequently in special education classes, and less likely to be held back in a grade (Datta, 1979; Shipman, 1972a, 1972b; Abelson et al., 1974; Royster, 1977; and Weisberg & Haney, 1977).

Project Follow-Through

The need for continued intervention   The national Follow-Through program represents one of the largest, longest, and most studied *experimental* early childhood education intervention efforts conducted to date under the auspices of the federal government (Hodges et al., 1980). In 1967 the program was launched in answer to research findings that cognitive gains made by Head Start graduates over non-Head Start children disappeared when they entered the elementary grades. Short-term preschool programs clearly were not sufficient to overcome the effect of impoverished environments on the development and learning of young children. Because low-income children continued to live in those environments, effective intervention would require follow-up and support for children and their families beyond the preschool years. As Edward Zigler (1978), former Director of the Health, Education, and Welfare Office of Child Development, pointed out, "We can never inoculate children in one year against the ravages of deprivation; there must be continuity" (p. 5).

Recognizing the necessity for continuous intervention, President Lyndon B. Johnson proposed to the 90th Congress in January of 1967: "We should strengthen the Head Start program, begin it for children 3 years old, and maintain its educational momentum by following through in the early years of school" (Johnson, 1967). Project Follow-Through thus was created as an upward extension of Head Start into the elementary school—specifically into kindergarten and grades 1-3. In keeping with the philosophy of comprehensive services, Follow-Through incorporated the same multi-component services approach used within Head Start. Like its sister program, Follow-Through focused not only upon the child, but also upon the task of creating change in the school, the family, and the community, in order to minimize the adverse influences of poverty and to maximize the benefits of an intervention program.

Originally Follow-Through was planned as a prototype of Head Start—as another early childhood service program for low-income children in the primary grades. But it took on a new dimension when the anticipated budget of $120 million for the first year of Follow-Through was drastically cut by Congress to a mere $15 million. Such a major budget cut jeopardized the very existence of the program, so its planners went back to the drawing board. Their reconceptualization of Follow-Through resulted in its new identity as an *experimental research and development program* and the launching of one of the most significant educational experiments to date. Follow-Through was transformed from a service operation similar to Head Start to what has been called the *Planned Variation Experiment* (Haney, 1977). This is perhaps the single most distinctive feature of Follow-Through when compared to other compensatory education programs. The purpose of this new experimental emphasis was to study various approaches for raising the educational attainment of students, according to the Task Force on Child Development (U.S. Department of Health, Education, & Welfare, 1967).

Follow-Through united educational theory and practice by identifying, developing, and validating alternative approaches to the education of low-income children in the primary elementary grades. Thus, Follow-Through did not embrace one ideal approach to early childhood education and impose it upon public school systems. Instead, alternative approaches or *program models*, as they were called, were identified. Participating school districts selected the model they wished to implement in their own Follow-Through program. Nationwide research was conducted to monitor children's progress across the various programs over a period of years to determine which approach worked best under what circumstances. Robert L. Egbert served as director of this unique educational experiment.

Follow-Through program models   Under the planned variation experiment, various program models were created by prominent educators, psychologists, or researchers who had previously operated experimental programs for young children. The U.S. Office of Education invited the participation of these various educational specialists, who became known as *model sponsors*, to assume responsibility for working with a group of school districts designated as Follow-Through sites. Initially 13 model sponsors were selected; others were added later, making a total of 22 sponsors.

Each of the 22 Follow-Through models differed in one or more aspects, such as in its philosophy and values, theoretical underpinnings, instructional goals, teaching methodologies, instructional materials, or curriculum emphases. Each applied its own unique approach to foster what it considered most important to the future academic and life success of low-income children. Although every model is different, the various approaches can be roughly characterized under three broad groups (Stebbins, St. Pierre, Proper, Anderson, & Cerva, 1977): (a) models that focus primarily upon the teaching of basic skills in academic areas (math, reading, language, etc.), (b) models that focus upon cognitive/conceptual skills or upon the processes by which children become efficient learners, and (c) models that focus first upon children's attitudes toward themselves and toward their performance in school and only secondarily upon cognitive or academic skills. (In chapter 9, Program Models for Early Childhood Intervention, selected Follow-Through models are described in detail, including an analysis of the specific components that make up a program model.)

After the model approach was introduced under Follow-Through, other programs began to experiment with various alternatives for serving the needs of special groups of children. Demonstration programs, funded by the federal government for handicapped young children under age 5 though the Handicapped Children's Early Education Program Act (HCEEP Programs) of 1968, also used program models. Head Start, too, experimented with alternative models, and selected centers adopted some of the Follow-Through models as a part of the Head Start Planned Variation Program.

Project Head Start and Follow-Through were not the only compensatory education programs created by the federal government to intervene in the lives of young children who were considered to be at-risk for developmental delay or underachievement. Other notable programs were created during the 1960s and early 1970s for children from low-income families (Valentine, 1979):

- *Parent and Child Centers (PCCs)*. Initiated in 1967, these programs were aimed at children from birth to age 3 *before* they entered Head Start. The intent of the Parent Child Centers was to provide enrichment programs and medical services early in life to disadvantaged children to head off the incremental damages imposed upon them by living in poverty-stricken homes. Basic elements of the PCC Programs were aimed at providing stimulation activities for the children, along with activities for parents.
- *Home Start*. Created in 1972, the purpose of this program was to provide within the home the same child development services available in Head Start centers. The unique feature of the Home Start program was the use of a "home visitor"—a community resident trained in the principles of child development and the goals of Home Start. Home visitors worked with low-income parents to teach them how to provide educational stimulation to their infants and preschool-aged children at home.
- *Head Start/EPSDT Collaborative Projects*. These projects were developed in 1974 as a means for aiding children from low-income families to gain better access to services

provided under the EPSDT program. EPSDT refers to Early Periodic Screening and Developmental Testing, a program created in 1967 as a part of Medicaid (Title XIX of the Social Security Act) and the Maternal and Child Health Program (Title V), which mandates that all children enrolled in Medicaid should be screened regularly during their infant and preschool years to assess their health status and assure appropriate referral for medical care and treatment as needed.

Head Start, Follow-Through, and other compensatory education programs played a major role in turning the attention of American citizens and educators alike to the notion of intervention. More important, these programs brought attention to the need for early intervention in the lives of children *before* reaching school age. And they demonstrated that intervention is a continuous process, not simply a one-shot solution to any child's special needs. Other important outcomes have come from compensatory education programs:

1. They provided the vehicle for involving politicians, professionals, parents, the federal government, and numerous state and local agencies in a nationwide effort to plan and implement social-educational programs aimed at intervention. The availability of funds, the demand for leadership at both national and local levels, the need for policy making to administer funds, and creation of numerous jobs brought about the involvement of citizens from all sectors of society into implementation of these programs.

Our first educational intervention programs focused upon preschoolers from disadvantaged homes and neighborhoods, to prepare them for more successful entry into kindergarten and first grade.

2. They brought millions of federal dollars into educational intervention programs for at-risk populations of children in communities throughout the country and simultaneously created a powerful advocacy group that has lobbied quite successfully since then to maintain these programs.

3. They established a particular philosophical orientation toward early intervention that embodied a comprehensive approach including parents and representatives of many different professional disciplines. In essence, this helped to create the beginnings of the interdisciplinary team approach to early intervention.

4. They established a particular point of view that no one educational approach is necessarily the right or best one for all children and that alternative approaches should be created and encouraged. Follow-Through particularly helped establish the notion of program models and fostered the development of several carefully designed approaches to early childhood education.

5. They fostered a major shift away from traditional early childhood education practices that focused upon a socialization/mental health function and toward a greater concern for intellectual/cognitive stimulation in young children. These programs also established a pattern of greater accountability within educational programs for the intellectual and cognitive outcomes achieved by the children they serve.

In conclusion, the compensatory education movement carried the concept of early intervention into public school programs, into early childhood preschool and day-care programs (as in Head Start), and into professional circles throughout the nation and documented the benefits for children and their parents. Because early childhood education had become an established practice with normally developing preschoolers and special education was established as a means for helping handicapped students in the public schools, attention inevitably turned to a final group of children needing all three kinds of services—special education, early childhood education, and early intervention. Early intervention for handicapped and at-risk preschoolers and infants was a frontier that educators and citizens alike could no longer ignore.

SUMMARY

Three major educational movements were forerunners to EC-SPED or in essence stand as "parent fields": special education as it developed for school-aged students, regular early childhood education, which encompassed several separate but parallel movements (kindergarten, nursery school, and day-care movements), and the compensatory education movement (Head Start, Follow-Through, Home Start, etc.). Each of these parent fields contributed in significant ways to the beginning of a new focus upon educational needs of preschoolers and infants with handicapping or at-risk conditions.

The *special education* movement established the notion that handicapped children can learn and should be entitled to the opportunity for appropriate education alongside their nonhandicapped peers. The *early education* movement brought acceptance to preschool education and day care as worthwhile (and not harmful) experiences for young children. The *compensatory education* movement gave reality to the notion of education intervention by initiating programs designed to prevent children from what seemed to be inevitable failure in our public schools. More important, the compensatory education movement demonstrated that early intervention can make a difference in children's lives and can enhance their chances for success in school. Had these important milestones not been reached, educators probably would not have turned their attention to the needs of handicapped children before reaching school age.

An understanding and appreciation of these historical roots offer some valuable insights into the social-economic-technological forces that have molded the practices now characterizing those parent fields. These practices represent a rich set of traditions that now influence the thinking of professionals who are in a positon to define what EC-SPED will be as a field and what it will offer to young children in its service programs. Many of the issues and problems that professionals have encountered in those earlier movements are the same ones that now must be confronted as early childhood-special education continues to grow in visibility as a new field and as an educational priority in the 1980s and 1990s.

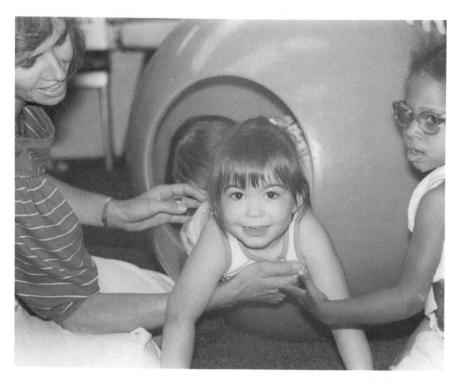

Isn't it fortunate that EC-SPED has finally come of age for young handicapped and at-risk children who, with special training and stimulation, can look forward to a more promising future!

II
SPECIAL CHILDREN
WITH SPECIAL NEEDS

4
Young Children At-Risk
For Developmental Disabilities

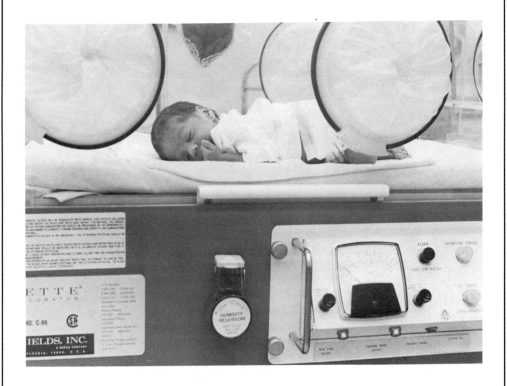

No parents anticipate that they will give birth to a child who is anything less than their ideal image of what a new son or daughter should be. Parents look for and hope for normalcy in their offspring. And for the most part the 20 million* children under age 6 in America today do fulfill those parental expectations. Most are born with intact, strong

---

*From U.S. Bureau of the Census (1983).

bodies. Most grow into healthy, normal children who are capable of learning, thinking, and adapting successfully to the world in which they live. Parents may fuss over the minor imperfections of their offspring—the blue eyes that should have been brown, the hyperactive temperament when a more quiet child would have been preferred, the crooked teeth that someday will require braces, or the stocky, short build when dad was hoping for a future basketball star. Despite those few disappointments, however, most parents still have the assurance that their children are normal and healthy. They can look forward to each phase of childhood and adolescence with confidence that the pains and trials of growing up will pass. Their sons and daughters will grow up, become independent, and some day will leave home to take their places as responsible citizens and parents of a new generation.

But some children's lives do not begin in a normal manner, and their welfare is threatened by conditions that can thwart normal development. Their future is not so certain. Of approximately 3.4 million* children born in the United States each year, over 7% have congenital abnormalities involving genetic, physical, or biological defects. Approximately one-third of those children have congenital abnormalities observable at birth. Their impairments are likely to be the most severe. Disabilities for the remaining two-thirds will become apparent as they grow and develop (or fail to do so) during infancy and the early childhood years.

An even larger percentage of newborn babies is delivered to parents who face serious limitations in their abilities, for whatever reasons, to meet the needs of their children. This latter group of children will grow up in impoverished home environments that may not provide the care and stimulation they need. Many parents from low-income homes do provide adequate care and stimulation for their children in spite of economic limitations, but children of low socioeconomic groups compared to those reared in higher socioeconomic homes show greater risk for disease, poor general health and nutrition, reduced motivation and poor learning habits, and delayed development. Over 4.42 million children under age 6 live in environments like these.* Still other children acquire disabilities as a result of disease, accident, or abuse and neglect by adults (National Center on Child Abuse and Neglect, 1980).

WHEN A CHILD IS AT-RISK

Sometimes an infant or preschooler is described as "at-risk." What does this mean? All children, upon conception and then birth, become subject to the hazards of human existence and of the environment in which they live. Some individuals face greater risks than others that certain factors will alter their physical, mental, or developmental futures. Generally speaking, *children are considered* at-risk *when they have been subjected to certain adverse genetic, prenatal, perinatal (at birth), postnatal, or environmental conditions that are known to cause defects or are highly correlated with the appearance of later abnormalities*. The presence of these risk factors is not necessarily an indication of an impending and inevitable disability. The probabilities simply are increased that these factors are precursory to other difficulties. Given the heightened probabilities, early intervention and prevention become of major importance.

*From U.S. Bureau of the Census (1983).

Tjossem (1976) described three groups of vulnerable infants and young children who are at-risk for developmental disabilities:

1. *Children at established risk*—those with diagnosed medical disorders (usually of known etiology) for which expectancies for physical and developmental insults are known. At least, the range of potential symptoms is known. Children with genetic abnormalities (e.g., Down syndrome) are at established risk because the conditions are known to produce certain abnormalities such as mental retardation, physical stigmata, and various growth deviations. Although some abnormality is inevitable, the ultimate impact upon a youngster's developmental status is variable because the conditions can be tempered somewhat through medical, educational, and therapeutic intervention.

2. *Children at biological risk*—those with prenatal, perinatal, or postnatal histories signaling potential biological insults or underlying problems. Singly or collectively, these conditions increase the probability that aberrant development or learning problems will appear later. At least, the presence of these conditions is highly correlated with the occurrence of various disorders. No clear abnormalities may be detected initially. Examples include complications during the mother's pregnancy (injury, diseases, or infections such as German measles), maternal dysfunction such as diabetes, or complications in labor. Prematurity, low birth weight, serious infections of the nervous system (e.g., encephalitis), and ingestion of toxic substances are other conditions that can render a young child at-biological-risk.

3. *Children at environmental risk*—those who are biologically and genetically normal and intact at birth but whose early life experiences and environmental surroundings impose a threat to their physical and developmental well-being. These conditions relate to the quality of maternal care and stimulation, nutrition, medical care, opportunities for social-educational-sensory stimulation, and the availability of a healthy, psychological environment for the child. Children reared in unnurturing, depriving, and substandard environments are more likely to develop poorly and to show depressed intellectual, language, and academic performance.

These at-risk conditions are not mutually exclusive. They often occur in combination, interacting to increase the probability of delayed or aberrant development in children or to increase the degree of their impairment as a result of some primary physical disability. Tjossem (1976) explained it this way:

> Sources of such interactions are readily evident . . . in biologically vulnerable, premature, and low birth weight infants born to adolescent mothers themselves living in and victims of poverty . . . in the placement, in infancy, of Down's Syndrome infants in the impersonal care of some custodial institutions. They are manifest in the hearing impaired infant born into a poverty stricken home deficient in language stimulation without systematic health care and without knowledge of and motivation to seek corrective resources. They function subtly in affluent homes in which an infant's early problem is met by low parental involvement, nonacceptance, and withdrawal of relationship by the parents. (p. 5)

This interaction among the various at-risk factors often confounds early diagnosis with mixed or unclear etiology and poses a more difficult problem for intervention. For example, treatment of just one problem may not be sufficient to remediate and overcome the total problem.

Adverse pre-, peri-, and postnatal conditions are associated with a tremendous range or continuum of potential outcomes (Knobloch & Pasamanick, 1960, 1967; Spreen, Tupper, Risser, Tuokko, & Edgell, 1984). Outcomes range from no impact and apparent normalcy to severe casualty. A specific disorder may produce any number of abnormalities including congenital malformations, neurological dysfunction, mental retardation, sensory defects, or behavior disorders. The problems that result from pre- and perinatal insults seem to be diminished or intensified by the favorability of the postnatal environment (Braine, Heimer, Wortis, & Freedman, 1966; Drillien, 1964; Hardy, Drage, & Jackson, 1979).

Sameroff and Chandler (1975) used the phrase *continuum of caretaking casualty* to describe this phenomenon. They noted that all pre- and perinatal difficulties do not invariably lead to later problems in that socioeconomic, environmental, and familial factors tend to overshadow the effects of some early difficulties. For example, high socioeconomic status tends to reduce the effects of low birth weight, and poor environmental conditions tend to amplify the effects. Given favorable environmental conditions and caregiving, reproductive complications are less likely to have later disruptive, debilitating consequences, but given unfavorable circumstances, children at-risk may turn out to have developmental disabilities and impairments.

A conservative estimate (10%) suggests that over 2 million children in the U.S. under 6 years of age have one or more conditions in their lives that place them at established, biological, or environmental risk. Their chances of developing normally or achieving their full potential are decreased unless adults take responsible action to intervene.

This chapter will review the major prenatal, perinatal, and postnatal hazards known to cause physical, developmental, and learning problems. Chapters 5 and 6 then examine some of the impacts of at-risk conditions on early development; there we will review how various handicapping conditions are manifest in young children and how those disabilities, in turn, influence learning and early development.

THE MIRACLE OF EARLY DEVELOPMENT

An understanding of handicapping conditions and abnormal development in young children must begin with an understanding of normal human development. The early years of life, beginning with conception until about age 5, constitute a time of phenomenal growth and development—the most rapid in the entire human lifetime. Fertilization of a single egg cell in the mother begins a process of rapid cell division that repeats itself billions of times. In 9 short months, a few delicate cells evolve into a human being complete with all bodily organs and well synchronized metabolic systems that are needed to sustain life.

After birth, physical growth continues to progress at an impressive rate. With the added benefits of learning and maturation, parents witness the metamorphosis of their helpless newborn into a person who can walk, talk, understand the meaning of words and symbols, and engage in surprisingly efficient problem solving if a cookie or toy is to be retrieved. By age 3 or 4, preschoolers have learned a great deal about their environment and will come to expect and anticipate certain responses from parents and significant others. White (1975) described the 2- to 3-year-old child as an already complicated, firmly established social being. By then most youngsters have developed a sense of their own position and worth. Prerequisite cognitive tools for higher forms of thinking also are being established. Some experts suggest that by age 3 or 4, children have been exposed to and acquired most of the receptive language they will use in ordinary conversation for the rest of their lives.

Developmental and maturational processes during these initial years are crucial because they form the foundation (motorically, neurologically, psychologically, and cognitively) for the development and learning yet to come. Accomplishments during these early years provide the child with basic tools to move ahead to more complex forms of learning. But what happens if these developmental processes do not evolve so smoothly?

The interaction of hereditary and environmental factors

The course of human development is a product of three powerful forces: (a) the unique genetic endowment passed on to each individual from the parents, (b) environmental conditions, both physical and psychological, under which an individual is reared, and (c) the individual's evolving behavior, which plays an increasingly important role in determining how one responds to and interprets life experiences.

Heredity once was believed to be the sole determinant of human potential, but experts now acknowledge that the interactive effects of hereditary and environmental elements are more important than either one alone. We also know that as human beings, we are not passive recipients of external forces that mold our lives. Each of us molds and influences our own destiny by our behavior, attitudes, decisions, and interactions with our environment. Our own behavior is a reflection of both heredity and environmental inputs. The quality of that input affects our evolving capacities to cope with life and to engage in behaviors that promote successful life adjustments. Young children are just beginning to develop the skills they need to cope with their environment. They are dependent upon nurturing, caring adults to act as their advocates and protectors. Only as children grow older and become more competent and independent does their potential for affecting their own destiny increase.

Although the old controversy as to whether heredity *or* environment determines human characteristics is gone, we do not clearly know *how* the two forces interact to shape the course of human development. The concept of a *range of reaction* is used extensively to explain the interaction (Scarr-Salapatek, 1975; Hirsch, 1971; Ginsburg & Laughlin, 1971; Gottesman, 1968).

In brief—the genetic endowment inherited from one's parents (one's *genotype*) has a unique range of possible reactions that can be manifest depending upon environmental conditions. A person's actual characteristics, as manifest in appearance, sex, behavior, bodily chemical idiosyncrasies, and mental abilities (the *phenotype*), are shaped jointly by hereditary and environmental factors. Two individuals with the same genotype or inheritance (i.e., identical twins) can develop quantitatively different phenotypes given varying environmental conditions. And persons wtih different genotypes can develop different phenotypes when they are reared in the same environment. Or, given a uniform environment but differing genotypes, many persons develop similar phenotypic characteristics.

The range of reaction concept thus suggests that a restricted or enriched environment will have differing effects on different people depending upon their genetic makeup.

Some genotypes hold a much wider range of reaction than others. For example, persons with reduced inherited mental capacity possess a much smaller range of reaction. Their ultimate level of ability is less subject to environmental influences than someone who inherits higher levels of intellectual ability. Using this interpretation, it is incorrect to suggest that heredity sets the limit on development while environment determines the extent to which one's potential will be realized. Both represent half truths—and they ignore the fact that environmental and genetic factors exert constant interactive effects on development.

The genetic blueprint underlying development

Some basic principles of genetics are helpful in understanding how genetic abnormalities occur. Fertilization of the female ovum combines 23 chromosomes from each parent to create the normal endowment of 46 chromosomes in each human being. This genetic blueprint, contained in the nucleus of the fertilized egg and duplicated thereafter in every cell, dictates a person's physical/growth characteristics and overall developmental potential throughout life. A *chromosome* is a giant molecule of deoxyribonucleic acid (DNA) that looks something like a coiled ladder. A *gene* is simply a segment of the large DNA molecule containing enormous quantities of data. These data are in the form of a code that triggers biochemical processes in the individual cells and organs of the body.

Scientists have determined that the genetic code is spelled out by precise quantities and sequences of four basic chemicals—adenine, thymine, quanine, and cytosine. This can be thought of as sort of a four-letter alphabet that spells out instructions for various physical characteristics a person will have, as well as basic chemical and growth processes that will occur in the cells. The four chemicals also spell out the blueprint for how the DNA, starting from a single fertilized egg, will reproduce itself exactly and repeatedly in every cell of a living organism (Lerner & Libby, 1976; Jacobson, 1978).

If something is wrong with the chemical code contained in a gene, errors in a child's physical growth can occur before or after birth. Sometimes the code itself is incorrect, which triggers inappropriate growth processes or simply fails to stimulate them at all. For example, a defective gene can trigger excess secretion of certain body chemicals, which in turn cause illness or disrupt metabolic functions. A defective gene may fail to activate the production of an enzyme needed for glands to function properly (e.g., the pituitary or the thyroid gland). Digestion and absorption of certain foods can be impaired by the absence of an enzyme needed as a part of the metabolic process. If this happens, certain food nutrients remain unassimilated in the body, causing a deficiency that can affect growth or general health. Improper metabolism of food also can lead to retention of certain toxic substances, which can cause illness, changes in the functions of body organs, or even mental retardation from an accumulation of toxins that damage the brain and nervous system (Wortis, 1980).

In summary, genes direct and control developmental and growth processes in each body cell through several biochemical actions: (a) Genes contained within the nucleus of each cell dictate the structure of proteins produced by the cell and the rate at which they are synthesized; (b) proteins in turn act as enzymes or catalysts for hundreds of different chemical processes that occur in each living cell, including growth; and (c) every enzyme (or protein subcomponent of an enzyme) is created according to the genetic code spelled out in the thousands of genes contained in the 46 chromosomes within each cell. The accuracy of that code or its mere presence (or absence) determines if normal growth processes are initiated.

Some other basic principles of genetics explain hereditary influences on growth and development:

1. The 23 chromosomal pairs we receive from our parents differ in shape and length. These differences allow specific chromosomes to be identified by their size and shape and by differences in their staining properties just before cell division. This is how geneticists identify the extra chromosome in the cells of children with Down syndrome. The first 22 chromosome pairs are called *autosomal chromosomes*; the 23rd pair consists of the *sex-linked chromosomes*, which determine the sex of each individual.

2. The sex-linked chromosomes are duplicates in the female (XX). They are different in the male (XY). The male Y chromosome functionally is barren of genes, whereas the X chromosome carries genetic instructions. This is why males face a greater risk for being affected by a defective gene. Because both sex chromosomes of the female have a full complement of genes, a recessive gene from one parent will be manifest only if a matching recessive gene is inherited from the other parent. With the male, this is not so. Since the Y chromosome is barren of genes, any defective gene on the X chromosome from the mother will be manifest in her son because there is nothing to counteract its effect.

3. Genes are either dominant or recessive. Each chromosome pair includes one from the father and one from the mother. When genes opposite each other carry the code for the same trait, they are called *homozygous genes* (such as genes for brown eyes). If the genes differ (one coding blue eyes and the other brown), they are called *heterozygous*. In heterozygous gene pairs, one gene dominates and determines the manifest characteristics (or phenotype) of the individual. Brown eyes, for example, are dominant over blue. Black skin is dominant over a lighter skin. A few known disorders resulting in physical impairments and retardation are caused by dominant genes. Although recessive genes may not be manifest as one's phenotype, they are still carried as one's genotype and can be transmitted to some, but not necessarily all, offspring. Some disorders are caused by recessive genes.

4. Though a person's phenotype (manifest characteristics) depends in large part upon a genetic base, or genotype, it is also dependent upon a set of environmental circumstances. A particular genotype, for example, can create a propensity for freckled skin, but exposure to sunlight is a prerequisite for its expression. Likewise, an inherited susceptibility to certain mental disorders such as schizophrenia may be equally determined by the person's psychological status, learned means for dealing with emotions and stress, and stresses imposed by the environment (Kaplan, 1971).

Prenatal development—the creation of new life*

An amazingly rapid growth process begins the moment the mother's egg cell, or ovum, is fertilized by the male sperm. In the 36 weeks that follow, a single cell transforms into

---

*Information sources: Gasser (1975); Ingelman-Sundberg (1966); Moore (1977); Hamilton and Mossman (1972); and O'Rahilly (1973).

a human being capable of surviving outside the womb—that is, if everything proceeds normally. A complex network of body organs, glands, muscles, nerve tissue, and circulatory systems is formed and becomes ready to function in a delicate balance that can sustain life. Fetal development proceeds along predictable metabolic and physiological gradients. Growth in the head and upper region occurs earlier and more rapidly than that in the lower part of the body; this is called the *cephalocaudal gradient of growth*. Growth also is more rapid in the center of the body than at the periphery—the *proximodistal gradient*. The same pattern of growth continues even after birth. This is demonstrated as an infant first learns to control head movements, then masters movement in the arms, and then the lower extremities (cephalocaudal growth). Proximodistal growth is illustrated in the child who masters gross motor movement in the shoulders, arms, and legs before mastering fine motor tasks requiring use of the hands and fingers.

In just 3½ weeks after conception, the foundation for major body parts has been laid. Delicate embryonic tissue, which looks more like a tiny mass of spongy material than a baby, actually contains the beginnings of major body organs: eyes, spinal cord, nervous system, thyroid glands, stomach, liver, kidneys, and intestines. A primitive heart begins beating haltingly on about the 18th day. Even tiny buds of arms are beginning to form. Yet, at this point, the *embryo* is only 1/10 of an inch long.

By 5 weeks the embryo is about ⅓ of an inch long. At this point a human embryo cannot be distinguished from any other mammalian embryo. Eyes are beginning to develop. Stumps of arms and legs are visible. A skeleton, made only of soft cartilage, is beginning to form. During this second month nerve cells develop rapidly in the spine so that early, although primitive, signs of behavior can be detected (e.g., the embryo will respond to touch). This is a critical time because major bodily systems are being formed and the embryo is vulnerable to chemicals, bacteria, and viruses. Risks are even greater because the mother likely does not know she is pregnant. This is the time when arms and legs can be deformed by thalidomide (a drug used to control morning sickness). Other drugs can be equally harmful. From 1-3 months the embryo is vulnerable to the effects of German measles, which can cause a number of birth defects although the mother may not show symptoms of having the virus herself.

At 8 weeks the developing organism is no longer referred to as an embryo, but a *fetus*. At this point the first real bone cells begin to form, replacing the cartilage that has acted as a skeletal mold. Bone tissue begins forming in the middle of the long bones in the arms and legs and the middle of the ribs and proceeds outward in both directions. By now, just 2 months into the pregnancy, the expectant mother likely will be going to the doctor to confirm that she is pregnant. This is the point when most expectant mothers begin to be concerned about health and nutrition. They are likely to be more alert to their consumption of medicines, drugs, alchohol, or other substances that could be injurious to the baby. Yet, impressive development has already occurred (or has failed to occur). All major bodily systems and internal organs found in the adult body are in various states of development. *Only now is the unborn baby less susceptible to damage from outside sources.*

Although the fetus weighs a mere 1/30 of an ounce and is only about 1 inch long at this 8-week mark, its sex and reproductive organs are forming. It has a mouth with lips, buds for 20 milk teeth, and a rudimentary tongue. As the fetus progresses on to its third month of development (8-12 weeks), signs of behavior increase as various reflexes begin to appear. If the fetus drops a few centimeters, for instance, its muscles automatically contract. Electrical stimulation causes the limbs to move. The heart beat also becomes more regular and patterns somewhat characteristic of adults can be noted.

Between the fourth and fifth month (16-20 weeks) the fetus fills out considerably and becomes recognizable as a human baby. It measures more than 8 inches from crown to rump, weighs about 10 ounces, and has begun to occupy all the room in the mother's pelvis. A permanent skeleton made of real bone, which began forming at 8 weeks, continues to grow. Fingernails and toenails are growing rapidly. The baby can easily scratch itself because its skin is so thin and transparent. The nervous system and muscles are synchronizing so the fetus is active and energetic. The mother can plainly feel the baby's frequent punches and kicks. By now the fetus' head moves independently from the rest of its body (it can nod, tilt, retract, and rotate), and all limbs are movable at every joint. At this stage the 4- to 5-month-old fetus can make most of the responses that can be elicited from a newborn baby. Yet, in spite of the striking physical and behavioral resemblance of the fetus to the newborn infant, it is not likely to survive outside the uterine environment. Babies born prematurely at this point generally do not thrive.

By 27 weeks, or 7 months, the fetus' overall physical development is complete. Some premature babies are born at this stage. (In fact, some born at 6 months have survived, but only because of intensive medical support.) A baby born at 27 weeks is only about 2½ pounds and 12 to 15 inches long. The remaining months of uterine life produce major changes in size and weight, along with continued refinement of body structure and functions. The respiratory apparatus, particularly the lungs and nostrils, become stronger. Premature babies often have respiratory distress because of the immaturity of that system. Most important, the brain continues to develop in the last months of pregnancy. In fact, the brain of the fetus has been claimed to begin to technically "live" at about 28-30 weeks (Purpura, 1975). Important connections between nerve cells are made, making possible more complex and better integrated activities.

The final weeks in the uterus allow the baby to acquire immunity to disease from its mother. From her blood the fetus receives antibodies against diseases including measles, chicken pox, scarlet fever, mumps, small pox, and polio. These antibodies provide protection to the fetus for about 6 months after birth. A baby born prematurely fails to gain this protection and is highly vulnerable to disease and infection. Thus, premature babies are kept inside an incubator in a controlled, bacteria-free environment. During the remaining weeks in utero, the fetus grows rapidly in overall size—from about 14 to 21 inches in length and about 2½ pounds to somewhere between 6 and 7 pounds. Larger babies may weigh as much as 8 or 9 pounds.

Birth—the transition into a new world

In the uterus the fetus exists in a dark, low gravity, warm and protective environment. This changes abruptly as the fetus is pushed into a world where it must adjust to the light, gravity, cold, noise, and a buzzing array of environmental stimuli. The birth process may be easy or difficult, depending on several variables: size and structure of the mother and child, physical condition of the mother and the elasticity of her muscles, the mother's mental attitude and readiness for delivery, and the position of the baby. Labor and full delivery usually take between 12 and 25 hours with the first child. Sometimes a normal delivery though the birth canal is not possible. The fetus may be positioned incorrectly (such as breech, or buttocks first, or a transverse position), the mother's birth canal may be too small, or medical complications may threaten the mother's or baby's condition. Surgical delivery (a caesarian section) is then used. Immediately following birth, a baby typically cries, indicating that the lungs have inflated and are beginning to function. When breathing starts, the valves of the heart alter the path of circulation for the blood so that it flows into the lungs instead of the placenta.

The birth process obviously is strenuous and exhausting on a newborn child. Most babies do not suffer undue trauma although they may be bruised and their heads misshapen from the tight squeeze through the birth canal. Unfortunately, some babies do suffer excessive stress and possible injury. Neonatal mortality is greatest in the first 24 hours after delivery. Rupture of the amniotic sac, or placental membranes, earlier than 24 hours before delivery carries a risk of infection from the mother's uterine content. Prolonged, difficult labor increases the pressure on the baby's skull. In an uncomplicated delivery the risk of neonatal death is approximately 0.3%, but in labors that last over 24 hours, risk is increased sixfold. The risk for neonatal death is 6% in deliveries over 30 hours. An overly short, tumultuous labor, with precipitous delivery, also increases the risk of intracranial hemorrhage. The baby's head simply does not have enough time to mold to the shape of the birth canal so that it can move through gently and without injury. If separation of the placenta occurs prior to delivery, or if the umbilical cord becomes compressed, the chances of brain damage or fetal anoxia are increased (Behrman & Vaughan, 1983).

Infancy and the preschool years—building a foundation

Two terms define the major occupation of the child's early years: *growth* and *development*. These terms describe two interrelated processes characterized by a series of progressive, systematic changes that occur over time as a young child matures and learns new skills through experience and interaction with the environment. *Growth* refers to biogenetically based changes in a child's physical characteristics, including changes in weight, height, skeletal and muscular features, and maturation of the circulatory, respiratory, and nervous systems. Growth, however, involves more than mere enlargement or increases in size. Parts of the body change in relative size, glands take on new functions, and innumerable changes in the body's microanatomy and biochemistry result from growth processes. *Development* refers to progressive and orderly changes in a child's motor, cognitive, linguistic, social, and adaptive abilities that result in the organization of complex and interrelated systems of competencies. These competencies evolve as a result of interactions between growth and maturational factors, environmental influences, and learning.

Following birth, growth and development continue to be exceedingly rapid in a normally developing infant. During infancy (the period from birth to age 2), a child undergoes a gradual but significant transition from horizontal to vertical posture, from passive to active mobility, and from helplessness to the early beginnings of independent functioning. Physical growth continues rapidly. An average weight, full-term baby (7½ pounds) will double the birth weight in 5 months, triple it by 12 months, and quadruple it by 2½ years of age. Body length will increase rapidly, too, from approximately 20 inches at birth to 30 inches by age 1 (Wasserman & Gromisch, 1981).

Development of the nervous system continues to be important, especially during the first two years. At birth the brain is only about one-fourth its adult weight, but by 6 months it will have reached half the adult brain weight, and by 2½ years it will have attained three-fourths of the adult weight. Though the number of brain cells appears to be established at birth, this rapid increase in brain size results from increases in size of the brain cells, which come to assume their characteristic adult shapes.

Few living creatures are so helpless at birth as the human infant. Compared to what older children and adults do, the list of things the newborn cannot do is endless. Not surprisingly, then, adults have tended to view babies as passive and unalert to their surroundings. For years adults made the mistake of thinking that infants' experiences were not important as long as they received sufficient food, warmth, affection, and sleep.

Today we know that view is grossly wrong. Infants are capable of performing a variety of visual, olfactory, auditory, and perceptual discriminations, but they must have stimulation to develop normally (Als, Tronick, Lester, & Brazelton, 1979; Als, Tronick, Adamson, & Brazelton, 1976; Brazelton & Robey, 1965; Carpenter, 1974). For instance, infants are capable of form perception and discrimination (Salapatek, 1975). They can make auditory discriminations between sounds of different duration, which is a basic ability requisite for distinguishing spoken language (Clifton, Graham, & Hatton, 1968; Eisenberg, 1965). Infants demonstrate an early sensitivity to odors and show differential taste to salt, lemon, or even to different carbohydrates (Rieser, Yonas, & Wikner, 1976; Engen, Lipsitt, & Peck, 1974). Babies show early face perception, including an awareness of distortions (Gibson, 1969; Hershenson, 1964) and an ability to generalize from a real face to a color photograph of the same person (Dirks & Gibson, 1977; Fagan, 1976). Evidence of concept formation is shown by infants as young as 30 weeks (Cohen & Strauss, 1979).

Initially a baby acts purely as a physical being who learns about the environment through bodily acts—touching, throwing, seeing, tasting, feeling. Gradually the child learns to represent physical actions with symbols. He or she learns to point to a picture and say "doggie eat," as well as point to a real dog and label it "doggie." Learning, perceptual experience, and stimulation are crucial in the first months and years of life. As early as 18 months, differences are apparent between children who have had a rich, stimulating environment and those who have not. Children lacking early stimulation begin to fall behind their peers on tests of general intelligence and language development (White, 1975). Already the subtle undermining of development caused by inadequate experience shows its effect. Burton White, a recognized authority on early development, maintains that to begin thinking about a child's educational development and learning at age 2 is already too late; the fact is that learning processes begin at birth and perhaps even before (White, 1975).

During the preschool years a child's physical growth in size and weight is slower, compared to the rapid changes of infancy. The notable change during these years is the high rate of learning, the acquisition of new skills, and the maturation that quickly transforms a baby into a unique person. Preschoolers become increasingly able to understand and use language, solve problems, and engage in reciprocal social interactions with adults and peers. The years from age 2 to 5 or 6 are particularly important for mastery of a tremendous array of basic skills across a broad spectrum of what educators refer to as the *developmental domains*. These include: motor development (fine, gross, and sensorimotor skills), language development (receptive and expressive communication), sensory and perceptual development, cognitive and intellectual development, social development (formation of reciprocal relationships with caregivers and then peers, and the acquisition of play skills), emotional and personality development, and finally, development in self-care and adaptive behavior. Achievement of specific skills in each developmental domain provides the stepping stones for all subsequent achievements. A child's progress typically is described in terms of his or her mastery of *developmental milestones*, or what Havighurst (1953) has called "developmental tasks."

To provide an in-depth review of child development in each developmental domain is not within the scope of this text. Entire books are devoted to these topics. The orderly, predictable changes that occur in the first 5-6 years of life, however, can be described under several basic principles of development:*

1. All children proceed through the same developmental sequences or stages, but at different rates, and they achieve differing levels of proficiency at each stage. Development results from both learning and maturation and is a function of the interaction between environmental stimulation and biogenetic factors.
2. An individual child's development does not necessarily proceed uniformly across all domains. Individual progress, in large, is highly variable and is characterized by accelerations, regressions, and plateaus.
3. Children begin to show individual differences at a very young age. These differences are apparent across all aspects of behavior and development, such as in temperament, activity level, physical development, and even overall speed of development.
4. All aspects of development are interrelated in that progress (or lack of it) in one area affects progress in other skill areas. Thus, development of speech and language facilitates thinking and cognitive development, which in turn is helpful in promoting social interaction.
5. Early development is characterized by increasing levels of *differentiation* and *integration*. Differentiation means that a child's skills become increasingly more distinct and specific. For example, early motor movements initially are more random, gross, and sweeping; hence, the task of picking up an object is accompanied by much effort and unnecessary motor movements. Gradually, skill improves so that the child can quickly locate the object, reach out, and grasp it. *Integration* involves coordinating several behaviors simultaneously so that they form a well synchronized combination of actions.
6. Early developmental achievements pave the way for subsequent, more complex learning. Because development is sequential, mastery of earlier stages is essential before a child can progress to more advanced ones.
7. Experience has a cumulative effect. That is, experience affects a child's expectations and reactions to the next similar situation. A single success tends to make the next

---

*Resources: Falkner and Tanner (Vols. 1-2)(1978a, 1978b, 1978c); Clarke-Stewart, Friedman, and Koch (1985).

success more likely. A failure increases the probability of a subsequent failure.

8. At certain periods young children show a maturational and psychological readiness for learning certain skills, such as speech, motor skills, and various cognitive skills. These periods sometimes are referred to as *critical* or *formative periods*. Although the same skills can be acquired before or after these formative periods, learning often seems to be more difficult and perhaps less rapid.

For further detailed explanations of child development, see: Clark-Stewart, Friedman, and Koch (1985); Falkner and Tanner (1978) (Volumes 1 and 2); Gabel and Erickson (1980); Huston (1984); Mussen, Conger, Kagan, and Huston (1984); and White (1975).

THE ETIOLOGY OF DEVELOPMENTAL DISABILITIES

For most children the developmental and growth processes just described all unfold in due time. Yet, while parents and society at large acknowledge the exceedingly rapid growth and developmental achievements of early childhood, they can easily be taken for granted. Educators and parents alike rely on the "magic" of early development on the assumption that, with time, most youngsters will develop and grow like their agemates. Given an even moderately supportive, nurturing environment, most children do just that. But this developmental process is not so straightforward for a small percent. In some cases the reasons for their slow development are not even apparent. For others the diagnoses are clear and perhaps painful realities. These are the children whose parents will face another new reality: Their child's development cannot be taken for granted. Each step along the developmental continuum may be affected in some way by their child's special problem.

To rear this individual, caregivers cannot fall back on the "wait-and-see" approach to determine whether each important milestone will be reached at the appropriate time. If the child's development is to be optimal, parents may have to pace their youngster through experiences that other children access readily. Furthermore, they may have to specifically teach their child skills that other children seem to acquire almost spontaneously.

What is a developmental disability?

Several terms are used to refer to children with special problems that require educational intervention. A person may be described as *disabled*—one who is structurally, physiologically, psychologically, or neurologically different from a normal person as a result of accident, disease, congenital abnormality, or developmental problems. The term *disability* refers to a variety of conditions that can interfere with a person's ability to perform in the same way a normal person can. This may involve an injury or incapacity in one or more areas of functioning including: sensory disabilities (a hearing impairment or a visual impairment), physical disabilities (motor impairment arising out of neurological damage, orthopedic impairment, and health impairments), speech and language disabilities, cognitive disabilities (mental retardation and learning disabilities), and behavior disabilities.

The term *developmental disability* refers to conditions originating during the developmental years (before age 18) that may impede an individual's ongoing developmental progress.

Sometimes the term *impairment* is used to refer to the damage, injury, or incapacity that a person has. Thus, we refer to cognitive impairment as the outcome of injury to the brain after a serious accident, or to physical impairment as the result of a congenital deformity. Sometimes the term is used synonymously with disability.

The term *handicap* (or *handicapped*) has a more restrictive meaning. A *handicap* refers to the consequence(s) of a disability that renders a person less able to function or to perform tasks in the way a normal person can. Some disabilities produce inconvenience and discomfort for a person but are not ultimately handicapping. For example, many individuals have vision problems that result in reduced visual acuity and limited vision, but with eye glasses or contact lenses, these people can function adequately and are not considered handicapped. A child is handicapped *if* the disability interferes with normal functioning so that performance is affected and possibly limited by the condition.

One final term often used in regard to handicapped individuals is *exceptional*. This term is more encompassing than those described previously. It includes individuals at both extremes of the continuum who differ from what society regards as "normal." That is, exceptional children are those with intellectual, emotional, or physical attributes that fall *above* or *below* so-called normal individuals. This term includes those who are gifted and talented as well as those who are handicapped.

A great deal is known about the causes of developmental disabilities in young children, including what factors are highly correlated with their occurrence. At the same time, identifying the specific cause in individual cases is often difficult. The next section discusses why pinpointing precise cause-and-effect relationships is so difficult. In any case, the cause can be clearly established in only about 30%-40% of identifiable cases of developmental disabilities (of all types) in young children. In another 20%-30%, an "educated guess" can be made about the probable etiologies, based upon a child's medical and developmental history and on information about the home and family background. Unfortunately, in the remaining 35%-50% of children with disabilities, the etiology or cause remains unknown (Crome & Stern, 1972; Milunsky, 1975).

Basic concepts

Several basic concepts are useful in understanding the causative factors underlying the physical and developmental inpairments we observe in young children and the kinds of impacts they have:

1. Abnormalities resulting from multiple causes are increasing, whereas those resulting from singular causes are decreasing. Singular causative factors, as well as singular disabilities, are better understood now and can be treated so that many no longer are debilitating. For example—hydrocephaly (excessive fluid in the brain caused by blockage or inappropriate drainage or absorption) can be corrected surgically, averting serious brain damage by placement of a shunt in the head. A cleft palate can be closed through corrective surgery.
2. Severe abnormalities or disabilities can be diagnosed earlier and more easily than can mild disorders. A definitive diagnosis of mild problems in very young children sometimes is difficult because early symptoms can be attributed to many causes including

normal variations in development among children. Furthermore, some disabilities become evident only as children begin to engage in more complex, higher order cognitive behaviors or when they fail to do so.

3. The full impact of an abnormality or a condition known to interfere with growth and development may not be manifest immediately. Physical or behavioral symptoms develop over time to become of sufficient magnitude that they can be readily observed and diagnosed by a specialist. Abnormalities or various harmful conditions internal or external to a child may affect his or her welfare at any state in the life span—at conception, during development in utero, or after birth. Or their effects may be continuous and progressive.

4. A particular pathological, genetic, or harmful environmental condition that causes disabilities in young children may produce different symptoms and degrees of impairment across individuals (*variable expressivity*). The frequency with which a particular condition actually results in diagnosable abnormalities also may vary from person to person (*variable penetrance*).

5. Some disabilities are a direct or primary result of an abnormality or injury (such as cerebral palsy, blindness, or deafness). Other impairments are secondary in that they occur when the primary disorder interferes with development and growth processes that otherwise would have proceeded normally. If unchecked, secondary problems can progress to a level at which the child becomes handicapped in another way.

6. The impact of a condition upon an individual and its severity depend, in many cases, upon (a) the interaction between the original cause (if it is biological or genetic in nature) and the environment, or (b) between the environment and the unique psychological-temperamental-physical characteristics of the individual that make him or her more or less vulnerable to the disorder.

7. The symptoms produced by an abnormal or harmful condition (internal or external to a child) depend partially on the timing of the assault. The earlier in life the disability occurs, the broader is the potential impact upon other areas of growth and development.

CONDITIONS THAT RENDER A CHILD'S FUTURE AT-RISK

Whenever concerned others encounter a child who looks different, who acts strangely, or whose development is not up to par, several questions automatically arise:

● What is the problem?
● Is the problem progressive, and is it continuing to impose injury or impairment upon the child?
● Can the disorder be treated to prevent further disruption of the child's growth and development?
● Will the child's condition now interfere with future development and produce additional difficulties such as mental retardation and social maladjustment?

Knowledge about the causes of disabilities helps answer some of these questions. In examining some causes of developmental disabilities, we will proceed chronologically by looking at conditions that impose their initial insult upon a child prenatally, perinatally, and postnatally.

Prenatal risk factors

Conditions that signal an at-risk pregnancy   Some women begin their pregnancy with a higher risk than other women for producing offspring with developmental defects. Conditions that signal a risk include:

1. *Parents of low socioeconomic status who live under impoverished, substandard conditions.*

Higher rates of mental retardation and other developmental disabilities are found among children from low socioeconomic homes. Hazards that more frequently endanger the welfare of an unborn fetus in this population include: undernutrition of the mother during pregnancy and undernutrition of the child after birth; frequent exposure to and contraction of bacterial and viral infections by both mother and child; and poor medical care and hygiene. Premature birth and neonatal death occur much more often in babies of low soicioeconomic parents than those from middle to upper economic groups (Bauer, 1972; Fomon & Anderson, 1972). Mothers from more favorable socioeconomic backgrounds tend to seek out more reliable obstetrical information and care, to have better health and nutritional status when they begin their pregnancies, and to have babies at a more favorable age. All these conditions bear a relationship to the occurrence of complications during pregnancy and to the incidence of prematurity, congenital deformities, brain damage, and death among newborns (Hardy, Drage, & Jackson, 1979; Reed & Stanley, 1977).

2. *Maternal age of under 15 or over 40.*

Risks for chromosomal abnormalities, prematurity, complications during pregnancy, and congenital abnormalities in offspring are greater in older mothers. Young mothers (under age 15), whose reproductive systems are still immature and whose bodies are still growing, also face a greater risk for defective offspring. Highest risks for mental retardation are among children from mothers who have borne three children before age 20, and children from mothers over age 35 and whose pregnancy was their first (Lillienfeld and Pasamanick, 1956). Occurrence of genetic defects increases significantly with age. For example, incidence figures on Down syndrome are 1 in every 2,000 births for 20-year-old mothers, and 1 in every 20 births for mothers over 45 (Miller & Erbe, 1978). MacMillan (1982) reported average incidence figures on Down syndrome per 1,000 births of .76 for the 20- to 24-year-old range of mothers, rising to 29.52 for those over 45.

3. *Mothers with a history of difficulties with previous pregnancies.*

Women with a history of miscarriage, stillbirths, premature deliveries, or previous births involving genetic defects or congenital abnormalities run a much higher risk of complications than do other mothers. For example, a mother who has delivered one child with spina bifida (abnormal closure of the spinal cord resulting in paralysis of the lower extremities) has 12 times the standard risk. Mothers who have children with cerebral palsy have a greater risk (2 times) of stillbirth or neonatal death than usual (Lansford, 1977).

4. *Mothers with one or more chronic health disorders or physical conditions that can interfere with pregnancy.*

Women with diabetes, untreated syphilis or other venereal diseases, hyperthyroid condition, heart defects, drug addiction, and alcoholism all place their unborn babies at higher risk for developmental or physical abnormalities. Many of these women deliver babies prematurely or with lower than normal birth weight. Both prematurity and very low birth weight are correlated with heightened incidence of disease, infant mortality, neurological defects, and other types of developmental impairments (Behrman & Vaughan, 1983).

5. *Parents (mother or father) with family history of congenital abnormalities.*

Parents whose own families and relatives show a high rate of disorders are at greater risk for giving birth to children with similar kinds of problems. Families with a history of genetic deafness, metabolic disorders such as PKU, muscle or neurological disease such as muscular dystrophy, or Tay–Sachs disease are more vulnerable (Lansford, 1977; Behrman & Vaughan, 1983).

Prenatal risk factors of genetic origin   Genetic disorders are transmitted in three ways: (a) by abnormal chromosomal conditions (an extra chromosome, a missing chromosome or part of a chromosome, or bits of one chromosome tacked onto another), (b) by a pair of defective recessive genes resulting when both parents are carriers, and (c) by a defective dominant gene inherited from just one parent. Statistics indicate that as many as 3% of all newborns have some genetic birth defect and 20% of all infant deaths are attributable to genetic defects (Porter, 1977). Approximately 1 in 200 has a chromosomal abnormality, 1 in 250 has a single-gene defect, and at least 1%-2% has abnormalities arising from multiple genetic factors (Epstein & Golbus, 1977).

The effect of a genetic abnormality may be immediate in that the initial formation of body structures, organs, the central nervous system, or the brain is altered from the very beginning. Some effects are *metabolic* in nature and involve no manifest changes in the physical structure of the individual—at least not initially. Metabolic processes simply are altered or prevented as a result of an error in the genetic code that triggers chemical actions in the cells. This causes damage to the brain or central nervous system or disrupts normal growth processes. The damage is progressive once the metabolic process is triggered. The effect of still other genetic disorders may not be observed until later in life as particular environmental conditions or developmental stages (such as puberty) come into play to activate them. If a genetic disorder is recessive and is inherited from just one parent, the child will become only a carrier of the condition and it will not be manifest at all.

The more common genetic disorders that may be diagnosed in early childhood are described here briefly. More extensive information on these and other genetic disorders can be found in Spreen, Tupper, Risser, Tuokko, and Edgell (1984); Behrman and Vaughan (1983); Carter (1978); and Plomin, DeFries, and McClearn (1980).

Down syndrome, or trisomy 21—a chromosomal abnormality   Young children with Down syndrome are prime candidates for early intervention because their condition presents an *established risk*. That is, the condition is known to result in mental retardation, physical abnormalities, and delays in other areas such as motor functioning, speech, and language. Infants who have Down syndrome can be diagnosed at birth by their physical appearance, with confirmation by a microscopic analysis of the child's chromosomes. A baby with this disorder has an extra number 21 chromosome—hence the name *Trisomy 21*. Of children with moderate to severe mental retardation, Down syndrome accounts for over 10% (Hansen, 1978; Stein & Susser, 1977).

The extra 21st chromosome results from improper division of the DNA in the cell nuclei. This occurs most commonly in the division of the egg or sperm cells. The result is a gamete (an egg or a sperm cell) with 24 chromosomes instead of the normal 23. If, for example, a defective egg is fertilized by a normal sperm, the fetus will have one too many chromosomes (47). This error is called *nondysjunction*. Occasionally the error occurs after fertilization in the second or third division of the embryo (mitosis) and produces a more rare form of Down syndrome called *mosaicism*. Because at least one cell division already has occurred when the error in chromosomal division happens, two parallel lines of cells develop—some with the normal genetic endowment of 46 chromosomes and some with 47. A child with this form of Down syndrome tends to manifest less severe retardation and fewer physical stigmata (Koch & de la Cruz, 1975; Smith & Wilson, 1973).

Is Down syndrome inherited? Parents do not pass this abnormality along to their children as an inherited trait in the same sense that eye or hair color is transmitted. Rather, the error in cell division causes an otherwise normal genetic inheritance to produce an abnormal fetus. But a third type of chromosomal abnormality associated with Down

The fact that Emily has Down syndrome places her in the category of established risk. But the big question for her is the same as that of any child: How far can she go? How much can she learn to achieve her full potential?

syndrome, called *translocation*, is associated with a higher risk that parents may conceive another child with the same defect. In this condition all or a part of one chromosome becomes attached to another. Translocated chromosomes sometimes are found among adults who are physically and mentally normal and have the normal amount of DNA in their cells. The problem is that the translocated chromosome increases the chances for improper division during meiosis (before fertilization) so that the resulting egg or sperm has the extra 21st chromosome. Parents who give birth to a child with Down syndrome can have genetic tests to determine if they are carriers of a translocated chromosome.

In addition to mental retardation, children with Down syndrome may have other distinguishing characteristics (Smith & Berg, 1976) such as:

— distinctive facial characteristics (e.g., slanting, almond-shaped eyes; a unique fold of skin in the upper corner of the eyes, called *epicanthal folds*; small head and ears).

— short physical stature (including small hands and short, stubby fingers).

— poor muscle tone, physical impairments (e.g., heart defects, vision problems, and susceptibility to respiratory ailments because of underdeveloped sinus and nasal cavities).

Metabolic disorders caused by defective recessive genes

A child with phenylketonuria (PKU) is not able to metabolize the protein phenylalanine into tyrosine. The lack of an essential enzyme causes phenylalanine to build up in the blood until it reaches a toxic level, which results in progressive damage to the brain. If undiagnosed and untreated, severe retardation occurs. A baby who inherits the defective recessive gene that causes PKU from both his or her parents appears normal at birth, but when the infant's own metabolic processes are set into action to digest food, phenylalanine builds up and causes damage.

Most hospitals routinely screen for PKU in newborns, using urine tests with ferric chloride or blood tests. Early diagnosis and immediate treatment are essential to avoid damage. A diet low in phenylalanine, along with vitamin supplements, appears to reduce the damage shown in nontreated PKU children. Although the effects of dietary treatment are still being studied, treated children seem to show less retardation and may have IQs similar to unaffected siblings (Fuller & Schuman, 1971; Dobson, Kushida, Williamson, & Friedman, 1976; Williamson, Koch, Azen, & Chang, 1981). How long the low-phenylalanine diet must be continued is a somewhat controversial and undetermined issue. Some research shows that school-aged children have discontinued the diet without effect (Holtzman, Welcher, & Mellits, 1975). Other evidence suggests that termination of dietary control allows phenylalanine levels to rise again, which can cause behavioral change and interfere with learning (Berry et al., 1977). Females who later become pregnant, without continuing dietary control, may bear childen who are mentally retarded (Sells & Bennett, 1977).

Many other metabolic disorders—some of which are not clearly understood—are caused by recessive genes. *Galactosemia* is a disorder of carbohydrate metabolism in which a baby is unable to properly metabolize lactose, a primary sugar in milk, into galactose. Given the typical milk diet, the baby develops jaundice, vomiting, cataracts, malnutrition, and high susceptibility to infections. As with PKU, toxic substances that are damaging to the brain, liver, and other tissue build up. Early identification and dietary treatment, however, can prevent damage.

Tay–Sachs disease is a disorder in the metabolism of fatty substances called lipids. The disease usually begins to be manifest at about 6 months of age in what appears to be a normal infant. Listlessness, weakness, feeding difficulties, hypotonia, hypersensitivity to sounds, and visual difficulties are a few of the symptoms. Regression occurs, with death usually by age 3 (Behrman & Vaughan, 1983). Possibly, many other undiagnosed disorders resulting in progressive deterioration are metabolic in nature. Much has yet to be learned about the underlying causes and the means for preventing these types of inherited metabolic disorders.

Prenatal risk factors of biological origin   Conditions that interfere with biological processes in the mother and her unborn child include pathological or infectious diseases that can damage the fetus by (a) direct invasion or (b) indirect toxic effects that in turn cause injury.

Young children whose mothers contracted one or more infectious diseases during pregnancy (especially during the first 3 months) are at-risk for possible damage and later developmental problems. Although the placenta serves as a barrier to protect the fetus from disease in the mother, infections can be passed on to the baby and can result in serious congenital abnormalities. Sometimes a pregnant woman is not even aware that she has contracted a disease. Some viruses produce a few mild symptoms or none at all in the adult but have profound effects on a developing fetus. The Collaborative Perinatal Study (Hellman & Pritchard, 1971; Hardy, Drage, & Jackson, 1979) indicated that approximately 5% of pregnancies are complicated by one or more clinically recognizable viral infections.

A number of viruses have been known to pass through the placenta to the fetus (examples: those causing measles or rubella, chicken pox, small pox, poliomyelitis, hepatitis, encephalitis, and mumps). Most seem to cause only transient symptoms in the unborn baby, although sometimes spontaneous abortions or stillbirths result. *German measles*, or rubella, appears to be the major *acute* maternal infection that causes congenital defects in a fetus. Several *chronic* infections also are culprits in cases of congenital abnormalities and mental retardation. *Toxoplasmosis, syphilis*, and infection caused by *herpes virus hominis (Type II)*, discussed here briefly, are among the more known ones.

Rubella (German measles) usually produces only mild symptoms in an adult, but of mothers who contract rubella during the first trimester of pregnancy, some 50% have babies with notable abnormalities. If the disease occurs in later stages of pregnancy, the risk is much lower, though still present. Although rubella may appear to be of brief term for the mother, the virus can be harbored in the infant's cells for an extended period after birth, even if antibodies build up.

The effects of rubella on a fetus are highly variable, depending on the point of fetal development when the disease was contracted, what organs or body parts were developing at that time, the severity of the disease, and its duration. Some fetal cells are literally destroyed by the virus. Temporary or permanent growth deficiencies can result. Other possible effects include mental retardation, heart abnormalities, microcephaly, cerebral palsy, cataracts, skeletal abnormalities, blindness, and deafness. Deafness is the most common result, although mental retardation also is frequent. Some 30%-60% of infants with congenital rubella manifest neurological effects ranging from severe cerebral palsy to mild retardation (Hardy, McCracken, Gilkeson, & Sever, 1969; Vernon, 1969a; Sever,

1970, 1971; Dudgeon, 1976). In other cases, postnatal symptoms from rubella are subtle and appear over time. Some children show only "soft signs" of neurological dysfunction. Behavior disorders have been reported to be more common among post-rubella children than among a contrast group of deaf children (deafness being the major postnatal symptom of rubella), but establishing that these symptoms are the direct result of rubella is difficult (Vernon, 1969b; Gotoff & Gotoff, 1978).

Extensive use of rubella vaccine has drastically reduced its incidence and the accompanying congenital defects. The greatest tragedy about rubella today is that although it is preventable, it still occurs because of ignorance or negligence. Too many women of child-bearing age do not know whether they have had German measles or if they have been exposed and do not seek immunization. After a female becomes pregnant, immunization is powerless to build resistence to the virus. In fact, precautions are advised to avoid any accidental vaccination of a female who may not know she is pregnant. Those who are immunized should not conceive for at least 3 months because the virus will still be present in their bodies and could damage the fetus.

Toxoplasmosis is caused by a protozoan infection. Normally it is of little more consequence than the common cold to an adult, but it can be devastating to an unborn child. Cats are a major host for the protozoan organism that causes toxoplasmosis, although it also is found in other mammal species, some birds, and reptiles. The disease appears to be transmitted by ingestion of uncooked meat and through contact with contaminated cat feces in litter boxes and flower beds. Pregnant mothers are encouraged to avoid these kinds of contact and to eat well prepared meat. An analysis of a mother's antibodies in her blood is the only way to verify if she has been exposed to the disease. Exposure prior to pregnancy is not dangerous, but it is during pregnancy. Blood tests are helpful only if a baseline is taken early in pregnancy to allow subsequent comparison. Elevated levels of certain antibodies would then suggest that the mother has been exposed to the organism.

About 50% of the infections contracted by a pregnant mother will affect the fetus, and only primary maternal infections during the first 6 months are likely to damage the fetus. The prognosis for those with symptomatic neonatal toxoplasmosis, however, is poor, resulting in death for some 10%-15%. Nearly 85% of the survivors are mentally retarded and show severe vision impairment and neuromotor disorders. The largest number of newborns with congenital toxoplasmosis show no symptoms during the neonatal period. If early symptoms are apparent, they may include convulsions, cerebral calcification, inflammation of the choroid coat of the retina of the eye, microcephaly, and hydrocephaly.

Some youngsters show no symptoms until after the first year of life, so early detection can occur only by previous careful monitoring of the mother's status during pregnancy. If it is established that she contracted toxoplasmosis during that time, her baby is at biological risk and should be observed carefully for subsequent vision impairment or damage to the central nervous system (Alford, Stagno, & Reynolds, 1974; Desmonts & Couvreur, 1974). Screening of newborns for specific antibodies also can aid in early detection. Drug treatment is possible upon identification, although its effectiveness in alleviating symptoms or their level of severity is not yet fully determined (Gotoff & Gotoff, 1978).

Syphilis, a common venereal disease, once was the cause of a significant number of neonatal deaths. Compulsory blood tests for marriage licenses and for pregnant women,

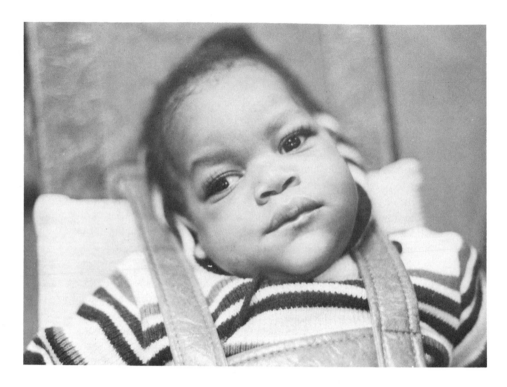

The effects of low birth weight and other prenatal complications on the development of this bright-eyed little girl are yet to be seen. She is a child at biological risk.

coupled with advances in treatment methods, reduced its incidence dramatically. The disease continues to be a threat, however, in spite of effective treatment methods.

The spirochete bacterium causing syphilis in an infected pregnant mother can be spread to her unborn baby in two ways: (a) The bacterium can pass through the placenta after about the fifth month of gestation and invade the fetus as it develops, or (b) the baby can contract the disease at birth when it passes through the birth canal. Manifestations of the disease are highly varied and depend in part upon when it was contracted. The disease can disrupt development of the fetus' nervous and circulatory systems. Cataracts, heart defects, deafness, kidney disease, bone deformities, small size for the gestation period, and enlarged liver and spleen are among the many possible symptoms.

About 10% of the children who have the disease show no clinical evidence either at birth or in early infancy but develop symptoms in late infancy, the early childhood years, or even later. In these cases one early symptom is meningitis at around 4-5 months, followed by paralysis, blindness, hydrocephaly, and mental retardation. When onset occurs between 1 and 2 years of age or when the child is in school, symptoms may begin initially with forgetfulness and apathy. Motor regression begins to affect speech and writing, then walking, and progresses to increasingly more severe abnormalities that suggest damage to the central nervous system.

Successful treatment of syphilis is possible even prenatally, since penicillin can cross the placenta. Congenital damage can be prevented if the disease is diagnosed and treated promptly, but once damage occurs—regardless of subsequent treatment—its physical-neurological effects are irreversible. A woman can be infected with syphilis before or during pregnancy and be unaware of it, so blood tests as part of prenatal care are important to detect and prevent the dire effects of this disease (Carter, 1978; Behrman & Vaughan, 1983).

Herpes virus hominis infection causes a variety of pathological symptoms that affect newborn babies and older persons as well. Effects range from only local manifestations (cold sores and ordinary fever blisters) to vaginal inflammation in the female (now classified as a venereal disease). Meningitis—inflammation of the outer covering of the meninges of the brain—also can result from this virus. The latter has been known to cause serious brain damage, and even death, in adults. The herpes virus is now classified as Type I and Type II. Type II is transmitted through sexual contact in adults and is acquired by a baby as it passes through the birth canal of an infected mother. Approximately 40%-60% of all babies born to women with active Type II herpes infections become infected (Sells & Bennett, 1977). Type I herpes virus hominis is not sexually transmitted.

Prenatal herpes infections appear to be caused by the Type II virus. The outcome is fatal for many fetuses. Among those who survive, about half show manifestations of neurological damage (e.g., mental retardation and motor impairment). Research on the Type II herpes virus suggests that once contracted by adults, the virus remains in the body even though it may become inactive as a result of treatment. Affected adults thus can experience intermittent recurrences of the disease. In pregnant mothers known to be infected, delivery by caesarean section is recommended if their infection has been active within 3 weeks of labor (Carter, 1978; Behrman & Vaughan, 1983).

Cytomegalic inclusion disease may sound unfamiliar, but it is the most frequent viral cause of brain damage and mental retardation in unborn children, even surpassing the rubella virus. Estimates suggest that 1 of every 1,000 infants is affected—or nearly 3,000 children a year in the U.S. alone who are retarded as a result of congenital infection from the cytomegalovirus, or CMV (Scheiner, Hanshaw, Simeonsson, & Scheiner, 1977). The virus can be carried by a healthy mother and passed through the placenta to the baby. Most healthy individuals who acquire the virus after birth, including adults who acquire it through sexual contact, show no symptoms at all; yet the virus may be present in their body secretions for months.

Effects on the fetus range from no symptoms to severe neurological manifestations to fatality. The virus also is associated with neonatal complications including blindness, deafness, cerebral palsy, blood abnormalities, and enlargement of the spleen. The children who show no apparent physical abnormalities still are at-risk for subtle abnormalities that will appear later. For example, in a follow-up of children who had been infected prenatally, some 50% were found to have some degree of sensorineural hearing loss (Gotoff & Gotoff, 1978; Behrman & Vaughan, 1983). Others showed microcephaly in later infancy (Dudgeon, 1976).

Prenatal conditions that create an adverse intrauterine environment The most basic condition of a nurturing environment, either pre- or post-natally, is that it protects the physical safety of the child from harmful elements and provides the necessary nutrients to sustain life. Four broad kinds of conditions can undermine the physical security and nurturing qualities of the uterine environment: (a) maternal dysfunction, in which the mother's bodily systems do not function properly, thereby failing to sustain biological and metabolic processes necessary for a healthy prenatal environment, (b) maternal sensitization, in which the mother's body reacts to the fetus as foreign matter and builds up antibodies that pass through the placenta and attack the fetus, (c) exposure of the fetus to toxic or injurious substances through the mother's voluntary consumption or accidental exposure, and (d) maternal undernutrition.

Maternal dysfunction   A mother's overall health and well-being directly affect how smoothly her pregnancy proceeds. The degree to which her bodily systems deliver sufficient oxygen and other critical nutrients to the fetus, remove waste material efficiently, and resist disease determines how optimal the uterine environment is for the fetus.

Some maternal dysfunctions occur because of the additional stress placed upon the mother's body during pregnancy. Some conditions may be present before she conceives but are activated or exaggerated by her condition. In other instances, such as with diabetic women, the bodily dysfunction is one with which they begin pregnancy and which requires careful monitoring. Other *noninfectious* maternal conditions such as anemia or heart disorders can cause biological dysfunction by reducing the capabilities of the mother's circulatory system to sustain the needs of her own body as well as that of her fetus. Impairments in liver and kidney functions can reduce the efficiency of waste disposal.

The three most common forms of maternal dysfunction are toxemia, diabetes, and hypertension (high blood pressure). *Toxemia* is a common complication of pregnancy involving swelling of the mother's body and limbs and dysfunction of her kidneys and circulatory system. It is accompanied by high blood pressure. What triggers this condition generally is not known. Its heightened incidence among lower socioeconomic women suggests that nutrition may play some role. Toxemia appears to interfere with nutritional support to the fetus and with efficient disposal of wastes. Cornblath (1967) reported a high incidence (50%) of hypoglycemia (low blood sugar) in infants whose mothers had toxemia during pregnancy. Pasamanick and Knobloch (1966) reported higher rates of cerebral palsy, cognitive disorders, epilepsy, and hyperactivity among children born of toxemic mothers, including those who had experienced unexplained vaginal bleeding during pregnancy. They suggested that toxemia and vaginal bleeding may cause oxygen deprivation in the fetus and cautioned that conditions causing toxemia also may contribute to possible fetal damage.

Diabetic women are able to bear children today because of insulin and current medical advances that allow blood sugar and insulin levels to be monitored and controlled. Years ago, before this medical treatment was possible, about 25% of these mothers died in childbirth and about 50% of their fetuses and infants did not survive (Hellman & Pritchard, 1971). Nonetheless, the condition still carries greater risks for the well-being of diabetic mothers and their babies. The likelihood of severe hypertension disorders, for example, is increased fourfold above that of nondiabetic mothers. The risk is greater for contracting infections, and if they occur, they are usually more severe. Infants of diabetic mothers have heightened rates of neonatal or prenatal death. If a mother's diabetes is not well controlled with insulin or monitored carefully throughout her pregnancy, risks are especially high for respiratory distress and possible death of the baby.

Newborns of diabetic or prediabetic mothers have distinctive physical characteristics. They either are born small for their gestational age or, more frequently, their bodies are swollen with fluid. The latter condition complicates their birth, making passage through the birth canal more difficult and often necessitating caesarean section. Post-partum hemorrhage is common. Behrman and Vaughan (1983) have noted that the newborn babies of diabetic mothers tend to be jumpy and trembly after the first 24 hours of life. Hypoglycemia and respiratory distress are common. Congenital malformations of many different kinds occur twice as frequently as in babies of nondiabetic mothers. Neurological and intellectual defects also are more frequent (Churchill, Berendes, & Nemore, 1969; Behrman & Vaughan, 1983). Whether the diabetes and its effects upon bodily processes cause these disorders directly or whether the secondary problems, such as prematurity or hypoglycemia, are the culprits is open to question.

Hypertensive disorders (high blood pressure) occur in 6%-7% of all pregnancies during the last trimester and account for some 20% of maternal deaths in the U.S. (Moore, 1977). In mothers with continuous hypertension, fetal loss is frequent. This is especially unfortunate because good prenatal supervision and monitoring by a competent doctor could prevent it. The specific role hypertension plays in causing certain abnormalities that appear later in surviving infants is not clearly apparent. High blood pressure often is accompanied by other complications of pregnancy, all of which are associated with later difficulties in the young child. Often these are mild in nature and are difficult to diagnose.

Maternal sensitization Occasionally a mother's body reacts to her fetus as foreign matter by forming antibodies that cross the placenta to attack red blood cells in the fetus and cause damage in a variety of ways. A number of blood-type and biochemical incompatibilities can cause rejection. One of the most common is *RH blood incompatibility*.

If a female with Rh negative blood conceives a baby with an Rh positive father, the probability is high that their baby will inherit an Rh+ blood type. (Rh+ depends on whether the father's genes for blood type are homozygous or whether he carries a recessive gene for Rh- blood type.) When an Rh- mother bears an Rh+ fetus, her body can become sensitized against the Rh+ blood cells of her fetus. The Rh+ blood contains antigens that can cross the placenta into the mother's blood. There they trigger production of antibodies, which cross the placenta into the fetal bloodstream and destroy red blood cells. This rarely happens with a first pregnancy unless the mother previously has received Rh+ blood accidentally through a blood transfusion. But if fetal Rh+ blood cells leak into her system during delivery of the first and perhaps a second child, her body's immune system will build up an army of antibodies to protect itself.

The danger comes with a subsequent pregnancy involving an Rh+ fetus. Antibodies in the mother's blood will attack the red blood cells of the young fetus, causing anemia (called *erythroblastosis fetalis*). Jaundice occurs as bilirubin is released into the fetus' bloodstream. The fetus' liver is still immature and unable to metabolize the bilirubin. If the bilirubin builds up to a toxic level, the baby's brain is damaged.

Several techniques are used to treat maternal sensitization and prevent damage to the fetus. One method involves injecting the Rh- mother with gamma globulin immediately after delivery of an Rh+ baby. Rh+ fetal blood cells are most likely to enter her own circulatory system during labor and delivery. The gamma globulin destroys the foreign fetal blood cells in the mother and prevents further production of lethal antibodies in her system. This injection, known as *RhoGAM,* must be given within 72 hours after delivery of an Rh+ baby. A second method is an actual intrauterine blood transfusion and is used if bilirubin reaches dangerous levels. Or a complete blood exchange can be made immediately upon the baby's birth. Transfusions can save the life of the fetus, but residual brain damage is possible.

The threat of Rh incompatibility is controllable if the parents and their physician recognize the possibilities of this condition early and undertake appropriate monitoring and treatment. In addition, blood incompatibilities may occur in A, B, or O blood types, producing similar antibody production in the mother's body (Behrman & Vaughan, 1983).

Build-up of toxic substances or exposure to radiation

Build-up of toxic substances or exposure to radiation   Various chemicals and other environmental agents, in sufficient dosages, can be destructive to an unborn child. Norris (1978) noted, "The fetus in its intrauterine environment was thought to be protected from mechanical injury by the amniotic sac and from toxins in the maternal blood by something called a placental barrier. The amniotic sac does do a commendable job, but the placental barrier is largely a myth" (p. 441).

Alcohol has been implicated as a damaging chemical agent for unborn children. The more a pregnant woman drinks, the greater are the risks for her having an abnormal baby (Furey, 1982). Jones, Smith, Ulleland, and Streissguth, (1973) and Jones, Smith, and Streissguth (1974) first brought attention to the *fetal alcohol syndrome* when they, and later Russell (1975), reported that children born to chronically alcoholic women manifest some alarmingly consistent symptoms such as:

- Low birth weight—less than 2,500 grams or 5.5 pounds.
- Prenatal and postnatal growth deficiencies—linear growth rate of only about 65% that of normal children; weight about 40% less than normal.
- Mental retardation—IQs in the mild to moderate ranges; frequent microcephaly (Streissguth, 1976).
- Distortion of facial features—narrow eye slits; sunken nasal bridge, giving a flat face appearance; drooping eyelids; very thin lips.
- Deformities in body organs and other structures—depending on when the damage occurred—malformed arms and legs; defective body organs, including frequent occurrence of heart defects.
- Behavior problems—hyperactivity or "extreme nervousness"; poor attention span.

Perinatal mortality in babies of alcoholic mothers may be as high as 17%. Furthermore, up to 32% of the offspring from mothers with high alcohol consumption during pregnancy show identifiable symptoms. This does not include youngsters with more subtle, mild symptoms that cannot be clearly tied to alcohol consumption alone (Hanson, Jones, & Smith, 1976; Jones, Smith, Streissguth, & Myrionthopoulos, 1974; Ferrier, Nicod, & Ferrier, 1973; Jones & Smith, 1975). The National Institute on Alcohol Abuse and Alcoholism (NIAAA) gives a conservative estimate that the syndrome affects 1 in every 2,000 babies born each year, placing it among the top causes of birth defects that result in both physical and mental impairment (Witti, 1978).

That chemical substances such as alcohol and drugs can cross the placenta and damage the fetus is clear. What is not clear is how much alcohol is too much. Alcohol passes through the placenta in the same concentration as is present in the mother's body, but the ratio of alcohol to body weight is drastically higher for the fetus. If the mother is drunk, the fetus will be *very drunk*. The problem is complicated for the fetus because its liver (the key organ for removing alcohol from the blood) is not fully developed and is unable to metabolize the chemical. Thus, alcohol must be removed from the fetus' body primarily through diffusion back into the mother's system. Because this cannot occur until the mother's blood alcohol level goes down, the fetus retains a potentially high level of alcohol for what can become a lingering period of time. A normal adult liver metabolizes about ½ to 1 ounce of alcohol an hour. If the mother continues to drink, the liver simply will become even more overloaded, producing a heightened blood alcohol level for the fetus (Rosett & Sander, 1979).

The NIAAA warns of a definite risk for any pregnant mother who drinks 3 or more ounces of alcohol per day. One to 3 ounces a day may be risky.* Social drinking is such a traditional and widespread practice in the U.S. that the potential for birth defects resulting from alcohol consumption is great. A couple of beers during the day, a martini before dinner, and a glass of wine during dinner are routine for some women. Weekend social events may involve heavier drinking. When these women become pregnant, they may not be aware that they have conceived until 4-6 weeks into their pregnancy. In the meantime, they probably have continued their usual pattern of alcohol consumption. When they finally become aware of their condition and could curtail their use of liquor, they already have subjected the fetus to constant dosages of alcohol during its most critical, vulnerable phase of development.

Drugs and other chemical substances pass freely through the placenta to the fetus. The effect is much the same as alcohol on the body of the rapidly growing fetus, and damage can ensue. According to Barnes (1968), voluntary ingestion of chemicals in the form of medications, stimulants, food additives and preservatives is epidemic in Western society. And hidden contaminants—pollutants in our air, water, and food—are present. Even the cumulative effect of chemicals added to processed food is something of which consumers may not be aware. Involuntary ingestion of these chemicals is staggering. Taken collectively with chemicals voluntarily ingested, the average American is exposed continuously to a great number of chemicals.

Drugs have variable effects depending upon how much is taken, for how long, and at what period during pregnancy. Consequently, isolating exactly what effect each drug has on an unborn child is difficult. Over 600 drugs are known to produce congenital deformities in laboratory animals. Their effects on humans are less clear because experiments that impose potential risks upon pregnant mothers are not possible. Scientists have pinpointed defects in the human fetus caused by a number of specific drugs (Blatman, 1974; Crain, 1984; Heinonen, Slone, & Shapiro, 1977; Wilson, 1973).

The potentially devastating impact of drugs was clearly shown when the drug *thalidomide* was used briefly as a mild tranquilizer and sedative to prevent morning sickness in pregnant women. The most tragic manifestations of the drug were deformities in the formation of arms and legs. Women who took thalidomide between 28 and 42 days of pregnancy were highly vulnerable since that is the period when tiny limb buds are just forming on the human embryo. Many children whose mothers took thalidomide

---

*Two mixed drinks, each containing about 1 ounce of 100-proof whiskey, for example, equals about 1 ounce of alcohol. (Alcohol content for distilled spirits such as whiskey, gin, or vodka is indicated by dividing the "proof" number on the label in half.) Two 5-ounce glasses of still (not fortified) wine or two 12-ounce glasses of regular beer yield about 1 ounce of alcohol.

were born with arms and legs that developed little past this stage. Others lacked arms or legs, or both. Other babies had small flappers as arms or partially developed limbs with a few rudimentary fingers or toes at the end (Decarie, 1969; Lenz, 1962). Some babies also suffered from malformations of the heart and digestive tract. Apparently some women who took the drug in the later part of their pregnancy gave birth to normal babies.

Other drugs known to produce fetal damage are listed below.

- LSD, a hallucinogen, is known to produce chromosomal damage (Cohen, 1968). Mothers ingesting it during pregnancy are at risk for delivering newborns with various abnormalities (Maugh, 1973). But some controversy remains about the specific effects of this drug on unborn babies.
- Heroin, morphine, and methadone addiction of a pregnant mother produces withdrawal symptoms and other behavior effects in the baby at birth (Strauss, Lessen-Firestone, Starr, & Ostrea, 1975; Rothstein & Gould, 1974).
- Cocaine has been cited increasingly by the electronic and print media as a life-threatening drug for both the pregnant mother and her baby by causing premature birth and other complications, including cerebral palsy, even though the baby may look normal at birth.
- Nicotine exposure from a mother who smokes during pregnancy appears to increase the chances for a premature or small-for-date baby, and a clear relationship exists between prematurity and low birth weight with developmental disabilities, including impairments in mental ability (Pasamanick & Knobloch, 1966). Specific kinds of defects that can occur from maternal smoking, however, remain unclear. Fetal heart rate increases when the mother smokes, apparently because of oxygen deprivation (Quigley, Sheehan, Wilks, & Yen, 1979; Fechter & Annaw, 1977).
- Quinine is known to produce deafness.
- Thyroid drugs, including potassium iodides in cough medicines and radioactive iodine, can cause congenital goiter. Prophylthiouracil, a drug inhibiting synthesis of thyroid hormones, can cause goiter and other abnormalities such as cretinism as a result of loss of thyroid hormones (Wasserman & Gromisch, 1981; Wright, Schaefer, & Solomons, 1979).

Environmental pollutants in our air and water are highly suspect causative agents for genetic abnormalities, stillbirths, cancer, and heightened rates of congenital defects in newborns (Wilson, 1974, 1977). Lead and mercury, known to gradually accumulate in the body over time, can cause mental retardation, neurological damage, seizures, and overall lethargy. The destructive effects of mercury are well documented by what happened in the Japanese village Minimata. Fish and fowl, which were consumed by local villagers, had absorbed mercury from industrial wastes dumped in the water. Before the cause was isolated, many villagers showed progressive deterioration resulting in severe physical and mental impairment. An excessively high number of babies showed early signs of neurological damage and blindness, and many died during infancy. A similar incident occurred in Iran in 1972 when wheat was contaminated with antifungal mercury compounds. Pregnant women who ingested the wheat showed excessively heightened fetal blood levels of mercury. Severe brain damage was reported in a high percentage of their infants (Casarett & Doull, 1975).

Radiation has been known to cause genetic mutation that can disrupt early cell division in the embryo and thus produce abnormal growth of the brain and other organs. The risk of spontaneous abortion and chromosomal abnormalities is increased notably as a result of maternal exposure to radiation (Sells & Bennett, 1977; Wald, 1979). Even therapeutic X-ray or radium doses in pregnant women were found years ago to cause congenital brain defects, microcephaly, and central nervous system damage in their off-spring (Goldstein & Murphy, 1929; Murphy, Shirlock, & Doll, 1942). Vulnerability of the human fetus to damage by radiation appears to be particularly high during the first three months in utero (Atomic Energy Commission, 1975). Physicians and dentists now use lead aprons to cover a woman's abdominal area when administering radiation therapy or X-rays.

Maternal undernutrition   The effects of maternal nutrition on an unborn fetus are well documented through research with both animals and humans. Diet influences the pregnant mother's own health and resistance to disease. This in turn affects her own body's efficiency in sustaining metabolic processes that contribute to a healthy prenatal environment for her fetus. Caloric intake, as well as the nutritive value of her diet, is important. Calories alone do not offer the proper nutrients required for optimal development of the fetus. Proper growth and functioning of the placenta, which are closely related to diet, are critical to the unborn child's well-being. When the placenta functions inefficiently, impairment in fetal growth can occur (Birch, 1971; Spreen et al., 1984).

Research with rats and other mammals in which maternal diet has been systematically manipulated during pregnancy has demonstrated that undernutrition can produce severe impairment in the health and brain functions of offspring. Brain cells can be reduced in number by as much as 15% (Winick & Rosso, 1973; Zamenhof, VanMartens, & Margolis, 1968; Zamenhof, VanMartens, & Shimomaye, 1976). Nutritional deprivation among human beings (particularly women in the U.S.) generally is not as severe as that imposed upon laboratory animals for research purposes. Neither is undernutrition likely to be sustained at exactly the same level in a fetus for a prolonged time during both its prenatal and postnatal life. Thus, the effects of more subtle forms of mild to moderate undernutrition are difficult to pinpoint. Effects are more variable and complex because of interactions between prenatal undernutrition, diet after birth, and other environmental conditions.

One measure or indicator of prenatal nutrition is birth weight of the newborn. Research shows a much higher incidence of abnormalities in full-term newborns who are of low birth weight (less than 2,500 grams or under 5½ pounds). Prenatal malnutrition can result in growth retardation and interfere with normal development of the brain (Chase & Crnic, 1977). Knobloch, Rider, Harper, and Pasamanick (1956) compared 500 low birth weight infants to a control group and found that the low birth weight babies were intellectually inferior and manifested neurological abnormalities more frequently. As birth weight decreased, the occurrence of impairments, and their severity, increased. Numerous studies have demonstrated specific relationships between the mother's protein intake during pregnancy and the incidence of prematurity and neonatal death (Bergner & Susser, 1970; Jeans, Smith, & Stearns, 1955; Spreen et al., 1984).

A second method of studying the impact of prenatal undernutrition has been through research on development of the placenta. Information on the weight and DNA content (number of cells) of the placenta helps explain why a newborn is underweight. Poor nutrition in the mother or any factor that limits nutritive supplies to the fetus also affects the supply to the placenta. As a result, the placenta, too, will weigh less than normal. Analysis of DNA content in the placenta thus provides some indication of when undernu-trition occurred. The placenta is fully developed by about the 34th week of pregnancy, so if DNA content is below normal, undernutrition would have occurred prior to that time. Low birth weight can be caused by several factors: congenital or genetic disorders, prematurity, or nutritional deficiency. The condition of the placenta, however, helps to decipher which variable is the major cause. An extremely small newborn with congenital abnormalities usually has a placenta of normal weight and DNA content. Likewise, a premature baby born at 34 weeks, give or take a few weeks, also is likely to have a relatively normal placenta.

How does nutrition affect the placenta, and subsequently the physical growth and development of the brain and other organs in the fetus? Growth usually is measured by weight gain, but it also can be assessed in terms of cell proliferation, which can be monitored by measuring DNA content. Thus, if DNA content of an organ doubles, this would imply that the number of cells also must have doubled. Weight gain in an organ may reflect either (a) an increase in cell number or (b) an increase in cell size (Culley, 1978). Extensive research reported by Winick (1970a, 1970b, 1970c; 1971) indicates that organs first grow (gain weight) as a result of cell proliferation. This is followed by a stage in which cell proliferation and increases in cell size occur simultaneously. In a third growth stage, cell proliferation ceases and weight gain is solely a result of increases in cell size. This sequence is significant when we look at prenatal development in the human infant and the effect of nutrition during that time. In the prenatal period most organs, including the brain, grow as a result of increases in cell number. Therefore, organs are most vulnerable at that time to the adverse effects of undernutrition.

Chloe's congenital orthopedic impairment affects her physical growth and mobility and imposes continuing medical concerns. The parents, along with teachers/therapists of this little girl, monitor her condition carefully so they can minimize the effects of these disorders on her development and learning.

Research indicates that the lower number of cells resulting from undernutrition is not easily corrected. In fact, it will cause a permanent defect in cell numbers if not corrected by the time cell proliferation normally stops for the organism. Undernutrition that occurs after cell proliferation ceases in an organism will not affect cell number, but it can result in decreased cell size. Smaller cell size resulting from malnutrition can be reversed, however, through nutritional rehabilitation (Winick & Rosso, 1969, 1973, 1975).

In summary, the timing of undernutrition is particularly significant in relation to brain development. The vast majority of neural cells in the cerebral cortex is formed prenatally. Thus, defects in the number of cells formed prenatally as a result of nutritional limitations are not correctable through improved postnatal nutrition. Other brain cells do continue to divide postnatally but generally cease during the first year of life. After that, growth occurs primarily in terms of an increase in cell size. Of course, the mere presence of cells does not ensure that they are functioning normally. Undernutrition not only can impair cell growth, but it also can alter to some degree how cells function.

Methods to detect abnormality   Several methods are now in use with pregnant mothers to obtain information about the presence or absence of abnormality in their unborn fetus (Cowart, 1983, 1984; Daker, 1983; Loeffler, 1984). These include:

1. *Ultrasound scans.* Sound waves are used to produce a picture of the fetus by recording tissue densities pictorially as shadows. This allows determination of placental placement, physical deformities, and central nervous system abnormalities.
2. *Amniocentesis.* Amniotic fluid is drawn through a long needle inserted into the mother's womb, then cultured for several weeks so a chromosomal analysis can be made on fetal cells and the amniotic fluid can be analyzed for hormones, amino acids, enzymes, and metabolic wastes.
3. *Chorionic villus biopsy* (a newly developed alternative to amniocentesis that can be done earlier, during the first 8 weeks of pregnancy). A tiny sample of placental tissue is suctioned out via a catheter, using ultrasound guidance. An analysis then is made on fetal cells in the placenta, placental DNA, and other elements in the tissue as is done in amniocentesis.
4. *Fetoscopy.* An endoscope is placed surgically into the uterus, enabling diagnosis of cranial abnormalities, physical deformities, and other defects.
5. *Blood analysis.* Samples of the mother's blood are used to sort out embryonic cells (trophoblasts) that migrate from the fetus into the mother's bloodstream, where they appear to prevent her immune system from rejecting the fetus. These cells then are analyzed for genetic disorders and other abnormalities.

Perinatal hazards that place a newborn at-risk

Birth is a significant biological event that tests the resiliency and strength of a newborn baby to survive apart from the protective uterine environment. Some conditions related to the occurrence and process of birth increase the risk for neonatal death or developmental disability later on. Certain injuries resulting from the birth process are apparent immediately. What functional impairment these injuries will have upon a youngster's ability to learn and perform tasks like other children becomes apparent only over time. In examining some of the perinatal hazards, we must look first at conditions relating to the developmental status of the newborn that render it at-risk. These include prematurity and low birth weight. Then we will review some of the factors associated with the birth process itself that increase the risk for developmental disabilities, including perinatal asphyxia, and excessive physical trauma resulting in mechanical injury.

Prematurity and low birth weight   The term *premature* actually encompasses two groups of infants—those with:

— shortened gestational age—less than 37 weeks from the first day of the last menstrual period. These babies are developmentally and physically immature, but if they are merely preterm, their size and weight are appropriate and normal for their gestational age.
— low birth weight—improper growth of the fetus during gestation, resulting in a birth weight of under 2,500 grams (5½ pounds) for a full-term baby or a lower than normal weight for gestational age in babies delivered prematurely.

Thus, a newborn may be premature but of normal weight for the gestational period; the baby may be full-term but have a lower than normal birth weight. Or a baby may be both premature *and* of low birth weight for the length of gestation.

Prematurity and low birth weight usually are concomitant, particularly among newborns weighing 1,500 grams (3½ pounds) or less at birth. Both factors are associated with increased risk for congenital abnormalities, biological dysfunction, and death (Behrman & Vaughan, 1983). Most research, unfortunately, does not differentiate between the two groups. Studies of "premature" babies typically use weight as the sole criterion. Only in recent years has the distinction been made between premature infants and low birth weight infants.

The type of prematurity, however, *does* make a significant difference in research results. For example, Niswander and Gordon (1972) and Chase (1977) reported data from the Collaborative Perinatal Study indicating that perinatal death is 25% higher among infants with low birth weight than those with higher birth weight. Developmental outcomes and mortality also were compared between (a) babies who were born prematurely but of normal weight for gestation and (b) babies who were underweight for their gestation period. The latter had a lower incidence of death, but they showed a higher ratio of notable developmental problems later on.

What causes babies to be born prematurely or show inadequate rates of prenatal growth and thus low birth weight? Usually no one factor causes either prematurity or low birth weight. A complex interaction of several variables is more likely the case. Nonetheless, the occurrence of these conditions in newborns is highly correlated with a number of maternal, sociocultural, and biological factors.

Prematurity is associated typically with conditions that render the mother's uterus incapable of retaining the fetus. For example, premature separation of the placenta triggers delivery before full term. Multiple pregnancies usually result in premature delivery. Interference in the course of the pregnancy through trauma or serious injury to the mother or some stimulus that prompts uterine contractions before full term also results in early delivery.

Low growth rates in the fetus, resulting in lower than normal weight for gestation, are associated with an even greater variety of conditions, including:

1. *Conditions that interfere with circulation and placental efficiency for delivering oxygen and nutrients to the fetus and/or exchange of metabolic waste products* (Vorherr, 1975). Maternal conditions that seem to influence these mechanisms are: heart disease, toxemia, smoking, use of drugs, viral infections, and structural features of the uterus and placenta. These latter conditions are related, in turn, to the mother's ethnicity, physical size, general health, nutritional status before and during pregnancy, and socioeconomic class (W. DeMyer, 1975; Gruenwald, 1975; Ounsted & Ounsted, 1973; Korones, 1976).

2. *Conditions that interfere with growth and development of the fetus.* In addition to the factors just cited that affect placental efficiency, and thus fetal growth, chromosomal and congenital anomalies in the fetus influence birth weight. Marked reductions in weight often are found in infants with metabolic and other genetic abnormalities. Down syndrome babies, for instance, have birth weights below normal compared to controls of the same gestation age (Robson, 1978; Polani, 1974). Pregnancies involving twins or multiple fetuses typically are characterized by reductions in the size of the babies and preterm delivery (Shanklin, 1978).

3. *Conditions that affect the overall health and nutrition of the mother.* According to Battaglia and Simmons (1978), almost all serious diseases in the mother are associated with an increased incidence of premature delivery. The degree of impact is determined in part by the nature of the disease and its severity. Maternal nutrition, as discussed earlier, affects the fetus and produces reduced size of all organs and overall body size.

What are the consequences of premature birth or low birth weight? In themselves, prematurity and low birth weight cannot be cited as the cause of developmental disabilities or even death in young children, but they are indicators of other possible underlying problems. The fact that a baby is born prior to term and is physically and biologically immature or underweight makes the infant susceptible to additional stresses after birth. These babies are more subject to: (a) respiratory and cardiac failure or complications, which interfere with delivery of oxygen to the tissues (since the nervous system is still developing until the 42-46 week of gestation, the central nervous system is particularly vulnerable), (b) hemorrhage, (c) more frequent infections because they lack normal mechanisms for fighting common diseases (they also do not show many of the typical signs of infection, which complicates diagnosis and the timely application of treatment), and (d) overdemands upon the baby's bodily systems and organs, which are too physically and biochemically immature to sustain life processes. Each of these conditions is associated with later manifestation of physical and mental impairments (Kopp & Parmelee, 1979; Reed & Stanley, 1977; Hardy, Drage, & Jackson, 1979).

What is the prognosis for preterm and low birth weight infants? Many do grow up to be normal, healthy youngsters and adults, but the incidence of developmental problems still presents an alarming picture. The prognosis suggests that active intervention, rather than a passive wait-and-see approach, is important. The mortality rate of low birth weight infants who survive the first few weeks or months of life to be discharged from the hospital is approximately 3 times that of full-term infants during the first two years of life. Congenital deformities are present in some 25% of live-born infants with birth weight under 1,500 grams, 12% of those between 1,500 and 2,500 grams, and 6% with birth weight over 2,500 grams.

Follow-up studies show a high incidence of physical and mental handicaps, including a high incidence of behavioral and personality problems (Behrman & Vaughan, 1983). A noteworthy follow-up study on psychological and educational sequelae of premature and low birth weight infants was conducted by Rubin, Rosenblatt, and Barlow (1973). They found that: (a) low birth weight rather than gestation age correlated highly with the occurrence of neurological, educational, and psychological impairment, (b) low birth weight males and low birth weight full-term infants of both sexes had a significantly higher incidence of school problems that required special school services than children who had full-term prenatal histories and normal birth weight; (c) low birth weight youngsters, compared to a control group of children with normal birth weights, showed lower scores on all measures of mental development, language, school readiness, and academic achievement through 7 years of age, and (d) at age 7, low birth weight children were of smaller stature and had a higher incidence of diagnosed neurological abnormalities than did controls.

Though prematurity and low birth weight continue to pose problems, advances in neonatal intensive care methods are reducing the rate of mortality and morbidity in at-risk newborns. Physiological functions now are monitored routinely. Diet is more carefully tuned to the neonate's bodily needs. More effective feeding methods (such as tube feeding) are now used, and greater attention is given to maintaining consistent body temperature. Because of these and many other advances, Kopp and Parmelee (1979) have noted that risks in these newborns for moderate to severe intellectual and neurological abnormality are being reduced; whereas some 10%-40% of low birth weight infants showed such impairment in the past, the current rate in industrialized nations is more accurately around 5%-15%, based upon their calculations and other reports (Davies & Stewart, 1975; Dweck, Saxon, Benton, & Cassady, 1973; Hagberg, 1975).

Asphyxia   Lack of oxygen before, during, or immediately after delivery can cause brain damage and even death. Children known to have had major oxygen deprivation may show the effects of damage relatively soon after birth, especially if the resulting impairments are severe. Other children manifest no symptoms until later, and then may show only "soft signs" of neurological damage (subtle, minor manifestations suggesting *possible* neurological damage). Definite diagnosis, however, is usually difficult, if not impossible.

Among the numerous conditions that can interfere with passage of oxygen to the fetus just *prior* to birth are: (a) inadequate oxygenation of maternal blood because of hypoventilation by the mother after she has been given anesthesia for delivery, or through cardiac failure, (b) low maternal blood pressure, (c) premature separation of the placenta, (d) disruption of blood flow through the umbilical cord as a result of premature compression and knotting of the cord, and (e) placental inadequacy resulting from a variety of causes such as postmaturity or toxemia. Oxygen deprivation *during* the birth process itself is a major risk and can occur for a number of reasons. Sometimes excessive pressure on the baby's head during birth ruptures blood vessels in the brain. Blood clots then form, which in turn deprive other brain cells of oxygen and cause them to die. If blood clots are numerous or if a clot impinges on a major or critical section of the brain, the outcome can be functional impairment. The exact outcome depends upon the section of the brain involved and the extent of the damage.

Another cause of asphyxia, or *anoxia,* is prolonged delay between the time the baby ceases getting oxygen through the placenta from the mother and the time breathing begins on its own. Abnormal suspension of breathing is called *apnea.* Use of sedatives or anesthesia with the mother before delivery can affect the newborn by reducing the ability to begin and maintain strong respiration immediately after birth. Failure of newborns to begin breathing upon birth or to maintain satisfactory respiration in the period shortly thereafter is one of the most common emergencies in the delivery room (Behrman & Vaughan, 1983).

Regardless of the cause, perinatal asphyxia sometimes leads to deficits in the functioning of a child later on. The manifestations are highly variable and often are difficult to pin down as a clear abnormality or impairment. Furthermore, the resiliency of the human brain and body compensates for some forms of damage, making a clear prediction or prognosis of a child's later functioning difficult. Some professionals suggest that learning disabilities in children have their origin in subtle brain injuries or subtle forms of oxygen deprivation during birth.

Physical trauma resulting in birth injury   Sometimes delivery is so difficult and traumatic that the baby's head, brain, or a vital organ is injured. This is more likely to happen if the baby's head or body is relatively large in comparison to the size of the mother's pelvis or if the baby is incorrectly positioned for passage through the birth canal. When labor begins, the most favorable position is head first with the face downward (to the mother's back).

The *breech position* (buttocks presented first instead of the head) can cause serious difficulties because the infant's body mass that must pass through any point in the birth canal is wider and larger than in the normal birth position. This places greater stress on the mother and greater pressure on the baby. More effort likely is required to move the baby through the birth canal. If the head is presented last, it reaches the pelvic girdle (the bony hip structure of the mother) during the latter stages of labor when contractions are more rapid. The head may have less time to mold to fit the birth canal than would occur under normal birth conditions, which might force reshaping in abnormal ways and be subject to atypical pressure. Damage may occur if parts of the brain are crushed from the rapid compression. Or hemorrhaging within the skull could endanger oxygen flow to brain tissue.

Similiar kinds of problems occur if the baby is presented for birth in a *transverse position* (baby is lying crosswise in the womb so the back is presented first to the birth canal). Obstetricians do attempt to move the fetus into correct delivery position, and if this is unsuccessful, they resort to delivery via caesarean section (National Institute of Health, 1981).

In summary, physical injuries resulting from the birth process can be classified into four main types: (a) cranial injuries involving actual crushing of brain tissue, (b) hemorrhage in the brain that disrupts oxygen flow to brain cells, and subsequent clotting that further blocks blood circulation, (c) damage to the spine or spinal cord through fracture or separation of the vertebrae, and (d) damage to internal organs (usually the liver or spleen). Only occasionally are bones broken (Vaughan, McKay, Behrman, & Nelson, 1979).

Postnatal conditions that threaten normal development

Hazards that jeopardize normal growth and development in children are not limited to prenatal and perinatal periods. After infants enter the world outside the mother's womb, they are subject to a whole new array of possible hazards and environmental influences with which they must cope. In the uterus the fetus relies upon the mother's body for oxygen, nutrients for growth, warmth, and removal of metabolic wastes. After birth the infant's own physical mechanisms must provide sufficient oxygen and nourishment. Bodily organs must carry out metabolic processes that heretofore were inactive.

More important, the newborn is rendered into the hands of parents who may or may not be prepared or ready to assume their new role. The environment they create provides whatever protection, nourishment, and stimulation their child will get to allow him or her to grow and flourish. Ideally, parents want to and have the capacity to respond to the needs of their offspring. But if conditions in the new environment are poor or if the quality of care given the child is less than adequate, the child's subsequent development may be at-risk.

A brief overview of the major types of postnatal hazards is given here under five broad categories: (a) postnatal diseases and infections, (b) toxic or poisonous substances, (c) accidental or inflicted injury through abuse and neglect, (d) malnutrition, and (e) substandard and depriving environments.

Postnatal diseases and infections.   Measles, mumps, and chicken pox are familiar infectious diseases that a majority of children contract in their early childhood years if they have not been immunized. These infections usually are of short duration with no lingering aftereffects. Occasionally complications become precursory to other, more serious illnesses. If infection continues with a persistent high fever, physical damage can occur. For example, hearing loss, or even deafness, is a possible outcome of complications with mumps, measles, chicken pox and influenza. Some viral diseases can result in malformed body parts, mental retardation, congenital heart disease, and central nervous system damage. Given proper treatment and timely attention when problems first arise, the chances for lasting negative effects are reduced. But parental neglect, poor environmental conditions, general poor health—and, hence, greater susceptibility to disease—can complicate matters.

Meningitis and encephalitis are two infections known to cause mild to severe neurological damage. *Meningitis,* a bacterial infection, is an inflammation of the meninges (protective covering of the brain) and spinal column. Different microorganisms cause various forms of the disease, but all can potentially leave the victim with neuromotor disabilities, mental retardation, seizures, speech disorders, or hearing defects. Meningitis occurs mostly in children below age 5. The risk for serious damage is greatest if the infection is contracted during infancy (Gotoff & Gotoff, 1978). The illness is accompanied by high fever and various signs of brain infection—convulsions, headache, delirium, paralysis, and even coma. The effects are highly variable. Some children show no permanent effects; others show clear signs of neurological damage, including impairment in learning.

Encephalitis is an infection in the brain itself. It, too, is caused by a number of different viruses and can occur after complications from other infectious diseases such as measles, chicken pox, whooping cough, and influenza. Symptoms are highly varied and, thus, easily misdiagnosed. The impact of encephalitis ranges from no ill aftereffects, to brain damage, physical or mental impairment, to death.

Innumerable other diseases pose potential threats and may cause physical or neurological impairments. These are summarized in Table 4.1.

Toxic or poisonous substances

Risks imposed by prenatal exposure to drugs, poisonous substances, and other toxic elements were described earlier. Children continue to be subject to similar kinds of hazards after birth. They not only are vulnerable to toxic substances in the air, water, and food they eat but also to toxic things they accidentally ingest. Curious infants and preschoolers are especially prone to accidental poisonings. The greatest number of poisoning cases treated in hospitals and clinics are between 1 and 4 years of age. Poisoning in children under age 5 typically involves (in order of frequency): aspirin, soaps, detergents, cleansers, bleaches, vitamins, minerals (including iron), insecticides, plants, polishes and waxes, hormones, and tranquilizers (Vaughan, McKay, Behrman, & Nelson, 1979). Younger children are more likely to ingest common household products; older children are more likely to ingest medicines.

Symptoms of acute poisoning often are similar to those of acute diseases such as appendicitis, meningitis, or encephalitis. Effects are highly varied, depending upon what and how much was ingested, the child's size and weight, and over what period of time the chemical was ingested. Depression of the central nervous system resulting in lethargy or coma is the most dangerous complication from poisoning. Destruction of tissue, cardiac failure, or kidney damage may also occur.

Certain drugs or medications, taken without proper medical supervision or by accidental ingestion, can be injurious. Streptomycin and other members of the *mycin* group of antibiotics, for example, can cause permanent hearing loss. The drug destroys or damages hair cells in the cochlea of the inner ear (Green, 1981).

Toxins in the environment (e.g., lead and mercury) can be especially damaging to young children whose nervous systems and bodies are still developing. Paints and plaster used in many old slum dwellings contain over 50% *lead*. Paint on some toys also contained lead in the past, and children who ate that paint sometimes suffered neurological damage. Use of lead-based paint for indoor use and on children's items has since been prohibited. Now a major source of lead poisoning seems to be through air pollution (Landrigan et al., 1975); about 98% of lead now comes from automobile exhausts that contaminate the air and soil. Other sources of lead to which children are vulnerable are: (a) lead shot in fishing weights, (b) contaminated fruit juices that have been mixed and stored in the refrigerator in lead-glazed earthenware, and (c) lead-soldered cooking containers. Vaughan et al. (1979) reported that 10% or more of the children ages 1-6 in the U.S. have absorbed excessive amounts of lead.

Lead poisoning produces initial symptoms such as anemia, tiredness, irritability, and constipation—all symptoms that could suggest any number of illnesses. With increased dosages of lead, vomiting and convulsions occur. With severe build-up of lead in the blood over time, blindness, convulsions, spasticity, and brain damage can result.

Mercury is another dangerous pollutant found in excessive proportions in major waterways where fish and fowl have become contaminated. If humans eat these foodstuffs, they risk mercury poisoning, which can cause neurological damage (ranging from mild to severe palsy), seizures, mental retardation, memory loss, and visual disturbances (Amin-Zaki et al., 1974; Bakir et al., 1973; Matsumoto, Goyo, & Takevchi, 1965; Snyder, 1971).

Table 4.1

Diseases That Can Interfere With Normal Growth and Development

Disease	Description and Potential Impacts
Cystic Fibrosis	Chronic disorder caused by a defective gene, which affects the lungs, pancreas, or both. Mucus in lungs does not drain properly and thus inhibits breathing. If pancreas is affected, digestion is impaired and malnutrition may ensue. Results in frequent coughing, possible respiratory tract infections or pneumonia. Growth can be impaired, and child may show increased appetite but low stamina. Disease often is fatal, with average life expectancy 15-19 years.
Infectious Hepatitis	Caused by a virus in contaminated food or water. Also can be contracted through direct contact with an infected person. Results in jaundice, fever, enlargement of liver, and liver damage, in severe, prolonged infection. Death can result if treatment is not initiated soon enough.
Juvenile Arthritis	Among several forms of this disease are juvenile rheumatoid arthritis (cause unknown) and infectious arthritis (most common during infancy), usually affecting shoulders, hips, and other large joints and causing destruction of cartilage. Juvenile rheumatoid arthritis has two high incidence peaks—one between ages 1 and 4. It, too, produces swelling and stiffening of joints and spine, growth disturbances, and destruction of joints.
Leukemia	Cancer of bone marrow, resulting in massive or abnormal production of white blood cells. Disease may be acute or chronic. Symptoms include fatigue, fever, weight loss, pain in joints, and excessive bruising. Treatment can increase survival time from 6 months to as long as 5 or more years, and sometimes the disease goes into remission. Drugs can produce side effects. Children with leukemia face greater risk for infection and bleeding.
Muscular Dystrophy	A progressive weakness of muscles, resulting from degeneration of muscle cells and their replacement by fat and fibrous tissue. Cause is unknown, although it appears to have genetic origin. Childhood form (Duchenne or progressive muscular dystrophy) is found primarily in males. Early symptom is slow motor development; thus, clear diagnosis may not occur until some time during preschool or early primary years. Mild mental retardation can be associated with Duchenne. Disease produces progressive disability, including overall weakness, skeletal deformities, and ultimately death.
Nephritis	Exact cause is unknown, but disease usually follows a streptococcus infection. Symptoms include puffy eyes and body parts, fever, anemia, high blood pressure, vomiting, possible convulsions, liver damage, and enlargement of heart.
Otitis Media	Acute or chronic infection of middle ear, common among preschool and early school-aged youngsters. Secretions are discharged from middle ear. Blockage of eustachian tube may result in excessive inner ear pressure, rupture of tympanic membrane, and then possible scarring of ear. Children with cleft palate have high incidence of otitis media.
Poliomyelitis	Viral infection that destroys certain cells in the spinal cord. Causes paralysis of muscles (but not sensory paralysis), possible spasticity, and skeletal deformities. Salk polio vaccine has almost eradicated this disease.

Table 4.1 (continued)

Rheumatic Fever	Cause is unknown, but disease usually follows a streptococcus infection. Results in fever, arthritis and inflammation of joints and connective tissue, and skin rash. Continued or prolonged attacks can cause permanent heart damage. Treatment with penicillin and other antibiotics has helped reduce occurrence of this disease.
Sickle Cell Anemia	Blood disease caused by a recessive gene affecting largely Black children. Sickle shape of red blood cells interferes with circulation. Causes anemia, swelling of hands, feet, and joints, severe pain in abdomen and limbs, weakness, impairment of liver functions, and slow healing. Fainting and overall lethargy also occur.

Note. From Bleck and Nagel (1975); Haslam and Valletutti (1975); Behrman and Vaughan (1983); Blackman, 1984.

Other potentially threatening chemicals are found in *food additives* and *pesticides*. The younger the child, the greater is the susceptibility to permanent damage. Just one episode of severe toxicity involving the nervous system can be enough to cause permanent damage, even when the toxin is subsequently eliminated (Behrman & Vaughan, 1983).

Accidental or inflicted injury   Accidents are one of the leading causes of death among children in the U.S. today. Some 50% of structural abnormalities in the limbs of young children has a congenital origin, but the remaining half is accidentally acquired (Myers, 1975). Similarly many head injuries resulting in brain damage accrue through car accidents, anoxia from near drownings, or other asphyxiating events. The most common sources of serious head injury in young children are automobile accidents and child abuse (MacMillan, 1982). The end result can be some degree of mental impairment, learning disabilities, visual or perceptual defects, hearing impairments, seizures, and other kinds of motor difficulties. Serious burns from fire, hot water, or other thermal agents are not uncommon among young children. These can produce serious scarring, severe limb contractures, and disfigured appearance. Emotional trauma resulting from the accident itself, from extended hospitalization, or from the social impacts of disfigurement can undoubtedly interfere with a child's overall well-being and healthy development.

Inflicted injury resulting in psychological, emotional, physical, or even neurological damage to a young child usually is the result of *parental abuse or neglect*. The frequency of child abuse is difficult to ascertain since parents typically deny or hide the fact that they abuse their child, but the incidence is estimated to be high, and particularly so with very young children and infants (Friedman, Sandler, Hernandez, & Wolfe, 1981). The Joint Commission on Mental Health of Children (1970) estimated at that time that 2,000 - 3,000 children were injured each month by abusive parents and approximately two youngsters were killed each day in the U.S. from physical abuse. In a survey of 140 children below age 16 in facilities for the retarded, Buchanan and Oliver (1981) found that 3% definitely—and a possible maximum of 11% probably—had been rendered mentally handicapped by child abuse. In another 24%, neglect was considered a contributing factor to their retardation.

What is the effect of abuse upon children? Abusive homes place a child at-risk for emotional trauma, as well as for potential physical injury, mental retardation or other cognitive disorders, and a variety of other developmental difficulties. Studies indicate that abused children are similar behaviorally to children deprived of normal maternal stimulation (Elmer, 1977; MacCarthy, 1977; Ramey, Starr, Whitten, Pallas, & Reed, 1975). Normal cognitive and motor development are threatened in the abused young child (Martin, 1976).

In a 13-year longitudinal study on the psychological and physical status of 20 abused children, 90% showed some residual damage (Elmer & Gregg, 1967). Over half were mentally retarded, and more than half were designated as emotionally disturbed. Growth abnormalities, speech disorders, and other forms of developmental delay were present to the extent that only two of the children were considered "normal." In another follow-up study, by Morse, Sahler, and Friedman (1970), 70% of the 25 children were found to be below normal in either intellectual, emotional, social, or motor development. About 43% displayed symptoms of mental retardation or motor hyperactivity. The cause-and-effect of abuse is not entirely clear (i.e., whether the abuse caused the disabilities or whether they were present before the abuse). In any event, environmental conditions surrounding abuse, or characteristics associated with abusive parents, are factors that can seriously jeopardize the healthy development of children who must live and develop under those conditions (Morse, Sahler, & Friedman, 1970; Johnson & Morse, 1968; Friedrich & Boriskin, 1976; Kempe & Kempe, 1978).

Abusive homes often are neglectful homes, but the two conditions—abuse and neglect—do not necessarily go hand-in-hand. Abuse and neglect appear to occur more frequently in low socioeconomic homes but also are found among parents of middle and upper classes (Steele & Pollock, 1974). Parents may be physically present but psychologically unavailable to their children. Neglect may come in the form of poor nutritional care or minimal parent-child interaction. Neglect also may involve a parent's failure to protect the child from environmental conditions that are potentially harmful. Or parents may fail to mediate the child's interactions with the environment in ways that promote learning and adapt experiences to the child's level of functioning.

Postnatal nutrition   The critical role of nutrition in development of the brain and central nervous system (described earlier) does not stop at birth. The newborn's brain is still immature, having about 40%-50% of its adult cells and only about 25% of its adult weight. Because brain development continues rapidly until 6 months to 1 year of age, good nutrition during infancy continues to be critical. By 6 months of age, 66% of the brain cells will have developed, and 90%-95% by age 1; by 1 year, the brain will weigh 3/4 that of an adult (Chase, 1973; Chase & Crnic, 1977). When division of the neuro cells ceases and the number is thus fixed, growth thereafter involves a change in cell size. Dendrites, the connections between neuro cells, become more elaborate and synapses are formed. Enzymes required for making chemical neurotransmitters are synthesized as well. This maturational process is what increases brain mass from ages 2 to 6 years (Lipton, 1976).

Thus, major increases in weight and the remaining postnatal growth of the brain are in (a) development of glial cells that form a supportive framework for the central nervous system, (b) increased size and morphological complexity of the existing neuro cells, and (c) development of the myelin sheath that coats the axons of the neural cells. Myelin is a fatty, protective covering of the nerve fibers that facilitates transmission of the nerve impulses. Myelinization is highly dependent upon adequate protein in the diet. Over 50% of the myelin sheath is formed between 12 and 24 months of age (Lipton, 1976), and neuro fibers linking the cerebellum and the neocortex are not fully sheathed with myelin until about age 4 (Spreen et al., 1984).

Various parts of the brain develop at different rates and thus are affected differently by malnutrition. For example, at birth the cerebral cortex and brain stem are about twice as advanced as the cerebellum. *Postnatal malnutrition* is more likely to affect development of the cerebellum, which controls motor coordination and postural control. Diet affects myelinization, and hence the efficiency of the central nervous system in transmitting electrical impulses back and forth from the brain to various body parts. Damage to the cerebellum thus is likely to be shown in impaired motor function. In contrast, *prenatal undernutrition* may affect development of the cerebral cortex, which controls higher thought processes including learned behaviors and integrated sensory motor behavior such as speech. An infant suffering from prenatal malnutrition is likely to have fewer brain cells, and thus to show broader intellectual impairment (Winick, 1976; Winick & Rosso, 1973; Brockman & Ricciuti, 1971).

Postnatal malnutrition rarely occurs in isolation from a number of other variables known to cause greater risk for developmental deficiencies. Malnutrition often is associated with low socioeconomic status, higher incidences of infection, a variety of pre- and postnatal hazards associated with later impairments, and low parental education. Chase and Cyrnic (1977) have suggested that the interaction between environment and nutrition is so complex as to be inseparable; they used the term *environutritional deprivation* to describe the impacts of nutrition on human development. Given the environmental context in which nutritional inadequacies occur, postnatal effects operate at several levels, as depicted in Figure 4.1.

What are the outcomes associated with postnatal malnutrition? Studies indicate that poorly nourished children show physical growth deficits, as well as depressed performance on tests of cognitive ability (Galler, Ramsey, Solimano, Lowell, & Mason, 1983a, 1983b; Lester, 1975; Monckeberg, 1975; Birch & Cravioto, 1968; Falkner & Tanner, 1978c; Stoch & Smythe, 1963). Other neurological and physical consequences are listed as follows:

- *Iodine deficiency* can result in improper functioning of the thyroid gland and cause growth abnormalities, changes in facial appearance, and, in its most severe form, mental retardation and cretinism.
- Protein deficiency can cause reduced brain growth and physical symptoms such as weakness, irritability, digestive disturbances, dry skin, and, in its most severe form, kwashiorkor (excessive bloating of the stomach).
- *Vitamin B_6* and *Vitamin D* deficiencies can cause seizures or convulsions.
- *Vitamin B_{12}* deficiencies can result in mental retardation, motor impairment, and general weakness.

Are the effects of prenatal or postnatal malnutrition reversible if proper nutrition is reinstated? Research suggests that the younger the child is when malnutrition occurs, the more severe and irreversible are the effects. Severe malnutrition during the first 6 months of life generally produces irreversible damage manifest in decreased ability to learn and possible neurological-motor impairments. Later nutritional deficiencies, after development

Figure 4.1
Interrelationships Between Primary and Secondary Effects of Undernutrition

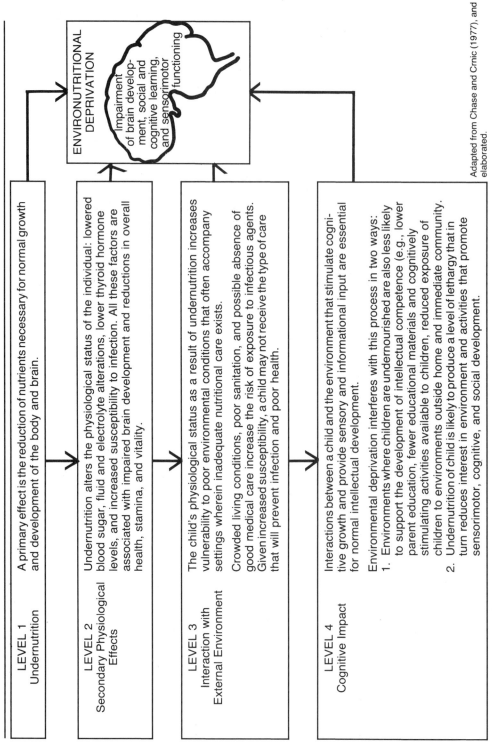

ENVIRONUTRITIONAL DEPRIVATION

Impairment of brain development, social and cognitive learning, and sensorimotor functioning

LEVEL 1
Undernutrition

A primary effect is the reduction of nutrients necessary for normal growth and development of the body and brain.

LEVEL 2
Secondary Physiological Effects

Undernutrition alters the physiological status of the individual: lowered blood sugar, fluid and electrolyte alterations, lower thyroid hormone levels, and increased susceptibility to infection. All these factors are associated with impaired brain development and reductions in overall health, stamina, and vitality.

LEVEL 3
Interaction with External Environment

The child's physiological status as a result of undernutrition increases vulnerability to poor environmental conditions that often accompany settings wherein inadequate nutritional care exists.

Crowded living conditions, poor sanitation, and possible absence of good medical care increase the risk of exposure to infectious agents. Given increased susceptibility, a child may not receive the type of care that will prevent infection and poor health.

LEVEL 4
Cognitive Impact

Interactions between a child and the environment that stimulate cognitive growth and provide sensory and informational input are essential for normal intellectual development.

Environmental deprivation interferes with this process in two ways:
1. Environments where children are undernourished are also less likely to support the development of intellectual competence (e.g., lower parent education, fewer educational materials and cognitively stimulating activities available to children, reduced exposure of children to environments outside home and immediate community.
2. Undernutrition of child is likely to produce a level of lethargy that in turn reduces interest in environment and activities that promote sensorimotor, cognitive, and social development.

Adapted from Chase and Crnic (1977), and elaborated.

of the central nervous system is relatively complete, may not cause as serious outcomes. Recovery of deprivation through improved diet, if it occurs after age 2 and particularly after age 4, is more likely (Lipton, 1976). More nutritious diets have produced changes in general alertness, energy and vitality, and cognitive functioning (Birch & Gussow, 1970; Freeman, Klein, Townsend, and Lechtig, 1980). (For more information, see a summary review by Spreen et al., 1984.)

Substandard and depriving environments   A large percentage of young children who have prenatal or perinatal complications and whose development reflects real or potential problems come from impoverished homes. Physical, social, and psychological conditions characterizing these settings correlate highly with the prenatal, perinatal, and postnatal hazards discussed earlier in this chapter. Conditions known to enhance children's development may be diminished or lacking altogether (Kugel & Parsons, 1967). Young children are totally dependent and in no position to escape from or alter their own surroundings. Thus, they are easily made victim to whatever life conditions adults impose upon them or to adverse elements in the environment in which they must live.

The link between poverty, disadvantaged environments, and the risks imposed upon children and their well-being is well documented by data represented by the following:

- The incidences of prematurity and neonatal death are higher among infants of low socioeconomic status (SES) than among babies of middle- to upper-class parents. Death resulting from birth complications is about twice as frequent in babies of low-income mothers compared to those from more prosperous families (Bauer, 1972; Foman & Anderson, 1972; Hood, 1971; Reed & Stanley, 1977).
- The incidence of low birth weight is highly correlated with low SES. Conditions connected with reduced fetal growth (such as poor maternal nutrition, anemia, frequent infectious and noninfectious diseases, pregnancy in mothers under age 15, or maternal histories of frequent and closely spaced pregnancies) are additional variables found with higher frequency in women of low SES compared to those from upper social classes (Behrman & Vaughan, 1983; Osofsky, 1979).
- Health care of children from low-SES environments typically is inferior to that of children from affluent families. They suffer greater health risks and infections during their early years (Robinson & Robinson, 1976; North, 1967).
- Young children with early developmental deficits as a result of prenatal or perinatal trauma are less likely to overcome them if they are from low-SES homes. Willerman, Broman, and Fielder (1970), for example, followed up infants who scored in the bottom 25% on a developmental evaluation at 8 months. When retested at 4 years of age, those from low-income homes were 7 times more likely than children from higher SES families to obtain IQ scores below 80.
- Incidences of mental retardation are higher in poverty stricken urban areas compared to more affluent urban areas. Conditions characterizing those environments show high correlations with poor physical, mental, and developmental status in children (e.g., overcrowded conditions, increased maternal and infant mortality rates, poor infant care, reduced access to medical services, social disorganization, increased incidence of infectious diseases) (Campbell, 1976; Cassel, 1973; Jackson, 1968).

Low SES by itself cannot be tagged as the cause of developmental disabilities or poor performance among children. Many parents of poor economic circumstances do cope exceedingly well and are successful in rearing healthy, normal children. Likewise, families with seemingly better economic circumstances may subject their children to neglect and depriving, nonstimulating environments.

Figure 4.2 depicts some major variables associated with low SES that seem to increase the chances for poor development in young children. These variables can be clustered into four broad categories. Note that every variable listed under each category is not necessarily characteristic of every low-SES home. Probabilities simply are greater that one or more of these variables exist in poor homes as compared to more affluent settings. First, *parental variables* are often associated with low SES. Second, certain *environmental elements* related to health and family well-being are more prevalent in low-income homes.

Third, the cumulative effects of the prior two sets of variables undoubtedly take their toll as *psychological variables* upon parents and families. To families with limited resources, life can easily become a seemingly endless parade of nagging problems. Costs for car repairs, an unexpected illness, or other basic expenses may mean a choice between a car to get to work or no food. If the family is to receive medical care, parents may have to take time off work without pay. Again parents may be forced to choose between medical services for their children and earning money to put food on the table. Unwanted pregnancies, loss of work, poor health, and a myriad of other problems continually add new stresses. Problems considered small ones for families with good support systems and financial resources can become major when parental resources are stretched to the limit. No wonder adults then feel overwhelmed, discouraged, and helpless. Given the many other problems confronting these parents, their children's needs (beyond immediate care) may receive little attention. Fourth, the cumulative impact of the previous clusters of variables affect parent-child interactions and the home environment, creating *adverse impacts on the children*. In the end, all these conditions influence children's development and learning, their own self-concept and motivation, and life expectations.

Some of the unique dynamics shown by research to characterize many marginal living environments include the following:

1. Many homes lack toys, educational materials, paper, crayons, and other items that promote learning and forms of constructive play that promote language development, conceptual learning, and thinking at increasingly more complex, sophisticated levels (Bradley & Caldwell, 1976a, 1976b; Elardo, Bradley, & Caldwell, 1975, 1977).
2. Home is more likely to be a disorganized, chaotic, noisy place where children learn to cope by simply "tuning out." Some children from impoverished homes may be understimulated; others may be overstimulated with a disorganized and nonmeaningful barrage of things that do not necessarily promote real learning (Radin & Weikart, 1967).
3. Fewer adults tend to be available to children of low-SES families compared to more affluent families. Larger families or the absence of one or both parents contributes to this. Fathers often are missing, and if they are present, they are less apt to assume a major role with their children (Hess & Shipman, 1965; Lewis & Wilson, 1972).
4. Child-rearing patterns tend to rely more heavily on punishment as a means for controlling behavior. Less attention is likely given to teaching children why certain behavior is desirable, with more emphasis upon blind compliance to external, adult-imposed

controls (Brophy, 1977; Karnes, Studley, Wright, & Hodgins, 1968; Wilton & Barbour, 1978).

5. Language stimulation may be reduced since low-income parents are less likely to interact verbally with their children. They are less likely to reward and then shape the early vocalizations in their children or to model appropriate language patterns. Furthermore, mothers seem to engage in less verbal game-playing with their young ones, and to provide less verbal mediation of their child's experiences.

6. Parents in economic despair tend not to have high educational aspirations for their children. Achievement in school and striving for success are likely to be less rewarded and less emphasized by parents, compared to middle-class homes (Heber, 1978; Kagan & Freeman, 1963; Radin & Weikart, 1967).

The impacts of the four clusters of variables depicted in Figure 4.2 are interrelated in complex ways that promote what is called "the vicious cycle of poverty." Children from poverty stricken homes are at higher risk than their counterparts from more affluent homes for developing learning problems, health disorders, and a variety of cognitive and language impairments. In a sense, a poor environment may serve to squelch many of the capabilities and talents they do have.

SUMMARY

One of the first questions parents, professionals, or people at large ask when they encounter a child with a handicap or disability is, "What caused this problem? . . . Could it have been prevented?" Knowledge about developmental disabilities in young children thus begins with an understanding of the factors contributing to or interfering with normal growth and development. Fortunately, most children are born with intact, healthy bodies and develop normally during their infancy and preschool years. A small percent of children (whom we call at-risk), however, are subjected to adverse genetic, prenatal, perinatal, and postnatal conditions or environments that are known to cause certain disorders or to be highly correlated with the later appearance of developmental and learning problems. Children at-risk generally fall into one or a combination of three broad groups—those with (a) *established risk* (having diagnosed medical disorders in which the range of physical and developmental outcomes is known), (b) *biological risk* (having prenatal, perinatal, or postnatal histories that include genetic, biological, or infectious conditions that increase probabilities for abnormal development), and (c) *environmental risk* (in which life experiences and environmental surroundings present a potential threat to a child's developmental well-being).

In regard to causes (etiologies) of developmental abnormalities, a continuum of potential outcomes can result from any adverse condition, ranging from no impact upon a child to a severe impairment. A single disorder does not always produce the same symptoms or degree of impairment in every individual. Neither do all conditions invariably lead to disabilities that are indeed handicapping for a child, Medical treatments, surgical procedures, and prosthetic devices now alleviate many disorders that once were seriously debilitating. For these reasons, one should not be overly quick to predict what the outcome of a particular disorder will be upon a child's performance or developmental well-being. Further, although much is known about causal factors underlying physical and develop-

Figure 4.2
Substandard Environments, Poverty,
And Their Effects Upon Children's Development

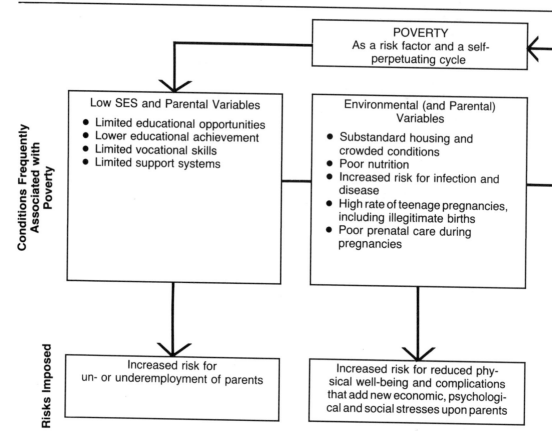

Psychological Impacts on Parents and Families

- Atmosphere of depression, discouragement, alienation, and helplessness
- Attitude of fatalism and powerlessness to change circumstances
- Absorption of psychological and physical energies in tasks of mere survival
- Less emphasis on educational activities and intellectual pursuits at home

Increased risk for continued economic entrapment, social failure, and psychological defeat of family

Impacts on Children

- Increased infant mortality and morbidity
- Higher rate of prematurity and low birth weight in newborns
- Higher incidence of pre-, peri-, and postnatal conditions known to threaten normal development
- Increased probabilities for lower maternal competency in recognizing child needs and providing adequate care
- Absence of, or reduction in, parent behaviors that foster language, cognitive, and school readiness skills in children
- Lack of reward and encouragement for cognitively oriented forms of activity
- Increased probabilities for child abuse and neglect
- Poor development of cognitive and intellectual abilities

Increased risk for developmental delay, including physical, neurological, and cognitive impairments, and school failure

Given these conditions, children may grow up to perpetuate the poverty cycle

mental impairments, the exact etiology may remain unknown in 50% or more of children diagnosed as disabled.

Nonetheless, by being aware of conditions that cause children to be born with congenital abnormalities or to develop problems early in life, expectant parents can be more alert to actions they might take to enhance their own chances for bearing healthy, normal offspring. Professionals and parents alike can be more alert to conditions for which medical, environmental, or educational intervention should be sought to prevent a disorder from progressing. Many disabling conditions can be prevented or minimized *if* adults recognize the problem early and take steps to gain appropriate treatment.

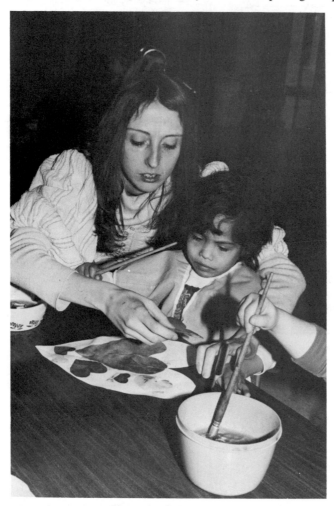

What is the ultimate effect of an adverse condition or abnormality upon a child's development and performance abilities? The potential outcomes can be highly variable and are greatly influenced by what medical, educational, therapeutic, and environmental interventions are rendered to the child and his or her parents.

5
Handicapping Conditions: Sensory, Orthopedic, and Health Problems

All at-risk conditions, like those described in chapter 4, do not invariably lead to developmental problems that persist into childhood, teenage, and adult years. At the same time, early medical and developmental histories of many handicapped school-aged students and adults reveal that one or more at-risk conditions, precursory to or symptomatic of their disability, were apparent early in life.

Children with *established risk*, you will recall, have clearly diagnosable neurological, physical, sensory, genetic, or metabolic disorders. Although these conditions present real or potential secondary threats to a child's development, some can be controlled through medical treatment, surgery, or corrective/prosthetic devices. Some at-risk conditions will alter growth and development, but the outcome may or may not ultimately lead to what is considered a "handicap," or render the person unable to engage in normal life activities. Consider, for example, how many persons you know who wear glasses or contact lenses. If you ask them to remove their glasses or lenses, several undoubtedly would be unable to read regular print in books or newspapers. Without glasses they are handicapped people. Without medical treatment or eye surgery, some people may otherwise have become blind.

In short, three basic principles describe the relationship between at-risk conditions manifest early in life and the diagnosis of "handicapped" during the school years:

1. An at-risk condition does not imply that a child will invariably end up being diagnosed as a "handicapped person"; it simply increases the probability. How much that probability is increased above children not considered at-risk depends upon: (a) the nature of the at-risk condition, (b) whether it is treatable or untreatable, (c) whether it is organic or psychological or environmental, and thus changeable over time, and (d) whether the child's symptoms or the conditions to which he or she is subjected are considered mild or severe.
2. Early treatment or correction of at-risk conditions (through medical or educational-therapeutic intervention) can bring many conditions under control so that the threatened outcomes are prevented or diminished in their severity. Some at-risk conditions may continue to exist, but early treatment often can hold the condition in check so as to minimize the impact upon a child's growth, development, and learning.
3. Because of the increased probabilities that at-risk conditions impose for aberrant development and because intervention can help reduce those probabilities, action should be taken when a child clearly is at-risk. To assume a "wait-and-see" attitude is to gamble with the life and future of a child.

In chapter 4 we looked at the factors that place a child at-risk. Now we will look at the consequences. This chapter deals with sensory and physical handicaps that can be diagnosed medically—hearing and vision impairments, orthopedic and neurological impairments, and health-related disorders. Chapter 6 deals with handicaps that concern developmental and learning processes, typically diagnosed through psychological, clinical, and educational testing and observation of the child's behavior (behavioral disorders and problems, speech and language disorders, and cognitive impairments). Each handicapping condition in these two chapters is discussed by looking at (a) early signs and symptoms of the disorder that might be noted from birth to age 5, (b) the nature of the handicap itself, including its definition and diagnostic criteria, and (c) the impact of that handicap upon early development and learning.

SOME OBSERVATIONS ABOUT DEVELOPMENTAL PROBLEMS

The following observations are germane to the discussion of manifestations and impacts of handicapping conditions. They provide a foundation for understanding the specific handicapping conditions, discussed later in this chapter.

1. *Developmental irregularities in the formative years may not appear problematic.*

The seriousness of physical, sensory, or congenital abnormalities may not be as apparent in an infant or preschooler as in an older child or adult. Toddlers and preschoolers are given considerable latitude in the behavior expected of them. Consequently, they often do not engage in activities that make their problem particularly visible. Irregularities in behavior or development of a seemingly normal youngster can be overlooked easily because they do not interfere significantly with the child's overt behavior or in the usual caregiving required of parents. Because young children are still dependent and are just acquiring skills that will lead to independence, adults naturally take over tasks their children are not yet able to perform.

Parents often are quick to compensate when a youngster's behavior is immature, inept, or inappropriate, but in doing so they can adapt to a child's inadequacies so readily that they may fail to recognize (at least initially) some potentially serious deficiencies. In fact, some mothers indicate that their child can perform a task when in reality the child is able to perform because she helps or prompts each step of the task. This is not to suggest that all parents are oblivious to irregular or abnormal behavior in their children. Mothers often sense something is wrong long before professionals make formal diagnoses. At the same time, weeks and months or even years may pass before parents act on their intuitions. They may be unsure that their concerns are warranted or may not understand the potential long-range seriousness of the symptoms they observe.

2. *School environments present demands that make a child's strengths and weaknesses more apparent.*

Upon entering kindergarten or first grade, children suddenly meet with a new set of expectations. A new kind of structure is imposed on their lives. They are expected to listen, sit quietly, understand and follow teachers' instructions, and work in a setting with many other children. Independence is important. Children must be able to attend to their own needs or to make requests for help. Within a given time frame they are expected to acquire reading, writing, and arithmetic skills, as well as to master concepts in subject areas such as science and language arts. They must demonstrate evidence of learning by answering questions, reciting facts, solving problems, or producing tangible products.

No wonder learning and behavioral problems become more apparent to parents and teachers at this juncture! Limitations imposed by physical impairments become an obvious reality in a child's performance. Teachers quickly become aware of each youngster's strengths and weaknesses and note the difficulties that lead them to conclude "something is wrong." For children with known and already diagnosed disabilities, school activities further define the impact or seriousness of their handicap as it affects learning and school performance. Manifestations of difficulties among school-aged students are more clearcut than the irregularities shown during their early preschool or toddler years. Cognitive problems can be seen specifically in performance of reading, math, or problem solving/ thinking tasks. Performance can be examined further by standardized tests. The fact that many handicapped children are not identified until the elementary grades is not surprising.

Of school-aged students, some 10% are identified as handicapped and enrolled in some kind of special education program. In 1985 over 4.3 million students in our nation's public schools required special education. When so many school-aged students are determined to be handicapped, one must ask some probing questions:

- Where did all those handicapped students come from? Did their problems really emerge suddenly at age 6, 7, 10, or 12, or were warning signs of their impending difficulties present before those children started school?
- Is the need for special education, regarded as so critical for the success of school-aged students, also not present in those individuals before they begin kindergarten or first grade?
- Would the 4.3 million handicapped students or a smaller percentage of them have the problems they present in school if special education and training had been provided to them earlier?

3. *Many young children show signs of emerging difficulties long before the kindergarten round-up.*

A significant number of handicapped students requiring special education during their school years did not suddenly become disabled the day they started kindergarten. The limitations of those labeled as visually impaired, deaf or hard of hearing, orthopedically handicapped, multiply handicapped, and moderately to severely retarded undoubtedly were apparent during their early childhood years. But many of those problems have not been officially diagnosed before age 5 or 6. School-aged students labeled as mentally retarded (particularly mildly retarded) and emotionally disturbed probably showed developmental delays or behavioral irregularities that caused their parents intermittent concern long before they started school. Over time, their difficulties probably became more apparent as the gap widened between them and their normally developing peers. Students identified as learning disabled may have shown fewer clear-cut symptoms when they were young. Yet, in retrospect, some warning signs probably were there. Delays in overall development or in specific areas (e.g., speech and language, motor skills), or warning signs in their prenatal, perinatal, and early developmental histories may have suggested that they were candidates for future learning problems.

The point here is that individuals who become candidates for special education during their school years have special needs during their early childhood years that are equally critical. Yet the U.S. Department of Education (1980) reported that only 2.6% of children in the U.S. between 0 and 5 years of age received any form of early intervention. The U.S. Bureau of the Census (1983) reported some 20 million children in our country and its territories under age 6. Estimates from the Department of Education suggest that 8%-10% of children in this age group have handicaps (U.S. Department of Health, Education, & Welfare, 1979). If 10% of them are handicapped, that would translate to 2 million infants, toddlers, and preschoolers in need of special education intervention.

Even an estimate of 10% may be low. It does not include youngsters who are simply at-risk for developmental disabilities and who do not, in their early childhood years, show deviations of sufficient magnitude to warrant a clear diagnosis. As many as 17% or 18% of children in the 0-5 or 6-year-old range may be at-risk for developmental disabilities and therefore in need of early intervention if they are to develop optimally (Garland, Stone, Swanson, & Woodruff, 1981).

AN OVERVIEW OF HANDICAPPING CONDITIONS

Handicaps traditionally have been categorized by the following labels as set forth in the Rules and Regulations of Public Law 94-142 (Section 121a.5):*

Handicapped children: those evaluated in accordance with provisions of the law (age-appropriate, nonbiased tests) as being mentally retarded, hard of hearing, deaf, speech impaired, visually handicapped, seriously emotionally disturbed, orthopedically impaired, other health impaired, deaf-blind, multihandicapped, or as having specific learning disabilities, who because of those impairments need special education and related services.

Deaf: having a hearing impairment so severe that the child is impaired in processing linguistic information through hearing, with or without amplification, which adversely affects educational performance.

Hard of hearing: having a hearing impairment, whether permanent or fluctuating, that adversely affects a child's educational performance but that is not included under the definition of "deaf."

Deaf-blind: having concomitant hearing and visual impairments, the combination of which causes such severe communication and other developmental and educational problems that special education programs solely for deaf *or* blind children cannot accommodate them.

Visually handicapped: having a visual impairment that, even with correction, adversely affects educational performance. The term includes both partially seeing and blind children.

Orthopedically impaired: having a severe orthopedic impairment that adversely affects educational performance. The term includes impairments caused by congenital anomalies (e.g., clubfoot, absence of a limb, or paralysis), impairments caused by disease (e.g., polio, muscular degeneration), and impairments from other causes (e.g., cerebral palsy, amputations, and fractures or burns that cause contractures).

Other health impaired: having limited strength, vitality, or alertness, as a result of chronic or acute health problems, such as heart conditions, tuberculosis, rheumatic fever, nephritis, asthma, sickle cell anemia, hemophilia, epilepsy, lead posioning, leukemia, or diabetes, that adversely affects educational performance.

Speech impaired: having a communication disorder, such as stuttering, impaired articulation, a language impairment, or a voice impairment, that adversely affects a child's educational performance.

Mentally retarded: having significantly subaverage general intellectual functioning (2 standard deviations below the mean on one or more standardized tests of intelligence), existing concurrently with deficits in adaptive behavior and manifested during the developmental period, that adversely affects a child's educational performance.

Specific learning disability: having a disorder in one or more of the basic psychological processes involved in understanding or in using language, spoken or written, that may manifest itself in an imperfect ability to listen, think, speak, read, write, spell,

---

*Source: *Federal Register* (1977, August) *42* (163). 20 U.S.C. 1401(1), (15).

or do mathematical calculations. The term includes conditions such as perceptual handicaps, brain injury, minimal brain dysfunction, dyslexia, and developmental aphasia. The term does not include children who have learning problems that are primarily the result of visual, hearing, or motor handicaps, of mental retardation, or of environmental, cultural, or economic disadvantage.

Seriously emotionally disturbed: exhibiting one or more of the following characteristics over a long period of time and to a marked degree that adversely affects educational performance:

— an inability to learn that cannot be explained by intellectual, sensory, or health factors;
— an inability to build or maintain satisfactory interpersonal relationships with peers and teachers;
— inappropriate types of behavior or feelings under normal circumstances;
— a general pervasive mood of unhappiness or depression; or
— a tendency to develop physical symptoms or fears associated with personal or school problems.

The term *seriously emotionally disturbed* includes children who are schizophrenic or autistic. The term does not include children who are socially maladjusted, unless it is determined that they are seriously emotionally disturbed.

In looking at the preceding definitions, they obviously were formulated primarily with school-aged students—not infants or preschool-aged children—in mind. Each definition interprets the condition of being handicapped in relation to its effect upon *educational performance*. You also may have noted that specific learning disabilities are defined in regard to performance in more advanced cognitive/academic skills—speaking, reading, spelling, and mathematical calculations (criteria that are impossible to apply to children from birth to age 5). Educational performance is not typically a point of reference one can use to evaluate the status of preschoolers or infants.

Each definition would be more appropriately applied to this young population if the words "educational performance" were replaced by the phrase "development and learning." That is, a physical/sensory/cognitive/psychological/emotional condition is handicapping for an infant or preschooler if it interferes with (a) normal physical *growth* processes, (b) *development* or maturational processes, and (c) *learning* processes achieved through stimulation and exposure to the environment. A young child's status thus is measured not through what is commonly defined as educational performance or achievement but, rather, by attainment of the expected growth and developmental milestones during the formative years.

HEARING IMPAIRMENTS

Early signs and symptoms of hearing loss

If an infant is born deaf or acquires a hearing loss very early in life, few symptoms initially signal a problem. Early behavior of an infant with even a severe or profound loss is much like that of a nonimpaired infant. Even though parents may observe occasions of unresponsiveness to sound, the infant probably gives enough random responses that appear to be in response to external stimuli to suggest that he or she may hear just fine. Only as these infants begin to respond more consistently to their environment, and as babbling begins, are more symptoms likely to become apparent. If a child has some *residual hearing*—which is true in the majority of cases—the lack of clear-cut symptoms may mean that several years could pass before a hearing loss would be suspected and confirmed.

Alertness to potential hearing loss in a young child is important. Usually the parents' sensitive, keen observations over time to the child's responses to environmental stimuli are what lead to the question, "Is this child hearing normally?"—and thus to a subsequent diagnosis (Shah & Wong, 1979). After surveying parents who have deaf children, Horton (1976) reported that in 70% of the cases she studied, the parents were the first to suspect their child's hearing impairment. Approximately 50% of them became concerned before their child reached 1 year of age. In only 7% of the cases was a physician the first to note the problem (because of physical or medical symptoms).

Early detection of the signs or symptoms of hearing impairment begins with a preventive approach. Rather than waiting for symptoms to appear that are of sufficient abnormality or severity to be noticed, three categories of risk factors might alert concerned adults to potential hearing disorders in young children: (a) factors identifiable in the family history, (b) factors associated with the mother's medical history during pregnancy and the child at its birth or during early childhood years, and (c) factors identifiable through observation of the child over time or through discussion with the mother about her child's overall behavior. The first two categories encompass variables that the National Joint Committee on Infant Screening now recommends be used to establish a *high-risk register* of children at-risk for hearing impairments. Basically, the major variables on the register define what Downs and Silver (1972) have labeled the "High Risk Register A, B, C, D's":

A— Affected family—a history of sensorineural and inherited hearing losses in child's immediate family.

B— Bilirubin levels above normal—in prematurely born infants, levels greater than 15 mg/100 ml, and 20 mg/100 ml in full-term newborns, or hyperbilirubinemia caused by Rh blood incompatibility during neonatal period.

C— Congenital rubella—mother's contraction of rubella or other infections such as herpes or cytomegalovirus infections during pregnancy.

D— Defects in the child's ears, nose, or throat—as revealed by physical examination, malformed, lowset, or absent pinna (external ear); cleft palate or any other structural abnormality of the otorhinolaryngeal system.

s— Small at birth—lower than normal gestation weight (less than 5.5 pounds for a full-term baby).

The final set of danger signals is associated with the child's behavior itself, as listed below:

Age	*Symptoms Suggesting Possible Hearing Impairment*
Birth to 6 months	• Child does not startle, blink eyes, or change activity in response to a sudden, loud noise.

- Child is not soothed by mother's voice or shows no response to voice.
- Child does not imitate gurgling and cooing sounds or show some response to noise-making toys.
- Child does not turn eyes and head in direction of sound that comes from the side or from behind.

By 10 months
- Child does not make some form of response when his or her name is called.

By 12 months
- Child does not respond to normal household sounds (dog barking, voice of a family person, footsteps from behind, etc.).
- Child engages in loud shrieking and sustained production of vowels.
- Child does not respond to another's voice by turning to look directly at speaker.

By 15 months
- Child does not imitate sounds and simple words, or if imitation does occur, sounds do not progressively become more similar to the model's.

15 months to 4-5 years
- Child does not give attention unless people raise their voices.
- Child frequently says "huh" and "what" when spoken to.
- Child responds inconsistently to sound, sometimes seeming to hear and other times failing to respond (this behavior tends to be excused by attributing it to stubbornness, preoccupation with a toy, or other activity).
- Child shows preference for high or low sounds.
- Child shows delayed acquisition of speech.
- Child produces abnormalities in voice tones and excessive mispronunciation in vowel and consonant sounds.

The nature of hearing impairments

The ear is a well designed instrument for conducting sound to the brain. The external ear collects sound waves and directs them into the ear canal. Sound waves pass through the ear canal to the eardrum (tympanic membrane), where they are converted to mechanical vibrations. These vibrations then are transmitted through the middle ear by a series of three small bones—the malleus (hammer), incus (anvil), and stapes (stirrup). The middle ear also contains the eustachian tube. This tube, which extends from the back of the throat to the middle ear cavity, opens and closes to equalize air pressure on each side of the eardrum.

In the inner ear, sound is transformed from mechanical to electrical energy. The cochlea, a snail-shaped structure with three chambers, allows hearing to occur. The outer and inner chambers contain fluid; the middle chamber contains the organ of Corti. Inside are thousands of delicate hair cells (12,000 in the human ear) that together constitute the nerve that carries electrical impulses to the brain. The movement of these hair cells, caused by waves in the fluid of the outer and inner chambers of the cochlea, produces nerve impulses that are sent to the brain. Another structure in the inner ear, the vestibular apparatus, helps us maintain balance.

When a child is said to be hearing impaired, exactly how is hearing affected? If a 3-year-old boy is described as having a severe 70-decibel loss, what impact will this have on his ability to hear speech? Textbooks on the subject define hearing losses in several ways—by the type of loss or the physical origin, the degree and range of loss, and the functional-educational effect.

Types of hearing losses   The type of loss is a major factor in how hearing is affected. Losses are classified by three different types—conductive, sensorineural, or mixed.

1. *Conductive hearing loss.* Malformation or damage in the outer or middle ear interferes with normal transmission of sound waves to the inner ear. A leading cause of conductive loss is middle ear infection, or otitis media, resulting in malfunctioning of the eustachian tube. Excessive ear wax impounded in the ear, lodging of foreign objects (such as candy, beans, pebbles) in the ear canal, or excess fluid in the eustachian tube are additional sources of problems.

   Conductive impairments reduce one's ability to hear air-conducted sound. Sounds transmitted through bone conduction, which bypasses the outer ear, are heard normally. Most conductive hearing losses can be corrected through medical treatment or surgery. Amplification with a hearing aid can be beneficial. Most hearing impairments from conductive problems are not severe enough to entirely prevent a child from hearing speech. Certain sounds or conversations may be difficult to hear if they are not loud enough. Thus, young children may show delays in speech and language development.

2. *Sensorineural hearing loss.* This type of loss involves damage to the inner ear and auditory nerve (i.e., the cochlea or its delicate hair cells, which transform physical sound waves into electrical impulses that go to the brain). These losses can be caused by illness, extended high fever, medicines that destroy or damage the hair cells of the cochlea, and congenital defects. Extended exposure to very loud noise can be damaging. In this type of loss the outer ear and middle ear are structurally and functionally normal, but because of the neurological damage to the inner ear, sounds are distorted. Unlike conductive losses, impairments associated with sensorineural damage are not treatable either medically or surgically. Though sounds can be amplified, they are still unclear and distorted to the listener.

3. *Mixed hearing loss.* Both conductive and sensorineural impairments are present in a mixed hearing loss. This produces the combined problems of sound distortion and reduction in the individual's ability to hear sounds below a certain decibel level, or loudness. Only the conductive elements of this type of loss are treatable medically. Treatment may pose some unique problems if a hearing aid is used. Treatment of the conductive problem without attention to the sensorineural damage may be ineffective and possibly incompatible, inasmuch as amplification can only intensify the difficulty produced by the sensorineural impairment.

Degree and range of hearing loss   Impairments alter a person's hearing in terms of the loudness (intensity) of sound necessary before it can be heard or the pitch (frequency) of sounds that can be heard. Loudness of sound is described in decibel (db) units. Human hearing extends to 130 decibels. Sounds louder than 130 db can actually produce pain. Continued exposure to sounds above this level may produce sensorineural damage. Ordinary conversational speech usually falls between 50 and 80 db. Impairments in hearing also can alter the pitch levels of sound that can be heard. Pitch levels are described on an audiogram as hertz (Hz) units. Human beings can hear a wide range of pitches, extending from low tones at 16-20 Hz to very high-pitched sounds of 20,000-30,000 Hz. Children have a higher range of tone sensitivity, but this decreases with age. A normal adult probably does not hear frequencies much greater than 10,000-12,000 Hz. Normal speech tones in ordinary conversation generally fall between 500 and 2,000 Hz.

A person's hearing loss is assessed for each ear, since each ear can have a different degree and range of loss. Further, a person could have a sensorineural loss in one ear and a conductive loss in the other, or a combination of both in one ear.

Functional-educational effects of hearing loss Impairments in hearing affect auditory reception of sound in different ways. To reflect these differences, children typically are described in regard to (a) the severity of loss as it affects their ability to hear speech and learn speech, and (b) the age of onset. Levels of severity are simply described as mild, moderate, severe, and profound. Hearing impaired persons are grouped according to the age of onset as:

— *congenitally deaf:* those who are born deaf and have never had the benefits of normal hearing. Basically, their hearing is nonfunctional for purposes of acquiring speech and language.
— *adventitiously deaf:* those born with normal hearing who incurred damage later through injury or illness. These individuals have the benefits of having heard speech and having had some time to acquire speech and language through normal means. The impact of hearing loss for these persons is much less severe than for those deaf from birth.

The age of onset and severity of impairment (which govern how much functional hearing remains) are of major importance in a child's speech and language development. Even personality and emotional adjustment are affected significantly by the age of onset and the severity level. The earlier the onset and the more severe the hearing loss, the greater is the developmental impact. Children born deaf will grow up without acquiring functional speech skills unless they receive special training. Language skills will likely be reduced, especially if early intervention and training during the critical periods of language acquisition do not occur. Children who have a brief exposure to speech and language before becoming deaf have a greater chance of developing more proficient communication and language ability than those who are deaf from birth. That short exposure provides a crucial foundation upon which subsequent language development can be based (Carhart, 1970; Lenneberg, 1967; Northern & Lemme, 1982).

Table 5.1 summarizes the various levels of impairment that can occur within the pitch range (hertz) normally used for speech, and the functional-developmental impact of those losses on a child.

The impact of hearing loss on development and learning

The cumulative effect of deafness or of varying degrees of hearing loss is shown in studies

Table 5.1

Description of Various Degrees of Hearing Loss

Average Hearing Loss in better ear (500-2,000 Hertz)	Ability to Hear Speech	Nature of Communication Handicap
0-25 db Insignificant	Has no significant difficulty with normal conversation or faint sounds.	None.
26-54 db Mild hearing loss	Understands conversational speech if face to face but has some difficulty hearing normal conversation; frequently misses faint sounds (e.g., whispered speech, unvoiced consonants).	Possible mild language delay. May leave out voiceless consonants.
55-69 db Moderate hearing loss (hard of hearing)	Has difficulty hearing normal conversation, especially with background noise. Conversation must be loud to be understood.	Some difficulty with auditory learning. Language and speech delays evident, including articulation problems.
70-89 db Severe hearing loss (includes hard of hearing and deaf)	May hear loud voices if 1 ft. from ear but has difficulty hearing even loud speech. May be unable to understand even amplified speech.	Severe speech/language disorders highly probable, including evidence of learning delays. May lack intelligible speech.
90 db or more Profound hearing loss (deaf)	Usually cannot hear speech even if amplified.	Severe speech and language disorders. Probably no oral speech. Notable impact on general learning.

Sources: Report of the Ad Hoc Committee to Define Deaf and Hard of Hearing (1975); American National Standards Institute (1969).

describing academic achievement among hearing impaired children in school. Studies have shown deaf students to be educationally retarded as much as 3-5 years, a deficit that increases with age (Scheir & Delk, 1974; Trybus & Karchmer, 1977). Furth (1971, 1973) reported that the average reading level of deaf students is about third grade, with only about 10% of the deaf attaining reading skills above fourth-grade level. Similarly, Karchmer and Trybus (1977) found that the average hearing impaired student in the ninth grade was reading at the fourth grade level. Typically, educational retardation is less apparent in more mechanical skills such as arithmetic computation and spelling. Deficits are more prominent in areas dependent upon language and conceptual skills.

Scheir and Delk (1974) further reported that only about 12% of the deaf population ages 25-64 have gone to college. Only half of those completed baccalaureate degrees—a rate of about one-third that found in a normal population. The diminished educational achievement of deaf and hearing impaired students may be attributable partially to the excess amount of school time required to teach speaking skills and to remediate language deficiencies.

A higher frequency of emotional problems, compared to that found in hearing populations, is also reported. Jensema and Trybus (1975) found that over 8% of a population of 44,000 hearing impaired students in school special education programs had educationally significant emotional and behavioral problems.

Recognizing the long-term effects of hearing loss, what then are the effects upon young children during infancy and their preschool years? Auditory impairments affect young children in many ways, but the most obvious is in the initial acquisition of speech and language. Experts suggest that language acquisition is a time-locked function tied closely to certain maturational periods in a young child's life. At certain developmental stages a child is particularly sensitive to auditory stimulation. Once this period passes, effective utilization of auditory signals declines and auditory stimuli have diminished potency for effecting development in that area. Language input thus must be experienced at certain stages or it will be decreasingly effective in promoting the emergence of language skills (Ling, 1976a, 1976b, 1984; Northern & Downs, 1974; Tervoort, 1964; Lenneberg, 1972).

Hearing loss affects speech and language development during the early years in several critical ways:

1. *Reduction of sensory input available to a child.*

Auditory input is one of the first ways in which a child becomes aware of his or her surrounding environment and learns about things and people in it. Sounds and words come to have meaning. Mother's voice takes on significance. Sounds and objects become associated. Simply by listening to others, a young child acquires an impressive receptive vocabulary long before acquiring equal mastery of expressive language skills. When a child has limited or no auditory input, other modes of imput, such as vision, must be used instead. But stimulation from the environment likely is reduced substantially. No doubt this reduces the rate at which a child learns about his or her environment and acquires knowledge.

2. *Interference in speech and language development.*

Hearing impairment quickly reveals its impact upon a child's speech development. During the first few years of life, children repeatedly hear thousands of words, which they gradually attempt to reproduce themselves. During the second year of life, they show a particularly rapid increase in learning object names and putting together nouns and action words (such as "daddy go," "doggie eat"). By age 2 a child normally has a speaking vocabulary of nearly 300 words. This expands to about 900 words at age 3, about 1,500 words at age 4, and over 2,000 words at age 5.

According to Ling (1984a, 1984b), preschool children with hearing impairments fail to progress at this rate. Because auditory input is the major vehicle for this kind of learning, its impaired efficiency undoubtedly slows developmental progress.

3. *Interference in acquisition of linguistic tools for thinking.*

Young children begin to engage in "thinking processes" only as they acquire the mental tools to do so. This involves, in part, mastering a system of symbols representing ideas. Language is such a tool. Although the development of cognition is relatively unimpaired in hearing handicapped children (at least to a certain age level), measurement of mental abilities beyond the sensorimotor stage is highly related to linguistic competence and the child's ability to communicate ideas. As a result, hearing impaired individuals often do less well than normally hearing youngsters in cognitive performance. When tested on standard IQ tests, deaf or significantly hearing impaired children do less well.

Over time, if language development is not facilitated in ways that compensate for the lack of auditory input, a secondary outcome will be diminished cognitive development.

4. *Interference in acquisition of speech and normal speech production.*

Deaf and hearing impaired children can and do learn to speak, but the quality and intelligibility of their speech typically is different. The degree to which speech is affected depends on the severity and type of hearing defect, the age of onset, and the training these children receive. In many cases their speech requires the listener to have considerable patience and attention. It requires a sensitivity that peers and others, who may be unaware of the problem or lack understanding of the child's limitations, do not always extend.

5. *Social isolation.*

Hearing impaired children may experience considerable social isolation (Meadow, 1984). Even at young ages a child can easily be left out of interactions among family members merely because of his or her failure to know what is going on and an inability to enter into the rapid verbal exchanges that transpire between others. Unless someone takes responsibility for helping the hearing impaired child understand the content of interactions between people, the child tends to be ignored and left a silent observer. Parents can inadvertently fall into the trap of not talking to their hearing impaired child. This is especially a problem with very young children because of their limited behavioral repertoires and inability to respond in meaningful ways.

Experts emphasize the importance of early language stimulation and speech training for hearing impaired children. Ling (1984a, 1984b) has pointed out that much of the language deficiency found in these children is the unfortunate result of failure to initiate language learning until after age 2, 3, 4, 5, or even 6, when hearing losses are known to exist. Some evidence indicates that the longer language stimulation is delayed or the more it is reduced, the less efficient language development will be. Even mild hearing losses have been shown to cause measurable and permanent loss in language ability if steps are not taken to prevent this (Ling, 1976; Northern & Downs, 1974; Northern & Lemme, 1982; Stark, 1977).

VISION IMPAIRMENTS

Early signs and symptoms of vision problems

Total blindness, originating prenatally or perinatally, usually can be identified in the first year after birth simply by the absence of visual responsiveness. Partial vision losses are more difficult to identify in young children and can go unnoticed until a child enters school. These vision problems are more likely to be noted in school because academic tasks demand close visual work, precise visual perception, and visual attentiveness. In fact, academic tasks, as traditionally presented at school, place a high premium on vision for learning reading, writing, and arithmetic skills. Difficulties in learning these skills and other behavioral signs appear quickly when vision problems interfere with learning. With infants and young preschoolers, however, vision disorders are not so readily apparent. Because young children have no concept of what they *should* be seeing, they do not recognize their own inability to see clearly.

Parents, preschool teachers, or other child-care workers must be alert to subtle signs of visual disorders in young children. This includes alertness to possible conditions in a child's prenatal, perinatal, or postnatal history, such as those described in chapter 4, which place a child at greater risk for developing visual disorders.

Some potential signs of vision impairments in children are:

Possible Signs of Vision Impairment in Infants

- Pupils of the eyes do not react to light.
- Baby seems inattentive to visual stimuli unless it is very close or some noise accompanies its presentation.
- Baby does not gaze or stare at surroundings.
- Baby does not follow a moving object with eyes.
- Eyelids are red, encrusted, watery, or swollen. The eyes have visible deformities including drooping of eyelids.
- Baby seems excessively sensitive to light.

Possible Signs of Vision Impairment in Toddlers and Preschoolers

- Child frequently rubs eyes.
- Child squints or frowns when attempting to look at an object.
- Child stumbles a lot and seems more hesitant than usual to move about.
- Eyes are visibly out of alignment and do not focus together.
- Child holds toys up close to face.
- Child has frequent sties, watery or red, inflamed eyes.
- Child may seem unresponsive, lacking in curiosity, or unalert to surroundings.
- Child assumes postures—such as head bent down—that give impression of disinterest or unresponsiveness.

The nature of vision impairments

Loss of vision has legal, medical, and educational implications for the person, society at large, and specialists responsible for dealing with the impairment. It is not surprising, then, to find numerous definitions, each describing different aspects of visual handicaps. The legal-medical definition emphasizes *visual acuity,* or clearness of vision at various distances. The educational definition emphasizes the *extent to which vision can be used* for reading printed material and learning. A more recent, functionally oriented definition emphasizes *what a person actually can see*. These various definitions are summarized in Table 5.2.

A great variety of disorders can affect the eyesight of young children. The impact on vision can be described on several dimensions: (a) how intact and structurally normal the physical mechanisms of the eye are (*physical integrity*); (b) how clearly the child sees at various distances (*visual acuity*); (c) how well the two eyes work together to allow proper focusing upon stationary objects or tracking of moving objects, and to produce binocular vision (*muscular efficiency*); and (d) how well the child uses vision or the degree of functional efficiency by which visual stimuli are integrated, organized, and interpreted to allow accurate perception of what is seen (*functional visual perception*).

Table 5.2

Definitions of Vision Impairments

The Legal-Medical Definition
(National Society for the Prevention of Blindness, 1966)

Blind	Visual acuity of 20/200 or less in the better eye with best possible correction or field of vision reduced to the degree that its widest diameter subtends an arc of 20 degrees or less.
Partially Sighted	Visual acuity between 20/200 and 20/70 in the better eye with the best possible correction.

The Educational Definition
(American Foundation for the Blind, 1957)

Blind	Visual loss is severe enough that it is not possible to read print, necessitating that the child be educated through use of braille and other tactile and auditory materials.
Partially Seeing	Residual vision is sufficient to allow a child to read large print or possibly regular print under special conditions and to use other visual materials for educational purposes.

The "Functional Efficiency of Vision" Definition
(Barraga, 1976)

Blind	Vision allows only light perception, thus requiring other sensory modes to be used for sources of input from the external environment.
Low Vision	There are limitations in distance vision, but the child can see objects and materials if they are a few inches to a maximum of 2 feet away.
Limited Vision	Visual defects are correctable with eye glasses, contact lenses, or surgery, and though vision problems may present occasional inconveniences, the child can function basically as a normally sighted person.

Exactly how vision is impaired differs with the various conditions, but in every case the impact is a loss in functional use of this sensory organ.

Damage to the physical integrity of various parts of the eye affects how well light rays pass through the cornea and lens, through the aqueous chamber (middle of the eye) to the retina, where electrical impulses then are transmitted through the optical nerve to the occipital lobe of the brain. Infectious and noninfectious diseases, inherited degenerative disorders, injury, drugs, and various environmental agents toxic to eye tissue can damage or alter eye structures in ways that cause vision loss. Here are some of the more common examples:

Cataracts: clouding or opacity of the lens, which interferes progressively with passage of light into the eye. Prenatal insults from maternal infections, metabolic disorders, and disease such as rubella are primary causes. Cataracts can be treated only by surgical removal. Substitute lenses can be implanted through surgery, and contact lenses/eye glasses can be worn after surgery.

Retrolental fibroplasia: formation of scar tissue and fibrous material behind the lens of the eye as a result of exposure to excessive concentrations of oxygen by premature infants placed in incubators. Permanent blindness can result.

Glaucoma: gradual destruction of the optic nerve, caused by build-up of pressure in the inner chamber of the eye when aqueous fluid fails to circulate properly.

Impairment in visual acuity is most often caused by a refractive problem. It is determined by measuring what a child can see on a Snellen chart positioned 20 feet away. A person with normal vision is said to have 20/20 vision. The top number of the acuity index represents the 20-foot distance between the person and the vision chart. The bottom figure represents the distance at which a normally sighted person could distinguish the same line of letters on the chart that the testee was able to see clearly at 20 feet. An individual having 20/70 vision thus sees at 20 feet what someone with normal vision could see readily at 70 feet.

Refractive disorders are generally of three types:

Myopia (nearsightedness): the eyeball is too long, causing light rays to focus in front of the retina, which makes objects more difficult to see at farther distances.

Hyperopia (farsightedness): the eyeball is too short, causing light to focus behind the retina, thus affecting near vision.

Astigmatism (blurred vision): uneven curvature of the cornea or lens, preventing light rays from focusing correctly on the retina.

In all but extreme cases, refractive problems are correctable with glasses or contact lenses. Tests can be given to detect and measure these types of problems in older children, but obtaining a clear assessment of younger children's vision is more difficult because they are less able to communicate to adults what they do see. Visual assessment typically requires that the child be trained first to respond reliably to visual stimuli in ways that allow an examiner to determine what the child sees.

Muscular inefficiencies or irregularities affect how well the eyes focus and how well both eyes work in synchrony to produce clear, binocular vision. Single binocular vision occurs through fusion of the two images projected by the right and left eyes into a visual perception. Perfect fusion is dependent upon two conditions: (a) The visual axes of the two eyes must be straight, and (b) movement of the extraocular muscles for both eyes must be coordinated so that they move together in proper alignment as they focus upon a particular object. When the visual axes are misaligned, several possible problems can result. The most common difficulties include:

Amblyopia: suppression of one eye results from dimness in vision or muscle imbalance, or other defects in that eye (sometimes referred to as "lazy eye").

Strabismus: improper muscle action in the eyes causes various degrees of cross-eyedness. Because the visual axes of the eyes are not in alignment, the eyes are not directed simultaneously on the object in a way that allows proper fusion of the two images from both eyes into one. In strabismus the eyes turn inward. "Wall-eye" refers to a condition in which the eyes turn outward.

Nystagmus: quick, jerky, side-to-side or up-and-down movements of the eyes produce marked visual inefficiency.

Muscular imbalances impair effective fusion of the images from each eye or the focusing required to obtain a clear visual image. They also can result, over time, in loss

Courtney attempts to get Michael to play with her. Now 1½, Michael has been blind since birth (because of maternal ingestion of ac-cutane, a drug used to treat severe acne). Michael needs a lot of stimulation through other senses to help him discover and learn about a world he cannot see.

of vision in one eye. The brain will compensate for double images or the inadequacy of one eye by suppressing or ignoring the sensory input of one eye. Continual suppression of one eye leads to a loss of functional vision. Muscular imbalances or dysfunctions are frequent in children with cerebral palsy and other neurological disorders. Diminished vision from muscular disorders usually can be reversed if treatment is initiated before age 5 or 6. After that, however, correction and maintenance of normal vision are difficult and often unsuccessful. Early treatment is important.

Visual perception, the cognitive reception and understanding of visual stimuli, is not always discussed in textbooks in regard to potential visual impairments. Sensory processes involving vision usually are discussed from the viewpoint of the physical apparatus of the eye or the clarity of visual images a child sees. Nonetheless, visual perception cannot be separated from all other aspects of the act of seeing. As mentioned previously, whether perceptual difficulties are actually impairments in vision itself, in thought processes controlled by the brain, in learning, or in a child's experience itself is not clear. Whatever the cause, however, perceptual difficulties represent a disorder of sensory processes involving vision.

Some evidence suggests that although visual acuity and binocular vision may function properly, certain children have difficulty in how they perceive visual stimuli (Colarusso, Martin, & Hartung, 1975; Guthrie & Goldberg, 1972; Snyder & Freud, 1967; Strauss &

Lehtinen, 1947). Typically, these difficulties go unnoticed until a child begins school and is expected to perform more precise visual tasks than those of the earlier childhood years. Visual perception tasks play a significant role in school learning—in reading, writing, and arithmetic. These disorders have come to be labeled within the "learning disabilities" classification, probably because they interfere most with just that—learning.

Difficulties in visual perception usually are described in relation to several component skills. Examples include difficulties in (Lerner, 1981):

Spatial relations: perception of position and interrelationships of objects in space (i.e., the placement of objects in space and the spatial relations of one object to other objects surrounding it).

Figure-ground discrimination: differentiation between an object from the background surrounding it so that relevant and irrelevant stimuli are sorted out and attention can be focused upon the focal point of a visual image or upon the important stimuli.

Visual discrimination: differentiation of one object from another by distinguishing features that make them similar or different on some dimension.

Visual closure: recognition of an object when the full stimulus is not presented. When given stimuli concerning familiar objects in which parts of the visual stimulus are missing (such as an unclosed circle), it would normally still be perceived as a circle.

Object recognition: recognition of an object when it is viewed even if it is viewed from different angles or if various aspects of the object (such as size and shape) change.

See Cress, Spellman, and Benson (1984) for information on vision screening for preschoolers with handicaps.

The impact of vision impairments on development and learning

Loss of vision, especially if it is severe, is a handicap of potentially great magnitude in the life of a developing child. Vision is such a powerful mechanism for learning! Just think of how much you learn through vision alone when you go to an unfamiliar place. In a matter of minutes, you can scan the new environment to see what things and people are there. Imagine how long a person, especially a small child, with limited or no vision would take to gather the same amount of information. Children learn so much by watching the behavior of others, by imitating them, and then noting the consequences. If we have vision, even direct contact with things we learn about is unnecessary. We can observe objects or events from across the room or from the grandstands of a baseball stadium. We can watch television, look at pictures, or see a movie. All these experiences and sources of sensory input are reduced significantly when functional vision is impaired.

The degree to which sensory input is diminished is, of course, directly proportional to the degree and type of vision loss. Nevertheless, visual impairment is a good example of a handicap that not only impairs sensory input but affects development in other areas as well. Limitations are imposed on a child's language, motor, conceptual, and personal-social development in three rather global ways (Lowenfeld, 1973; Rogers & Puchalski, 1984):

1. The range and variety of experiences accessible to the child are reduced. Furthermore,

the amount of information/learning that can be assimilated from a single experience is reduced because the child likely will require more time to explore and learn about things given the reduction in efficiency of just one sensory input mode.

2. The child's ability to move about the environment freely and to enter into new experiences is restricted. Lacking awareness of what is "out there," a child will not be enticed into moving around, reaching for an object, or engaging in activity in response to a toy or some interesting event nearby. Visually impaired children, especially the very young, are highly dependent upon adults to bring experiences to them.

3. The child's ability to interact with the environment and with people in meaningful ways is diminished by a serious vision impairment because the child is less likely to (a) recognize the presence of meaningful stimuli, (b) see the consequences of actions, and (c) enter readily into new situations because of difficulties in coping with and understanding the meaning of sounds or things.

Gesell, Ilg, and Bullis (1949) in their well known studies of child development, emphasized the role of vision in children's early learning. They concluded that vision is eminent among the sensory modalities because it plays a highly directive role in normal development. Vision serves as an integrator of a child's developing action systems and experiences. The source of sounds or smells can be located and associated with certain objects simply by "seeing" where one particular stimulus is coming from. The functions and characteristics of objects can be learned quickly as a child makes visual associations between events and things that go together. Vision thus represents not only a sensory modality, but an added qualifier of sensations and of experience as well.

Other impacts of vision impairments on early growth and development are summarized as follows:

1. *Impacts on language development.*

Language and speech development are not seriously affected during the first 8-10 months of life in a blind or severely visually impaired baby. Hearing seems to be the most important input channel for prelinguistic skills during the early months. Beginning around age 1, however, language development involves understanding and using object labels. A child must have a concept of an object before he or she can label it. Without visual stimuli this labeling process is more difficult. Fraiberg (1977) noted that a blind child faces two dilemmas: (a) Without visual experience he or she must rely solely on experiences with things touched or heard, resulting in a deprived experiential base, and (b) mobility is significantly delayed. Experiences with objects in the environment and the opportunity to learn about them so they have meaning are greatly hampered.

A blind child may require at least a year longer than normal children to acquire concepts of concrete objects and thus to attain a truly linguistic level of language (Sonksen, 1979; Willis, 1979). Once a blind child begins to acquire an understanding of objects, language development can proceed more rapidly, although without visual input that child always will have difficulty understanding his or her environment. Although words for things in the environment may be learned, the child may have a distorted concept of what he or she is trying to discuss. Alonso, Moor, Raynor, Saaz von Hippel, and Baer (1978) noted that a blind preschooler may seem very verbal but will continually use words and phrases out of context.

2. *Impacts on motor development.*

Studies indicate that blind children who are otherwise neurologically and physically normal show early delays in motor development compared to their sighted peers. Postural and stationary motor milestones such as sitting and standing are normal in visually impaired infants. But the more severe the vision loss is, the more delays are present in self-initiated behaviors such as reaching, crawling, and walking. Until sound has meaning, a blind child remains quiet and rather passive to auditory stimuli or frightens easily. The act of attending to a sound stimulus requires a higher level of cognitive functioning than that used to simply move toward a visual object. A blind child will not develop the ability to respond to a sound by moving in its direction until the end of the first year (Fraiberg, 1977).

That these children are delayed in gross motor development and in skills such as running, hopping, jumping, and skipping is not surprising. In a study of 66 neurologically intact blind children, Norris, Spaulding, and Brodie (1957) found that only half were walking independently by age 2. Sandler (1963) suggested that the prolonged period of immobility experienced by blind children increases the probability that they will be left alone more often than otherwise would be the case. This promotes passive self-centeredness and a lack of striving toward mastery of skills at later ages. Blind children often engage in self-stimulating, rhythmic, purposeless movements, called *blindisms,* of which rocking, swaying, and twisting of the body are examples. Adelson and Fraiberg (1974, 1975) have suggested that delays in self-initiated mobility need not exert a lasting effect on a blind child's overall motor development, but these delays can have an effect on personality, initiative, and a child's overall rate of learning.

3. *Impacts on cognitive development.*

A substantial amount of research indicates that blind and partially sighted children lag behind their sighted peers in cognitive and conceptual abilities (Gottesman, 1973, 1976; Witkin, Birnbaum, Lomonaco, Lehr, & Herman, 1968; Zeibelson & Borg, 1967). Visually impaired children are more likely to deal with their environment in concrete terms and do less well in abstract thinking. Spatial concepts are often deficient. They tend to lag behind their sighted peers in school. Children with partial vision are found to be average in grade placement but somewhat below grade level in academic achievement (Rapin, 1979). Birch, Tisdall, Peabody, and Sterrett (1966) studied school performance in 903 fifth and sixth graders with partial sight and found they were about 2½ years behind academically; yet all students were of average intelligence.

Kephart, Kephart, and Schwartz (1974) noted that blind children often have distorted understandings of simple, straightforward concepts. Though they may give correct responses on standardized test items, further probing often reveals an incomplete understanding and conceptualization of the world around them. Kephart et al. asked 5- to 7-year-old blind children to name the parts that should be included in drawings of a house and a person. Compared to the sighted youngsters, the blind children had less knowledge both of body parts and of house components. In over 50% of the cases, the 7-year-old visually impaired children did not mention fingers, ears, or eyes. Their responses showed a fragmented, distorted view of many objects and things that they seemed at times to be able to talk about with understanding.

Cognitive development clearly is slowed by the reduction in sensory input and direct experience with people and things. Learning becomes dependent upon an increase in stimulation through other sensory modes (auditory, kinesthetic, motor, olfactory, and tactile). Input through these sensory systems must be increased significantly to make up for what cannot be received as visual input. Safford (1978) noted that developmental delays are apparent in children with notable visual impairment during the first three or four years of life in almost every developmental domain. But with appropriate stimulation during the first year of life and with continued attention to the child's special needs in the years that follow, a blind child with no other cognitive or neurological impairments can approach behavioral norms for sighted children in these areas by about age 5 or 6.

One final point should be made about the impact of vision loss on young children: *Their learning requires more time, more practice, more verbal mediation, and more encouragement from adults.* Children learn by doing. They profit greatly by being able to imitate an action they have first watched someone demonstrate. Although visually impaired or blind children may be less able to "watch" a model, they still need the same experience and practice. Because a preschooler cannot watch someone else put on a coat or button a shirt, these skills will be more difficult to master. The blind child cannot see that a coat has two arms and a front and a back. The child must learn the parts of a coat by touch and by cognitive understanding before being able to totally master that task and perform it independently. Given the added complexity of that task, it simply will take longer to learn.

ORTHOPEDIC/NEUROLOGICAL IMPAIRMENTS

Early signs and symptoms of orthopedic/neurological disorders

Identification and diagnosis of these disorders is primarily a medical task. Early signs or symptoms may be clear-cut, as in the case of orthopedic or crippling disorders. In other instances symptoms may be more subtle and apparent only through sophisticated medical analyses. Sometimes early symptoms of neurological damage are simply not apparent in the early years. Signs of orthopedic/neurological disorders include:

Structural abnormality: No guesswork is involved here. A physical deformity that affects motor behavior or locomotion is clearly apparent and immediately diagnosable.

Signs of motor dysfunction: Although a child's physical body structures may appear normal and intact, more subtle signs may suggest problems in motor function originating from neurological damage, muscle disorders, or other damage as a result of disease. Motor dysfunction may be suggested by:

— abnormal reflex patterns, including absence of appropriate reflexes, persistence of primitive reflex patterns, or abnormal manifestations of reflex patterns.
— lack of appropriate coordination and integration of motor movements for chronological age.
— occurrence of strange or repetitious motor patterns; unexplained pauses or disruptions in a motor sequence, which may be precursory to or evidence of seizures.
— poor balance, poor equilibrium, or weakness in a child that makes running, climbing, or postural control overly difficult.

— poor muscle tone (lack of firmness); stiffness or excessive flaccidity in muscles.

— excessive movement when child reaches, walks, or responds with excitement or with a startle.

Signs of motor regression: Child's motor skills or muscular strength or tone may seem to be deteriorating instead of becoming more mature and sophisticated.

Signs of neurological dysfunction: In young children, early symptoms of brain damage include abnormalities in sucking, grasping, posture, reflexes, and muscle tone, as well as clumsiness or delay in locomotion. Although these signs are often associated with neurological dysfunction, this is not invariably true. Kennedy, Drage, and Schwartz (1963) followed 10,000 children who had low APGAR scores (0-3 on a 10-point scale). At age 1, one-fifth showed signs of possible neurological abnormality (abnormal gait, posture, and muscle tonus). A subsequent follow-up at age 4 showed that a large number of those children had poor fine and gross motor control (Drage, Berendes, & Fisher, 1969).

Prenatal/perinatal histories suggestive of possible neurological damage: Alertness to at-risk conditions in the child's early developmental history or in the mother's pregnancy can signal children who are potential candidates for neurological/motoric dysfunction and who should be monitored carefully.

A common misconception is that most neurological disorders that result in orthopedic impairments are apparent at birth. The fact is that a diagnosis is not easily made in the immediate postnatal period. Clinical symptoms of a brain lesion may not be apparent for weeks or months after birth because the voluntary motor center of the brain is not involved in the reflexive behavior typical of an infant during early postnatal life. Certain symptoms, however, are reported to be shown in infants who later manifest signs of cerebral palsy or neurological dysfunction (Batshaw & Perret, 1981; Denhoff, 1976; Scherzer & Tscharnuter, 1982):

● General depression of all or most of the primitive reflexes (Moro, blink, rooting and sucking, palmar and plantar grasps, traction from supine position, placing, stepping, and supporting).

● Excessive reactiveness to visual or tactile stimuli with heightened jitteriness or tremulousness.

● Convulsions.

● Asymmetry of various primitive reflexes.

● Motor or sensory neurological signs pointing to localized lesions (a less frequent symptom).

The nature of orthopedic/neurological disorders

A large number of disorders (inherited, infectious, and noninfectious) cause motor impairments that interfere with movement and locomotion. Some of the major ones are described here.

Cerebral palsy Cerebral palsy is one of the most common crippling impairments found in children. Estimates suggest that 7 children per 100,000 are born with cerebral palsy. The term actually encompasses a group of disorders of varied etiology resulting in paralysis, weakness, or incoordination of the motor system as a result of intracranial lesions (Scherzer & Tscharnuter, 1982). The causes are prenatal (e.g., rubella, Rh incompatibility, toxemia), perinatal (e.g., birth injury due to prolonged labor, obstetrical complications, or asphyxia), or postnatal (e.g., encephalitis, anoxia, head injury). According to Behrman and Vaughan (1983), more than one-third of children with cerebral palsy are low birth weight babies. If both prematurity and low birth weight are considered, Bleck (1975b) has suggested that 33%-60% of all cases of cerebral palsy are accounted for by these two factors alone. Anoxia and mechanical injury to the brain at birth are the most frequent types of trauma causing the disorder.

As a nonprogressive condition, cerebral palsy involves various types of impairment in gross and fine motor coordination. The disorder is no longer regarded as only a pure motor dysfunction but, instead, a multidimensional disorder. The type and distribution of motor impairment is a neurodevelopmental marker for underlying and associated neurological, cognitive, and perceptual impairments. Cerebral palsy is associated with other disorders including convulsions, speech disorders, sensory defects, and disorders in intellectual functions (Bleck, 1979).

Cerebral palsy can be described in several ways—most commonly by the physiological impairment and the nature of motor interference. Using this type of classification system, the seven different types of cerebral palsy are: *spastic* (the most prevalent), *athetoid, rigid, ataxic, tremor, atonic* or *hypotonic,* and *mixed* (a combination of the other types—usually spastic and athetoid). Characteristics of each type are summarized in Table 5.3.

A second way to describe cerebral palsy is in terms of what limbs are affected (Bleck, 1975, 1979; Capute, 1975; Behrman & Vaughan, 1983):

Monoplegia: one limb affected (this condition is rare).

Hemiplegia: arm and leg on one side affected (usually of a spastic type; sensory involvement frequent).

Paraplegia: legs affected only (almost always spastic or rigidity type).

Triplegia: three limbs affected—typically both legs and an arm (usually spastic).

Quadriplegia: all four limbs affected (those with greatest involvement in legs usually spastic; those with greater arm involvement usually athetoid).

For an excellent discussion of these and numerous other physical disorders, two excellent volumes are: *Physically Handicapped Children: A Medical Atlas for Teachers* by Bleck and Nagel (1975), and *Medical Problems in the Classroom* by Haslam and Valletutti (1975).

Spinal cord damage   Several *medical disorders* result in deterioration of the spinal cord (such as spinal muscular atrophy or polio) or in congenital malformation of the spinal cord (as in spina bifida). Spinal cord *injuries* represent another type of impairment. These injuries to the spinal cord, resulting from accidents in the environment, are not discussed further as their characteristics and degree of damage vary according to the specific injury. *Spinal muscular atrophy* produces progressive degeneration of the motor

Table 5.3

Types and Characteristics of Cerebral Palsy

Types of Cerebral Palsy	Characteristics
Spasticity (Most prevalent—50%-60% of children with CP)	Loss of voluntary muscle control. Limb muscles are tight from too much muscle tone (hypertonic), attempts to move produce opposite result than intended (muscles contract and flexion occurs). Voluntary movements are slow, tense, jerky, and limited in range. If child is startled, rigid muscle extension or flexion occurs, placing child in a fixed, rigid position. As growth occurs, spastic muscles tighten, drawing muscles into more flexion and causing limb deformities unless therapeutic intervention occurs.
Athetosis (Second most prevalent— 15%-20% of children with CP)	Excessive involuntary, purposeless movements of the limbs; uncontrolled writhing and irregular movements. Throat and diaphragm muscles are usually affected, causing drooling and labored speech. Two types of athetosis are: (a) nontension athetosis (contorted movements without tightening of muscles), and (b) tension athetosis (muscles are tight).
Rigidity	Constant diffuse tension of both flexor and extensor muscles, which produces severe spasticity. Affected limbs are rigid and extremely hard to bend. Bending child's arm or leg is like attempting to bend a lead pipe. These children are usually quadriplegic.
Ataxia	Lack of balance, uncoordinated movement, and lack of a sense of position in space. Gross motor movements are poor. Child walks with a staggering gait "like a sailor on a rolling ship at sea"—feet apart and weaving of the trunk. Arms are extended for balance.
Tremor	Shakiness of the affected limbs apparent only when a specific movement occurs. Shakiness is caused by alternating contractions of the flexor and extensor muscles. Tremors differ from athetoid movements in that athetoid movements are large and changeable while tremors are small and rhythmic.
Atonia or Hypotonia	Lack of muscle tone and inability to move or maintain postural control (child is "floppy"). As child matures, however, clinical symptoms tend to change and characteristics of another type of cerebral palsy evolve. Hypotonia generally is nonexistent by the time the child reaches school age—usually evolving into athetosis. Thus, the atonic or hypotonic child often is described as *pre-spastic, pre-athetoid,* or *pre-ataxic.*

nerve cells in the spinal cord. The most apparent symptom of this disease is a progressive weakness and atrophy of muscles in the trunk of the body. The effect upon the child can be delayed motor development, fatigue, and clumsiness. This disease is inherited, with no known cure. The infantile form progresses rapidly, causing death before age 5 or 6. The juvenile form develops more slowly, first causing atrophy in the leg muscles and, later, affecting muscles of the shoulders, upper arms, and neck. Children with this form of the disease may have a normal life span and may remain mobile as long as 20 years (Koehler, 1975).

Spina bifida is a condition characterized by an opening in the spinal column resulting from abnormal fetal development in the first 30 days of pregnancy. For unknown reasons, the neural tube fails to develop completely and close properly. The deformity can be at any point along the spine from the head to the lower end, but usually it occurs in the lower end. Its incidence is .1 to 4.13 cases per 1,000 live births. The fact that this deformity is apparent from birth allows medical intervention and motor therapy to begin early. The three types of spina bifida are (Batshaw & Perret, 1981):

Myelomeningocele (myelo = cord; meninges = coverings of the spinal cord, cele = sack; pronunciation: mi'-el-lo-men-ing'-go-seal): This form of spina bifida is distinguished by a protrusion of the spinal cord through the gap in the vertebrae of the spine into a sac-like structure. Contained in the sac are the nerve roots and portions of the spinal cord. Paralysis of the lower limbs and trunk occurs, the extent of which depends upon the site of the sac along the vertebrae.

Meningocele: This deformity is the same as the previous one except that the protrusion or sac contains only the coverings of the spinal column. The sac may contain cerebrospinal fluid, but no neurological impairment is present. Myelomeningoceles occur four to five times more often than meningoceles.

Spina bifida occulta: In this form, the least severe, the back arches of the vertebrae have failed to develop. Neither the meninges nor the cord itself (including its protective covering) protrudes. The bony defect is covered with skin and often is identified only by a growth of hair covering the area of the deformity.

Several related problems may be present in children with spina bifida (Bleck & Nagel, 1975; Blackman, 1984; Myers, 1975):

- Hydrocephalus (occurs in 90%-95% of children with myelomeningocele). Spinal fluid circulation in the brain is blocked. Typically, a shunt (a tube with a pressure valve) is implanted in the brain to allow proper circulation and drainage of fluid. If this is done before pressure builds, brain damage can be prevented. If hydrocephalus is allowed to develop, mental retardation, seizures, and spastic paralysis can result.
- Bladder and bowel paralysis. The location of the sac is almost always above the major nerve to the bladder. Most children are incontinent (unable to control emptying of the bladder). Similar problems with bowel control may occur.
- Paralysis of the trunk and lower limbs. When paralysis occurs, the extent depends on location of the sac. For example, if the spine is damaged at the 12th thoracic vertebra or above, paralysis of the trunk and of the lower limbs results; if damage is at the third or fourth lumbar level, trunk muscles are not affected and part of the hip and thigh muscles are functional. Paralysis occurs primarily in the leg, foot, and ankle. Sensation in the skin to temperature, touch, or other sensory stimulation is also lost.
- Bone deformities. The partial or total paralysis in lower limbs also results in muscular imbalance (contractions of muscle groups), which results in progressive deformation of the feet, legs, and hips. Contractures cause rotation of the legs or feet or spinal curvature. Surgery, bracing, and other medical procedures can help correct some of these problems as they develop, although they present continuing problems.

Muscular dystrophy   MD is characterized by progressive degeneration of the voluntary muscles (e.g., those in the arms and legs). Muscle cells gradually are replaced by fat and fibrous tissue. This produces general weakness and increasing difficulties in movement. The disease is caused by a sex-linked recessive gene transmitted by the unaffected mother to her sons. Occasionally the disease occurs in girls, in which case it is believed to be transmitted through an autosomal recessive trait inherited from both parents.

Early symptoms of this disease may appear in children as young as 3 years of age. Parents may note that their son appears strangely awkward and clumsy and runs "funny." Another early sign is walking on tiptoe—a problem caused by early weakness in the muscles that pull the foot up. Postural abnormalities may appear (e.g., sway back with protrusion of the abdomen, caused by increasing weakness in the abdominal muscles). Initially, mobility is hampered in running or walking up stairs. As the disease progresses, the child has difficulty walking even on flat surfaces. Skeletal deformities develop as unopposed weaknesses in muscle groups cause shortening of other muscles and contracture of the joints. Severe curvature of the spine can occur.

The course of this disease is steadily downhill as muscles continue to degenerate and secondary problems develop. Most children are in wheelchairs by age 10. Death usually occurs in the late teens. The heart muscles become so weak that the heart fails, or weakness in the breathing muscles makes lung infection probable and subsequently lethal (Bleck, 1975c; Behrman & Vaughan, 1983).

Less common orthopedic disorders resulting from disease   Muscular dystrophy is by far the most common orthopedic disorder caused by disease, but of other, less prevalent ones, *juvenile rheumatoid arthritis* is well known. Rheumatoid arthritis is relatively uncommon in children, affecting only an estimated 3 children per 100,000. The cause is unknown, but the inflammation and swelling of joints characterized by the disease are believed to result from an attack of the body's immune system against normal body cells or tissue.

Arthritis usually is associated with the middle-aged and elderly, but some notable differences are found between the disease in adults and that in children. According to Miller (1975), 60%-70% of rheumatoid children will be free of the disease after about 10 years (only 20% have adult remissions). The length of time a child is ill varies from a few months to several years. Miller suggests that teaching and all therapy should be based on the assumption that a permanent remission will eventually occur (hence, development of functional mobility skills and motor skills is important). With good care, only 10% of affected children should be left with functional physical limitations.

The three types of juvenile rheumatoid arthritis are: (a) *systemic arthritis*, in which abnormal health symptoms (fever, rash, enlarged spleen) are predominant and arthritic or joint inflammation is a minor symptom; (b) *pauciarticular arthritis,* which produces only a couple of swollen joints—otherwise, the child neither looks nor feels ill; and (c) *polyarticular arthritis,* affecting the largest proportion of children (50%-60%). Here, the symptoms are more diffuse. Joints in the knees, ankles, feet, wrists, and fingers are severely affected.

This latter form of arthritis is very painful, and the afflicted children are often in misery. They tend to sit as still as possible, with joints in a flexed position because this is most comfortable and least painful. Joints lose their range of motion and develop contractures. Growth is affected. Accompanying symptoms may be fever, irritability, and poor appetite. As a result of the arthritis, the heart, liver, spleen, and eyes also may become inflamed—all requiring careful medical management. Major complications for children with severe arthritis are the permanent changes that can occur in the joints. Inflammation damages cartilage and destroys the smooth surface of the ball in the joint, which produces scarring and tightening of the surrounding soft tissue. The degree to which these conditions are treated and controlled determines the extent to which permanent or crippling damage occurs (Miller, 1975; Myers, 1975).

Arthrogryposis is a congenital disease that begins to affect a developing fetus long before birth. The muscles simply fail to function, resulting in lack of early movement of the joints. Thus, a newborn has stiff, deformed joints. Children with this disease resemble wooden puppets; their limbs are fixed in almost any position. The newborn typically has flexed, stiff elbows, flexed wrists and fingers, and stiff knees. Fingers are curled into the palms, and hips are flexed and turned outward.

This condition requires continuous and extensive surgical correction simply to keep the limbs somewhat functional and to control growth so that abnormalities do not become even more severe. Most children require a wheelchair. The disease does not directly affect mental capacities. Some associated impairments, such as congenital heart disease, urinary tract abnormalities, and respiration problems, do occur (Bleck, 1975a).

Osteogenesis imperfecta, or brittle bone disease, is characterized by imperfect bone formation. Although the exact cause is unknown, it has been established that this disease is inherited through a dominant gene. In the two forms of the disease, one is congenital and the other form appears later in life. The bones of a child with osteogenesis imperfecta do not grow normally in length or thickness and therefore are brittle. The joints are excessively mobile or lax. For example, the thumb can be bent back to almost touch the forearm. Limbs are small and usually bowed in various contortions as a result of repeated fractures and healing. Dwarfism and deafness are common secondary handicaps.

A child with this disease is quite recognizable because of characteristic physical changes. The eyes have a blue tint. Soft skull bones result in broadening of the forehead and bulging of the temple as the child grows older. The chest is barrel-shaped, with protrusion of the breast bone. The spine becomes rounded (Batshaw & Perret, 1981).

Absence or deformity of limbs   Some young children lack arms or legs as a result of congenital malformations or amputations by accident or surgery. Occasionally a major deformity of the limbs results in limited function, if any at all. Drugs such as thalidomide have been responsible for some cases of congenital absence of limbs. Metabolic disorders also are believed to be possible causes. Congenital malformations usually occur some time during the 4-8 weeks of gestation when the limb buds are just developing in the fetus (see chapter 4).

The absence of one or more limbs presents obvious problems. These can be solved partially with the use of prosthetic devices (e.g., artificial arms), although this is not always possible, especially with a very young child. Sometimes prosthetic devices are not fitted on infants or preschoolers in preference to waiting until they are older, when they perhaps will be better able to learn how to maneuver the device. Limb-deficient children tend to perspire heavily, because of limited body surfaces, and thus may be sensitive to temperature changes. Fear of falling is common. Associated problems for a child with an amputated limb are irritation or breakdown of tissue and skin over the bony end of the stumps, resulting in ulcers that are very sore and slow to heal. A poorly fitting prosthesis or a stump end that is not kept clean can promote the development of ulcers.

The impact of orthopedic/neurological disorders on development and learning

When a young child becomes mobile by crawling and then walking, a whole new world opens up. No longer is the child totally dependent upon adults to bring experiences or place stimulating toys and objects within reach. Through mobility the child becomes capable of seeking out new experiences and can (to some degree) change his or her own environment! Young toddlers and preschoolers do just that—getting into cupboards, drawers, mom's closet, or any other place that offers something new to explore. As a result of this broadened experience, learning accelerates rapidly. Mobility not only multiplies the potential sensory and experiential input, but it also exposes youngsters to new risks and potential dangers. If a child has a physical impairment that restricts mobility or motor activity, this important transition into an expanded world is restricted or deterred totally.

As Caldwell (1973) described it, if a child has any kind of motor dysfunction, "he cannot get up and move himself to find something better, or at least cannot move himself to a situation where the environment might make a better match with his own developmental state. It is a clear situation of the old rule of the 'haves' and the 'have nots.' The have nots continue to get less" (p. 7). Because children learn by doing and physical action, by manipulating, feeling, touching, and activating objects in their environment, motor development plays an important role in early experience. We know that early experience and interaction with the environment promote learning across all domains—speech, language, cognitive, and social development.

To make broad generalizations about the impact of physical or neurological handicaps on a child's development and learning is difficult because this varies with the nature and severity of the condition. Furthermore, a child's development and mastery of adaptive skills, which affect how well he or she copes with a physical abnormality, are heavily influenced by experience and treatment after birth. For example, Willerman, Broman, and Fiedler (1970) found that physically impaired infants with early signs of slow cognitive development were more likely to show continued slow rates of development if reared in a working-class family. In contrast, delayed children in middle-class families were more likely to show normal cognitive development by age 4. This evidence suggests that although physical disorders have many direct impacts on the developmental status of a young child, environmental factors also are at work, interacting with, and perhaps even overriding, the impact of a child's physical disorders.

Several broad kinds of impacts *potentially* affect a young child with some type of physical impairment. Obviously, the more severe the physical abnormality is, the more likely these impacts will be seen.

1. *Medical procedures needed to correct or treat physical problems are often painful and frightening to a young child and may require hospitalization, which can have further impact on the child's development, as well as on parent-child attachments.*

   One young child with spina bifida known to the author was admitted to the hospital for operative procedures an average of once every 5-6 months following her birth until age 6. A small, 2½-year-old girl with cerebral and spinal deformities required such extensive corrective and emergency surgery that she was hospitalized 23 times by the time she was 3. Although these are extreme cases, the fact remains that many physically handicapped young children who require extensive medical treatment experience a very different kind of caregiving during their early lives. Given their young age, the necessity of sometimes painful and frightening treatment is incomprehensible to them and can be traumatic to children who are unable to understand why adults are hurting them.

These experiences can impact upon children in other ways, too. Hospitalization may separate a child from parents during times when attachments are forming. Parent-child interactions may be interrupted or altered because the child is heavily medicated or too weak and ill to respond in ways that promote positive, reciprocal forms of interaction. Crankiness, dependency, and lack of responsiveness may result. Some children regress to more infantile forms of behavior and may lose skills they had previously mastered (such as toilet training). Temper tantrums or resistance to treatment may be intensified, especially when the children have undergone much pain or discomfort. Although these reactions in a young child are understandable and somewhat expected, caregiving still becomes difficult and stressful for parents. Some of the potential impacts described in the section on health impairments apply also to children with orthopedic and neurological disorders.

2. *Abnormal reflex patterns that interfere with proper movement and with the progression to more mature and complex levels of motor functioning may be manifested.*

Neurological maturation and integration are essential for normal physical development. If a child is to achieve normal developmental milestones in the motor area, basic reflex patterns and postural mechanisms must be continuously integrated into higher level movement patterns. Children with neurological dysfunction have brain injury that inhibits neurological maturation. In fact, one of the signs of cerebral palsy is the persistence of primitive reflexes when normal children no longer have these reflexes after a given age. Certain reflexes are termed "primitive" because they are present in infants and are controlled via primitive parts of the nervous system (spinal cord, labyrinths of the inner ear, and brain stem). Through maturation of the cortex and nervous system, reflexes are gradually integrated into voluntary movement. During early infancy, reflex action dominates movement, but by about 6 months of age, integration of the primitive reflexes is fairly complete (Capute, Accardo, Vining, Rubenstein, & Harryman, 1978).

Some of the most influential reflexes that can interfere with achievement of normal motor milestones are tonic labyrinthine reflex, asymmetric tonic neck reflex (ATNR), symmetrical tonic neck reflex (STNR), grasp reflex, and Moro reflex. (For detailed explanations of these reflexes, see Fiorentino, 1973, 1981.)

When certain reflexes do not develop or fail to be integrated into higher movement patterns, a child has difficulty in developing more sophisticated motor skills. For example, Utley, Holvoet, and Barnes (1977) have described some of the problems associated with an abnormal asymmetric tonic neck reflex (ATNR): (a) Rolling over is difficult, if not impossible, (b) if placed on all fours, the child will collapse if the face is turned to either side, (c) the child may be unable to bring both hands to the midline for motor activities, and (d) the child has difficulty mastering normal motor tasks such as self-feeding and

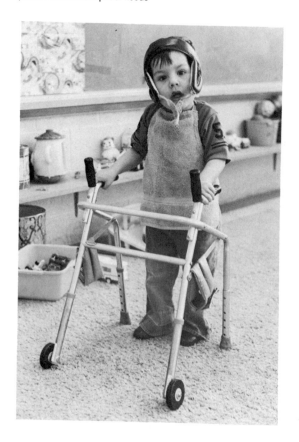

This youngster gets around his preschool classroom quite well with his walker in spite of his orthopedic impairments. His helmet protects him from injury should he fall from seizures or as he tries to keep up physically with his peers.

walking. Handling these children in ways that minimize abnormal or disruptive motor responses and maximize movement potential requires that caregivers know how to handle and position the child.

3. *Muscle tone may be altered through neurological impairment or extended immobility or lack of postural change because of physical impairment, which in turn thwarts movement patterns and even physical growth.*

Motor development proceeds through a complex sequence of interlocking stages, which are dependent upon reflex activity and which are modified by a child's motor experiences. Initially a young infant's reactions to stimuli are with total movement. Gradually this global response is modified into appropriate, more specific, and efficient motor movement. Thus, a child learns to move one body part independently of other parts. Motor development is not complete until a child is age 5 or 6, although significant milestones are achieved during the first 1-2 years. The culmination of this developmental process is a child who is able to right himself or herself against gravity, maintain a stable posture against gravity, and move against gravity without losing postural stability or balance (Conner, Williamson, & Siepp, 1978; Finnie, 1975; Ford, 1975). This whole process of motor development is accomplished as lower, more primitive motor patterns are developed, inhibited, or modified into new motor responses.

Physical disorders causing muscular atrophy or neurological impairment such as cerebral palsy produce changes in muscle tone that greatly affect reflexive and voluntary movement. For example, a child with excessive muscle tone has spastic muscles, which cause the limbs to be reflexed or extended rigidly most of the time. If action is not taken to counteract the effects of chronic extension or flexion, the child will develop *contractures* (the permanent shortening of muscles and connective tissue). If this happens, movement becomes even more difficult, if not impossible. The child is "locked" into certain postural positions, or limbs are immobilized. Skeletal deformities, too, result as the child grows in size (e.g., curling of feet or crossing of legs, or tight clenching of arms or hands against the body).

Any type of abnormal motor pattern, especially if it is severe, can have a profound effect on a child's daily life. Children with fluctuating muscle tone (such as athetosis in children with cerebral palsy) produce uncontrolled movements when they attempt a motor response. Thus, grasping and holding a toy or manipulating play materials with some degree of control are exceedingly difficult to do. The child is more likely to knock every object off the table as he or she attempts to work with materials. If the lower extremities are affected, walking with a smooth, steady gait may be literally impossible. Unless steps are taken to help restrain excessive movement, the child's attempts to engage in purposeful physical activity are extremely difficult and frustrating.

A child with a lack of muscle tone and the "floppiness" that results (hypotonia) may have difficulty learning to hold up his or her head, sit, and stand. Reflex actions likely are missing. In contrast, excessive muscle tone (hypertonia) results in certain exaggerated reflex actions. For example, a child may be unable to sit up because of insufficient hip flexion and flexion or extension of the legs is such that it interferes with positions that allow sitting. A spastic child who is laid on his or her back will have restricted movement; because of the rigid extension of the child's body, he or she cannot freely turn the head and view the surroundings. Rigidly flexed arms with fisted hands cannot reach forward to grasp toys. A child with this disorder cannot even explore his or her own body or suck on fingers and toes. If placed on the stomach, the same child will be unable to lift the head to see activities around him or her. When bathed or cuddled, the child is restricted in responses. This apparent unresponsiveness, in turn, interferes with the normal give-and-take in a reciprocal parent-child relationship.

Impaired motor development, even of a milder nature, may affect children's social and emotional development. Conner, Williamson, and Siepp (1978) have noted that many spastic children show a rather passive affect. They often are viewed as "lazy" because their movements are slow and labored. In reality their movement simply requires great effort. Children who experience difficulties in motor activity or who are insecure in their balance or stability in locomotion may be so frustrated and limited in movement that they lose the motivation to mobilize themselves.

4. *Restrictions in movement, including locomotion and voluntary gross and fine motor actions, can occur and interfere with the further mastery of motor and other development skills.*

Children with physical impairments that interfere with movement or make movement laborious are faced with limitations in their ability to access their environment. An infant or toddler, who normally could move freely from room to room in the home, may be restricted to one room and the stimuli available there unless an adult takes the initiative to move the child to other places. Normal preschoolers are constantly expanding their physical environment as they move about and explore new places and things, but physically handicapped children are slowed in this process, reducing significantly their experiences and exposure to the outside world (Rosenbloom, 1975).

As Langley (1979) noted, the ability to move is basic to all life-skill activities. It affects communication and experiences through which the child can relate to other people. It affects the formation of concepts since the child's direct experience with things, through exploration and manipulation, is the primary means for conceptual learning. The ability to move is prerequisite to independence and the development of self-care skills that allow children to care for their own needs. Rosenbloom (1975) noted that infants as young as 6 months who were deprived of upright positioning, so they could view activities around them, tended to show evidence of perceptual disorders.

Movement in all its many forms is altered or prevented by physical disabilities. An absence of limbs or a restriction in range of motion in one or more limbs because of paralysis or deformity can make even basic tasks of eating, dressing, object manipulation, play, or locomotion tedious and tiresome. Children with physical or neurological impairment may have abnormal balance reactions that further impede equilibrium and righting responses, which in turn hamper movement and mastery of motor skills. For example, certain postural reactions that develop in 6- to 18-month-old infants aid them in learning to sit and then stand (Wilson, 1977). A normal *protective extension reaction,* for example, occurs when a person is pushed off balance from a sitting or standing position. The arms automatically extend outward to block a ball and protect the head. When children lack this protective response, they are more vulnerable to injury from falling because they are less able to counteract a loss of balance or to protect their head from hitting the floor.

Some children with physical impairment show abnormal *staggering reactions.* Though they are able to stand or walk without assistance, they fail to cross-step when pushed sideways. Likewise, they are not able to counter a forward or backward loss of balance. Again they are apt to fall, to be less agile or quick in their movements, and to be uncertain or unsure of themselves since equilibrium is so easily threatened whenever they attempt to move.

Because cerebral palsy is one of the most common types of physical impairment, some impacts of this neurological handicap should be noted in addition to the impacts already described:

1. Movement is a foremost disability among children with cerebral palsy, but this is often accompanied by associated disabilities. Approximately 60% of these children are mentally retarded (Robinson, 1973). Children with hemiplegia, the most common type of cerebral palsy, typically have the best intellectual outcomes, and many have normal cognitive abilities. Fewer than 30% of children with spastic diplegia, the form of cerebral palsy most often associated with prematurity, have normal intelligence (Crothers & Paine, 1959). Of those with abnormal cognitive abilities, some 15% are mildly retarded, 35% show moderate retardation, and 50% or more are severely to profoundly retarded (Robinson, 1973).

2. Vision problems are common as well. More than 40% of children with cerebral palsy have visual defects (Black, 1980). Hearing and language deficits are reported to occur

in about 20% (Robinson, 1973). Mecham (1966) reported that 70%-80% have some speech involvement. The oral musculature may be either hypotonic or hypertonic depending upon the form of palsy. Epilepsy, too, is often associated with cerebral palsy. Figures suggest that 35% of all CP children will develop seizures some time during their lives (Bleck, 1975b, 1979).

3. Children with cerebral palsy generally have delays in acquisition of normal developmental milestones. Some of those delays, noted by Denhoff (1967, p. 25) in a majority of cerebral palsied children, include:

Developmental Milestones	General Age of Achievement by Normal Child	General Age of Achievement by Cerebral Palsied Child
lifting of head	1-3 months	12 months
reaching	3-5 months	14 months
sitting	6-8 months	20 months
crawling	8 months	26 months
walking (without assistance)	13 months	27 months
	18 months	33 months

4. Prespeech skills are often abnormal. A number of interrelated factors may interfere further with speech production. For example, uncoordinated and abnormal oral responses caused initially by abnormal reflex patterns or muscle imbalances can interfere with swallowing; cerebral palsied children commonly have an open mouth and protrusion of the tongue. This reaction is the opposite of normal swallowing, in which the tongue moves forward and the lips close. As muscle tone increases, this abnormality can become even stronger.

Babies with abnormal reflexes and poor muscle tone may be unable to get their hands to the mouth or to provide oral stimulation. Feeding becomes increasingly difficult, and oral stimulation through feeding thus is diminished or even absent. This, in turn, prevents development of the oral musculature and can interfere later with successful production of speech sounds that are essential for articulation of words, and later sentences (Davis, 1978; Buch, Collins, & Gelber, 1978; Mysak, 1971).

5. Abnormal movement patterns also have an enormous impact on speech development, particularly upon the development of normal respiration patterns. Irregular or abnormal breathing affects voice production, shown in the child's difficulties in sustaining and varying vocal production. Children with cerebral palsy often talk with an excessively quiet, whispered voice or may produce outbursts of loud, uncontrolled sounds. When children are unable to sustain voice production, their length of utterance is restricted even though they may have cognitive knowledge of syntactic structures and may be able cognitively to produce a sentence.

HEALTH IMPAIRMENTS

Early signs and symptoms of health disorders

Every health disorder carries its own set of symptoms. At the same time, physical symptoms observed in children (fever, nausea and vomiting, pallor, earaches and headaches, rash) are common to many illnesses. The question here is: How does a parent, early childhood teacher, or caregiver recognize the early signs of poor health in a young child?

Parents and other caregivers do not have to be diagnosticians, but they do have to be alert, consistent observers of a child's physical state and healthiness. These people are in the best position to note sudden changes in a child or to see changes that might be detected only by someone who knows what a child's past behavior and physical appearance were like. Occasionally parents or caregivers are just too close to a child to see subtle signs of disease. This is where the objective eye of a specialist is helpful. Some signs and symptoms suggestive of potential health problems in young children to which we should be alert and seek medical attention include:

1. Changes in behavior or overt physical signs that suggest a child is not feeling well or is coming down with a disease (e.g., behavioral signs—excessive crankiness, lack of energy, whiny, not hungry; onset of strange or unexplainable behavior; physical signs—fever, clammy skin, rash, dull eyes when they are typically bright, paleness or change in coloring, upset stomach and vomiting, complaints of sore stomach, headache or earache).
2. Changes in body functions or excretions that suggest something is not functioning right (e.g., diarrhea; notable changes in color, shape, or odor of bowel movements, or in color/odor of urine; excessive or difficult urination; unusual or excessive bleeding or poor clotting of blood with minor scratches).
3. Observable irregularities in the child's physical appearance (e.g., rashes, discolorations of skin, sores; poor coordination and muscular weakness; size notably larger or smaller than agemates; emaciated look, excessive skinniness, or bloated appearance).
4. Worrisome patterns of illness or poor physical health/stamina over time (e.g., constant colds or discharge from sinuses and lungs; repeated sore throat or earache; overly frequent bouts of diarrhea or constipation; high susceptibility to every cold or disease that siblings or peers contract; longer recovery time or extended loss of energy after common illnesses; labored and wheezy breathing patterns).

Regular health check-ups, regular immunizations, and monitoring of growth by a physician are especially important during infancy and early childhood. Consistency in health care and physical check-ups are the best ways to detect early disorders and allow treatment to be given before damage and secondary problems occur.

The nature of health impairments

Common diseases of early childhood, such as measles, chicken pox, and mumps, typically come and go. Children and their parents survive the rashes, fevers, runny noses, upset stomachs, and temporary discomfort of these infectious diseases. Other diseases are chronic, continuously affecting youngsters' physical well-being, including their energy level, general vitality, overall development, and psychosocial welfare. For this reason, some health disorders are of educational and developmental concern as well as medical concern.

To describe all the acute or chronic health disorders that can pose serious threats to ongoing developmental processes in young children is not possible. Those encountered most frequently are summarized here.

Leukemia This malignancy of the bone marrow is one of the most common forms of childhood cancer. It involves an overproduction or abnormal formation of white blood cells. Though the disease was usually fatal years ago, chemotherapy has extended the life expectancy of children by several years. Sometimes leukemia can be brought into indefinite remission, lasting a few months to many years before the disease reappears. Medication often is continued even if no outward symptoms are present.

Children with leukemia may show a variety of symptoms: fatigue, pallor, fever, weight loss, pain in the joints, and excessive bruising. Drugs used to treat leukemia can produce a variety of side effects, the most apparent of which are a moon-shaped face, obesity in the trunk of the body (from the drug cortisone), and loss of hair. A tendency for infection and excessive bleeding is apparent. The basic symptoms of this disease are common to many other diseases, so the possibilities of leukemia sometimes can be overlooked. A diagnosis can be made only by a thorough medical evaluation, several blood tests, and analysis of the bone marrow. Other forms of cancer also are found in young children, the other most common being tumors of the brain, eye, and kidneys (Myers, 1975; Behrman & Vaughan, 1983).

Cystic fibrosis Cystic fibrosis involves a generalized dysfunction of the exocrine glands. It is caused by a defective recessive gene inherited by a child from both parents. Abnormally thick, gluey mucus is secreted in the pancreas, lungs, and other body organs. Mucus in the pancreas blocks the various ducts to the intestines, preventing pancreatic secretions from reaching the intestines. This interferes with digestion, and malnutrition may ensue even though a child eats adequately. The blocked ducts in the small glands surrounding the pancreas fill with mucus, swell, and develop into cysts, causing further damage to the organs. Mucus in the lungs interferes with breathing and can damage lung tissue.

Children with cystic fibrosis cough frequently because of lung congestion, and they have increased risk for respiratory infection or pneumonia. Affected children have more frequent and larger bowel movements because of the alterations in digestive functions. This creates intestinal gas, causing the abdomen to be distended and to protrude. Growth can be affected, too. The physical appearance of these children varies depending upon the severity of the disease. Because of hyperinflated lungs, the chest may have a big, rounded appearance.

Treatment requires multiple medications and continual physical therapy to relieve the bronchial obstruction resulting from accumulated mucus. No cure is yet known. Treatment is generally aimed at slowing some of the secondary effects and complications of the disease, but cystic fibrosis is generally fatal. Children have a life expectancy of 15-19 years at most (Harvey, 1975; Myers, 1975).

Congenital heart defects   Heart defects occur at a rate of about six in every 1,000 live births. If stillbirths were counted, the rate would be even higher. Any structural defect of the heart or circulatory system at birth is called a congenital heart disease. If the disorder develops after birth, it is called an acquired cardiovascular disorder. Congenital defects originate during the first 1-3 months of embryonic development, when the heart and circulatory system are being formed. These defects generally are caused by genetic abnormalities, diseases such as rubella, and toxic prenatal conditions such as those discussed in chapter 4.

Early symptoms suggesting possible heart defects include shortness of breath, fatigue, poor growth and development, and pain in the chest. Blueness of the lips and nail beds, pale coloring in general, fainting, and chest deformities are additional signs. Numerous types of structural defects can develop, each producing different irregularities in blood circulation through the heart, in reoxygenation of blood, or in removal of carbon dioxide from blood that has passed through the body.

Heart defects affect a young child's development to varying degrees, depending upon the severity and nature of the problem. In many cases, overall development proceeds normally, but children with severe defects can have such a loss of energy and such limited tolerance for exercise that normal activities of early childhood are significantly reduced. Over time, development can become delayed to the extent that a significant gap appears in achievement between the child and agemates (Baum, 1975; Behrman & Vaughan, 1983; Myers, 1975).

Sickle cell anemia   A defective recessive gene causes this severe, chronic blood disease. It is particularly prevalent among Black children, although it is not limited solely to them. The disease results in production of defective hemoglobin, in which the shape of the red blood cell is a distorted crescent, or sickle. Because these cells do not pass easily through the blood vessels, the blood supply to body tissue can be cut off or reduced significantly.

Symptoms, which usually appear in childhood, include severe pain in the abdomen, legs, and arms. Also, swelling of the joints, weakness and fatigue, high fever, skin ulcers on the legs, and jaundice occur. These symptoms come and go, reappearing at irregular intervals. A period of recurrence is referred to as a sickle cell "crisis." Youngsters with this disorder fail to grow properly. They tend to have a short trunk and spindly legs. The risk or damage to tissue because of the loss of blood supply is high. Degeneration of the joints and related orthopedic problems are common, as are fainting and overall lethargy. Many children with this disease die before age 20 from complications such as cerebral hemorrhage or kidney failure. No cure is known. Treatment usually involves rest, medication for pain, blood transfusions, and oxygen inhalation therapy (Walker, 1975).

Juvenile diabetes mellitus   An inherited disorder, diabetes is characterized by the inadequate and improper metabolism of sugar (glucose) and starches (carbohydrates), caused by inability of the pancreas to produce insulin. Insulin allows glucose to enter body cells and create energy. When it is lacking, glucose levels in the blood increase, eventually reaching an excess that cannot be extracted by the kidneys. Glucose then is excreted in the urine. Several symptoms typify diabetes. First, glucose carries water with it, and hence the amount of urine expelled is increased significantly. Excessive urination is one of the first signs of the disease. As a result, a diabetic child tends to be constantly thirsty and to drink huge amounts of fluid. Second, because glucose cannot enter the cells, the body acts as if it is starving and begins to use body fat as an energy source instead. A child may eat a lot of food but show weight loss, tiredness, and weakness. If the diabetes is not diagnosed and the glucose level is not brought back to normal, a person can go into a diabetic coma and, if untreated, will die.

Development of these symptoms in the early stages of diabetes takes several weeks, but once insulin treatment begins, failure to take injections can produce symptoms in just a day or two. A difficulty in treating diabetes lies in monitoring glucose levels and administering appropriate doses of insulin. Too little insulin is harmful; too much insulin can produce a shock reaction. When this happens, the sugar level in the blood drops too far. Organs such as the brain must have glucose. If glucose is lacking, various symptoms quickly appear: headache, dizziness, nausea and vomiting, blurred vision, profuse sweating, heightened heart rate. Convulsions and death can ensue if action is not taken to counter-balance the excess insulin. Ingestion of a concentrated sugar (candy or fruit juices) usually suffices. In addition to the risks of diabetic coma or insulin reaction, a child with diabetes is more reactive to illness or infection. Sore throat, disease, or infection can make the diabetes worse and change insulin needs, thus requiring careful and sensitive monitoring of glucose levels in the urine (Behrman & Vaughan, 1983; Christiansen, 1975; Katz, 1975).

The impact of health impairments on development and learning

Each chronic health disorder likely affects the lives of young children and their families in unique ways. Chronic or severe illness during the formative years not only threatens life and physical health, but a child's overall developmental progress is vulnerable, too. Watch a young child who is very ill. He or she is likely quiet and listless or excessively fussy and cranky, more interested in sleeping, being cuddled and comforted by a parent, and being entertained by an adult. Small children may feel insecure when they are ill, clinging and being more dependent than usual on their caregivers. The discomfort or pain inflicted by the illness is likely to be distracting to the extent that it interferes with activities in which the child would normally be engaged. The child may be less responsive and interactive with people and less enticed to play or attend to events in the environment. Only as children grow older do they become more capable of coping with illness in a way that they can be sick and engage in other activities at the same time.

Health impairments, per se, cannot be said to cause problems in the development of cognitive, speech, motor, and social skills. Nevertheless, extended illness can create conditions that in turn interfere with learning, with the child's ability to participate in and profit from experience, and with normal developmental processes. Furthermore, hospitalization and medical treatment sometimes impose additional restrictions on a child's life. These secondary effects of extended illness are what makes a health impairment potentially handicapping.

To what extent chronic illnesses produce secondary effects in young children depends on the interaction of several variables: (a) severity of the illness, including the particular physical symptoms it produces, (b) its duration and whether it is terminal, (c) the child's age, (d) the degree to which symptoms cause discomfort and pain, (e) the degree to which the illness or its treatment interrupts normal activities of daily living for either the child or the parents, and (f) the parents' reaction to the illness, and their methods of relating to their sick child and coping with the illness. Summarized below are some of the potential impacts of a serious health problem on a young child:

1. *Social isolation and disruption in normal life experiences that promote early learning.*

Extended periods of bed rest, medical treatment, or hospitalization can isolate a child from many normal social experiences and the ordinary experiences of everyday living. Optimal times for learning new skills may come and go. Because a child is too ill to be responsive or because medical treatment must come first, a child may be prevented from getting stimulation at a time when it is most crucial for learning.

2. *Physical limitations and reduction in energy level.*

Illness can sap a child's energy and vitality. Even though the environment may offer rich stimulation and caregivers are nurturing and responsive, a child simply may not feel well enough to be responsive or interested. Listlessness, inattentiveness, and unresponsiveness are common in a seriously and chronically ill child. The less severe the physical impact of the illness, the less these behaviors are likely to be shown. Some chronic diseases, once under control through medical treatment, will not affect how the child feels and thus may not affect daily activities at all.

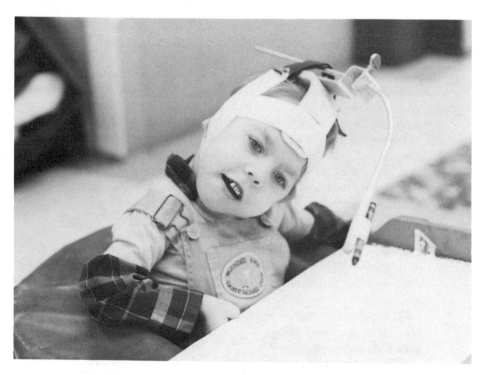

Like other preschoolers, Sammy loves to draw pictures. It just takes some creative adaptations by his teachers and therapists to help him cope with the limitations imposed by cerebral palsy.

3. *Potential disruption in interpersonal relationships.*

Chronic illness can alter the relationships between the child and parents or siblings. If the disorder appears early and results in extended separation from parents, affectional bonding between them can be disrupted. Some parents may be prone to divorce themselves psychologically from the child, especially if younger children in the family demand attention and care, too. Other parents focus all their attentions on the sick child; family life becomes centered on the child's illness. Overaccommodation and indulgence then occur. In either instance, psychological implications for a child's self-concept and emotional well-being are not healthy.

4. *Effects upon parent's child rearing practices.*

Normal child-rearing practices may be altered when a child is ill, or disrupted when a child is away from home because of hospitalization or medical treatment. Parents cope with these changes in various ways. Some hesitate to put pressure on a child who is not feeling well and thereby change their usual expectations for behavior. Ordinary teaching, disciplining, and shaping of desirable behavior may be deemphasized or even skipped for a time. Some parents have difficulty disciplining a sick, helpless child, but in doing so they fail to expose the child to age-appropriate standards of behavior. Some parents respond to a sick child with unrealistic expectations, imposing demands to prove to themselves and others that the disease really doesn't matter. Overprotection or overcontrol, like lack of discipline, can become deterrents to a child's healthy social-emotional adjustment.

5. *Alterations in a child's level of dependence/independence.*

Illness itself renders a child more dependent upon adults. A very young child is likely to have an extended "infancy" or period of dependency when illness restricts activity and requires more careful monitoring by parents. Thus, the illness not only imposes a form of dependency during times when a child should be growing more independent, but a child also may learn to behave as a dependent person who fears independent activity.

6. *Side effects of medications.*

Medical treatment can have its own side-effects, causing drowsiness, lessened energy, or associated health problems such as diarrhea or nausea. These may further inhibit activity. Added onto the other symptoms, the child may appear even more "out of it."

7. *Potential emotional effects of illness.*

Illness is not only physically threatening, but it also can be psychologically-emotionally traumatic. Some medical treatments are painful and frightening. Hospitalization can be distressful. Young preschoolers are not likely to understand fully why they are being taken to a strange place and why so many strangers are doing something to them.

Suran and Rizzo (1979) have suggested that young children do not understand the causal relationship involved in illness. They experience illness subjectively or egotistically. If they have sufficient language to describe their condition, they provide psychologically oriented reasons for not feeling good. The pain, medical tests and treatments, and separation from parents are often seen by a young child as punishment for real or imagined misbehavior. Mattsson (1972) described a child with a heart defect who explained he was ill because he had "run too much," a young child with colitis who explained he was sick because he had "eaten something dirty," and a child with diabetes who explained that her sickness came because she had "eaten too much candy."

SUMMARY

Diagnosis of handicapping conditions in young children presents a unique set of problems. The initial identification of disorders in preschoolers or infants is particularly difficult because their behavioral repertoire is so limited. What behaviors are truly deviant is not always clear because of tremendous differences in growth patterns and early behavior of young children. To further complicate matters, early developmental delays initially may be quite mild and not of sufficient severity to allow definite diagnosis. Young children typically are not placed in structured situations where they must perform certain tasks, so their difficulties may not be visible even to adults. For these reasons, many children's disabilities become apparent only when they enter school and specific demands are placed upon them to perform under a rather standardized set of conditions. A large majority of children who are eventually identified as handicapped are so labeled when they have difficulty performing in the classroom and learning academic skills.

Indicators of developmental disorders in young children are often only subtle ones and may be manifest only as slight developmental delays or irregular patterns of behavior. A further complicating factor in identifying young children with developmental problems is that current definitions of handicapping conditions, as contained in PL 94-142, are written primarily in reference to handicapping conditions in older, school-aged students and tend to define the condition of being handicapped in regard to academic performance. Educational performance, however, is not an appropriate point of reference for evaluating the developmental status of preschoolers and infants. Thus, most definitions have limitations as descriptors of the conditions that call for intervention with children under age 5. A more appropriate approach would be to consider a physical, sensory, cognitive, or psychological-emotional condition as handicapping if it interferes with (a) normal growth processes, (b) developmental or maturational processes, and (c) learning processes that occur if a child is able to experience and interact with his or her environment in a normal manner.

Conditions of a physical or sensory nature that can be diagnosed medically or clinically include hearing and vision impairments, physical, orthopedic, and neurological impairments, and health impairments. One of the most important questions to be considered for each handicap is: What are the impacts of this impairment upon the development and learning of young children? This question is of particular significance because those effects are what early intervention programs are designed to prevent or diminish.

In considering physical and sensory impairments, every disorder does not invariably cause a child to be handicapped. A condition is handicapping only if it interferes with a person's ability to learn and function as a normal person might. Medical treatments, surgical procedures, and prosthetic devices alleviate many conditions that once were considered debilitating. Furthermore, children with sensory and physical handicaps can be taught skills that allow them to cope with their disabilities. If adults are supportive to children and help them gain access to experiences that otherwise might be thwarted by disability, other more debilitating outcomes can be averted or minimized.

6
Handicapping Conditions: Behavioral, Speech/Language and Cognitive Problems

Handicaps described in this chapter concern irregularities in children's behavior or performance that may or may not be accompanied by physical abnormalities that can be diagnosed medically. Identification of young children with behavioral problems, speech and language disorders, or cognitive disorders is complicated by lack of clarity as to what is normal and what is abnormal. Societal values play an important part in defining what one labels "abnormal." What is considered subnormal behavior in one culture may be viewed as normal in another. Several issues thus emerge when labeling social behavior, speech and language, or cognitive performance as impaired:

- To what degree must a child's social behavior, speech and language, or cognitive performance be deviant or differ from that of agemates to be considered "impaired" or "abnormal?"
- To what extent must behavior interfere with growth and development in a young child to be considered sufficiently handicapping to warrant referral to an early intervention program and eligibility for services in that program?
- How can abnormality of behavior (and the degree of deviance) be objectively measured and diagnosed in young children? Can reliable diagnoses be made in which several specialists operating independently of one another arrive at the same conclusion? How can early diagnoses of abnormal behavior and performance be kept free of bias from cultural values or from child-rearing practices of ethnic and sociocultural groups?

As you read about various handicaps described in this chapter, keep in mind that no single symptom in itself is indicative of abnormality. A *cluster* of behaviors and poor performance is what gives weight to any diagnosis.

BEHAVIOR PROBLEMS AND DISORDERS

Signs and symptoms of behavior disorders

Whether a young child's behavior is suggestive of emotional disturbance, abnormal or delayed social-emotional development, or simply a transient behavior problem is not easy to determine. Compared to the diagnosis of physical or sensory impairments, in which symptoms are relatively clear-cut and measurable, the designation of emotional or social behavior in young children as abnormal is fraught with difficulties. To label behavior as abnormal involves a subjective judgment of its appropriateness or inappropriateness. On what basis can one make that judgment? Several factors make this task particularly elusive with children under age 5 or 6:

1. *Behavior considered "normal" in young children has a tremendous range.*

What differentiates normal behavior from problem behavior or from truly abnormal behavior is a matter of degree. Normal children reveal the same behaviors as children described as disturbed. Both groups exhibit fears, tantrums, antisocial acts, problems with bowel or bladder control, withdrawal, aggressiveness, or behaviors parents see as troublesome. What distinguishes the two groups are primarily differences in (a) situations in which the behaviors are exhibited, (b) developmental ages at which the behavior appears and continues to be manifest, (c) intensity of the behavior (representing a significant *excess* or *deficiency* compared to other children), (d) duration or persistence of the behavior, (e) extent to which others can alter the behavior, (f) how much the behavior interferes with progress in other areas of development, and (g) how much the behavior interferes with the lives of others.

The difficulty in defining what represents a serious disturbance is this: Because there is such a wide range in what is regarded as normal behavior, there is no clear-cut standard of behavior against which very young children can be judged. Furthermore, many children considered normal do show some "disturbed" behaviors at some time during their formative years (MacFarlane, Allen, & Honzik, 1954; Thomas & Chess, 1977, 1980; Thomas, Chess, & Birch, 1968).

2. *Differences in children's behavior during the formative years are a manifestation, in part, of variations in parents' child-rearing practices, expectations for behavior, and cultural values.*

Parents' styles of child rearing and the models they provide for their children have a tremendous impact on socialization and emotional-personality development in their offspring. Parents from various socioeconomic, religious, cultural, and age groups differ greatly in how they care for and deal with children in matters such as:

— the degree of permissiveness exercised with a child, including the amount of teaching, directing, structuring, helping, and shaping of desired behaviors.

— the manner in which children are allowed to express anger and frustration, including what models parents themselves provide for expressing and controlling aggression.

— the degree of parental control exerted over child behavior, including the extent to which parents are permissive, indulgent, or strict in their tolerance of certain behaviors.

— behavioral and performance expectations placed on young children, including the pressure parents exert on their offspring to master skills in feeding, dressing, toileting, self-control, and independence at various ages.

— the degree to which warmth, physical and verbal affection, and acceptance are communicated in the interactions between parent and child.

— the type of discipline and reinforcement parents use, including the degree to which parents expect blind compliance or evidence of the child's understanding the consequences of his or her own behavior.

Child-rearing practices account for many differences in children's behavior. For example, aggressive parents tend to have aggressive children (Hess, 1970). Children often express and control aggressive behaviors in ways that their parents model (Feshbach, 1970; Jacob, 1975). Parents who tend to be lax, uncaring, and rejecting toward their children but who also apply harsh, hostile, and inconsistent discipline tend to have hostile, aggressive children (Martin, 1975). The effect of any one style of child rearing is shaped by its interaction with the child's psychological-temperamental and biological idiosyncrasies, behavioral repertoire, and developmental stage (Kauffman, 1981).

3. *Children's behavior is especially individualistic during the early years, before they are placed in structured situations that press for conformity to parental and societal standards of conduct.*

Once children begin school, they all share in a common social-education experience that consumes nearly 8 hours of each week day. This common experience allows certain assumptions to be made about what children have been exposed to, what they should be able to do, and how they should behave in social situations. Given these standards and assumptions, defining behavioral deviance among school-aged students is easier. But for preschoolers and infants, few common experiences can be assumed. Given the highly diversified lifestyles in our country, along with regional and cultural differences in child care, assumptions cannot always be made about what very small children should be able to do. Developmental milestones associated with motor, language, cognitive, and self-help skills are the only markers one can use. Even here, however, children show considerable variation.

Individuality and behavioral differences in young children also result from their unique temperamental characteristics. *Temperament* is a child's behavioral style or characteristic way of responding to situations within the environment or to encounters with people. Children's temperament greatly affects how others respond to them.

Results of a 20-year longitudinal study conducted by Thomas and his associates (1963, 1968, 1977) suggested that children generally fall under three temperamental categories. Some youngsters are described by their parents as "difficult"—hard to care for, hard to manage, and sometimes hard to tolerate. *Difficult children* evidence irregularity in biological functions, negative withdrawal responses to new stimuli, frequent and loud crying periods, slow adaptability to change, and frustration expressed through frequent tantrums. Other youngsters are described as "easy" to care for. *Easy children* are characterized by adaptability, approach responses to strangers or new situations, biological regularity, predominant positive moods of mild to moderate intensity, and some tolerance of frustration. A final group is composed of *slow-to-warm-up-children*. These youngsters show initial mild negative responses to new stimuli that become positive if given time, slow adaptability, and some irregularity in biological functions (eating, sleeping, or elimination).

The Thomas study noted that children described as "difficult" seem at greater risk for developing behavior problems and disorders. Some 40% of the "difficult" children, compared to 18% of those described as "easy," experienced behavior problems requiring psychiatric attention. This does not mean that certain behavior styles in a young child in themselves lead to behavior problems. The study concluded that the key factor is in the interaction between temperamental styles and the child's environment. For example, an outgoing child who repeatedly is subjected to negative experiences and punished for being socially assertive likely will become more withdrawn.

4. *Social-emotional and personality characteristics of young children are evolving and are highly influenced by their particular stage of development.*

Children's behavior should be evaluated in terms of the particular stage of growth and what is considered developmentally appropriate for that stage. Many difficulties in adaptation manifested by children are stage-specific and often self-corrective. Every child's development typically progresses and lags unevenly across the various areas. Consequently, defining a problem behavior as an overriding personality trait or behavioral pattern is difficult.

One of the most plaguing problems in defining disorders among children under age 5 is that traditional labels and diagnostic approaches are derived largely from approaches used with adults. Hobbs (1975) argued that generalizing from the adult system for diagnosing and categorizing psychological disorders to children carries two questionable and harmful implications. First, it implies that children are miniature adults—a perspective that ignores developmental considerations in defining what behaviors are actually abnormal in young children. Second, it implies that disorders or behavior problems in early childhood are preliminary stages to analogous adult pathological conditions, and hence are precursors to later difficulties. Research does not support this conclusion. Many behavior problems in early childhood do not carry on into adulthood (except in cases of severe disorder).

A second problem is that many evaluations of deviant behavior are based upon adult expectations for acceptable patterns of behavior. Thus, classifications of behavior disorders are based to a large extent on *adult judgments* of social transgressions or deficiencies in social performance (Achenbach & Edelbrock, 1978). These diagnostic labels fail to reflect the developmental status of children or the variations in behavior that are so typical of them. Interpreting a young child's behavior is highly dependent upon the developmental stage he or she is in at the time.

All this points to a major dilemma—the lack of an appropriate system for evaluating and describing behavioral problems and disorders among preschoolers, toddlers, and infants. How does one sort out what are truly disturbed behaviors that warrant treatment from what are natural developmental "traumas" of children who are struggling to master expected social and personal skills? Because of the uniqueness of behavior difficulties that concern young children (i.e., high situational specificity, fluctuations, and interweavings with developmental stages), more descriptive diagnostic systems are needed. Pragmatically, information on a young child's overall social-emotional status is at least as important as a broad label defining real or supposed pathology. Simply stated, *the need to describe the behavior of young children accurately is greater than the need to label it.*

5. *Many behavior problems or disturbed behaviors of young children are transient difficulties associated with a particular developmental period and are not likely to continue into later developmental stages.*

Some behaviors, such as destructiveness, shyness, somberness, and attention-demanding behaviors, tend to persist into the teenage years *if* they are apparent at age 6 or 7 (Robins, 1972). But problem behaviors prior to that time are not good predictors of children's emotional-social status years later (Kauffman, 1981; Rutter, Birch, Thomas, & Chess, 1964; MacFarlane, Allen, & Honzik, 1954). Some behavior difficulties arise simply as a child attempts to master early developmental milestones (e.g., establishing independence and developing a separate identity from the mothering figure). Toilet training and feeding bring their own unique traumas or intermittent crises, which most children and parents survive! Children normally experience fears that they gradually overcome as they become more secure and familiar with the object or things feared. Approximately 40%-50% of all children reveal some types of fears. Many fears are age-specific. Fears commonly found among small children, according to Miller, Barrett, and Hampe (1974) and Sroufe (1977), include:

Common Childhood Fears	*Approximate Age of Appearance*
loud noises, loss of support	0-6 months
strangers	6-9 months
separation from primary caregiver, injury, or situations associated with toileting	12 months (1 year)
imaginary creatures, robbers, and death	24 months (2 years)
dogs, being left alone	36 months (3 years)
darkness	48 months (4 years)

A historical study by MacFarlane, Allen, and Honzik (1954) on developmental problems in children from 21 months to 14 years revealed that most children display certain developmental problems at various age levels. Their data, presented in Table 6.1,

Table 6.1

Manifestations of Various Problem Behaviors
in "Normal" Children at Various Age Levels

Problem	Sex	Percent of Problem Incidence				
		Age 1¾	Age 3	Age 5	Age 10	Age 14
Disturbing	B	16	29	20	33	6
dreams	G	13	29	29	47	4
Nocturnal	B	75	18	8	11	11
enuresis	G	73	31	10	6	0
Soiling	B	32	4	3	0	0
	G	20	0	0	0	0
Tics and	B	0	0	5	0	0
mannerisms	G	3	4	5	0	0
Nail biting	B	5	8	8	18	33
	G	3	10	17	32	22
Thumb sucking	B	21	18	5	0	0
	G	33	35	19	6	0
Excessive	B	29	37	46	26	11
activity	G	17	33	35	15	0
Speech	B	30	24	18	11	0
problems	G	17	18	8	3	4
Lying	B	0	14	49	15	6
	G	0	12	42	12	0
Stealing	B	7	12	10	4	0
	G	3	18	4	0	0

Note. Adapted from *A Developmental Study of the Behavior Problems of Normal Children Between Twenty-One Months and Fourteen Years* (pp. 66-67) by J.W. MacFarlane, L. Allen, and M.P. Honzik, 1954, Berkeley: University of California Press. Used by permission.

indicate that many children considered "normal" exhibit behaviors at some time in their lives that could be considered pathological or indicative of underlying difficulties. These behavior problems usually are transitory and disappear within a few weeks or years unless they are severe and involve hostile, aggressive, and destructive elements (McCaffrey & Cumming, 1969).

6. *Behavioral manifestations of various impairments or disorders during the early years have considerable overlap, which causes difficulty in determining whether a behavior is indicative of a certain disorder.*

The symptoms manifested by children considered mildly mentally retarded, learning disabled, or mildly or moderately disturbed have more similarities than differences. Because children with severe retardation or emotional disturbance share many common characteristics, distinguishing between them is not easy. Neither is the distinction clear between some behaviors of a severely disturbed child and behaviors of one who is deaf, blind, or brain damaged (Balthazar & Stevens, 1975; Wing, 1966). The younger the child is, the more difficult this becomes.

Perhaps what really matters most with young children is not the labeling but, rather, what adults must do to aid a child in moving through difficult stages of growth. Debating whether a youngster is emotionally disturbed or retarded seems useless. And to spend valuable time attempting to apply a categorical label that still fails to describe the deviant behaviors is equally nonproductive. In essence, the author questions whether a diagnosis of "emotional disturbance" is even appropriate for very young children (except perhaps in very severe cases).

Distinguishing between disturbing behavior, behavior problem, and disordered behavior

So how does one recognize symptoms that suggest disturbance and separate those from the everyday problems that are a normal part of children's early social-emotional development? First, remember that all children—especially very young ones—vary in their behavior from day to day. Second, remember that preschoolers and infants are highly influenced by conditions in their environment that create insecurity, cause discomfort, disrupt bodily functions, or arouse anxiety. Many inappropriate, troublesome behaviors are merely temporary reactions to physical states or frightening experiences. Youngsters who observe parents fighting or overhear a heated adult discussion often react with anxiety and fear. Tiredness, hunger, or illness can disrupt normal patterns of behavior. A 3- or 4-year-old can be overly aggressive and quarrelsome with peers one day and then become ill the next day. If a child is frequently ill or suffers from chronic allergies that interfere with overall feelings of well-being, problems might be more frequent.

Disturbing behavior is usually disruptive to others and bothersome to adults, but it generally does not suggest a serious emotional problem. Disturbing or bothersome behaviors are simply more apparent and less controlled in young children than they are in older children and adults. Disturbing behavior can become a more prevalent pattern in children's acts if it is reinforced or if it brings attention that a child cannot get through appropriate behavior. Disturbing behaviors also can be actions that are characteristic of a child's own temperament but that represent a mismatch with a parent's behavior styles. For example, a child who is energetic, aggressive, exceedingly curious and into everything can be disturbing to a parent who is less active, easy-going, and lacks the energy to trail after the child to provide supervision.

A true *behavior problem* not only is disturbing to those who supervise and care for a child but also is disruptive to the child's own activities and those of siblings and peers. Behavior problems are often learned behaviors. Or they may be attributed to immaturity, lack of social skill, or a child's inability to deal with frustration or anger in socially appropriate ways. Problem behaviors are usually situation-specific and are not necessarily indicative of personality "patterns." A 4-year-old boy may behave acceptably when his older sister is present, but when his sister is elsewhere, he may become noncompliant and overly aggressive with playmates. Another child may play satisfactorily when she has her own toys and is not expected to share with others, but if other children attempt to share the same toys, she may withdraw and simply let the others take over. Problem behaviors are usually malleable through adult guidance and reinforcement for more desired forms of behavior. If problems have become habitual, change requires more time and effort and may even necessitate change in parents' own actions toward their child or require professional intervention.

Finally, *seriously disordered behaviors,* suggestive of a real emotional disorder, are manifest in more pervasive modes of behavior and moods that interfere more broadly with interpersonal relationships. With very young children, seriously disturbed behavior is more likely to be manifest in failure to establish meaningful interactive social behaviors and in the presence of persistent maladaptive behaviors. If continued, these behaviors likely will interfere with development and learning experiences that a child needs to move on to more mature stages of development. Bizarre or purposeless activities that can become physically harmful to others or to the child himself or herself are prevalent here. The most significant characteristic of children with disordered behavior is that it typically involves a pattern or cluster of *many* inappropriate behaviors. Usually children with seriously disturbed or disordered behavior manifest deviance across such a wide array of situations that it can be considered a characteristic trait or pattern of behaving (Kauffman, 1981; Phillips, Draguns, & Bartlett, 1975; Rhodes & Paul, 1978).

In summary, several questions should be asked to help clarify if the symptoms a child exhibits are suggestive of serious emotional disorder, a behavior problem, or just a disturbing behavior that is largely an inconvenience to adults:

Developmental appropriateness:	Are the behaviors inappropriate for a child at this developmental stage, and are they significantly different from those observed in other children at this level?
Degree of deviation:	Is the behavior excessive or exceedingly limited compared to that of other children at the same developmental level?
Generalizability of behavior:	Is the problem specific to certain situations, or is it pervasive across most activities in which the child engages?
Duration of behavior:	Is the behavior(s) persistent and resistive to modification?
Pervasiveness of behavior:	Are just one or two problem behaviors of concern, or does the child show a pattern or cluster of behaviors that are deviant for his or her developmental level?
Functional impact of troublesome behavior:	Are the child's behaviors disruptive to his or her own ability to learn, to participate in the normal activities in which peers engage, and to form age-appropriate social relationships? Or are the behaviors primarily troublesome because they are inconvenient to adults or represent a mismatch in behavioral-temperamental style with the primary caregivers?

The nature of behavior problems and disorders

Most textbooks on emotional disturbance or psychopathology focus primarily upon disorders and symptoms manifested in school-aged students or in adults. Few address problems unique to children under age 5, except in cases of extreme disturbance such as early infantile autism and childhood schizophrenia. To give an overview of problems encountered in youngsters of preschool age and younger, brief descriptions are given here of (a) severe emotional disorders that are pathological, and (b) developmental behavior problems that can be considered deviant or normal depending on other factors.

For more detailed information on childhood emotional disorders, see Schwartz and Johnson's (1981) book *Psychopathology of Childhood;* Samuels' (1981) book *Disturbed Exceptional Children;* and Erickson's (1978) book *Child Psychopathology: Assessment, Etiology, and Treatment.*

Severe emotional disorders   Childhood psychosis is the most severe form of behavior disorders because so many aspects of behavior are affected. Several diagnostic labels are used interchangeably to refer to psychosis in children: childhood schizophrenia, autism, and psychosis. In recent years the trend has been to recognize two distinct forms of childhood psychosis: autism and childhood schizophrenia. Because of inconsistency in terminology and in the criteria for diagnosis, the incidence of childhood psychosis is not precisely known. Data do show that it occurs more frequently in boys than girls during childhood—three boys to one girl (Rosen, Bahn, & Kramer, 1964; Rutter & Lockyer, 1967). This ratio becomes more equal during adolescence. Werry (1972) has estimated that the incidence of psychosis during childhood is between .008% and .06% but noted that it accounts for 3%-9% of children seen in clinics. The onset of psychosis may occur at any age from birth on. The most severe forms of psychosis begin during the early preschool years. Actual diagnosis, however, often is made several years after symptoms are initially manifest.

Infantile autism is believed to originate very early, with onset of symptoms before 2½ years of age and usually during the first year. Parents describe their infant as uncuddly and socially unresponsive. These infants fail to make postural adjustments to being held and may seem deaf even though their hearing is normal. They seem happiest if left alone, and they engage in excessive repetition of body movements. Rocking and head banging are common. During the second year the child's lack of social responsiveness is more glaring. Autistic children do not make eye contact and are not particularly responsive to the sound of a person's voice. Speech is absent or delayed at the time when other children are rapidly learning names of objects and people in their environment. Gross deficits in language development (e.g., in functional use of language) are apparent.

Psychologists report that autistic characteristics become especially pronounced around age 3-4 years. This is when most autistic children are referred and diagnosed. Other characteristic behaviors of these children include: difficulty in playing with other children, failure to relate verbally to adults, echolalic speech (an "echoing" response, repeating what someone else says), insensitivity to sound and sometimes pain, a general aura of aloofness, obsessive insistence on sameness of routines or surroundings in the environment (a change may produce extreme tantrums), preoccupation with mechanical objects or use of those objects in strange and stereotypic ways. Stereotyped body movements, such as spinning objects, rocking, whirling, or hand waving for extended periods, are common (Wing, 1969, 1976; Rimland, 1964, 1971; Kanner, 1965)

Considerable controversy surrounds the issue of what causes infantile autism. Explanations range from psychological factors such as a disturbed mother-infant relationship (Speers & Lansing, 1964; Bettelheim, 1967) to organic abnormalities (Ornitz, 1978; Rimland, 1964). Perceptual impairment also has been suggested as a cause of autism (Ornitz & Ritvo, 1968; Schopler, 1965; Ornitz, 1974). A biological explanation seems logical for three reasons: (a) Symptoms appear shortly after birth, making a psychological or environmental explanation less likely, (b) the disorder occurs more frequently in boys than girls, which is consistent with a biogenic explanation, and (c) the presence of autistic-like behavior in children with known brain damage and the remarkable similarities between autistic children further support a biogenic explanation.

Childhood schizophrenia is manifest in children through symptoms similar to those of adult schizophrenia—thought disorder, delusions, hallucinations, and altered mood. Schizophrenic children usually seem relatively normal until the symptoms of disturbed thinking begin to appear before age 6. Onset may be gradual, with the child showing initial symptoms of neurotic behavior.

Specific symptoms of schizophrenia vary. Diagnostic criteria, originally presented by Potter (1933), typically are based on a combination of characteristics including:

— withdrawal of interest in the environment and deficits in emotional rapport with peers or adults (Potter, 1933; Hingtgen & Bryson, 1972).
— decreased speech output, even mutism (Potter, 1933).
— repetitious language in which content and affect are unrelated or the child may revert to the use of some private language (Erickson, 1978; Clarizio & McCoy, 1976).
— moods, actions, and thinking that are inappropriate and unrelated to reality; voice may show little emotion (Goldfarb, Braunstein, & Lorgo, 1956; Potter, 1933).
— bizarre and repetitive movements and possible hyperactivity or underactivity for age (Potter, 1933).
— normal or exceptional intellectual skill concurrent with intellectual awkwardness (e.g., child may show extraordinary ability to remember dates or events while simultaneously showing inability to connect thinking with reality) (Werry, 1972).

Rimland (1964) and Prior, Perry, and Gajzago (1975) noted several differences between schizophrenia and autism in children. A most apparent one is that schizophrenic children have more varied symptoms and engage in more human contact than do autistic children. Other differences are: (a) Autism appears shortly after birth whereas schizophrenia is manifest following a period of more or less normal development; (b) autistic youngsters usually are described as physically healthy and good looking; schizophrenic children are sickly or nondistinctive physically; (c) autistic children or infants are not responsive to being picked up and cuddled; schizophrenic youngsters rarely are described this way; (d) the need to preserve sameness in the environment or in routines is unique to autism; (e) echolalia is common to autism but not to schizophrenia; (f) autistic children often show remarkable manual dexterity in tasks requiring fine motor coordination; schizophrenic children are more likely to be uncoordinated; and (g) the autistic child's language is grossly impaired and is characterized by prenominal reversal (saying pronouns as they are heard so that the child refers to himself or herself as "you" instead of "I," etc.); the schizophrenic child displays normal developmental speech, although it is often used to produce noncommunicative content.

Common developmental behavior problems   Some difficulties are common to most children at certain ages, whether they are considered normal or emotionally disturbed. These difficulties come and go and typically do not endure over a very long time. In severely disturbed children the same behaviors are manifest in greater numbers and in more exaggerated, severe, and perseverative forms. Common developmental problems present a challenge to every parent even though they are normal accompaniments to a child's passage through various phases of growth, maturation, and learning. A few of the more typical ones are discussed here.

Eating problems are frequent among young children. They eat too little or refuse food, eat too much, or ingest inedible substances (a behavior called *pica*). Finicky eating can be a problem in infants and preschoolers. Sometimes eating problems evolve out of poor modeling by parents and siblings. Adults' eating habits may be viewed as appropriate for adults (e.g., gulping food or using their hands instead of utensils as they race to catch the bus), but if imitated by a small child who is expected to sit in a chair at the table and eat with a spoon, the behavior is considered troublesome. The great majority of children are simply reflecting normal developmental patterns in eating or learned behaviors, but parent and child can readily create tug-of-wars over what, when, and how much food is eaten.

Several factors may be operating when young children develop eating problems. Illness causes a decrease in food intake. An overly anxious or upset child often refuses food or goes to the other extreme and eats excessively. Fatigue, overstimulation, and inadequate exercise are additional factors. Vomiting of food is common in young children, especially infants, as a result of swallowed air, overfeeding, allergies, or illness. Riding in cars produces nausea in some children. Persistent regurgitation in infancy may suggest an obstruction in the digestive system. Some young children are more prone to vomit than are others. This can be triggered by highly stimulating events or stressful experiences associated with food. Given the variety of conditions in which young children can become nauseated, previously neutral stimuli can become the conditioned stimuli for vomiting.

Behavior modification programs can be helpful in eliminating these conditioned problems and other eating difficulties. Consistent routines for eating, avoidance of rushed mealtimes during which a child is pressured to eat—and eat quickly—and maintenance of a pleasant, reinforcing atmosphere during meals all help in teaching young children appropriate eating behaviors. Control of continuous snacking between meals also can help parents gain better control over their child's eating behaviors.

Fears, especially mild ones, are common among children (as described earlier). Most youngsters work through and overcome their fears as they move on to new developmental stages and new levels of personal competence. In fact, children without any fears are highly unusual and likely would be of concern to a parent because of their increased vulnerability to danger. Fears of falling and of loud noises are present in normal infants at birth. Fear of strange persons, objects, or new situations appears during the first year and is replaced with new fears during the preschool and primary years. Some fears appear to have a survival function and are considered normal and adaptive, not deviant.

Most experts suggest that adults should recognize fears as a normal phenomenon that simply requires reassurance and support by parents and caregivers. If activities become unnecessarily inhibited by a child's fearfulness, intervention is needed. Extreme irrational fear that is disproportionate to the reality of the situation (a *phobia*) requires helpful support from adults to allow children to learn more about the objects they fear and to gain confidence. To force confrontation or belittle a child because of his or her fears likely will increase the intensity of the fear and diminish the child's feeling of self-worth and competence. Given time and reassurance, most fears are transient and pass within a few weeks or months. A few fears may continue beyond a year. Adults should be careful to not allow a child's fears to become instrumental in manipulating others or avoiding things he or she does not want to do. In such cases, parents may inadvertently reinforce the fear. Children with fears that are actually pathological typically show additional symptoms that suggest deeper emotional difficulties.

Temper tantrums and aggressive behavior are sometimes displayed as children learn how to express anger and how to manifest appropriate forms of aggression. This is a normal part of early development and socialization. Parents should teach and model to a young child how to handle frustration or anger in ways that are not unduly inappropriate. At the same time, parents should not try to totally inhibit the expression of aggressive behavior. Assertiveness and competitiveness are healthy derivatives of aggressiveness and are necessary behaviors for effective functioning in our society—provided they are exhibited in socially accepted ways.

Temper tantrums are violent outbreaks of anger expressed by crying, screaming, and bodily movement that may involve hitting, kicking, throwing, or destroying property. Infants initally express anger and frustration in physical ways, such as kicking and screaming. As they become mobile and begin to interact with others, they vent frustration in more social ways, striking out at other people or making verbal outbursts such as "I don't like you!" or "I hate you!" As a child strives for autonomy and becomes more independent, clashes with parents are inevitable. As social interactions with agemates increase, inevitable frictions arise between peers. This is a normal part of learning and growing up. Although frictions are not necessarily desirable outlets, they do not mean that a child (especially a very young child) is a "bad person."

Parents can play an especially important role in helping a youngster learn how to express anger and solve conflicts with playmates. Their own behavior serves as a major role model for their child. Some parents punish their child for an outburst of aggressive behavior by flaring up themselves, screaming an angry retort, and showing excessive aggressiveness toward the child through harsh physical punishment. Unfortunately, they are modeling the very behavior they punish in their own child. Physical punishment of aggression may actually increase, rather than decrease, undesired behavior in a child (Bandura, 1973).

Withdrawal and social isolation is not an all-or-nothing problem. All youngsters exhibit withdrawn behavior under some circumstances. Social responsiveness varies, too, among young children. Two types of withdrawal are relevant to young children: (a) social isolation, and (b) more profound withdrawal, as is often found with severe emotional disorders. Closely allied with withdrawal behavior are two other behavioral deficiencies— immaturity and inadequacy.

Overly shy or withdrawing behavior is usually of less concern in young children until they are placed in social situations such as preschool or kindergarten classes. In those settings, withdrawing behaviors can interfere with participation in group activities or social interactions that promote the learning of social skills. Social withdrawal or isolationism in young children can arise from or be maintained by several factors: (a) constraints of over-restrictive parents, punishment of social approach responses or inadvertent reinforcement of nonsocial behavior, (b) lack of social experience or opportunities to practice social reciprocity with other children, (c) lack of exposure to people outside the immediate family and, hence, shyness or fearfulness of unfamiliar social situations and people, (d) anxiety or fearfulness associated with interactions with others resulting possibly from previous experiences that were threatening or unpleasant, and (e) temperamental qualities that cause a child to be more quiet, withdrawing, and perhaps less adaptive in behavior style.

Some children show more severe forms of withdrawal evidenced by an inability to relate to parents or peers and by unresponsiveness to social stimuli. Mild forms of shyness are not abnormal. Most young children show separation anxiety when they are away from their parents for the first time. Withdrawal is usually transitory as a child becomes more familiar with the situation and the people in it. But withdrawal and social isolation, if they persist, can result in cumulative worsening of the condition. By not interacting with others, a child misses experiences that lead to greater social competency and confidence. This leads to more social isolation. By failing to learn play skills that allow young children to hold their own in the play group and to protect their own interests, they are easier targets for aggression and can be bypassed by more assertive, skillful peers. Gottman, Gonso, and Schuler (1976) suggested that this cycle can be broken only by specific intervention aimed at teaching social skills to these withdrawing children.

Problems with elimination vary considerably because children differ greatly in the ages when they attain bowel and bladder control. According to Erickson (1978), almost 70% of all children achieve bowel control by age 2, and 90% by age 4. Control over urination comes more slowly, and day-time control is achieved earlier than night-time control. Roughly 75%-80% of 4- to 5-year-olds have achieved nocturnal control (Schaefer, 1979). These figures suggest that a child can be expected to display day- and night-time bladder control by age 5 or so and to have bowel control somewhat earlier. Successful toilet training is the result of learning and of sufficient maturation in the nervous system to inhibit strong natural reflexes. Sometimes progress is delayed because of immaturity in nervous system development, inadequate learning, or emotionally linked reasons. Although all young children do have accidents and can be inconsistent in their toileting skills in early stages of learning, more serious difficulties sometimes occur.

Enuresis is the failure to develop control over urination after an age when the majority of children have done so. Diagnostic criteria for enuresis outlined by the American Psychiatric Association (1980) *DSM III Manual* are:

— repeated, involuntary urination day- or night-time.
— at least two such events per month for children ages 5-6 and at least one per month for older children.
— not due to physical disorders such as diabetes or a seizure disorder.

Chronic enuresis involves cases in which the child never learned to control urination or to urinate only in appropriate places. In *regressive enuresis*, a child achieved control at one time but has reverted back to day- or night-time wetting.

Encopresis refers to the failure to control defecation after age 3 or 4. Diagnostic criteria defined by the American Psychiatric Association (1980) *DSM III Manual* include:

— repeated voluntary or involuntary passage of feces of normal or near normal consistency in places not appropriate within a child's sociocultural environment.
— at least one such event a month after a child is 4 years old.
— not due to a physical disorder.

Encopresis often involves periods of excessive fecal retention alternating with periods of soiling. Extended bowel retention over time can result in internal hardening of fecal matter. Stools can become so impacted and large that defecation is painful. Once this happens, a child may withhold bowel movements even more to avoid pain. If this continues, a child may be physically unable to eliminate the large, compacted stools and medical or therapeutic intervention is necessary.

Ross (1980) noted that difficulties associated with defining psychological disorders in young children are also true in regard to defining what is a real problem in elimination. Whether bed wetting in a 4- to 5-year-old represents a true "psychological-emotional" problem is an arbitrary decision and must be made individually with each child. The family-home environment must be taken into consideration in assessing the seriousness of these events. In some families, bed wetting at any age is accepted as an expected, unremarkable occurrence. Other families are concerned if a 3-year-old is unable to sleep without wetting. In the final analysis, the child's social-cultural environment determines if a behavior is problematic. Once a behavior is viewed as unacceptable, the response of the environment to the behavior makes it a behavior problem.

Difficulties associated with elimination easily become overlaid with emotional-behavioral reactions—by the child as well as the parents. When these children come to the attention of professional psychotherapists, they likely have already acquired some conditioned anxiety to the stimuli associated with wetting or fecal soiling. These stimuli (such as sensations associated with sphincter release or actual urination or defecation) are the same whether elimination is done appropriately or inappropriately. Anxiety reactions become associated with these stimuli, creating an incompatible response when it is elicited while a child is on the toilet.

Part of the treatment involves discrimination training so that toilet cues do not elicit anxiety responses and toilet-avoiding behaviors. A further problem associated with encopresis and enuresis is the image children build of themselves. Having failed at learning "what any baby can learn" or to please their parents in what is an obviously important accomplishment (to "be dry" or to "use the potty"), these children can learn to see themselves as inadequate, bad or naughty, dirty, worthless, or not a "good boy" or "good girl." The child may interpret parents' reactions to their soiling or wetting as "they don't love me," thus increasing feelings of insecurity.

Hyperactivity is a behavior characterized by restless motor activity, short attention span, impulsiveness, and distractibility (Chess & Hassibi, 1978; Kauffman, 1981). Hyperactive children seem to have little tolerance for frustration. They may show rapid mood changes ranging from withdrawal to aggression. Their short attention span is shown in a lot of seemingly random, erratic behavior. A young child appears to "flit" around a preschool environment, working at any one task for only a short time before moving on to something else. Play with a toy is started but usually left unfinished. Also, perseveration (continuation of behavior after it is no longer appropriate or functional) is often associated with hyperactivity. The combination of restless-impulsive activity along with the short attention span, erratic emotional state, and low frustration tolerance reduces the child's ability to engage in constructive learning. Furthermore, the child's behavior serves to fragment and disrupt experience in ways that do not allow pursuit of more complex tasks or learning sequences.

What represents excessive activity and a true "problem" is again an arbitrary decision.

The tolerance level of the child's environment, the values and priorities of adults within it, and the situation(s) in which the hyperactivity is manifest are perhaps the best criteria. Young children typically are very active. Child-rearing practices at home influence how much children learn to control and focus their behavior. Relatively few restrictions or rules of conduct are placed upon some children during their toddler and preschool years. Their behavior is likely to be quite different from children who are expected to follow adult instructions, sit quietly, and play at a task for an extended time.

Werry et al. (1972) speculated that a so-called hyperactive child is a problem only because adults place a high value on other kinds of behavior. The demand for controlled, quiet, and focused behavior increases when a child enters preschool and later moves into the elementary grades. Because classroom environments impose greater structure, the number of children described as "hyperactive" not surprisingly increases in the primary grades.

Hyperactivity in young children represents another kind of problem in that it can place them at greater risk for accidents because of their lack of skill or inability to anticipate the consequences of their actions. Adults become more frustrated by an excessively active, impulsive child who must be watched constantly. Whether hyperactivity is indicative of neurological problems or minimal brain damage is difficult to ascertain in young children unless they have other symptoms. But the behavior itself may be problematic and thus will require training and reinforcement of more desired behavior patterns.

The impact of behavior problems/disorders on development and learning

Severe emotional disorders in young children are not common. If they are present at such a young age, the possibility of underlying organic or biochemical abnormalities and other disorders is high (Rutter, 1972; White, 1974). In these cases, the disturbance is often pervasive and disruptive to every aspect of development. For example, children with childhood schizophrenia or autism may show difficulties in basic functions such as digestion and elimination, motor coordination, cognitive functions, emotional responsiveness, independence skills, and functional use of language. Most experts view the prognosis for improvement in children with severe emotional disorders at such a young age to be rather dismal (M. DeMyer, 1975; Ornitz, Guthrie, & Farley, 1977; Rhodes & Paul, 1978; Rutter, 1974).

The impact of problematic behaviors on a child's development can best be understood if we remember that children live and grow in the context of a social environment. Children play an active part in their own socialization. Just as parents are (to some degree) molders of children, children mold the behavior of their parents. A child with troublesome, maladaptive behavior can make caregiving tasks more difficult and less reinforcing for parents. An engaging, happy child who smiles and responds readily to adults is often the one who gets a great deal of positive attention.

As for the majority of children with mild social-emotional problems, no single set of impacts applies to all children. Effects of problematic behavior are individual for each child. Some *potential* consequences of emotional difficulties upon development, learning, and social relationships are:

1. *Potential disruption in the establishment of reciprocal patterns of social interaction with caregivers.*

When a child's actions are maladaptive, socially inappropriate, and include problematic behaviors, chances are greater for a "mismatch" between the child's temperament and that of parents' temperament and caregiving skills. Given a mismatch and lack of synchrony in parent-child interactions, probabilities are higher that parents will deliver more negative feedback, less positive social praise, and reduce their level of social interaction with the child.

Young children, including infants, are not passive recipients of their caregiver's attentions. From an early age, infant-caregiver interactions are reciprocal as they engage in what is termed "behavioral dialogues" (Bakeman & Brown, 1977). Behavior of one elicits certain responses in the other, and a reciprocal system of responding is created with each participant shaping and modifying the behavior of the other. The result is a mutual interaction system of adaptation (or lack of one) and a set of expectations that develop over time. As a active participant in an interaction, an infant or young child helps to sustain interaction sequences, which in turn promote increasingly more complex forms of social exchange. Thus, the child's own behavior acts as a stimulus for the caregiver and helps shape the nature of the interactions that occur (Thoman, 1980; Green, Gustafson, & West, 1980).

2. *Potential disruptions in attachment and the development or affectional bonds.*

An important social milestone early in life is the attachment or affectional bonding between infant and caregiver. Usually this is the mother, although attachment can occur with any person who is particularly sensitive or responsive to the child's needs. This reciprocal attachment is important to a child's social-emotional development, as well as the development of a nurturing parent-child relationship. Attachment is equally important for the parent since it appears to promote more positive interactions and greater competence in the child's social behavior (Ainsworth, 1969; Tracy, Lamb, & Ainsworth, 1976).

When a child's own behavior makes caregiving trying, excessively tiring, and lacking in the reinforcement that brings satisfaction to the caregiver, normal attachment may be absent or delayed. Parents may protect their own feelings about themselves as people or as parents and deal with their disappointment and hurt by withdrawing emotionally to invest their efforts in other family members. (See chapter 10 for a further discussion of attachment and parent-child interactions.)

3. *Potential negative influences upon the formation of self-identity and self-concept.*

A child's own negative or problematic behavior may be mirrored back to him or her in ways that affect the evolving sense of self. Interactions with others, their reciprocation, and the messages others convey to a child about his or her worth bear tremendously upon the concept of self. Most basic to a child's sense of self is the acquisition of a physical self-concept or body awareness. This emerges during the second year and is evidenced as a child learns to point at body parts, such as "my nose," "my tummy," and to show self-recognition in a mirror. Social feedback contributes to a child's view of self as others give positive or negative responses. These messages communicate expectations of the child and judgments about him or her. A child then forms concepts about himself or herself (e.g., I'm a good boy or I'm a bad boy; I'm smart or I'm stupid; Mama likes me or Mama doesn't like me; I'm pretty or I'm not pretty).

A final contribution to self-concept is a child's own experiences of success or failure, pleasure or punishment, criticism or praise. As children meet the expectations of others, rewards and other forms of pleasure, which help them feel good about themselves, are forthcoming. Success—and clear, consistent recognition of that success—is an important ingredient for a healthy self-concept. Children who fail to meet others' expectations begin to associate unpleasant feelings and anxiety with the situation and the people involved. Page and Garwood (1979) suggested that an attitude of high self-regard and competence guides children's behavior toward increasing competence (or at least maintaining that competence). Children who learn to view themselves as bad or incompetent are more likely to be self-defeating and pessimistic about their potential for success. They then may avoid situations that require cognitive or social achievement. As a result, they miss the very opportunities that could change their growing negative self-image.

4. *Potential interference in the mastery of social skills and in the development of security and confidence, which help a child enter readily into activities that promote further learning.*

Problematic behaviors can interfere with the growth of appropriate attentional and social behaviors that promote efficient learning. Motivation to learn also may be altered. Children who acquire effective social interaction skills have an advantage over those who are less skilled. Waldrop and Halverson (1975) noted that children considered socially competent at 2½ years of age are likely to be socially skilled at 7½ years of age. Those described as friendly, socially involved, and skilled in dealing with peers at 2½ are described at age 7 as socially at-ease, and more involved in peer interactions and group decision-making processes with peers. In contrast, socially isolated, unsociable youngsters are more likely to develop behavior problems.

In short, a circular relationship seems to exist between a child's behavior and his or her own development. Problem behaviors can interfere with skill learning. A lack of social competency, in turn, can promote social-emotional problems. Through social experience beginning in early childhood, children soon build expectations of themselves and others. These expectations affect a child's behavior style, motivation, and willingness to venture out into new experiences. Children are believed to acquire an expectancy for success or failure depending upon the previous success-to-failure ratio (Rotter, 1954; Bandura, 1977; Bandura & Harris, 1966). Ross (1980) suggested that children as young as age 2 or 3 become aware of the judgments others make of them in comparing them to agemates. They soon become capable of making these same comparisons themselves.

Children's own behavior can be helpful or disruptive to good parenting. Erickson (1963) postulated that these social dynamics shape children's development as they move through several stages during which they acquire a basic sense of trust or mistrust (infancy), a growing sense of autonomy or shame and doubt (around 1½-3 years of age), and initiative versus guilt (around 3-5 years). How parents react to and interact with their offspring affects whether the child acquires a sense of trust, autonomy, and initiative.

SPEECH AND LANGUAGE DISORDERS

Early signs and symptoms of speech and language impairments

Speech and language are part of a complex and interrelated *communication process*. Although acquisition of these skills proceeds in predictable sequences, the rate of learning and the sophistication or use of communication tools vary greatly among children. The quality and quantity of children's communicative development are affected by many variables: culture, experience, richness of the early environment, and the speech/language patterns of adults around them. Compared to hearing and vision impairments, which can be measured precisely, or to physical-organic disabilities, which are manifest in concrete ways, assessment of how normal or abnormal a young child's speech and language skills are is much less objective.

What is the difference between speech and language?   Signs and symptoms of evolving communication difficulties may involve three separate but closely related entities: language, oral speech, and the functional-practical use of communication as a social tool. _Language_ refers to an arbitrary code system or set of rules involving grammatical structures used to transmit meaning from one person to another. The most common code system is spoken language, but others include computer language, sign language used by deaf persons, and Morse code. When we speak of a child's language development, we mean the child's comprehension of meaning from words and ability to apply grammatical structures to express meaning.

Children acquire _receptive language_ first; they learn the meaning of what others say to them before they become skillful in communicating back. _Expressive language_ is the ability to communicate meaning in a way that another person can understand. To acquire expressive language, children first must master some receptive language—words or labels for objects, events, and processes in their environment. Gradually they must learn to combine and order symbols or words in ways that orally express concepts and feelings. _Oral speech_ involves the actual articulation of consonant and vowel sounds and the production of those sounds in sequences to produce words, phrases, and eventually sentences. Oral speech is the major means that young children use for expressive language, but it is not the only way. As children grow older and become more skillful, they learn to employ other methods of expressive language. Gestures, pictures, written words, secondary languages, and visual or auditory codes such as musical notation represent other communication mediums.

Finally, the _functional use of language (pragmatics)_ refers to the user's intention and the relationship between communication and the context in which it is used. It also involves an individual's conversational skills. A person may have language skills and be capable of speaking, yet fail to use language in functional, adaptive ways as a means for relating to other people. An autistic child, for example, typically can understand what is said and can speak in clear, understandable sentences, but the autistic child typically fails to use language as a functional tool for social communication.

Understanding developmental sequences in speech/language acquisition
To identify children whose language and speech skills are not evolving as expected requires an understanding of normal developmental stages of speech and language learning. Table 6.2 summarizes the sequence and approximate age levels when key speech/language skills develop. As shown in the table, foundations for speech and language proficiency begin to form very early in life. By age 5 or 6 most youngsters have achieved a functional understanding of language and have mastered the basics of oral speech. Although their speech will become increasingly more articulate and fluent, and their language structures

Table 6.2
Development of Speech and Language Production
In Young Children

Age of Child*	Speech Production	Language Production	Usable Speaking Vocabulary**
0-3 months	↑	Differentiates cries to show discomfort, pain, and hunger.	
4-6 months	Vowel sounds are learned	Babbles.	
9-12 months		Combines consonants and vowels into words such as "mama."	1-3
12-14 months		Can say a few recognizable words, such as "ball."	
18 months	↓	Starts combining two words together, such as "Mommy go."	18-22
2 years	(h,p,b,m,n)		270-300
	(k,d,f,ng,y)		
2½ years		Begins combining words into short phrases. Starts asking primitive questions such as, "Where milk go?" Begins using early forms of negation such as, "Wear mitten no."	450
	(t,w)		900
3 years	(g,s)		
3½ years	(r,l)	Is able to use simple sentence structures. Starts inverting subject and verb when asking a question, such as in, "How that open?" Increases ability to use negation. Begins using pronouns and placing endings on words.	1,200
	(sh,ch)		
4 years	(th)		1,500
4¼ years		Is able to use a variety of sentence structures. Becomes proficient in use of pronouns and different verb tenses. Language structures are well on their way to mastery.	
	(v)		2,000
5 years			
	(z,j)		
6-8 years			2,600+

*Age at which 75% of children master sounds.
**Number of words.

Information sources: Byrne and Shervanian (1977); Cole (1982); Prather, Hedrick, and Kern (1975); Holland (1984).

and vocabulary more sophisticated and varied, their foundation for functional communication has been formed. In fact, by age 5 or 6 most youngsters have mastered language well enough to produce sentence structures and apply grammatical principles similar to those used by adults with whom they live.

Because school-aged students should have well developed speech communication and language systems, identification of a disorder is a relatively straightforward task. Taking the criteria of standard speech used by older children and adults, we simply examine existing speech/language patterns and identify any omissions or irregularities in articulation of speech sounds, voice abnormalities, poor fluency, or immature forms of speech and language competence. Diagnosing irregularities in speech and language in young infants, toddlers, or preschoolers is not so simple. Receptive and expressive language, including speech, is just evolving, and hence is incomplete and inadequate. When talking begins, vowel and consonant sounds are not articulated clearly and accurately. Words are not always organized into meaningful sequences. Sentence structures do not necessarily follow consistent grammatical rules. Only gradually will children use more and more sophisticated language systems to communicate with others. Thus, the idiosyncrasies and errors in early speech and language of young children are normal characteristics of their evolving skills.

If we are to accurately identify symptoms in young children that suggest real problems, we have to distinguish between normal omissions/distortions in speech and normal deficiencies in language from what are real abnormalities. The example of Ronnie illustrates that important distinction.

> Four-year-old Ronnie has difficulty pronouncing several consonant sounds clearly. He says "fwarowite" for favorite, "sort" for short, and "shimney" for chimney. Concerned about Ronnie's baby talk, his teacher referred him to a speech therapist. Basically Ronnie had some difficulty articulating consonant sounds such as r, f, v, and z and the consonant blends of sh and ch. Is his speech disordered? If you look at Table 6.2, Ronnie's inability to say these sounds clearly is not abnormal. Although some of his peers may have learned them, these sounds typically are not mastered fully until around 6-8 years of age. Though Ronnie's difficulties with these sounds might have been a little more apparent, his speech is developing normally.

Conditions that signal a child at-risk   Three types of information are useful indicators of children who may have difficulty developing intelligible speech (McDonald, 1980): (a) injury or physical at-risk conditions in the child's prenatal, perinatal, and neonatal history, (b) the child's early development of speech compared to the expected developmental milestones, and (c) the child's physical status in regard to the presence or absence of normal physical structure and neuromuscular movements that affect speech production.

Developmental history may reveal conditions suggestive of pending difficulty. Conditions associated with brain damage and delayed or abnormal development (e.g., maternal disease or complications during pregnancy, birth injury or excessive trauma, low APGAR scores) may suggest future difficulties (Denhoff & Robinault, 1960; Alderman, 1972).

Findings on a sample of 20,137 children studied as a part of the Collaborative Perinatal Project (Lassman, Fisch, Vetter, & LaBenz, 1980) revealed the following variables as related to the later appearance of speech/language problems:

— children whose mothers were under age 18.
— children whose parity (number of children born to the mother) was high.
— children whose mother's weight gain during pregnancy was less than 15 pounds or greater than 25 pounds.
— children who were delivered prematurely, breech or with forceps, or who were of low birth weight.
— children whose mothers are mentally retarded.

Results from the Collaborative Perinatal Project also concluded that psychological, social, and environmental variables were stronger predictors of later speech/language performance than were perinatal factors. Youngsters from low socioeconomic homes or whose parents had little education, for example, generally performed more poorly on speech/language assessments than did a comparison group of children from higher socioeconomic homes. Other studies suggest that children with histories of anoxia, seizures, feeding difficulties, atypical crying, hyper- or hypoactivity, and respiratory dysfunction show increased risk for speech/language problems (Denhoff & Robinault, 1960; Alderman, 1972).

Developmental lags in the acquisition of neuromotor behavior associated with the oral apparatus, in the progression of reflex patterns, or in acquisition of beginning speech/language skills also may suggest future difficulties. Speech and language proficiency is the cumulative outcome of a long sequence of maturation, learning, and experience. Speech development and language learning proceeds rapidly from birth to about age 3 or 4. If a child shows signs of a neuromotor or cognitive disorder, concern about lags in speech or language development of a few weeks may be justified.

Physical-neurological status, as assessed in a physical examination, is a good indicator of potential speech/language difficulties. Several factors are of particular interest. First, the normalcy of reflex patterns is one means for identifying children at-risk for possible speech difficulties. Abnormal tonic reflexes usually suggest delays or abnormal development of the central nervous system. Resulting abnormalities in the distribution of muscle tone can interfere with respiration, phonation, and articulation required for good speech (Bobath, 1965; Fiorentino, 1973; McCormick & Schiefelbusch, 1984; Mysak, 1963). Second, abnormal neuromotor movements, such as in swallowing, chewing, or sucking, may suggest possible speech difficulties. Immature oral-motor functions beyond the ages listed below may interfere with the development of intelligible speech (McDonald, 1980):

Oral-Motor Behavior	*Usually Normal To:*
deficient sucking behavior	1-2 weeks
tendency to choke on fluids	1-2 weeks
jaw clonus	6 weeks
choking on semi-solids	28 weeks
excessive air swallowing	40 weeks
mouth held open; drooling	40 weeks
failure to chew	18 months

Third, the presence of conditions known to be highly correlated with unintelligible or poor speech is an obvious warning sign. Children with known brain injury, genetic or biological disorders causing mental retardation, cerebral palsy, or physical deformities such as cleft palate likely will have difficulties in both speech development and language acquisition. Children with hearing impairments undoubtedly will have some difficulty developing both speech and language. Blindness does not necessarily interfere with speech production, but it likely will restrict early experience in ways that delay language acquisition (Darley, Aronson, & Brown, 1975; Sparks, 1984).

In identifying children with language disorders who do not have related physical or cognitive handicaps, professionals and parents must be alert to more subtle signs of difficulty. These signs are often apparent in relationships between a child's comprehension and production of language in a social context. Or the signs may be apparent in the cognitive level at which a child functions. Rice (1978) has suggested four primary identifier characteristics that may signal a young child who is developing a language deficit:

1. Child does not interact verbally with peers or adults in a social context.
2. Child does not follow verbal commands or seems not to comprehend the specifics of a verbal instruction.
3. Child does not talk much but uses a lot of other methods for communicating (hand gestures, vocal inflections, facial expressions, etc.). This means that the child may not have adequate expressive language for what he or she has to say.
4. Child seems to have well developed comprehension and can produce socially appropriate responses, but expressive productions are limited in both quality and quantity. Language responses, when produced, may be accurate, but given the child's age and maturity, the responses are too restricted and lacking in sophistication.

Environmental factors, including the psychological, social, and physical conditions to which a child is continually exposed, have a major impact on the learning of speech and language skills. An environment that offers little exposure to educational experiences or materials and lacks intellectual and verbal stimulation can affect cognitive and language development. In fact, environmental variables have been shown to have greater impact than prenatal or perinatal factors on later speech and language abilities (Kluppel, 1972; Hardy, 1965). Children from impoverished homes, for example, seem to perform less well than children from middle-class homes where parents are more educated and place greater emphasis upon verbal communication. Jensen (1968) identified a number of environmental situations that seem to bear upon language development of children in impoverished homes:

1. Early babbling and vocalizations of infants are less likely to be reinforced.
2. Parents engage in less verbal interaction and verbal play with their young children.
3. Parents are involved in less shaping of speech sounds, words, and sentence structures into productions that become increasingly more like adult speech.
4. Language models are not necessarily good ones, nor do they promote the kinds of linguistic skills that transfer to school learning.
5. Early question asking by young children is discouraged when adults are focused upon other concerns and thus fail to take advantage of questions as an educational opportunity for a child.

The nature of language disorders

Language disorders manifested by young children vary tremendously. Consequently, what might be said about one child with language deficits may not be true about another. A further complicating factor in describing these problems is that professionals' interpretations of children's language disorders are highly divergent. A review of various textbooks on the subject will reveal a great variety of perspectives.

Some basics on language development Both child factors and environmental factors enter into early language learning. First, to acquire language, a *child* must possess certain characteristics: (a) an intact sensory system for detecting stimuli in the environment, and (b) capabilities for processing those incoming stimuli to receive, interpret, store, and retrieve information. Second, the *environment* must provide certain inputs: (a) stimuli that the child's sensory system(s) can detect, and (b) selective reinforcement of appropriate responses the child gives to the stimulation. The child's interactions with the environment give rise to experiences that are the building blocks of language.

Problems or abnormalities within the child or in the environment can interfere with language learning. Furthermore, an inappropriate match in the timing of environmental stimulation and the child's maturational readiness level can hamper language acquisition. McDonald (1980) explained that when a child's sensory system does not allow detection of stimuli in the environment because of sensory impairment, language learning will be more difficult. Likewise, learning of language is impaired if a child's cognitive systems are inefficient, as in the case of mental retardation or brain damage, and the child cannot encode sensory input (perception), store it (memory), and attach symbols to it (association, discrimination, and abstraction).

Environmental limitations, on the other hand, restrict experience and learning. A cerebral palsied child who is unable to explore the environment and whose response repertoire is severely limited may be further deprived by an environment that offers inadequate stimulation. A child's own inability to respond reciprocally to adults may reduce their responsiveness. A mother, for example, is reinforced as she talks to her child and the child reacts with a smile, with babbling, or with words or gestures that communicate a response. If her child responds, she is more likely to continue the stimulating behaviors. The reinforcement a mother gets from a severely handicapped child may be minimal. The child may give no vocal response, unpleasant and meaningless sounds, grimaces, or other bizarre responses. When this happens, the mother tends to reduce activities that enhance language development in her child. For these reasons, many handicapped children do not get the stimulation they need at the time it matters most in the development of language.

Types of language disorders As pointed out earlier, disorders in language among young children are *developmental* in nature. That is, a child who has a disorder does not acquire language normally from the very beginning. This is in contrast to adult disorders in which the problem is present and is to be treated *after* basic language skills have been acquired. Developmental language disorders typically are described in terms of behavioral *characteristics*—not causes. For our purposes here, these difficulties will be discussed according to (a) deviations in the acquisition or mere timing of language learning, and (b) deviations in the qualitative aspects of language.

Deviations in the acquisition rate or timing of language learning may be manifest in:

1. Failure to acquire verbal language by age 3.

   Some children appear not to understand language even by age 3. They manifest no spontaneous speech, nor do they attempt to communicate verbally at a time when peers are learning new words and rapidly gaining in the ability to communicate with others. Although these children hear normally, they do not attach meaning to what they hear. Some may make utterances, but these are mere jargon and void of meaning. Some children who fail to acquire language have limited intellectual abilities. Sensory and motor handicaps are frequent as well.

2. Delay in the rate of language learning.

   Language development in some youngsters follows normal patterns, but it falls much below that expected for their age and apparent cognitive abilities. These delays may suggest that a child is simply at the lower end of the normal distribution but will ultimately achieve an adequate level of language proficiency. For others, delays may be cumulative and over time result in significant deficits.

   Delays in language acquisition may be general or specific. General delay involves all dimensions of language development. In essence, the child's language proficiency is immature and characteristic of a much younger child. Other children have specific difficulties in one or more dimensions of language, such as syntax, semantics, or pragmatics of language. (These are discussed next.)

3. Interrupted progress in language learning.

   Some children, whose language development is normal initially, experience an event that interrupts this learning process. Illness, an accident resulting in injury, emotional trauma, or an acquired handicap are examples. The result may be an overall delay in the progression of language learning or a loss (temporary or enduring) of certain qualitative aspects of language. If the damage is sufficiently severe, a child may fail to develop functional language skills at all.

   To what extent these interruptions can be overcome depends upon (a) the child's age when the interruption occurs, (b) the extent of organic damage, (c) language skills mastered prior to the event, and (d) the educational intervention the child receives. Generally, the younger the child is, the better are the chances for recovery (Lenneberg, 1972; Costello, 1984).

Deviations in the qualitative aspects of language are described in regard to three dimensions of communication: (a) syntax, (b) semantics, and (c) pragmatics (Holland, 1984). As children progressively develop language proficiency, they master skills across each of these dimensions. They are learning all these aspects of language simultaneously, but progress may be greater in one area or another at any given time.

Syntax involves the ordering or arrangement of words to communicate an idea. If children use language normally, they must learn linguistic structures to convey their intentions or ideas. Initially, they learn single words to express meaning, but soon they begin to combine words to express relational meanings (examples: big dog, pretty dolly, baby eat). Children then begin to use grammatical words to modify the basic meaning of their utterances. They add inflections to nouns and verbs, prepositions, articles (the, this, an), or auxiliary verbs to give more specificity to the meaning they want to express. They learn sentence forms and begin to select the types of sentences that best convey the message they want to communicate.

According to Cole (1982), when children's mean utterance length (average number of words they typically include in a statement) approaches three words, they begin to use more creative sentence structures: negations, yes/no questions, what and where questions, and commands. This usually occurs around age 3. The more sentence forms children learn to use, the more effective they are in expressing their intents. They also are more able to adjust their communications to fit the situation appropriately.

What types of syntax errors or problems do young children exhibit? Errors in syntax are classified in four ways (Byrne & Shervanian, 1977): (a) lack of syntactic structure in speech, (b) limited mastery of syntactic structures for a given age or developmental level, (c) incorrect grammatical structures, and (d) omission of syntactic structures where they should be used. Byrne and Shervanian noted that syntactic errors are expected when children are initially learning language. A 1-year-old is not expected to use more than one-word utterances, but the lack of syntactic structures such as noun-verb phrases at 30 months of age suggests a possible problem. If that same child has limited syntactic structures and cannot join words together to form a sentence by age 3, we would consider him or her below average.

Speech/language disorders and learning disabilities are not always easy to diagnose during the very early years. Delayed development *in speech/language or cognitive learning is much more likely to be observed in young children.*

As toddlers and preschoolers learn correct grammatical forms, they make many errors, saying things such as, "Daddy do," "Kitty eat food," "Me likes candy," "Them wants ice cream." As children learn proper relationships for noun-verb combinations and as parents model appropriate syntactic rules, errors of this nature gradually disappear. These errors are a normal part of the learning process as children experiment with different word combinations. But when these kinds of errors persist, continuing beyond the age when grammar should begin to follow structural rules characterizing adult language, a problem may exist. During the developmental phases of language acquisition, children need to hear correct syntactical forms from adults and older children around them. If adults use poor or incorrect syntax, young children will imitate those same patterns.

Semantics involves the acquisition of vocabulary and use of words to refer to objects, people, processes, actions, or conditions (Cole, 1982). As children master the semantics of language, they learn that words are symbols or representations of real things in their environment. They learn to associate words with their referents (objects or processes or persons) through experience with things and persons in the environment. Mastering the semantics of language is a process that continues throughout life. Unlike the other basic components of language, in which the task is to master some basic rules, people continue indefinitely to enlarge their vocabulary to learn more about the meaning of words.

The mastery of semantics is manifest in two ways: (a) in the comprehension or understanding of what others communicate (receptive language), and (b) in one's expression of ideas and intents to others through the appropriate selection of words that will convey the desired message (expressive language). When a child fails to acquire the semantic aspects of language, this interferes greatly with communicative skill and can result in deficits in acquiring other components of language (Aram & Nation, 1975). Age is an important factor in assessing a child's progress in learning semantics. A 6-month-old child is not expected to have mastered very many words in terms of either receptive or expressive vocabulary. Yet, by 3 years of age, most children will have mastered a speaking vocabulary of around 900 words and will have an even larger receptive vocabulary. A 2-year-old who calls all fuzzy animals "kitty" would not be unusual, but a child at 3 who still calls all small animals "kitty" would cause some concern.

Children with language difficulties in semantics either do not learn the meaning of words or are unable to interpret the meaning of a series of words that collectively convey meaning. Byrne and Shervanian (1977) noted that deficits in expressive language resulting from semantic difficulties range along a continuum from a total lack of symbols to partial deficits. A child's mastery of expressive or receptive vocabulary may be nonexistent, incorrect, inappropriate, or simply limited. In the latter case, limited vocabularies sometimes result from a lack of experience and poor environments in which a child gets inadequate stimulation. It also may suggest other cognitive difficulties that interfere with the child's ability to learn the names of objects and things in the environment.

Pragmatics involves the functional use of language as a social tool for communication and as a tool for learning, directing behavior, or generating new ideas. A child's pragmatic competence can be assessed in regard to the variety of purposes for which he or she uses language. As children master the structural and content components of language, they also must learn to use language in appropriate and functional ways in various contexts. If language is functional, a child must learn to adapt its use to the situation or to the listener. Autistic children are a good example of those who may master the basic structural and syntactic components of language but fail to use it in any functional way. They characteristically fail to use language to communicate ideas to others, ask for something they want, or manipulate their environment. Although most children do not show such extreme deviance in their ability to use language functionally, parents and teachers do observe considerable variation in how young children use language socially.

Deficits in the pragmatic applications of language among young children are manifest in many ways, especially as they grow older. Two of the more common difficulties among very young children are (Snyder, 1984):

— *problems in expressive intentions.*   Some children are restricted communicatively because they use language for a limited variety of purposes. They may use it to get something they want but fail to use it to regulate others, learn about their environment, or express feelings. Some youngsters do not recognize that language can help them interact with other people or aid them in getting something they want. Because they do not know how to use language to accomplish these purposes, they may not progress normally in other aspects of language learning.

— *difficulties in maintaining a flow of conversation.* Between ages 2 and 3, children begin accepting greater responsibility for maintaining a dialogue with another person. Some youngsters, however, fail to acquire normal interactional-communicative skills at a prelinguistic level and are ill prepared to use language in conversation. They may be successful in a monologue, but prerequisite skills may be deficit: They do not understand how to take turns or engage in reciprocal interactions necessary for conversation, or they may not attend to the content of the other person's remarks or understand their role in continuing the discussion.

The nature of oral speech disorders

Speech disorders are among the most frequently reported handicapping conditions among school-aged students. Speech problems (or, more broadly, communication problems including language) also have been cited most often as a problem among preschoolers. An important distinction must be made, however, between what is considered a speech disorder for school-aged students and what is a disorder in children 5 or 6 years of age and younger. We expect school-aged students to be talking and exhibiting speech patterns that are generally similar to those of adults. Thus, in determining speech disorders, we compare their speech to the adult standard and notice behaviors that are inappropriate, irregular, or simply missing. *Speech that is not understandable, calls attention to itself because of its deviance from that of others, interferes with communication because of its deviance, and causes its user to be maladjusted is considered defective* (Van Riper, 1978).

Some basics on speech production and learning   Speech involves the physical production of sound and the willful shaping of sound, using the oral mechanism, into specific vowel and consonant utterances. (The oral mechanism includes the tongue, teeth, oral cavity, and voice box, or larynx.) Speech also involves the learning of sound sequences that form words, phrases, and eventually sentences. Basically, speech production involves three systems or processes:

1. The *respiratory system* must provide a source of power in the form of a controlled airstream. Speech requires the control of certain respiratory patterns to produce speech sounds that are intelligible, sequential, and rhythmic. These patterns are of a higher level of neuromuscular integration and coordination than needed for regular breathing. Some children with neuromuscular disorders (such as cerebral palsy) do not have enough respiratory control to develop intelligible speech (Darley, Aronson, & Brown, 1975).

2. The *vocal tract* (throat, nose, and oral cavity) must be structurally intact and functionally operative so that speech sounds can be produced accurately. Children with structural malformations (such as cleft palate) or neuromuscular disorders (such as cerebral palsy) have a difficult time producing intelligible speech sounds (i.e., vowels and consonants). Youngsters with cleft palates, for example, often have hypernasality and misarticulation problems. Over 50% of children with cerebral palsy have speech defects including voice and articulation problems caused by poor neuromuscular control of the apparatus needed for production of speech sounds (Morley, 1967).

3. A child must learn to coordinate the fine motor movements of the *articulators* to produce various sounds. Through modeling and imitation, practice and feedback, he or she must learn how to use various parts of the oral mechanism to articulate intelligible speech. Certain sounds are made by the teeth and tongue (dentals, such as t, s, d), some with the lips (labials, such as p, b, m), and others by pressing the tongue against the roof of the mouth (velars, such as k, g). Gradually children learn that sounds can be distinguished by differences in (a) how much air is needed to produce them, and (b) the amount of voice required (e.g., b, d, and g are voiced, whereas s, f, and p are not voiced) (Darley, Aronson, & Brown, 1975).

Some children are subjected to conditions, such as poor models with inarticulate speech, that interfere with this learning process. Some youngsters lack sufficient verbal stimulation and feedback from adults in the environment to help them become more skillful and accurate in speech production. Children who cannot hear sounds or discriminate the differences in sounds also have difficulties during this phase of speech production. Or simply poor learning, in which children fail to initially acquire correct patterns of sound production or articulation, can produce defective speech. If these patterns are not reshaped through modeling by adults and older children or through corrective feedback, they will become a matter of habit. Once they become habitual, speech patterns are more resistive to change.

Speech disorders and normal characteristics of evolving speech   Speech disorders involve one or more of the following kinds of difficulties:

Articulation disorders: irregularities in oral production of the 46 vowel and consonant sounds in the English language or whatever language a child speaks as the mother tongue.

Voice disorders: inappropriate pitch, volume, or voice quality for communicating effectively.

Oral fluency disorders: irregularities in the flow or rhythm of speech outputs involved in formation of sounds, words, or sentences.

But what specifically constitutes a speech problem in a 2-year-old, a 4-year-old, a 6-year-old? Since their oral speech skills are still evolving, adult standards of good, intelligible, fluent speech are not appropriate. From infancy to the late preschool years, children go through a period of incredibly fast speech and language development. The newborn begins with only a few distinguishable crying sounds, but in just one or two years that same child will learn to produce many of the basic sounds (*phonemes*) of the English language and how to string those sounds together in ways that convey meaning (*morphemes*). By age 4, the child will be talking in phrases and sentences that reflect an impressive mastery of some basic syntactical rules governing grammar and sentence structure. What a tremendous change in just a few short years!

This developmental process in speech and language acquisition means that a young child's speech will be immature, incomplete, and at times inarticulate compared to that of adults. This points to an important principle for judging whether a young child's speech is normal or abnormal:

★ *The appropriate standards against which a child's speech should be judged are (a) the developmental sequences of speech acquisition for young children, (b) the speech of agemates (keeping in mind the range of individual differences in speech/language acquisition among children), and (c) the social and cultural context in which the child lives.*

Remember that as children learn to produce speech and use oral language to communicate, errors are common until they become more skillful and precise in their communicative actions. Here are a few of those normal errors that are to be expected:

1. Young children are just learning to articulate certain phonemes and sound combinations and sequences. They will not be able to articulate all of the sounds correctly. (See Table 6.2 for sounds that are not typically produced with consistent accuracy until ages 4, 5, 6, or even 8.)

2. Children's early use of speech is not always socially appropriate or "tuned in" to the requirements of the situation. It may leave the listener puzzled and confused. Early speech (and even up to age 5 or 6) is egocentric. The child is not concerned about whom he or she is speaking to or even if the other person is listening. Children talk to themselves for the pleasure of the activity. Only gradually does speech become more socially functional. In socialized speech the child begins to consider the listener's point of view. If one looks at the speech of 2½-year-olds, their speech may not make sense and may at times seem to be more random "word play." Here is an example:

> Sally: My sister has a birthday today.
> Shaun: My dog bit me.
> Sally: (playing with a doll) Drink your milk—drink (followed by gurgling, drinking sounds).
> Shaun: My blocks . . . see (as he arranges the blocks on the floor).

3. Dysfluency is often characteristic of a child's speech during the preschool years. Preschoolers may have a hard time saying what they want to say, as shown in this example of a 4-year-old describing a visit to the zoo to his teacher:

Teacher . . . teacher . . . (pause and big breath) uh-uh . . . . We went . . . we went . . . we went to the zoo yester . . . yesterday and uh-uh-uh-uh-uh we . . . we saw a big bear and uh-uh-uh-uh Gweg (for Greg) . . . Gweg fed popcorn . . . he-he threw popcorn in i . . . i . . . its cage (laugh). They had uh-uh-uh-uh giraffes, too.

As many as 85% of all children 3-4 years of age have hesitations such as these in their speech. Young children are building a hearing vocabulary faster than they have learned to put words together into coherent, connected, conversational speech. Thus, they must stall for time until they can form the proper mode of expression. Children ages 2-5 may repeat as many as one of every four words in part or in whole. Repetitions decrease as they grow older and gain competence in their speech and language skills.

4. Excitement, situational pressures, and emotional stress seem to increase hesitancies and repetitions in the speech of preschoolers. These are usually temporary if adults handle the situation skillfully by providing support and reassurance to the child and by simply being patient listeners. Excitement over activities, attempts to gain attention, and social-emotional adjustments, such as when a new baby comes home from the hospital, are sometimes associated with periods of increased speech dysfluency and inarticulate speech.

Given the unique qualities of children's early speech, adults should be cautious in interpreting a child's inarticulate and sometimes dysfluent speech as deviant. Many of the inadequacies of speech in young children are not to be interpreted as a "problem" or disorder or defect in speech. These inadequacies simply represent *skills yet to be learned.* But when these speech patterns continue beyond the ages when they are considered normal and when more advanced skills do not appear, a child's speech might truly be considered disordered.

Regardless of whether a speech pattern is considered normal or inappropriate for a child's age, the adult's task is the same: to model appropriate speech and language behaviors, and to provide opportunities for the child to learn language and then to express ideas through oral communicative methods. Adult feedback to a child should shape increasingly more accurate and complex speech behaviors. If adults become tense and upset about a child's speech during the years when the youngster is just learning to talk and express ideas, they are likely to contribute to his or her anxieties. By putting pressure on a child to perform speech tasks he or she is yet unable to do or by making a child overly self-conscious about what is said, an adult is possibly laying the groundwork for real problems to develop.

Types of speech disorders   Young children's speech difficulties usually do not fall neatly into categories of articulation, voice, or fluency disorders. Therefore, we will review each of the major classes of disorders only briefly so you will be acquainted with the various types of problems that *can* develop. Developmental difficulties in speech production among preschoolers usually are broader in nature.

Articulation disorders can easily become a matter of habit. Because articulation habits are formed early, children should be taught good speech habits from the beginning. Constructive adult models help children learn to produce correct speech sounds. Shaping utterances by repeating in correct form what a child has said, and by playing word games that allow children to practice saying words and sounds are an important part of adult-child interactions during the formative years of oral speech. Articulation errors are generally classified according to four types of deviations:

Omissions: pronouncing only parts of words. (Example: omitting a sound at the beginning of words—"I ove my ittle dog" for "I love my little dog"; "abbit" for "rabbit.")

Substitutions: replacing one sound with another. (Example: commonly, b for v — "bery" instead of "very"; w for r — "wabbit" for "rabbit" or "woad" for "road.")

Additions: adding extra sounds to words. (Example: "summber" for "summer"; "sawr" for "saw"; "warsh" for "wash.")

Distortions: approximating correct pronunciation but deviating slightly, usually because child does not use the tongue, teeth, or oral cavity correctly to produce the sound. (Example: "ts" or "th" for "t.")

Children with other disorders that interfere with sound production or with the oral-muscular movements involved in articulation likely will have difficulty in clearly pronouncing speech sounds. Children with cerebral palsy and with cleft palate are prime examples.

Voice disorders generally involve:

— *a problem in loudness or softness of voice production.* This may be caused by a lack of control in voice production resulting from impaired hearing, cerebral palsy, or faulty learning. Some children learn to scream or speak loudly to gain their parents' attention. Other children begin to speak too softly but are never taught or expected to do otherwise; over time they establish the habit of speaking quietly and not using air properly to produce a stronger voice.

— *a problem in voice quality.* This may involve excessive or insufficient nasality, breathiness, harshness, or hoarseness. Insufficient nasality can result from colds, allergies, or enlarged tonsils, in which normal resonance in the sinuses and oral cavity is blocked. Excessive *nasality* is usually the result of organic-physical defects (e.g., cleft palate). *Breathiness* can result from poor vocal habits or physical-organic disorders that prevent the vocal cords from coming together properly to allow air to pass. *Hoarseness* or *harshness* usually results from vocal abuse.

Fluency disorders are commonly referred to as stuttering. *A stuttering disorder involves abnormal repetitions, hesitations, prolongations of speech sounds or syllables involved in speech production.* The speaker may produce grimaces, tics, or bodily movements along with the blocking of speech. Most cases of stuttering begin in early childhood—usually between ages 2 and 4 (Van Riper, 1971). Because dysfluencies during this early period are normal, tagging a child as a "stutterer" when he or she exhibits dysfluency is unwise and probably unrealistic. Most children (over 80%) who exhibit dysfluency during this developmental period ultimately develop normal speech. Only a small proportion of children fail to outgrow this early stage and to develop a real stuttering disorder (Prins, 1983).

The impact of speech/language disorders on development and learning

A major achievement of children during the years from their birth to the time they begin elementary school is the development of an effective, highly elaborated language and communication system. Though they master other important motor, social, and cognitive tasks, language offers one of the most crucial tools for all subsequent intellectual and social learning. Without question, language plays a pivotal role in children's learning. *First,* it is the mechanism through which children relate to their environment by expressing ideas, taking a social position with others, and communicating actions that allow them to manipulate their environment and affect how others deal with them. Language also is the means by which children communicate to others what they know or want.

Second, language provides a system or tool for thinking. Words and symbols have meaning that allow organization of stimuli in a conceptual way. Experience can be labeled and categorized, allowing children to generalize from one experience to another, draw inferences from a group of similar observations, solve problems, and create new and original ideas. Without language or a symbolic system for labeling ideas and concepts, real thinking and cognitive activity may not occur. Experts such as Piaget see language as an expression of cognitive development. Although the relationship between language and cognitive or intellectual development is controversial, everyone seems to agree that cognitive performance and language are highly intertwined.

Children whose development does not progress normally often show delays in language/speech development. What do these delays mean for them, expecially if they persist? What impact do deficit language skills, poor speech or oral communication skills, or both, have upon a child's performance and subsequent development in other areas? The developmental consequences of both speech and language disorders are a function of the nature and the severity of these problems. Social and educational demands placed upon a child temper the degree to which these difficulties affect other areas of development. A mild articulation problem may present minimal problems to a child and may persist through adulthood with few truly negative consequences. A severe language delay, however, will likely affect every aspect of development. Furthermore, it can have potentially far-reaching impacts upon a child's educational/emotional/interpersonal achievements (Aram, Ekelman, & Nation, 1984; King, Jones, & Lasky, 1982; Vetter, Fay, & Winitz, 1980).

Other potential impacts of difficulties in language or speech, or both are:

1. *Absence of a functional or age-appropriate communication system.*

Children whose language skills are inadequate or poorly developed have a communication system that simply will fail to serve them in all the ways that children with more adequate language enjoy. Inability to understand or interpret language inputs from others definitely places these children at a disadvantage. First, they are less able to understand what is going on around them, especially if others are using language systems to exchange information. Second, they miss many opportunities to learn new concepts or to receive information from others, because these children do not comprehend what others are saying to them.

2. *Interference with social interactions.*

Difficulty in using language to communicate with others (expressive language) places children in a less advantageous social position. They are less able to take part in their social environment because they cannot engage skillfully in reciprocal communicative interactions. This makes them more dependent on adults. With limited communication skills, children are less able to negotiate their needs and less able to apply their ideas with peers by making suggestions, posing questions, or carrying out dialogues that direct or mediate play activities.

3. *Interference with the nature and quality of interpersonal relationships.*

Language disorders undoubtedly affect interpersonal relationships since they require a give-and-take interaction. If children are unable to respond appropriately to an adult or peer, their own responses (or lack of them) are likely to affect the nature of subsequent communications. Parents of children with poor communicative abilities are at a disadvantage because the burden of communication is placed largely upon them. Although parents readily assume this position with infants, they are less likely to do so with older preschoolers. Communication with a noncommunicative person can be frustrating. At times it can become intolerable for even the most conscientious, resourceful parent or peer.

4. *Limitations on ability to communicate needs or ideas.*

Difficulties in using language to communicate render a child less able to capitalize upon other people and the environment as a means of learning. Young children extend and clarify their experience by asking questions. In fact, they are notorious for their unending parade of questions: "Where did he go?" "Why are you doing that?" "Why is the grass green?" "What is that?" "What are you doing now?" By listening to others, children glean information about things unseen and from experiences others have had. Without a good grasp of language, limitations are imposed upon what a child can learn in this way.

5. *Added frustrations for the child and effects upon self-image.*

Language difficulties are undoubtedly frustrating to children themselves, especially when they want to express themselves but repeatedly find they are misunderstood. Watch a young child with poor articulation attempt to communicate, and you will likely see the social effects of the communication problem. When adults do not understand what a child is saying, they often respond in one of two ways:

a. by asking the child to repeat the statement. This sometimes produces a clarification but often results only in another request for the child to "say that again." If the adult still fails to understand, repeated requests to "tell me again" become frustrating to a child.
b. by reacting with a tolerant "yes" or "is that so" response, which may or may not fit what the child has said. Responses like this communicate to the child (who knows what he or she intended to say) that no one really listens to him or her. Attempts at communication thus fail to serve the purpose.

These consequences can extinguish a child's efforts to communicate and add to the child's growing lack of confidence in the ability to express himself or herself. Since communication may not seem to work, the child may be less motivated to use speech or oral communication as a means to interact with others.

6. *Effects upon learning and performance of cognitive tasks.*

Language is fundamental for academic learning. Research is limited on the eventual developmental levels attained by children who exhibit early language impairment, but research does suggest that expressive language deficits are associated with delay in both nonverbal and verbal mental abilities (Moore, 1967; Stevenson & Richman, 1976; Weiss & Lillywhite, 1976). Aram and Nation (1982) noted that many children who experience difficulties in school learning have histories of delayed speech development or difficulties with language as preschoolers. Also, considerable evidence suggests that language skills are highly correlated with academic achievement and with student scores on tests of mental ability.

COGNITIVE DISORDERS: MENTAL RETARDATION, LEARNING DISABILITIES, AND NOTABLE COGNITIVE DELAYS

Signs and symptoms of cognitive disorders

Children with cognitive impairments do not constitute a homogeneous group. The nature of a cognitive disorder, its severity, and the child's ability to cope with the problem all affect how visible this disability is to an observer. The environment in which a child lives, including expectations for performance there, also color how functional or dysfunctional a person's behavior appears. Some environments accentuate a child's weaknesses. Others deemphasize those weaknesses. To explain the tremendous range of characteristics among children with cognitive impairments, these disorders can be clustered into four broad groups:

1. *Cognitive disorders associated with brain or neurological damage.*

   Children in this group fall into two subcategories:

   a. Cases in which the origin of the damage is known and the condition is medically diagnosed (established risk). Evidence of physical damage to the brain, malformation, or neurological dysfunction (e.g., paralysis, abnormal reflexes, or other motor impairments) is there. The damage can be confirmed through medical evaluation using techniques such as a CAT scan, an EEG, tests of motor and pupillary reflexes, and other neurological measures. These are "hard signs" of neurological damage. Children is this group are typically labeled *brain damaged, neurologically impaired, mentally retarded,* or all of these.

   b. Cases in which brain damage cannot be confirmed directly by medical evaluation but the child's behavior or developmental status raises questions about possible damage (biological risk). Abnormal or sluggish reflexes, poor motor coordination, impaired visual-motor coordination, clumsiness, and other irregularities in psychomotor performance are examples. These are called soft signs of neurological impairment. Children in this group generally show developmental irregularities rather early, but their difficulties usually are not severe enough to allow a definite diagnosis. When these children enter school, where they must perform more complex cognitive tasks, their difficulties become more apparent. They ultimately will be diagnosed and labeled as *mentally retarded (MR)* (probably mild), *learning disabled (LD),* or possibly even *emotionally disturbed.* Some experts apply another label to these children, too—*minimal brain damage (MBD).* Considerable debate surrounds the use of this label and what it represents. Also, some children who show "soft signs" of neurological damage will not manifest the same symptoms later and will be considered normal. All cases in this second group are difficult to officially diagnose early in life. In fact, labeling them during infancy or the preschool years is tenuous and perhaps premature.

2. *Cognitive disorders known to occur in connection with other diagnosable medical disorders* (genetic abnormalities such as Down syndrome, metabolic disorders such as Tay-Sachs disease, or degenerative neurological disorders).

Given the primary disorder (which often is identified during the preschool or infant years), some degree of cognitive impairment is known to result. In this group are children who are obviously abnormal but the exact etiology of the abnormality is not known, though possible causes are apparent. Their physical abnormalities and developmental status are such that no doubt exists that they are also cognitively impaired. Many of these children are handicapped from birth. Others simply will fail to develop as expected, so the cognitive disorder will become evident soon after the first year. In most cases, these individuals will be diagnosed and labeled as *mentally retarded* during their early childhood years.

3. *Cognitive disorders that have no apparent organic cause and that seem to evolve over time.*

Children in this group seem normal initially. Their early progress may be slow but not atypical enough to cause real concern or make them seem that different from other agemates. Gradually over the preschool years the gap between the developmental level of these children and that of their normally developing peers widens. Unfortunately, many of these children are not identified as handicapped until they reach kindergarten or even the elementary grades. Their difficulties become evident primarily within the educational context. Outside of school they function more adequately, and their parents consider them to be quite normal. Teachers often describe these children as immature, lacking in readiness skills, slow, deficient in language and preacademic skills, and poor learners. Many come from impoverished, substandard home environments. Probably the best term to describe these children during their preschool years is *developmentally delayed*. When children in this group are ultimately diagnosed and labeled, as school-aged youngsters, they are typically labeled as *mildly retarded*. A few will be classified as *learning disabled*. Some may even be termed *emotionally disturbed*, with the implication that their depressed cognitive performance is a secondary outcome of emotional difficulties.

4. *Cognitive disorders that become evident primarily after a child is in school and attempts learning tasks such as reading, writing, arithmetic, and spelling.*

Like the previous group, these children tend to appear normal during their early years. A few may manifest behaviors that cause parents to describe them as "hard to manage." Cognitive disorders become apparent when they enter school and face new demands to participate in more structured learning activities that place a premium on higher-order cognitive and thinking skills. They experience difficulties in one or more of the psychological/learning processes involved in mastering academic subjects. For example, these children may have problems with visual perception tasks such as those involved in reading. Difficulties in analyzing problems, abstracting, generalizing, classifying, and thinking through a learning task may be apparent. Writing may produce only a messy, disorganized page of unreadable garbage despite the student's best efforts. Speech may be halting or "funny." Receptive language may reveal strange misconceptions and poor memory for long sequences of information or material that most other children master quickly. Difficulties in mathematical calculation and other conceptual tasks also may become apparent.

The overall intellectual abilities of these children are within the normal range, falling anywhere between borderline and gifted. But there are noticeable *discrepancies* and *inconsistencies* in their performance abilities. Children in this group show no evidence of other disorders (such as mental retardation, hearing impairment, emotional disturbance) that could explain their academic learning problems. Individuals with these types of cognitive disorders are generally diagnosed and labeled as *learning disabled*.

Identifying cognitive disorders in young children A great many handicapping conditions originate from physical or organic disorders. The signs and symptoms for each can be described concisely and in observable, concrete terms. When we begin to deal with behavioral abnormalities of an educational or a psychological nature, however, the symptoms are not as clear-cut. (As noted in the earlier discussion on emotional disturbance, to precisely define what constitutes abnormal behavior is difficult. The determination of normality is, in part, a *value judgment.*) Sociologist Jane Mercer (1973) pointed out that in defining what behaviors are indicative of mental retardation, a person's social system determines whether he or she is normal or retarded. In one social context or culture a person may be considered retarded, but in another, normal. This difference in diagnostic perspective is demonstrated by the reality that large numbers of children labeled as mentally retarded are not regarded as such until they are in school, where they fail to perform adequately. After being "mentally retarded" or "learning disabled" for 8 hours at school, they return to their homes and neighborhoods, where they are still regarded as normal. Later in life many of these same individuals will shed that label and blend into society as just another person on the block.

Identification of cognitive disorders is more difficult with infants and preschoolers than school-aged students. This is particularly true with children who eventually are diagnosed as mildly handicapped. School-aged students have accumulated a developmental history that we can look back upon to find evidence of abnormal development or slowed progress in attaining major developmental milestones. By the time a youngster is in school, certain skills should be mastered and certain mental processes should be in place. Standardized tests can be used to objectively assess whether these skills have been mastered. If a student has deficits of sufficient magnitude to place him or her below average for the age group, we have diagnostic evidence to suggest a cognitive disorder. Furthermore, diagnosis with school-aged students is simplified by the fact that they are in a standardized environment at school, where their behavior can be observed over time and compared to that of agemates.

When dealing with very young children, however, we are not able to obtain a range of data comparable to that used in diagnosing the disabilities of school-aged students. We have no extended developmental history to examine. Of even greater import is the fact that many of the behaviors we would examine to evaluate cognitive competence are not yet developed or are just in the process of developing. We do not expect infants or preschoolers to be able to perform sophisticated mental acts that demonstrate their abilities for higher-order thinking and problem solving. This means that a child's cognitive abilities cannot be compared to those of an adult or even an older child.

Signs of cognitive disorder in children are highly unique to each individual. A number of behaviors are potential indicators of a problem, but no one behavior alone can be interpreted to mean that a child has a cognitive impairment. Furthermore, we cannot always distinguish between those who are cognitively impaired and those who are simply immature (Eaves, Kendall, & Crichton, 1972). How can one really discern, so early in a child's developmental history, whether a problem reflects a real or potential handicap or whether it is only a temporary difficulty?

The effects of labeling   Diagnosis of specific cognitive disorders in young children by categorical types has further limitations. An infant or preschooler whose development seems irregular may exhibit characteristics shared by children who are visually impaired, hearing impaired, speech delayed, or seriously emotionally disturbed. For these reasons, hasty labeling of a young child as mentally retarded or learning disabled on the basis of a small sample of behavior or only a short developmental history should be avoided. Except in cases of severe disability or when medical diagnosis clearly indicates existing or imminent cognitive impairment, a diagnosis of MR or LD for a young child can be premature and presumptuous. As Lerner, Mardell-Czudnowski, and Goldenberg (1981) explained:

> Premature categorization of the child's problem can result in a destructive, self-fulfilling prophecy. By placing a label on the child, teachers and parents set up expectations based on that label, and the child often fulfills that prophecy by becoming like the child with that label. (p. 27)

To search for young children who need early intervention by attempting to identify and label them by categorical types is not always a good idea. A noncategorical approach, evaluating a child's status on the basis of of physical, developmental, neuromotor, social, and linguistic characteristics, seems more sensible. If worrisome delays or diagnosable physical disorders that imply a child is at-risk for developmental disorders are present, intervention should be initiated. We are interested in signs of *existing problems* as well as *potential future disabilities*. By using a noncategorical approach, we can avoid the pitfalls of premature and inaccurate labeling. At the same time, children needing early intervention can be identified.

The nature of cognitive disorders

What is mental retardation?   Professionals have debated for decades on the definition of retardation. Early definitions were arbitrary, often citing the condition as incurable. As we have learned more about retardation, the controversy has focused on how to define it, how to diagnose it, and under what circumstances the label of "mentally retarded" should be applied. The fact that a definition of mental retardation implies that we know what intelligence *is* further complicates matters. Since deficits in intellectual functioning are what lead us to say that a person is retarded, the two definitions go hand in hand. The problem is that professionals also do not agree on what constitutes intelligence. This controversy becomes particularly clear in trying to explain the application of the two concepts—mental retardation and intelligence—with regard to young children. What is mental deficiency in an infant? In a preschooler? What is intelligence in a child who is just learning to roll over, to walk, to talk?

Cognitive functions in young children, compared to cognitive processes in older children and adults, are the least understood by professionals. A child under age 5 is in the initial stages of developing the thinking and cognitive skills that are typically measured to evaluate a person's intelligence. Any diagnosis based on those yet incomplete, evolving behaviors seems tenuous and premature. This does not relate to the diagnosis of children who are unquestionably retarded and who would be unanimously defined as such by everyone, no matter what the definition of retardation. But for the majority of young children whose development is marginal, an evaluation of their mental functioning and a diagnosis of normality or retardation is greatly dependent on what definition of mental retardation is used.

The most widely accepted definition is one from the American Association of Mental Deficiency, the major organization representing professionals in the field of mental retardation. According to its classification manual (Grossman, 1983), a retarded person is one who has:

1. *Significantly subaverage general intellectual functioning.* Intellectual functioning is assessed by one or more standardized tests of intelligence, and significantly subaverage refers to an IQ of approximately 70 or below. This is 2 standard deviations below the mean or average of the tests.

2. *Impairments in adaptive behavior.* This concerns the degree to which a person is able to meet standards of personal independence, social responsibility, and functional skills for daily living expected of his or her age and cultural group. Adaptive behavior generally is assessed by standardized tests, developmental checklists, or the clinical judgment of a qualified expert.

   Expectations for adaptive behavior vary with age groups. Thus, what is considered a deficit in behavior or intellectual functioning varies also. Adaptive behavior in infancy and early childhood focuses on behaviors that are part of normal developmental sequences and maturational processes. Delays in achieving expected developmental milestones such as crawling, walking, or talking represent potential deficiencies in adaptive behavior. Specifically, areas of adaptive behavior in young children include:

   —sensorimotor development.
   —communication skills including receptive/expressive language.
   —self-help skills.
   —social skills (the ability to interact with others as appropriate for age).

   Areas of adaptive behavior in childhood and early adolescence focus more on learning processes including basic academic skills and other functional skills needed for independence. These include:

   —basic academic skills for daily life.
   —appropriate reasoning and judgment in interactions with the environment.
   —social skills for dealing effectively in group and interpersonal relationships.
   —vocational performance and social responsibility.

3. *Manifestations of the disorder during the developmental period.* For a condition to be diagnosed as mental retardation, it must be identified between birth and 18 years of age.

Mentally retarded individuals typically are classified according to the severity of their problems. Table 6.3 summarizes the most common classification systems used to describe the various severity levels.

Characteristics of children who are mentally retarded   The most obvious characteristic of children considered retarded is their slower rate of development and reduced ability to learn. Early signs of mental impairment in young children typically are manifest as developmental delays. The child does not show a rate of maturation or learning commensurate with age norms. Early reports of children who are ultimately diagnosed as mentally retarded are filled with descriptions of delays in development of age-appropriate skills such as rolling over, standing up, crawling and walking, saying first words, talking in short phrases, or mastering toileting skills or early feeding skills.

This slower rate of development accumulates over time into major deficits and a deviance of sufficient magnitude that a label of retarded can be assigned. The implications for this reduced rate of developmental progress are explained by Capute (1975) in describing a child diagnosed in the schools as EMR (educable mentally retarded). He noted that the EMR child will develop at a rate of 1/2 to 3/4 of the normal expected rate. This means that by approximately age 16 the person will reach a mental age of only 8-12 (given that the same rate of development continues). In the case of a child diagnosed as TMR (trainable mentally retarded), developmental progress is even slower—a rate of 1/3 to 1/2 of the normal rate. Thus, by adulthood a mental age of only 4-8 years will be achieved.

Considerable research has been devoted to describing the characteristics of mentally retarded children. Although not all children exhibit the same characteristics, some of the most frequently noted problems are (Robinson & Robinson, 1976; Ellis, 1966-1974, Vols. 1-7):

— a reduced ability to learn. This seems to be the result of many factors including deficiencies in memory, discrimination abilities, abstract thinking, generalization skills, and a lack of learning strategies.
— deficits in attentional abilities. This is shown in the inability to identify and attend to relevant stimuli in a learning task, short attention span, and high distractibility.
— language deficiencies and impairment. These are frequent in MR children. Language skills are typically below the level expected for a child's mental age. Speech problems such as articulation disorders are more frequent among the mentally retarded than among normal children.
— sensorimotor handicaps. When damage to the brain has occurred, sensorimotor disorders are some of the earliest signals. Many mentally retarded children, especially those with moderate to severe impairments, have problems of this nature.
— deficits in functional skills of daily living. These problems are typical of those with moderate to severe impairment. The moderately to severely handicapped are particularly dependent upon special training if they are to master skills in this area and be brought to a more independent level of functioning.
— deficits in social skills commensurate with age group. This problem may not characterize those with mild cognitive impairments. In fact, the mildly retarded are often indistinguishable from their normal peers in social skills. With the moderately to

Table 6.3

Classification Systems for Describing
Severity Levels of Mental Retardation

Classification System Used by the American Association on Mental Deficiency

Level of Severity	IQ Score on Stanford Binet	IQ Score on Wechsler Scales
Mild	52-67	55-69
Moderate	36-51	40-54
Severe	20-35	25-39
Profound	Under 20	Under 25

Classification System Used by Public Schools

Level of Severity	IQ Range
Educable Mentally Retarded (EMR)	50-70 or 75
Trainable Mentally Retarded (TMR)	30 or 35 to 50 or 55
Severely Multiply Retarded (SMR)	below 25 or 30

severely retarded, however, difficulties with social skills are apparent. The lack of appropriate play and social skills is especially noticeable in young preschool and primary-aged children with moderate to severe retardation.

What are learning disabilities? Considerable confusion and debate continue among professionals as to what constitutes a learning disability (Turner & Wade, 1982). For some, the term includes a broad range of youngsters who experience problems in learning academic and cognitive skills at school, for whatever reason. Some view learning disabilities as applying to children who are slow to learn but whose difficulties cannot be classified under any other category (e.g., mental retardation, emotional disturbance, hearing impairment). Others see learning disabilities as a more specific type of disorder, such as irregular perceptual processes that interfere with learning. Still others suggest that school problems are the result of faulty learning and that LD children are those who have failed to acquire strategies for thinking and problem solving. They lack awareness of their own thinking processes. The absence of deliberate methods for approaching a mental task cumulate into thinking and learning habits that interfere with their learning in certain areas. These problems become apparent when children come under the structure of a school classroom where they are expected to learn and perform in specific ways and are held accountable for doing so.

Across the various perspectives on learning disabilities run some threads of commonality. Hallahan and Kauffman (1976) noted five major concepts found in most descriptions of LD:

— academic retardation or underachievement.
— an uneven pattern or discrepancy in achievement across the various developmental areas.
— may or may not be central nervous system dysfunction.
— learning problems not attributable to psychosocial disadvantage.

— learning problems not attributable to other handicapping conditions such as mental retardation or emotional disturbance.

Questions about the nature of learning disabilities remain. In the meantime, the definition used nationwide is one contained in Public Law 94-142 (*Federal Register, December 29, 1977, Part 3*):

> "Specific learning disability" means a disorder in one or more of the basic psychological processes involved in understanding or in using language, spoken or written, which may manifest itself in an imperfect ability to listen, think, speak, read, write, spell, or to do mathematical calculations. The term includes conditions such as perceptual handicaps, brain injury, minimum brain dysfunction, dyslexia and developmental aphasia. The term does not include children who have learning problems which are primarily the result of visual, hearing, or motor handicaps, of mental retardation, of emotional disturbance, or of environmental, cultural, or economic disadvantage.

Guidelines in the *Federal Register* further note areas in which a severe discrepancy between ability and achievement may be found: (a) oral expression, (b) listening comprehension, (c) written expression, (d) basic reading skills, (e) reading comprehension, (f) mathematics calculation, and (g) mathematics reasoning.

Given this definition of learning disabilities and the specific kinds of problems it details, one would be hard pressed to diagnose a preschooler as learning disabled. With an infant, it would be an impossible diagnostic category to apply. At the same time, children who are possible candidates for developing learning problems of this nature might be helped through early identification and educational intervention. Keogh and Becker (1973) explained the diagnosis and intervention dilemma surrounding learning disabilities in this way:

> When we seek to identify preschool or kindergarten children whom we fear may become learning failures, we are, in fact, hypothesizing rather than confirming. That is, the conditions which we view as atypical, namely, learning disability and failure in school, have not yet developed. Our concerns are that these conditions will develop. Yet children who have not been exposed to a reading program cannot really be said to have reading problems; children who have not participated in a first grade program cannot be classified as first grade failures. (pp. 5-6)

Keogh and Becker suggested that professionals, before applying categorical labels such as learning disabilities to young children, should recognize an important distinction: the difference between identification and labeling of "in-child conditions" that already exist and identification of children based instead on a *hypothesis or prediction* that a condition will develop.

Characteristics of children who are learning disabled   What are LD students like? A national task force surveyed the literature for descriptors of learning disabled students; over 99 characteristics were reported (Clements, 1966). The eight most frequently described ones are listed below. These characteristics describe school-aged students. To what degree the precursors to these behaviors are evident in preschoolers is not clear. Also, remember that not every child shows every one of these characteristics:

Hyperactivity: constant motion that is generally purposeless/nonproductive activity.
Perceptual motor impairments: difficulties in organizing, discriminating, and interpreting visual or auditory symbols.

Emotional lability: frequent shifts in mood, such as being high-strung and nervous or showing low tolerance levels for frustration.

General coordination deficits: physical awkwardness and incoordination that make ordinary movements seem clumsy.

Disorders of attention: inability to maintain attention and to be distractible, so a teacher has difficulty gaining a child's attention and sustaining it or switching the child's attention from one activity or stimulus to another.

Disorders of memory: deficits in auditory or visual memory attributable to lack of strategies for learning or poor language skills. Thinking deficits often involve difficulties in applying certain thought processes and a lack of awareness of one's own thinking, as well as a lack of conscious awareness of one's own thinking processes.

Specific learning disabilities: inability to perform in certain areas of academic learning or in specific mental functions involved in academic tasks such as reading, writing, or arithmetic.

Language problems: deficits that affect receptive or expressive language, such as a limited verbal repertoire or faulty sequencing of words in a sentence to convey meaning (syntax).

If children who may be potential candidates for developing the behaviors just described are to be identified for early intervention, what indices can be used to find them? Lerner (1981) suggested several possible at-risk signals:

1. The presence of biological and environmental at-risk conditions that are correlated with later developmental problems (e.g., prematurity, low birth weight, complications during pregnancy or a stressful birth, low APGAR scores at birth, or high-risk status during the first months of life).
2. Delays in achieving normal developmental milestones or specific difficulties in mastering basic skills in areas of motor, perceptual motor, language, or speech, or in engaging in tasks that involve memory, discrimination, and simple thinking sequences.
3. The presence of or an evolving pattern of behaviors that are not conducive to effective learning—particularly when the child eventually will be in more structured, controlled situations (e.g., inability to persist with a task, inability to attend to a stimulus for very long, hyperactivity and impulsiveness, distractibility).
4. The absence of a growing repertoire of skills needed to succeed in kindergarten. This may include cognitive skills that are precursory to reading and mathematical thinking, social skills that help a child function within a group setting (e.g., waiting and sharing, cooperation, and organization of play activities to achieve some end), and tools for being an effective learner (e.g., ability to listen and comprehend, ability to speak clearly and be understood, ability to communicate ideas in a relatively coherent fashion).

The impact of cognitive disorders on development and learning

The very nature of cognitive impairments implies either one or both of the following learning difficulties:

1. *Reduction in rate of learning.*

Learning is slower, resulting in developmental achievements that are less than what normally might be expected. The acquisition of normal developmental skills is delayed, and certain behaviors may not emerge at all. Given this decreased rate of learning, a lower level of cognitive sophistication will be reached in a year's time and over the entire life span. The individual will function like a younger child and may even be labeled "mentally retarded."

2. *Increase in difficulties associated with learning processes.*

Learning is more difficult and less efficient because of limitations that hamper integration and interpretation of sensory input, thinking and problem-solving processes, or output through various response modes. Learning in a person of otherwise normal intelligence thus requires greater effort if the child is to master certain skills or attain his or her true potential. These specific learning problems are most apparent in academic learning tasks at school and may result in a child being labeled "learning disabled."

In either of these two types of learning problems, the effect upon a child's life is a potential reduction in the *quantity of learning* (the amount of information assimilated in a period of time and the speed at which it is mastered) and in the *quality of learning*. Quality of learning is reflected in the degree of understanding, versus rote memorization, that occurs. It includes the ability to draw upon past learning and apply it in daily living, to generalize learning to new situations, and to use information previously mastered as a tool to solve problems and generate new, original ideas. Limitations in mental capacity influence all aspects of a person's life and adaptive capabilities. Obviously, the more severe the cognitive impairment is, the greater is the potential gap between how a person functions and how a person might have functioned. This discrepancy between achievement and what a child might have achieved had the cognitive impairment not been present is perhaps what gives parents and teachers the greatest sense of loss when dealing with a child who is cognitively handicapped.

The impact of cognitive impairments upon development and learning varies greatly from person to person. This is true even for children whose cognitive disorders originate from similar etiology. Furthermore, because the term *cognitively impaired* encompasses such a variety of problems and levels of severity, attaching blanket generalizations about the life achievements of any person so labeled is presumptuous. Environmental conditions, opportunities for learning, and other home/family variables affect a child's progress. To predict what any person—whether normal, retarded, or learning disabled—will achieve in his or her lifetime can be restrictive, even to the extent of promoting treatment by others that contributes to a self-fulfilling prophecy.

In past years professionals made the mistake of defining levels of retardation in terms of what that individual could achieve. For example, trainable retarded persons once were described as being able to achieve only rudimentary self-care skills and not able to master functional academic skills. Given these expectations, educational training in academic areas was withheld simply because TMR children were considered unable to benefit from it anyway. As expected, most retarded persons, given the absence of appropriate educational opportunity, lived up to those preconceived notions. Many trainable retarded children since have proven that preconception to be wrong. Today we are shedding those unfortunate stereotypes of what retarded persons can achieve and have adopted a more positive posture of "let's see what this child can learn." Many children progress much further than we had expected.

Each person's ability to cope with his or her limitations and the degree to which his or her environment supports continual learning is a highly individual matter. Two children with similar IQs may demonstrate very different strengths and weaknesses and may function quite differently in the same environment. The following descriptions exemplify the variable effects that cognitive disorders have on different individuals. Consider the contrasts between these persons and the impact of cognitive impairment upon their lives.

Cassey and Angela are 5-year-old kindergarteners who attend the same special education classroom. They share the same diagnosis—Down syndrome and mental retardation—but they are as different in their abilities as two normal children whom one might pick at random. Cassey is tiny for her age, slender, and with a physique much like that of a normal 4-year-old. Although she has the characteristic facial features of Down syndrome, her appearance and alertness are such that she can almost pass as a normal child. In contrast, Angela's physique is short, stubby, and stereotypic of children with Down syndrome. She lacks muscle tone, strength, and coordination. She tends to breathe through her mouth, with her tongue protruding. Angela's appearance clearly conveys the impression that she is not normal.

Cassey and Angela differ significantly in their abilities to function independently, with peers, and in the classroom. Cassey has good communication skills, a vocabulary equal to that of a 3½-year-old, and her speech can be clearly understood. Angela's voice is hoarse and raspy, and her speech has been slow in coming. Though she is a skillful imitator and often mimics her teachers' behaviors, she rarely attempts to imitate oral speech on her own. At the same time, Angela's receptive vocabulary appears comparable to Cassey's, and she follows instructions accurately when she is not being stubborn and noncompliant. Cassey is socially skillful and is a favorite playmate of both her handicapped and nonhandicapped classmates. Angela engages primarily in solitary play and does not know how to interact with other children except to steal toys or attack. She often sits alone doing something repetitiously until a teacher intervenes. Though the skills of these two little girls are very different, their composite IQ scores on the WPPSI (Wechsler Preschool and Primary Scales of Intelligence) put them within 10 points of each other.

Tobin and Amy were diagnosed in the third grade as learning disabled, but for different reasons. The impact of their cognitive impairments during the early childhood years cannot be described since no one imagined then that either child had any real or potential problems. Tobin was a super-energetic "typical boy," as his parents described him—always on the go, always involved in rough-and-tumble play. He shied away from any of the "sissy" activities such as looking at books or sitting at a table working on a quiet task. No one pressured him to quiet down or insisted on more variety in his play. No one expected that he would have so many problems learning to read in school. Amy, too, seemed like any other preschooler. Her mom recalls that she seemed a little disoriented at times, got lost easily, or forgot where she had put things. Amy never was athletically inclined; she took a while to learn to ride her tricycle and never attempted to learn to ride a bike.

Sometimes she seemed a bit "tuned out," resulting in many reminders to pay attention. But none of those little things added up to any reason for concern because Amy obviously was a bright child.

Now, as third graders, Tobin's and Amy's special problems affect their lives in very different ways. Tobin is called hyperactive. He gets frustrated easily and explodes in anger or simply refuses to try. He is considered a behavior problem in both his regular class and in his special resource room. He often gets in fights with peers. Tobin hates school and sneaks away from the building if not watched closely. His parents don't think he should be forced to do anything he doesn't want to do but aren't sure how to handle his bad attitudes about school. By the end of the day, Tobin can't wait to get on his bike, which he rides until nearly bedtime. Amy, on the other hand, is a "plodder." She works hard and reacts to a poorly graded assignment with a look of frustration but then proceeds to do it over again. When she finally gets 90% or 100% (usually after several tries), she takes the work home, where her parents pridefully display it on the refrigerator. Amy's handwriting is messy, too, and sometimes her writing is hard to read. But she works on that at home with her parents' help. She thinks that she has that problem licked, however— she is learning to type. Amy excels in some of her other academic areas and has several A's on her report card. Her dream is to be a college professor like her father. She tries so hard and does so well in so many other things that a person sometimes forgets her clumsiness, her propensity to get lost even in the school building, her forgetfulness, poor handwriting, and poor grades in math.

Jerode and Ted are "grown up" now. Both are 32 years old. In their early childhood and school years each was diagnosed as trainable mentally retarded with unknown etiology. Both had IQs in the 40-50 range, and both were educated in special classes for TMR students. Today, as a 32-year-old retarded adult, Ted works as a janitor in a local business as part of a vocational sheltered workshop program for the retarded. He earns a wage and uses part of it to pay rent on an apartment (a semi-independent, supervised living arrangement operated by the sheltered workshop), which he shares with two roommates. Ted gets around on his own by walking or riding the bus. He shops for his own groceries (though he needs help to pay the proper amount of money) and fixes his own meals with his roommates. For recreation he goes to movies or the local swimming pool. People in town know Ted and stop to say hi. He greets them with a smile and hello and carries on a simple conversation about his activities. If you were to meet Ted for the first time, you would not perceive him as a "trainable level" retarded person.

Compared to Ted, Jerode's life is very different, even though his measured mental abilities initially were described in terms quite similar to those used to describe Ted. Jerode lives in a nursing home, where he is constantly surpervised. He can talk but responds only when spoken to and lacks much interest in things around him. Jerode must be prompted a lot to get him to use his time constructively. He has to be reminded to zip up his pants, take a bath, or wipe his face after a meal; yet he is able to perform all of these tasks. If Jerode would wander away from the nursing home, no one is quite sure whether he would be able to find his way back.

These descriptions, contrasting Cassey with Angela, Tobin with Amy, and Jerode with Ted, emphasize what different impressions each individual gives and how differently their mental handicaps affect their lives. Children with mental retardation or any type of cognitive impairment are not a homogeneous group. They have just as many individual differences among them as any group of so-called normal individuals.

Caution also should be exercised in using the construct of "mental retardation" or "learning disabled" to explain learning problems. Circular explanations, such as, "Joshua's speech and language development is delayed because he is mentally retarded" or "Patrick can't do his math very well because he is learning disabled" should be avoided. Explanations such as these are inappropriate and counterproductive when the emphasis belongs on what a child needs to continue learning—not an explanation for why he or she cannot.

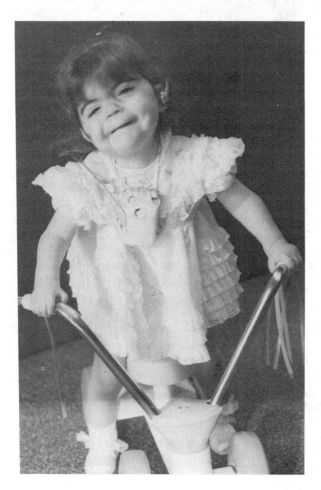

Tara has Cornelia de Lange syndrome, which is characterized by mental retardation, hearing impairment, and vision impairment. Nonetheless, her family and the professionals who work with her simply ask, "How much can we teach this little one?"

Mental handicaps often are accompanied by other handicapping conditions, such as those described earlier in this chapter and in chapter 5. Thus, earlier descriptions of the potential impacts of sensory, health, physical, neurological, and emotional disabilities on development and learning may affect the lives of children described as cognitively impaired. Rather than presenting any further generalizations on potential outcomes of cognitive disorders in young children, some of the kinds of specific learning difficulties frequently encountered in such children are listed briefly.

1. Because learning rates may be slower in children with cognitive impairments, the gap increases between the age when specific skills ordinarily would be acquired and the age at which a child actually learns the skills. As a result, the environment may be less stimulating and supportive of skill learning at the times when the child is ready and most receptive. For example, parents readily engage in babbling and reciprocal cooing with an infant—a type of interaction that facilitates early sound production and prespeech learning. Adults, however, are less apt to engage in the same behaviors with a 4-, 5-, or 7-year-old retarded child who may just be reaching a stage of maturity to begin acquiring those skills.

2. The more severe the cognitive impairment is, the greater are the chances that other handicaps are present. Cognitive disorders such as mental retardation go hand-in-hand with deficits in other developmental areas such as speech, language, motor development, and emotional/social/adaptive behavior. Which is the primary or secondary handicap is not always clear. Nonetheless, mental handicaps may render a child less able to compensate or overcome the limitations imposed by other types of handicaps. The other associated handicaps may create limitations, such as limited sensory input or mobility that reduce the rate of learning in ways that further complicate learning and cognitive development.

3. Children with cognitive impairment often lack many thinking tools that otherwise would help them learn how to learn. Thus, initial deficits make the learning of other new skills more difficult, and the absence of those skills further hampers learning at the next level. For example:

   - Mentally retarded children tend to rely on rote memory to recall items as opposed to applying more systematic organization of concepts (Spreen, 1965; Spreen et al., 1984; Stephens, 1972, 1973).
   - Children with mental retardation seem to have more difficulties with short- and long-term memory than normal children of the same chronological age. This seems more pronounced with abstract materials than with concrete information. These memory deficits may interfere with efficient learning, recall, and use of learned material (Butterfield, Wambold, & Belmont, 1973; Detterman, 1979; Ellis, 1970).
   - Children with cognitive impairment appear to develop speech and language functions in the same sequence as normal children, but their rate of attainment is slower. This is evidenced in regard to the development of increased vocabulary size, sentence length, and complexity of sentence structures. Given the reduced proficiency in language, a child is less equipped for further learning because he or she lacks the tools to initiate, mediate, and perpetuate learning events (e.g., asking questions)(Graham & Graham, 1971; Buium, Rynders, & Turnure, 1974; Sitko & Semmel, 1973; Spradlin, 1968).

- Children with cognitive impairment show more difficulty in identifying and attending to relevant stimuli in a learning situation. They seem to have a propensity for selecting cues or stimuli that are not relevant to the learning task and to take longer to focus upon the dimensions upon which appropriate discriminations can be made (Zeamon & House, 1963; Fisher & Zeamon, 1973).

SUMMARY

The handicapping conditions described in this chapter all deal with irregularities in children's behavior or performance that may or may not be accompanied by physical abnormalities that can be diagnosed medically. Compared to the physical and sensory disorders described in the previous chapter, the diagnosis of emotional problems, speech and language disorders, or cognitive abnormalities is even more complicated. What represents normal or abnormal behavior in each of these areas is particularly ambiguous. Any diagnosis of these types of disorders involves a judgment of the degree to which a child's behavior deviates from some standard of normality and whether the degree of variance is of sufficient magnitude to be considered abnormal or pathological. How one judges deviance, normality, and hence pathology in a young child, however, is highly influenced by social values and by the perspective of the individual who attempts to make that determination.

Because considerable controversy surrounds the judgments made in diagnosing young children as emotionally disturbed, learning disabled, or mentally retarded, and because of the risks that the determinations may be premature and inaccurate, caution has to be exercised in the use of these labels. The diagnosis of language and speech impairments may be less cumbersome, but parallel kinds of problems still are present in defining the point at which speech and language behavior is disordered. Professionals should avoid being too hasty in attaching any diagnostic label of mentally retarded to a child. Concerns over the misuse of diagnostic labels and the potential stigmatization with school-aged students should be sufficient warning that these problems should not be repeated again with young children. The risks that a child will be treated in a way that an early diagnosis will only become a self-fulfilling prophecy are serious enough that early childhood-special educators should consider alternative systems of designating young children who need early intervention programs.

III
DELIVERING SERVICES
TO YOUNG CHILDREN
WITH SPECIAL NEEDS

7
Assessment and
Evaluation Processes

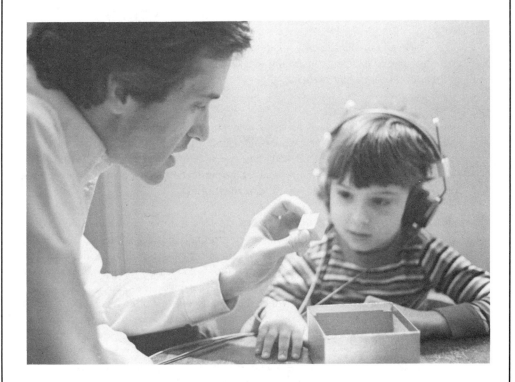

Now that you are acquainted with early childhood-special education as an field and with the young children who need intervention, we turn to a new topic: the actual *delivery of special education services* to infants and preschoolers who are handicapped or at-risk for developmental disabilities. The intervention process begins with *assessment,* wherein the children we want to help are identified through a process of information and data gathering, using testing instruments such as checklists, standardized tests, criterion-referenced tests, and direct observational methods. Assessment procedures are continuous

This chapter was authored with John Meier, whose contribution is much appreciated.

throughout the entire intervention, serving as a guide for everything that happens to a child. Given the pivotal role that assessment plays in delivering services to young children with special needs, the purpose of this chapter is to:

— review basic concepts underlying the measurement of children's behavior and the use of various testing approaches.
— examine the various assessment processes applied in special programs for young children.
— discuss some special considerations and issues associated with the assessment of behavior and developmental problems in young children.

SOME BASICS ON EDUCATIONAL ASSESSMENT: A REVIEW

Before one can talk intelligently about assessment procedures with infants and preschoolers, some basic concepts concerning measurement must be understood. These concepts and the terminology that describes them are reviewed first.

Approaches to assessment

A variety of approaches can be used to evaluate development and learning in young children. One's choice of method depends upon (a) the purpose of the measurement and the kind of information desired, (b) characteristics of the children, including their ages and the types/severity of disability, and (c) the particular behaviors or skills to be targeted. Some of the possible approaches are described briefly.

Formal versus informal assessment   As the term implies, *formal* assessment involves the use of instruments that have been formally developed, tested, and refined by their authors. What distinguishes formal from informal tests is that formal tests typically (a) have been improved and refined as a result of field testing, and (b) have some measure of reliability and validity. *Informal* tests are teacher-made tests that are less refined and usually specific to the situation in which they are used. Most often this involves measuring a child's daily or weekly progress as a result of a particular learning sequence. The reliability and validity of informal assessment tools are not usually known. Informal tests are often directly related to learning objectives in a child's individualized education program (IEP) and serve an ongoing instructional, informal diagnostic, or evaluative function. In contrast, formal tests generally are global in their content.

Norm-referenced versus criterion-referenced assessment   Children's learning can be evaluated from two perspectives: (a) in comparison to the performance of others, and (b) in comparison with themselves and their own progress in learning a set of defined skills or behaviors. Testing instruments using a *norm-referenced* approach compare a child's skills with a *norm group*. Results are expressed in terms of a child's standing among a group of peers of the same age or who have some characteristic in common (e.g., gender or a type of handicap). Results are in the form of (a) a *developmental score,* usually given as age equivalents (year and month) or grade equivalents (grade and 1-9 months), (b) a *percentile score,* reflecting a child's relative standing among the norm group (e.g., 40th percentile would indicate that 40% of the norm group falls below the child's score), or (c) a *standard score*, such as a developmental quotient or IQ. *Criterion-referenced* tests, on the other hand, do not compare a child to any group of individuals. Performance simply is compared against a standard indicating whether the child has mastered certain skills or met targeted learning objectives.

Standardized versus nonstandardized assessment   *Standardized* testing implies a formalized procedure. Standardized measures are based on (a) a fixed procedure for administering and scoring the test, including specific instructions to be given a child, (b) standard apparatus, materials, or stimulus items to be used in administering the test, (c) empirical testing of the items in the instrument and refinement of the test based upon results, and (d) norms against which a child is compared (Aiken, 1985; Salvia & Ysseldyke, 1981). In standardized testing, exact procedures must be followed if test results are to be valid. This assures that the test is given to all children in exactly the same way, to provide a basis for comparing their performance. *Nonstandardized tests,* in contrast, generally entail informal, teacher-constructed evaluation procedures. Methods of administering the instrument usually are defined more loosely.

Direct versus indirect assessment   *Direct* observation implies that the determination of what a child can do or the documentation of his or her behavior is made by watching that child in action. *Indirect* assessment methods imply that an intermediate person provides information about the child. The information source is typically a person (parent or teacher) who knows a child well and is in a position to provide the necessary data. Methods used to gather information from the secondary source person may involve checklists, rating forms or questionnaires, and interviews of either a formal or an informal nature conducted by the evaluator. Direct observation may take place in structured or nonstructured situations. Structured observation is akin to formalized testing methods in that a well developed procedure is used to gather data. The child may be allowed to engage in regular activities for the observation, or may be asked to perform specific tasks.

Basic concepts and terminology in assessment

Regardless of the type of behavior to be evaluated, any assessment tool or procedure must have both validity and reliability if it is to provide meaningful, accurate information. Definitions of these terms and an explanation of the methods educators use to establish validity and reliability are described below.

Reliability   The consistency with which a test measures what it is supposed to measure is termed *reliability*. It is a measure of a test's *dependability, accuracy, stability,* and *predictability,* which are essential if the test is to be of any value to its users (Wiersma & Jurs, 1985). In direct observational procedures in which a person watches a child's performance and records continuous data, those data have credibility if a second person is able to observe and record the same events. High agreement between the observers should be manifest. Reliability with formal tests usually is expressed in the form of a *correlation coefficient*. This describes the degree of relationship between two sets of scores. A correlation coefficient ranges from -1.00 to $+1.00$. A correlation of 1.00 indicates a perfect relationship. This means that as performance on one measure goes up, it also goes up on the second measure, or if one score goes down, so does the other. A perfect negative correlation (-1.00) means that an inverse relationship exists. As performance on one measure goes up, performance on the second one goes down. When a coefficient approaches .00, no recognizable relationship or pattern exists between scores on the two tests.

Reliability of assessment instruments or procedures is determined in one of four ways:

1. *Test-retest reliability.* An assessment tool is administered and then administered again in a relatively short time. Agreement between the two measures is compared and expressed as a correlation coefficient.

2. *Alternative form reliability.* Two equivalent forms of the same instrument, assumed to be of equal and comparable difficulty, are given. A correlation coefficient then is computed to determine the concordance between children's scores earned on both forms.

3. *Split-half reliability.* Test items are divided into two parts (usually by grouping odd- and even-numbered items), children's scores on each half are calculated, and then the correlation between the two scores is determined to gain an index of reliability.

4. *Interobserver reliability.* This comparison is made for data gathered through direct, ongoing observation of a child's behavior. In this case, reliability is determined by a second, independent observer who takes simultaneous data. Data then are compared by counting the number of recordings on which the observers agree or disagree. Finally, reliability is calculated in terms of a percent of agreement. Usually a standard of 85% or 90% agreement is a minimal level of acceptable reliability.

The question often is raised: What is the minimum reliability that is acceptable? This question has no one answer because "good reliability" depends on (a) how one test's reliability compares to that of other similar tests, (b) what type of approach was used to establish reliability (e.g., test-retest, equivalent forms, split-half), and (c) what type of behavior or performance is being measured (e.g., achievement, development, personality, or ability). For an in-depth discussion on acceptable levels of reliability, see Shertzer and Linden's (1979) *Fundamentals of Individual Appraisal* (pp. 87-100).

Validity   How well an assessment instrument measures what it purports to measure is called *validity*. This means if a test is purported to tap a child's language skills, it should contain items that systematically evaluate various aspects of behavior considered to constitute what we call "language." The several types of validity are:

Content validity: The adequacy with which an instrument covers a representative sample of the behaviors it supposedly measures. A test is inspected to see if the test items actually tap the behaviors that are intended to be evaluated. This is done by logical analysis and comparison with other accepted tests that measure the same behavior.

Criterion-related validity: The degree to which a testing instrument effectively relates behavior to some specific criterion. Two methods are applied here to determine if an instrument is acceptable on this dimension. First, results of the test are compared with those of another accepted test that measures the same behavior. A high correlation between the two suggests good criterion-related validity. This is sometimes termed *concurrent validity*.

The second method involves a determination of how well a child's real performance can be predicted from results of the evaluation instrument. (Example: A kindergarten readiness test successfully estimates children's probability for success in first grade. A high correlation between the test and performance in first grade suggests the test does predict well). This second type of criterion-related validity is called *predictive validity*.

Construct validity: An index of the extent to which an evaluation tool actually measures a psychological quality or construct such as intelligence, creativity, or cognition. A *construct* refers to an abstraction or idea used to explain some aspect of behavior we observe. Construct validity is determined through rather complex procedures that will not be elaborated here. Basically, however, construct validity is determined through three major steps (Gronlund, 1985): (a) identification of the constructs presumed to account for a child's test performance, (b) derivation of hypotheses regarding test performance from the theory underlying the construct, and (c) verifying those hypotheses through logical or empirical means.

When reviewing a new testing tool and considering its use with children, the manual and other literature should be referred to for reliability and validity information. Any instrument or observation procedure that has no measure of reliability or validity may be questionable.

> For more information on principles, basic measurement, and evaluation, see: Goodwin and Driscoll (1982); Gronlund (1985); Sabatino and Miller (1979); Wallace and Larson (1978).

Theoretical orientations affecting early childhood assessment

A person's views on the nature of human development and learning greatly affect how one goes about the evaluation process and how one interprets the behavior (or lack of behavior) in an infant or preschooler. The theoretical position one assumes will dictate (a) what behaviors are considered most important to measure, (b) what procedures are applied to accurately measure and describe those behaviors, and (c) what explanation is given to interpret results. Fewell (1983) reviewed four major theoretical points of view that have dominated the thinking of professionals in regard to testing and evaluation processes with young children. Those four perspectives are:

1. *The developmental perspective.*

This approach views behavior in terms of its natural progression through stages of normal skill development in areas such as cognitive development, fine and gross motor development, language, and social behavior. Thus, a child is evaluated in terms of his or her mastery (or lack of mastery) of basic developmental skills. This type of assessment usually is based upon normative data on a large population of children. These norms are used to establish (a) what skills children typically master at various age levels, and (b) the general sequence of skill learning under each developmental domain. A child's developmental status or performance on various learning tasks is interpreted by comparing his or her performance with peers in the norm group. Some of the most widely known developmental scales and checklists are developed on the basis of this orientation. An example is the Gesell Developmental Schedules created by Arnold Gesell (Gesell, 1925; Gesell & Amatruda, 1947). Cattell's Infant Intelligence Test draws heavily from Gesell's scales. The Bayley Scales of Infant Development (Bayley, 1969) are based upon a combination of Bayley's own normative data and the Gesell norms.

2. The cognitive stages perspective.

This orientation derives primarily from Piaget's theory of intellectual development. Piaget explained development as a series of hierarchical stages, qualitatively and quantitatively different, that show horizontal and vertical change over time as a result of a child's interaction with the environment (Piaget, 1950; Piaget & Inhelder, 1969). A child's progression from one stage to another is influenced by four major variables: (a) maturation, (b) experiences with the physical environment, (c) influence of the social environment (i.e., interactions with peers and adults), and (d) the child's fluctuating state of equilibrium, which acts as a self-regulating, self-correcting process of adaptation. Through this latter process, a child assimilates new information into existing cognitive structures, or existing cognitive structures are modified to fit the new, incoming experiences and environmental influences. A child's own press for equilibrium and internal motivation move him or her ahead from one stage to another.

This view of development has resulted in development of numerous cognitively oriented, or Piagetian-based, evaluation devices. The *Infant Psychological Development Scales* developed by Uzgiris and Hunt (1975) are an example. These scales contain an ordinal progression of cognitive processes through the various stages and substages described in Piaget's theory. A degree of controversy surrounds the application of Piagetian-based scales with retarded persons. Some experts note its usefulness (Dunst, 1981; Robinson & Robinson, 1965, 1976; Rogers, 1977); others question its applicability to more severely mentally retarded individuals (Switzky, Rotatori, Miller, & Freagon, 1979).

3. The behavioral perspective.

Development, from the behavioral point of view, occurs as a result of learning and interaction with the environment. It is not simply a phenomenon that unfolds spontaneously as a result of maturation or from any inherent characteristics within the child. Learning comes about as a child practices new behavior, finds it functional, and experiences reinforcing consequences. The behavioral perspective prescribes a functional approach to assessment involving four major steps. *First,* behaviors that are absent, of insufficient frequency, excessive frequency, or simply inappropriate are noted. *Second,* objectives are set down to define what behaviors or skills should be developing. These objectives define observable behaviors and are written in precise, measurable terms. *Third,* criteria for performance, defining mastery of each new behavior, are set. *Fourth,* performance or developmental progress is measured systematically through direct observation and precise methods of data collection.

Evaluation procedures from this theoretical perspective do not compare a child's performance with that of agemates as do approaches based upon a developmental perspective. Development simply is compared against the initial criteria. Evaluation of this kind often is referred to as criterion-referenced, child-referenced, or curriculum-referenced testing (Hamilton & Swan, 1981). Examples of this type of evaluation include the Brigance Diagnostic Inventory of Early Development (Brigance, 1978), the Learning Accomplishment Profile or LAP (Sanford, 1981), or the Portage Developmental Checklist (Shearer & Shearer, 1977).

4. *The adaptive-transactive perspective.*

This view does not focus on the individual per se as do the other theoretical orientations. It emphasizes interactions or transactions between a child and external stimuli such as social stimuli provided by a parent or agemate, or environmental stimuli. From this perspective, behaviors of greatest interest are a child's response patterns to auditory stimuli (Wilson, 1976), visual stimuli (Cohen & Salapatek, 1975), and environmental events (Cicchetti & Scoufe, 1976). This perspective holds that behavior change cannot be explained purely in terms of biological or psychological phenomena. Instead, it must be explained and evaluated in the context of environmental conditions in which it occurs or in relationship to the interactions surrounding its occurrence (Sameroff & Cavanaugh, 1979).

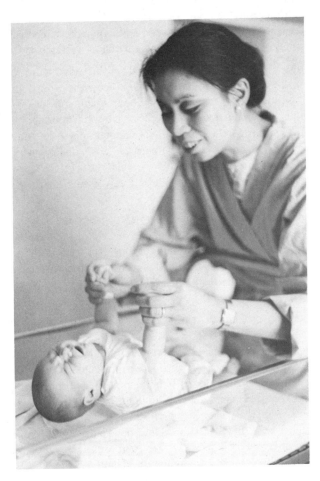

An early assessment is conducted on this newborn, using the Brazelton.

This theoretical orientation has been applied particularly in the evaluation of infant behavior and of reciprocal interaction between caregiver and child. Most assessment instruments developed from this perspective are new and still in experimental stages of development. Consequently, most are available only through their developers. Examples include the Home Observation for Measurement of the Environment (HOME), developed by Caldwell and Bradley (1978), and the Infant Questionnaire (Carey & McDevitt, 1978).

AN EVALUATION MODEL FOR EARLY CHILDHOOD-SPECIAL EDUCATION

The terms *evaluation* and *assessment* connote very different things to different persons— especially when they are applied to young children. Though professionals agree that assessment and evaluation are integral to early intervention programs, interpretations vary as to what this entails. The most plaguing source of confusion is the lack of a consistent terminology. Words such as assessment, screening, evaluation, identification, and diagnosis appear in the literature frequently, but their meanings are not standardized (Cross & Goin, 1977; Fallen & McGovern, 1978; Hare & Hare, 1977; Suarez, 1982). Thus, we find ourselves using similar terminology but referring to different concepts. No wonder so much confusion arises when we talk about assessment evaluation processes! For the discussion in this chapter, the definition of terms must be clearly established.

The term *evaluation,* as used in this chapter, is an all-inclusive word referring to the overall process of making judgments about a child's behavior or development, an instructional procedure, a program, or anything else about which conclusions are to be drawn. To *evaluate* implies that some value judgments or interpretations are made on the basis of information collected through observation, formal and informal testing, or other means. Evaluation is a part of literally every treatment and educational function we can carry out with young children. This emphasizes the fact that evaluation is a *process*—not just a single event that occurs before and after children receive some special intervention program.

Before one can begin to evaluate or make judgments about anything, information and specific data must be gathered. This ongoing process of collecting data for purposes of evaluation is what we call *assessment.* Various strategies are used in the assessment process: direct observation, testing with instruments such as criterion-referenced tests, standardized tests, or information gathering via interviews, surveys, checklists, and questionnaires.

Within early intervention programs a variety of assessment processes comes into play. Each assessment process is applied for a different purpose; each addresses a new set of questions that must be answered; and each produces a unique kind of information or end result. Expanding upon the system of evaluation presented by Cross and Goin (1977), we suggest a model of evaluation for early childhood-special education programs that entails six major stages of assessment, depicted in Figure 7.1. These are: *casefinding, screening, diagnosis, educational assessment, performance monitoring,* and *program evaluation.* All persons working directly with handicapped and at-risk children must understand these various assessment processes, their purposes, and outcomes. In the following pages each type of assessment is examined in detail.

Figure 7.1
An Evaluation Model for Early Childhood-Special Education

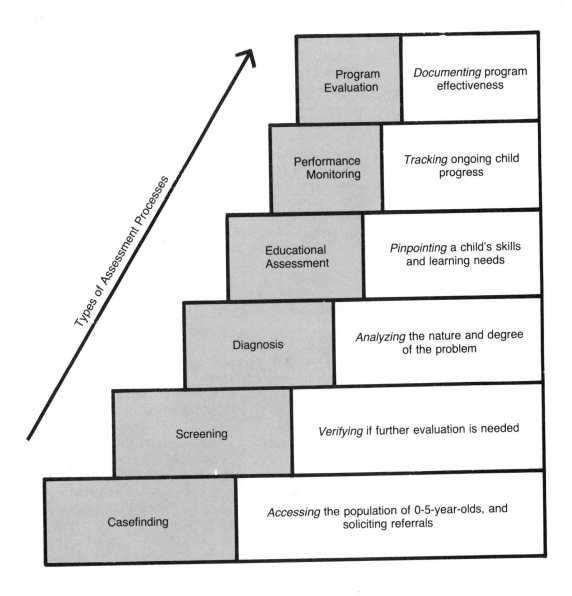

TYPES OF ASSESSMENT PROCESSES

Table 7.1 provides a detailed analysis of each type of assessment process: its major purpose, the underlying questions to be answered, and the individuals most likely to carry out that function. Note that these processes fall into an orderly sequence of events that parallel the steps taken to deliver special education services to young handicapped/at-risk children. Each type of assessment adds to the information base established by the previous assessment process. Each, in turn, provides the essential ingredients required to move ahead to the next phase of assessment.

Casefinding

Casefinding is the first step in locating infants and preschoolers who are possible candidates for early intervention. It is a means for *accessing* the target population of children and soliciting referrals. Although actual procedures of casefinding are not evaluative per se, casefinding activities stimulate a kind of informal assessment process. The goal is to get individuals and agencies to take a critical look at young children with whom they interact and to be sensitive to situations in which a referral for screening is appropriate. This means asking some probing questions about one's own observations during personal or professional contacts with young preschoolers and infants:

- Does this child seem to be developing normally? Is his or her behavior within the range one would expect of a child at this age?
- Does the child exhibit any behaviors that are of concern or that give any sense that maybe a problem is present?
- Do any circumstances in this child's medical or developmental history suggest a higher risk for possible problems that should be monitored carefully?
- Are conditions in the home environment conducive to healthy physical, emotional, cognitive, or linguistic growth, or do any circumstances suggest that the child may be receiving less stimulation and nurturance than needed for optimal development?

Casefinding as a means for gaining referrals or locating potential candidates for screening is a task unique to the field of early childhood-special education. Compare, for example, how different the task is when school-aged students are identified as candidates for special education services. School-aged students already are gathered together in one place—the local elementary, middle, or secondary school—where their teachers can observe them daily. These students learn and perform each day in a standardized environment where certain tasks are presented and common expectations are placed upon the students. The very setting allows a student's performance to be observed and compared with that of agemates.

Given these conditions, deviant behavior or lack of progress is more noticeable. Over time, each student builds a record of performance—one in which his or her ability to learn and to perform expected assignments becomes clear. This performance history and teachers' ongoing observations are what typically lead to referral of a student for testing and possible special education services. In a sense, casefinding and screening are combined with school-aged students. There is no need to go out into the community to find and recruit candidates for screening and observation.

Table 7.1

Evaluation and Its Sequential Processes

Assessment	Purpose	Underlying Questions	Who Typically Implements
Casefinding	To alert parents, professionals, and the general public to children who may have special needs and to elicit their help in recruiting candidates for screening	Does a child show any problems or unusual behaviors that are of concern to the parents or others around the child? Should some child be referred for screening because his or her development or behavior seems unusual?	Local preschool and day care personnel Physicians and other health professionals Clergymen Parents and interested citizens Social service workers
Screening	To identify children who are not within normal ranges of development and need further evaluation and who may be candidates for early intervention programs	Which children give evidence of potential problems or abnormalities? Which children show need for further diagnostic evaluations and case study? Which children suggest a possible need for intervention if they are to develop normally?	Interdisciplinary screening teams Program staff Specially trained volunteers

Diagnosis	To conduct an in-depth evaluation to verify if a problem exists; to determine the nature and severity of the problem and prescribe the treatment or type of intervention services needed	What exactly is the impairment or abnormality?
		
		How severe is the problem, and will it likely affect development and learning?
		
		What type of intervention or treatment is needed?
			Specialists from various disciplines:
			    Audiologist
			    Speech/language pathologist
			    Occupational therapist
			    Physical therapist
			    Educational diagnostician
			    Psychologist
			    Pediatrician or medical specialist

Educational Assessment	To identify a child's specific level of functioning across each of the developmental areas and to gather other performance data for developing the individualized education program (IEP)	What are the child's strengths and weaknesses? What skills have and have not been mastered, and in what areas is special instruction needed? What instructional/therapeutic objectives should be pinpointed, and what special services and curriculum should be provided?	Teachers, clinicians, parents, and other service providers

Table 7.1 (continued)

Assessment	Purpose	Underlying Questions	Who Typically Implements
Performance Monitoring	To track or monitor each child's performance and mastery of new skills as a result of the special instructional or therapeutic activities in the intervention program	Is each child making continuous progress as a result of individually prescribed learning activities? Is each child reaching the IEP goals that have been defined? Are teaching methods producing the desired learning?	Teachers, clinicians, paraprofessionals, parents, or anyone who assumes responsibility for instruction in a skill area relating to an IEP objective
Program Evaluation	To evaluate the quality of the overall intervention program and to document its impact upon the children or parents it serves	How effective is the program in intervening in the lives of children? What are the outcomes of the program in regard to child performance and developmental gains? Are parents, staff, and others associated with the program satisfied with its services and methods of operation?	Program staff Parents Outside evaluation teams The funding or sponsoring agency

Casefinding with children under school age is more complicated and is not accomplished so easily. This population is not found gathered together in one setting as are school-aged students. Canvassing neighborhoods to locate preschoolers and infants who should be referred for screening is a major task. It requires the cooperation of individuals who are in continuous contact with young children and can act as casefinders and referral agents (e.g., parents, caregivers, relatives, or professionals in service roles such as public health nurses, social workers, physicians, or clergy).

Considerations in conducting casefinding activities Scott and Hogan (1982) have pointed out that casefinding requires identification of three rather different groups of young children for potential inclusion in early intervention programs:

1. *Children with clear disabilities.* These children are easily identified by medical doctors, psychologists, or educators, and likely will be diagnosed early. The casefinding task here is not so much one of identifying the child with the problem as of helping people see the value of early intervention. Parents may think the damage has already been done and they must accept and cope with the situation the best they can. Casefinding with this population of children, then, is primarily one of getting parents or professionals to make the necessary referrals.

2. *Children with hidden handicaps.* These are children whose difficulties are not so apparent and who may leave an adult only with a general impression that "maybe something is wrong." Casefinding of infants and preschoolers in this category depends upon parents, caregivers, or relatives who are close enough to observe a child's behavior over time and are able to note subtle signs of irregular or questionable behavior. Effective casefinding is dependent upon getting these individuals to take action (even when they only have questions about a child's behavior) by referring the child for screening.

3. *Children at risk.* These children have no apparent disorders, but their life history or condition suggests that their developmental progress should be watched. Some are *medically at-risk.* If so, medical professionals are in the best position to counsel parents to seek early intervention programs or take advantage of screening programs. Some children are *environmentally at-risk.* These preschoolers and infants can be targeted by the neighborhood in which they live or by information available on their parents and older siblings. Social service and public health agencies, clergy, and neighborhood organizations are in a prime position to act as referral agents with these cases. Other children are *biologically at-risk* or have *established risk* even though specific disabilities may not be particularly notable (as described in chapter 4). These children, too, should be screened.

An effective casefinding strategy depends on several factors (L. Cross, 1977). First, the *age range* of children to be recruited for service has to be considered. Recruitment of infants is done best through contacts with pediatricians, neonatal and high-risk clinics in hospitals, and parent groups. Recruitment of preschoolers can be done more efficiently through contacts with nursery schools, day-care facilities, and churches, and through general public awareness campaigns.

The *type(s) of handicapped children* to be served (i.e., types of handicaps or levels of severity) represents a second variable affecting casefinding. Community agency workers and public health personnel often are aware of children with relatively severe handicaps (L. Cross, 1977). Contacts with these agencies and their personnel therefore can be helpful in locating those children. Finding children with mild disorders is more difficult. A solution is to recruit particular populations of children who are more likely candidates for developing special problems. To this end, Scott and Hogan (1982) have recommended that the following groups be targeted: (a) children from families at social risk (e.g., low-income families or families with established histories of neglect or abuse), and (b) infants from intensive care units.

A third factor affecting casefinding activities is the *geographical location.* How one would go about making contacts, what agencies should be contacted, and what organizations are most likely to bring responsive action from citizens depends on the local social system and communication network. Informal support networks often develop among neighbors in small communities or tightly knit neighborhoods within large metropolitan centers. These often are more powerful networks than the formal service system set up within public agencies.

Examples of strategies for casefinding   Innumerable strategies can be used to gain referrals and recruit children for screening. Table 7.2 summarizes some of the possibilities.

Table 7.2
Strategies for Casefinding

Task	Description	Strategies
Building Community Awareness	Purpose is to (a) educate the public about importance of early identification and intervention with handicapped and high-risk children, (b) alert the public of the availability of screening services and special early intervention programs, and (c) enlist assistance of public agencies, organizations, and local citizens in making referrals and in supporting services for young children with special needs.	1. Announcements alerting public about screening clinics and the importance of identifying children who need special help, through newspaper features, radio/TV spots, posters, or distribution of brochures/letters/information sheets to community leaders, service agencies, and professional practitioners. 2. Presentations to PTAs and other parent groups, church and civic groups, local professional organizations, special interest groups, and staffs of local service agencies. 3. Creation of an advocacy group among influential citizens and personnel in key positions within organizations who can bring visibility and local support to recruitment efforts.
Setting Up System for Referral and Eliciting Referrals	Purpose is to establish network of informed agencies and individuals who come into contact with a large number of children and who will take initiative to refer appropriate children for screening. Task is to (a) provide these persons or agencies with information on screening clinics and service programs for handicapped/high-risk children, (b) provide information and written literature on contact person and procedures for making referrals, and (c) establish working relationships between referral agents and intake/screening contact person.	1. Direct contacts with officials of key community agencies to establish formal linkages for sending and receiving referrals (e.g., public schools, local preschool and day-care programs, churches, mental health clinics, social service and welfare offices, health clinics, and agencies serving the handicapped—such as Easter Seal, United Cerebral Palsy, Association for Retarded Citizens). 2. Direct contacts with private practitioners who serve young children and their parents and who are in a prime position to make referrals (e.g., pediatricians and other medical professionals, dentists, psychologists and family counselors, psychiatrists, social workers, and therapists in private clinics, such as speech-language-hearing clinics or mental health clinics).

Table 7.2 (continued)

Task	Description	Strategies
Canvassing Community for Children Who Need Screening	Purpose is to conduct a systematic survey of children in the designated age range and geographical area to identify those for whom screening is needed and who may not be referred through other sources (often the mildly handicapped or developmentally delayed). The task is not only one of systematically canvassing the community to gain direct or indirect contact with the target population of children, but also to offer guides for helping parents and others identify child characteristics that suggest referral for a screening evaluation.	1. Direct observation of children or consultation with staff and parents associated with local preschool or day-care centers, local churches, parents' and women's groups, or any other major organization through which a large group of community members are brought together. 2. Direct door-to-door canvassing of community to share information on how to make referrals and to offer checklist guides for helping parents discern situations when a child should be referred for screening. 3. Distribution of information on screening services and referral procedures by sending materials home with school-aged students or under-school-aged youngsters enrolled in local preschool, day-care, and Head Start programs.
Maintaining Local Publicity and Contacts with Referral Sources	Purpose is to maintain a continual flow of referrals from various sources by (a) keeping the network of individuals and agencies continually informed about the screening system and the current contact person(s), (b) sharing information on the on-going activities of the screening/placement system, and (c) providing yearly reports on the number of children identified for early intervention, and on the success of the screening system in linking children with community services.	1. Yearly renewal of official contacts with key citizens, agencies, and organizations in referral network, to provide updated information on referral procedures for new persons who may become involved as a result of normal turnover in agency personnel and organization membership. 2. Replenishment of written materials disseminated to the network of referral agencies and citizens so that casefinding activities are continued and do not fizzle out over time. 3. Dissemination of year-end written reports summarizing data on the number of children referred, number screened, and percentage of children subsequently placed in special service programs, to allow referral sources to see the outcomes of their efforts.

Screening

This second phase of evaluation (as depicted in Figure 7.1) is a means of verifying whether a child needs further diagnostic evaluation. Its purpose is to identify children who do not fall within normal ranges of development as suggested by rough estimates of their current and remembered past behavior. Parents and professionals thus can be alerted to children who may have conditions considered to be handicapping or precursory to abnormal growth and development. These are the children who are potential candidates for special early intervention programs.

The population of children to be screened may be defined in any number of ways, such as: preschoolers 3-5 years of age, infants, children with potential speech and language difficulties, or children from low-income families. The parameters that define the group of children to be screened depend upon state laws, purposes of the screening, and the kinds of local programs for which children are being identified.

The comprehensiveness of screenings varies, too, as does the expertise of individuals conducting them. Screenings may be conducted by a team of professionals representing several disciplines, or screenings may be conducted by the teaching staff that later will be working with the identified children. Occasionally screening is done by a team of specially trained parents and volunteers. Usually the scope of screening activities is defined by the nature of the special intervention program and other special services for which children are being identified.

One very large school district—which we will call Middle City, U.S.A.—has a large, interdisciplinary early intervention program serving children 3½-5 years of age who have any type of handicapping condition. Middle City's screening approach is comprehensive in order to identify children with any disability or at-risk condition. The screening team is composed of members of its own interdisciplinary staff—nurse, social worker, psychologist, two preschool classroom teachers as the educational specialists, speech/language pathologist, occupational therapist, and consulting pediatrician.

A small town nearby has only one small, privately operated program serving handicapped young children. Its purpose is to provide speech/language training for hearing impaired children between birth and 7 years of age. The staff from that center (speech pathologist, preschool teacher, and consulting audiologist) makes up the screening team. Identification and recruitment efforts are limited to hearing impaired and speech/language delayed children, because those are the only areas in which services are provided. Although the staff does not screen for other special problems, it does make referrals to other professionals in the community if the need arises.

The ideal screening program is a comprehensive one—*if follow-up services are available*. Comprehensive screening ensures that all aspects of a child's growth and development are checked so that comparisons can be made within and across all domains. This ensures a much more sensitive examination of a child's overall well-being. On the other hand, if services are not available, comprehensive screening serves no functional purpose.

Screenings yield only general types of information, since the intent is to examine a large number of children quickly and simply. Screening tests are for *identification* and are not to be used for diagnostic purposes. Results should *not* be used to label a child. Screening simply answers one basic question in regard to each child: Does a potential problem exist that warrants further consideration?

Considerations in planning screening programs   Because special education-early childhood services vary greatly from state to state and from community to community, the screening programs needed vary considerably. What, then, should a comprehensive screening program include? The National Program for Early and Periodic Screening, Diagnosis, and Treatment (EPSDT) (a national program for children eligible for Medicaid as a result of chronic disabilities arising from handicapping conditions) suggests that screening should evaluate children from several key perspectives: biological, psychological, family context, and environmental and social/cultural variables unique to each child that impact upon development. Using this comprehensive approach, a screening program might include:

— pediatric examination.
— developmental history obtained through interview of the parent(s) or primary caregiver and possible use of a checklist or questionnaire to gather specific facts about the developmental history.
— parental or primary caregiver input regarding special problems or concerns about the child.
— evaluation of child's general developmental status using a screening instrument.
— specialized developmental reviews (as determined by the services available, the child population, and the individual subject) in four domains: (a) physical status, (b) psychological/developmental status, (c) family status, and (d) environmental, social/cultural status. The psychological-developmental domain may include a review of cognitive development, emotional development, speech and language development, auditory perception, visual perception, self-help and adaptive skills, and motor development.

Several special considerations and precautions should be taken when planning screening programs for young children:

1. *The procedures used for screening and the screening instrument procedures applied should be determined in relationship to several key variables: (a) age range of the population to be screened, (b) dispersion of the population in the geographical area to be served, (c) means for gaining access to that population, and (d) predicted prevalence of the conditions for which screening is to be done.*

Screening procedures will be different, for example, for infants and toddlers than for 4- to 5-year-old children. The former will require greater reliance upon the pediatric review and family and environmental factors than upon the psychological aspects of evaluation (Brooks-Gunn & Lewis, 1981; Sheehan & Gallagher, 1984; Trohanis, Meyer, & Prestridge, 1982). With preschoolers, evaluation of developmental skills becomes increasingly important. Screening programs for widely scattered rural populations must be organized so that testing and information gathering can be accomplished quickly and efficiently during a single contact with the parent and child. Children from more densely populated areas, where neighborhood clinics can be set up, can be screened through several contacts.

Finally, screening handicapping conditions of high prevalence among certain population groups may not be necessary because serving all children within that population may be best; emphasis should be placed upon locating the broad population group rather than screening individual children. For example, if developmental disabilities are a high-risk condition among low-income and minority families, screening activities should focus simply on locating those types of families.

2. *Screening programs always should be conducted as part of a continuum of assistance that includes diagnostic services and treatment or intervention.*

Hayden and Edgar (1977) noted that, "Screening without referral of children at-risk is dangerous not only because the child will be denied needed services, but also because it often results in labeling and parental anxiety. Assessment [meaning "diagnosis" as it is used here] without referral takes these dangers one step further. Thus, appropriate referral is the critical sequel to screening and assessment" (p. 89). Screening also should focus upon conditions that can be modified, prevented, or ameliorated through a treatment or educational program. Early intervention should begin as early as possible.

In determining where screening should begin, however, the continuum of services is important to consider. To institute screening and service programs for infants does not make sense if no services are available for preschool-aged children. A better idea is to work backward from the elementary-age level, where public school programs are available, initiating services for preschoolers, then toddlers, then infants—to assure that intervention will continue once it is started.

3. *Parents should be briefed about the screening process and given sufficient information to: (a) assure their input and participation in the screening of their child, and (b) assure that they fully understand the intent and potential outcomes of screening processes.*

Parents or primary caregivers have the greatest collection of observational information about and experience with their child. Variations in a child's behavior are most likely to be observed by the parent and least likely to be observed by the professional who sees the child for only a short time. The younger the child is, the more vulnerable the evaluation is to momentary changes in behavior and extremes in moods. Professionals must rely upon the experience of the parents or caregivers to gain a true and full picture of a child. Parents, however, must be prepared for this screening process. We cannot assume that they fully understand the purpose of screening. Some may not be ready to look for or accept potential problems. Like professionals, they must understand what screening is and what it is not. Parents commonly view screening as a diagnosis. If appropriate briefing precedes actual screening, problems of this nature can be avoided.

4. *Screening must be sufficiently sensitive to separate children who present potential abnormal or handicapping conditions from those with no potential problems.*

Identifying children with mild or moderate types of problems while not over-referring those who do not have these conditions is a challenge. Generally, referring a larger number of children for more extensive evaluation, some of whom will be found to not have any particular problems, is better than to under-refer. If children who need intervention are missed, the screening has failed to serve its purpose.

5. *Labeling children on the basis of results from screening tests should be avoided.*

Parents and professionals alike must clearly realize the purposes of screening and the meaning of its outcomes. Stigmatization of young children often occurs because of a lack of understanding about evaluation processes. Parents and others should recognize that identification of a potential problem is not the same as a definite diagnosis of a disability. They also must understand that future problems leading to diagnosis and labeling of a disability possibly may be prevented through early identification and intervention.

Examples of instruments used for screening   A number of instruments have been developed specifically for screening young children for early intervention programs. Table 7.3 outlines a few selected ones.

Diagnosis

Once children have been located through the screening process, another form of assessment becomes necessary to confirm or disconfirm the existence of a handicap or abnormality

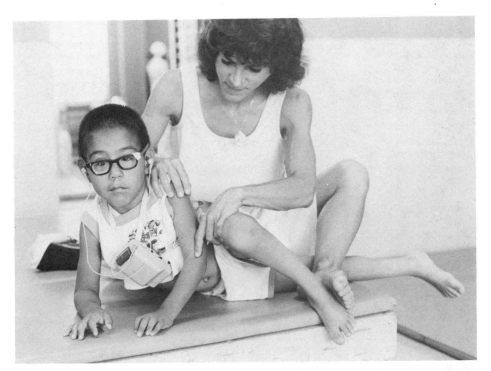

Meaningful diagnostic evaluations on young children with handicaps or at-risk conditions require the expertise of many disciplines. A physical therapist is conducting an evaluation here on the physical-motor status of this young boy.

Table 7.3

Descriptions of Selected Instruments Used for Screening

Test	Age Range	Description	Content Areas Evaluated
APGAR Rating Scale (Apgar, 1953)	1, 5, 10 min. after birth	Identifies infants needing special care and treatment Administered in delivery room	Heart rate Respiratory effort Reflex irritability Muscle tone Color
Assessment of Children's Language Comprehension (ACLC) (Foster, Giddan, & Stark, 1973)	3-7 yrs.	Determines understanding of semantic word classes Short form for screening Long form for educational assessment, IEP planning	Receptive vocabulary of syntactic elements
Del Rio Language Screening Program (Toronto, Leverman, Hanna, Rosengweis, & Maldonada, 1975)	3-7 yrs.	Identifies children whose language skills are inappropriate for age, language, and background Spanish/English	Receptive language
Denver Developmental Screening Test (Frankenburg, Dodds, & Fandal, 1975)	0-6 yrs.	Detects delayed development Quick, inexpensive Standardized	Gross motor Fine motor Personal-social Language
Developmental Indicators for the Assessment of Learning— Revised (DIAL-R) (Mardell Czudnowski, & Goldenberg, 1983)	2½-5½ yrs.	Identifies potential learning problems Standardized	Gross motor Fine motor Concepts Communication
Developmental Profile II (Alpern, Boll, & Shearer, 1980	0-12 yrs.	Estimates current level of performance through parent interview Norm-referenced/ standardized	Physical Self-help Social Academic Communication
Neonatal Behavior Assessment Scale (Brazelton, 1973)	0-1 mo.	Evaluates infant's responsiveness to environment Referred to as "Brazelton"	Stages of state (deep sleep to crying) Specific and general behaviors in response to stimuli

Table 7.3 (continued)

Test	Age Range	Description	Content Areas Evaluated
Parsons Visual Acuity Test (Spellman & Cress, 1980)	Children who have or can acquire a pointing response	Measures acuity of handi-capped children Training options to teach pointing skill	Near- and far-point vision for visual acuity
Preschool Attainment Record (PAR) (Doll, 1966)	0-7 yrs.	Yields attainment age scores and attainment quotients Parent interview format One behavior sampled per 6 mo.	Physical Social Intellectual
Vineland Social Maturity Scale (Doll, 1985)	Birth to maturity	Assesses progress toward social maturity, competence, or independence Interview format Yields social age, social quotient	Self-help Self-direction Occupation Communication Locomotion Socialization

Diagnostic assessment and evaluation by an interdisciplinary team is conducted to determine the exact nature and extent of a child's disabilities and to determine eligibility for special education services. Whereas the purpose of screening is to sort out children who *potentially* have a special problem, diagnostic assessment/evaluation involves analyzing a child's behavior to answer the question: What exactly is the problem, and how severe is it?

In-depth testing and information gathering provide the basis for recommending treatment or remediation measures, including possible placement in a special intervention program. Recommendations also may be made as to how therapists might best serve the child and what specific problem areas require attention. An audiologist, for example, conducts specific tests to determine if a child has a hearing loss and, if so, what type and degree. Based upon the diagnosis, a hearing aid may be suggested, along with language and speech training in a special preschool. A psychologist administers a battery of tests to measure a child's developmental status and cognitive abilities. Or an interdisciplinary team of specialists may conduct diagnostic evaluations and then jointly prescribe a comprehensive intervention plan for addressing a child's special needs.

The term *diagnosis* traditionally has been used by the medical profession, whose emphasis is on finding the cause of physical disorders and prescribing treatment to eliminate symptoms and cure the underlying illness. When viewing the full range of factors that must be considered in diagnosing handicapping and at-risk conditions in young children, this view of diagnosis is too narrow. In some cases the cause may not be the most important factor. The cause may be undeterminable and simply a matter of past history for a handicapped child. A perspective of the *nature* and *severity* of a particular disability and a prescription for treatment may be of greater value. Prevention of further impairment or disruption in development may be the most critical factor. This kind of assessment cannot be made from a medical perspective alone. Representatives of many disciplines must work together to make a full assessment and evaluation of a child's particular difficulties, as well as a measure of abilities that remain intact. Hence, a comprehensive interdisciplinary diagnosis allows an analysis of factors within and outside of the individual that are contributing to normal or abnormal development.

Diagnosis typically requires specialized techniques, special tools, and expertise on the part of each member in the diagnostic team. Specialists from various disciplines who conduct these evaluations may or may not be a part of the treatment or service activities. That is, diagnosticians often provide information that others use to make service and treatment decisions. Clear, complete reports by diagnosticians are therefore important, and recipients of those reports must be trained sufficiently to understand results or ask intelligent questions about them. On the basis of diagnostic findings, the intervention is determined. This may be a medical intervention, a social intervention (such as changes in caregiving arrangements or parents' child-rearing patterns), a psychological intervention (such as a behavior management program or therapy), or an educational intervention (such as enrollment in a special or regular early childhood program). Frequently, multiple intervention strategies that require the services of several disciplines are applied with very young handicapped children. (See chapter 11 for a discussion on the team approach.)

Diagnostic evaluations usually do not prescribe in detail what should happen to a child once recommendations are made for the type of intervention or placement deemed most appropriate. Practitioners working directly with children in early intervention programs sometimes become disillusioned because diagnostic evaluations do not provide more specific information that tells them "what to do with Johnny." For example, one teacher of preschool handicapped children complained because findings of the diagnostic evaluation were simply a verification of what she originally had thought: that a 4½-year-old boy in her class was mentally retarded and had mild motor impairments resulting from cerebral palsy. Clearly, more detailed information is needed to plan meaningful instructional programs for that child. This is where the purpose of diagnostic assessment and evaluation frequently is misunderstood. As explained earlier, diagnostic assessments are made to determine the exact nature and extent of a disability or handicapping condition. They are not to prescribe what a child should be taught or to suggest instructional strategies that likely will be most effective. What goes on within an intervention program is where diagnosis stops and the next phase—*educational assessment*—begins.

Considerations in obtaining diagnostic evaluations

Diagnosis should be a multidisciplinary process because of the diversity of expertise required by diagnosticians to detect abnormalities in the behavior, growth, and development of young children (Calhoun & Hawisher, 1979; A. Cross, 1977; Hayden & Edgar, 1977; Krajicek & Tearney, 1977; Meier, 1976). What specific disciplines should be included in a diagnostic team and what types of in-depth assessments are made on individual children depend upon at least three factors: (a) areas of concern pinpointed during the screening process, (b) types of services for which children are being screened, and (c) the age and characteristics of each child (Orlando, 1981).

A diagnostic team should begin its evaluation by asking two primary questions: What types of data are needed on this particular child? How much data can be considered sufficient evidence of ability or disability in the suspect area(s) (A. Cross, 1977)? Giving clear communications and instructions to a diagnostic team or to the team coordinator is critical here. Without this preliminary information, the effectiveness of a diagnostic team is decreased immensely. When requesting diagnostic evaluations, the following guidelines are helpful:

1. Requests should be specific concerning the type of diagnostic evaluation desired and the reasons for making the request. Brief explanations of observations and information leading to a request are helpful. A vague request such as "Please do a diagnostic work-up on James S." will leave any team at a loss as to what is needed. The team is left to conduct what amounts to a repeat of the screening. Time is lost, and money is spent re-identifying the areas in which further diagnosis is needed rather than moving ahead quickly to conduct the diagnostic evaluation.
2. Provide screening data and other available data to the diagnostic team to avoid duplication of effort. This information helps define the nature of suspected problems and can be used to determine exactly what diagnostic procedures are most appropriate. (Permission from the parent must be obtained to provide information of this nature to other agencies or diagnostic personnel.)
3. Prepare parents for the diagnostic process so they understand what will be occurring and can gather any information or records on their child that may be helpful.

Diagnostic evaluation involves much more than administration of a few tests. This is an important concept for professionals and parents who may equate diagnosis with testing. Although tests are heavily employed, a variety of information gathering and measurement devices are of value. The synthesis and analysis of all the assessment data are what leads to a diagnostic work-up that provides a fair, unbiased, accurate evaluation of the child's strengths and weaknesses, abilities and disabilities. No single diagnostic test or procedure will do the job. A battery of diagnostic tools representing four types of data collection is recommended (A. Cross, 1977):

1. *Interviews with parents or primary caregivers.* Formal and informal interviews comprise one method for gathering in-depth information about the child and about the community, home, and social environment. Child-rearing methods, discipline, and opportunities for learning in the home, along with parental attitudes and perceptions of their child's behavior, can be explored (Palmer, 1970).
2. *Information gathering to prepare the child's historical record.* Asking parents to recall past history or to draw from their own records on their child's development is another means of constructing the historical record. Parents are asked to provide information on when significant illness occurred and when the child reached major milestones (e.g. sitting alone, crawling, walking unassisted, saying first words). Medical records, and records from preschool or early stimulation programs that a child attended also offer perspective.
3. *Observation of the child's spontaneous and response-specific behavior.* Direct observation of a child's behavior in both structured and unstructured situations gives a perspective of developmental skills, social competency, communication skills, and general ability. From observational data, areas in which more formalized testing is needed can be identified. Qualitative judgments about behavior add further depth to the quantitative measures gained from standardized tests.
4. *Administration of standardized tests.* A battery of selected tests aids in objectively

measuring a child's abilities and testing potential problem areas identified during screening. Assessment instruments selected must be appropriate to the child's age and functioning level. Handicapping conditions that might influence a child's ability to perform should be taken into consideration when selecting tests.

Given these multiple sources of information, diagnostic evaluation requires more than a simple compilation of data. It involves a process of *analysis* and *synthesis*, defined by A. Cross (1977) as "bringing together the results of all the analyses [of each interdisciplinary team member] so that they form an accurate picture of the child's condition." Behavior must be interpreted in terms of the child's total functioning, including both abilities and disabilities. How the child performs in a variety of settings or contexts must be taken into consideration because behavior at home may be different from that observed by professionals during structured testing sessions. This synthesis typically occurs in the staffing or case conference. The diagnostic team (including the parents) should be involved in the synthesis process. From it should come a prescription for placement and the child's education programming. Due process procedures required under PL 94-142 (described in chapters 3 and 11), require that a conference be held and that parents be involved in the decision-making process.

What typically happens in a case conference or staffing? A. Cross (1977) outlined six general steps through which staffing should proceed:

1. Parents and others attending the case conference should be made aware of the procedures to be followed in the conference.
2. Significant findings should be reported by each disciplinary representative who has evaluated the child. Group members should ask questions as necessary to clarify findings or interpret the meaning.
3. Consensus must be reached on the "profile" of a child's major needs, as derived from the global and individual findings of the evaluation team.
4. Placement and treament options should be reviewed, with a discussion of the advantages and disadvantages of each option.
5. A decision on placement and treatment that provides the "best match" of the child's and family's needs with the service should be reached.
6. Responsibility should be designated as to (a) what agency is to be held responsible for services to the child and family, (b) what the parental responsibilities are, and (c) who is to assume responsibility for the transfer of records.

Examples of instruments used for diagnostic purposes   A variety of formal tests can be used as a part of diagnostic evaluations with young children. Most have been designed for normally developing children, but some can be adapted for use with physically or sensorially handicapped children. Others are not as useful when children's abilities to respond are restricted by some handicapping condition. Before using any test for diagnostic purposes, its adaptability to the particular child in question should be considered. Table 7.4 lists some of the more common tests used for diagnostic purposes with preschoolers and infants.

Educational assessment

To determine what specific instructional programs should be offered to each child on a day-to-day basis, the staff must identify exactly what skills a child has and what skills are yet unmastered in each area of development. A diagnosis may reveal that 5-year-old Kim has Down syndrome, no apparent secondary handicaps, and is functioning at a 4-year-old level, but this tells us little about what Kim needs in her preschool classroom. If Kim's teacher and the other disciplinary team members at her preschool center have done an adequate educational assessment, they will have a clear picture of what specific skills Kim has mastered and what skills are missing or need remediation. Instruction for Kim therefore can begin at the level at which she is functioning—not where the "middle" of her class appears to be.

Educational assessment thus concerns questions such as: What are the child's specific strengths and weaknesses? In what skill areas are special instruction or therapy needed? What instructional objectives should be pinpointed for this child, and what kinds of curriculum activities should be provided? On the basis of this information, individualized instructional objectives are set for each child.

To the practitioner who works with handicapped children, educational assessment is one of the most critical assessment processes. Without it, the staff will have difficulty developing individualized curriculum that truly matches a child's developmental level and learning needs. Otherwise, a program can be based only upon some good guesses and subjective assumptions about what an individual child needs. The educational assessment process, however, often is given the least attention by some practitioners. This may occur because of:

— the expectation (and misconception) that persons who conduct the diagnostic evaluation are also responsible for providing prescriptive information. This creates the frustrating situation of everyone waiting for everyone else to provide specific information and recommendations on what to do for a child—a predicament Meier (1976) appropriately called the "paralysis of analysis."
— practitioners' lack of familiarity with assessment tools and procedures for gathering specific assessment information that leads to instructional prescriptions. Some may view the assessment process as much too complicated, too difficult, and too complex to include as part of the classroom or special therapy program.
— practitioners and program administrators fail to recognize the critical relationship between assessment procedures and a curriculum that meets the special needs of young handicapped and at-risk children. Too often, "needs" are assumed on the basis of blanket characteristics assigned to children on the basis of their label: "preschooler," "4-year-old," "deaf," "language delayed," "mentally retarded." Individual needs must be determined systematically through ongoing educational assessment and observation of each child.

The difficulties just described deter practitioners from discovering that assessment procedures need not be that difficult. With training (and a willingness to embrace a positive attitude about the assessment process as an integral part of teaching), anyone working with children can learn some useful assessment techniques. Effective educational assessment depends upon careful planning and appropriate measurement tools. It also requires thorough analysis and evaluation of test results and observational data, followed by sensitive application of that information to ongoing program planning for each child.

Educational assessments can be made through a variety of tools: observational

Table 7.4

Descriptions of Selected Instruments Used for Diagnostic Evaluations

Test	Age Range	Description	Content Areas Evaluated
Battelle Developmental Inventory (Newborg, Stock, Wnek, Guidubaldi, & Suinicki, 1984)	0-8 yrs.	Nationally standardized screening and diagnostic test Yields age equivalent scores Determines relative developmental strengths and weaknesses	Personal social Adaptive Motor Communication Cognitive
Bayley Scales of Infant Development (Bayley, 1984)	0-30 mos.	Evaluates infant developmental status Standardized	Cognitive functioning Motor skills Social behavior
Bracken Basic Concept Scale (Bracken, 1984)	2½-7 yrs. (diagnostic scale) 5-7 yrs. (screening test)	Standardized test Norm-referenced and criterion-referenced interpretations Useful for IEP planning	11 categories of basic concepts: colors, letter identification, numbers/counting, comparisons, shapes, direction/position, social/emotional, size, texture/material, quantity, time sequence
Developmental Test of Visual-Motor Integration (Beery & Buktenica, 1967)	2-15 yrs.	Evaluates ability to integrate visual perception and motor behavior Yields a Visual-Motor Integration Age	Integration of visual perception and motor behavior
Frostig Developmental Test of Visual Perception (Maslow, Frostig, Lefever, & Whittlesey, 1964)	3-8 yrs.	Measures visual-perceptual skills through paper-and-pencil tasks Raw scores from 5 subtests can be converted to Perceptual Age	Eye-motor coordination Figure-ground discrimination Form constancy Position in space Space relations
Goldman-Fristoe-Woodcock Test of Auditory Discrimination (Goldman, Fristoe, & Woodcock, 1974)	4-8 yrs.	Measures discrimination ability through response to tape-recorded stimulus	Discrimination of speech sounds

Table 7.4 (continued)

Test	Age Range	Description	Content Areas Evaluated
Illinois Test of Psycholinguistic Abilities (Kirk, McCarthy, & Kirk, 1978)	2-10 yrs.	Measures "psycholinguistic abilities" (understanding, processing, production of verbal and nonverbal language) Norm-referenced, good reliability and validity	Auditory-vocal behaviors Visual-motor behaviors Receptive and expressive language processes Automatic and representational levels of language
Leiter International Performance Scale (Leiter, 1948)	2-18 yrs.	Measures intelligence through nonverbal, block pattern-matching response Lacks normative data, reliability, and validity	Generalization Discrimination Analogues Sequencing Pattern completion
McCarthy Scales of Children's Abilities (McCarthy, 1972)	2½-8 yrs.	Determines general intellectual level, strengths, and weaknesses Norm-referenced/ standardized	Verbal Perceptual-performance Quantitative General cognitive Memory Motor
Nebraska Test of Learning Aptitude (Hiskey, 1966)	3-16 yrs.	Special intelligence test for deaf and hearing impaired children Pantomime and practice exercises included to train child for performance	Visual memory Fine motor skills Spatial relations Pictorial analogies and association
Peabody Picture Vocabulary Test (PPVT)—Revised Edition (Dunn, 1981)	2½-18 yrs.	Measures receptive vocabulary through pointing task Easy to administer Good reliability, validity	Receptive vocabulary
Receptive-Expressive Emergent Language Scale (REEL) (Bzock & League, 1971)	0-3 yrs.	Measures early language through parent interview Yields Receptive Language Expressive Language Age, and Combined Language Age scores Adequate reliability and validity	Receptive language Expressive language (in vocal, symbolic, and communicative behaviors)

Table 7.4 (continued)

Test	Age Range	Description	Content Areas Evaluated
Scales of Independent Behavior (SIB) (Bruininks, Woodcock, Weatherman, & Hill, 1984)	0-adult	Structured interview format Standardized Tests normal to severely handicapped persons Early development scale measures adaptive behavior, 0-3 years	Motor Social and communication Personal living and community living skills
Southern California Sensory Integration Tests (Ayers, 1972)	4-8 yrs.	Detects sensory integration problems through 17 subtests	Perceptual and psychomotor performance
Stanford-Binet Intelligence Scale (Terman & Merrill, 1972)	2-18 yrs.	Measures IQ Useful for predicting academic achievement Norm-referenced/ standardized	Language Perception Fine motor Reasoning
Uzgiris-Hunt Ordinal Scales of Psychological Development (Uzgiris & Hunt, 1975)	0-2 yrs.	Provides description of cognitive development Based on Piagetian theory	Sensorimotor development
Wechsler Preschoool and Primary Scales of Intelligence (WPPSI) (1974)	4-6½ yrs.	Yields verbal, performance, and full-scale deviation IQs Standardized	Verbal IQ Performance IQ Full-scale IQ

techniques, criterion-referenced tests (including informal teacher-made assessment devices), and (when appropriate) norm-referenced tests. Observational techniques may consist of anecdotal records, informal observation notes of a child's behavior, or precise observational data in which predefined behaviors are counted during set time intervals. Criterion-referenced tests are particularly helpful because they allow a child to be described simply in terms of his or her own behavior. Such concrete, practical information on a child's skills can easily be translated into learning objectives.

Considerations in conducting educational assessments   Those who work directly with children are the individuals responsible for conducting educational assessments. These are the persons who will use the information to plan individualized daily programs for each child. Typically, they include classroom teachers and therapists (e.g., speech therapist, occupational therapist, perceptual-motor therapist, music therapist).

Educational assessments are planned to survey each child's developmental status and skill level across the following areas:

- Motor Development (gross and fine)
- Language (receptive and expressive) Skills
- Self-Help Skills
- Social-Emotional Development
- Cognitive Development and Preacademic Skills
- Skills of Daily Living (play skills, adaptive skills, safety skills, functional living skills).

Specific skill areas usually are assessed in further depth by individual therapists within their own treatment domain. A perceptual-motor therapist, for instance, may do further reflex testing and may check posture, mobility, visual perception, and a number of other perceptual and motor functions. An occupational therapist may examine feeding and dressing skills and sensory functions that also are of concern to the perceptual-motor therapist. No matter who conducts these evaluations, the outcome should be a clear picture of a child's skills, strengths, and weaknesses in each of the developmental areas (Bagnato, 1981; DuBose, 1981; Fewell 1983a; Horowitz, 1982).

The timing of educational assessments is critical. Evaluations should be completed *after* diagnosis but *before* a child's IEP and specific program objectives are planned. The educational assessment provides the basic information upon which individualized education programs (IEPs) are built. Early intervention programs, however, may differ in their timing of educational assessments in relationship to placement of a child in a program. For example, some programs arrange for temporary placement of a child in a center or home-based services to allow more extended observation and educational assessment. This short-term "diagnostic placement" allows additional time to assess the child's needs and determine what kind of programming and early intervention are most appropriate. This procedure works especially well for young children who are not easily evaluated through a few brief encounters with a stranger. Over time (as much as 8-11 weeks) and as the children become more at ease with the professional staff that works with them, a more complete diagnostic evaluation and educational assessment can be made. On the basis of that information, the final IEP is written.

Other intervention programs have less extensive evaluation procedures; thus the initial IEP is written prior to a child's placement and is based upon evaluative information gained through each child's initial evaluation. The staff makes additional educational assessments once a child is enrolled in the intervention program.

How is this assessment information used in preparing the IEPs? Three basic steps describe the process. *First,* on the basis of assessment information, a list of each child's strengths and weaknesses is developed, with notations in each of the curriculum or developmental areas, such as:

"Skills need remediation" (with a listing of those skills)

"Skills are delayed" (with a listing of delayed or deficit skills)

"Skills are within normal ranges."

Second, skills that will be targeted through special instruction are noted. More skills likely will be identified than can be worked on simultaneously with the child. Priorities therefore must be assigned as to which skills will be addressed first. Attention must be given, of course, to the sequence in which those skills should be taught. *Third,* long-range and short-term objectives are defined on the basis of the target skills and the priorities assigned to them. (See further discussion on development of the individualized education program in chapter 11.)

The following general guidelines are suggested for conducting educational assessments to ensure that they provide worthwhile information and fulfill the function for which they are conducted:

1. Educational assessment tools that are selected should be compatible with the philosophy and theoretical orientation of a program. For example, a program emphasizing a Piagetian orientation should use assessment tools that evaluate children's behavior from that point of view.
2. Educational assessment is not a one-shot occurrence but, rather, should be done at regular intervals after the initial assessment has been completed. Goals and objectives for each child must be updated regularly, and progress should be reviewed objectively on a regular basis.
3. Every effort should be made to obtain an accurate picture of each child's skills, assets, and deficits. This means drawing upon, if necessary, several resources for assessing what the child can do, and not necessarily relying totally upon one observation or the report of one person. Multiple checks on a child's ability to perform certain tasks can prove fruitful.
4. Since a child's at-home behavior and at-school behavior may differ, assessments might sample behavior across more than one setting. Sometimes parents report that their child has mastered a task, while the teacher insists that the child has not. Both can be right. Conditions under which the behavior is performed may be different in each setting. This emphasizes the importance of parental input in educational assessment.
5. All members of the disciplinary team providing direct services to a child require information from educational assessments. Planning within the team how these assessments will be conducted is important to avoid unnecessary duplication. Assessment responsibilities can be delegated across the team, and findings can be presented and synthesized during the IEP meeting. (In chapter 11 the IEP planning process and the steps for using assessment data to prepare IEPs are discussed in further detail.)

Examples of instruments used for educational assessments A number of assessment tools have been developed specifically for instructional planning with young handicapped children. Some of the more familiar ones are described in Table 7.5. Some of the tests used for diagnostic purposes, described earlier in Table 7.4, yield information that also can be useful for instructional planning. (This is especially so if an analysis is made of a child's specific responses on individual test items or on subsections of a test in particular skill areas.) The most functional tools for ongoing, day-to-day instructional planning, however, are those created specifically for that purpose, such as those listed in Table 7.5.

Performance monitoring

Performance monitoring involves tracking each child's continuous progress over several days or weeks in conjunction with special instructional programs. This type of assessment involves ongoing data collection by teachers, paraprofessionals, or clinicians concurrent

Table 7.5

Descriptions of Selected Instruments for Educational Assessment

Test	Age Range	Description	Content Areas Evaluated
Brigance Diagnostic Inventory of Early Development (Brigance, 1978)	0-6 yrs.	Yields developmental age levels in each area Criterion-based tool with norm-based qualities Useful for targeting instructional objectives	Preambulatory motor skills Gross and fine motor Self-help Pre-speech, speech and language General knowledge and comprehension Readiness, basic reading, writing, math
Callier-Azuza (Stillman, 1982)	0-9 yrs.	Assesses deaf-blind and multihandicapped children Useful for targeting instructional objectives	Motor Perceptual Daily living Language Socialization
Carolina Developmental Profile (Lillie & Harbin, 1975)	2-5 yrs.	Exposes weaknesses in each area Criterion-referenced checklist Useful for targeting instructional objectives	Fine motor Gross motor Perceptual reasoning Receptive language Expressive language
Early Learning Accomplishment Profile for Infants (Early LAP) (Sanford, 1981)	0-3 yrs.	Facilitates programming for severely handicapped young children Criterion-referenced measure	Gross and fine motor Cognitive Language Self-help Social Emotional
Hawaii Early Learning Profile (HELP) (Furuno et al., 1979)	0-3 yrs.	Based on developmental milestones model Curriculum-referenced tool	Cognitive (with receptive language) Language Gross motor Fine motor Social-emotional Self-help
Learning Accomplishment Profile— Diagnostic Edition (Revised) (LeMay, Griffin, & Sanford, 1981)	0-6 yrs.	Generates profile of fully acquired, absent, and emergent capabilities Criterion-referenced, with normal sequence of skills Useful for targeting instructional objectives	Fine and gross motor Language Cognitive Self-help Social

Table 7.5 (continued)

Test	Age Range	Description	Content Areas Evaluated
Minnesota Child Development Inventory (Ireton & Thwing, 1979)	1. (MCDI) 0-6 yrs.	1. Minnesota Developmental Inventory (MCDI) Diagnoses atypical development Standardized	1. MCDI General development Gross motor/fine motor Expressive language Comprehension-conceptual Situation comprehension Self-help Personal-social
	2. (MPI) 2-6 yrs.	2. Minnesota Preschool Inventory (MPI 2-6) Screening instrument Profiles current functioning levels	2,3. MPI Developmental Scales self-help, fine motor expressive language, comprehension,
	3. (MPI) 3-4 yrs.	3. Minnesota Preschool Inventory (MPI 3-4) Shorter version, similar to MPI	memory, letter recognition, number comprehension Adjustment Scales immaturity, hyper-activity, behavior and emotional problems
	4. (MIDI) 0-15 mos.	4. Minnesota Infant Development Inventory (MIDI) Provides a developmental review of infants (as opposed to screening)	4. MIDI Gross motor Fine motor Language Comprehension Social behavior
Portage Guide to Early Education (Shearer et al., 1976)	0-6 yrs.	Assesses current level of performance through checklist Includes manual and 580 activity cards for skill development	Infant stimulation Socialization Language Self-help Cognitive Motor
Preschool Language Scale (Zimmerman, Steiner, & Pond, 1979)	1-7 yrs.	Evaluates strengths and deficiencies in each area Provides "language age" description of performance Spanish version available	Verbal ability Auditory comprehension Language
Uniform Performance Assessment System (UPAS) (White et al., 1981)	0-6 yrs.	Assesses skill levels through criterion-referenced tests Good reliability and validity data	Preacademic Communications Social Self-help Gross motor

with their delivery of special instruction. Its purpose is to monitor the progress of each child across major instructional areas in which IEP goals and behavioral objectives have been defined. The focus of this assessment process is upon three basic questions: (a) Is each child making continuous progress in specific skill areas as a result of the learning activities? (b) Is each child reaching the goals defined in his or her IEP? (c) Are the teaching techniques selected for each child working?

Data collection strategies are planned to answer each of these questions for each handicapped child. Translating the questions into specific ones for an individual child, a teacher might ask: "How many new names of objects has Val mastered to date in his language training program? What is his rate of learning this week compared to last week? Is our contingent reinforcement procedure decreasing the frequency of Val's tantruming? Is he reaching his IEP goal that he will be able to identify each of the body parts?" Using these data, teachers and other program staff can make wise instructional decisions for Val's subsequent learning programs based upon a clear, objective picture of his performance under present instructional procedures.

Performance monitoring is different from educational assessment in that the latter identifies what a child should be taught, and monitoring is designed to measure what is happening once instruction begins. Monitoring involves keeping tabs on (a) the *performance* of individual children as a result of the instruction they receive, and (b) the *effectiveness* of instructional methods in helping children acquire the desired skills. Careful analysis of these data allows one to see what types of response errors a child is making and to plan new teaching procedures to correct them.

Several forms of data are useful here: samples of children's work, daily counts of correct and incorrect responses during learning sessions, and brief probe data or "mini-tests" administered at the end of learning sessions to check performance independent of special prompting and teacher assistance. These latter data may be computed into a percentage correct, a rate of performance (e.g., five responses per minute), or a frequency count of the occurrence of a behavior during a certain time interval.

General approaches to performance monitoring

Efficient monitoring of a child's ongoing performance involves four basic steps: (a) planning and designing data collection procedures (including preparation of data collection forms), to monitor each learning objective for each child, (b) collecting data on a systematic basis (daily, every other day, or weekly) in the targeted areas, (c) summarizing and analyzing data regularly to derive some judgments about each child's progress and about the effectiveness of the instructional approach, and (d) using that information to make decisions about subsequent instructional strategies.

This type of assessment is not always done consistently by staffs that work directly with children. Some see the task as overwhelming in the face of other demands for supervising a group of youngsters. But this kind of data collection is much easier than it seems. With practice, it can become an act almost simultaneous with teaching. The secret is that adequate planning must occur beforehand on what data will be recorded and what methods will be used. Once this is done, data collection is simply a matter of placing a mark on a piece of paper. Most teachers and clinicians find that systematic data collection helps them to better organize their teaching. It makes objectives clearer and clarifies what exactly is to be accomplished with children. Most important, it leaves no "guessing game" as to how well a child is doing or what skills should be the target of learning activities.

Several questions typically arise when we talk about performance monitoring with practitioners in the field. They may shed light on some of the most pressing of concerns—how to make performance monitoring a worthwhile activity for the adult and a means for improving instruction for young children.

Aren't one's general impressions sufficient to evaluate the effectiveness of instruction on a day-to-day basis?

Subjective impressions can be helpful, but when one must keep track of the performance of many children across several individual learning programs, "impressions" lack the precision to ensure that our judgments are accurate and reliable. Progress for very young children, and often handicapped young children, often is made in small increments. Collectively and over time those increments lead to mastery of significant developmental skills. Taken singly, success in mastering one small step may be reflected by little daily change in a child's broad behavior patterns. We have a tendency to obtain our impressions on the basis of broad, general patterns of behavior. Thus, a small child may appear to be making little progress. When the training of a very young or severely handicapped child requires the breakdown of tasks into small, sequential steps, there may be an illusion of no progress when indeed progress is being made. Parents and teachers alike can become discouraged if left to those subjective impressions. Ongoing data collection provides a better picture of what actually is happening. Slight, step-by-step progress can be documented nicely with good performance monitoring. This can bring great satisfaction to parents and teachers who see the results of their efforts in the data. The following example stresses the point that subjective measures can camouflage what is really happening when highly visible outcomes draw attention away from more subtle instructional outcomes.

Janet A. was a parent educator in a parent-toddler home program. As a part of her program, she devised a series of lessons to help parents use more appropriate instructions with their young children to elicit the desired behavior. The intent of the program was to increase the number of appropriate instructions given by mothers (i.e., specific instructions as opposed to general ones, simply worded instructions, and special prompts paired with instructions) and to decrease inappropriate instructions (nagging, overly complex and long commands, use of vague or abstract words).

At the end of her 8-week training program, Janet reported to her colleagues that the program was a success. Parents had changed their instruction-giving behavior with their young children and praised the training she had provided. This report was based upon her subjective impressions. When Janet began to analyze the probe data that she had collected during the last 5 minutes of each training session, she gained a different perspective of the program outcomes. Alas, the program had not produced the results she had thought. The data showed that inappropriate instructions had actually increased while appropriate instructions had decreased. Janet's subjective impressions were distorted because of the overall increase in the number of instructions parents gave during training.

Two lessons can be learned here: Impressions are not always accurate, and they can camouflage what is really happening. Careful data collection provides a more accurate picture. Second, data should be reviewed and summarized regularly throughout the instructional process if it is to provide worthwhile feedback. Janet's analysis at the very end told her that she had failed. Had she known earlier that her goal was not being met, instructional procedures could have been modified to improve her chances for success.

Must data be taken on literally everything we teach each child? How can that task possibly be managed within a classroom of 8-12 children?

Data need not be taken on everything we do with children. Performance monitoring should be done for a purpose. Data should be collected to be used—not to be stored in a file for analysis at the end of the school year. Because staff time is limited for analyzing and reviewing large amounts of data, data collection should be applied selectively where it will be of most use. How much data should be collected depends upon the amount of time available for analysis and use of data.

Two general rules of thumb are: (a) *Be selective* about when data are taken and on what behaviors or learning programs, targeting *high priority* training areas that have been set as major goals in each child's IEP or major instructional activities in the classroom for which specific outcomes in the children are expected; and (b) take data on the major skills defined in each child's *short-term objectives in the IEP* (documentation of progress on these goals is required under Public Law 94-142).

How does a person make sense out of all those data? Can this information really help one make better instructional decisions?

Data in raw form may not have any inherent meaning. It must be translated into some type of meaningful summary to give a picture of a child's overall pattern of performance and of the success of the instructional procedure. Data can be summarized in several ways. Two examples are:

— transposing response data into percentages or ratios and plotting each day's or week's data on a graph or table.
— standardizing the number of potential responses that will constitute a probe or mini-test of the child's skill. With this standard number of potentially correct or incorrect responses, the number correct can be recorded on a summary chart, a bar graph, or some other record form.

Summarized data are useful in decision making, whereas stacks of unsummarized data provide no more information than one's general impressions. Data can reveal if a child is nearing criterion for a new skill and if instruction should move on to new tasks. Performance monitoring data also can show where a child's errors are being made and can help identify where special help should be focused to improve learning. Data also will show erratic or inconsistent performance and provide the stimulus to look further for factors that may be interfering with learning.

How can I possibly keep track of and manage that amount of data—especially when it may be different for each child?

Effective performance monitoring does require good organizational skills and planning. No one can decide suddenly, "Today I will take data," and expect it to come off smoothly. Several general strategies can be employed to help manage the various tasks involved in implementing this process. First, as learning programs are planned to address each child's IEP objectives and deal with other general curriculum goals as well, data collection procedures can be planned at the same time. Second, parallel data collection procedures sometimes can be used across children or within a particular skill area. Although the particular criterion for performance may be different for different children, the general monitoring procedure often can be the same. Teachers and clinicians usually master three or four types of data collection procedures that they find most useful in their programs. These can be applied again and again with minor adaptations according to the specific skill being taught and the particular child.

Third, a standard way of keeping track of major ongoing instructional programs for each child, including the data on that program, is desirable. A folder, clipboard, or three-ring binder, containing summary tables and charts on the learning program for each child, works nicely. Or a display of charts and tables in one corner of the room could provide a constant visual display of programs. Fourth, a specific time each day or week should be set to summarize data—and this should be done consistently. Finally, a precise time for staff members to meet, to review and interpret data, and to discuss its implications for subsequent teaching should be scheduled. This is best done at least once weekly, or even daily. If done consistently, these review times can be fun, productive sessions.

Examples of strategies for performance monitoring   Strategies for performance monitoring are highly specific to the teacher's or therapist's style of teaching, the child's learning objectives, and the nature of the specific skill being taught. Many different types of data can be gathered to track a child's progress. Table 7.6 summarizes some broad types of data one could collect as a means for monitoring child progress. (For other information on performance monitoring systems, see Bagnato & Neisworth, 1981; Bricker & Gumerlock, 1985; White & Haring, 1980.)

Program evaluation

This is the only assessment process that focuses upon the intervention program itself rather than upon individual children. Its purpose is to measure the quality and impact of an intervention program on children and their families. It involves judgments about three aspects of a program: (a) the efficiency and quality of program operations, including staff performance, (b) overall child outcomes, and (c) consumer satisfaction. Program evaluation is designed to answer questions such as: Did the program have an impact upon children and their families? Is the program cost-effective in that children showed sufficient gains to warrant the cost of the special services? Were the goals and objectives of the program achieved, including those specifically defined for the individual children who participated? How effectively and smoothly are internal program operations carried out? What do parents of children enrolled think about the program? Answers to these questions provide an index of the quality and success of an early intervention program.

This type of evaluation is most important to the future of intervention programs or

Table 7.6
Alternative Methods of Data Collection
For Monitoring Child Progress

Monitoring Device Or Method	Description of Data Collection Procedure
Developmental Checklists	Teacher uses a formal or informal developmental checklist to record child's continuous progress in mastering developmental milestones or skills and to track a child's progress in comparison with the age level at which most normally developing children acquire each skill. Some teacher-made checklists allow for recording the date on which the child attains each new skill, as well as some measure of the level of proficiency (or independence) with which the skill is performed (e.g., brushes teeth independently, with physical prompts, verbal prompts, or only graduated guidance).
Behavior Rating Scales	Teacher rates child's behavior at regular intervals by means of a checklist or rating scale on which presence or absence of certain behaviors or skills is noted (either appropriate or inappropriate behaviors). A child's behavior may be rated on a *dichotomous* measure (yes-no), a *continuum* (always-frequently-sometimes-never), or a *qualitative* judgment (poor, acceptable, excellent). Rating scales help a teacher identify problematic behaviors, behavioral deficits where more experience should be given to improve skills, or good behaviors that should be given more attention and praise.
Permanent Product Samples	Teacher obtains samples of a child's work at regular intervals for qualitative comparisons with later products and to provide concrete examples of the child's progress over time (e.g., drawings of a person, writing of name or numbers, art work, sample worksheets on preacademic work). Audiotapes of a child's speech or videotapes of social behavior or performance on a task provide a good indication of a child's skill. This method of data collection is especially useful in showing parents what their child can do and concrete evidence of progress.
Anecdotal Recording or Diaries	Teacher makes notes on significant events concerning a child's behavior and activities or records observations of the child's physical or emotional state on a given day—which may be factual or an interpretive form of data. If information recorded is a teacher's subjective interpretation, this could be made clear in the written narrative. Anecdotal records may entail written notes on specific behaviors, including events that preceded and followed each behavior observed (e.g., what words a child uses during certain activities and in what situations a child engages in spontaneous verbalizations). Or anecdotal records may involve more lengthy written narratives describing the sequence of events when a child exhibits a certain behavior (e.g., temper tantrum, seizure, accident involving the child). Anecdotal records usually focus on the content or style of behavior or situations in which behavior occurs rather than its frequency or duration. Anecdotal recording is most helpful and accurate if an "ABC" analysis approach is used by recording behavior as events occur rather than at the end of the day; notations are recorded in terms of: A = antecedent events, B = the behavior exhibited, C = consequent events after the behavior occurs.

Table 7.6 (continued)

Monitoring Device Or Method	Description of Data Collection Procedure
Collection of Ongoing Performance Data	
• Frequency Data	Behavior is monitored in regard to the number of occurrences. Teacher takes a simple count of the number of discrete events of a particular behavior as it occurs during a given observation period (e.g., how many tantrums a child has in a day; how many colored blocks a child sorts during fine motor period; how many times a child asks a question).
• Percentage Data	Behavior or skill learning is monitored in terms of the proportion of correct to incorrect responses. Teacher takes a count of the number of discrete events of a specific behavior against the number of opportunities the child has to perform the behavior (e.g., a child labels 12 objects correctly out of a total of 20 objects: 12/20 x 100 = 60%).
• Rate Data	Behavior is monitored in regard to how fast a child performs a given skill. Teacher takes a count of the number of responses given in a specified, timed observation period (e.g., a child prints 6 lower-case alphabet letters in 1 minute; a child discriminates 18 red objects from other colored objects in 2 minutes).
• Duration Data	Behavior is monitored in regard to how long it lasts. Teacher uses a stopwatch to measure the total amount of time a child engages in a specific appropriate or inappropriate behavior (e.g., how many seconds a child can balance on one foot; how many minutes a child spends in self-stimulating behavior).
• Latency Data	Behavior is monitored in regard to the time that elapses before a child gives a response. Teacher uses a stopwatch to measure how long it takes the child to begin a task after instructions are given (e.g., how many seconds the child takes to begin putting away toys after being told to do so; how many minutes the child takes to move toward the sink when told to wash his or her hands).
• Interval Recording	Behavior is monitored in terms of whether defined behaviors occur or do not occur within specified time intervals. Teacher establishes a specific observation period and divides the session into a number of predetermined time intervals (e.g., 30-second intervals or 15-second intervals). Using a stopwatch, the teacher or a staff person observes the child and records the presence or absence of the behavior during each interval. At the end of the observation period, the number of intervals in which the behavior occurred is counted and divided by the total number of intervals observed to obtain a ratio of total intervals in which the child exhibited the specific behavior. (Example: A child is observed to be engaged in cooperative play in 5 of 15 intervals observed when the child had the opportunity of exhibiting social behavior; 5 divided by 15 shows a rate of 33% of cooperative play.)
• Time Sampling	Behavior is monitored by observing a child at designated time intervals to note presence or absence of specified behaviors. Teacher predetermines the length of time between observations (e.g., 5 min., 30 min., 1 hr.) and observations are taken exactly at the defined time intervals. At the end of the observation session, teacher counts the number of observations during which the child exhibited the behavior, dividing

Table 7.6 (continued)

this count by the total number of observations to obtain a percentage measure. (Example: A child's whimpering behavior is observed by means of a 5-minute time sample. Every 5 minutes the teacher observes whether the child is whimpering and makes a tally on the observation form if the behavior is noted. The number of observations when the child was whimpering is divided by the total number of observation events; 6 whimpering observations divided by 30 total observations = 20%.)

of any educational endeavor because it provides the means for *accountability*. Programs should be able to give evidence of their effectiveness, including proof that staff time and project funds are being expended wisely to meet the needs of individuals for whom the program was established. This documentation serves several critical functions. First, it provides evidence for decision makers who want some measure of the utility of a program. Second, it provides data to justify requests for funds to operate a program and gives evidence that funds are benefiting the children and families being served. It also gives proof of the effectiveness of early intervention. Legislators and advocates need these data to argue for allocation of state and federal monies for these purposes and to support legislation for programs. Finally, the documentation provides the basis for making changes and improvements in actual services for children and their families and in overall management of the program.

Program evaluation typically is conducted in a much different manner than the other forms of evaluation discussed. Usually two approaches are applied: (a) *internal review* (that conducted within the program by those who are participants in some way, such as staff, and parents), and (b) *external review* (that conducted by outsiders not associated with any aspect of the program and who can provide an objective, unbiased view of the program's merits and weaknesses).

Within each of these two approaches, a variety of strategies may be employed to gather data: questionnaires, direct observations of program operations, interviews, administration of evaluation instruments such as checklists, informal criterion-referenced tools, or standardized tests. In some cases pre-post measurements are taken to document gains within the targeted population of children or with parents. Comparisons can be used to show gains by those served by the program in comparison to the gains reflected among those who did not participate.

Considerations in planning program evaluations   A good program evaluation design provides for feedback from two perspectives—one from an internal point of view and one from an external point of view. Internal reviews yield a much different perspective of a program than do external ones. The staff within a program usually places different emphases upon services and program operations than do individuals who are not directly associated with the program.

Program evaluation also should include both formative and summative forms of review. *Formative evaluation* includes activities that provide feedback as a program is being developed. This kind of feedback can be used to make changes or modifications in program content or operational procedures before they have become formalized. *Summative evaluation* refers to the measurement of terminal outcomes or overall program success and usually is made at the end of a year, or possibly a longer block of time. Both formative and summative forms of evaluation are important, as are internal and external reviews.

Anastasiow (1981) and Caldwell (1977) have suggested that greater emphasis should be placed upon formative evaluation during a first year of operation. Measurements of child progress, for example, may be made for purposes of planning appropriate curriculum and developing effective instructional techniques, and for giving feedback to teachers, aides, and parents. The second year should continue to stress the formative evaluation mode to further refine, modify, and adapt instructional methodology and curriculum. Summative evaluation may not be until the third year, when a project is sufficiently robust to validate a clear intervention approach.

In planning and implementing this type of evaluation, several general guidelines are offered:

1. The program philosophy, program objectives, and program evaluation approach should be a close "match." The type of evaluation required is determined in part by the program's philosophical and theoretical foundations. Objectives should define, in part, the content of what is to be evaluated. In reverse, the factors to be evaluated define the kind of documentation needed to demonstrate effectiveness (Zigler & Balla, 1982; Sheehan & Gallagher, 1983).

2. Selection of assessment instruments and strategies should reflect a carefully planned evaluation design (Sheehan, 1979) rather than random selection of assessment tools simply because they are available or because they look interesting. Following the formulation of a plan, instruments then should be selected that (a) address the major issue that must be confronted to justify the program and to document its results, (b) document whether program objectives were met, (c) represent evaluation strategies that are a "best fit" for the population under consideration, and (d) comprise a well-rounded review of the overall program (Ramey, Campbell, & Wasik, 1982; Keogh & Sheehan, 1981).

3. The feasibility and practicality of program assessment and evaluation strategies should be kept well in mind as the evaluation design is prepared. Limitations in staff time, the expertise of internal and external reviewers, the mechanics of implementing the evaluation design, and the cost should be considered (Suarez, 1982). In planning such an evaluation, it is often easy to become idealistic and over-ambitious, only to find when the time comes to implement the plan that staff members "bit off much more than they could chew."

4. Some overlap derived from the six types of assessment (depicted in our model in Figure 7.1) may be present. Assessment procedures for one phase of evaluation may in some cases be applicable to another. For instance, assessments conducted on individual children as a part of the in-depth interdisciplinary diagnostic review and educational assessments can be used as pretest data for the program evaluation. Ongoing formative evaluation as a part of overall evaluation of the program also may serve as performance monitoring data for some instructional programs. Although dual uses for data should not be taken for granted, evaluation data often can be applied toward two

or more types of evaluation processes. The key to effective use of this kind of overlap is *careful and prior planning*. Opportunities for overlap should be noted early so that requirements surrounding each type of assessment process can be met to assure validity and reliability of results (Cross & Johnston, 1977; Garwood, 1982).

Considerable discussion in the literature and differing viewpoints complicate the issue of what constitutes appropriate program evaluation in early childhood-special education. Issues generally center on the following questions:

- What variables and outcomes measures should be assessed to document the efficacy of early intervention programs? (Zigler & Balla, 1982; Wolery & Bailey, 1984)
- What child behaviors should be assessed to determine if progress has been made? (Sheehan & Keogh, 1981; Simeonsson, Huntington, & Short, 1982; Sheehan, 1982)
- What testing instruments or assessment procedures are appropriate to use with such a diverse population of children and to evaluate the outcomes of intervention programs with them? (Garwood, 1982; Ramey, Campbell, & Wasik, 1982; Bailey & Bricker, 1984)
- What criteria should be applied to determine the "success" of a program? (Wolery, 1983; Bricker, 1978a; Zigler & Trickett, 1978; Bricker & Littman, 1972)
- What evaluation designs should be used to determine program outcomes with very young and difficult-to-test children? (Sheehan & Keogh, 1982; Carta & Greenwood, 1985; Odom & Fewell, 1983)

In summary, assessment and evaluation are central to every phase of service delivery to young handicapped children. This does not mean simply test giving. Program evaluation is not a simple procedure that occurs at one point in time, after which the real intervention program begins. Ongoing assessment is a crucial part of child and program evaluation and is at the heart of effective decision making.

Examples of strategies for program evaluation   Table 7.7 lists some of the questions and alternative strategies for evaluating the effectiveness of an early intervention.

SPECIAL CONSIDERATIONS IN ASSESSMENT

Most professionals are trained to apply the assessment tools of their own discipline to populations of school-aged students or adults. Because early childhood-special education is a relatively new service area, many teachers and clinicians have had little or no experience in assessing preschoolers and infants—especially those with handicaps or significant developmental irregularities. Evaluators' understanding of behavior patterns and development in young children may not be commensurate with their expertise with older children. This is not surprising in light of the fact that "formal education" historically has concerned only children after age 5 or 6. Furthermore, the public school has been the setting where the focus of the testing movement has been placed. No wonder the field of evaluation has been based primarily upon principles and assumptions that assume an older, more competent subject! For these reasons, caution should be taken in assuming that traditional assessment techniques can automatically be applied to preschoolers,

Table 7.7

Examples of Strategies for Evaluating Program Effectiveness

Evaluation Task	Possible Questions to be Asked	Potential Data Collection/ Evaluation Strategies
Evaluation of Efficiency and Quality of Program Operations	*Formative and Summative Questions* • Are program purposes, goals and philosophy clearly defined and understood by all staff members? • Are operational procedures clearly defined and followed by staff? • Are staff activities organized and well coordinated? • Are individual staff members performing their jobs effectively and showing continuous growth in their own professional skills? • Are programs planned for individual children and based upon objective evaluation information? • Does daily curriculum reflect children's IEP objectives, and are individualized programs carried out according to plan? • Does staff have objective means for assessing how well children are doing? • Are records up-to-date, readily available, well organized, and used in effective ways? • Do staff members communicate on program matters in timely way and work together effectively as a team with children and in solving program issues? • Are things staff members say are important reflected in daily operations and services? • Is program in compliance with local and state regulations for education and for early childhood programs?	*Internal Review Strategies* • Regular staff business meetings to address issues and review progress • Regular consultations and interviews with individual staff by program director or coordinator • Formal review procedure for giving individual staff feedback on job performance at least once or twice a year • Formal staff evaluation of program operations via —round table discussions —checklist or questionnaire evaluation on program —questionnaire or checklist for self-evaluation of job role and performance • Informal staff or client feedback via —personal conferences —suggestion box —presentations by individual staff on activities or procedures, with discussion and reactions *External Review Strategies* • Observations and review by outside evaluation team • Comparison of program operations with those of other similar programs staff may visit • Review of program by state and local officials to determine compliance with regulations • Examination of program documents, records, and operational procedures by a consultant, advisory board members, representatives of funding agency, colleagues from other similar programs, or experts in the field

Table 7.7 (continued)

	Formative and Summative Questions	Formative Evaluation Strategies
Evaluation of Child Progress and Developmental Outcomes	• What is the rate of progress shown by each child in learning activities? Is this below what the child is capable of doing? • Are each child's needs being met within the program, and is child being responsive to activities/therapy given? • Is each child progressing steadily toward learning objectives and mastery of new skills under current teaching methods? • Are children meeting IEP goals and objectives as defined, and in the projected timeline? • What are overall gains made by children who participate in the program? • Are children maintaining new skills and generalizing them to new situations and settings? • What other benefits are occurring for the child and parents as a result of their participation in the program? • Is the program producing the expected outcomes for children and parents that are considered important?	• Collection of performance data during learning activities with graphing/charting of data daily or weekly • Weekly or biweekly review of child's progress on learning objectives • Recording of child behavior or incidents via direct observation and data collection, anecdotal records, rating scales, or checklists *Summative Evaluation Strategies* • Individual child and group data on standardized tests, developmental checklists, or other objective measures of progress collected as part of a pretest-posttest design or posttest only design for comparison with a control group • Feedback from parents and others familiar with child on progress as reported by formal or informal checklists or assessment instruments • Summarized observational data showing cumulative change over time for individual children and for group of children in program • Samples of children's work before and after intervention, such as drawings, worksheets, videotapes of behavior, or audiotapes of speech/language performance

	Formative and Summative Questions	Formative Evaluation Strategies
Evaluation of Consumer and Staff Satisfaction With Program	• How do parents view the program, its staff, and its methods of operating? How do staff members view themselves and their own activities? • How do parents rate the program, the services they receive, and the manner in which staff deals with them and their child? Are they satisfied with the program? How do staff members rate themselves on the same variables?	• Appointment of parent advisory council with intermittent meetings with staff for purposes of input and program review • Suggestion box for staff and parent input or feedback • Requests to individuals or groups for input on program practices at beginning of year or as need arises, via questionnaires, checklists, or roundtable discussions

Table 7.7 (continued)

- Do parents feel welcome, fairly treated by the program, and view their role as an important member of the intervention team? How do staff members view their relationships with parents?
- Do parents understand the program and have sufficient information about is operations? Does staff think parents are given enough information and understand what the program is about?
- Do parents have suggestions on how the program can be improved? What do parents view as strengths and weaknesses in the program?
- Do staff members have suggestions on how the program can be improved? What do they view as program strengths and weaknesses?
- How do other agencies who refer children to the program view its services and relationships with parents and with the community at large?

- Formal and informal meetings between parents and staff, among staff members, or between staff and administrative personnel, for purposes of program review and problem solving

Summative Evaluation Strategies

- Formal evaluation/feedback questionnaires or rating scales for parents and for staff
- Formal interviews with parents or staff concerning perceptions of program and own role in program
- Formal feedback via rating form from referring agencies
- Review and data collection by outside party via observations, interviews, or questionnaires

toddlers, and infants. It would be a serious mistake to assume that evaluation procedures that work for the 10-year-old are equally as applicable to the 3-year-old.

Several contrasts highlight the difference in assessment processes as we have applied them with school-aged students and those that are now needed with very young children.

★ *The manner in which screening and diagnostic processes are used differs on several counts between students already attending elementary and secondary schools and children under age 5 who may or may not be participants in any formal early childhood education program.*

First, screening/diagnostic processes with young children are a means for bringing them *access to educational services* from a position of having no services. Assessment and evaluation procedures rarely, if ever, pose the possibility of excluding or removing preschoolers or infants from any "regular" educational experience since no standard preschool education system exists for all children. This is in direct contrast to the situation with school-aged youngsters who are participants in a regular education track. Evaluation processes with school-aged students opens the door to possible removal from the educational mainstream and placement in special education classrooms. The possibility of unfair, biased testing leading to inappropriate exclusion of elementary or secondary students from the educational mainstream has been a valid concern. Similar concerns in regard to preschool children do not exist.

Second, diagnostic procedures with school-aged students typically are initiated *after* a student has been in school for some time, *after* the child has generated a history of failure to perform in academic subject areas, and usually *after* teachers have had a period of time to observe and document a student's learning problems. Diagnostic evaluation in these circumstances is done to determine if the problem is of sufficient deviance to warrant labeling and placement in special education. In contrast, screening and diagnosis with preschoolers or infants must occur *before* the child has a long developmental history or *before* the youngster has a clear record of "failure" or "success." Because the goal is intervention, assessment procedures with young children are applied not only to identify diagnosable disorders, but also to catch impending developmental disorders *before* they compound into more serious problems that are truly handicapping.

★ *The content of assessment processes with preschoolers and infants is somewhat different from that used with school-aged students. Content is different both in the breadth of behavior assessed and in the types of behavior measured.*

Diagnostic tests for elementary and secondary students focus primarily upon measurement of learned academic skills (reading, writing, arithmetic, basic information in various subject areas, general mental ability or intelligence). If more in-depth testing is pursued, it generally focuses upon underlying cognitive skills and mental processes required for success in various academic areas. Testing of this nature is appropriate for identifying

Not every young child is as responsive in a testing situation as this 4-year-old. Those with handicaps, limited skills, and communication difficulties can present a real challenge if accurate assessment information is to be gathered.

problems in school-aged students because they have a common history of educational experience. This history is used as a basis for comparing students to identify those whose performance is sufficiently discrepant to suggest a problem.

In contrast, assessment and evaluation of preschoolers and infants cannot assume a common experience base. Early experience, stimulation at home, and opportunities for learning preacademic skills vary greatly across families. To assume that certain learning should have occurred at a particular age is more difficult given the differences in the early experiences of young children. Performance in a narrow range of academic subject areas such as reading and math concepts is obviously of no use. Assessment of young children therefore must rely on behaviors of even greater variability—the achievement of basic developmental milestones in areas of fine or gross motor development, speech and language, cognitive development (such as memory, discrimination, attention, and generalization), self-help skills, and socioemotional development). Professionals also must rely on much smaller performance repertoires in young children to gain a picture of functioning level and cognitive abilities.

The pitfalls that thwart attainment of valid and reliable measurement data are applicable to any age group of children. But certain constraints that ordinarily are not of concern with older children are unique to preschoolers and infants. These factors influence how assessment procedures are carried out. They also insert caution in what inferences can be drawn about a child's abilities and future performance on the basis of early assessment data.

The mere age factor, and lack of developmental sophistication, greatly affects assessment processes with infants and preschoolers. Simply put, their linguistic skills are only evolving, which limits communication between examiner and child. Their behavioral repertoires are small. Thus, the responses a child can make to a task are limited and highly affected by previous experience at home. A young child's potential inability to understand instructions, if they are too complex or abstract, does not always enable an examiner to elicit behavior on command. Simply the presence of a stranger or someone who talks differently and uses a vocabulary unfamiliar to a child can cause a preschooler or infant to become unresponsive.

Greater reliance must be placed on overt, physical actions as indicators of what young children can do and as manifestations of their cognitive processes. Older children, in contrast, can orally tell the examiner what they are thinking or can describe actions they would take if circumstances do not allow them to actually carry out the actions. Young children are not that verbally skillful. Assessment with young children entails the tapping of *evolving* skills, and often these are insufficiently complete to allow a child a workable set of tools to communicate what he or she actually is able to do.

The literature contains numerous citations on the difficulties of assessing young children, with suggestions as to how one can work toward fair, more accurate measures of performance. Some of those pointers are:

1. *Keep in mind the unique characteristics of young children that impinge upon their ability to perform well in formal testing situations.*

Testing procedures should be conducted with a keen eye toward the effects of the following variables in young children's behavior (Bayley, 1969; DuBose, 1979, 1981; Dunst & Rheingrover, 1981b; Harbin, 1977; Johnson-Martin, 1985):

a. *A high fatigue factor:* inability to maintain attention for a long period of time or to tolerate a prolonged period of structured, intense activity.

b. *Lack of motivation:* absence of sufficiently developed social awareness to want to do his or her best or to please the examiner.

c. *High distractibility:* tendency to turn attention to things that are interesting, novel, or simply a change in routine, which interferes with maintaining constant attention to assessment tasks given by the examiner.

d. *Lack of attentiveness:* inability to hold attention on a task for an extended time, or the propensity of a young child to refuse to respond if a task or material is uninteresting or if the child simply seems to be not "in the mood."

e. *Uncooperativeness:* the propensity of a young child to assert his or her independence by noncompliant behavior and unwillingness to follow commands or instructions— especially if given by a stranger.

f. *Fear of strangers or strange situations:* extraordinary stranger anxiety, shyness, or fear over separation from mother or familiar people; fear of a new situation or an unfamiliar setting that may result in inattentiveness, distractibility, and poor responses to tasks on which a child usually might perform quite well.

2. *Avoid one-time assessments since the behavior of young children is highly variable from day to day, from situation to situation, and even from minute to minute.*

The younger the child, the more evident is the situational variability. External environmental conditions (such as the presence of a stranger, distractions, or unfamiliar surroundings) or internal states (hunger, bodily discomfort, sleepiness, illness) greatly influence a child's overt behavior at any given time. This variability in turn affects test reliability and validity since assessment must in some way measure either "typical" or "best" behavior. With a very young child one has difficulty knowing if this has been attained (Vane & Motta, 1980; Lidz, 1977; Flapan & Neubauer, 1970).

3. *Recognize the performance limitations imposed by a physical, sensory, or neurological disorder and that adaptations in testing procedures may be necessary for a true measure of what a child is able to do.*

At times, changes in what are supposed to be fixed, standardized testing procedures will have to be made. One of the important tasks of assessment is to determine how a child's handicaps have influenced the sequence and pattern of development (DuBose, 1979; Kopp & Parmelee, 1979; Simeonsson & Wiegerink, 1975; Bagnato & Neisworth, 1981; Downs, 1977).

4. *Select testing tools that fit your purpose for assessment and evaluation and the actual process you plan to accomplish (screening, educational assessment, etc.).*

Evaluation tools also should be examined to assure their appropriateness for (a) the child's age level, and (b) the child's performance capabilities. No matter how good an instrument is, a fair, meaningful measure of the child's developmental abilities will not be achieved if the instrument places a premium on certain response modes or skills that a child is not yet able to perform (either because of immaturity or a disability) (Mendelson & Atlas, 1977; Karnes & Lee, 1978; MacTurk & Neisworth, 1978; DuBose, 1981; Kemper & Frankenburg, 1979; Hamilton & Swan, 1981).

5. *Be cautious in interpreting test results, and do not be too hasty in attaching labels or using test data for making definitive statements about a child's future* (Chase, 1975; Dunst & Rheingrover, 1981a; Shonkoff, 1983).

Several realities should temper what confidence is placed in assessment data as to how much they represent an accurate, stable measure of young children's capabilities:

a. *Growth patterns in young children are characterized by rapid and uneven developmental change, which affects the stability of performance on assessment instruments.* What may appear at times to be a deficiency in skill learning and possible irregular development may only be a part of a child's unique growth pattern (Ciminero & Drabman, 1977; Evans & Nelson, 1977; Olweus, 1979; Mash & Terdal, 1981).

b. *Age is very much a factor in determining the meaning and significance of certain behaviors.* Some behaviors (such as temper tantrums) are an expected and rather normal pattern at certain ages but at other ages would be considered inappropriate. Developmental characteristics of children at various age levels (including social behaviors, cognitive styles, responses to structured tasks) differ, and hence affect one's interpretation of what is "normal." Any interpretation of test data should be based on a basic understanding of child development and early behavior (Mash & Terdal, 1981; Harbin, 1977).

c. *Predictive ability of early intellectual or performance tests on young children is limited.* Correspondence between scores on developmental scales in infancy and later IQs is very poor (Dunst & Rheingrover, 1981b; Keogh & Becker, 1973). Tests during the first year of life are particularly weak predictors. Only in cases of extreme scores do measures in infancy or early childhood show greater correlation with later developmental status (Knobloch & Pasamanick, 1967; Smith, Flick, Ferriss, & Sellman, 1972). Several studies indicate that one of four young children who are judged to be mentally retarded under age 3 will not be judged so later in life (Holden, 1972; Koch, 1963).

6. *Recognize that the logistics for testing young children will, of necessity, be somewhat different from strategies involved in testing older children.*

Young children cannot be expected to function well in highly structured situations for extended periods. A series of short testing sessions is more realistic. Young children are reactive to new and unfamiliar situations. They will not necessarily be responsive to a stranger. Extended rapport building will have to be a part of the evaluation procedure. Parents likely will be present and may even be needed to assist in the actual assessment process—especially with infants. Testing environments that are more natural or familiar to a young child are more likely to increase his or her responsiveness. Strange and overly structured settings are more likely to cause a young child to be fearful or simply to "clam up" (DuBose, 1979; Colvin & Zaffiron, 1974; Sheehan & Gallagher, 1984).

7. *Look at the child in the context of his or her environment, and be alert to external surroundings that impinge upon the nature of the performance.*

Avoid isolated, piecemeal information that describes behavior out of context. With young children, that approach increases the chances for gaining an inaccurate view of their strengths, weaknesses, and developmental abilities (Erickson, 1976; Barnes, 1974).

8. *Be sure that the examiner who tests a young child not only is competent in administering tests for this population but also has personal experience and skill in managing a preschooler or infant.*

The ability to interact with a young child, establish rapport, and gain and maintain the child's attention to tasks is a big part of successful assessment and evaluation (Gotts, 1979; Hare & Hare, 1977).

9. *If secondary sources of information about a child are used for estimating a child's abilities and skills, recognize the limitations in placing reliance upon what someone "thinks" or "remembers" a child can do.*

Many of the instruments used with young children call for parent or teacher reports. Studies have shown that parents and teachers are not always in agreement and that some parents tend to either overestimate or underestimate their child's abilities (Gradel, Thompson, & Sheehan, 1981; Mealor & Richmond, 1980; Mantle, 1982).

SOURCES OF INFORMATION ABOUT EVALUATION TOOLS

Teachers and other disciplinary personnel frequently ask, "Where can I get information about what testing tools are available for use with young children—especially the handicapped?" Following is a list of some of the best resources currently available.

Preschool Test Matrix: Individual Test Descriptions
Publication of CORRC (Coordinating Office for Regional Resource Centers), University of Kentucky, Lexington, 1976.

> Provides a detailed, descriptive analysis of 127 tests, including intelligence tests and developmental tests covering language, social, cognitive, self-help, school readiness, and other areas. The volume includes a descriptor matrix on which all tests are classified in regard to (a) who can administer test, (b) how it is to be administered (group or individual), (c) age/grade covered, (d) time required to administer, (e) response mode (verbal or nonverbal), (f) test type (criterion- or norm-referenced), (g) content of test, (h) type of evaluation (e.g., screening, diagnostic, achievement), and (i) population focus (type of handicapped children on which device could be used).

Tests and Measurement in Child Development: Handbooks (Volumes 1 & 2)
O. G. Johnson, San Francisco: Jossey-Bass Publishers, 1976.

> Volume 1 is a resource book of unpublished measures covered in the literature from 1956 to 1965. Volume 2 is an extension of Volume 1, covering literature from 1965 to 1974. Measurement instruments were located by a search through journals and research reports to identify instruments being used. The two volumes give descriptive information on each test, including age range, type of instrument, variables measured (often with sample items), and information on reliability and validity. Tests are divided into groups, including those that measure (a) cognition (intelligence, readiness, language, etc.), (b) personal and emotional characteristics, (c) perceptions of the environment, (d) self-concept, (e) qualities of caregiving and home environment, (f) motor skills and sensory perception, (g) physical attributes, (h) attitudes and interests, (i) social behavior, and (j) vocational.

Measures of Maturation: An Anthology of Early Childhood Observation Instruments
E.G. Boyer, A. Simon, and G. Karatin (Eds.), Philadelphia: Research for Better Schools, 1973.

Reviews instruments that quantify the behaviors of children and those who interact with them (teachers, parents, etc.). Observational systems are categorized into those assessing individual behaviors, social contacts, physical environment, and child's developmental level in areas of neurological, physiological, affective, cognitive, and interpersonal-social.

Socioemotional Measures for Preschool and Kindergarten Children
D. K. Walker, San Francisco: Jossey-Bass Publishers, 1973.

Contains listings of measures suitable for preschool-aged and kindergarten children ages 3-6. The book reviews 143 measures drawn from a variety of sources including journals, standard reference books on tests, government evaluation reports on Head Start/Follow-Through and other early childhood programs, annotated bibliographies of published and unpublished measures, and published books on tests. Evaluation measures are divided into six socioemotional areas: (a) attitudes, (b) general personal and emotional adjustment, (c) interests and preferences, (d) personality or behavior traits, (e) self-concept, and (f) social skills or competency.

A Bibliography of Screening, Diagnosis, and Assessment Instruments
L. Cross and S. Johnston, in L. Cross and K. Goin (Eds.), *Identifying Handicapped Children: A Guide to Casefinding, Screening, Diagnosis, Assessment, and Evaluation* (First Chance Series), New York: Walker & Co., 1977.

Contains a bibliography of evaluation instruments used with young handicapped children, including many developed as a part of HCEEP (Handicapped Children's Early Education Programs). Descriptions are given of each test and its content. Addresses from which test can be obtained and published costs (1977) are listed. A matrix listing categorizes all tests in terms of age range covered, type of test (screening, diagnostic, or assessment), the performance factors measured (language, perception, fine motor, gross motor, reasoning, school readiness, social-emotional, etc.).

Buros Ninth Mental Measurements Yearbook (2 volumes)
Buros Institute of Mental Measurement, Lincoln, NE: University of Nebraska Press, 1985.

The most recent of a series of volumes that serve as one of the best known and most used reference volumes for standardized tests. Includes summaries about a wide range of standardized tests that comprise the whole spectrum of tests for all age levels, not just early childhood. Summaries of a wide range of standardized tests are given, including a critical review of each. Strengths and limitations of each test are noted, along with technical information concerning reliability, validity, and the norming sample. Tests reviewed include intelligence, achievement, ability, personality, and vocational instruments.

SUMMARY

Evaluation and assessment procedures traditionally have not been used with children before they enter kindergarten. The rise of early intervention programs for children with handicaps or at-risk conditions, however, has created the necessity for formal assessment of some children during their infancy or preschool years to ascertain their developmental status. Evaluation in early intervention programs is a *continuous process,* not a single event, which encompasses six rather different kinds of measurement activities: (a) casefinding, (b) screening, (c) diagnosis, (d) educational assessment, (e) performance monitoring, and (f) program evaluation. Each of these processes is applied for a different purpose, and each addresses a unique set of questions that leads to a unique end result.

Casefinding is a means for *locating and accessing* the target population of children and soliciting referrals. It does not involve assessment activities in the traditional sense, but it does require adults to recognize children who should be referred for screening.

Screening is a means of *verifying* if a child needs further diagnostic evaluation. Children who do not fall within normal ranges of development, as suggested by broad estimates of their behavior, are identified as potential candidates for early intervention.

Diagnostic evaluation is a means of *analyzing* the nature and degree of a child's developmental disabilities or behavioral limitations using assessment data obtained through in-depth testing, observation, and information gathering. As a result of this evaluation, eligibility for services is established and treatment measures are recommended, including what kinds of services a child should receive.

Educational assessment involves *pinpointing* a child's skills and learning needs for purposes of planning his or her curriculum or daily instructional and therapeutic activities. To practitioners working directly with children, this evaluation process is one of the most critical, and its timing is of utmost importance. Educational assessments should be done after diagnosis but before a child's IEP and instructional program are firmly set.

Performance monitoring involves the continuous *tracking* of each child's behavior to see if progress is being made toward IEP goals and objectives. If adjustments in teaching techniques are needed, these are noted.

Program evaluation involves *documenting* program effectiveness as a means for accountability. It involves a measure of the quality and impact of a program upon the children and parents it serves.

A communication board is used with this nonverbal child to allow him to respond in this assessment situation. Even verbal preschoolers will often respond more readily when asked to point to pictures rather than give verbal answers.

Effective, sensitive assessment of young children requires special skills on the part of professionals, including an understanding of development and behavior in preschoolers or infants. Persons who are skilled as evaluators of school-aged students are not necessarily prepared to perform meaningful evaluations on young children, nor are methods of assessment traditionally used with other students appropriate with infants and preschoolers. The manner in which screening and diagnostic processes are used and the behaviors assessed differ greatly. These differences should be kept in mind when planning and carrying out any one of the six assessment processes described in this chapter.

Application of formalized assessment procedures with very young children raises a number of critical questions for professionals: How can meaningful assessments of infants and preschoolers be made in view of the variability in their behavior from day to day and the difficulties involved in getting a sample of their "best performance?" How can professionals avoid the pitfalls of premature diagnosis and labeling with young children and still identify those needing early intervention programs? How should assessment data on young children be interpreted, given the questionable relationship to a child's later performance on formalized tests (particularly on tests of cognitive ability)?

8
Service Delivery Approaches

Because the major focus of public education is upon some 43 million* youngsters who attend our nation's elementary and secondary schools, most Americans think of education primarily in terms of the familiar classroom in the neighborhood school. If asked to describe educational programs for children, you probably would conjure up images from your own school experiences—a classroom filled with desks or tables, textbooks in reading

---

*From *Statistical Report on the Condition of Education*, National Center for Educational Statistics, Washington, DC: U.S. Department of Education, 1980.

and math, workbooks and duplicated worksheets, and a teacher (possibly assisted by an aide) working with 15 to 35 students. This familiar classroom represents the type of setting and service delivery approach used to educate the majority of American youths. Because education is mandatory for students from age 5 or 6 through high school, this is the age group around which the heart of our system of American education has been built.

As public education now expands to include handicapped preschoolers and infants, educators must consider a much broader concept of education. What is an appropriate education for children so young? What kinds of educational environments work best with preschoolers and infants who need early intervention? These children do not sit at desks. Their educational task is not one of reading and writing. They are not independent and cannot work in large groups with just one teacher. Unlike older, school-aged students, they cannot walk to school, board a bus alone, or even travel long distances on a bus without direct supervision and care. An appropriate education for them does not mean textbooks, workbooks, and quiet seatwork on tasks that produce tangible products.

Preschool children are only beginning to learn skills that are considered prerequisite for enrollment in kindergarten or the elementary grades. They are just learning to walk, talk, listen, follow instructions, and interact with peers. They are not yet able to work independently for long periods on structured activities. They may not be able to communicate their needs to others. At this young age, many are yet unable to toilet or feed themselves without help. Most need constant attention and supervision by an adult. The optimal school day for these young learners is probably 2½-4 hours, after which they will spend the major part of their waking hours under the care of a parent or alternative caregiver. How, then, can special education services or early intervention programs be delivered in ways that meet the special needs of this unique group of children?

A PREVIEW OF EARLY CHILDHOOD-SPECIAL EDUCATION PROGRAMS

If you were to tour the United States and visit early intervention programs for handicapped infants and preschoolers, you would find tremendous diversity in the services they offer and in how the staff goes about offering services. This variation is a result primarily of one major factor: *Early childhood-special education programs have evolved in different ways from site to site and from state to state.* Here are just a few of the many observations you would make in visiting some of these programs:

- *Programs for young handicapped and at-risk children are based in many different types of physical settings.*

Unlike standard forms of education for school-aged students, which invariably operate within elementary and secondary school buildings, early childhood-special education programs often are housed in nontraditional kinds of settings. These include the children's own homes, community centers, public or private clinics, university- or college-based service centers, churches, day-care centers, commercial facilities, and hospitals. Some programs also are found in elementary school buildings and special schools.

- *The administrative sponsorship of early childhood-special education programs differs from state to state and from program to program.*

Local school districts and state education agencies sponsor some programs for handicapped and at-risk preschoolers or infants. These agencies are legally responsible for services in states where legislation mandates special education services for children under school age. Other sponsors include private organizations, religious and civic groups, nonprofit agencies formed by parents or community advocacy groups, universities, and governmental agencies. Because the purposes of these organizations vary, the services they offer likely differ as well.

Funding sources for programs vary, too, imposing different kinds of standards and regulations to which each center or program must adhere. For example, a program funded by private donors and public contributions may have few external regulations imposed upon it. Program policies, therefore, may be left primarily to the discretion of the administrative agency. A program supported by a state or federal agency must comply with specific guidelines that dictate staff qualifications, admission procedures, eligibility criteria for children to be served, and the type of program offered.

- *The recipient of services may be viewed differently across programs.*

All programs do not necessarily focus upon the child alone. Services may be offered to the parents, siblings, or a primary caregiver other than the parent. In programs in which parents are the major recipients of special help, staff activities may center on helping parents become more skillful in meeting the special needs of their handicapped child at home. On the other hand, if children are the primary target for services, the staff spends its time designing learning activities for each child to provide special therapy and education.

- *The types of children served within each early childhood-special education program may differ from site to site.*

Within public schools, elementary-aged students who receive special education services typically are grouped *by disability* type (e.g., mentally retarded, learning disabled, emotionally disturbed), *by level of impairment* (mild, moderate, or severe), and *by age*. Groupings of youngsters in early intervention programs usually are not standardized in the same way. Some centers are cross-categorical; they enroll children within a given age range without regard to their particular type or level of disability. Other programs offer specialized services only to children with certain disabilities, regardless of age. For example, they may serve only visually impaired, deaf and hearing impaired, or orthopedically handicapped youngsters. Some programs include both handicapped and nonhandicapped children. In short, early intervention programs have little consistency in the way children are grouped.

- *The type of services offered (including the weekly and monthly schedule of services provided by an agency) varies significantly across programs.*

State laws influence the comprehensiveness of educational programs for children under the mandatory school age. In states with permissive laws, state education agencies (SEAs) and local school districts (LEAs) or other agencies are free to organize programs if they so choose. In those states, many different organizations are likely to be involved in operating programs, with each pursuing its own interpretation as to what constitutes an appropriate and quality early intervention program.

Centers likely offer their own unique "menu" of classroom curriculum, services, and special therapies. One program will operate daily, 11 months a year, whereas another will operate three mornings a week, 9 months a year. One program will offer comprehensive educational, social, and therapy services; another will offer only selected kinds of therapy and no real classroom program. In contrast, states where services are mandated by law likely have early intervention services that are more standardized, fall under the jurisdiction of just one agency (which is given the management responsibility), and present less variability in their administrative organization.

● *Staff composition within early childhood-special education programs differs from center to center.*

Whereas elementary schools follow a rather standard staffing pattern, staff composition in early intervention programs does not necessarily follow a standard plan. Programs differ markedly in the number and types of personnel employed, depending upon (a) the nature of the organization sponsoring the program, including its purpose and philosophy about educational services, (b) the source and amount of financial support, and (c) the types of children served. Thus, in one center, trained personnel from a variety of professional disciplines will be employed. Another program sponsored under a different agency may be staffed largely by paraprofessionals and lay volunteers.

In summary, conditions unique to each community and state determine the particular characteristics of early childhood-special education programs. The potential for variation is tremendous. One of the most exciting aspects of the field of early childhood-special education is that so many innovative educational approaches are possible. In fact, flexibility has been critical for some programs to exist.

To understand the possible service delivery options and gain a perspective of traditional approaches with which educators are familiar, we will look at service delivery approaches used with two related populations of individuals: (a) school-aged special education students in elementary and secondary schools, and (b) preschool-aged children in regular nursery, preschool, or day-care programs. With that background, we then will review some issues and considerations that affect the planning of service delivery strategies for handicapped preschoolers and infants. First, however, we will define and discuss some concepts essential to an understanding of service delivery.

A DEFINITION OF SERVICE DELIVERY APPROACHES

Special educators use the term *service delivery approach* to refer to administrative arrangements for delivering instructional assistance to exceptional students. Over the years the emphasis of this definition has shifted in ways that reflect a changing perspective of what special education is and how it can be best provided. Service delivery approaches traditionally have been defined simply by a type of setting (e.g., regular mainstreamed classroom, special class, resource room, special day school, residential school, or home-based program setting). This approach encouraged educators to attend more to the issue of *where children should go* than to *what should happen* to them in that setting once they are placed there.

Dunn (1973) offered a more expanded interpretation of service delivery approaches by adding to potential placements for children the possible *types of provisions* educators can use to help exceptional students. He emphasized that if special education is to offer something special, something extra or unusual must be provided beyond that available within regular education. Four types of special provisions identified by Dunn include:

1. *Specially trained professional educators* who work with exceptional children and offer special services that are not normally available in a regular classroom. These include special teachers with expertise in mental retardation, learning disabilities, and the like, speech therapists, adaptive physical educators, and many others.
2. *Special curricular content* that replaces or supplements the regular curriculum for nonhandicapped students. Examples are mobility training and braille for blind individuals, special speech and language training for the deaf.
3. *Special methodology* designed to facilitate learning and circumvent problems that thwart learning in a handicapped child. This may include breaking learning tasks into smaller steps and sequencing them to promote continuous progress, using alternative sensory modes for learning, and applying behavior modification procedures.
4. *Special instructional materials/equipment* that provide helpful supports for learning. Special typewriters, communication boards, large-type books, devices to aid hearing, programmed materials, prosthetic devices, adapted toys, and simplified response materials for learning tasks are a few examples.

All family members play an important part in delivering the early stimulation and care required by a handicapped infant. When service delivery systems for early intervention are planned, efforts should be made to attend to the needs of the family as well as to those of the infant.

The limitation of these first two approaches to service delivery is that they emphasize only a place or a type of service and do not call attention to the real *actions* and *processes* by which services are delivered. A more functional view of service delivery, reflected in the regulations of PL 94-142, is emerging. That law goes one step further by describing service delivery in terms of *what special educators must do* to assure that exceptional students are placed in an appropriate educational setting and receive an appropriate, individualized special education program.

This view can be summarized in what the author offers as a functional, *process-oriented definition* of service delivery approaches. That is, service delivery approaches are those selected strategies and processes used to plan and implement a quality individualized education program (IEP) for a handicapped individual. This approach defines *where* a child will be placed for educational purposes, *what* special kinds of assistance are to be rendered, plus the *mechanism* to be used *to deliver special services*. A process-oriented service delivery approach connotes ongoing processes and actions that are not simply one-time decisions. Table 8.1 contrasts the three definitions of service delivery and provides a summary of the author's process-oriented definition.

The term *service delivery approach* is sometimes confused with another concept used frequently in educational circles—the *education program model*. The latter term is a broader one that refers to a comprehensive plan for an entire educational program. A program model includes the unique service delivery approach to be employed, plus other distinguishing features of the program. Chapter 9 is devoted to a detailed discussion of education program models and descriptions of several exemplary program models for handicapped children.

The need for alternative service delivery approaches

The concept of alternative modes of service delivery is an important cornerstone of special education today. As you learned in chapter 3, alternative strategies were of little concern to special educators at one time. Handicapped students who did not fit into existing public school programs were simply terminated, referred to institutions, or removed from regular classes and placed in separate special education rooms.

Dissatisfaction with the widespread use of special classes in the late 1960s caused special educators to examine the legitimacy of segregating handicapped students in special classes. The result was a movement away from over-reliance on special education classes as the only method of service delivery. Educators began talking about other approaches, too, such as resource rooms and itinerant teachers. The premise underlying these new approaches was simple: *When alternative approaches are available to provide children with special instructional assistance, services can be matched to each person's unique problems and needs.* Because children's needs differ, so must administrative strategies for serving them.

Alternative service delivery approaches are necessary for other, more specific reasons. *First*, the special problems and needs of handicapped children are so diverse that no single administrative approach is universally appropriate for every exceptional individual. *Second*, certain educational environments are ideal for exceptional children with certain disabilities but less so for others. An educational environment that is most supportive for a severely, multiply handicapped 6-year-old is likely to be quite different from that needed to help a mildly hearing impaired 12-year-old. *Third*, some service delivery approaches

Table 8.1
Definitions of Service Delivery Alternatives

Place-Oriented Definition	Content-Oriented Definition	Process-Oriented Definition
Emphasizes placement of an individual for special services.	Emphasizes potential content or components of a special education program.	Emphasizes strategies and activities used to deliver special services to a group of children or an individual child.
Describes services in terms of where student should go to be educated.	Describes services in terms of what is possible or what should characterize special education.	Describes services in regard to what will happen in providing services a child requires, which encompasses previous two definitions and translates them into action steps.
Service delivery approach involves selection of one of the options of:	Service delivery approach involves selection of one or more of the following types of services:	Service delivery approach encompasses the planning of all steps/processes below; includes designation of:
• Regular classroom • Resource room • Combined regular/ special class placement • Special day school • Residential school	• Specially trained professional educators • Special curriculum content • Special teaching methodologies • Special instructional materials and equipment	• WHO will receive various types of special services for the purposes of helping the child • WHEN the services will begin and how long they will continue • WHAT services will be provided and what the broad program is, as well as specific child objectives they are designed to achieve • WHERE or in what type of setting services will be delivered • BY WHOM services will be delivered and what specially trained personnel will be deployed to work in various capacities with recipient(s) of the services • WITH WHOM services will be delivered so as to assure the individual recipient the most normalizing and least restrictive environment • THROUGH WHOM services will be offered in the sense of what departments, organizations, outside agencies, or other administrative units will assume responsibility for making possible the delivery of planned services

are more functional in certain school districts than others depending upon (a) the number of individuals to be included in special education and the types and severity levels represented among them, and (b) the geographical area and dispersion of children to be served. Some service delivery approaches are viable in an urban community but less desirable in a rural area. *Fourth*, instructional, social, and personal needs of children change as they grow older. Certain service delivery strategies may be more appropriate with selected age groups.

Principles affecting current special education practices

During recent years three concepts have emerged in special education that have a major impact upon its practices: *mainstreaming, least restrictive environment,* and *normalization.* To understand special education as it operates today, one must be familiar with these concepts and the rationale underlying them. An even more important consideration is the question: How should these concepts be interpreted and applied in practice to early intervention programs for handicapped preschoolers and infants?

Mainstreaming   The term *mainstreaming* is familiar to almost everyone, but it means different things to different people. Kaufman, Gottlieb, Agard, and Kukic (1975) have offered a helpful definition of mainstreaming:

> Mainstreaming refers to the temporal, instructional, and social integration of . . . exceptional children with normal peers based on an ongoing, individually determined, educational planning and programming process and requires clarification of responsibility among regular and special education, administrative, instructional, and supportive personnel. (pp. 40-41)

Several events led to the growth of the mainstreaming concept. For example:

1. Research began to suggest that EMR (or mildly retarded) students made no greater progress in special classes than those retained in regular classes (Dunn, 1968; MacMillan, 1971; Goldstein, 1967; Iano, 1972; Kolstoe, 1972; Cegelka & Tyler, 1970; Guskin & Spiker, 1968).
2. An overabundance of non-English speaking minority children was found in EMR classes. Diagnostic instruments often appeared to be culturally biased and thus contributed to inappropriate diagnosis and placement of some children in special classes for the retarded (Kirk & Gallagher, 1979).
3. Educators and other concerned citizens began to point to possible adverse and debilitating effects of labeling a child as retarded or handicapped, especially when the child was borderline or at a particular disadvantage because of cultural, ethnic, or language differences (Rosenthal & Jacobson, 1966; Hurley, 1969; Goldstein, Arkell, Ashcroft, Hurley, & Lilly, 1975; Mercer, 1973).
4. Social and political changes in our society brought increased sensitivity to the legal rights and privileges of children and their parents in regard to testing and diagnosis, educational placement, and rights to appropriate treatment.

Kaufman et al. (1975) suggested that successful mainstreaming must encompass three key components. First, *integration of handicapped students* must occur. True integration is manifest in several ways. A child must be *temporally integrated* with normal peers; that is, a significant and meaningful amount of time must be spent with nonhandicapped peers within the classroom setting. A child must be *socially integrated.* Social isolation and rejection of a handicapped individual in a regular classroom does not reflect appropriate mainstreaming. With true integration, handicapped and nonhandicapped peers associate and interact with one another in a manner that suggests social acceptance of the exceptional pupil within that educational environment. A child also must be *instructionally integrated* in the sense of sharing in the instructional environment of the regular classroom. If instructional integration is to occur, three conditions are necessary:

1. Learning characteristics and instructional needs of the student in question must be compatible with learning opportunities provided to the other, nonhandicapped individuals within that educational environment.
2. Learning characteristics and instructional needs of the student must be compatible with the regular teacher's professional capabilities and personal willingness to adapt and modify instructional procedures.
3. Special support services provided to the exceptional student must be compatible with or complementary to the goals that the regular teacher has identified for that student.

A second component underlying successful mainstreaming described by Kaufman et al. is that *an ongoing educational and programming process* must take place. Mainstreaming does not merely entail placement of a student in a regular classroom instead of a segregated special education class. Mainstreaming must incorporate an ongoing planning and instructional process to assure that a handicapped child's special instructional needs are met. If a student's needs are neither identified nor met programmatically, real mainstreaming does not occur. This ongoing educational and programming process includes continuous assessment of student needs, targeting of specific goals and objectives, preparation of an individualized education program (IEP), and commitment of resources that allow the required special services to be delivered. It also requires ongoing evaluation to determine the effectiveness of instructional programs.

A third and final component that must be encompassed within effective mainstreaming is *clarification of responsibilities* among administrative, instructional, teaching, and supportive consulting or clinical staff. Educational tasks must be defined and responsibilities clearly assigned among both regular and special staff members who will serve the student.

In summary, mainstreaming places considerable responsibility upon the persons and programs purporting to apply this concept in services to exceptional children. Too frequently practitioners view mainstreaming in an overly simplistic manner without sufficient attention to its programmatic implications. Over-zealous advocates may jump onto the mainstreaming bandwagon and insist upon placing handicapped children in regular classes without simultaneously making appropriate preparations to assure that children receive the instructional assistance they need. Educators must recognize that mainstreaming is no more the best alternative for educating all handicapped children than is the segregated special education classroom. The more important question is: Where can each child best be taught, and what educational setting will afford that child the greatest all-around opportunity to learn and to achieve his or her potential? The answer is the regular mainstreamed classroom for some youngsters. For others it is a special classroom or some other alternative.

Least restrictive environment   Like mainstreaming, least restrictive environment represents a philosophy about what constitutes an "appropriate" educational placement for exceptional children. Kirk and Gallagher (1979) explained the concept of least restrictive environment like this:

> The child should be taken from the regular classroom only when it is not possible to deliver the needed service within the regular classroom. . . . A special class should be established only when it becomes obvious that a part-time resource room or itinerant teacher program is not adequate to do the job, and . . . the child should be institutionalized only when all other efforts to provide good education within the framework of the local school system have failed. (p. 19)

The concept of least restrictive environment was applied in the courts long before it became a familiar concept among educators. There it was referred to as the *doctrine of the least restrictive alternative* and eventually was applied in cases involving the rights and privileges of handicapped persons. Over a series of court cases (summarized in Table 3.2 of chapter 3), some consistent values began to emerge: (a) Placement of the handicapped in regular classrooms is preferable to placement in segregated classroom settings; (b) a continuum of alternative services and educational environments for the handicapped is needed, with the degree of preference determined by the extent to which an alternative is most like a normal educational setting; and (c) in cases in which services are to be delivered to an individual or group of deviant individuals, the standard guiding its design should be the nature of services provided to all other persons (Kaufman & Morra, 1978).

Though the concept of least restrictive environment (LRE) may be clear, its application to children is not so clear-cut. Confusion surrounds the issue of what constitutes the least restrictive environment for individuals with various types and degrees of disability. Opinions differ on what a least restrictive environment is for a blind child of normal intelligence, or a moderately retarded child with Down syndrome, or a severely retarded, immobile 15-year-old boy, or a 4-year-old profoundly disabled child functioning at the level of a 2-month-old infant. In an attempt to reduce this confusion and to provide a continuum of services that professionals can use when considering placement options for a handicapped person, several models have been developed.

A continuum of special education services common to these models, ranking service delivery options from most restrictive to least restrictive, is depicted in Figure 8.1. Eight educational settings are listed, with those considered least restrictive at the bottom and those most restrictive at the top. The interpretation of what is most or least restrictive is based upon a standard set according to how and where school-age students generally are educated. The fact that this continuum of special education services focuses upon alternatives commonly applied with *school-aged students*, as opposed to a broader population including preschool and post-secondary groups, should not be a surprise. Until recently, special education involved only school-aged students. Later in this chapter we will look at applications of the concept of least restrictive environment to younger children not yet enrolled in public school programs.

As you can see from the array of services in Figure 8.1, educators have many options to consider when planning for a special student. The regular classroom is depicted on the continuum as the least restrictive environment, but what is least restrictive for one child may not be least restrictive for another. Two points may help clarify implementation of this principle.

1. What is least restrictive is a determination made *individually* for each handicapped child based upon the individual's needs, functioning level, performance capabilities,

Figure 8.1
Continuum of Special Education Services

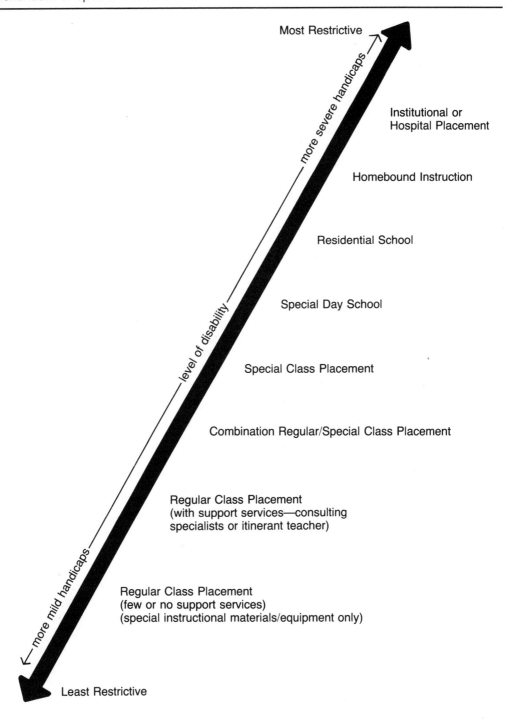

Most Restrictive

Institutional or
Hospital Placement

Homebound Instruction

Residential School

Special Day School

Special Class Placement

Combination Regular/Special Class Placement

Regular Class Placement
(with support services—consulting
specialists or itinerant teacher)

Regular Class Placement
(few or no support services)
(special instructional materials/equipment only)

Least Restrictive

more severe handicaps

level of disability

more mild handicaps

and other intellectual/social characteristics. This means that blanket placement decisions for all EMR students or all visually impaired students are not to be made by school officials, either to place all handicapped children in regular classes or to keep them out (Kaufman & Morra, 1978).

2. Placement decisions and selection of the least restrictive environment for an individual child must be made on the basis of the formally written individualized education program (IEP).

Normalization   Although the normalization principle first was applied to the mentally retarded, it has applications with all handicapped persons. As applied to services for the handicapped and the treatment they receive from persons assuming supervisory roles over them, the principle of normalization means that (a) the care of handicapped persons should be as culturally normative as possible, and (b) placement for a handicapped person and any educational service should establish and maintain personal behavior and characteristics that are as culturally normative as possible (Wolfensberger, 1972). Bengt Nirje, Director of the Swedish Association for Retarded Citizens, was instrumental in further extending the principle of normalization to the design and operation of residential facilities for the retarded. He defined normalization as:

> . . . making available to all mentally retarded people patterns of life and conditions of everyday living which are as close as possible to the regular circumstances and way of life of society. (Nirje, 1976, p. 231)

For the handicapped person, this may be interpreted to mean such things as:

— opportunities to be a part of the normal rhythm of the day, of a week, or of a year. This involves sharing the same privacies, activities, and responsibilities of nonhandicapped persons as well as having the freedom to go to school or to work and to participate in social/leisure activities within a community.

— opportunities to undergo the normal developmental experiences within a typical life cycle. This involves moving through the experiences and developmental steps of infancy and early childhood, and entering into school to participate in education experiences as do other children and youth. It also includes advancing to more independent stages of living. Advocates of normalization suggest that just as normal adults move away from the home and establish independence and new personal/social relationships, so should the handicapped.

— the right to understanding and respect for personal desires and needs for self-fulfillment. This means allowing the retarded or other handicapped persons freedom to enjoy some of the same forms of personal relationships and basic economic patterns of life experienced by other members of society. This might include relationships between the sexes, job and employment opportunities, leisure and social activities, etc.

(Nirje, 1976)

Nirje has argued that the normalization principle should apply to all handicapped persons, regardless of their degree of disability. Although it will not make handicapped or retarded persons normal, it does make possible a more normal and nonstigmatized life style.

To summarize, the three concepts we have discussed are closely interrelated. Although each concept focuses upon slightly different issues, all relate to an underlying value that *what is good for the nonhandicapped child is of value also to the handicapped. Social-educational traditions and approaches for serving nonhandicapped persons should be the standard model for designing programs for the handicapped.*

Implications for early intervention programs

Several issues are apparent in examining applications of *mainstreaming, least restrictive environment (LRE)*, and *normalization* to children under school age. How these concepts should be interpreted for preschoolers or infants is not clear. In fact, interpretations applied to school-aged exceptional students often are extended downward arbitrarily with the assumption that they can be implemented in similar ways in preschool and infant programs. This is not an appropriate assumption.

What is a normalizing or least restrictive environment for a handicapped preschooler or infant?   The question of what is the least restrictive environment (LRE) for a child at the preschool level or a young infant and the question of what kind of environment is most normalizing for these same children go hand-in-hand. Policy concerning implementation of the LRE concept, as stated in the *Federal Register* (August 23, 1977), indicates that:

1. Handicapped children should be educated to the maximum extent appropriate with children who are not handicapped.
2. Handicapped children should be removed from regular classes and placed in special classes or separate educational environments only when the nature or severity of the handicap is such that education in the regular classroom setting cannot be achieved satisfactorily.

This interpretation of LRE obviously is based upon a standard set according to what treatment normally is given to nonhandicapped children in the elementary and secondary grades. Because all children are required by law to attend school beginning at age 5 or 6 and all are educated in local elementary schools in regular classes, the determination of what is "normal" for children once they enter the public education system is a simple matter. The regular classroom is the standard environment or least restrictive setting against which all other options are weighed. What, then, is least restrictive for a student is determined individually by weighing options against that standard for normal youngsters and the child's unique educational needs.

The question concerning interpretation of LRE with young infants and preschoolers is: What is a normal environment for children at this young age? What standard typically applied with normally developing infants and preschoolers is a basis for defining what represents a desirable and least restrictive setting for the care and education of young handicapped children? The point is: *No accepted, single standard exists regarding where infants and preschoolers should be cared for during the years prior to their entry into school.*

How and where young children are reared is a highly subjective matter influenced by the personal values of parents and the ethnic, religious, cultural, and socioeconomic groups from which they come. Perhaps the only point of agreement is that the setting and form of care should be nurturing and responsive to the child's emotional, physical, and developmental needs. How this is best achieved, however, is a matter of opinion.

What is the most "normal" environment for infants and preschool-aged children cannot simply be defined by a single setting. In interpreting the applications of LRE to preschool education, Turnbull (1982) suggested that the relative restrictiveness in specialized programs may be a necessary prerequisite to future freedom. Some children (e.g., blind, severely learning impaired, or physically disabled) may need training that is unavailable in many preschools for nonhandicapped children. By participating in an early intervention program that segregates them from nonhandicapped peers, specialized training can be given to help them acquire skills that will increase the chance of their participating in a regular environment more successfully later.

In the author's opinion, interpretation of the least restrictive environment for a young handicapped child should rest upon three important criteria:

- Can the setting provide an effective "intervention" through special services and individualized programs that will increase the chances that the child will be developmentally more capable of functioning later in a less restrictive environment?
- Is the setting culturally compatible with the values and practices of the community or subculture of which the parents and family are a part?
- Is the setting equipped to provide the forms of stimulation and care that are age-appropriate for the child and in harmony with the child's unique caretaking and educational needs?

What are the obstacles in operationalizing preschool mainstreaming? The rationale for mainstreaming preschoolers may be self-evident, but implementation of the concept is not as easy as it may appear. Contrast, for instance, the task of mainstreaming elementary school students with that of mainstreaming preschoolers. Public schools, as a single administrative unit, operate both the special classes for handicapped students and the regular class in which mainstreaming will occur. They hold administrative authority over both programs, the staff, and the services provided under each. Both regular and special classes may be located in the same building and supervised by the same principal. Because the entire staff is responsible to the same employer and system of supervision, the same set of program policies and decision-making structures applies. In short, schools hold jurisdiction over all options they might exercise to serve a handicapped student. To mainstream an elementary student simply means activating the existing system and moving the student to a different placement. To mainstream handicapped children under school age and simultaneously assure that adequate special services are provided is much more complicated.

First, in the absence of any standardized system of nurseries or preschools within our communities, programs fall under the auspices of many different organizations. Services offered by each agency differ greatly, as do their administrative structures. Agencies serving young handicapped children are not likely to be the same ones that operate regular nursery and preschool programs where a youngster could be mainstreamed. This necessitates making agreements, planning services, and coordinating between two or more agencies. The mere logistics of working with several agencies to mainstream large numbers of children can become overwhelming. To complicate matters, someone must decide what preschool settings should be selected as mainstreaming sites and what criteria are to be used.

Second, the availability of appropriately certified and trained staff may be an issue. Many preschools do not have enough funds to employ professionally qualified personnel. Yet, to deliver the kinds of special training programs handicapped children need, the staff must be well trained and skillful in planning and implementing individualized special education programs.

Third, the degree to which regular programs are educationally oriented, rather than designed as settings for general child care and social enrichment, also varies. The extent to which programs meet the intent of PL 94-142 differs across regular early childhood centers. This does not mean that quality early childhood programs do not exist. It does mean that not all programs are equipped to offer the special services handicapped children require. These statements are not in criticism of regular early childhood centers. The purpose of many centers has been to serve normally developing children, who require different kinds of programs and different kinds of services. Programs that offer quality early childhood education for normally developing preschoolers cannot necessarily offer the special education a handicapped child needs without major adaptations in curriculum, teaching methods, and physical environment.

How, then, can widescale mainstreaming be implemented? This question represents a major issue that educators face as they arrange community-based services for handicapped preschoolers and infants. The questions raised earlier point to a serious reality. Mainstreaming a large number of children is more difficult when it involves several independently operated preschools. It cannot be implemented as easily as mainstreaming within a public school system. Head Start offers a possible site for mainstreaming handicapped youngsters, but it serves only a select group of families below a certain socioeconomic level.

If large numbers of preschool handicapped children are to be mainstreamed, new systems are needed to arrange placements and coordinate between agencies who join in a cooperative enterprise. Criteria are needed for selecting regular preschools that have the capacities for serving as mainstreaming sites. Strategies must be developed for adding the necessary support services, training regular staff, and providing special equipment and materials across several sites that are operated under the auspices of different administrative structures. Finally, systems for monitoring children's progress once they are placed in mainstreamed settings, and for assuring that services are delivered as needed, are an important part of any large-scale early intervention effort.

What precautions should be exercised in preschool mainstreaming? When selecting any service option for a child with developmental disabilities, the advantages and disadvantages of every alternative must be weighed. Hasty placement of a handicapped preschooler in a regular preschool setting without attention to the child's special needs, and the *reasons* why services are being rendered, should be avoided. For example, one might ask: Is a child's integration with normal peers the major concern, or are intensive individualized services in a special program of greatest priority? Very young children are just becoming alert to their social environment and are only beginning to interact with peers. As long as a stimulating social environment is available, who is included in that environment may not be as critical as the quality of training and stimulation given to the child. For very young children, a one-to-one relationship with a nurturing, skillful adult may be more crucial.

Educators would be foolish to assume that mere experience or social participation in activities with other children is sufficient to serve the special needs of a handicapped child. No matter how fun or enriching the experience is (and no matter how many attractive toys and learning materials are available to create a stimulating preschool environment), this does not assure that handicapped young children will acquire the skills needed to cope with or overcome a handicapping condition. Effective intervention implies that the child is *taught* critical developmental skills and that time is not wasted waiting for skills to emerge.

When placing young handicapped children in mainstreamed settings, several precautions thus should be exercised:

> ★ *Regular early chldhood programs that serve as mainstreaming sites must have the capabilities for providing appropriate educational services for handicapped enrollees.*

Educators should not assume that all early childhood programs are educationally oriented or apply instructional and teaching methods that focus on individual learning objectives of each child. Placement of a handicapped child in a regular educational environment presumes that, with some minor adaptations or additions in support services, an appropriate educational program will be provided. In mainstreaming young handicapped children, one must assess the setting into which the child is to be placed.

First, can the setting provide quality educational training for the child? Most handicapped children require more than just enrichment and social experience, which rely heavily upon incidental and spontaneous learning. Second, can an individualized program actually be carried out within the context of that regular preschool setting and its practices? This depends on staff expertise and willingness, the equipment and materials available, the organization and scheduling of children's ongoing activities, and priorities as reflected in the teaching methods and curriculum.

Some programs do not purport to be educational in nature. Some do not conduct activities that would be considered structured enough to provide the systematic training that handicapped children need. The staffs of some programs are not prepared to meet the demands for supervision and special instruction that handicapped children would place upon them.

> ★ *The meaning of mainstreaming must be kept in mind since effective mainstreaming implies an instructional and treatment process involving systematic planning and goal setting; a mainstreaming site should have the staff capabilities for carrying out this process.*

Including a handicapped youngster within a group of children so that he or she is not a bother or so that he or she fits in without disrupting ongoing classroom activities is possible. This type of inclusion is not necessarily effective mainstreaming. It does not address the fact that the child is handicapped and that unless something more than inclusion occurs, the child will continue to be handicapped. Because the intent of early childhood special education programs is one of intervention, a primary objective is to (a) help the child acquire skills that otherwise might be delayed or not acquired at all because of the handicapping condition, (b) help the child acquire special skills to cope with the handicapping conditions and to function as effectively as possible, and (c) prevent "spillover" from one handicap into other areas of development that will lead to secondary impairments or disabilities.

This means that special educational services and special training are an essential part of the handicapped child's preschool experience. If a mainstreaming site is to meet this challenge, it must have the service capabilities to do something more than simply including the child in the existing program.

★ *The more severely handicapped the child is, the more specialized are the services required.*

Not all regular early childhood programs have the resources to serve a moderately to severely handicapped child. Reliance upon consultive services and referrals of the child for intermittent services at another location may not offer sufficient support to make a mainstreamed setting the most appropriate alternative. Although enthusiasm and desire to help handicapped children may not be lacking, realistic estimates should be made of the ability of a preschool staff to meet the needs of moderately to severely handicapped children. Given the absence of many service alternatives in some communities, to rely upon mainstreaming as *the* means for serving handicapped preschoolers may be tempting. But mere inclusion might be confused with real mainstreaming or integration.

A very severely handicapped child can be included in classroom activities quite easily by being held in someone's lap and helped constantly. The child can be made to go through the motions of participating with everyone else if an aide is there to move and carry him or her about, and even to move his or her arms for the fingerplays during music time. The child can be included readily in group activities of a regular preschool. These things, however, do not constitute effective intervention.

TRADITIONAL SERVICE DELIVERY APPROACHES IN SPECIAL EDUCATION

An understanding of the service approaches with which special educators have become accustomed in public school settings will be helpful as we think about what strategies will work best with younger children from birth to age 5 or 6. As you read about these approaches here, ask yourself: What applicability does this have to younger children? Can this service delivery approach be applied in programs serving handicapped infants and toddlers? Are other new service delivery options needed to address the unique needs of this new population and to fit into the administrative systems under which early childhood-special education programs are operated?

Service delivery alternatives for school-aged youngsters generally are described in special education textbooks according to the first definition presented earlier in the chapter—by the settings where special education takes place. Authors refer to these alternatives as "administrative plans," using various terms such as service delivery models, alternative learning environments, or placement options. Basically, they encompass four broad service delivery alternatives: *regular classroom placement or mainstreaming with special support* (having several levels of possible support), *special class placement, special day or residential schools,* and *hospitals or homebound instruction.* (Refer back to Figure 8.1.)

Regular classroom placement with special support

Mainstreaming exceptional students into regular classes implies that the exceptional student is served primarily in the context of the normal school environment where other normal peers are educated. This approach works best with mildly handicapped students who can function adequately in the regular class with supplementary help. Some exceptional youngsters require no real assistance or special adaptation in the regular classroom. They can work successfully with the same materials, curriculum, and learning activities provided to other children. They simply require extra assistance by the teacher in the form of frequent feedback, more carefully sequenced instruction, and extra practice to master new skills. Any necessary special assistance may be provided through the options described earlier in Table 8.1.

Maintaining a handicapped child in the regular classroom has distinct advantages because it possibly offers a child the best of both regular education and special education. First, a child who needs help beyond what a regular teacher can provide but who does not require extensive special education can receive services without drastic changes in placement or in overall educational programming. Second, itinerant teachers can supplement and support the work of the regular class teacher. This is especially beneficial in rural areas. One teacher traveling from school to school is more cost-effective than attempting to transport children long distances to group them together for special services.

A potential problem associated with the itinerant teacher option is the possibility of case overload. Inappropriate assignment of children to an itinerant teacher can reduce the amount of time that could be spent with individual children and thus diminish that person's ability to provide quality, individualized instruction for each child. For example, an itinerant teacher may be asked to serve severely handicapped children who need the kind of intensive help that could best be provided in a special class. If this occurs, excessive demands are placed upon a teacher whose purpose is to provide help only on an intermittent basis.

Special class placement

Special classes are used most often with moderately and severely handicapped children who require continuous and intensive special education programs. For school-aged youngsters, special classes typically are organized by disability areas: special classes for the mentally retarded (subcategorized by severity levels and referred to as educable and trainable classes or level 1, 2, 3 classes); classes for the emotionally disturbed (sometimes called personal-social adjustment or behavior disordered classes); classes for the hearing and visually impaired; and classes for the severely multiply handicapped. If special classrooms provide "special" educational opportunities for exceptional students as intended, they should provide the most individualized and most concentrated form of special education.

Advantages of special classrooms are: (a) The entire classroom is organized around curriculum and teaching methodologies geared to the special needs and limitations of children with a certain disability; (b) children are served by a teacher specially trained to deal with their disability; (c) special adapted equipment, instructional materials, and aids are available to create a supportive environment for handicapped children; and (d) children are in an environment among peers with similar difficulties and thus enjoy a more accepting, supportive atmosphere than might be available in a regular classroom.

A criticism of special classes is that they have not measured up to this ideal standard. Critics suggest that special classes have failed to provide special curriculum or instructional methodology but instead have offered a watered-down version of what occurs in regular classes. This may be a legitimate criticism in some schools. It may be the result of unqualified or poorly trained teachers or failure among special education personnel to carry out the spirit and intent of the special class. Two other commonly cited problems are the stigma associated with special classes and the segregation from normal peers when the long-term goal is to integrate the handicapped into society. Despite these criticisms, special classes do serve a purposeful function and offer a beneficial learning environment for children who are unable to function effectively in a regular classroom even with the help of resource personnel.

Special day and residential schools

Special schools typically have served students with one type of disability. Most common are schools for the blind, for the deaf and hearing impaired, and for orthopedically/ neurologically handicapped children. The prime purpose of special day schools and residential schools is to provide special education services that are perhaps qualitatively and quantitatively superior to those offered in local communities.

Special schools offer several advantages. They are able to assemble a faculty of highly trained and specialized teachers and ancillary personnel and to create physical plants that are adapted to the populations they serve. They accumulate specialized equipment and materials far beyond the financial capabilities of a single school district. Special schools generally are able to provide much more intensive, long-term training, as well as more curricular continuity from year to year, than can be provided elsewhere. Another advantage of residential schools is that they have the capabilities for providing comprehensive programs of instruction that not only span regular school hours but also provide training and recreation covering the entire day, an entire week, and an entire year.

A potential disadvantage of special schools is the isolation of handicapped children from their nonhandicapped peers, and hence the loss of opportunities to observe peers who can model age-appropriate skills and social behaviors. Another disadvantage is the isolation from the real world environment in which children with disabilities still must learn to function and adapt.

Hospital and homebound instruction

For children confined to hospitals, convalescent centers, or their own homes because of medically or physically related problems, special education can be provided through one of two possible service delivery methods: (a) A homebound or itinerant teacher from the child's home district can visit the home regularly to provide tutoring; or (b) some hospitals, such as regular inpatient hospitals or state hospitals for the mentally ill, often have their own education unit with teaching staffs. This type of special education may involve children normally being served in a regular class, as well as handicapped youngsters who need special educational assistance for the time they are under medical treatment. The obvious benefit of this form of special education is that it provides a means for minimizing interruptions in a student's education as a result of short-term or long-term confinement.

Disadvantages that may exist for hospital or homebound instruction depend greatly on the student's age, the conditions that resulted in using this service delivery approach, and the duration of services in that setting. For a very young child, homebound or hospital-based educational services may be highly appropriate, whereas for an older student, this option may result in isolation from peers and from the educational and social mainstream. With older, school-age students, however, this option typically is a short-term necessity because of the student's condition that prevents his or her participation in other school options.

TRADITIONAL SERVICE DELIVERY APPROACHES IN REGULAR EARLY CHILDHOOD EDUCATION

Unlike special educators, early childhood educators have not been faced with the legal or legislated responsibility of creating alternative methods of service delivery for preschoolers or infants. Nor are they required to guarantee each child an appropriate, individualized, educational program in the least restrictive environment.* Instead, their challenge has been to establish quality nursery, preschool, and day-care centers and maintain their programs through means much different than that used by public schools.

The absence of a single authorized agency to administer preschool and nursery programs in the United States has hampered development of a single set of educational standards common to all, or a standardized system of alternative modes of service delivery parallel to those in special education. This is not to imply that alternatives in the types of early childhood education programs are limited. To the contrary, regular preschools and day-care programs vary greatly. But these variations result more from different sponsorship and funding of programs than from any deliberate attempts to arrange alternative modes of service delivery.

Early childhood educators have no standard classification system to describe the service delivery approaches they use. At the same time, professionals use a variety of familiar terms to describe program types. *Nursery school, day care, play school,* and *kindergarten* are a few examples. Unfortunately, practitioners use these terms inconsistently and interchangeably to refer to very different programs. The result is a lot of confusion.

For purposes of our discussion here, regular early childhood programs can best be described on the basis of six program dimensions: (a) age groups of children served, (b) the purposes and objectives for which programs operate, (c) temporal features of a program as to the portion of the day for which services are offered, (d) sponsorship, (e) the kinds of services or curriculum offered, and (f) location of services.

Early childhood programs as distinguished by age groups served

Regular early childhood programs often are organized around age clusters of children and are described in that manner. If you look around at programs in your own community, each is geared to serve infants, toddlers, or preschoolers, or possibly a combination of these. The terms used to identify these age clusters are not always applied consistently. The most common distinctions by age group are:

- *Kindergartens:* generally serve children who are just one year away from entry into the first grade. State legislation differs for kindergarten programs. Mandatory kindergarten education is legislated in some states and is a standard part of public elementary schools, but in other states it is not.
- *Nursery schools and preschools:* serve children in so many different age clusters that associating them with any single age group is impossible. These terms, in fact, often are used interchangeably, with similar types of programs enrolling children anywhere

---

*Preschool, nursery, or day-care programs usually are required to meet state licensing requirements. These regulations are concerned most with items such as health, safety, physical space, and staffing of centers. Less attention is given to the specific nature of the program provided for children.

between ages 2½ or 3 to 5 or 6 years. In some instances, *nursery school* designates programs for the youngest age group of children (such as 3- to 4-year-olds), while *preschool* designates the older age group.

- *Infant and toddler programs:* generally serve babies and young children up to 2 or 2½ years of age. Centers for toddlers usually include children between 18 months and 2½ or 3 years of age. Prior to the 1960s, programs for children so young were largely designed as child care for working mothers. In the late 1960s and 1970s infant and toddler programs emerged to provide additional stimulation for disadvantaged children in order to counteract the effects of impoverished home and environmental conditions.

Early childhood programs as distinguished by purposes for operation

Because early childhood centers are operated by a variety of agencies or private organizations, their purposes differ also. Some programs operate for multiple purposes, but most can be classified under one of five categories describing their *primary* objective (Hess & Croft, 1975; Hildebrand, 1985). That is, a program may be operated primarily to provide:

— educational enrichment or compensatory education for young children.
— social experience and exposure to other children of the same age.
— day care for children of working parents.
— a laboratory setting for personnel training and research within universities or child study centers.
— a vehicle for profit making for a commercial or franchise business in child care or preschool education.

Educational enrichment and compensatory programs are offered as a form of readiness training to prepare children in basic skills areas and perhaps give them an early start on tasks required in kindergarten or first grade. *Compensatory education programs* are designed to make up for experiences children may have missed and to help them catch up in areas where their skills are not up to par. These programs emerged primarily when children from low socioeconomic backgrounds were found to lack many basic experiences and skills that peers from more affluent homes had mastered by the time they entered school. Thus, compensatory education programs stress prerequisite skills considered important for success in the early years of schooling. Curriculum usually focuses on readiness skills in the areas of language, math, reading, basic concepts, and other cognitive operations.

Social development programs are designed to provide children with social and play experiences outside the home. Parents often seek out this type of program to expand their child's experiences outward from the family and to provide opportunities for play with children of their own age. Churches, community groups, parent cooperatives, and some recreational organizations offer these kinds of programs.

Child day care is an increasingly important service as more women pursue careers and as single-parent families increase in number. Programs designed primarily for purposes of child care may operate for just a few hours to as long as 8-10 hours each day. These settings provide a substitute home environment for children when the parent(s) works or cannot provide home care for other reasons. Day-care programs vary considerably in the content and quality of service provided. This depends in part upon the number and expertise of the staff, the day-care environment and activity schedule, the availability of appropriate educational materials and play equipment, and the philosophy of those operating the center. Child-care programs in some instances include a formalized educational component along with play and general child care and supervision. Others provide less structured supervision for more play and socially oriented activities.

Training and research programs typically are found within university and college settings. Their purpose is to provide laboratory settings wherein university students receive supervised training in child care and preschool education, and specialized training in areas of language, physical development, and so on. In addition, some programs operate for purposes of research and demonstration and are supported by state and federal funds. University and college laboratory schools or nursery schools have been a well known source of early childhood services for many years.

Commercial or franchise programs are operated as a profit-making enterprise. Services offered to clientele vary greatly from program to program and usually are designed not only to benefit children but also to be convenient and attractive to potential customers in a competitive business market. Program content generally is prescribed by the owner-investor or by the staff within the organization that grants the franchise.

Early childhood programs as distinguished by temporal qualities

Programs for young children can be described according to the temporal features of services offered. These include (a) short-term or drop-in programs, (b) part-day or half-day programs, (c) full-day programs, and (d) extended-care programs (Day & Parker, 1977).

Short-term or drop-in type programs typically are located at resort or vacation sites, shopping centers, or large stores for the convenience of parents who patronize them and whose business is encouraged by the immediate availability of child-care services. These programs are designed to provide only short-term supervision with no expectation that the client will return. Because emphasis is upon brief care of children, activities are planned to fulfill the task of constructively occupying a child's time while the parent is away, providing general supervision, and caring for a child's short-term needs.

Part-day or half-day programs are typical of the services offered by nursery schools, preschools, and kindergartens. Half-day programs are considered to be 2-4 hours in duration. The purpose for which an early childhood program is operated is a major factor in determining the length of a program day. Part-day programs are often educationally oriented, and the staff works with children for a shorter, intensive time focused upon specific educational goals. Classes may be brief (2-2½ hours) for very young children who are just being phased into nursery school activity, and a child may be enrolled only 2-3 days per week.

Those who advocate half-day programs as most appropriate for preschool-aged children commonly cite four advantages of half-day sessions compared to full-day programs: (a) Children are most attentive and do not get as tired with shorter program sessions, (b) the staff has more time for curriculum planning, program evaluation, and work with parents, (c) arrangements do not have to be made for lunch services and rest activities (lunch services impose additional financial burdens and require additional equipment and staff); and (d) children still have a significant part of their day left to spend in the home environment with the family (Decker & Decker, 1976).

Full-day programs are usually 4½ to 6 hours in duration and are designed for older children who can handle longer periods of work and play activity. Full-day programs serve the dual role of providing educational programs plus day care for children with working parents. Growing numbers of working mothers have increased the demand for both preschool educational services and day-care services. This has generated some controversy about the benefits or harmful effects of longer program sessions. A report of the Education Commission of the States on Early Childhood Program Alternatives in 1977 stated that there is no evidence that 3-, 4-, or 5-year-old children benefit more from programs longer than 3 or 4 hours. On the other hand, there is no evidence to suggest that children will not benefit from such programs or that any harmful effects result.

Extended-care programs usually offer more varied child-care services emphasizing both education and day care. These programs operate as long as 10-12 hours a day, allowing parents to deliver their children to the center on the way to work and pick them up as late as 5:30 or 6:30 in the evening. These programs are not abundant in the United States, but franchised day-care businesses offering extended care are beginning to appear across the country.

Early childhood programs as distinguished by sponsorship

No standard system across the U.S. for providing day care or early education for children under school age exists to parallel educational programs for school-aged students operated through state education agencies and public school districts. As explained earlier, governmental support for early education has been an important but intermittent stimulus for growth of nationwide programs. When governmental support at the federal, state, or local level is not available or is insufficient, responsibility for early education falls back upon private organizations, churches, small businesses, or upon parents themselves. Sponsorship of regular early childhood programs can be classified under three broad categories: (a) public sponsorship, (b) private sponsorship, and (c) special agency/organizational sponsorship.

Public sponsorship of programs for young children comes from (a) states or federal agencies that administer funds allocated by Congress or state legislatures, or (b) agencies within a county, city, or community funded through state or local taxes. This includes public school systems, which in some cases have administered Head Start programs and other special compensatory education programs. Other public sponsors include universities, colleges, and social service agencies.

Private sponsorship for early childhood programs comes from many different sources that vary greatly from community to community. Sources of private support include groups such as churches, parent cooperatives, businesses, and industries that provide child care for employees or for clientele (as in the case of ski resorts that provide day care or early childhood programs for short-term residents or weekend vacationers). Both private profit-making and nonprofit organizations are represented in this category.

Special agency/organizational sponsorship overlaps the other two categories but is presented separately here since this category represents special purpose agencies that provide an administrative "umbrella" under which an early childhood program may be financed and administered. Under the supervision of a board of directors or an advisory committee, special purpose agencies provide a means for raising funds, obtaining the support of private or corporate foundations, and contracting with appropriate parties to operate the desired service programs. Special agencies become involved in early education programs for various reasons. Some are public service agencies charged with the specific responsibility of identifying community needs and responding to them. Other agencies represent citizen advocacy groups that have organized for purposes of creating programs to meet some need. These may be profit or nonprofit organizations.

Early childhood programs as distinguished by services or curriculum offered

Any parent who goes shopping for a preschool for a 3- to 5-year-old son or daughter knows what tremendous differences exist in the curriculum offered within early childhood centers. To classify these differences or to cluster them in some way is difficult because programs vary in so many ways, and possible combinations of curricular content for a program are endless. Learning activities or the curricular focus of early childhood programs may differ on five basic dimensions:

1. The degree to which *structured* and *nonstructured learning activities* are scheduled.
2. The degree to which curriculum and learning activities are *individualized* or geared to a set of *learning experiences considered good for all children* of a certain age level.
3. The degree to which the *curriculum* includes specific instruction in academic and developmental skills or more socially and experientially oriented activities.
4. The particular emphasis upon a *theoretical approach* to curriculum and teaching methodologies (e.g., Montessori approach, Piagetian approach, psychodynamic-developmental approach, behavioral approach).
5. The degree to which activities are *child-oriented* or *teacher-oriented.*

Early childhood programs as distinguished by location of services

Several early childhood experts classify programs by the site where services are delivered (Leeper, Witherspoon, & Day, 1984; Siegel, 1972):

- *Home-based programs*: generally are operated at the home of the child served, at the home of one of several participating mothers, or in the home of the person offering the service as part of a profit- or nonprofit-making arrangement.
- *Center-based programs*: usually are located in a center where one or more preschool or day-care classrooms are organized. Centers for early childhood programs are found in numerous kinds of settings—churches, community centers, elementary schools, specially built and designed child-care facilities, community buildings, commercial centers, and so on. These programs are more common than home-based programs.

In summary, regular early childhood services reflect tremendous diversity from center to center. The unique styles of service delivery that have evolved in regular education must be considered as educators plan how to best serve the special needs of handicapped preschoolers and infants. As educators develop early intervention programs for the handicapped and attempt to blend these new services with existing public school special education service systems or with regular early childhood programs, some questions will inevitably arise. Because traditions of service delivery are so different in each of these "parent" fields, a number of issues concerning what methods of service delivery are most appropriate will become evident.

ALTERNATIVE SERVICE DELIVERY APPROACHES IN EARLY CHILDHOOD-SPECIAL EDUCATION

Now that we have examined how special education is delivered to school-aged youngsters and how regular preschool services are organized, we are ready to look at service delivery approaches for handicapped preschoolers and infants. In serving this young population, opportunities for variation among programs are great. In fact, flexibility is critical for several reasons:

1. Characteristics of children from birth to age 5 are significantly different at various age levels, and so are their needs for stimulation, social experience, and basic care. What represents an appropriate intervention program for an infant is not the same as that required by a handicapped toddler or preschooler.
2. Early childhood-special education concerns young children with all types of disability and at-risk conditions, as well as all levels of disability. Characteristics of the population to be served can differ considerably from community to community. Hence, the means for best serving them also will be different.
3. Sponsoring agencies and funding sources behind intervention programs differ and therefore dictate to some extent the nature of services offered. As the purposes and philosophies of those agencies vary, so does the nature of the programs they sponsor.
4. Resources within individual communities vary greatly. These include the availability of trained teachers, physical facilities to house a program, and the availability of agencies from which the services of various professional disciplines can be obtained.
5. The geographical characteristics of an area served by an intervention program affect what type of service delivery approach is most applicable. What works well in one area with a high population density and children in close physical proximity may not represent a viable alternative for a rural, sparsely populated region. A service delivery approach that fits the lifestyles and child-rearing patterns of a traditional small town environment may not work well in another community.

In attempting to answer the question of what approach to service delivery works best for young handicapped children, educators are in general agreement: *No single "best approach" can be taken for delivering early intervention programs.* As a result of the HCEEP demonstration programs described in chapter 2, a number of very different service delivery alternatives have been demonstrated to be effective. Lacking a "best approach," what then are the alternatives to consider when planning an early childhood-special education program? If you were asked to help design an intervention program for hand-icapped preschoolers in your community, what options would you suggest for implementation? If you were the parent of a year-old child with Down syndrome, what types of special services would be most beneficial to you and your handicapped child now and in the next four years?

Service delivery alternatives for early intervention can be described best in relationship to seven key decisions that educators must make in planning programs for young children. These decisions concern several interrelated issues for which the answers collectively define the parameters of a particular service delivery alternative. These issues make up the *who, when, what, where, by whom, with whom,* and *through whom* questions underlying a service approach. The possible options for each of these questions are detailed in the Early Intervention Service Delivery Decision Matrix depicted in Table 8.2.

Target of services (who)

Any service delivery approach depends first upon a delineation of the specific population of individuals to be served. As shown in the first column of the Decision Matrix, the initial question is: *Who* is the major recipient of services offered under the early intervention program? In public schools, the student is the focus of service, although teachers occasionally may be targeted as the recipient of special consultative help to aid planning instructional programs for children. In planning an intervention strategy for young handicapped preschoolers and infants, several other persons may be targeted: one or both parents, a surrogate parent or substitute caregiver, or possibly the entire family.

Because young children spend a major part of their waking hours under the care of a parent or substitute caregiver, the greatest impact is achieved if parents are included in the intervention. At times, intervention with the entire family may prove to be advantageous. For example, the family of a severely hearing impaired child will have to learn sign language or some alternative form of communication to provide adequate language stimulation for the young member. As handicapped children grow older, programs begin to target them as the primary recipient of services, with less emphasis upon significant others. If resources, program staff and expertise, and financial support are available, a combined approach serving *both* the child and parents can be advantageous.

Beginning age of intervention (when)

A second decision, shown in the second column of the Decision Matrix, defines *when*, or at what point in a handicapped child's life, services are to be rendered. Will services be initiated at birth? At 2½ years? At 3-4 years of age? Some early intervention programs have a limited range of services and establish arbitrary limits for the age groups to be served (e.g., only children between 3 and 5 years of age). Others offer services from the point of identification and therefore include service options designed to meet the special needs of infants, toddlers, and preschoolers.

Much debate has centered on the question: At what age should early intervention begin? Questions have been raised as to whether children who participate in early intervention programs for 3-4 years show greater gains than those enrolled only 1-2 years preceding kindergarten. To date, data are inconclusive as to the best age for initiating an intervention, but experts generally agree that the earlier, the better. Most experts contend that infancy is the most crucial time for intervention to begin. To wait is to ignore the obvious needs of a handicapped child and to invite problems to develop. Once an intervention begins, it should be continued up to and possibly beyond the point of entry into public school kindergarten and primary grades.

As suggested by research data from Head Start and Follow-Through programs, developmental gains are less likely to be lost if some form of support continues. To

Table 8.2
Early Intervention Service Delivery Decision Matrix

Service Delivery Alternatives

(WHO) Target of Service	(WHEN) Beginning Point of Intervention	(WHAT) Services to be Provided	(WHERE) Setting for Intervention Program	(BY WHOM) Primary Intervention Agent	(WITH WHOM) Social Context of Services	(THROUGH WHOM) Agencies Providing Service(s)
Child	Birth	Casefinding and screening services	Home-based	Paraprofessional	Individual program	Public schools
Mother	Infancy	Diagnostic services	Center-based Classroom Clinic	Parent	Group program Segregated Mainstreamed	Private schools
Father	Toddler years	Education program		Teacher	Integrated Reverse-mainstreamed	State/local government agencies
Both Parents	Preschool years	Therapy services	Combination of center-based and home-based	Therapist		Churches
Family	Kindergarten	Speech and language Physical Occupational Other special therapies		Social services personnel		Nonprofit service organizations
		Parent education and training		Multidisciplinary team		Profit-making agencies
		Family counseling		Combination of intervention agents		Multi-agency consortium
		Social services				
		Nutritional services				
		Medical services				
		Transportation				

Elements Defining a Service Delivery Approach

initiate services for a short time and then terminate them when a child continues to need assistance is not programmatically sound. When funds limit the scope of a program, making it impossible to serve all children from birth to age 5, it is better to offer continuous services for a selected population of children once intervention is started than to offer programs for infants with no preschool program as a follow-up.

Types of special services offered (what)

The *what* issue, shown in column 3 of the Decision Matrix, refers to decisions about the nature and scope of services offered as a part of the early intervention program. After the target of services has been identified, and it has been decided when intervention is to begin, educators must determine what type of service will best meet the needs of the targeted population individually and collectively.

Some programs serve only a selected group of children (e.g., language delayed, deaf, or orthopedically handicapped), thereby restricting services to just one or two options, as listed in the Decision Matrix. Other programs serve a more diverse population of children and thus offer six or more different types of services (e.g., parent-infant home-based training, several preschool classrooms supplemented by a variety of therapy services, and a parent involvement program). Many combinations of services are possible. Early intervention programs frequently offer services that extend much beyond those

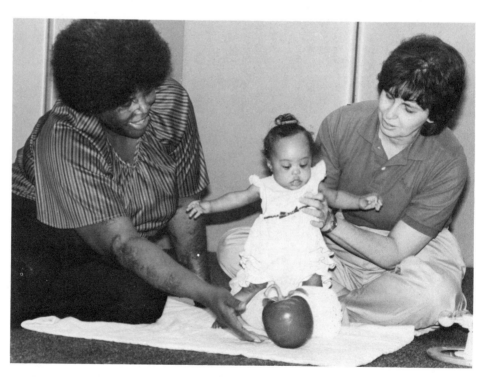

Shelby's mom and an occupational therapist make up the intervention team that provides special training and stimulation for her as part of a home- and center-based parent/infant program.

traditionally provided to school-aged youngsters. Head Start is an excellent example of a comprehensive, multi-service early intervention program. In any case, what services are rendered depends particularly upon the needs of the target population and the age at which intervention begins. Of course, choices always are influenced by the funding realities and by the resources available in a given community.

Setting for the intervention program (where)

A fourth decision that further specifies the nature of a service delivery approach concerns the issue of *where* the early intervention service is to be delivered (column 4 of Table 8.2). Intervention programs for young children generally are one of three types (Karnes & Zehrbach, 1977): home-based, center-based, or a combination of home- and center-based. Special education programs for school-aged students typically are center-based (although in cases of serious illness, home-based services may be rendered on a temporary basis). Because all students of school age are served in the traditional elementary or secondary school setting, this is considered to be the most normalizing, least restrictive environment. When we think about the characteristics and needs of handicapped preschoolers and infants, however, a group setting or a central facility where everyone assembles is not always the best setting.

Home-based programs are located in the children's own homes, where services are delivered on an individual basis to each child (or parent). Occasionally several families join together and designate one home as the meeting place. Home-based programs have several advantages: (a) They lend themselves to sparsely populated areas, rural communities, or towns having a low-incidence population of handicapped children scattered over a wide area; (b) they are useful with very young infants who are too young to profit from the social setting of a center and whose immediate needs are associated with the care and stimulation the primary caregiver or mother is able to provide; and (c) they are helpful with parents who are somewhat reluctant to send their young children away from home to participate in a center program, and with parents from cultural groups in which the absence of mother and child from the home is not encouraged.

In most home-based programs, the strategy is to train the mother or primary caregiver to work with the child. The mother or primary caregiver is viewed as the primary intervention agent for the child, and the staff works in ways that help in this role. Occasionally the staff may provide direct training or tutoring to the child.

Some limitations associated with home-based programs are that (a) the one-to-one training requires a great deal of staff time and reduces the numbers of children who can be served; thus, home-based programs can be expensive; (b) the staff may be required to travel long distances—even spending more time in travel than in direct service; and (c) because the staff must be itinerant, contact with the parent and child is reduced considerably compared to what might occur with a center-based approach. Reliance must be placed upon the parent to be conscientious in maintaining consistent, quality training with the child. Some parents carry through with the program conscientiously, but others are not able or willing to do so.

Center-based programs are practical in more densely populated areas or in neighborhoods where centers are relatively accessible to parents. Center-based programs may be located in early childhood centers, churches, elementary schools, commercial buildings, clinics, or facilities on college/university campuses. Advantages of center-based programs are that (a) they offer availability and easy access to all staff members and their expertise if the child or parent needs it; (b) the staff is able to give intensive and consistent training to a child who participates in a 1- to 4-hour program several days a week and possibly up to 5 days weekly; (c) the center offers social exposure to the child (who will be around other children) and to the parent, who can interact with other parents and observe other children at the center; (d) part-day programs can provide added support for working parents who are not in a position to work with their child during the daytime but who want special educational services for their child; and (e) the greater availability of special equipment and materials adds to the quality and intensiveness of training for the child.

Some limitations or special problems associated with center-based programs include:

— problems associated with the transportation of children to the center and back to their homes, especially if mass transportation is used for groups of youngsters.
— higher costs and additional management responsibilities for staff because physical facilities must meet regulations concerning safety, health, availability of appropriate space, and equipment (e.g., toilet facilities, drinking fountains) for the population served. If children remain at the center for long periods, lunch service is necessary; with that come regulations concerning kitchen facilities, food preparation and storage, and sanitation.
— additional administrative requirements to operate a center since it includes not only management of the program operations, but also of a physical plant.

Combination home- and center-based programs offer the advantages of both program settings. They provide the flexibility that allows children and their parents to be matched to the service delivery approach most appropriate for them. Some combination programs provide a home-based service for young children from birth until they reach about age 2½ or 3 years, followed by a center-based program that allows the child to participate in a nursery or preschool. In more elaborate programs this may be supplemented by a continuing home-based program for either or both child and parent. In other cases, a parent involvement component is continued but may not include direct services in the home.

Several considerations are important when selecting the setting for an early intervention program. First, the geographical location of a program is important, and the population density should be taken into consideration. A second factor centers on the age level and the characteristics of the children to be served. The younger the children, the more advantages home-based programs have. Ackerman and Moore (1976) analyzed the types of service delivery approaches represented among the BEH First Chance Demonstration Programs or HCEEP Projects. Center-based programs were employed most frequently, although home-based programs were used more often for very young children.

Primary intervention agent (by whom)

Who will play the major role in working with the person(s) designated as the target of intervention if that individual is the parent, the child, the family, or some combination of these? The services will be administered primarily *by whom*? Column 5 of the Decision Matrix lists several persons who can act in this important role. In both public school and regular early childhood nursery or preschool programs, the child traditionally has been the primary target of services and the teacher has acted as the key agent or pivotal point for all service activities (i.e., case manager, coordinator of services, instructional programmer, communicator with parents, and record keeper). Administrative structures and service delivery approaches commonly employed in these programs put the teacher in the best position to act as the primary service delivery agent. Other personnel then function in supportive roles to that of the teacher and thus are called "support staff."

Early intervention programs offer alternatives for several persons to assume the role of primary intervention agent. This role can be filled by a teacher or another professional such as a speech or occupational therapist, social worker, or early childhood specialist. The intervention agent can be a child's own parent, another parent trained specially to fulfill the role of interventionist, a paraprofessional, or a volunteer. Or a number of individuals working together as a team (with no single person having a predominant role) can constitute the intervention agent. In the latter case, one person usually assumes coordinating responsibilities to assure that the team operates smoothly and information is clearly and efficiently communicated within the team.

Selection of the person(s) who will be intervention agent(s) is influenced primarily by the answers to other decision issues in the Matrix—*who, when, what,* and *where.* These decisions define the nature of the actual services to be offered, and thus the skills and levels of expertise needed by the person(s) responsible for delivering them.

Social environment for intervention (with whom)

If handicapped children are the primary target for intervention, *with whom* are they to be grouped? To what extent will they have contact with other handicapped and nonhandicapped peers? As indicated in column 6 of the Decision Matrix, some children—such as those who receive only special therapy from a therapist, or developmental specialist (e.g., speech therapist, physical therapist, occupational therapist)—are served on an individual basis. Typically, handicapped infants and toddlers are served on an individual basis. Because they are not yet engaging in social interaction with peers and will benefit most from stimulation given on an individual basis by a responsive, nurturing adult, their social contact with agemates is of less immediate concern. As these youngsters grow older and become more aware of their social environment and peers, the social setting where intervention occurs becomes more important. Group or classroom-based programs work well for children at about age 3. When considering group intervention strategies, three service delivery options are possible:

1. *Segregated special early intervention programs*: intended solely for handicapped children; curricular and instructional methods are designed around the special needs created by the children's disabilities.
2. *Mainstreamed regular early childhood programs*: created primarily to serve a majority of normally developing youngsters but accept a small minority of handicapped children (usually 10%-20%).
3. *Integrated special early intervention programs*: created primarily for handicapped youngsters but enroll a small number of nonhandicapped children who serve as "models." Nonhandicapped enrollees usually constitute 20%-50% of the classroom enrollment. Sometimes educators have described these programs as a type of "reverse mainstreaming."

Segregated early intervention programs such as special preschools are a common approach for serving young handicapped children. This is particularly the case for children with moderate to severe handicaps. Despite the widespread emphasis on mainstreaming, segregated programs for children under age 5 are common for several reasons.

First, the lack of a standardized system of regular preschool education or a single administrative agency in charge of all regular preschool services makes widescale mainstreaming a cumbersome and difficult management task. Many small communities simply lack regular early childhood programs where handicapped children could be mainstreamed. In communities where regular preschool programs are available, the issue becomes one of whether they have adequate professional staff and facilities to accommodate handicapped children and their special educational needs.

Second, funding sources for early childhood-special education programs typically support only services for children diagnosed as handicapped or in some cases "at-risk." In fact, some funding sources allocate monies on the basis of the number of handicapped children served. If nonhandicapped youngsters are included in programs having a limited enrollment, they reduce the funds that can be received to cover costs. Consequently, current funding patterns encourage segregated programs.

Third, though some school districts are expanding their special education services to include children under age 5, they are not responsible for serving normally developing preschoolers and therefore may not want to involve them. School administrators may hesitate to have regular preschoolers attend early intervention programs, even as special "models," because it raises issues about which nonhandicapped children should be accepted and on what basis others are to be denied admission. Some administrators are concerned about what precedent might be established if regular preschoolers were to be included and whether this might create pressure to serve larger numbers of normal children.

Segregated intervention programs have several advantages. An obvious advantage is the opportunity to design curriculum and instructional methods wholly around the special needs of handicapped children. When intensive, treatment-oriented programs are delivered, educators have a better chance of effecting change in children's development and achieving a successful intervention. In a regular program the staff may have more difficulty offering a handicapped child enough intensive services and specialized help to bring about significant change in his or her developmental status. If preschoolers can achieve skills prerequisite for later success in a mainstreamed or regular kindergarten program by attending a special early intervention program during their early years, a segregated environment may be the best alternative. One disadvantage of the segregated intervention environment, however, is the lack of exposure to normally developing peers during a time when imitation/modeling is an important vehicle for learning.

Mainstreamed early intervention settings are designed primarily for normally developing children while integrating a few handicapped children (usually 10%-20%). Curriculum and teaching methods are designed around the enrichment and social needs of the nonhandicapped majority and ideally are adapted as necessary to accommodate the handicapped enrollees. Mainstreaming of handicapped preschoolers has been emphasized a great deal in the literature and among professional groups. This has probably been an outgrowth of the popularity of mainstreaming, as implemented in the elementary schools (Wynne, Ulfelder, & Dakof, 1975). Head Start was particularly instrumental in bringing visibility to mainstreaming as an alternative for serving young handicapped children. Other private, church-sponsored, or community-based nursery and preschool programs are beginning to admit handicapped applicants.

What are the arguments for mainstreaming preschool handicapped children? Major arguments presented by a number of experts (Klein, 1975; Guralnick, 1976; Peterson & Haralick, 1977; Bricker, 1978b; Wynne, Ulfelder, & Dakof, 1975; DeWeerd, 1977; Peterson, 1980; Snyder, Apolloni, & Cooke, 1977; Fredericks et al., 1978; and Karnes & Lee, 1978) are:

1. Legal and legislative precedents emphasize placement of handicapped children in the most normalizing environment. What the most "normal" environment is for early intervention programs serving infants and toddlers when the purpose is one of *intervention*, however, is unclear.

2. Mainstreaming can be an economical and money-saving alternative by using existing early childhood programs as resources to reduce some of the overall cost of serving young handicapped children. Despite major expenditures of federal dollars for special education programs, resources are still limited. Because many handicapped children under age 5 remain unserved, to create entirely new programs for them could be costly and perhaps prohibitive.

3. Efforts to mainstream young handicapped children early may discourage temptations to isolate and separate these children from the social mainstream that their normal peers enjoy. Early integration gives handicapped youngsters equal visibility with the majority population—a position that encourages awareness among the general public that handicapped children are a part of the community and of our public education system.

4. As handicapped children learn to function in an integrated group during the early years, they also learn the ways of the world in which they are to be a part. Separation can create distance, misunderstanding, and rejection. It can result, too, in being over-protected and failing to learn the skills necessary to function in the social mainstream. Inclusion with normal peers from the very beginning can help handicapped children make social adjustments more easily. When children are kept in environments different from those where we hope they will eventually function, the shock of reentry and the necessary relearning can be overwhelming.

5. Integrated programs create a more stimulating, responsive, and normalizing environment for a handicapped child than does a setting that includes only other handicapped peers who also have limited behavioral repertoires. The presence of normally developing children adds a form of social structure that elicits involvement from less skillful peers in class activities. A more demanding environment may push the child ahead to develop appropriate behavioral repertoires. This kind of peer group is likely to exhibit a greater variety of play and exploratory behavior, to engage in verbal interaction, and to participate in more constructive social interchange.

6. Integration allows handicapped children the opportunity to observe, interact with, and imitate other children who may provide developmentally more advanced and skilled models of behavior. If placed in preschools with only handicapped children who have similar developmental deficits, a child's own disabilities can be compounded by the lack of appropriate behavioral models.

7. Integrated programs offer benefits to teachers, other professional staff, and parents by giving them opportunities to observe mixed groups of children. This provides a framework for gauging child behavior along the developmental continuum and can help teachers and parents establish more realistic expectations for a handicapped child.

Many of the arguments just summarized are philosophical and propositional in nature. They are based upon many assumptions about what actually will happen if handicapped and nonhandicapped preschoolers are placed in a single educational environment. Research is needed to verify the validity of these assumptions as arguments for mainstreaming.

Some limitations or concerns are frequently raised about mainstreaming as an alternative for serving young handicapped children (Tawney, 1981). A major concern is that handicapped children will not receive the intensity of services needed to bring about the desired outcomes. Because an early childhood program for handicapped children is intended to be an intervention and not merely an opportunity for enrichment, the question arises as to whether services will be of sufficient quality and intensity to bring about enough change in the child's development status to improve the prognosis. Another concern is whether a regular preschool staff has sufficient expertise to recognize a handicapped child's special needs and implement meaningful educational and training programs. Regular early childhood teachers may be unfamiliar with special education concepts, assessment procedures, individualized education plans, or procedures for developing an IEP. They may not be experienced in how to individualize instruction for a handicapped youngster.

Still another concern relates to the potential isolation a handicapped child may experience in a mainstreamed class, where he or she is in the minority among individuals who are likely to be more skillful, more independent, and more articulate in expressing their needs. A handicapped child (especially one with moderate to severe disabilities) may be brushed aside by other children. The teaching staff may not give adequate help. As long as handicapped children are not disruptive and aggressive toward peers, a teacher may be prone to allow them to just "follow along," without special attention to their instructional and developmental needs. In fact, many handicapped children tend to be passive, to not initiate activity, and to exhibit limited behavioral repertoires. As pointed out earlier, simple inclusion is not true mainstreaming. The programmatic and teacher responsibilities that come with true mainstreaming can easily be forgotten once a child is admitted.

Integrated early intervention programs are designed for handicapped and at-risk children but include a few nonhandicapped children who are enrolled as "models." Sometimes these are referred to as *reverse-mainstreamed* programs. This approach has emerged as educators have attempted to create more normalizing environments for handicapped preschoolers who are served in segregated early intervention programs. In these settings nonhandicapped children are the minority (usually 25%-50%) of the enrollment. As participants in a classroom emphasizing individualized instructional programs, the normal models also are recipients of carefully planned early education programs. This service delivery alternative perhaps offers the best of two worlds—the benefits of the segregated special early intervention environment and the advantages of a mainstreamed setting in which handicapped and nonhandicapped children have the opportunity to associate and play with each other. Funding patterns promote the development of segregated programs, at times creating difficulty in operating traditional forms of mainstreamed programs. Reverse-mainstreamed preschools offer a means for adapting these segregated programs into settings in which those valued aspects of regular educational environments can be created.

The strategy of integrating early childhood-special education classrooms is relatively new. Educators and parents raise many questions about the effect of this approach on the handicapped and nonhandicapped children. From one point of view, why would parents of nonhandicapped children want to enroll their preschoolers in a program with a majority of handicapped youngsters? Where and how are nonhandicapped models found? Are the nonhandicapped preschoolers who participate in such a program challenged? Can normally developing youngsters benefit cognitively and developmentally by working and playing in an environment designed primarily for handicapped children? Won't the normal children pick up "retarded-like" or undesirable forms of behavior from their handicapped class-mates? Will teachers pay attention to the normal models if their primary concern is for the children who need early intervention?

From an opposite point of view, parents of handicapped children who experience the transition from a segregated program to an integrated, reverse-mainstreamed one express similar concerns. Their questions reflect parallel reservations about the effects of the normal children upon their special children. Will the nonhandicapped youngsters ridicule and tease their handicapped child? Will a skillful, aggressive, nonhandicapped child draw the teacher's attention away from the children who need extra help? Will the nonhandicapped children be too rough with handicapped peers who may be less adept at play and less able to protect themselves?

These questions reveal real concerns among teachers and parents upon first encoun-tering the idea of integrated early intervention programs. Experiences of the author in operating a reverse-mainstreamed program at the University of Kansas and of colleagues around the country suggest that these concerns need not be serious. Like any program in which a minority of children (be they nonhandicapped, gifted, handicapped, or non-English speaking) presents some special needs, the quality of their educational experience is dependent upon what teachers and other staff members do. It depends upon their attitudes and efforts to identify and accommodate the needs of every child. If teachers assess child needs, plan individualized curriculum, and implement instructional and play activities that focus upon specific objectives for individuals as well as groups of children, both handicapped and normal children can benefit from inclusion in the program.

One caution or potential limitation of the reverse-mainstreamed approach is that effective curriculum planning and individualized programming require skillful teachers and program staff. This approach also is dependent upon the availability of good interdis-ciplinary team support from speech therapists, occupational or physical therapists, and other specialists. If reverse-mainstreaming is selected as a part of the service delivery strategy, careful planning of curriculum and coordination of services across staff is crucial because of the extreme range of abilities and needs represented within one group of children.

Agencies providing services (through whom)

Now that the basic characteristics of the intervention approach have been defined in regard to the questions of *who, when, what, where, by whom, with whom,* one final decision completes our description of an early intervention program service delivery approach. That final decision concerns *through whom*—what agencies are to become a part of the mechanism for delivering services. This has not been an issue within special education for school-aged students, or for that matter within regular early childhood programs. The school district is the authorized agency responsible for delivering services. An early childhood center typically acts singularly as the sponsoring agency of its own preschool or nursery program. Each plans and delivers its own services. Involvement of outside agencies is not required, although in some cases public school districts contract for special services with another school district, a private school, or an outside agency.

In the field of early childhood-special education, however, many agencies are involved in providing services. In states with no mandate requiring school districts to serve this population, no single designee is responsible for coordinating between agencies who offer services to these children. Several questions thus arise: What agencies should be involved in serving these children? How can the services of various agencies be coordinated? Who should do the coordinating? How can unnecessary duplication of effort be avoided? How can services be provided so that young children at-risk are not unnecessarily segregated from their normally developing peers?

Given these questions, the need for interagency collaboration is obvious. The very nature of early intervention programs, and the mixture of professionals and agencies with responsibility or interest in serving this population, encourages some form of interagency cooperation. Otherwise, duplication, fragmentation of services, and confusion are likely to occur. The economic and political conditions of this decade create an even greater necessity for devising economical, efficient methods of service delivery. Several factors argue for interagency linkages to be formed as early intervention programs are initiated or expanded to serve all young handicapped infants and preschoolers (Peterson & Mantle, 1983). They include the need for (a) multidisciplinary expertise, (b) a broad array of

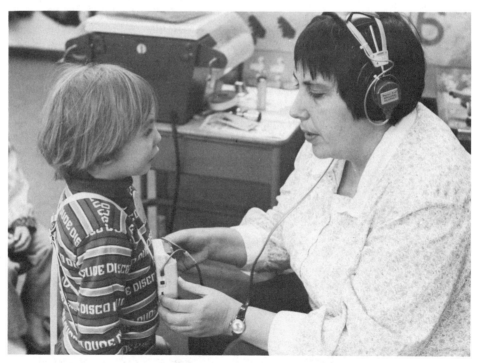

Speech and language training is an important part of the intervention program provided to this preschooler by the speech pathologist, who works with him and his teacher both in the classroom and in a one-to-one setting, as shown here.

services to meet the needs of a diverse population of handicapped children, (c) coordination of activities across multiple service providers, and (d) expansion of services, in spite of financial restrictions, through more creative strategies for resource sharing across agencies.

How can agencies cooperate to prevent duplication and to improve methods of service delivery to young handicapped children and their families? Here are just a few of the ways (Peterson & Mantle, 1983):

- Collaboration on basic standards for the operation of early intervention programs by various agencies.
- Collaboration in the use of financial resources, facilities, material resources, and manpower resources for achieving mutually agreed-upon objectives.
- Collaboration by use of uniform procedures, processes, or activities for delivering services, such as (a) common intake and referral systems, (b) a common set of information forms, and service calendars, (c) coordinated community-wide planning meetings, (d) coordinated staff inservice training activities, and (e) a common record-keeping system to coordinate services rendered to children.
- Collaboration by pooling resources to operate a single program in which each agency contributes its expertise, services, and part of its financial resources to support a common multi-agency-sponsored early intervention program.

CONSIDERATIONS IN SELECTING AN EARLY INTERVENTION STRATEGY

The definitions earlier summarized in Table 8.1 collectively define the nature of a service delivery approach in early childhood-special education. The possible combinations are almost limitless. But we cannot assume that every option is always appropriate for every group of children. Neither is every option functional or economically sound for certain communities or geographical locations. Several factors influence what options are most viable, and each should be considered carefully in planning a new program (Ackerman & Moore, 1976; Ellis, 1977; Karnes & Zehrback, 1977a, 1977b; Mori & Neisworth, 1983). In the remainder of this chapter, we will look at six of the most important considerations.

State legislation and local policies

Certain service delivery options or program limitations may be imposed upon the agencies that arrange early childhood programs for handicapped youngsters under school age. Local policies within a county or township also may impose certain regulations. When professionals and their respective agencies begin to plan new programs, several legislative questions should be answered (Ellis, 1977):

- Does legislation make you responsible for specific services to a specific client group or generally accountable for an ill-defined client group?
- Does the legislation mandate or suggest cooperation among agencies to deliver services to children?
- Does the legislation specify the program components to be delivered by agencies other than the education agency (e.g., identification and screening to be done by public health)?

- Does the legislation specify the scope of services to be offered?

States with mandatory legislation authorizing the creation of early intervention programs for children under school age usually have regulations stating what service delivery strategies are most feasible. Because each state differs, all the kinds of provisions that exist cannot be summarized here. Any person involved in planning a new early childhood-special education program should become familiar with state legislation and local policies within the specific school district(s) and local township.

Geographical characteristics of the area to be served

Rural, suburban, and urban areas each pose unique issues affecting the cost and feasibility of service delivery strategies. Simply the dispersion of children across a geographical area influences the desirability of certain approaches such as center- or home-based programs. Where population density is high in large metropolitan areas, larger numbers of young children with special needs are likely to be found within a smaller area, so transportation and access to the children are less likely to be of concern. This fact alone allows greater flexibility for planning programs because larger numbers of children are available for participation, allowing them to be grouped and subgrouped so that several service delivery strategies can be applied. For example, some children can be served in preschool classes in neighborhood centers. Or staff members can travel to their homes to conduct home-based, parent and child training programs. The close proximity of children to one another and to the center where they can be served makes this a feasible alternative. If children are in close proximity, a tremendous savings can be realized in the cost of transportation or in staff time consumed in traveling.

Rural settings, in contrast, present a number of special issues affecting service delivery. Families typically are scattered over a wide area, and young children with handicapping or at-risk conditions represent only a small proportion of the larger population. Some rural programs serve as much as a 2- to 3-county area spanning as many as 50-200 or more miles from end to end. They are small programs and consequently limited in both funds and staff. Only one type of service strategy may be used to serve all children (e.g., a classroom program or a home-based program), but it must be flexible enough to meet the needs of children across a wide age range and with all types and levels of disability. When selecting an appropriate service delivery strategy for rural programs, transportation alone is a major issue.

If children in a rural program are brought to a central facility, some of the important considerations to weigh are the long hours in transit from home to center; care and supervision of very young children in buses or cars; and the value of a center-based educational program for children who may be tired and hungry after long periods of travel. If, instead, the staff travels to provide home-based programs, other advantages and disadvantages must be weighed: the unavailability of special equipment and materials that cannot be transported easily; the reduction in the number of children whom the staff can serve when working on a one-to-one basis; the reduced frequency of contact and the length of time spent with each child and the parent when the staff must travel around from home to home; and the major responsibility upon parents to carry out and maintain training programs when they have other responsibilities inside and outside of the home. This latter item can present particular limitations for working parents. Another consideration is the high cost per child in home-based programs, because expensive staff time must be spent on the road. Children in rural areas served under a home-based program likely will work with just one specialist, but if they can be brought together in a centralized location, a whole team of special teachers and therapists can work with a child intensively and on a daily basis.

Estimated number and characteristics of children to be served

Would you plan differently if you knew the target group would consist of 15 children or 250 children? How would you design a service delivery approach if the population of children were between 1 and 36 months of age or if it were to include children 3-5 years of age? If both populations were to be served, how would this affect your selection among various service delivery options? The number of children to be served and their characteristics represent a critical consideration because it affects all subsequent decisions outlined in the Decision Matrix (Table 8.2) Child characteristics of particular significance include: (a) the age range of children to be served, (b) the types of handicapping conditions represented among them, and (c) the severity levels and range of severity of disabilities within the population to be served.

The number of children to be included in a program influences the complexity and scope of services that will have to be arranged. If the target group is large, subgroups of children (such as those with orthopedic/neurological impairment, vision or hearing deficits, or only mild developmental delays) possibly can be assigned to programs or classes specifically geared to them. Programs for large numbers of children often encompass several service delivery alternatives, such as special classes for children with particular types of handicapping conditions, noncategorical mainstreamed classes for mildly impaired youngsters, and maybe home-based services for parents, infants, and toddlers. If the target group is small, however, one well chosen strategy will have to do the job. Thus, broad child characteristics and the number of children to be served constitute a primary consideration in decisions about the *who, when, where, by whom,* and *with whom* issues outlined in Table 8.2

Cultural and ethnic values within a community

All too often, cultural and ethnic values of the families to be served are overlooked in selecting service delivery strategies. Exuberant advocates of early intervention sometimes are so tuned into their own professional values and convictions that they forget to acknowledge the cultural traditions and values of the persons to be served. If patterns of child care and local attitudes about early education are recognized in program planning, many problems in getting parents to accept a new program can be avoided. We must remember that although school attendance for children of legal school age is mandatory, early childhood education for normal or handicapped preschoolers and infants is not. Parents hold the right to choose whether they and their handicapped child will participate in an early intervention program. If parents do not perceive any benefit in the services offered, or if they view the program as incompatible with their own needs and values about child rearing, they will not participate and the program will fail.

Some neighborhoods do not have a predominant set of values and traditions concerning child care and early education, but others do. Some cultural, religious, and ethnic groups have strong values about family and parental responsibilities for the care of their young and the acceptability of others' assuming responsibility for their children.

> Some years ago the author observed a new program being planned for handicapped 1- to 3-year-olds on an Indian reservation. In its enthusiasm the small staff given responsibility to develop the program had forged ahead by itself and designed a well organized center-based program. But it failed to work with the Indian community being served. When the program was launched, parents were not responsive to the staff's recruiting efforts. Children were not referred. Parents resisted taking their infants and toddlers to the center.
>
> Had the cultural values in that community been examined, the staff would have found deep-rooted attitudes about the responsibility of families to care for their own young children at home. Taking a child, especially a handicapped youngster, elsewhere for training and special education was viewed as a form of rejection. Families traditionally had protected and accepted their handicapped members. They did not separate a deformed or disabled child out from others or consider him or her as different. Perhaps if the community had been consulted and if services had been taken to mothers in their own homes, the early intervention program and its services would have been received more positively.

A good rule of thumb is that a quality early intervention program must not only be well planned and implemented but also must be viewed by its recipients as supportive to their own values and child-rearing needs. Cultural and ethnic values within a community definitely influence choices in the Decision Matrix (Table 8.2) in regard to the variables of *who, when, where,* and possibly *by whom.*

Sponsoring agencies and regulations governing their program operations

The feasibility of certain options within the Decision Matrix for early intervention programs in Table 8.2 may be controlled to some extent by the agency or agencies assuming administrative responsibility for early intervention. Education and social service agencies at both state and local levels are governed by established rules and regulations. Those regulations affect an agency's mode of operation, including the nature of service delivery it selects. Private agencies and nonprofit groups formed by interested citizens usually have greater freedom to define a new style of operation for a program and to choose the nature of services they will offer. They may be required to comply only with state health, safety, and licensing regulations. All of the types of regulations with which various agencies are expected to comply cannot be detailed here, but the wise planner of an early intervention program will be alert to the guidelines and limitations under which various organizations operate.

Public schools, as an example, must adhere to guidelines outlined in their State Plan for Special Education and other state regulations outlined by the State Department of Education. Early childhood-handicapped programs are sponsored and operated by a variety of agencies, some of which operate under a different set of regulations for administering programs of this nature. In interagency cooperatives, each agency brings to the newly formed consortium its own precedents and methods of administration, including regulations to which each must continue to adhere. Issues in regard to what regulations are to be enforced have to be resolved. A working set of guidelines that the new program must follow has to be clarified. Otherwise, too many regulations, some of which may be contradictory and incompatible with one another, can paralyze an operation.

Available resources

The nature and extent of a community's resources determine how comprehensive services can be and how large a program can become. In order to select what single or multiple service delivery options realistically can be implemented, resources available to the agency involved in a program should be identified early in the planning process. These resources include program funds, staff, physical facilities, auxiliary services, equipment, and supplies. Funding alone determines how many children can be served adequately and what dollar-saving tactics must be exercised. Programs with strong financial backing are in a better position to consider more elaborate, sophisticated service delivery options than are programs with limited funds. Well capitalized programs can employ professional staffs and build programs that enjoy some continuity from year to year. When funds are not abundant, other resources such as volunteers and donated services must be used. Unfortunately, this makes continuity tenuous from year to year and thus may result in more simplified service delivery approaches.

Resources within most communities or within other agencies usually are abundant *if* they are sought out and *if* program planners take the initiative for arranging cooperative use. When funds are limited, assistance possibly can be gained through volunteers, linkages with existing community programs, cooperative agreements with universities and colleges seeking training experiences for advanced students, and service projects for local civic groups. Service delivery need not be totally dependent upon the cash budget of a new program. Many innovative, creative early childhood intervention programs have been built with small budgets and skillful coordination of existing community resources.

SUMMARY

Understanding traditional approaches to service delivery for school-aged students and regular early childhood programs enables recognition of the alternatives (and issues) that educators must face in considering how best to serve the special needs of handicapped/at-risk preschoolers and infants. Of course, the styles of service delivery traditionally practiced with older handicapped students in public schools or in regular early childhood education programs for normally developing children may not always be practical for early intervention programs. The unique characteristics of handicapped infants and preschoolers and their needs sometimes dictate new service delivery approaches to fit the particular community, the resources at hand, and the particular population of young children to be served.

Two important points should be emphasized. *First*, EC-SPED programs differ greatly from community to community (as do regular early childhood programs). Variability is essential because conditions within each community or state dictate what services are needed and what service delivery systems are most practical. *Second,* no one "best approach" is recommended for serving all young children with special needs. Some approaches are more functional than others for a given community. Factors that must be taken into consideration in selecting a service delivery approach include: (a) state legislation and local policies, (b) the number and ages of children to be served, including the types of handicaps they present and the severity of their disabilities, (c) the geographical characteristics of the area (rural or urban) and the dispersion of children to be served within that area, (d) cultural and ethnic values within a community, (e) the agencies who will sponsor the program and the regulations that govern their activities, and (f) the financial resources, personnel, facilities, and other resources available.

The Service Delivery Decision Matrix in this chapter helps identify the many alternatives to consider when planning how services will be delivered to young children. The several key questions in that matrix are: *Who* will be the target of services? *When,* or at what age, will the intervention begin? *What* type of service(s) should be offered? *Where* will be the setting for the intervention program? *By whom* will the children be grouped? *Through whom* will services be rendered, or what agencies are to be involved? By working through each of these questions, service delivery approaches can be designed to best fit a given population of young children and a particular community.

9
Program Models for Early Childhood Intervention

Suppose you are part of a planning committee that wants to organize an intervention program for handicapped young chidren. You are responsible for planning the service delivery approaches to be applied, as well as all other features that will distinguish the new program, such as its philosophy and theoretical orientation, curriculum, teaching methodologies, and staffing pattern. Consider each of the following situations and ask yourself: What type of early intervention program could I develop that would be effective for children and most feasible to operate in this community?

The author acknowledges and appreciates the contribution of Jane DeWeerd to this chapter.

A large city school district serving 50,000 school-aged students wants to start an intervention program for handicapped 3- to-5-year-olds. Over 3,000 preschoolers need special services. Because few programs are available, most children are at home unserved. The new program is to serve all handicapped preschoolers regardless of their handicapping condition or level of severity.

The city contains a mixture of ethnic groups, some of which are sensitive about caring for children outside their own homes. Also, large economically depresed sections of the city contain large numbers of handicapped preschoolers (although some of the children come from more affluent sections of the city). How could you organize and implement an early intervention program to serve the needs of this diverse group of children and these sociocultural groups?

A private foundation has offered funds to support an early intervention program for deaf and hearing impaired children from birth until kindergarten age. Some 45,000 citizens reside in the town, which is the home of a state university. Children from some surrounding farming communities also are to be included. The university operates the largest regular early childhood nursery school serving the area.

Because hearing impairments represent a low-incidence disability, you estimate the number of children with such impairments to be low. But youngsters with significant language and speech delays can be included in the program as well. Because the program will serve infants, toddlers, and preschoolers, you must plan services to match the unique needs of each age group and their families. What would be an effective approach to use in this community?

A survey covering a sparsely populated, three-county farming area indicates that 25 young children between 5 months and 6 years of age need special education-early intervention services. Special programs are unavailable unless parents drive over 250 miles to the nearest large city. It is not clear what agency should assume responsibility for serving these youngsters or how services might be arranged. The target population includes children from birth to school age who have all types of disabilities, but there is a high concentration of two types of youngsters—those with multiple handicaps and those with significant delays in language and cognitive development. No regular preschools are available locally. How would you serve these families in view of their dispersion over such a broad area? Given the diversity of the population to be served and the lack of resources in this rural area, how should services be arranged?

You may find yourself searching for the "right" program model to serve the children and families in each of the situations described. No doubt you would want to select an approach that would be most effective. Although several variables influence what approaches are more desirable and more feasible than others for certain communities, educators generally agree on one important point: *There is no single best model that all early childhood programs should follow; neither is one approach equally effective with all children.*

What defines an "effective program model" is guided by the values and philosophy about education to which you adhere. What one person considers a successful program may not be so regarded by another. Educators agree there is no one best approach, but different schools of thought emerge concerning what represents an *appropriate* intervention program for young children. Heated debates have been waged among educators with very different philosophical and theoretical backgrounds. Their arguments stem from differing values about what young children need, what the long-term goals of education should be, and how one should teach. What constitutes *learning* on the part of the child is another point of contention. Given these differences in opinion, variation across programs is inevitable.

At the same time, variation is an expected and important part of free enterprise in American education. As the needs of children vary, so should the freedom of parents and educators to define their values and translate them into models for educating young children, including those who are handicapped. Differences across programs today are thus recognized as a useful and a healthy source of variety in American education.

Exemplary models have been developed as a part of Follow-Through, Head Start Planned Variation Programs, and the Handicapped Children's Early Education Programs (HCEEPs). These models have been created to serve communities like those just described. In chapter 8 you learned about service delivery alternatives and the unlimited combinations of strategies one can use to offer special help to handicapped young children and their parents. This chapter goes one step further, to look at the total design for all aspects of an educational program, including some of the key dimensions on which programs differ. As you will see, the service delivery approach one selects is but one part of a total, well planned early intervention program model.

Knowledge of nationally recognized early childhood program models can be useful to you in several ways. *First,* if you become involved in planning a new program, these models provide excellent examples of how others have tackled similar problems to create workable, successful programs. *Second,* as a practitioner working with young children, the models represent a valuable resource for information, instructional materials, curriculum guides, assessment tools, teacher training materials, and guides for organizing programs. *Third,* you and the program with which you may eventually be employed may wish to affiliate with one of these national models and adopt its approach rather than developing a new one. The models described in this chapter are operating in centers around the country. Staffs often are available on a contractual basis to provide training, consultation, materials, and other helpful services for communities that want to replicate their model. *Finally,* by understanding what components comprise an exemplary model, you have a useful guide toward designing an early intervention program of your own (Karnes, Kokotovic, & Shwedel, 1982).

WHAT IS A PROGRAM MODEL?

★ *An* educational program model *refers to a program for children in which its content and operational strategies are clearly conceptualized and defined in a manner that assures internal consistency and coherence.*

All aspects or components of a program model are organized to reflect the same set of values, the same theoretical base, and the same set of goals and objectives. Spodek (1973) characterized a program model as an *ideal* construction of a program in which its essential elements, both practical and theoretical, have been specified in a way that the program can be copied or replicated by another. Models highlight the essential elements and eliminate the nonessential or situation-specific elements that are neither generalizable nor replicable in other sites. The ideal model, according to Spodek, provides a standard against which actual practices of a program can be compared. It has a clear statement of the philosophical and theoretical framework to which it adheres. Practices are standardized so they can be implemented consistently by the entire staff. This clarity of purpose would be apparent if you were to ask staff members about the model. Each would describe it in similar ways, using the same concepts, emphasizing the same key features, and describing the same instructional strategies. A program model, therefore, is:

— based upon a philosophy, theory, or educational strategy that gives continuity to the goals and objectives of the program, to its curriculum and instructional methodology, and to all other components that characterize the program (Egbert & Brisch, 1979).

— defined by a number of program components that fit together philosophically and operationally; relationships between each component are delineated clearly and reflect that common set of values, assumptions, and goals.

— defined in sufficient detail so that the same program approach can be clearly understood and implemented by others who want to replicate it in another location.

A program model also shows evidence that it works. Fully developed models have been tested in actual classrooms or at service sites, with data indicating that goals and objectives of the model can be achieved if its prescribed components and procedures are implemented. Not only are outcomes of the model clear, but evidence also shows that those outcomes result from the model's own procedures and not merely from the influence of a dynamic personality within the staff or an unusually talented teacher. If replicated in other comparable locations with populations of children similar to those with whom the model was developed, results should be predictable.

NATIONAL EFFORTS IN MODEL DEVELOPMENT

Educators who started the first intervention and compensatory education programs in the early 1960s were truly pioneers. Exemplary models for early childhood education at that time were lacking. Little was known about what educational experiences and instructional strategies would deter the failure for which so many children seemed destined when they entered elementary school. This is not to suggest that philosophies about what education should be were nonexistent. In fact, many different instructional strategies were being touted as "the way to teach children." The problem was that few educational innovators had organized their ideas into well defined, complete prescriptions for educational programs. At least, their ideas about the design of educational programs were not written down in sufficient detail so that educators could replicate them across other locations.

There is no single "best" approach for teaching and stimulating these little ones as they move on into their toddler and preschool years and as their needs change.

Concern over this lack of exemplary models and recognition of the need for systematic experimentation with alternative models led leaders in the field to take action. They sought legislation to support federal programs that would emphasize the development and dissemination of viable models for early intervention. In the late 1960s several programs that embraced the concept of planned variation were initiated through experimentation with different educational models. Three of the most notable programs were Project Follow Through, the Head Start Planned Variation Program, and the Handicapped Children's Early Education Demonstration Programs (HCEEPs).

Follow-Through model programs

Project Follow-Through (described in chapter 3) was one of the most influential national programs to apply the concept of educational models. Follow-Through became an experimental demonstration effort to develop, refine, and evaluate alternative approaches for educating young disadvantaged children. Its purpose was to unite educational theory and practice by putting several different models into operation in various cultural and environmental settings across the country and evaluating their effectiveness (Egbert, 1973). Models traditionally tested under controlled conditions of a laboratory or demonstration school thereby could be subjected to the test in the pragmatic, "real world" conditions found in community and public school settings. Each model was to be monitored by its implementors as well as by an external evaluator to ascertain the overall impact on children and their families. This approach was referred to as *planned variation.*

To select the models used in the Follow-Through planned variation experiment, experts across the country were invited to apply for funds to try out their ideas at selected program sites. Those selected became known as *program sponsors.* They assumed responsibility for (a) developing their ideas into well defined, carefully planned prescriptions and writing them in a form that could be disseminated to educators in programs around the country; (b) training staff and working with representatives in a community to implement the model, (c) providing support, training, and continuing supervision of teachers and administrative staff at sites to assure accurate replication of their model; and (d) monitoring the children's progress throughout the life of the program (Maccoby & Zellner, 1970). Some 22 model sponsors became a part of the Follow-Through experiment.

Introduction of the planned variation and sponsorship concepts as means for introducing an external change agent into public education represented the most "ambitious educational experiment ever carried out on a national level at that time" (Cherian & Associates, 1973). Follow-Through's application of the concept of planned variation was repeated by Head Start in its own experiment with alternative models and by the Bureau of Education for the Handicapped with its HCEEP Projects.

The planned variation experiment in Follow-Through was not intended to identify a single best method for educating disadvantaged children. Its planners recognized from the beginning that outcomes of each model would vary. The models emphasized different things, placed priority upon different educational objectives, and approached learning in different ways. Simply, the intent of Follow-Through was to identify the outcomes, benefits, and conditions that affected implementation of a given approach and influenced its ultimate success. Given this type of information, more appropriate matches could be made between a particular educational approach and the school/community setting into which it would be placed.

Brief descriptions for six of the better known Follow-Through models are given in the following pages. Although Follow-Through targeted children in kindergarten through third grade, its models are relevant to early childhood-special education and to our discussion here, for several reasons. *First,* many Follow-Through models evolved from the work of researchers who developed their programs first with *preschool* disadvantaged populations. *Second,* the Follow-Through models were the ones that Head Start applied as a part of its Planned Variation Experiment. *Third,* some Follow-Through models are now being used with young handicapped children (e.g., Weikart's High Scope or Cognitively Oriented Model). *Finally,* the Follow-Through models offer some of the best examples of well conceptualized, well developed models.

Descriptions are a composite of information taken from the authors' contact with the models, along with the following sources: Maccoby and Zellner (1970); Klein (1971); Stanford Research Institute (1972); Bissell (1973); Cherian and Associates (1973); Nero and Associates (1975, 1976); Day (1980); and Rhine (1981).

Bank Street Developmental-Interaction Approach

Original Developer/Sponsor: Elizabeth Gilkeson, Bank Street College of Education, New York, NY

Basic Premises

- Education should be based upon a developmental approach in that the classroom is the child's workroom, where he/she should be free to explore, discover, make choices, and seek out his/her own means for learning.

- A productive learning environment is one that is constantly rearranged to fit the child's changing interests and needs. Teachers' role is one of building trust, being responsive to children's needs and feelings, and sensitizing them to sights, sounds, feelings, and ideas to help build positive images of themselves as learners.

- Education should focus on the whole child, with the purpose of enabling the child to become deeply involved and self-directed in his/her own learning. A child learns best through direct experience and active participation. Adults should support the child's autonomy while extending his/her work by introducing opportunities for new experience and then helping the child understand and express the meaning of that experience.

Curricular/Instructional Approach

- Model emphasizes a philosophy of "open education" rather than specific teaching and curricular methods applied arbitrarily. Children are viewed as self-activated learners. Teachers should provide an array of materials and create opportunities for experiences from which children have freedom to choose.

- Activities are child-initiated and child-directed, with teachers acting in roles as interpreters of experience. Teaching is carried out on basis of child's response by elaborating upon and interpreting the experience and feelings. Activities create opportunity for children to engage in tasks that are satisfying in terms of their own goals and that simultaneously encourage cognitive and affective development.

- Teachers arrange planned activities or events by providing materials and creating options for the children. Activities originate from classroom themes (such as cooking, organizing chores, or block-building) and eventually extend into community themes (such as food marketing, vocational roles such as a baker or nurse). Academic skills are acquired through practical experience in context of the ongoing classroom life experience.

Classification of Model (Descriptors)

- Child-oriented

- Discovery program

- Open education approach

Behavior Analysis Model Approach

Original Developer/Sponsor: Don Bushell, University of Kansas

Basic Premises

- Principles of applied behavior analysis provide an effective guide for instructional procedures in the classroom. Children learn best when systematic positive reinforcement follows the desired behaviors and they are praised and rewarded for their efforts. Extrinsic rewards may be necessary to support children's early learning until they reach a level of mastery that allows them to enjoy new skills for their own intrinsic reward.

- Effective intervention with disadvantaged children should emphasize mastery of basic skills in reading, math, spelling, and handwriting, using individualized, programmed materials and methods of teaching.

- Criticism, verbal or physical punishment, and coercion do not encourage learning or teach desired behavior. They have no place in the classroom.

Curricular/Instructional Approach

- Model focuses on teaching methods in the classroom and desired child outcomes using principles of behavior analysis. Systematic reinforcement is given, using a token-exchange system, to provide immediate consequences for desired learning and social behaviors. Inappropriate behavior is ignored. At the end of learning sessions, tokens are exchanged for special activities or materials. Instructional-work periods alternate with special activity/token exchange times throughout the day.

- Curriculum emphasizes daily instruction in reading, math, spelling, and handwriting, via small rotating groups taught by the teacher, an aide, and two parent aides employed on a rotating basis with other parents.

- Instructional procedures call for clear definitions of objectives and desired outcomes for the child. Programmed, sequential learning materials are used to permit each child to work at his/her own pace. Teachers keep specific records on child performance and progress through learning sequences.

- Emphasis is placed on use of programmed instructional materials that are carefully sequenced and provide immediate feedback (if possible) to the child.

Classification of Model (Descriptors)

- Behaviorally oriented

- Academically oriented

- Structured teaching approach

- Emphasis on basic skills

Engelmann/Becker Model for Direct Instruction

Original Developer/Sponsor: Wesley Becker/Siegfried Engelmann, University of Oregon

Basic Premises

- Disadvantaged children are academically behind middle-class children and in order to catch up, they must learn basic skills at a *faster rate* than middle-class peers.

- Student failure is instructional failure. The rate and quality of a child's learning are functions of environmental events. Teaching via structured, carefully sequenced lessons based on behavior and reinforcement principles and task analysis of concepts/skills that elicit frequent responses from the child will increase learning.

- Effective teaching should be based on behavioral learning theory and principles of reinforcement (behavior that is reinforced is strengthened, and behavior that is not reinforced becomes weaker). Desired behavior in the child should be systematically reinforced by praise and pleasurable consequences. Antisocial or unproductive behaviors should be ignored.

Curricular/Instructional Approach

- Model focuses primarily on methods of instruction in the classroom and curricular content. Academic learning in reading, arithmetic, and language using programmed sequences specified in *DISTAR Instructional Materials* is emphasized.

- Instructional approach used by teachers involves well planned, small-group sessions involving face-to-face, rapid-fire drills between teacher and children. Children must maintain high level of attention and respond verbally in response to questions/tasks teacher presents.

- Teacher role is to present programmed learning tasks specified in detail in preplanned and pretested *DISTAR* materials. Teacher is viewed as instigator of learning—who elicits responses, reinforces correct responses, and quickly corrects mistakes or incorrect responses.

- Reward and praise are used to encourage desired patterns of behavior.

Classification of Model (Descriptors)

- Classroom instructional procedures

- Academically oriented

- Structured teaching

- Learning of basic skills

Florida Parent Education Model

Original Developer/Sponsor: Ira Gordon, University of Florida

Basic Premises

- Parents play a key role in the emotional and intellectual growth of their children. Any intervention should provide ways to involve parents in educating their own children and a means for motivating parents to provide a stimulating home environment that encourages better performance from the child.

- Mothers in low socioeconomic, disadvantaged homes often do not provide good models of abstract thinking. They have difficulty organizing their own existence and thus provide disorganized home environments for their children. They evidence feeling of low self-esteem in that they have little control over their own lives. An effective intervention program should aid parents by teaching them how to teach the child, by establishing a sense of importance and purpose within the parent in regard to the child's future, and thereby raise parent esteem as well as child performance.

Curricular/Instructional Approach

- Model focuses primarily upon home-based training of parents as teachers of their own children by "parent educators" who visit the homes regularly. Mothers of project children are hired as "parent educators" who are trained by program personnel. Parent educator works in the classroom half-time as a teacher's aide and then travels to children's homes weekly to work with the mother.

- Training of mother centers on learning tasks taught in the classroom, which the parent also learns how to teach to the child at home. The intent is to get parents at home and teachers at school to work as instructional partners. Weekly tasks emphasize cognitive skills.

- Curriculum is not standardized, although it does emphasize a Piagetian approach. This is used flexibly, and lessons are varied according to the needs of individual children/classes.

- In addition to the instructional role of parent trainer, the parent educator serves as a liaison between the school and home to bring about better communication between parents of professionals. This key person also acts as a referral agent for medical, dental, psychological, or social services. He/she communicates news from school and information about school/community functions and organizes parent meetings in which parents should be involved. This important role, played by a parent paraprofessional, is a crucial part of the Florida Model.

Classification of Model (Major Emphases)

- Home-based parent training

- Cognitive-discovery oriented curriculum

- Parent-implemented

High Scope Cognitively-Oriented Curriculum Model

Original Developer/Sponsor: David Weikart, High Scope Education Research Foundation, Ypsilanti, MI

Basic Premises

■ Emphasis in education should be to develop children's thinking skills, as well as teach academic subject area competencies. Active experience with real objects, experimentation, exploring, and talking about experiences are more effective in teaching children than telling and showing them what to do. Thus, instructional strategies should stress the "process of learning and thinking."

■ Classroom environment should provide an open framework that encourages each child to pursue his/her own interests and ideas through key experiences that develop his/her ability to (a) make decisions about what he/she is going to do and how to go about doing it, (b) express self in ways that communicate that experience to others, (c) work with other children and adults so that tasks are completed through group planning and cooperative effort, (d) exercise self-discipline by identifying personal goals, by pursuing and then completing selected tasks, and (e) embrace a spirit of inquiry and openness to various points of view.

■ Children should acquire a wide range of intellectual and physical abilities, and particularly processes for thinking and learning.

Curricular/Instructional Approach

■ Model emphasis is primarily upon curricular and instructional processes in the classroom along with learning processes within the child, based upon Piagetian theory. Classroom activities and instructional methods are designed to foster intellectual development through experimentation, exploration, and constant verbalization and dialogue between teachers and children and among children. Children are expected to generate much of their own learning—but through structured processes shaped by teacher questions and planning/implementation steps through which children move.

■ High Scope classrooms have learning centers for language, math, science, and art, which include a variety of materials and equipment. At the preschool level, centers include playhouse area, block area, art area, and quiet area. Other areas may be created as needed.

■ Daily activities are organized around a cycle of planning-working-representing-evaluating. In *planning time,* children plan individually, or in a group, activities or project of interest to them—what will be used, who will be involved, what steps will be taken, and what problems are to be solved. During *work time,* children go to learning centers, select materials to produce products or performances, and carry out plans. During *representation time,* children transform their direct experiences into concepts by describing activities in the form of written or pictorial reports, graphs, charts, drawings, dramatizations, or answers to questions. During *evaluation time,* children evaluate the success of their projects by comparing the original plan to the work and its outcome.

   In addition, large-group time provides opportunities for general class meetings, dramatic performances, games, physical exercise, or presentation of class projects. Small-group time provides additional opportunity for the teacher to conduct carefully sequenced activities in academic skill areas such as language arts, math, science, music, art, and drama.

■ Teacher's role is defined as one of facilitator and catalyst for children's learning. Teacher must create an environment wherein children will engage in active learning and where a variety of materials, resources, and objects are available. Teacher helps children in planning and implementation processes by asking open-ended questions, helping children to elaborate on their initial conceptualization of a task or to extend ideas and discover solutions to achieve task completion. Teacher also asks probing questions to help children identify the sequence of steps they must follow to carry out a project and to identify what responsibilities must be assigned to allow successful group activity.

   During representation and evaluation periods, teacher interacts with children, offers suggestions and help as needed. Teacher also provides direct instruction for small groups, using methods consistent with developmental learning principles in that they emphasize mental processes, learning by doing, representation of actions, and communication.

Classification of Model (Descriptors)

■ Cognitive discovery
■ Child-oriented
■ Process-oriented

Tucson Early Education Model (TEEM)

Original Developer/Sponsor: Marie Hughes and Ronald Henderson, University of Arizona

Basic Premises

- Language and intellectual development are intertwined. Education must build upon language competence along with broad intellectual and academic skills and positive attitudes, to prepare children to function effectively and confidently as adults. (The model was developed originally with Mexican-American children who were deficient in Spanish and English, had little experience with objects and little sense of time as an ordered sequence of events. TEEM was created to remedy these deficiencies. It was adapted for use with children of all cultural and socioeconomic backgrounds.)
- Children should not be forced to learn. If an environment is sufficiently interesting, provides alternatives, and is based on the experiences/interests of children, it will demand by itself (without teacher prodding) that children learn.
- Children learn language skills by imitating peers and adults. Teachers should elaborate and explore with children their own interests and ideas, in order to develop language, thinking skills, and skill in learning how to learn.
- Social reinforcement such as praise and attention should be used liberally. Children's work should be displayed with mistakes left unchanged.

Curricular/Instructional Approach

- Model emphasizes a language-experience approach to instruction in the classroom. Classroom is arranged to allow experience-based learning, giving children choices of activities and materials throughout the day. Curriculum is carefully structured but is also flexible to allow choices in children's activities and behavior.
- Curriculum focuses on four areas of instruction: (a) language competence, which is considered the major technical skill a child should acquire; (b) development of intellectual skills necessary for learning (e.g., ability to attend, recall, organize and sequence events, make choices, and evaluate alternatives); (c) development of a motivational base (e.g., positive attitudes toward school, an expectation for success, and ability to persevere); and (d) development of societal arts and skills (e.g., reading, writing, math, and social skills for cooperation and planning). These four curriculum areas are developed simultaneously through functional activities.
- TEEM classroom is organized into interest centers for small groups to encourage interaction of children with their environment and peers. A unique feature of the model is the instructional-learning process used. Committees of 3-5 children (heterogeneously grouped) are organized by the teacher or voluntarily by the children themselves, who operate with or without an adult leader to accomplish specific tasks. Children read and write instructions for the activity and carry it through to completion. Teacher prints or draws pictorial instructions, questions, or messages on cards to add to the language-reading stimulation for the children. In addition, as part of the emphasis on language training, children's stories are recorded and some are represented in writing or pictured in illustrated books.
- Instructional materials are selected for their functional value for learning by doing. Household items, raw materials, and various tools (e.g., measuring instruments, household utensils, vocational tools) typically are used. Many activities are arranged around teacher-made *intellectual kits,* which are collections of "stuff"—all of which have one characteristic in common. Children examine the materials and extract the common principle as a means for developing problem-solving and how-to-learn skills.

Classification of Model (Descriptors)

- Process-oriented
- Cognitive discovery
- Child-oriented

Head Start Planned Variation models

Like Follow-Through, Head Start's Planned Variation Program was an effort to experiment with alternative program models. Head Start centers had been in operation approximately four years when its Planned Variation Program began in 1969. Several issues were explored (Bissell, 1973):

- The effects of various well defined educational strategies on Head Start children and their families.
- The nature of experiences provided by different program models.
- The mechanisms of curriculum implementation.
- The benefits of continuous, sequenced intervention following the same educational strategy over several years. (p. 66)

Eight preschool models were selected for the Head Start Planned Variation Program on the basis of two criteria: (a) The model had been tested in a laboratory school and represented a well formulated approach for preschool education with disadvantaged children, and (b) the sponsor of the model had implemented the model as a part of Follow-Through. Communities already implementing those models as a part of their Follow-Through project were invited to participate in the Head Start experiment. In those communities, the models then were extended into the Head Start centers in selected classes, and outcomes were compared with those of children who participated in traditional Head Start comparison classrooms. Generally these classes were from the same communities. Results from the Head Start Planned Variation Experiment are summarized by Bissell (1973) in a report entitled *Planned Variation in Head Start and Follow-Through*.

The important point here is that Head Start further established the practice of using program models in its own experiments with planned variation. Staffs in selected centers around the country became part of these model programs and were trained to implement the model with disadvantaged preschool children. As noted earlier, the Head Start Planned Variation models came from those used by Project Follow-Through. The six Follow-Through models described earlier are among those used for the Head Start Planned Variation Program.

HCEEP model programs

The Handicapped Children's Early Education Program Act (PL 90-538), described in chapter 2, initiated another major effort in 1968 to experiment with alternative early childhood-special education intervention models. This time the target was not disadvantaged children from low socioeconomic neighborhoods; instead, the focus was on handicapped children from birth to age 8. Recognizing the paucity of services for handicapped children in this age group and the absence of exemplary models upon which services could be built, Congress allocated monies to develop demonstration projects. The purpose was to design innovative approaches or models for serving young handicapped children and their parents. Like model programs created under Follow-Through, HCEEP projects have designed strategies for training staff, evaluating children's progress, and assessing the outcomes. Methods for coordinating with local public schools and other related agencies and disseminating information about the project also have been a part of the model programs (DeWeerd & Cole, 1976; DeWeerd, 1977).

Since 1968, over 500 HCEEP models have been developed. Several models have been validated as successful programs by the Joint Dissemination Review Panel (National

Diffusion Network, 1975). To receive such a distinction, programs must present evidence of their effectiveness before the JDRP, a special board appointed by the U.S. Commissioner (now Secretary) of Education. This board analyzes the program model for its clarity of content and procedures, as well as its outcomes in terms of child gains and general program effectiveness.

The brief descriptions of several HCEEP Program models here do not reflect all aspects of the complex program designs. They provide only a sketch of the philosophical orientation, methodologies, and curriculum/materials that typify each model.

Additional information on the models can be found in several other volumes: Day and Parker (1977); Evans (1975); Gordon and Breivogel (1976); Hanson (1984a); *HCEEP Overview and Directory* (1979, 1984); Jordan, Hayden, Karnes, and Wood (1977); Maccoby & Zellner (1970); and Weber (1970).

PEECH Project (Precise Early Education for Children with Handicaps)

Location: Champaign, Illinois

Target Population: Children 3-6 years of age who are mildly to moderately handicapped

Type of Program: Combination home- and center-based

Description:

Intervention program includes a preschool class, operating 2½ hours daily, in which children participate in large- and small-group activities and individual training activities. An instructional model emphasizing language, derived from the Illinois Test of Psycholingusitic Abilities (ITPA), provides a guide for curriculum development. A curriculum (Game Oriented Activities for Learning, or GOAL), developed for disadvantaged and normally developing preschoolers, also has been modified for use with handicapped youngsters.

PEECH model emphasizes a systematic, individualized instructional process including systematic assessment, defining behavioral objectives, instructional programming for individual children, and reinforcement. Follow-up lessons using a game format also are used. Each child's progress is systematically recorded daily. Instruction is developmental and focuses on gross motor, fine motor, social-emotional, self-help, math, language, and cognitive skills.

A multidisciplinary team provides input in planning delivery of special services. The staff team delivers an individualized parental involvement component encompassing a variety of potential activities: classroom observation, large- and small-group meetings, participation in screening, policy making, and classroom instruction, a toy lending library, and home-based teaching.

UNISTAPS (a family-oriented noncategorical program for severely handicapped children)

Location: St. Paul, Minnesota/Minneapolis Public Schools

Target Population: Children 0-6 years of age with hearing impairments, other sensory and
      developmental impairments

Type of Program: Multiple program options in homelike and center-based settings

Description:

> Multiple service options for parents and children—a significant part of this model—include: (a) an infant
> program for children from birth to 3½ years, (b) a parent-child nursery, and (c) a primary program for
> children 3½-6 years old.

> The primary program encompasses half-day nurseries, regular nurseries, half- and full-day kindergartens,
> a kindergarten for hearing impaired youngsters, a readiness program, and an integrated program. The
> infant program provides direct services to hearing impaired or other handicapped children while a
> tutor-counselor works simultaneously with the parent and counselor. The tutor counselor also meets with
> the parent and child weekly in a homelike setting where the parent is trained to provide language
> stimulation for the child.

> Parent involvement also includes parent participation in nursery classes, family workshops, couples
> evening meetings, and "men only" meetings. Particular curricular emphasis is given to the language
> and communication needs of hearing impaired youngsters to develop aural/oral communication skills,
> social skills, and optimal use of residual hearing.

Rutland Center (developmental therapy model for treating emotionally disturbed children)

Location: Athens, Georgia

Target Population: Children 2-14 years of age with severe emotional or developmental problems

Type of Program: Center-based

Description:

> Intervention focuses on use of the "developmental therapy curricula," a psychoeducational treatment
> approach designed to reduce children's social and emotional difficulties. Curriculum emphasizes
> communication, socialization, academics, and behavior, each arranged in five developmental stages
> requiring a different psychological emphasis as well as different teaching techniques and materials.
> Greatest importance is placed upon academic and communication skills as they relate to a child's
> functioning in social situations.

> Children are enrolled in the intervention program on a flexible basis, ranging from 1-2 hours daily and
> from 2-5 days a week. Time spent in the special classes decreases as attendance is increased in a regular
> day-care, nursery, or preschool program.

> Special services to parents, another important component of the model, are provided by the treatment
> team. A follow-up program facilitates reintegration of children into regular educational programs.

Portage Project (a home approach to the early education of handicapped children)

Location: Portage, Wisconsin (Public School Districts and
    Wisconsin Department of Public Instruction)

Target Population: Children in rural areas from birth to age 6 with any type of handicap

Type of Program: Home-based

Description:

Intervention approach focuses upon teaching parents to train their own handicapped children using behavior modification techniques. A home teacher visits each home approximately 1½ hours weekly to help parents acquire skills to: (a) assess their own child's skill in areas of cognition, self-help, motor development, language, and socialization; (b) target emerging skills for training; (c) apply appropriate teacher technique with their child; and (d) evaluate their child's progress. Parents are trained to apply an instructional program based upon an assessment tool outlining developmental sequences and a set of corresponding curriculum cards that make up the *Portage Guide to Early Education*.

Instructional procedures with both parent and child follow a *precision teaching model*. Home teachers use modeling to train parents and provide precise weekly prescriptions for the parent to follow in teaching the child. Baseline and continuous data are collected and charted on the child's progress. All instruction and special programming occur in the child's home, with the parents holding major responsibility for maintaining the intervention program between visits by the home trainer.

**Model Preschool Center for Handicapped Children:
Down Syndrome Program**

Location: Seattle, Washington (University of Washington) Experimental Education Unit

Target Population: Children from birth to age 6 with Down syndrome

Type of Program: Center-based

Description:

Program strategies are designed to accelerate and maintain development in children with Down syndrome and to begin intervention as soon after birth as possible, using parent training. Several programs offer a complementary sequence for training:

1. The *Infant Learning Program* gives 1-1 training in motor and cognitive areas through weekly, 30-minute sessions with the parent, child, and staff trainer. Parents continue training process at home. It begins at birth or upon identification and continues to 18 months of age.
2. *Preschool and then kindergarten classes* operate 2 hours daily, 4 days per week, and provide both group and individual training in areas of physical, personal-social, communication, and cognitive development. Individualized instruction in preacademic and academic areas also is given daily.
3. *Center-based parent training* continues during preschool and kindergarten years. Parents remain involved through roles as teacher-aides and data-takers. Parents are taught methods for reinforcing new skills learned at school and maintaining them at home.

COMPONENTS OF AN EXEMPLARY MODEL

An education model can be understood best if it is analyzed in terms of its component parts. A diagram depicting the overall design of a program model is shown in Figure 9.1. Collectively, 11 components build a complete prescription for the content and instructional priorities of a program, its implementation strategies, materials and facilities, and its expected outcomes. As shown in the figure, three components create the foundation or basic premises of a model upon which all other components are built. A *set of values or a philosophy* and the *theoretical orientation* define the underlying concepts from which decisions are made. From these, the third component, *program goals and objectives*, is derived. These goals and objectives define the purpose of a model and what is to be achieved for children, their parents, and the community at large. The remaining seven components deal with internal characteristics and working mechanisms of a model. Each defines how the basic values, theoretical orientation, goals and objectives are translated into actual practices for delivering services and teaching the client.

Understanding these model components can be of great help to you. If you were to design an early childhood-special education program model of your own, a good approach would be to work systematically through each component to plan what unique features will characterize your program. A conceptual system such as this makes model planning (which could be a confusing, overwhelming task) much more manageable. It helps you think through groups of interrelated issues to plan—for example, the curriculum and corresponding instructional procedures. It provides a structure through which you can check for internal consistency among parts of the model. It also offers a system for organizing information in a way that can be communicated clearly to others. Delineating a model by its component parts also provides a means for analyzing existing models and comparing them. Because the terminology and the choice of features used to define various models differ widely, comparisons between them are difficult and sometimes confusing. In identifying features by component and making comparisons on that basis, the unique qualities of individual models become more apparent.

The development of so many new model programs in the past decade offers an abundance of choices to educators. How does one go about selecting a model without being swayed by attractive, but perhaps superficial, features? Colorful, fun-looking instructional materials can attract attention and yet be a very peripheral part of a model. Likewise, dynamic presentation of a model by an inspiring speaker can generate enthusiasm and convince educators to adopt a particular model before they truly understand its implications for them and know it is compatible with their local needs and educational values. A component-by-component analysis of a program model offers a means for determining exactly what a model advocates and what its primary features are.

Each component within a program model is examined in the following pages, including what specifications each typically contains and the different points of view or approaches each component may embrace. All models do not place equal emphasis upon every component. Sometimes a model has elaborate descriptions, materials, and procedures for certain components but makes little mention of other component parts. The absence of information about a component can be confusing when trying to understand a model, but the omission tells something about the priorities and values of that model. A model may place less importance on a particular component (such as curriculum) but

Figure 9.1
Components of a Program Model

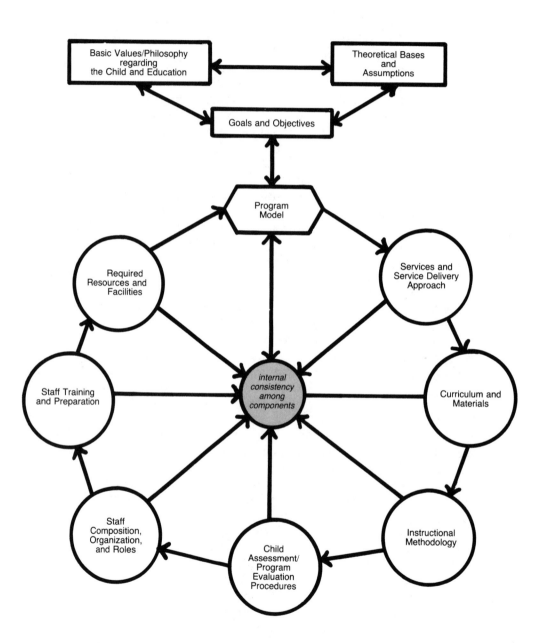

give greater emphasis to instructional methodology. Because the content of certain components is still a necessary part of an ongoing education program, however, it may be left to the teachers or staff to plan as long as it remains in harmony with the overall values and framework of the program model.

Basic values and philosophy

A program model embodies a basic set of values defined by its developer. These include:

1. *Values concerning the child.*
   - What does a child need? What additional needs do children have if they are disadvantaged? Handicapped? At-risk for developmental disabilities?
   - What are young children capable of doing? What should we expect them to be able to do cognitively, socially, and motorically if they are handicapped?
   - What is most important for children to learn? When should they begin to learn it, and who should assume responsibility for helping them achieve important developmental milestones, especially if the children are handicapped?

2. *Values about education.*
   - What is the role of education within our society, and what are its responsibilities to children, including handicapped/disadvantaged youngsters under school age?
   - What constitutes education for children at various age levels? On what activities/ learning should greatest emphasis be placed?
   - What child outcomes do we want as a result of education? In the case of early childhood-special education programs, what do we want to achieve with the child by providing early intervention services?

3. *Values about the educative process.*
   - How does one determine what a child should be taught? Who should be included in this decision-making task?
   - To what extent should teachers and other staff impose structure on the child and determine what he or she is to do versus leaving the child free to learn in his or her own unique way and pursue his or her own interests?
   - What role should the teacher play in education? Does the teacher act as a leader and decision maker or as a supporter and facilitator who lets the child follow his or her own interests and thereby determine both the style and content of his or her own learning?

In developing a program model, one can start with a set of values about the child, about education, or about the education process and translate those values into operational procedures in the classroom. Or one can focus first upon a theory of learning or a favorite curriculum design to build a model. In doing so, a set of values is derived. Whatever approach is taken, every model reflects its own unique set of values.

Educators constantly struggle with the question of values. These same issues are confronted in designing a program model or in selecting an existing one. Most heated arguments about what education should be or what it fails to be boil down to a question of basic values. Should children have the freedom to pursue their own interests and select their own activities, or should teachers set objectives and structure learning accordingly? Should the curriculum stress mastery of basic skills, or should it emphasize discovery learning, thinking skills, and the process of learning? Should parents be involved in selecting curriculum priorities or is this the educator's prerogative? Whether these questions are faced directly or indirectly, our values influence our decisions about education.

Here are a few of the major ways values affect programs for children:

1. Values help define curriculum priorities. Values help educators decide, in part, what will be the "core" of an educational program and what will be peripheral. With the handicapped, our values determine whether we stress academic skill learning or self-care and basic survival skills. Our values determine whether we regard the traditional academic skills taught to normal children as valued competencies for handicapped youngsters who may be limited in their capacity to master them.

2. Values affect how narrowly or broadly education is defined and whether we consider ourselves, as educators, responsible for all aspects or for only certain aspects of children's development and care.

3. Values help establish teacher expectations for children, which in turn affect what learning opportunities are arranged and what skills are taught. If adults value self-sufficiency on the part of the handicapped, certain types of educational goals are implied. On the other hand, if independence is not valued or expected, education will have a much different flavor.

4. Values shape the teacher's view of a child as a human being and what is important for that individual's self-fulfillment. This, too, affects educational practices in many ways. The kind and intensity of services we offer to a particular group are influenced by our values. How we regard the rights of the handicapped to gain access to the same privileges and opportunities others enjoy reflects our attitudes and values about them as people.

In summary, how values are defined is a very individual matter. They can be defined objectively on the basis of *empirical data* documenting what works with children. Values also come from *cultural traditions*—the way things have always been done. *Religious beliefs, personal feelings,* and *simple preferences* are other sources from which values are derived. No position is right or wrong, because values represent personal priorities that evolve through each person's unique life experiences.

Theoretical basis and underlying assumptions

A well developed model includes a clear definition of its theoretical orientation about development and learning in children. Programs differ, however, in how much theoretical concepts influence them and how theory is used to plan various other components (e.g., the curriculum, instructional methodology, or instructional materials to be used). Follow-Through and HCEEP models subscribe to a number of basic theories of learning and development. Most lean heavily toward one view, although some borrow from several theories.

In reading some descriptions of models, a clearly defined theoretical position is not always apparent. Sometimes theoretical concepts receive little mention. This may be because the developer(s) has taken an eclectic point of view, drawing bits and pieces from several theoretical positions and fashioning them into his or her own unique philosophy. An eclectic position usually places greater emphasis upon *values* or some other component (such as curriculum) and less importance upon theory as the basis for the model.

The theoretical basis of a model is what Spodek (1973) called its assumptions or "basic givens." These include:

1. *Theoretical viewpoints concerning development.*
   - How does development occur? Is it the unfolding of capacities inherent within the child and dependent largely upon maturation? Or is it a function of environmental influences and learning?
   - Does development proceed in predictable, orderly stages, or does development proceed differently in every child based upon his or her own experiences and abilities?
   - What factors facilitate development or interfere with its progression? Do direct teaching and training facilitate development?

2. *Theoretical viewpoints concerning learning.*
   - What is learning, and how is it manifested by the learner? How does one go about helping children learn most efficiently? What kinds of educational experiences foster optimal learning?
   - What variables influence a child's ability to learn? What conditions facilitate, and which ones interfere with, skill acquisition?
   - What is the relationship between intelligent behavior and learning? Can instruction

The teacher presents this young learner with one set of materials in a series of instructional tasks that make up his cognitive skills curriculum. Some programs reflect an emphasis upon curriculum and very specific types of instructional materials as the focal point of the intervention model.

enhance intellectual capacities? What are the implications for children who have physical, sensory, or mental handicaps? Can they be taught? How?

Program models differ significantly in the basic assumptions or theoretical position from which they operate. In comparing the Follow-Through/Head Start Planned Variation models, Stanford Research Institute (1972) grouped models into clusters that represent four basic points of view: behavioristic, environmental, personal-social (psychodynamic), and genetic-maturationist.

Behavioristic point of view   Those who adhere to a behavioristic theoretical orientation contend that children develop and become what they are through complex stimulus-response interactions with their environment. The behavioristic position assumes that all behaviors are learned. Educational failure occurs when children do not acquire the specific preacademic, social, or developmental skills necessary for learning other skills. If these skills are to be learned, they must specifically be taught, because they will not emerge spontaneously. Learning, then, is achieved by identifying the specific objective to be attained, arranging appropriate stimuli to elicit the responses, programming learning sequences in small steps, and reinforcing the desired behaviors. Withholding reward or attention as a consequence for undesirable behavior will diminish and eventually eliminate it.

Educational programs based on behavior theory usually are meticulously planned. Goals and objectives are defined in observable behavioral terms for the program as a whole, as well as for the children. Instruction is highly individualized, based upon initial assessment of a child's baseline behavior or skills and defined by specific objectives stated in observable behavioral terms.

Environmental point of view   The environmental theoretical orientation sees the child as one who acts upon his or her own environment and learns best from direct experiences. Through direct interaction and manipulation of the environment, the child becomes progressively more skilled in basic developmental tasks and moves ahead to greater levels of cognitive competence. Early interactions are largely sensory experiences, but as a child matures physically, these give way to more complex forms of interaction with the environment. A child begins to internalize experiences, uses symbols to represent those experiences or to manipulate ideas, and employs language as a means for organizing experiences. Thinking processes begin to be manifest as the child discovers relationships and uses them to interact in more complex ways with the environment.

Educational programs based upon this theoretical orientation usually focus on the quality of the instructional environment and stress that it should be arranged to respond to the child's interests and individual level of ability. Education should provide opportunities, from which the child can choose, to interact with and explore the environment. Children usually are allowed to seek out their own activities within prescribed limits and to undertake projects that help them learn how to learn. Although instructional procedures used to operationalize this viewpoint vary, they usually focus on children as self-guided learners. Direct experience, experimentation, learning by discovery, and active participation through a variety of opportunities from which the child chooses what interests him or her most are viewed as important. Learning is facilitated most when children's level of cognitive competence matches the kinds of experiences available to them.

Personal-social (or psychodynamic) point of view   Human development and learning from the personal-social perspective are viewed as a mastery of impulses and appetites that are basically innate. Learning is the means by which the individual passes through various stages of personal and social growth until achieving maturity. The emotional crises that occur in each stage influence a child's skill acquisition and mastery over the environment. Programs that operate from this point of view place top priority upon children's emotional growth and stability, feelings of self-worth, self-expression, and self-image. Emphasis is placed on what educators should do to create a "supportive" learning environment that minimizes emotional upheavals and allows children to pursue conflict-free learning.

Instructional methods derived from this orientation focus upon the quality of interpersonal relationships and creation of an environment wherein a child can seek self-actualization. Children's freedom to select their own activities and pursue their own interests is especially critical. The premise is that "the child knows what is best" and is quite capable of determining what he or she needs for learning to occur. Teachers must not interfere with this process but are to follow the child's lead. Models based upon a psychodynamic point of view usually are less specific in defining instructional methodologies, giving more attention to describing what atmosphere should be created in the classroom and what kind of person a teacher should be in relation to the children.

Genetic-maturationist point of view   The genetic-maturationist position holds that human development is determined by genetic factors. Because development is governed largely by innate forces and physical maturation, the environment and experience are only of secondary concern. They simply serve to shape maturation and possibly may interfere if extreme conditions are introduced. Educational programs stemming from this perspective stress readiness for learning and self-expression in a supportive, nurturing environment. Instructional methods are designed to attract and create interest in the child rather than to compel or force involvement. The approach is based upon one basic rule: Give children a nurturing, stimulating, interesting environment, and they will learn through their own activities and develop according to whatever potential is inherent within them.

Irrespective of whether the theoretical assumptions underlying a model are determined through deliberate planning, no one can design an educational model or implement an instructional strategy without making some assumptions about learning and about human development. Whatever those assumptions are, they influence the approaches a teacher uses to facilitate learning.

The theoretical position one takes is especially important in the instruction of handicapped young children because handicapped children may not reach major developmental milestones simply as a matter of course. If left to their own interests, they will not necessarily explore and interact spontaneously with their environment in ways that promote learning. They will not acquire every important skill simply through their interactions with the natural environment in the same time frame as nonhandicapped children acquire them. If teachers merely wait for behaviors to emerge spontaneously by providing primarily an "enrichment" curriculum, as they might do for a normal child, handicapped children likely will fall farther and farther behind.

Educators who work with the handicapped often take a behavioristic/environmental point of view, suggesting that developmental skills are best learned through direct intervention, systematic teaching, and contingent reinforcement. Although reliance may be placed upon inherent learning capabilities and the simple "unfolding" of development in a normal child, to wait for a young handicapped child to manifest the same growth under similar conditions is considered risky. This is especially true when obvious impairments or at-risk conditions are known to interfere with a child's development and learning. The implication is that the theoretical position behind programs serving handicapped children, especially those with moderate to severe disabilities, has to be different from bases for serving nonhandicapped youngsters. *What works with a normally developing child is not necessarily best for a young handicapped child.*

Goals and objectives

Stated goals and program objectives comprise an essential part of a well formulated program model. Goals are typically more general than objectives because they define the broad intent of the overall program model. Objectives, on the other hand, are likely to be more specific because they state the desired outcomes with children. The values and philosophy underlying a model, combined with whatever theoretical orientation(s) one embraces, provide the basis for defining its goals and objectives. A program's intent is summarized in its statement of purpose and its goals. These consist of both long-term and short-term goals, with the accompanying questions:

1. *Long-term goals.*
   - What are the broad, long-term goals the program seeks to achieve for the community, the children being served, or any other individuals who are targets of the service?
   - What broad skills and child outcomes does the program seek to attain with the children who participate?

2. *Short-term goals.*
   - What steps (action steps) must be taken to achieve the long-term program goals? What are the intermediate goals and objectives?
   - What short-term achievements are children to make in order to reach the long-term objectives?

In defining objectives for a model, some educators use a different terminology, referring instead to *product or performance objectives* as the long-term or terminal goals. *Process objectives* are the short-term goals or action steps to be taken to reach the terminal goals. A model's goals and objectives typically reflect its own set of values and theoretical foundations defined in earlier components. Theories and values in themselves, however, do not dictate goals. How theory is translated into goals and instructional practices requires good judgment, planning, and drawing out implications of theory to prescribe classroom procedures. Goals are thus derived when the model developer draws inferences from theoretical points of view, and implications for practices from a set of values. These, then, provide the basis for drafting a statement of goals and objectives for a program model.

Programs differ greatly in what they state as major goals and objectives. Stebbins et al. (1977), in analyzing the Follow-Through and Head Start Planned Variation models, found they could be clustered into three major types in terms of these basic goals:

1. *Basic skills emphasis.* Many models have goals stressing program activities that teach

children basic developmental competencies (e.g., language, motor, self-help, preacademic) or academic skills (e.g., reading, arithmetic, spelling).

2. *Cognitive-conceptual emphasis.* Some models define goals that emphasize processes as outcomes rather than mastery of specific content. Goals and objectives may focus on thinking skills, problem-solving skills, and learning how to learn.

3. *Affective-cognitive emphasis.* Another group of models stresses neither subject areas/developmental competencies nor process skills. Rather, goals and objectives focus upon outcomes in terms of attitudes, experiences, personal traits, and feelings. Secondary emphasis is given to strengthening cognitive abilities or thinking skills.

Although the classification of goals and objectives set forth here relates primarily to those for the child, its authors note that program objectives additionally may define outcomes that span more than what children are to learn. Long- and short-term goals may be defined in regard to (a) benefits and outcomes for parents as caregivers and teachers of their own children, and (b) goals for the program as a coordinator of services and a mechanism for social change in the community.

Day (1977) suggested another set of criteria on which goals and objectives for educational models differ: (a) their *emphasis upon content or process*, (b) their *specificity*, and (c) their *breadth*. Some models are *content-oriented* in that they emphasize mastery of a body of information, facts, or concepts by the child or other target of services. In a sense, this parallels what we also have called the *basic skills orientation*. The Kansas Behavioral Analysis Model, the Engelmann/Becker Model for Direct Instruction, and the Portage Project are examples of models with a content emphasis. *Process-oriented* goals and objectives, in contrast, focus upon processes of thinking, problem solving, and conceptualizing, with less attention to the specific subject matter used in mastering these processes. Several models described in this chapter have objectives that reflect this process orientation, including the High Scope Cognitively-Oriented Model, the Tuscon Early Education Model (TEEM), and the University of Illinois PEECH Project Model.

In the second criterion, *specificity*, "specific" means that goals and objectives define outcomes in terms of observable, measurable phenomena. Behaviorally oriented models value explicitly stated objectives. In fact, their objectives represent a task analysis of the steps required for the program or for the children involved to reach their terminal goals. In contrast, models with an affective/cognitive emphasis, including some that have a cognitive/conceptual emphasis, are often less behavioral in their statement of objectives, and therefore probably less specific in their definition of outcomes.

The final criterion, *breadth*, refers to how many different types of achievements are considered within the domain of the model (and thus are included in its statement of goals and objectives). How broad are curriculum objectives? How many different services are offered, and what objectives are set for each of them? How many different targets of service are being considered, and what short- and long-term goals are they to achieve? Programs differ considerably on this dimension. The important point is that the goals and objectives for some models are narrowly defined while others provide broad definitions of the short- and long-term outcomes. Most of the HCEEP models described earlier contain a set of objectives that are much broader than those in the Follow-Through models. This is principally because the HCEEP projects represent comprehensive service programs for handicapped children under school age whereas the Follow-Through programs are based on instructional models piggy-backed on top of existing elementary school programs.

Services and service delivery approaches

Every program model encompasses its own unique menu of services for children, their parents, or the community, and every model features its own service delivery strategies. As discussed in chapter 8, this component defines a model in terms of:

— *who* is the primary target(s) of service.
— *when* educational service or early intervention begins.
— *what* types of services are offered.
— *where* or in what settings services are carried out.
— *by whom* services are delivered (who is the primary intervention or educational agent).
— *with whom* services are offered (the social context in the classroom or setting where services are offered).
— *through whom* services are delivered (what agencies or departments within an organization are to assume responsibility for delivering services).

Because each of these elements was described at length in chapter 8, they will not be discussed again here. You may want to go back to the descriptions of the HCEEP and Follow-Through models and compare them on the who, when, what, where, by whom, with whom, and through whom types of questions. Then you will see just how creative people can be in designing service delivery approaches!

Curriculum and materials

All educational models are designed ultimately to enhance the development and learning of children. The actual curriculum and what is to be taught to children to achieve this end constitute another issue that model developers must confront. After curricular areas have been defined, the question of whether equal attention shall be given to all areas or if higher priority shall be given to certain ones has to be addressed. Once the basic curriculum has been determined and priorities set, instructional materials must be selected. What types of materials will implement the curriculum best and maintain the basic values and philosophy, theoretical orientation, and goals and objectives of the model? This component within a model is especially important because it *defines* what children are to be taught—specifically:

1. *Competencies to be taught to (or acquired by) the child or target of services.*
   • What skills/competencies does the model emphasize? To what degree will the curriculum emphasize *content* as the focus of learning activities or learning/thinking processes? How flexible is the curriculum?
   • What developmental areas (e.g., motor development, cognitive development, language development, social-emotional development, self-help) are emphasized? Are selected subject areas (e.g., science, math, preacademics, music, art, dramatics) to be a formal part of the curriculum?
   • How is the curriculum organized? Are activities organized to integrate all curricular areas, such as in class projects and functional daily living tasks? Or is curriculum organized into topical units, developmental emphasis areas, or some other system?

2. *Types of instructional materials.*
   - What types of child and teacher materials are needed to implement the chosen curriculum? What criteria are used to select materials?
   - Are materials of a type that children and teachers can use flexibly, or must materials be used in prescribed ways?

We have already discussed how models differ in their philosophical and value systems, theoretical underpinnings, and consequently the types of goals and objectives they embrace. These same differences are carried on into the curriculum designs of those models. One critical factor that influences curriculum, especially in models used with handicapped children, is the nature of that population—the age level and the nature of the disabilities. In their examination of a number of HCEEP models from the standpoint of curriculum, Wood and Hurley (1977) found five basic curricular approaches or emphases:

1. *Amelioration of deficits approach*: based upon children's problems or deficits and what curriculum is necessary to remediate those deficits. Content for the curriculum is based upon an assessment of each child's problems or deficiencies. Terms such as *remedial, compensatory, rehabilitative, prescriptive,* or *behavioral analysis* may be used to describe the curriculum.
2. *Educational content areas approach*: based on a scheme defining the areas in which it is believed children should have experiences or *basic skills* that children should master. This usually encompasses academic content areas such as reading, math, language, writing, and spelling for older children. Content areas for younger children may include prereading, music, story-time, social studies, nature, art, dance (body movement), and dramatic play.
3. *Basic skills approach*: based on skills children use in the learning *process*, such as language, sensory processes (auditory and visual), memory, problem solving, gross motor and fine motor skills. Curricula are organized around activities that encourage development of these process skills.
4. *Developmental tasks approach*: based upon *normal sequences* of human development in areas of fine and gross motor, speech and language, cognitive, social learning, and self-help and independence. Curriculum begins from hierarchical sequences of tasks, skills, or content derived from one of two sources: (a) normative information on how children develop, or (b) developmental analyses of skills based upon estimates of the chronological age or sequence in which the skills emerge.
5. *Psychological constructs approach*: based upon a *theoretical framework* about what elements facilitate learning and development of the whole child. Curriculum built from some psychological constructs often emphasizes one or more of the following themes: self-concept, creativity, primary mental abilities, cognition, need gratification, or self-identity. Instructional activities are created to foster the development of these psychological constructs in the child and hence to pave the way for other learning to occur. Rarely is a curriculum based solely upon this particular orientation; it most often is combined with other approaches.

Instructional methodology

Instructional methods represent one of the most visible parts of a model. Were you to visit a preschool or primary classroom where a model is being used, you undoubtedly would look for evidence of what makes that classroom different from any other. You would watch to see how the teacher interacts with the children and what he or she does to "teach." You would note the kinds of activities in which individual children engage and what the teacher views as good work. Most of all, you probably would watch to see what responses children are making and what tasks they are doing in order to learn.

Instructional techniques and teaching style are the very heart of some program models. Elaborate instructions are given to guide teachers on how to go about implementing curriculum, interacting with children, and preparing materials. Other models do not prescribe instructional methods per se but instead place emphasis on the values and philosophy underlying classroom instruction as they should be manifest in what teachers and children do. This implies that a certain "atmosphere" of learning must be created in the classroom and provides some general principles from which teachers work. Specific methods of teaching, however, are left to the teacher's preferences, creativity, and style.

No matter how elaborately detailed, the instructional methodology of a model can encompass these important dimensions:

1. *The nature of the teacher's role in the classroom.*
   - To what degree does the teacher control children's ongoing activities? Where is the locus of control between the teacher as leader and initiator in the instructional process and the child as determiner of his or her own needs and learning style?
   - To what extent does the teacher assume responsibility for determining what individual children need to learn and how they will spend their time?
   - What style of interaction does the teacher use in interacting with children? What kind of work atmosphere is created in the classroom during instructional/work times?

2. *The nature of the child's role in the classroom.*
   - To what extent are children free to initiate their own activities and select their own style of learning?
   - What behaviors should children exhibit as learners? What is considered appropriate classroom behavior? What kinds of responses should they be making as they engage in learning activities? To whom or to what should these responses be made?

3. *The nature of the instructional process, including use of materials.*
   - What is the typical daily schedule for the children? To what degree are daily schedules and teaching itself arranged around group needs versus individual needs? How flexible is the daily schedule?
   - Are children grouped some way for instructional activities? If so, what is the basis for that grouping?
   - To what extent are learning activities and children's modes of using materials and making responses structured? Are desired responses narrowly or broadly defined? To what degree are instructional activities didactic or discovery-oriented?
   - What methods, if any, are used to motivate children? Is any system for rewarding good behavior and handling inappropriate behavior specified?

Because models show differences and similarities on so many instructional dimensions, to summarize them all here is not possible. Attempts have been made to create taxonomies for classifying instructional procedures (Bissell, 1971; Emrick, Sorensen, & Stearns, 1973; Lambie, Bond, & Weikart, 1975; Day, 1977; Parker & Day, 1977; Stebbins,

St. Pierre, Proper, Anderson, & Cerva, 1977). But no single system accounts for all potential variations. Most key variables that distinguish instructional techniques represent dichotomies on which programs take some position along a continuum. To describe some of the potential dimensions along which instructional methods may vary, several key variables are defined briefly in Figure 9.2.

Child assessment/program evaluation procedures

What mechanisms are used within a model to determine whether its goals and objectives are being met? What evaluation/assessment procedures are specified as a working part of the model? Formalized models typically have some built-in methods for conducting one or more (and ideally all) of the assessment processes described in chapter 7. As you will recall, those assessment processes include: (a) casefinding, (b) screening, (c) diagnostic evaluation, (d) educational assessment, (e) ongoing performance monitoring, and (f) overall program evaluation. In a well conceptualized model, evaluation is not happenstance; it is planned right along with the goals and objectives, curriculum, and instructional methodology components. A model must have objective evidence of its effectiveness. All models require some means for teachers to assess if children are learning and making progess. This component thus encompasses some very crucial aspects:

1. *Assessment procedures with the child.*
   - What assessment procedures or tests are used to identify and screen children enrolled in the model program?
   - What child assessment procedures (if any) are used for planning curriculum or prescribing individual instructional programs? What instruments or procedures are used? How often are assessments made, and by whom?
   - How is children's progress on short-term goals assessed? What information is used to make this assessment?
   - What measures are used to evaluate children's overall gains? What child behaviors are evaluated as an index of child progress? When and by whom is this evaluation done?

2. *Evaluation of overall program success.*
   - How is the program's achievement of its overall goals to be evaluated? What criteria are used as indicators of the program's effectiveness?
   - What assessment instruments are used and what information is gathered to evaluate program effectiveness?

The important thing in describing this model component is not to point out the various approaches one can take or to show how models differ in evaluative techniques. They may differ significantly or may use similar evaluation techniques. The point here is that *internal consistency* between and among each of the component parts of a model is critical in the development of a strong evaluation component. If values and philosophy, theoretical orientation, goals and objectives, and all other subsequent components of a model that lead to this one are defined, free choice among all potential methods of evaluation does not exist. The method of evaluation should be compatible and in harmony with other parts of the model. Thus, all previous components of a model dictate largely *what should be evaluated, what styles or processes* of evaluation are most compatible

Figure 9.2
Dimensions for Variation in Instructional Methodologies

Teacher-Directed ------------ vs. ------------ **Child-Directed**

The degree to which the teacher determines how children spend their time, selects, and then orchestrates the tasks they undertake *versus* the degree to which children assume these responsibilities and make decisions for themselves.

Teacher as Initiator ------------ vs. ------------ **Teacher as Responder**

The degree to which the teacher's role is defined as one of initiating, directing, evaluating, and terminating children's activities *versus* a definition of the teacher's role as one of following the children's lead, reflecting and clarifying their experiences, and acting as an aide and resource to the children.

Children as Responders ------------ vs. ------------ **Children as Initiators**

The degree to which children are expected to respond to tasks predefined both in content and in response mode by the teacher or by the instructional materials they use *versus* the degree to which children are free to initiate their own learning, choose from among many alternatives, and pursue their own styles of learning.

Programmed Instructional ------------ vs. ------------ **Open Instructional**
Framework   **Framework**

The degree to which instructional processes must follow a carefully planned step-by-step sequence designed to lead children to specifically defined behavioral outcomes *versus* the degree to which instruction is activity-oriented, in which children experiment, question, explore, and thereby engage in processes out of which learning occurs.

Extrinsic Motivation ------------ vs. ------------ **Intrinsic Motivation**
and Reward System   **and Reward System**

The degree to which external, tangible rewards (e.g., tokens, praise, edibles, privileges, or special activities) are used to motivate children's learning *versus* the degree to which reliance is placed upon learning for the sake of learning and children's own intrinsic motivation to learn.

High-Structure ------------ vs. ------------ **Low-Structure**
Instructional   **Instructional**
Methodology   **Methodology**

The degree to which teacher behaviors are predetermined by the model and set into prescribed roles *versus* the degree to which teachers are free to act on the basis of their own feelings, educational philosophy, and intuitions, provided they are congruent with the overall goals of the model.

Didactic, ------------ vs. ------------ **Experiential, Discovery-Oriented**
Drill-Oriented

The degree to which learning is fostered through drill and repetitious practice of specific skills *versus* the degree to which learning is promoted through direct experience with functional tasks that promote discovery learning and experimentation.

Individualized Teaching ------------ vs. ------------ **Teaching to Groups**

The degree to which instruction is based upon an analysis of what individual children need and is delivered accordingly *versus* the degree to which instruction is oriented toward the needs of the group as a whole.

with the theoretical orientation and instructional approach, and *what criterion* should be used to determine "success" on the part of the program and the children.

Educators sometimes approach the task of planning evaluation procedures without first looking at other components in the model program. They may be inclined to start right off with the question, "What tests shall we use?" Or they may make the mistake of simply picking a battery of tests that "looks good." What may appear to be a reasonable selection of age-appropriate tests may end up being disappointing, especially if they test skills and behaviors that children were not taught because they were not considered important in the model. Good evaluation plans or components thus can be threatened by several "traps" in which teachers/administrators or children themselves get caught without systematic planning of an evaluation component. Some of those traps are:

Trap #1   Lack of agreement between the model's goals as stated and the goals that are assessed as an indicator of program and child success.

Trap #2   Absence of agreement on the criteria for "success." What the model emphasizes as important (as implied or stated in its values/ philosophy, theoretical approach, curriculum, and teaching methods) is different from skills/behaviors assessed by the kind of data being collected.

Trap #3   Assessment procedures that require child behaviors and response patterns very different from those encouraged and taught in the educational setting. Thus, children are expected to do their best and demonstrate competency through modes of behavior unfamiliar to them.

Trap #4   Lack of continuity within the model—between the program's goals and what then are used as curriculum and instructional methodologies. When goals/objectives stress something different than do curriculum and teaching procedures, conflict exists in what should be assessed. If evaluation is based on the stated goals, it will not assess what really is being taught. On the other hand, if evaluation is based upon what actually is being taught, it does not assess whether the program and the children are meeting the intended goals and objectives. Sometimes these discrepancies are not immediately apparent to staff, but evaluation results may be confusing and frustrating to personnel when their efforts are being assessed.

In summary, four critical features of the child assessment/program evaluation component should be noted in planning a model or examining an existing model for possible adoption. *First*, evaluation procedures should be in harmony with the values, philosophy, and theoretical framework of a model. If evaluative methods are used to make comparisons across programs that differ in philosophy, and hence measure skills not valued in a particular model, this discrepancy should be noted because it will influence how results should be interpreted. *Second*, the goals and objectives of a model and its curriculum provide the basis for deciding what should be assessed, and how. *Third*, whether norm-referenced or criterion-referenced assessment tools are used depends upon what criteria are selected to ascertain children's "progress" and "success." Curriculum, to some degree, should affect the choice of assessment tools since what is taught is what should be evaluated. *Fourth*, the degree to which instruments and procedures should be used to measure behaviors such as attitudes, psychological constructs (e.g., intelligence, creativity, self-concept), basic skills, or developmental status goes back to the basic values, goals, and objectives of the model.

Staff composition, organization, and roles

This component and the remaining two (staff training, and required facilities and other resources) relate to the practical considerations and logistics involved in implementing a model. Models may show many similarities in how these three components are defined, although some differences may be apparent. This is where the "reality test" begins. How many staff members are required to implement this model? Who are they? What will they cost? What expertise must they have? What other resources are needed to put this model into operation and make it work well? These practical considerations often determine whether a specific model actually can be implemented at a particular site.

Program models may define their own unique staffing pattern and organizational structure, although many are designed to fit into existing structures in elementary school or preschool settings. Some redefinition of staff roles may be necessary. How this component is defined rests ideally on how all previous components in the model are designed. The goals and objectives, services, and service delivery approach dictate what personnel are needed, and how many. The theoretical framework, curriculum, and instructional methodology to be applied affect the level of training and expertise required by staff. Staffing patterns, too, are influenced by the number of children and their ages, handicapping conditions, and the needs of their families.

This component, then, defines the management system for implementing the model, including how the staff is organized to work effectively as a team. It requires designation of:

1. *Staff expertise and assigned responsibilities.*
   - What types of staff are needed to carry out the program model as defined in each of the other model components? What skills/experiences/personal qualities must staff members have?
   - What job responsibilities and roles are assumed by each staff member? In what settings and with whom are these roles carried out?

2. *Administrative/staff management procedures.*
   - What are the lines of authority within the staff? Who is responsible for supervising whom, and how? Who is to coordinate with whom, and when? What methods are used to supervise and provide feedback to staff?
   - Who makes decisions regarding program/classroom operations? On what basis are decisions made, and which staff members are to have input?
   - What are the lines of communication within the program staff? With parents and those being served by the program? With outsiders who have no direct relationship to the program?
   - Is an advisory board part of the program? If so, what is its purpose, and what are the roles of its members?

A well developed model usually specifies the content of this component through (a) job descriptions for each staff member; (b) an organization chart showing lines of authority, supervisory relationships, and lines of communication; (c) formally written program policies defining how operations are to be run, criteria for making important kinds of decisions; and formalized procedures for carrying out certain administrative functions; and (d) a set of operational procedures (often communicated by word-of-mouth) describing how daily or ongoing program operations are to be managed. This includes a designation of what meetings are to be held, how and when planning sessions are to be held, and how the staff is to coordinate activities.

Staff training and preparation

Because of the unique qualities and approaches that characterize program models, staff members must have not only the basic training that qualifies them for their specific disciplinary roles, but also training in the particular procedures of the model. A model based upon a behavioral approach that applies behavior modification procedures with children requires a staff schooled in behavioral techniques. If special materials or teaching strategies are an important feature of a model, the staff must be prepared to use those materials and carry out particular teaching approaches competently. Staff training is the means for preparing people for their roles within the model and for assuring that the integrity of the model is maintained and implemented according to plan. The staff training component thus involves:

1. *Preliminary orientation and training with the model.*
   - What information about the model is given *before* the staff begins implementation? What skills/competencies are required from the beginning? What kind of preservice training is necessary to assure that the staff is prepared to implement the model correctly?
   - What method of training is used to prepare the staff to implement the model? What kinds of materials are used in the training process?

2. *Inservice training on model implementation for participating staff.*
   - What kind of follow-up and continued training are needed? How frequently should inservice training occur?
   - What strategies are used to provide feedback to staff members on their own progress in implementing the model and to allow continuous refinement of the model as it is being implemented? What means are used to maintain the "purity" of the model and its principles?

Well prepared, enthusiastic staff members are ultimately what make a program work. Staff preparation to implement a model is a key link in its successful operation. Ideally, some preliminary orientation and staff training occur prior to implementation, continuing on a regular basis as inservice training. In reality, models often are not that well developed ahead of time. Only those with a long history of development have sophisticated preservice training. In most cases, training must proceed as the model is being developed and implemented.

Staff training for early childhood-special education programs presents a special challenge. Teachers must be skillful not only in working with young children but with all types of handicapping conditions, and possibly all levels of severity. In an ideal situation, each staff member would have a background in both child development or early childhood education and special education. Preservice training through universities, however, does not always produce people with this dual background. Therefore, inservice training must augment the missing training and experience in these key areas. Often, the training needs of staff members vary so widely that individual plans are best worked out by the person in charge of training. Staff members within a program, consultants, or auxiliary therapists can share information in their areas of speciality. Or outside courses at colleges and universities and special consultants might provide resources for staff members to acquire new skills. Parents can help in training sessions to raise staff awareness about parent needs and effective ways for parents and professionals to work together.

Required resources and facilities

This final component of a model is significant inasmuch as it determines, in part, how costly and how practical an idealized model plan really is. All other components of a model described thus far dictate what kinds of resources must be available. If these resources cannot actually be provided, the model becomes limited—sometimes necessitating compromises or redesign of the model into a less elaborate one. When resources needed to implement a model in its ideal form are lacking, one solution may be to give certain components higher priority and to place less emphasis on other components. This works for some models, but in other models, components are so interlinked that to change or eliminate one would destroy much of the model's integrity and strength and probably would alter its effectiveness. Required resources and facilities, then, constitute an important consideration in designing a model. This includes the following types of provisions:

1. *Required classroom facilities.*
   - What physical space (classrooms, clinic space, or home-based facilities) is needed to implement the program as defined in each of the other components? Are specific environmental features crucial for implementation of the model?
   - How is space organized? That is, if the program is implemented in a classroom setting, how should it be arranged physically?

2. *Required instructional materials, supplies, and equipment.*
   - What curricular materials, toys, supplies, or special equipment are crucial to model implementation? What materials/equipment are recommended but of second priority?
   - What assessment instruments and materials and what teacher materials are required? Again, which materials are a necessity, and which ones are useful but not essential?

3. *Additional manpower needs.*
   - What additional manpower requirements, beyond those provided through initial program staff, are required to implement the model? If additional manpower sources are needed, how are these arranged?
   - What are the criteria for selection?

In regard to facilities, program models often prescribe two requirements. *First*, they prescribe the particular type of service facility. In what kind of setting is the program to be implemented? What kind of and how much space is needed? Are classrooms designed for very young children, including adjacent bathrooms with fixtures at heights appropriate for 3- to 4-year-old children? Are clinic facilities with a large number of individual work spaces available for one-on-one training if needed? *Second*, program models may prescribe how the physical facilities, particularly classroom settings, are to be organized. One program model may require a classroom structure in which several learning centers are set up around the room. Another may specify a more open classroom where specific learning and instructional areas are not particularly distinguishable.

The resources necessary to deliver special programs for young handicapped children are numerous. In addition to instructional supplies and equipment, the staff is generally considered to be a most critical resource. Many of the different types of roles and staff positions that may be required have been described already. In addition, special circumstances dictate a need for even more kinds of experience and expertise. For instance, a bilingual Hispanic social worker may be of key importance to one project. A trusted long-time resident of an area where services for young handicapped children are new may be helpful in identifying children with handicaps and in getting their parents to bring them to the program for assessment.

School systems and other agencies may not be accustomed to the wide variety of staff expertise and low child-staff ratios needed in some early childhood programs. Since schools have focused only on the needs of students beginning at kindergarten and have created policies dealing with the needs of a more mature population, they may not perceive the needs of young children as different from those of older children.

Programs for young children, especially the handicapped, can be expensive, but alternative ways of generating manpower, materials, and service resources are possible while keeping costs within a defined limit. Program models can augment the staff by utilizing volunteers, older students, and parents. To obtain appropriate staff expertise, some agencies use what is called *time-sharing*, in which each agency contributes a part of its own resources to hire a full-time speech therapist or social worker who then provides services across several participating agencies. In some areas, educational service centers work with sizable regions, sharing experts that individual schools could not afford alone.

In summary, program models often are developed as ideals, which are shaped as the staff gains experience through implementing the model. Plans may be modified considerably during the initial years of a model's development as the ideal plan is balanced with what is feasible in actual operation. This testing period is the very purpose for which various federal agencies fund demonstration or experimental models. Through trial implementation of a conceptualized model, the original plan can be modified, ideas can be tested to see if they work as intended, and a balance can be found between the ideal model and what can realistically be implemented in a typical program setting.

THE RATIONALE FOR USING A PROGRAM MODEL

You may be asking, "What is the value of using a model approach in delivering educational programs to children? Why would one want to develop a program model or use a model developed by someone else?" Robert L. Egbert, former National Director of Follow-Through, and his co-author (Egbert & Brisch, 1979) examined the advantages of educational models and noted, "There is a special kind of beauty, integrity, and utility in educational models derived from a single philosophical/psychological perspective." Models, they suggested, are easier to understand, easier to work within, and easier to explain to others. In addition, educational models are more likely to produce unified, coherent, and consistent results in children than are eclectic programs that do not adhere to any single unified approach.

Centers may apply the program model approach in two possible ways. *First*, a model that already has been developed and tested in another site may be adopted. Models developed through the Handicapped Children's Early Education Program or through Follow-Through and Head Start Planned Variation represent a wide variety of alternative models from which to choose. When selecting an existing model, the model must match the conditions and needs of the community in which it will be used. The values, theoretical bases, goals and objectives should be compatible. The population to be served and the availability of resources at the new site also must match those of the model. A *second* strategy for adopting a model is for a center to develop its own model. The staff can work through the process of defining each component, developing procedures for each component, and developing or selecting appropriate materials for the program.

Sites that choose to adopt a model that already has been developed and tested by another center benefit in at least three ways:

1. Use of an existing model can save time. Building a quality model with all of its component parts is an arduous task, and not one that can be accomplished in a few hours, weeks, or even months. Full development, refinement, and operationalization of a model may require several years. For example, federal projects funded for the specific purpose of developing and demonstrating a program model are typically 3 years in duration.
2. Educators who select an existing model benefit from knowing, prior to implementation, the effectiveness of a model and its major outcomes. In developing one's own new program model, outcomes are not yet clear, and several years of program development and implementation are necessary to ascertain the efficacy of that new approach. The effectiveness of tested models is already known. These data can be used in selecting a model that is best for a particular community.
3. Adopting an existing model—if it approximates the approach a new program is to take—can reduce duplication of effort. Many communities have similar needs and operate similar programs. If procedures and materials already have been developed for a particular program approach, investing money and staff time to "reinvent the wheel" seems pointless. Materials, guidelines for implementing programs, and other products are often already available for use. In addition, the original model developers can be contacted for technical assistance and advice in setting up and operating a program.

Or, if the staff of a center decides to develop its own program model, another set of advantages comes into play:

1. Unique community values and needs, along with unique characteristics of the population of children to be served, may favor an original program model designed to precisely match community values and needs.
2. Some communities or individual centers have the expertise, resources, and staff that would suggest the potential of providing leadership for others in the field and, in fact, developing their own models. This may be particularly appropriate when experienced, seasoned people have worked together for some time and already have begun to develop a formalized program model.
3. Staff participation in developing a model may cause staff members to identify with

their model and thereby increase their investment in its success. It also may increase the chances for strong community support. This assumption, however, should not be used as an overriding argument for developing a new program model. Involvement offers an opportunity for input from the entire staff in the planning process, but it does not necessarily guarantee more support for the final product.

The argument that staff will be more informed and will present a better level of understanding of a model by participating in its development, as opposed to adopting some other model, is not necessarily true. Just as developing a model from scratch takes time, so does educating a staff about an existing model. If an existing model is adopted, steps must be taken to provide the staff with an orientation to the model and training on how to implement it. If this is accomplished, a similar level of understanding and competency can be achieved with either an original model or an adopted model. Educators at the local level must determine whether "ownership" of a model is an issue and truly an advantage.

From the foregoing discussion, the merits of using a formal program model may be apparent. The question of what value a formal model has for the individual teacher also arises. Does adherence to a single program model help the individual teacher work more efficiently with children? Consider the following teachers:

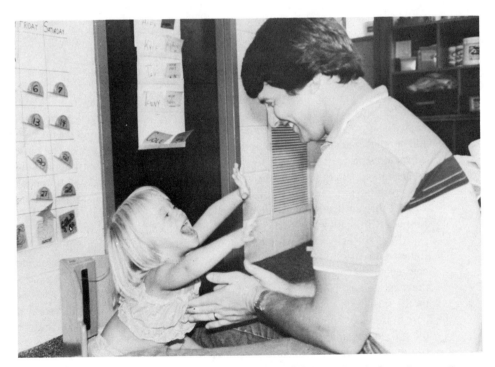

Jesse will get a big hug from the speech pathologist for her good work. Some intervention models place emphasis on reinforcement and other specific teaching strategies that should be used with young children.

Joan Finch is a preschool teacher of some 12 years. Her experience extends across several different preschool settings, where she has worked with a wide variety of children—disadvantaged, handicapped, and so-called normal. She is known by her colleagues as a seasoned teacher and often is sought out for ideas and advice. Her classroom reflects her own confidence and skill in carrying out a rather extensive curriculum program for the young children she teaches. She has many good ideas about what works and what does not work in teaching preschool children. What purpose would a formalized program model serve for her?

Mark Downs, a new teacher fresh out of college, was eager to tackle his first job as a teacher of handicapped 3- to 5-year-olds. Energetic and full of ideas, he could hardly wait to try out the things he had gathered during his university training. At first he was a bit overwhelmed with the task of getting everything planned and in operation during the first few months of school. His ideal had been to develop the kind of classroom he often had envisioned in discussions in his university classes. During Mark's first few weeks of school, however, he learned quickly that his task was more massive than he had anticipated.

Mark now works long hours each day after the children are gone, to develop the instructional programs, materials, and teaching procedures for his program. Would he gain any benefits by becoming involved in implementation of an already developed and validated early childhood model, or in working with other members of his school staff to develop a model program for the center where he works?

For teachers so different in background and expertise as Joan and Mark, what are the benefits of using the model approach? Wouldn't Mark and Joan and teachers like them be better off taking materials, teaching strategies, and curriculum from any available source and organizing them in their own unique curriculum program for children? One might argue that since no single approach is best, the most efficient strategy for designing educational programs is to pull together pieces and parts from other programs or theoretical frameworks that are most attractive. By taking the best from many different approaches, the resulting program might allow greater flexibility, and yet greater strength, in its content than in using only one approach. This type of reasoning, or the absence of any formalized principles and goals for a program, often has resulted in the *eclectic approach*.

Does the eclectic approach constitute a viable option for educating young children? Egbert and Brisch (1979) addressed this question in an article on singularity versus eclecticism in early childhood education. They suggested that although the strategy of drawing the best from several different approaches appears reasonable and open-minded on the surface, it is not as logical as it may seem. The individual program that takes the best from many approaches implies that each model has been studied carefully to select the procedures and materials that collectively build a program superior to any of those from which material was borrowed. This typically is not the case. According to Egbert and Brisch, a "trans-theoretical" approach may be an excuse for not fully mastering any single model, let alone a variety of ideas and models. This practice likely will lead to confusion of goals, and probably to less effective instruction:

By taking a piece from this model and a bit from that one, the educator assumes that instructional models are analogous to extremely simple mechanical models, and that if the various parts are selected carefully, they can be assembled into a neatly fitting, perfectly operating unit. But an instructional model is much more complex than even a sophisticated mechanical model such as an automobile, in which parts are not interchangeable across models. The bits and pieces from different instructional models, derived as they are from varying philosophies, will not necessarily operate effectively when put together. Indeed, a material or a procedure ideally adapted to one model may be so foreign to a basic value of another model that its use in the second model will prove counter-productive. (Egbert & Brisch, 1979, p. 30)

For teachers like Joan and Mark in the vignettes, informed versus uninformed eclecticism has important implications. Some individuals may have seriously studied alternative theoretical positions and have sufficient experience to analyze materials and then pull together those that are indeed compatible. These persons may be in a better position than a less informed individual to assume the eclectic position. To become competent and properly prepared in the eclectic approach is more demanding than to become competent in the operation of just one model. The easy road, if it represents a sound educational approach, is not the eclectic approach. Rather, application of a model that is compatible with the values and philosophy of a community and a program staff is perhaps the better route to a more unified, theoretically compatible set of program procedures (Egbert & Brisch. 1979).

Computer technology is being used in some innovative program models for early intervention. Computers offer new ways for helping children with severe physical impairments to interact with their environment and even to communicate with others.

SUMMARY

The field of EC-SPED is unique in that many of its services in communities around the country have been planned and organized around a formalized program model. Programs for young children funded under the Handicapped Children's Early Education Program (HCEEP) Act, and under the Follow-Through/Head Start Planned Variation Experiment all have been developed through a models approach.

A *program model* is a carefully developed blueprint or plan outlining the content and methodology for all components that make up the special services offered by a center to handicapped/at-risk young children and their families. A program model is based upon a well defined set of values, philosophy, and theoretical viewpoint about child development, education, and what a meaningful intervention must entail to help handicapped children. Specific goals and objectives are set, and each component of the model then is developed to achieve the defined objectives. The remaining components of a program model are: the services and service delivery approach; curriculum and materials; instructional methodology; child assessment/program evaluation procedures; staff composition, organization, and roles; staff training and preparation; and the required resources and facilities.

All components of a model must fit together in a coherent way and reflect an internal consistency in that all parts adhere to the same philosophy, focus upon the same objectives, and collectively provide the means for achieving defined outcomes. Further, a well designed program model has been tried and tested and has some measure of how well it works and if it succeeds in achieving the outcomes it claims.

Understanding program models and their component parts can be helpful in several ways. Information about the various models in operation today can be used in designing one's own community programs. If someone else has already developed effective procedures that can be adopted in one's home program, one doesn't have to start from scratch. Existing models provide useful ideas for planning new early intervention programs. Some centers actually select and replicate an existing model that another center program has developed and tested. In lieu of that, an understanding of the component parts of an exemplary model provides a framework for systematically planning and organizing one's own program.

The task of developing a quality early intervention program can be overwhelming given the complex needs of this young population and the service delivery alternatives (described in chapter 8) from which one can choose. But such an enormous task can be simplified by proceeding systematically, component by component, to plan a new program. A working knowledge of the component parts of a quality program thus can be most helpful to EC-SPED personnel who must develop effective programs for young children.

10
Parenting the Young Handicapped and At-Risk Child

While parents or primary caregivers play a central and crucial part in shaping any child's young life, caregivers of children with handicaps or at-risk conditions—which increase the chances their development will be irregular—must provide even more nurturance and special training if the children are to have an optimal chance to live as normal lives as possible. Burton White (1975), a renowned expert on early development, concluded from his extensive research that a child's own family is critical to achievement and developmental outcome in the first few years. In his book *The First Three Years of Life,* he stated:

. . . the informal education that families provide for their children makes more of an impact on a child's total educational development than the formal education system. If a family does its job well, the professional can then provide effective training. If not, there may be little the professional can do to save the child from mediocrity. (p. 4)

Effective parenting is not an easy task, nor is it one for which new parents are adequately prepared. White pointed out the irony that despite the tremendous impact parents have upon their children, society pays little attention to preparing its citizens for their parenting roles. Until a person faces the day-to-day demands of child rearing, few prospective parents fully realize the magnitude of that commitment or the changes parenthood will bring to their lives.

Fortunately, parents are initiated gradually into their caregiving roles. Pregnancy itself offers a time to psychologically prepare for the changes in family structure and new responsibilities (financial, temporal, and psychological) that the infant will bring. After birth, the neonates only gradually impose their presence and make their demands known. During the first weeks of life, a newborn sleeps most of the time, with intermittent periods of wakefulness for feeding and brief interactions with caregivers. Yet, the infant and caregivers are beginning a reciprocal interaction that is the foundation for an increasingly complex, intricate relationship. As the child grows and acquires a more varied behavioral repertoire, his or her needs become greater. This is turn places new demands upon parents' time and child-rearing competencies. Effective parenting demands an understanding of child development and behavior. As the child becomes more socially skillful and seeks out new experiences within the environment, caregivers must exercise sensitivity to the child's capabilities. In doing so, they mediate their child's experiences by adjusting them to a level commensurate with the child's abilities. This helps the child cope successfully and gain new levels of emotional, social, and cognitive competence.

Over time, parent-child interactions expand into increasingly more complex and extended chains of behavior, which contribute to the formation of primary emotional attachments. These in turn provide a cornerstone for subsequent growth and development. If for some reason the delicate balance and mutual sensitivity of their interactive system is not achieved or is interrupted, the parent-child relationship is disrupted. When a child is handicapped or at-risk, conditions created by the disability can disturb this important relationship and interfere with the quality and quantity of interactions. Effective intervention thus begins not only with recognition of the risks for abnormal or delayed development within the child, but also the risks for asynchronous relationships between the child and his or her caregivers. To ignore the dynamic interrelations between parent and child is to disregard one of the most important variables in planning effective intervention programs.

Sensitivity to the dynamics of the parent-child system (particularly when the child is handicapped, deformed, or abnormal in some way) begins with an appreciation for the myriad of feelings that parents confront when they learn that their child is handicapped or at-risk. Here are the feelings a few parents have expressed:

Raising a child who is profoundly retarded hasn't been easy, but on the other hand, it hasn't been as hard as it might have been . . . . But I have encountered some enemies . . . . One is fatigue, and the other is loneliness . . . . The fact of life for parents of handicapped children which is least understood by others is this: It is difficult and exhausting to live normally, and yet we must. To decide on the other route, to admit that having a disabled child makes us disabled persons, to say no to the ordinary requirements of daily living is to meet the second enemy—loneliness. It means drifting slowly out of the mainstream of adult life. In a very real sense, we are damned if we do make the extraordinary effort required to live normally and damned if we don't . . . . (Morton, 1978, pp. 143-145)

When I look back now, I realize I was so angry at this terrible thing that happened to us and so frightened. I was terrified that I wouldn't be able to cope and determined, on the other hand, to be a supermother. I was going to do it all! I was going to make Tim achieve the absolute most that he could if it killed me. I had this idea that if he didn't learn by the time he was three, all was lost . . . . Michael and Colette turned three and four the August we brought him, still sickly, home from the hospital. For the next three years, I don't think I heard a single thing they said to me, and I can only remember them in those years in terms of what was happening to Tim—a fact that still makes me want to sob. (Donna Lee, quoted by Kupfer, 1982, p. 67)

Tears still come to my eyes as I look at this handsome, blue-eyed, blond son of mine and think what he might have become had not something damaged his brain. I can rationalize that his life has had tremendous significance through his influence on our family, but the hurt is still there. Certainly he has changed our lives and helped make us into a family . . . . Robin's birth and the problems attendant to trying to find services and adequate care for him abruptly changed the pattern of my life, my attitudes, and my plans for the future . . . . My attitudes changed not only toward people with handicapped children but toward all people with problems. Now I know what it meant to be stared at, shunned, avoided. People became embarrassed when we brought Robin out in public or when we explained his condition—especially when they learned that he wasn't going to grow out of it or recover from it. (Helsel, 1978, p. 98)

The statement that evoked the worst emotional response in me was, "Don't worry, dear, everything's going to be fine." It took every ounce of will power and every lesson in tact and diplomacy that I had ever learned to contain myself and not shout back at anyone who said this, that I had reason to worry and that things were not going to be fine . . . . I remember . . . feeling that I had become a completely different person. I felt my ego had been wiped out. My superego with all its guilts had become the most prominent part of my personality and I had completely lost my self-esteem. I felt I was nobody. Any credits of self-worth that I could give myself from any of my personal endeavors meant nothing. Graduating from college and a first-rate medical school, surviving an internship, practicing medicine and having two beautiful sons and a good marriage counted for nil. All I knew at this point was that I was the mother of an abnormal and most likely retarded child. (Ziskin, 1978, pp. 74-75)

Who we are doesn't seem to change. After a few years [with] a good therapist, I am beyond the anger and anxiety attacks and am cruising along nicely with chronic depression and a return of childhood asthma. The rest of the world cannot fathom the suffocation of this life, but I think it's terribly appropriate that I have trouble breathing! Our Emily will be six in April—a beautiful, normal looking child who was perfect in every way at birth, but forever lost to an undetected, diagnosed-too-late, treated-too-late case of hypothyroidism. She functions at about fourteen to twenty-two months . . . . The gap between Emily and normal grows with every hour . . . . In the beginning I was labeled an "anxious first-time mother" who was expecting too much when at five months Emily was lethargic and passive. After two years of dealing with the medical world, I was beginning to have recurring thoughts of punching a pediatric neurologist in the face. . . . My emotional battery, I fear, is no longer rechargeable. What do I do? I love Emily, but living with her is making me a bad mother. I think I could love her more if I didn't have her here, if there were a light at the end of this tunnel. . . . Our family life is nonexistent. Nothing we do is normal. Worse, nothing we do is happy." (Denise, quoted by Kupfer, 1982, pp. 142-144)

The delivery was blessedly brief . . . . The next five minutes were the most difficult I have ever spent . . . . I recall the ambivalent feelings of detachment/attachment I felt . . . . A well meaning and much beloved relative had shared with us the hope she "might be taken soon," but I found myself hoping against hope that at least her heart would be within normal limits. I loved this little newborn and I no longer cared so much that she was a "Downs" as that she was "our Melinda." . . . It is now nearly a year since that June midnight and Melinda is more "Mindy" than she is a "Downs." . . . A *Little House on the Prairie* episode gave me a motto for surviving with Melinda. As I gaze with my clinically and medically trained eyes on our Melinda, . . . it is as if she says to me, "Love me with smiles and laughter . . . and if you can only love me with tears, then do not bother to love me at all." This is how I survive. (Durham, 1979, pp. 33-36)

As you proceed through this chapter, reflect upon these quotes, and the others scattered throughout, which describe parents' feelings and experiences. This chapter looks at the young handicapped child in the family context and examines the importance of interrelationships between child and parent, as well as those between parents and professionals. How does parent-child attachment occur, and what factors facilitate or interfere with this process? This chapter also takes a practical look at parent involvement in early intervention programs, its rationale, and some realities that bear upon meaningful parental participation. Everyone agrees that parent involvement is desirable, but what type and level are appropriate is not always clear.

THE RECIPROCAL RELATIONSHIP BETWEEN THE CHILD AND FAMILY

Parenting—a two-way relationship

Every infant grows and develops in a social environment. In past years this environment was regarded as one in which significant others acted upon newborns by providing care and stimulation, initiating interactions, and eliciting responses from the infants. Professional literature was filled with descriptions on how maternal behavior and environmental factors affected a child's development in positive or negative ways. Given this attention to external social factors that impinge upon a child's well-being, one can easily see how infants have tended to be regarded as passive organisms—constantly being affected but having no effect, constantly being changed by environmental conditions but producing no change themselves (Lewis & Rosenblum, 1974).

This one-way view of caregiver-child interaction is much too simplistic to explain the complexities of human relationships. Serious attention was not given to the infant's contributions to caregiver-child relationships and attachments until R. Bell (1968, 1974) and S. Bell (1971) published works proposing an interactional model that described the child's effect on the caregiver as well as the caregiver's effect on the child. Under this new perspective, interactions are viewed as part of a complex system in which the child's temperamental, biological, and genetic characteristics interact with those of the parent, with both contributing to an interdependent, reciprocal relationship. Through this interactive process, the infant increasingly is able to act upon and manipulate his or her own environment. This provides the basis for all subsequent learning and lays the foundation for cognitive, social, emotional, and psychomotor growth.

Research suggests that infants are social beings from the outset. They begin life with a range of behaviors that modify the quality and quantity of stimulation others deliver. Newborns behave in ways that promote contact and interaction with others through discriminative crying, gazing, and smiling (Ainsworth, 1973). Furthermore, newborns actively seek out stimulation, attend selectively to sensory stimuli, and show preferences for certain types of stimulus change. Rooting and sucking reflexes elicit contact and nursing behavior with the caregiver. Reflexive smiling (a behavior parents interpret as a sign of recognition and positive affect) is reinforcing to the adult and promotes increased efforts at caregiving and reciprocal stimulation by adults (Bennett, 1976). Eye contact, mutual gazing, postural adjustments (e.g., snuggling and holding up head) promote approaches from adults and encourage a certain positioning of the infant by adults that maintains visual contact and offers comfort (Korner & Thoman, 1970; Stern, 1974; Tronick, 1982).

Other "signaling" behaviors, such as those listed below, allow infants to maintain contact with their caregivers:

- Ability to discriminate the parent or primary caregiver from strangers. (Bell, 1974)
- Imitative behaviors and reciprocal play. (Stern, 1974)
- Prelinguistic communication and vocalization, such as elicited cooing, babbling, gestures, differential crying, and vocalizations. (Anderson, Vietze, & Dokecki, 1977; Bernal, 1972)
- Attentional behaviors and responsiveness to tactile, visual, and auditory stimuli. (Brazelton, Koslowski, & Main, 1974; Robson & Moss, 1970)

These infant behaviors also affect the caregiver's attitudes in that these acts suggest to the parent that he or she has special meaning to the child and reinforces the parent for responding to the infant's overtures. These "messages" are important to parents. As Bell (1974) pointed out, bearing and rearing children satisfies certain human needs. When a parent's psychological need for a cuddly, dependent child is met instead with an unresponsive or resistive infant, building a constructive, reciprocal interaction system can be difficult.

As parent and child elicit responses from each other and respond reciprocally, an interactive synchrony occurs (Ainsworth, 1979; Goldberg, 1977; Lewis, 1984). Whether a constructive or nonconstructive parent-child system is established depends upon two primary variables: (a) the timing (or synchrony) of their responses to each other, and (b) the nature or configuration of their responses (Lewis, 1972).

Synchrony in the interactive relationship is shown in mutual responsiveness as described in the following sequence: The infant gazes at the mother and smiles. She smiles back, talking and cooing to her baby, who in turn kicks and smiles with excitement. The mother responds with another smile, moves her face closer, and makes physical contact by touching and tickling the infant. He or she giggles, kicks with excitement, and reaches out to touch her face. In turn, she talks to her baby with exclamations about what a good baby he or she is and babbles with sounds that imitate his or her own vocalizations. The infant reacts by reaching (a gesture the mother recognizes to mean, "Pick me up"). The mother picks up the baby and pats him or her gently on the back. And so the exchange continues in a hierarchical fashion until one or the other terminates the sequence. Asynchrony in the parent-child relationship is shown in the infant who fails to respond readily to the caregiver's approaches. It also is shown by the caregiver who fails to respond in a timely manner to the infant's initiations for interaction or signals of some need (Snow, 1977).

Whatever characteristics caregiver and infant bring to their mutual interactions, an appropriate "match" is essential to establish a synchronous relationship (Ritvo & Solnit, 1958; Brazelton et al., 1974). This takes time and sensitivity by each partner to the other. Developmental changes in the child over time alter his or her behavior. And as the adult gains experience and maturity in the parenting role, the interactive system also must change, to maintain its positive qualities and reciprocal match.

In summary, Bell (1974) has explained the chain of reciprocal interactions between a young child and the primary caregiver in this way:

> The parent-child system is a reciprocal relation involving two or more individuals who differ greatly in maturity although not in competence, in terms of ability to affect each other. The relationship involves much more and longer-range intention on the part of one participant than on the part of the other. There is a certain balance of controls, in that the greater intentional behavior of the parent is offset by two features of the offspring's behavior: (1) the active short-range initiation of interactions, and (2) the organization of the behavior so that it is compelling and selectively reinforcing. Much of the modification of child behavior toward cultural norms occurs in the context of parental adjustments and accommodations to the initiations of the young. (p. 15)

Bonding and reciprocal attachment

During the early months of life, as the infant engages in reciprocal interactions with the caregiver, a primary attachment or *emotional bond* is formed. Most often this is with the mother, although any individual who nurtures an infant may become the attachment figure. Usually infants bond or attach to one primary figure, but studies indicate that young children ultimately attach to a *network* of other people including fathers and other relatives, friends, and even "social objects" (e.g., Linus' security blanket in the comic strip *Peanuts*) (Lamb, 1976; Weinraub, Brooks, & Lewis, 1977). These important primary relationships are the wellspring for all subsequent attachments and it is from these that the infant builds a sense of self. As Kennell, Voos, and Klaus (1979) have explained:

> Most of the richness and beauty of life comes from the close relationship that each individual has with a small number of other human beings—his or her parents, siblings, children, and a small group of friends. Much of the joy and sorrow of life revolves around attachments or affectional relationships: making them, breaking them, preparing for them, and adjusting to their loss . . . . Perhaps the parent's attachment to a child is the strongest bond in the human species . . . . The strength and character of this attachment will influence the quality of all future bonds to other individuals. (p. 786)

This early attachment between a specific caregiver and the infant is defined as an affectional bond manifest by the child's efforts to maintain some degree of proximity to the attachment figure (Stone, 1979). Behaviors such as fondling, kicking, cuddling, and prolonged gazing are indicators of attachment, all of which serve to maintain contact and express affection. The enduring qualities of the affectional bond are shown in an infant's behavior after prolonged separation from the attachment figure (Bowlby, 1973; Robertson & Robertson, 1971). Protest, despair, depression, withdrawal, and even weight loss and progressive detachment may be manifest in children when the primary caregiver is absent. When reunited, the sequence of ignoring, anger, and reproach the infant shows is further evidence of this attachment (Heinicke & Westheimer, 1966). Furthermore, attachment is shown in times of stress when the child retreats to the arms of the preferred person with whom he or she feels secure.

This baby's engaging look and her smile easily bring adults into interaction with her. She is a good example of how infants play an important role in soliciting and helping to maintain reciprocal interactions with their caregivers.

The importance of early attachment is emphasized by research on behaviors of infants with strong attachments and those with poorly developed affectional ties (Ainsworth, 1973; Bowlby, 1969; Joffe & Vaughn, 1982; Sroufe, 1979). Emotional and affective development is closely related to attachment. Early affectional exchanges between infant and caregiver promote the bonding process, which in turn affects the infant's emotional growth and psychological well-being. Like attachment, emotional development is intricately linked to a child's development of identity and self-awareness (Breger, 1974) and ego development (Loevinger, 1976). Furthermore, affective and cognitive behavior are highly intertwined. Piaget and Inhelder (1969) have suggested that affect and cognition are two inseparable aspects of the same process; no behavior patterns, however intellectual, exist apart from affective factors or motives. The quality of attachment appears to be related to a child's exploratory behavior in unfamiliar situations, mastery of the object world, and willingness to engage in interactions with strangers (Sroufe & Waters, 1977).

Research supports the view that the attachment figure provides a secure *base* from which a child orients himself or herself. This base provides security as the child ventures out into new surroundings and explores the environment (Bretherton & Ainsworth, 1974; Carr, Dabbs, & Carr, 1975). Individual differences are apparent in the quality of affectional bonds children attain, as well as in the consequences of those bonds upon their development. Studies show that toddlers who are insecurely attached to their caregivers are less cooperative, enthusiastic, persistent, and competent in problem solving than are securely attached children. Securely attached youngsters appear to be more compliant and more likely to have internal controls (Arend, Grove, & Sroufe, 1979; Londerville & Main, 1981). Furthermore, children classified as securely attached as infants have been found at age 4½ to be more flexible, resourceful, and curious than insecurely attached peers (Matas, Arend, & Sroufe, 1978). They also have been shown to score higher than insecurely attached children on tests of spatial ability (Hazen & Durett, 1982) and on developmental scales such as the Bayley (Main, 1973). Main also noted that securely attached infants play more intensely and for longer periods and show more positive affect in free play.

Securely attached infants generally are more socially and emotionally competent than are insecurely attached infants, and this advantage persists into childhood (Matas et al., 1978; Londerville & Main, 1981; Yarrow, 1972). Mahler and Pine (1975) interpreted this as suggesting a transfer of trust from the attached caregiver to a trust of others. They have an expectation that others (like the attachment figure) will be responsive to their needs and signals for help. Waters, Wippman, and Sroufe (1978) found securely attached infants to be more competent as preschoolers in their engagements with peers. Their ability to be involved in the object world, to seek out rewarding aspects of the environment, and to be affectively and verbally expressive seem to have a circular positive effect for the child. This kind of behavior likely attracts the attention and positive regard of other children and adults, who in turn interact positively with the child. (See Odum, 1983, for further literature review.)

Potential disruptions in the parent-child relationship

The unique stresses a young handicapped child places upon parents (such as separation at birth as a result of medical treatment, emotional responses to news of their child's handicap, and additional caregiving tasks because of the child's condition) jeopardize the development of normal attachments. The parent and child also are at-risk for developing an asynchronous interaction pattern. Because each plays a part in shaping their interactions, both are capable of behaviors that disrupt this process (Blacher & Meyers, 1983). Research shows that the maternal-infant relationship in the first few days and months after birth is indicative of their subsequent relationship, and thus the child's evolving personality (Broussard & Hartner, 1971; Thoman, Turner, Leiderman, & Barnett, 1970; Vietze & Anderson, 1981). Disturbances in parents' early attitudes toward their newborn can lead to chronic disturbance in their attachment.

Studies on the effect of a handicapped child upon parents suggest that mothers of mentally retarded children differ from mothers of normal children in that the former tend to have (a) increased depressed feelings, (b) more difficulty in handling anger toward the child, (c) feelings of increased possessiveness toward the child, (d) decreased sense of maternal competence, (e) decreased enjoyment of the child, and (f) feelings of rejection toward the child. Fathers of handicapped children, too, show differences from fathers of normal children. They report (a) more depression, (b) greater preoccupation with the child, (c) decreased enjoyment of the child, and (d) decreased self-esteem and other problems associated with their marital relationship (Blacher, 1984; Blacher & Meyers, 1983; Cummings, Bayley, & Rie, 1966; Cummings, 1976).

When parents are anxious and depressed about their handicapped child's condition and live with the feelings just listed, their interactions with the child undoubtedly will be affected. Out of grief, anger, shame, or guilt, one or both parents may reject their disabled child and fail to adequately respond to the child's needs. The child may be handled only when necessary and may be isolated from contact with people or experiences that a normal child would enjoy (Howard, 1978). Fraiberg (1974), for example, noted that parents of blind infants often are emotionally indifferent to their child because of the lack of facial expression and contingent smiling. A parent's inattentive behavior (such as lack of visual contact during feeding and lack of cuddling) promotes similar "turned off" behavior in the child who ceases attempts to engage the parent in interaction if the parent makes no response or lacks enthusiasm in responding (Klaus & Kennell, 1976; Korner, 1974).

Handicapped and at-risk infants frequently have physical and temperamental characteristics that interfere with development of reciprocal interactions with the caregiver. Or they may be deficient in the very behaviors known to facilitate attachment and reciprocal interaction (Hanson & Hanline, 1984; Ludlow, 1981; Walker, 1982). In an extensive review of literature, Ramey, Bell, and Gowen (1980) found evidence that handicapped infants may differ from normal infants in regard to:

— social responsiveness, including smiling, eye contact and gazing, and postural adjustments and responsiveness to holding.
— verbal and nonverbal communication, including crying and vocalizations.
— irritability, consolability, and adaptability, including the duration and frequency of crying.

These characteristics place greater responsibility upon parents to be adaptive and accommodating. If a parent is to successfully elicit appropriate responses from the infant, special caregiving efforts and skills become necessary (Kelly, 1982). Poor interaction patterns may result if a parent's own emotional state, level of maturity, or parenting skills are insufficient to allow the necessary adaptations. All these things can contribute further to developmental disorders in the child.

Children with physical handicaps or neurological impairment often have abnormal reflex patterns that prevent them from making appropriate postural adjustments to being held. These "noncuddlers" may seem so unresponsive that mothers resort to feeding them on a pillow, which perpetuates the lack of contact between parent and child (Lourie, 1971). A child with cerebral palsy may seem resistive, uncuddly, and unresponsive to parental approaches. An exaggerated Moro reflex (the startle response) can give parents the message that they are frightening the baby (Hanson, 1984b; Kogan, Tyler, & Turner, 1974; Stone & Chesney, 1978). Irritability or a passive temperament can be compounded by physical or cognitive impairment. As a consequence of these behaviors, greater strain is placed on the parent for patience, tolerance of less reinforcement, and less pleasure in caring for the child.

Young children who are blind or seriously visually impaired have reduced interest in their surroundings and are less socially responsive than sighted children. They fail to exhibit many behaviors that elicit interactions with adults, such as eye contact, gazing, facial expressions, and smiling (Bennett, 1976; Fraiberg, 1977). Given the absence of or reduction in these behaviors, parents may feel unrewarded by their child and may interpret this as evidence that the child does not reciprocate their caring.

Deaf and hearing impaired children face a problem in establishing interaction systems with their parents because of the absence of or delay in their verbalizations. A deaf infant babbles as normal peers do during the early months of life but ceases babbling around 6-9 months of age because of the lack of auditory feedback. This can be exceedingly disappointing to parents, especially when the hearing impairment has not been diagnosed. The child's behavior is likely to be viewed as withdrawal, obstinacy, and rejection of the parent. Harris (1979) noted that parents of these children often express a sense of incompleteness and dissatisfaction. Their interpersonal relationship with the child may be out of synchrony long before a diagnosis is finally made, and some parents may have given up attempts at interaction.

Children with emotional problems—especially severe disorders such as autism—fail to display functional communicative interactions. Autistic youngsters can be extremely frustrating to their caregivers. These children may not cry (a major signaling mechanism for infants) to communicate their needs, they may lack orienting and rooting reflexes to signal changes in their state, and they tend to avoid eye contact.

In summary, the interactive relationship between parent and child must be mutually satisfying if it is to be self-perpetuating and truly reciprocal. The child plays a powerful role in defining the nature of that evolving relationship by his or her own responsiveness to the parent and by the messages communicated to the caregiver directly or in subtle ways. As Rheingold (1969) described it, the child more powerfully socializes the adult into parenthood than the parent socializes the infant. At the same time, the parent's impact upon the child is of great importance. The parent provides the experiences and exposure

The birth of a handicapped child not only affects the lives of parents but all members of the family as well. Giving support and help to siblings and parents can be especially timely and beneficial during the early years of the handicapped child's life.

to stimuli that are necessary for social, emotional, cognitive, and psychomotor development to proceed. According to Yarrow, Goodwin, Manheimer, and Milowe (1973), the more sensitive parents are to their infant, the more socially effective the child will be judged 10 years later. Or the more punishing, critical, or controlling the parent is, the slower language acquisition will be (Nelson, 1973) and the poorer the child's performance on infant scales and tests of mental ability will be later in life (Bayley & Schaefer, 1964; Hazen & Durett, 1982).

THE IMPACT OF A HANDICAPPED/AT-RISK CHILD UPON PARENTS AND FAMILIES

> I don't think anybody can ever really *know* what it means to be a parent of a handicapped child . . . not until you've been there. You people can empathize; you can listen, but you can't possibly understand or even comprehend all the feelings that come like an avalanche at times . . . and only seethe inside you at other times. You have no idea of the desperate-saddening sense of loss, but the bit of hope . . . the resentment . . . the disbelief this could happen to me . . . the hopelessness . . . the helpless feeling that if only you could have made it different . . . the anger . . . the disappointment . . . the "what if" . . . but the "this is my kid—my own" feelings that reel through you. You run the whole gamut of reactions, positive and negative, that make you want to run away and forget it all but stay and fight at the same time.
>
> There's stuff you'd never believe you'd ever feel. Then there's some of the stuff you'd expect. Sometimes there's just nothing at all. When it's all said and done, there's just you . . . dealing with it all in your own alone way . . . as you have to. It never totally goes away. Maybe that's because your child is reality. He's there and will always be a part of you and your family. The reactions just change or the cycles run through again as you have new thoughts . . . as new things happen . . . as you have a new realization of what it all means . . . or doesn't mean.
>
> But then again, I'll also say . . . you're just another parent like everybody else . . . and it isn't all that different. You do what you always do as a parent. You go along . . . you deal with the ups and downs . . . the joys . . . the frustrations . . . the funny times that make you laugh and wonder "why do I make such a fuss over all this?" You take the good and fight with the bad. You go on being a parent and doing your best. Actually, you have no choice. And . . . you go on living.

This was the explanation given to the author by a parent during a discussion about parenting a young handicapped child. Afterward the parent added: "You know, it was hard for me to say all that. It brings up old feelings I've pushed away. I want to talk about it . . . . I need to, but then I don't . . . ."

As professionals working in a service role with parents of young handicapped children, and as friends and colleagues, we try to be sensitive and understanding of this unique parenting experience. Our role as interventionists and early educators is to provide support not only to the child, but to the parents and family as well. In our attempts to find ways to give appropriate kinds of service, recent literature shows considerable attention to discussions on the impact of a handicapped child upon parents and family systems. We will look at some of that literature here.

Parental reaction to a young handicapped/at-risk child

Discussions about parental reactions to the announcement, "Your child is not normal," typically refer to the "expected or fantasized child" that every expectant parent creates in his or her mind (Olshanksy, 1970; Chinn, Winn, & Walters, 1978; Heward, Dardig,

& Rossett, 1979). The months during pregnancy are a time of psychological-emotional preparation for the new family member. Preparations are acted out in a variety of ways—readying the baby's room, buying baby clothes, thinking about possible names, and talking about the changes that will be necessary in family schedules and roles to accommodate the new baby. Even grandparents, siblings, and, in some cases, close friends go through this preparation process with the expectant parents. Parents imagine what the new person will be like—whom the baby will resemble and what he or she might accomplish in a lifetime.

In this evolving "fantasy child," as Solnit and Stark (1961) call it, parents typically wish for and expect a normal child. Most parents envision healthy, physically fit newborns "with all their fingers and toes." Most parents imagine an attractive baby—someone they can show off with pride to family and friends. Their expectations are of an infant who is soft and cuddly, one who will elicit smiles and admiration and the much hoped for comment, "Oh, what a sweet, beautiful baby!"

The "new baby fantasy" has other elements, too. Parents want and expect others to like and accept their offspring. They hope for a child who will be bright and curious—a person to be proud of. Solnit and Stark (1961) suggested that the origins of these expectations are complex and deeply rooted. They embody elements of the parents' own self-image and ambitions. They embody a cumulation of family expectations incorporated from parents' own image and the values of other important people such as grandparents, the mate, or significant others in their lives.

Gabel, McDowell, and Cerreto (1983) pointed out that these images of the "expected child" serve two important functions for parents. *First,* the perfect child image may reflect a desire for the parents to have a second chance at life—an opportunity to have a better life than they have had. In a sense, the unborn child represents someone who can extend parents' own achievement beyond what they have been able to do and move ahead to greater heights. *Second,* the unborn child represents a means for a part of the parents to be continued forward in time beyond their own lifetimes. It gives a means for leaving something important behind as evidence of one's life and contribution to mankind. The new baby thus offers parents a means for living on—a sense of immortality.

The birth of a child with a congenital defect or an obvious abnormality abruptly shatters this cherished image. For parents who only gradually come to recognize that their child has a disability, the dream is chipped away more slowly, and perhaps more painfully. In either case, parents face a deep sense of loss and an adjustment process that requires letting go of the "expected child fantasy." They must create a new image of their child. They must even redefine to some degree their own roles as parents. Often this loss and the imposed adjustment have a profound impact on each parent's psychological well-being. Parents go through a series of emotional reactions to the reality they face, which is described as similar in many ways to the reactions adults experience in dealing with the death of a loved one (Chinn, Winn, & Walters, 1978). Just as the mourning process helps one adjust to the loss of a loved one, mourning also helps parents of a young handicapped child adjust to their losses. It moves them beyond the initial trauma of hearing that their child is not normal to acceptance of and realistic adaptation to their child's problem.

Parents appear to experience a series of emotional reactions: shock, refusal or denial, guilt, bitterness, envy, rejection, and finally adjustment (Blacher, 1984; Bristor, 1984;

Crnic, Greenberg, Ragozin, Robinson, & Basham, 1983; Farber, 1968; Cansler & Martin, 1974; and Love, 1970). Some parents have recurrent feelings so they never wholly work through and leave behind any of these stages. Chronic sorrow or intermittent feelings of inadequacy seem to be an underlying reality for some parents. Perske (1973) vividly described the various feelings parents have as "the glooms, the speeds, the blocks, the hurts, the guilts, the greats, the hates, and the give ups." Let's look briefly at some of these reactions.

Uncertainty   Many parents of young handicapped children do not get a definitive diagnosis of their child's problems until the youngster is a preschooler or even a student in school, but these parents often go through a period of uneasiness about their child. Though their child's physical appearance may be normal, they begin to notice that the child does not respond like other children. The parents observe a slowness to achieve developmental milestones such as sitting, crawling, walking, and talking. Often other family members or friends try to calm the parents' worries by saying, "He'll grow out of it" or "Every child is different." As the child grows older and falls further behind in development, however, parents' anxieties heighten until they obtain a professional evaluation of their child.

Shock   Parents' initial reaction to the news that their child is handicapped usually is shock. Discovering that they are indeed parents of a child such as this can be very intense and debilitating. Well meaning professionals may try to help the parents cope with the news and make logical plans and decisions for their handicapped child. When parents are experiencing this initial shock reaction, however, they may be so preoccupied with their own emotional feelings that they are unresponsive to any suggestions offered.

Denial   Once the shock over the child's handicap has worn off, parents may try to deny that the handicap exists. They may visit a series of doctors in anticipation of a miraculous cure or a more hopeful diagnosis. Parents of a child with more than one handicap may acknowledge the less stigmatizing handicap and deny the other handicap. For example, they may accept the child's physical handicap but deny the child's accompanying mental retardation.

Guilt   Parents often feel guilty, as if they are to be blamed for their child's handicap. Even when the parents have no reason to think they have caused the problem, this gnawing feeling of guilt sometimes persists. The parents may ask themselves, "What did I do wrong?" or "What is wrong with me?" Another way in which parents of a young handicapped child may experience guilt is through the mixed emotions they often feel toward their child. Although they love the child, they may have feelings of hatred or rejection toward the child because of the handicap. This sets them up to feel even more guilty for having such ambivalent feelings toward their own child.

Anger   Outright anger is another emotion that parents of a young handicapped child frequently experience. This emotion often goes hand-in-hand with a deep sense of injustice as parents wonder, "Why did this have to happen to me?" Some parents express their anger by lashing out at the professionals who supervised the birth of their child or who later treat the child. For instance, they may blame their obstetrician for improper prenatal care or carelessness in delivering the child. Other targets of a parent's anger may be the mate, other children in the family, or even the handicapped child.

Depression   As the reality of the child's problems begins to sink in, parents may feel depressed as they consider what the future actually holds for them and their young child. This sadness is often heightened when parents see neighborhood children accomplishing things they know their child may never be able to do. This reaction often is described as chronic; as the child grows older and misses out on normal activities during the various developmental periods of life, parents face this sadness again and again.

Acceptance   Ideally, once parents have worked through these previously discussed reactions, they can begin to reach a stage of acceptance of their child's handicap and can adapt to the child's needs. In the stage of acceptance, the parents begin to view their child's handicap more realistically and to make constructive plans for the child's immediate and long-term future. Some parents may reach this stage only temporarily. Then, when some new problem arises with their child, they find themselves working back through the earlier stages again.

In looking at these reactions, remember that emotional responses to the crisis of having a handicapped infant or young child are a very individual matter. Not all parents experience the same reactions, nor do they do so with the same intensity. Factors such as the age at which the child is diagnosed and the severity of the child's handicap can make a real difference in parents' reactions.

Sources of stress for parents and family systems

The addition of any new member into an already established family system requires the family to make adjustments, and the arrival of a handicapped child can present even greater adjustments. The effects of a handicapped child on the family and the sources of stress are not static, though. They vary as the child changes or as parents and siblings move on through the family cycle. At times, stress is acute but very situational. Other sources of stress are chronic and never go away. Sometimes stress may not be apparent at all. MacKeith (1973) has suggested four major points of crisis in families of handicapped children, where some of the greatest changes and overall family adjustments occur: (a) when the initial diagnosis takes place, (b) when the child begins to receive services, (c) when the child becomes of school age and enters the public school system, and (d) when the child leaves the home and moves out of the parents' direct care.

What are some specific sources of stress? Speaking about parents and families of handicapped children in general, various authors have identified several types of stressors (Beckman-Bell, 1981; Blackard & Barsh, 1982; Fredericks, 1985; Gallagher, Beckman-Bell, & Cross, 1983; Bray, Coleman, & Brackmen, 1981):

- Additional expenses and financial burdens.
- Actual or perceived stigma.
- Heightened demands on time as a result of caretaking requirements for the child.
- Difficulties with basic caretaking tasks such as feeding, bathing, dressing.
- Decreased time for sleep.
- Social isolation from friends, relatives, neighbors.

- Reduced time for leisure or personal activities.
- Difficulties in managing the child's behavior.
- Interference with routine domestic responsibilities.
- General feelings of pessimism about the future.

Additional stress-producing factors described by others include:

- Depression anxieties in one parent, adding to the pressure of the other, who may have been coping more effectively (Price-Bonham & Addison, 1978; Gath, 1978; McMichael, 1971; Wolfensberger, 1967).
- Expensive and continuing needs for medical care, possibly surgery and hospitalization (Caplan, 1964; Feldman & Scherz, 1967; Gabel, McDowell, & Cerreto, 1983).
- Constant fatigue and what sometimes seem to be endless caregiving demands upon parents (Gath, 1978; Dunlap & Hollinsworth, 1977).
- Marital discord that appears to arise over issues related to care of the child, guilt about the child, and dispersion of time relative to the child and mate (Boles, 1959; Gath, 1978).
- Sibling reactions or difficulties that are directly or indirectly related to the handicapped family member (Farber, 1959, 1968; McMichael, 1971; Tew & Laurence, 1973; Love, 1973).

How parents and families react to stress depends on the interaction of factors including severity of the child's handicap, stability of the family and its internal support system, and amount of external support to which the family has access. The availability of services or lack of support, such as medical, educational, counseling, and respite services, also alters the degree of stress parents report (Gabel, McDowell, & Cerreto, 1983; Schell 1981).

Most families eventually learn to cope effectively with their young handicapped child. Some families even feel they are drawn closer together in their efforts to deal with the child. Others are not as successful in their adjustment. For some families, having a handicapped child results in a breakdown of the family unit. Statistics reveal three times as many divorces in families with handicapped children (Schell, 1981). Child abuse is another frequent problem. Research by the Denver Department of Welfare showed that of 100 abused children studied, 70% had either a physical or mental handicap prior to their abuse. Of members of Parents Anonymous (an organization for abusive parents) surveyed, 58% of the members' abused children had developmental problems prior to their reported abuse (National Center on Child Abuse and Neglect, 1980, p. 2.). Children at-risk for developmental disabilities because of maturity or low birth weight also have been reported frequently in the population of abused children (Embry, 1980; Goldson, 1978).

In trying to explain the phenomenon of child abuse, researchers suggest that it results from the interaction of variables usually classified as *child characteristics, parent characteristics,* and *stressful elements* in the environment (Frodi 1981; Sandgrund, Gaines, & Green, 1974). Some young handicapped or at-risk children have characteristics that tend to cause parents stress and make them more susceptible to child abuse. As discussed earlier, many handicapped or at-risk infants and young children are more difficult to care for and less capable of reinforcing good "mothering."

Research on characteristics of abusive parents suggests that they frequently were abused as children themselves and thus lack good role models for appropriate child rearing

(Kempe & Kempe, 1978). Other traits of abusive parents often include immaturity, as seen in little impulse control and low frustration tolerance (Martin, 1976). And abusive parents often are found to hold unrealistic expectations for their child (Sandgrund, Gaines, & Green, 1974).

By viewing child abuse in terms of an interaction between and among these variables, it is difficult to determine whether a child's handicap caused the abuse or the handicap resulted from the abuse (Sandgrund, Gaines, & Green, 1974). For example, a normal child living in a stressful environment with an abuse-prone parent can become handicapped as a result of injury from abuse. On the other hand, a family with a handicapped child and without adequate support systems may incur enough stress to cause parents without abusive tendencies to abuse the child. In either case, awareness of the potential problem of child abuse is crucial for educators who deal with young handicapped children and their families.

Special needs of parents and families

Parents of handicapped children likely experience some of their most intense feelings and face some of the most difficult adjustments during the early years of their child's life. This may be partly because they are in the initial phases of coping with the fact that their child is handicapped. And if a clear diagnosis cannot be made but the child shows signs that something may be wrong, the early years can be particularly uncertain and stressful. In that situation, parents are caught between the question, "Is there a problem and, if so, what should be done about it?" and "Is this something that is only temporary, and I shouldn't make a fuss about it?" The vacillation of feelings under these circumstances easily can hold parents in a state of uncertainty between doing something and doing nothing. Dangling between hope for a healthy child and acceptance of a child who may be handicapped can be highly frustrating. Given the myriad of feelings, of decisions that must be made, and of adjustments that parents must work through during the first years of their special child's life, parents not surprisingly describe this as a time "when I needed help most!"

What parent needs can be served through parent involvement activities and parent-staff interaction? Who can better describe their needs than the individuals themselves who are parenting the handicapped infants and preschoolers? Who can better observe those needs than the staff that interacts on a day-to-day basis with those parents? The words of parents themselves vividly describe the realities of their lives and the kinds of assistance that we as professionals can offer to be of greatest value. In response to the author's questioning of parents about what kinds of help they value most and what early childhood-special education programs could do to best serve them and involve them in meaningful ways, parents' expressions of need were described in various ways, but their responses tended to fall under seven broad areas:

1. *Parents need information (of all kinds) to enable them to better understand the nature of their child's handicap and special needs, to help them set realistic expectations for themselves and their child, and to aid them in locating resources to help in their parenting responsibilities.*

> I was overwhelmed when we got the diagnosis that Monica had Cri du Chat syndrome. I didn't even know what it meant—if she was going to die, live, or grow out of it. All I had were some

fancy words—Monica's diagnosis (that made no sense to me)—and a desperate sense of fear. I didn't know what to do. There wasn't a soul around I could turn to. At least that's how I felt. I needed someone to explain it all to me . . . what it meant . . . what I could do . . . to give me some sense of her future. I needed help to know what the next step should be to move me out of my frozen state of dread.

The program here [the early intervention program] did that for me. The staff talked to me. They answered what probably seemed like stupid questions. They told me about handicapped children—showed me I wasn't alone at all. I learned about what could be done for Monica. If you ask me, that's where you can help new parents most—give them some information . . . talk to them. They need some place to go.

After serving as director of an early intervention program for handicapped children for many years, one person made this comment:

Our parents have a tremendous need for new kinds of information—about things they didn't think about and were not exposed to before their handicapped child came along. They ask where they can get reading materials and what they should read that will help them. They want to meet other parents like them and ask about organizations they can join. They want to know more about their child's condition. The questions are unending about how they can handle this situation . . . what to tell a sibling . . . what to tell the grandparents. . . . Parents of handicapped children are bombarded with a whole new jargon—medical terms, educational terms, medications—and they want to know what they mean. We've even had parents come to us asking questions I thought I'd never hear in this day and age. One parent asked when her son would grow out of Down syndrome.

2. *Parents need a support group of caring, understanding persons with whom they can share and discuss their feelings and enjoy a sense of friendship and camaraderie. Parents need someone who is an understanding listener and also has the experience/expertise to offer constructive help and information.*

In describing what she viewed as important parent needs, one parent commented about the staff and early intervention program with which she was associated:

The people here are a second family for me. I know they care, and I know they're here to help if I need them. I've shared pretty deep feelings with them—ones I couldn't even talk about with my family. There have been days I've come here and unloaded on Caryn [her child's teacher], even cried and said things I'd been feeling for a long time but couldn't talk about. I don't have many friends any more since Tammy came along—not ones who understand. Sometimes they act like Tammy's problem is going to rub off. I really needed a friend. . . . People around here have given that friendship to me. The things the staff has given me don't come through formal meetings . . .. It probably couldn't happen there. It's been the informal times—before school when I bring Tammy or after school—when we just talk . . .. Those are the important times.

Another parent said:

I think what I've needed most is someone to like Wendell . . . to love him and to show me that we're both okay. You may not believe this, but the thing that starts my day out right is to bring Wendell to preschool and watch people be glad to see him . . . to just talk for a minute with people who are so positive toward us. When I see you all work so hard with Wendell every day, it's inspiring to me. I see you [the teachers] get discouraged at times, too, but that tells me that my moments of desperation aren't times I should feel so guilty for. They're feelings I guess we all have. I really feel a lot of support from the people here, a lot of closeness . . . like people are rooting for me. I can't tell you how important that reassurance can be.

3. *Parents need relief from parenting duties and time off when others can assume respon-*
   sibility for teaching the child while parents have time to attend to their own needs
   and responsibilities to other family members and personal goals.

A mother of five children who is a full-time homemaker explained her needs and view
of parent involvement:

> It's a big sense of relief to leave Sam at preschool every day. I know he's in good hands, that
> he's learning. I don't have to feel guilty about taking time to do my own thing for a few hours.
> People with normal kids don't understand this, but those few hours are a godsend. They help
> me keep my sanity. Those few hours are the only times I have away from Sam. He's so severely
> handicapped . . . he takes 24-hour care. That kind of constant care is hard . . . tiresome . . .
> sometimes frustrating and discouraging—and something that never lets you forget you've got
> someone there demanding your attention.
>
> Sam's not very responsive at times. It's discouraging. I know people talk about the importance
> of parent involvement. I'm not indifferent . . . I care . . . I want to support a program that helps
> me. . . . I'll participate in things that have meaning for me. But don't expect me to be Sam's
> parent and his teacher. That's what I bring him to you for. Just let me be his parent—and help
> me be a good parent. Don't ask me to come back in and spend the few hours I have to myself
> working with him and the staff. I need this time just to clear my head . . . to think . . . maybe
> just to clean my house in peace. Don't tell me I ought to be doing more of what I already do
> the other 20 hours of every day of my life!

4. *Parents need special training that will help them manage a handicapped child more*
   skillfully at home or provide the kinds of stimulation that will promote development
   and learning in the child and better interactions between parent and child at home.

A parent who had participated in some parent training activities as a part of her involvement
had this to say:

> I think the kinds of things professionals can do to help us is such an individual thing. I've been
> to parent meetings that were terrible—a waste of my time. What has counted for me is the
> training the staff O.T. [occupational therapist] has given me on how to handle Jessica at home
> [Jessica has cerebral palsy]. She taught me things I never could have figured out alone. No
> doctor ever explained those things either. She showed me how to feed Jessica . . . how to move
> her . . . to sit her up in a relaxed position so she could use her arms and hands and not tighten
> up. Dressing Jessica was such a problem until Marilyn showed me how to reduce the muscle
> tension. I've learned so much. It's made my life so much more pleasant. That's the kind of help
> lots of us need—the practical, nitty-gritty stuff.

A father (of a hearing impaired 4-year-old son) who had worked through a series of
training sessions for parents of deaf children remarked:

> It's great to have people who say, "Here's how you can communicate with your son . . . here's
> how you can teach him to talk . . . here's what you can do to help him understand what you
> are saying." My wife and I had no idea what to do, and I had a hard time relating to Brandon.
> The staff has helped us in ways we can never repay. This is the kind of participation that has
> been useful for me. I don't care to be involved in many other things. I value the few evenings
> and weekends I have free. But these training sessions have given us something constructive to
> do at home. We have people we go to for advice when we need them . . . we know they are
> there to listen. A lot has been informal, but I like it that way. We both work . . . we can't go
> to lots of meetings. The time we spend with the staff here has got to be time that counts.

5. *Parents need informal opportunities for contact with the program and with staff members who work with their children.*

Two parents who frequently interacted with staff and other parents in their children's preschool program explained:

> If I had to choose between the opportunity to watch staff work with my child and attend a parent meeting, I'd take the observation booth any day. I learn a lot watching them work with Steffie. They get things out of her that I never can. It's exciting and encouraging to see that. Lots of us parents sit in here [the observation booth] and watch what goes on. Maybe you don't call that parent involvement, but I do. You'd be surprised at the discussions that go on here. Probably you'd be impressed. We talk a lot about our kids. Staff people come in and we talk . . . . They answer questions . . . . We get to know each other.

> The chance to talk with the staff informally . . . to visit with other parents every day is one of the things I appreciate most. I dread the day when my kid starts riding the school bus. Bringing Jed to the center every day and taking him home has given me a chance to really know this program. This program has become an important part of my life. We trade information. We talk a lot, and I know what Jed is working on so I can carry on at home. The staff shows me what to do with my son and gives me lots of suggestions. I need this kind of contact. I don't have to guess what's going on. I feel like I'm a part of the program. When they need help, I pitch in . . . cook . . . aide . . . health "checker-inner." I like to do that. I feel like I'm giving something back.

For other literature on family/parent needs, see: Bailey and Simeonsson (1984); Baker (1984); Benson and Turnbull (1986); Turnbull and Turnbull (1986).

PARENT-PROFESSIONAL TEAMWORK

Professionals agree that parent participation is a vital part of effective early intervention. Research suggests that professionals cannot make a meaningful and lasting impact on the lives of young children who have handicapping or at-risk conditions without cooperation and follow-through by parents. After reviewing outcomes of a number of early intervention programs with disadvantaged children, Bronfenbrenner (1974) concluded:

> Evidence indicates the family is the most effective and economical system for fostering and sustaining the development of the child . . . . Without such parent involvement, any effects of intervention, at least in the cognitive sphere, appear to erode fairly rapidly once the program ends (p. 55). . . . Intervention programs which cast the parent in a subordinate role or have the effect of discouraging or decreasing his participation in activities with the child are likely to be counter productive. (p. 56)

The most successful programs are those that support parents in their parenting efforts and strengthen their parent-child relationships rather than supplant them.

A new philosophy about parent roles in education

Parents have not always been a welcome party to educational activities concerning their children. The current emphasis on parental involvement represents a major shift in educational philosophy. Professional educators have not always believed that parents should be involved in formal educational processes involving their child, or that parents could even be involved meaningfully. Sometimes parents have been considered a hindrance, not a help, to the staff—which could work best if parents would just "stay out of the way." Even at times when lip service has been paid to the notion of parent involvement, actual practices have failed to reflect a true commitment. In past years, parent contact typically was limited to two or three brief teacher-parent conferences each year, when teachers told parents what they "needed to know" about their child's progress and alerted them to the problems. Further contact, unfortunately, usually related to problems or to requests to be made of parents. On occasion, moms and dads were invited to special events (e.g., programs in which their child performed, field trips, birthday or Christmas parties, or open houses).

This change in attitude about parent roles in education has come about only gradually. In chapter 3 you read about some of the forces that propelled the change. You will remember that when Head Start and then Follow-Through programs were launched, they were unique in including parents in educational and advisory kinds of activities. Those programs were built on the premise that change in the lives of disadvantaged children could be achieved only with concurrent changes in their parents, homes, and neighborhoods. All this occurred at a time when parent involvement was viewed rather skeptically—especially for low-income parents, who sometimes were believed to be indifferent and nonfacilitative to their child's progress in school. Head Start and Follow-Through demonstrated otherwise. Parents could and did help. Given some encouragement that their input was of value and that the staff wanted them to be involved, parents responded with enthusiasm. That parents needed guidance to work more effectively with their children also became obvious. Head Start and Follow-Through demonstrated what powerful outcomes are possible when parents are brought into educational programs as allies and not treated as outsiders.

You will remember, too, that the special education movement, which brought about appropriate educational services for handicapped children in the public schools, received much of its fuel from parent advocates. Their advocacy helped bring about the court decisions and legislation that opened the doors of education to handicapped children who previously had been excluded. When Public Law 94-142 was passed in 1975, Congress acknowledged the need for parents to be active participants in their children's education. That legislation officially extended parents' rights and duties from a role of passive observer to a role of educational decision maker in behalf of their child. This new role clearly represents a radical swing of the pendulum from practices that were common less than a decade ago (Turnbull & Turnbull, 1982).

The rationale for parent involvement

Why is parent involvement regarded as such a crucial component in effective early intervention programs? The professional literature cites a number of empirical, economic, legal, and even common-sense reasons. Here is a summary of the major arguments (Arnold, Rowe, & Tolbert, 1978; Bristol & Gallagher, 1982; Cartwright, 1981; Goodson & Hess, 1975; Hayden, 1976; Peterson, 1982a; Shearer & Shearer, 1972, 1977; Welsh & Odum, 1981; Yawkey & Bakawa-Evenson, 1975):

1. *Parents (or their substitutes) are the key teachers, socializing agents, and caregivers for children during the early years.*

A young child spends the greater part of his or her waking hours with parents or substitute parents—not a teacher who may provide early education services for 2 or 3 hours each day. The parent figure is the primary person who determines what opportunities, stimulation, general care, and nurturance children receive. Any support to facilitate good parenting thus benefits the child.

2. *Parents can be effective intervention agents and teachers of their own children.*

Parents have more to gain than anyone else associated with the intervention process. Their involvement—either as the primary change agent or as team members with professionals—is an economical and practical strategy for dealing with the young handicapped child in the context of the family.

3. *Parents are in a particularly strategic position to enhance or negate the potential benefits of an early intervention program.*

Parents are in a key position to first note irregular behavior or development in their child. Furthermore, their perspective on the child's special problems and their own knowledge of the child's strengths and weaknesses are exceedingly helpful in planning appropriate intervention procedures. Professionals have found that parents are more likely to respond to staff requests and to work on similar goals with their handicapped child if their input is included in planning that intervention process.

4. *Parents of young children with handicapping or at-risk conditions typically face additional demands and stresses that can test their coping abilities and parenting skills.*

Involvement in their child's intervention program offers parents a means for support and more ready access to people who can provide assistance. This assistance ultimately can help parents respond to and more successfully meet their child's special needs.

5. *Involvement offers a mechanism for helping parents build a positive perspective about their child and their position as parents.*

The support and fellowship of others can be of utmost importance during the early years when parents come to recognize, then understand, and finally accept their child's disability or "differentness." How parents work through this trying and often painful process and deal with their feelings greatly affects their attachment to and attitudes toward their handicapped offspring. Professional help can be made more accessible and opportunities can be provided for parents to meet others who have had similar experiences.

6. *The greatest and most lasting benefits of parent involvement occur in programs in which parents are part of the intervention process.*

Both the handicapped child and the parent benefit from parent involvement in early intervention programs. Studies also have shown that parent involvement and training can benefit siblings. Parents generalize their new parenting skills, gained through their involvement, in ways that enhance their interaction with all their offspring.

7. *Intervention works best when parents and professionals are working toward common goals for a child and when all are applying strategies that are compatible.*

The staff in early intervention programs cannot achieve alone what the staff and parents, working in tandem, can accomplish. Coordination does not occur magically, but parent involvement creates a mechanism for bringing about cooperative effort.

8. *Involving parents, and helping them be effective teachers/interventionists in their own children's lives, has obvious economies.*

Service for young children can be costly because it requires a small staff-to-child ratio. Parents' involvement is cost-efficient from three perspectives: (a) Their participation increases the chances for obtaining and maintaining the greatest child gains for the amount of money spent; (b) parents can help compensate for manpower shortages by assisting in various activities associated with planning, organizing, and delivering special services; and (c) parents offer a means for carrying out programs with children in sparsely populated rural areas, where distance and time limitations make center-based programs more costly.

9. *Involvement of parents in planning and implementing special services for a young child is a parental* right.

Parents have the right to be involved in the decision-making processes that involve their child's care and education. Public Law 94-142 guarantees parents' rights to be informed about and participate in the processes of identification, diagnosis, educational placement, and educational programming as they relate to their youngster. Parents also hold the right of consent—to agree or disagree with the educational placement and treatment plan for their child.

10. *Parent involvement is advantageous simply because a great many parents are interested in their child's care and educational activities.*

Most parents want a voice in what and how their child is taught. Furthermore, as consumers of a public education service, they pay for the cost (directly or indirectly) and do not want to be told to "stay away." Most want to support the efforts of program staff in ways that enhance their child's progress—at least to the extent possible within their own life and job demands.

11. *Involvement brings parents into contact with a great variety of resources that can help them in their parenting roles.*

When left to their own initiative, parents may be hesitant to seek help or to be assertive in organizing services from several agencies to get help for their child. Involvement programs can be a tremendous help to parents in gaining greater access to information about various community services, parent support groups, or other resources.

12. *Parent involvement helps build parent and community support for early intervention programs.*

Parents who are knowledgeable about the program in which their child is being served are its best advocates. They can be convincing spokespersons for the benefits of early childhood-special education services. In some instances, public policy and state laws supporting EC-SPED programs have been changed as a result of parent advocacy. Because early childhood-special education programs serve such a small minority, funding and continuation of the services are highly dependent upon ongoing support and advocacy by parents and concerned citizens.

The purposes of parent involvement

Now that ample evidence suggests that parents should be involved in the intervention process, the more pressing issues are:

- What goals are to be achieved through parent involvement, or what are the purposes for which we want parents to participate?
- How should parents be involved so that their participation is purposeful for them, their child, or the staff and program that serve them?
- To what extent should parents be involved, and what constitutes a meaningful level of participation?

To answer these questions, we will first look at the population of parents with young handicapped/at-risk children who are served by early childhood-special education programs and their characteristics.

Who are the target parents?   Parents of young children with handicapping or at-risk conditions come from all walks of life. They represent low-, middle-, and upper-income families. They come from all racial, cultural, and ethnic groups. Educational backgrounds vary, too. Many are well educated or skilled individuals. Some have professional training in education, special education, or related human service fields—career choices that sometimes are spurred by the presence of a handicapped child in the family. In essence, the parents we are concerned about represent a true cross-section of our society and, expectedly, they vary tremendously. They differ greatly in what personal resources they have to draw upon for support. And the capabilities of these parents for coping with a handicapped child and responding to his or her special needs cover the entire gamut. No two parents or families are exactly the same.

Parents whose children are served in early intervention programs for the handicapped differ markedly from the group of parents served by the early compensatory education programs (e.g., Head Start and Follow-Through). This is important to note because our notions about parent involvement in early education intervention were derived primarily from compensatory education programs. As Foster, Berger, and McLean (1981) have pointed out, early childhood-special education programs serve larger numbers of moderately to severely handicapped children, including multiply handicapped youngsters. Compensatory education programs, in contrast, dealt with parents and children from disadvantaged, low-income homes. Children in compensatory education programs were characterized by milder handicaps or simply a lack of the educational exposure common to children in middle and upper socioeconomic families.

Foster et al. suggested that many of the assumptions underlying parent involvement practices in early childhood programs as they evolved out of compensatory education may not generalize well to the broader population of parents with young handicapped children. Quite possibly, a new set of guiding principles is needed to define what represents appropriate (and effective) parent involvement in early childhood-special education.

Changing societal values and styles of living also affect the characteristics of parent groups now being served by early childhood-special education programs. The following figures describe some of those realities:

1. Ever increasing numbers of women are entering the labor force and pursuing careers. This means that mothers are spending less time in mothering, caregiving roles with their children and have less free time available for activities with programs that serve their children. In fact, labor force participation rates have increased most rapidly for married women with children of preschool age. Between 1950 and 1978, working mothers with preschool children tripled (U.S. Bureau of the Census, 1980). And 47% of all children under age 6 living in families in 1980 had working mothers; of those mothers, 70% were employed full time (U.S. Bureau of the Census, 1982).

2. Single-parent families are increasing in number. This is the result of several factors, including an increasing divorce rate and desertion within some families and the growing acceptance of single parents. Current divorce rates indicate that of individuals now marrying, some 40% of the marriages will end in divorce. Nine of 10 single-parent homes are headed by the mother (Glick & Norton, 1979). Single-parent homes are particularly common among Black families; census figures show that nearly half of all Black mothers have no husband in the home—about three times the number found among white mothers. Most often the single parent also is a working parent (U.S. Bureau of the Census, 1980).

Dads can get into the action, too. These parents are both highly involved in activities with their infant, and they meet regularly with other parents like them to share experiences and give support.

3. An obvious shift in male/female roles is altering patterns of child rearing. In husband-wife headed families, fathers are becoming more involved in the care of their children and in activities outside the home concerning them. Or both parents are relying more on day care or alternative caregivers for children so the parents can work outside the home (Singer, Fosburg, Goodson, & Smith, 1980; Lueck, Orr, & O'Connell, 1982; U.S. Bureau of the Census, 1980).

4. Increasing numbers of children are being reared by adults other than their own natural parents. Higher rates of divorce, illegitimate births (especially the increasing rates of teenage pregnancy), and other social changes are altering traditional family structures. As a result, more children are being reared by foster parents, members of the extended family, or persons other than their biological parents. Figures indicate that one of every eight children living with two parents lives with a natural parent and a step-parent (U.S. Bureau of Census, 1980).

Given these changes in living styles and the particular characteristics of the parent population with young handicapped children under school age, what are the implications for parent involvement? *First*, the fact that a large number of parents work poses a simple reality: Their time and energies for involvement are limited. *Second*, we cannot assume that mothers are always the primary caregivers for their young children or that they are the ones who spend the most time with their children, even with those under school age. Many children now are spending significant amounts of time with alternative caregivers, who may have an equal, or perhaps even greater, influence on the development and learning of some children.

Third, we cannot assume that all parents need or want a great deal of program support. Some parents may already have a support system and are dealing effectively with their handicapped child. They may seek services only intermittently. *Fourth*, we cannot assume that the care and early education of handicapped children is the foremost priority and concern of all their families. This is not to imply that parents are not interested in their children. The point is that the family likely has other valued members with needs to be met, too. Job responsibilities, commitments to community or church or other organizations with which a family is affiliated, other relationships, and personal needs demand time. The necessity that these be balanced and that time be apportioned among interests and obligations is a reality that a professional staff should remember when soliciting parent involvement.

What does parent involvement entail?   Morrison (1978) described parent involvement as "a process of actualizing the potential of parents; of helping parents discover their strengths, potentialities, and talents, and of using them for the benefit of themselves and the family" (p. 22). The term *parent involvement* covers an amazing range of possible services and activities relating to parents and families, which can be categorized under four broad kinds of involvement "processes":

1. Things that professionals do for parents or give to them.
   (*Examples*: services, information, emotional support or advice)
2. Things that parents do for the program or professional staff.
   (*Examples*: fund raising, dissemination, advocacy, information gathering)
3. Things that parents do with their child as an extension of the program.

(*Examples*: teaching and tutoring the child at home or at school)
4. Things that parents and staff do together, wherein both work on a common activity relating to the program.
   (*Examples*: planning, evaluating, working on joint projects; working together as trainer/trainee; discussing topics of common interest; working as co-therapists with a child).

The four broad kinds of involvement processes range from rather passive to very active kinds of parent roles. Because parent needs vary so greatly, to judge which type of involvement is more desirable than another may be presumptuous. Furthermore, parents' needs change over time as they grow and develop in their own parenting roles and as their children progress to new phases of development. Family circumstances and a myriad of other variables influence how practical various forms of involvement are for a given family at any particular point in time (Bailey & Simeonsson, 1984; Carney, 1983; Turnbull, Brotherson, & Summers, 1982; Wiegerink, Hocutt, Psante-Loro, & Bristol, 1980). Given all these factors, parent involvement assumes no one best approach. More important, no single type of parent involvement should be imposed on all parents. Professionals should not take the stance that they are the ones to decide what alternatives are more acceptable, as if to say to parents: "This is what is best for you. If you are a conscientious, cooperative parent, you will participate in the activities we plan for you."

This need for individualization in parent involvement is becoming an emerging theme in more recent literature (Turnbull & Turnbull, 1986). Karnes and Zehrbach (1975) have suggested the importance of matching family and services by making available viable alternatives for participation. Bricker and Casuso (1979) pointed to the extreme variability in families and suggested that professionals should individualize services for parents as they do for handicapped children. This dictates that no single strategy possibly can accommodate all individual family needs in so diverse a population. Turnbull and Turnbull (1982) stress the need for flexibility in programs involving parents in this statement:

> It is time—indeed, beyond the time—to consider the needs, abilities, and preferences of parents in regard to the demands of their child and expectations of the school. Rather than mandating that all parents be equal participants with the school personnel to make decisions jointly (*Federal Register*, 1981), public policy should tolerate a range of parent involvement choices and options, matched with the needs and interest of the parents. (p. 120)

Turnbull and Turnbull have suggested that parent involvement should offer numerous options ranging from allowing parents not to be involved if they so choose, to allowing full and equal decision making for parents who wish to participate at that level.

A definition of parent involvement and its goals   Parent involvement or parent services should be viewed broadly as a range of alternatives. Judging what is appropriate is best left to the discretion of the consumer—the parent. A functional definition of parent involvement is offered by the author:

> ★ *Parent involvement or participation denotes a process through which parents are brought into contact with (a) the staff that has responsibility for giving service to the handicapped child (and parent) for purposes of educational intervention, and (b) activities involving the child, which are created to inform parents and to facilitate parent roles with their own child. Involvement implies*

a variety of alternative activities that vary from program to program. Differences in the options available are affected by the unique features of a program, the geographical setting, the population of children and parents to be served, and the resources available.

The essential elements upon which this involvement process should be built include:

— *flexibility*—to allow changing levels and types of parent involvement over time.
— *individualization*—to match the style and amount of involvement to meet parent, child, family, and program needs.
— *alternative options*—to offer choices and the right of choice in order to achieve constructive and meaningful outcomes.

Involvement activities with parents should focus generally on one or more of the following goals:

- *Personal contact and interaction*: to provide a means for achieving communication beween parents and staff, among parents, and between parents and the ongoing service activities.
- *Information sharing and exchange*: to provide a means for ongoing interaction and sharing as a vehicle for building staff-parent rapport, camaraderie, and a sense of mutual understanding.
- *Social-emotional-personal support*: to build a system of mutual cooperation between staff and parents, as well as among parents, and to create a support system parents can turn to for encouragement, understanding, counseling, and simple friendship.
- *Coordination*: to create a means for staff and parents to work hand-in-hand toward the same goals so that continuity is maintained between parents and staff in education and training of the young child. This increases the chances for effective teamwork and reduces the risk that parents and staff will end up working in opposition to one another.
- *Assistance*: to provide a range of services that will facilitate parents in their roles, provide direct services to children, and aid families in ways that strengthen the overall family system.
- *Education and training*: to provide information or specific training, or both, to parents to (a) help them gain an understanding of their special child, his or her handicap(s) and needs, and (b) acquire skills that will enable them to manage their child at home, provide appropriate care and support, and be effective teachers of their own child.

Alternative roles and activities for parents

How can parents "participate?" Activities can be described in terms of various parent roles.

Parents as observers   A common strategy is to provide opportunities for parents to watch their own child in the classroom or to observe professionals in teaching-therapeutic roles. Though some authors stress the passive aspect of this role, it is a source of much incidental and vicarious learning whose value cannot be negated. One parent of a handicapped 3-year-old girl commented:

> One of the things I like most is sitting here in the observation room watching Caryn [the teacher] work with Laura. You know how much I'm here. I learn lots this way. She gets Laura doing

things I never believed she could do. It's a real boost to see that. I know you're thinking you ought to invite me to go into that classroom . . . but no. I'll be doing that the rest of the day. It's my time to sit here and watch . . . it does me as much good. I go home and try some of the things the staff does. Too bad every program doesn't have these booths so parents can see what goes on without their child knowing it.

Parents as an audience   "Audience" denotes a more formalized role of observer and participant, such as that found in these kinds of activities: (a) parents attending intermittent meetings where talks are given on topics of interest (e.g., health care of a handicapped child, legal considerations for handicapped children), or where demonstrations are given on strategies for working with a special child; and (b) parents attending short programs in which their child performs. This latter activity is familiar in most regular early childhood and school programs, but it is easily neglected in programs for young handicapped children. These performances are important to the children and their parents. To see parents' pleasure when their young child is part of an ever-so-small performance (a song, an acted-out nursery rhyme) is convincing enough that this kind of activity is an invaluable source of encouragement and reinforcement for parents.

Parents as providers of services and information   In the provider role, parents have a number of necessary functions that constitute valued forms of participation. These functions are part of what "greases the gears" for smooth delivery of services. For example, parents work with the staff to plan schedules for when and where they and their child will receive services. Parents usually are responsible for transportation and for seeing that the child arrives and departs from the designated location on time. They provide materials and various personal items the staff needs for the child.

Although this role often is not recognized as a form of participation, when a parent ignores the obligations of this role, professionals quickly become impatient. Some parents may be negligent in bringing or picking up the child on schedule. Some avoid contact, fail to provide information when it is needed, or simply are unresponsive to approaches by staff. Professionals typically view parents who behave in this way as failing to uphold their part of the service relationship. Active, responsive, mutually supportive consumer-provider interactions are what can make this linkage pleasant and successful for both parties.

Parents as decision makers and team members   Public Law 94-142 defined a set of principles and a philosophy about parent involvement that brought them into instructional planning, decision-making roles alongside professionals. In this role, parents are entitled to review educational records relating to their child, and ideally will do so. They attend IEP conferences and participate in several key functions related to planning their child's intervention program. Preparation for the conference and these responsibilities can lead parents into other activities such as informal assessment and observation of their own child, gathering additional information on the child, or giving the staff needed information. These processes extend parental roles into other areas, too. For example, parents are cast into the role of learners as they are exposed to new information and prepared for meaningful participation in the IEP planning process. (See details on PL 94-142 in chapter 2.)

Parents as policy makers and advisors   Parent involvement can take the form of membership in advisory or policy-making boards for the agency or program serving them. In this role, they are potentially in one of the most powerful positions to affect the nature of services they receive and program operations. It also places parents in a position of great responsibility as they become involved in the operational issues related to management, funding, policy, program philosophy, and content of services offered. As one father described his role in this capacity:

> This is a place I know I can contribute something to my son's program. I like having something to say about how the program is run. We've tackled some tough problems—ones that've plagued the program for years. It's made me understand why things are done the way they are. I have a whole new sense of what it takes to run this program for my kid. I've given them some good ideas, too. . . . We've made some progress. You know, it's hard for dads to be part of the teaching stuff during the day . . . wouldn't want to do that anyway. But I do know how to run a good business—and this is a sort of business. I can help behind the scenes. I feel some real ownership in this program.

Parents as liaisons or representatives   Interagency collaboration is increasingly important in public services because of diminishing funding resources and potential overlaps in services across agencies. Furthermore, many organizations have similar goals and hence seek ways to coordinate their efforts. In setting up their own advisory boards, some groups seek parent representatives from various service programs in the community. By participating as appointed or elected members, parents can act in a representative role for programs serving their child. For example, a parent whose child is enrolled in a preschool may represent that program on the local board for the Association for Retarded Citizens. As liaison, the parent carries information between the program and the agency, represents parent interests from the intervention program, and serves as advocate for the program when ARC support would be advantageous.

Parents as advocates, disseminators, and fund raisers   Parents can play an invaluable role in creating support for early intervention programs among local and state decision makers whose actions affect funding. Parents can disseminate information (formally or informally) about a program to friends, neighbors, legislators, and local governing officials. They can be involved in fund raising. Because early childhood-special education is not mandated in every state, funding for programs often depends upon local support. Parent power is a tremendous force in gaining support for early intervention services or preventing loss of support. The degree to which parents can play these roles effectively is dependent, in part, on how well administrative personnel keep parents informed and work cooperatively with them.

Parents as counselors, friends, and supporters   If a program creates opportunities for parents to come together, interact, and get acquainted, friendships and mutual support systems form almost spontaneously. Parents provide support to each other as they listen, share experiences, and give assistance (e.g., transportation, baby sitting, helpful information, and advice) to each other. As one mother confided:

> The other parents around here [those involved in a center-based infant and preschool intervention program] have become my best friends—sort of a second family to me. So many of my old

friends stay away since Leta was born. They seem uncomfortable. When Leta was in the hospital for her heart operation, it was the people here—the parents and the staff—who came to help. I didn't even have to ask . . . they understood.

These supportive roles can be formally created, too, through organized activities spearheaded either by the staff or through parent leadership. Parents in one program organized themselves so that when a new child entered the program, the parents personally were contacted by a welcome committee. Committee members went to homes to introduce themselves, share information about the program, and offer other assistance. In another city, parents assumed volunteer roles in a parent-to-parent program for new parents who delivered a baby with some kind of debilitating condition or impairment. Early contacts in the hospital offered support and informed parents about services available to help them and their new infant.

Parents as learners/trainees   The intent behind parent training is to provide opportunities for parents to acquire new skills that will facilitate their parenting roles with the special child. This may involve participation with staff in one-to-one training in which parents are taught specific techniques for caregiving, stimulating, and teaching their handicapped child. Or it may involve attendance at group meetings where various topics of concern are discussed. The major emphasis of some early intervention programs is upon parent training. Other programs target the child but include training for parents who indicate interest. A staff person may visit the home to work with the parent along with the preschooler or infant. Or parents might participate in classroom activities and learn teaching skills while acting in the role of classroom aide.

Parents as teachers/tutors of their own children   Some programs create official roles for parents as teachers/tutors to involve them actively in the intervention process. Parents implement all or part of the planned intervention by working with their child on specific skills at home or at the center. Involvement of this type can serve the purposes of:

— increasing the time parents spend in a helping, teaching role with their child.
— improving the quality of interactions between parent and child so that exchanges are more facilitative to learning.
— training parents in methods of instruction to help them be better teachers for their child, and to increase their ability to deal with stress or conflict situations.
— helping parents handle special needs related to the child's handicap (e.g., management of equipment such as braces or hearing aids, or dealing with feeding or other caregiving tasks).
— creating a structure so that parents will more likely reinforce the child's learning and provide more consistent carryover between home and school.

Parents as volunteers, aides, or assistants   The need for extra manpower in early intervention programs often brings parents into a variety of roles either as unpaid volunteers or paid assistants. Given limited budgets for staff, parents can be an invaluable source of help. In one center, mothers and even a few fathers took one-week turns at being "cook." They prepared lunches and snacks for the children—a service that was too costly for the center to support otherwise. In another early intervention program, parents and staff worked together to renovate a dilapidated playground; they now return each year for clean-up and repair work. Several fathers got involved in their youngsters' program by giving their time to do construction work for the center; they repair and paint furniture or do other handy work on a regular basis. The nice part about this form of activity is that it brings both parents and staff into informal, friendly contact.

Parents as people   The people role belongs on our list, too, especially because it is one that parents emphasize. Interestingly, however, it is rarely included in literature describing parent roles. When asked how parents could be involved meaningfully in an early intervention program, one young mother responded:

> See us as people. Treat me . . . accept me as a person, not as a "handicapped parent" just because I've got a kid with a problem. If I were any other parent—one with a normal kid—people wouldn't be so worried about how I'm involved. That's like an overprotective parent who's always finding things for a child to do and never letting the kid create something for himself. We parents can find some of our own ways to get involved. The staff doesn't have to do it all. Sometimes it's good just to be another interested person hanging around.

Barsch's (1969) research reiterates the point behind this mother's remarks. He noted that parents frequently express the desire to be recognized first as an individual person, the need to be treated with dignity as individuals, to be regarded first as people who seek acceptance and recognition in their own right. Parents do not want to be treated as "special." Neither do they wish to be treated impersonally as a member of that group or entity called "parents of a retarded child," "parents of a handicapped preschooler," or "mothers of at-risk infants." Perhaps one of the most important roles for parents is simply that of playing "themselves"—just regular people who have the same needs as the rest of us.

MAKING THE PARENT-PROFESSIONAL PARTNERSHIP WORK

Deterrents and facilitators to effective teamwork

When parents and professionals do not relate well to each other or when cooperation is lacking, each party tends to blame the other. One does not have to look far in the literature to find references to the shortcomings of professionals or mistakes in their interactions with parents (Roos, 1975; Stile, Cole, & Garner, 1979; Turnbull, 1983). And weaknesses in parents or conditions that deter them from meeting the expectations of professionals are cited, too (Heward, Dardig, & Rossett, 1979). Although these limitations or problems may be real, to hold one or the other party responsible for failure of parent-professional collaboration only ignores a more important point: *Parent-professional cooperation and teamwork involve a reciprocal relationship.* Each party affects the other. Each contributes to success or failure of the team effort. Each has an impact on outcomes of parent involvement efforts. Parents and professionals alike bring into the relationships their own assets and liabilities, skills and limitations, interpersonal and social skills, and attitudes.

Yet, regardless of what each party lacks or what each brings to the relationship, the goal is still the same: to interact, communicate effectively, and facilitate each other's role as it relates to the handicapped child. Parents and professionals make up a kind of system in which their roles and actions are interdependent. One's success is affected by the behavior and performance of the other. These reciprocal qualities of the parent-professional relationship, and the dual responsibilities of both that make it succeed or fail, must be recognized. As the saying goes: "It takes two to tango."

Although we emphasize the reciprocal nature of the professional-parent relationship, some realities that affect this unique partnership should be acknowledged. These realities sometimes compound the dissonance between parents and professionals and interfere with cooperation. They relate to the *allocation of time* and *responsibilities* of each party for input into the intervention process with a handicapped young child. Professional staff is employed specifically to carry out its part in an early intervention program. The reality is that parents are not. Parents' employment can consume their time in other activities totally unrelated to their child and special education. This means that the time they can devote to their child's formal intervention and educational program is limited. No matter how valued parent-professional teamwork and cooperative effort may be, this does not change the fact that the difference in time parents can devote to a program compared to the full-time professional is 400%. This imbalance in time affects the partnership in that it:

— gives the professional more power to influence what work is done with and for the child.
— places more responsibility on the professional to adapt to parent schedules and to the limitations of the parent's ability to devote time to the program and the child's education.
— places more responsibility on the professional to see that the agreed upon program (as specified in the IEP) is carried out.

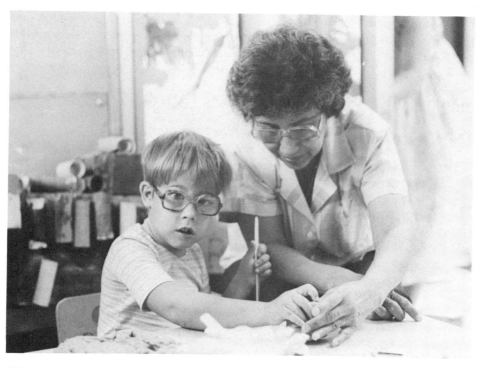

This mother assists in the preschool classroom as her way of being involved in her son's early intervention program. For some parents, other forms of involvement are more helpful and realistic given their work schedules and other responsibilities at home.

— weights success of the intervention program more heavily upon efforts of the professional, who has invested more and whose sense of professional achievement and competence is more tied to outcomes of the effort.

These realities need not create difficulties between parents and professionals if they are acknowledged and if realistic expectations are set as to what each is capable of giving.

The real deterrents to cooperative relationships are those in which professionals and parents must deal with basic differences that affect their common action and planning. Barsch (1969) pinpointed some of those differences, to which the author has added a few from her own experience. Dissonance between professionals and parents usually arises in regard to differences in:

— attitudes toward the handicapped child, his or her handicap, and treatment.
— expectations of what the program should do for the child and what the outcomes should be.
— values about the importance of education in allocation of the child's and parents' time.
— personal style in interacting with one another and style of communication and problem solving.
— values about what education should be for the child and where priorities should be set.

These sources of dissonance can be confronted, discussed, and resolved. Resolution depends upon communication, interaction, and willingness to share in decision-making processes.

Some guidelines

Trust and mutual cooperation between parents and professionals doesn't just happen. Parents do not become involved automatically because their child is part of a special education-early childhood intervention program. Opportunities must be created, be they formal or informal, for building mutual understanding and sensitivity that can lead to true parent-professional collaboration. How can programs be created for and with parents to elicit meaningful kinds of activity?

1. *Plan or provide alternative modes of parent activity, services, and support systems.*

   Parent needs are highly individual, as are their capabilities for involvement and their available time. Given the population of parents described earlier, alternatives must be flexible so parents can seek out the form of contact and involvement that best fits their needs. Professionals could define parents' involvement arbitrarily and then communicate to parents: "This is what you should do; this is where and when we want you around." But this approach would only add to the demands and expectations imposed upon parents and probably would increase their feeling of having little control over their own lives (a phenomenon that parents of handicapped children frequently describe). Such an arbitrary approach to parent involvement belies the very spirit and intent of parent-professional teamwork.

2. *Be realistic about what the program and staff can do to spearhead and support parent activities and services.*

   The staff (or any individual member) should avoid promising too much or creating expectations beyond what can be delivered. The goal of providing alternatives should be tempered with wise judgment of what options are most appropriate for a given group of parents at a given time. The underlying reality in organizing any quality parent activity or service is that an investment of staff time, as well as parent time, is required to make it work effectively. Failure to adequately judge the demands of an activity involving parents can lead to poorly implemented parent-staff activities, with resulting frustration for everyone. Professionals can end up appearing to give only lip service to the notion of parent involvement when in reality they ran out of time and energy.

3. *Invest time in building relationships with parents by getting to know them and letting them come to know you and other staff members.*

Mutual respect, trust, and caring are not transmitted by casual acquaintances or strangers, but these are the basic ingredients that make parent-professional relationships work and become mutually gratifying. Relationships develop through interaction, sharing, and association in activities that build some common base of experience. This is perhaps the foundation for strong parent-professional teamwork.

4. *Be available and willing to interact with parents informally whenever the chance presents itself, even if the exchanges must be brief.*

Informal exchanges—the brief, informal talks that truly build relationships—are the exchanges that parents comment on most. The staff should remember that parents are people who like to be acknowledged, too. Professionals tend to focus so much on their therapeutic-teaching roles that their approaches to parents are often formal, somewhat impersonal interactions relating to the handicapped child. Some parents have remarked, "I began to feel like the 'handicapped parent.'" Parents greatly appreciate the informal, person-to-person exchanges between themselves and the staff. Many prefer these over the formal interactions that occur in IEP meetings, staffings, or group training sessions. Warmth, caring, and real camaraderie require that staff and parents learn to see the person in each other, as well as the formal roles each play in their interactions.

5. *When designing parent activities and services, keep the total family system in mind.*

The parent not only is an individual with needs but also is a person who lives and functions within a unique family system. Services or activities must fit the parent, child, and family system. Every parent—from the single parent to the young parent who may be still struggling for a sense of independence and freedom from the "establishment," to the parent in an extended, multigenerational family living under one roof—is living in a special family situation. And within a family system the needs of mother, father, and siblings may be different. If separated parents share custody of the child, their needs and involvement with the program differ. At times, activities involving the whole family—not just parents—can be constructive. Program strategies should support parents and family members within the family system.

6. *View parent involvement broadly as encompassing a continuum of services/activities/ opportunities that bring staff-parent interaction, assist parents in their parenting roles, and involve them in the intervention process with their child.*

Parents' needs vary, and their interest in various forms of involvement changes over time. A balance should be attempted between (a) what staff does for parents, (b) what parents are asked to do for staff or the program, and (c) what staff and parents do in a joint or collaborative effort. All levels of activity have value, and at times a parent needs one type more than another. Assistance that encourages dependence and passivity and that which generates competency and independence in the recipient represents a delicate balance. Professionals can slip into a role of doing everything for parents and their child in their press to offer quality comprehensive services. They may make the mistake of promising too much and communicating, "Now I'm here—I'll take care of everything for you and solve your problems." Foster, Berger, and McLean (1981) have cautioned that because of real or presumed expertise, professionals run the risk of overriding and displacing parents' position as authorities in the family. Too much "doing for parents" can undermine their confidence in themselves as parents or as competent adults.

7. *Be both sensitive and realistic in the expectations you place on parents and in the tasks/activities on which they are asked to spend their time.*

Failure to recognize the differences between the professional role and the parent role can lead to conflict in expectations and misunderstandings between parents and staff. As educators and interventionists, we are *paid* to devote our full efforts to the needs of the children with whom we work. On the other hand, parents' sole obligation or commitment is not the handicapped child. Foster, Berger, and McLean (1981) have pointed out the assumption behind the professional's efforts: The more services, and the greater the effort expended on the child, the better. This point of view indeed benefits the child and family. But the assumption behind parental efforts cannot be exactly the same. It is not a matter of "the more the better" but, rather, a question of what effort is practical and realistic given the many other demands on parents' time. The more time parents expend on the handicapped child, the less time they have for other priorities.

Disproportionate emphasis on the needs of the handicapped family member compared to other family needs can disrupt family balance. Healthy family adjustment requires a balance of time across a variety of personal and family goals. Ideally, professionals are there to provide services in ways that help parents achieve and maintain this healthy balance, not to disrupt that balance by imposing unrealistic demands, expectations, and possible guilt upon the parent.

8. *Respect parents' right to ultimately choose their style of participation and to set their own values regarding their level of participation.*

When parents make decisions in regard to their handicapped child with which the staff does not agree personally, professionals may have difficulty accepting parents' rights. Yet, we must recognize and respect the autonomy of the parents of children we serve. We cannot dictate values, make decisions for parents, or attempt to live their lives for them. We should not impose our own personal system of values upon them and then label them as uncooperative if they do not agree. We can teach, educate, inform, advise, consult, and share our opinion when appropriate. But, most important, we are there to support, not to be the adversary.

Sometimes, in the spirit of dedication and commitment to the handicapped child and the educational/therapeutic part of his or her care, professionals become impatient with parents who do not conform to their wishes. These differences may arise when staff and parents are of different cultural, socioeconomic, or ethnic backgrounds. In any case, parents hold the right of choice and of consent to determine the course of their own personal and family life. Professionals must support parents in their choices, even when their own personal value system might have indicated another choice.

9. *Listen to parents as their concerns, priorities, needs, and ideas are part of the ingredients that go into effective program planning, implementation, and coordination.*

Parents may be unfamiliar with educational "jargonese" and may talk a different "lingo" than professionals. They may or may not be experienced with IEPs—or even know what they are. Most parents have never seen an IEP and are unfamiliar with the process of defining learning objectives for their child or deciding upon the most important instructional priorities. But they do know their own children. Whatever the case, parent input has a place in planning and implementing services for their child. Opportunity for parents to share their ideas and interact with staff about plans for their children should be available not only through formal IEP meetings and staffings but also through informal parent-staff discussions. Often, parents open up and express their feelings and ideas more freely in more informal situations.

10. *Recognize that parents' needs change over time as they grow and gain experience, their family changes, and their handicapped child moves on to new developmental stages.*

Parent involvement programs have to be dynamic and changing—evolving into new activities and opportunities for parents over time as they, too, change and enter into new stages of their parenting careers. The needs parents express at one point in time for information, assistance, or various forms of involvement likely will be different at a later time. Some children and their parents are part of an early intervention program for as long as 4-5 years if the intervention begins in infancy. The same menu of services and activities will grow old if it goes on year after year. Given the same continuing options for involvement, one cannot expect parents to maintain a consistent level of participation. This implies that: (a) parent needs should be assessed regularly (perhaps at the beginning of each year), and (b) parent input should be sought each year in making plans for parent activities. At times parents and their families will want a minimal level of involvment, and at other times pressures may be heightened and parents will want more help and staff support.

11. *Prepare parents for roles they will be asked to play, and give them ample time and assistance to assure their comfort and success in these roles.*

Decision-making/planning roles that parents play as a part of the IEP process or roles in which parents act as classroom aides or teachers of their own children require skills. For example, the IEP conference is an experience that most parents of young children are encountering for the first time. They have not participated in identifying long- and short-term objectives or evaluating their child's progress in an objective way. Meaningful participation is most likely if parents are oriented beforehand as to: (a) what will happen in an IEP conference, (b) what procedures will be followed, (c) what role they will play, and (d) what preparations they can make to be able to take a meaningful part in the discussion.

If parents are recruited into roles as teacher aides or tutors for their own child, adequate preparation is important to assure success. To throw a parent into a role like this without adequate preparation is to invite failure and frustration. The parent should receive assistance in what procedures to follow. As one parent remarked:

> I like it when the staff suggests some things I can do at home with my child—but don't assume I know how to do it. I'm not stupid, but I'm not a trained teacher either. Teachers maybe can do this stuff off the top of their heads without thinking about it, but I might not be able to do the same thing just "kaboom." You've got to show me what you want.

SUMMARY

All parents play a crucial role in shaping the lives and personalities of their children. The care and nurturance they give their children and the quality of parent-child interactions represent some of the most powerful environmental variables impacting upon the developmental achievements of young children. When a child is handicapped, the nature and quality of parenting are of particular significance. Parents may have to assume greater responsibility for initiating and maintaining interactions with their child since handicapped children are often deficient in the very behaviors that promote attachment and reciprocal interactions. Normal smiling, reaching, and other social behaviors that reinforce parents in their caregiving efforts often are delayed or absent. And handicapped children are likely to be more dependent upon parents to provide support and bring experiences to them that most other children could seek out for themselves.

If early intervention programs are to be optimally effective, they cannot operate in isolation of children's parents. Special education for just 2-3 hours each day when these children continue to spend the greater portion of their waking hours in the care of parents or other adults is not enough to deal realistically with the potential effects of a disability. Caregivers thus have to be brought into the intervention effort as team members to assure their child the best chance to benefit from special training and live as normal a life as possible.

Parents, too, need special support as they live with and care for their handicapped child. The demands of child rearing are not easy with any child, but they are compounded when a child is handicapped in ways that increase dependence and, consequently, caregiving/teaching responsibilities for parents. When a child does not achieve normal developmental milestones, parents may have to deliberately teach skills that most children acquire with little assistance. But parents do not automatically have the skills to handle the special needs of a handicapped infant or preschooler. Often they are left in a position of learning what to do by trial and error, or of not understanding what can be done until many precious years have passed and their child's disability has had a notable impact upon his or her functioning level. Early intervention programs thus can play a vital role in giving parents direction and assistance during the years when they are establishing attachments and patterns of caregiving with their special child.

No one prescription can be offered for how parents can best be involved in early intervention programs, but they can play a number of potential roles. Parents vary greatly in their individual needs, and programs likewise vary in their capacity to offer services for parents or to allocate staff time to parent activities. As professionals seek to involve parents in meaningful roles, several questions must be answered: To what extent should parents be expected to become involved in their child's intervention? What kinds of involvement bring the greatest benefit for parents and their child? What are the realistic expectations that should be placed upon programs and their staffs for offering services to parents and involving them in policy-making roles or educational activities with children?

11
Program Planning, Teaching, and Interdisciplinary Considerations

What do early intervention programs for young handicapped and at-risk children actually entail? What information do prospective teachers and other staff members need to plan and implement quality educational programs? We have narrowed our focus in this chapter to the special preschool classroom because such a large number of early intervention programs employ this service delivery approach. Of course, viable program models exist that do not provide services to young handicapped and at-risk children in

The author gratefully acknowledges the contributions of Barbara J. Thompson, K. Eileen Allen, and Barbara Brackman to this chapter.

classroom settings (e.g., home-based programs). In any event, many of the program features described here are shared by programs involving home-based and non-classroom service approaches. Furthermore, many of the educational and instructional processes with preschoolers discussed here are applicable to infants, toddlers, and older, primary-aged children as well.

Let's begin by considering three very different children who share one important characteristic—the need for a quality early childhood special intervention program.

> Mary is a 5-year-old child with Down syndrome. Her curly black hair and dark brown eyes make her especially appealing—as do her ready smile and friendly manner. Mary has already developed most of the self-help skills typical for a child of her age. Her speech and language development, however, has not progressed as rapidly and is more like that of a 3-year-old. She is just beginning to learn school readiness skills that most of her normally developing age-mates have mastered. Mary is not yet able to name simple shapes, colors, numerals, or to recognize her name in print. But she can identify objects by name and some by function, and she can do rote counting. She does not seem interested in or able to work puzzles or do simple matching activities. Her attention span is very short.

> Pedro appears to be a bright 4-year-old. If you watch him carefully, you will see how aware he is of everything that goes on around him. He is especially happy and obviously absorbed when someone shows him a book about animals, engines, spaceships, and dinosaurs. For a child so young, he has mastered an impressive number of facts on each topic. Pedro's physical activities, however, are dramatically altered by his handicap. He is severely physically impaired (athetoid cerebral palsy affecting all four limbs). He is unable to walk, sit by himself, or manipulate objects with his hands. In fact, Pedro is virtually unable to function motorically on his own.

> Connie, at first glance, does not appear to be handicapped at all. She is a pretty little 4½-year-old with red hair and blue eyes. She moves with confidence and seems unusually well coordinated—especially if you watch her on the playground jungle gym! If you spend much time with her, however, you will notice her quick temper outbursts, almost ritualistic behavior, and stilted speech. Connie refers to herself only as "the Connie girl" and never looks directly at a person when speaking. She has been diagnosed as autistic and never has shown normal social behavior patterns.

An early childhood-special education teacher who is well prepared to work with young handicapped and at-risk children must be able to plan for and instruct children with a wide variety of handicapping conditions in the same setting. Mary, Pedro, and Connie could be in the same classroom under the educational responsibility of one special education teacher. With this in mind, consider the following descriptions of three very different classrooms. Which one of these should you choose for Mary, Pedro, and Connie?

Classroom one is bright, large, and sunny. In one area is a large sand table; several children are gathered around it digging, making tunnels, and playing with miniature houses, cars, and people. In another part of the room is an area that looks like a small playhouse. Several children are dressed up in adult clothing and appear to be cooking dinner. Two dolls have been seated at a table set with red plastic dishes. Five children are building an intricate tower in an area designated for blocks. In the middle of the room is a large, round table filled with art supplies, where a number of young artists are busy with their creative endeavors. One of the teachers is in the book corner reading a story to several children. The other two teachers move from area to area, interacting quietly with the children and responding to their requests.

If you were to stay the whole morning session in this classroom, you would notice that although the same children do not stay in one area, essentially the same activities are ongoing. The only time the children are gathered into a structured activity as a whole group is for juice. If you were to ask the head teacher how she decided what the children would be doing, she would tell you that she selected the creative materials but that the children choose how they will use them. In fact, each child selects the area, the activity, and the length of time he or she will participate before moving on to a new area and endeavor.

Classroom two also is organized around several play areas. As in the first classroom, you immediately notice that more than one activity is happening at once. In one area, three children are naming animals shown in bright, colorful photographs held up by a teacher. In another area, one child is practicing buttoning with large buttons sewn to canvas fabric. Four children are playing quietly with blocks near a teacher, who calls them from this group one at a time and works with each child for 10-15 minutes. At the back of the room, one child is walking on a long, wooden board about 6' long and 12" wide. A paraprofessional is working with the child on balance as she counts each step on the board and praises the child for her efforts.

If you were to stay for an entire session in this classroom, you would notice that children change activities under teacher direction. The daily schedule paces the children through a sequence of specific learning activities. At several points, the children come together as a group. Once is for lunch, where careful attention is paid to the task of getting ready to eat, to some of the children's eating skills, and to cleaning up. The music time is for everyone, as is a brief outdoor play period, but most of the time is spent in small groups or one-to-one instruction. If you were to ask the head teacher of this classroom how he decided what the children would be doing, he would tell you that the decision was different for each child. He would explain that decisions were based on a battery of tests administered to each child to determine individual needs and by the daily recording of each child's progress in each instructional area.

> Classroom three is smaller than the other two but is equally attractive and inviting. Unlike the first two classrooms, you immediately notice that all of the children are together. They are sitting in chairs placed in a semicircle around a teacher. As the teacher holds up individual pieces of fruit, the children eagerly raise their hands, and when called upon, tell her what the piece of fruit she is holding is *not*.
>
> If you were to spend the whole session in this classroom, you would notice that activities change, and do so under teacher direction. Times for juice, story, outdoor play, art, manipulative materials, and preacademic training sessions are scheduled. You also would notice that all the children always participate in the same activity at the same time. If you were to ask the head teacher of this classroom how she decides what the children will be doing, you would be told that activities that teach readiness for kindergarten are planned for the group.

Which classroom did you select for Mary, Pedro, and Connie? We selected the second one. Let's consider the reasons why we made this choice, and then why we did not choose the first or third classroom.

● Did we choose the second classroom because it was better than the other two?

All three classrooms represent good, defensible programs, but the second classroom has some important features that make it better for Mary, Pedro, and Connie. These children each have different handicaps and different needs for intervention. A classroom that can accommodate all three of these children must be flexible enough to provide the directed and individualized instruction appropriate for each child. This means it must offer activities, materials, and equipment that fit a wide range of developmental and learning needs. Further, each of these children has serious and complex handicaps. Therefore, individual programs must be based on careful analysis of each child's developmental status and learning needs and then monitored to determine if instruction is effective.

The second classroom offers the flexibility and focus that all three children need. First, classroom activities and materials are chosen on the basis of individual children's needs for directed instruction. Second, these needs are determined by careful assessment. Third, each child's performance in each learning program is monitored to ensure that progress is being made.

● Why are the first and third classrooms not appropriate for these children?

The first classroom also represents an individualized environment, but the individualization is based on each child's self-choice. Fun, creative, and enriching opportunities are available in an open, free setting. Provided that a child does not have developmental problems and does not come from an environment with serious deficits or disadvantages, this type of program could provide an enjoyable and productive experience. Many children could learn a great deal about social interaction, independence, and decision making in this type of classroom. Our three handicapped children, however, do not have the resources to function well in this kind of setting or to benefit optimally from it. Mary lacks the cognitive skills and attention span to choose, participate in, or stick to nonstructured activities. Pedro lacks the motor skills needed to get around, use materials, and explore the environment by himself. Connie lacks the necessary social and interactive skills to benefit fully from the unstructured groups.

The third classroom offers more structure and directed teaching, but these aspects focus on group needs rather than individual needs. The assumption in this classroom is that all children profit from exactly the same activities and materials. Because the structure and directed teaching are aimed at skills and experiences needed to succeed in kindergarten, many children who have difficulty in kindergarten would profit from this classroom. Generally they are children who are immature, have only mild developmental delays, or come from environments that do not provide the experiences that most children have before kindergarten. Mary, Pedro, and Connie, however, have very specific and different needs, and their problems are far more complex. As with the first classroom, our three handicapped children lack the necessary behaviors to profit from the training provided in this classroom.

The children in our example do not have the behavioral resources to benefit optimally from either the first or the third classrooms, and the classrooms do not have the resources to meet all of their needs. Mary needs to learn to attend, develop more complex speech and language skills, and acquire basic discrimination skills for preacademic tasks. Pedro needs adapted play and work materials, special furniture and equipment, and physical and occupational therapy. Connie needs to learn more socially appropriate behavior and play skills. Each has special needs that classrooms one and three cannot meet without revision of their program philosophies, curriculum, and teaching strategies.

Mary, Pedro, and Connie are only three among many children who present a wide range of handicaps and might be brought together in a single early intervention classroom. Early childhood programs for young handicapped children typically serve children ranging from 0 to 5 or 6 years in age and may include some children up to age 8. Programs must be ready to serve children with all types of handicapping conditions and all degrees of severity, including multiple disabilities. Therefore, quality early intervention programs must be prepared to offer highly individualized activities to accommodate the variety of special needs in a diverse group of children.

FEATURES OF A QUALITY EARLY CHILDHOOD INTERVENTION PROGRAM

In chapter 2, several major concepts were described as cornerstones upon which special education programs for young children should be built. Programs for developmentally impaired or at-risk children must be somewhat different from special education as traditionally practiced with school-aged students and from regular early childhood programs as delivered to nonhandicapped preschoolers. In essence, programs must be a new blend of the two to create educational services and instruction that will effectively intervene when a young child's development is restricted by a handicapping condition. This blend calls for special teacher competencies. Although programs may vary in content, depending upon the handicapping conditions and specific ages of the children served, several features are generic to a quality intervention effort:

1. Individualized education goals and objectives for each child.
2. Individualized curriculum and learning activities based on child objectives.

3. Monitoring and evaluation of each child's progress.
4. Opportunities for interaction with peers who offer appropriate developmental models.
5. An adapted, supportive environment.
6. A healthful and safe learning environment.
7. Interdisciplinary involvement, coordination, and teamwork.
8. Parent participation and input.
9. Compliance with state education or preschool/day-care regulations.
10. Compliance with federal and state legislation for early childhood-special education programs.

Professional training programs generally devote a large portion of courses and practicum experiences to the topics addressed in this chapter. Several books could be written to describe the array of instructional methodologies, materials, and curricular approaches that make up a quality intervention program for young handicapped children. The intent here, therefore, is not to spell out *how* to teach children or how to carry out the nitty-gritty tasks of operating a program. The objective is to review each feature listed above and answer some practical questions about what competent teachers need to know to put that feature into practice in the classroom. Later, we will look at how teachers and other disciplinary staff work together as a team to create a quality program that encompasses the features described.

Individualized educational goals and obectives

★ *A quality early intervention program is one in which individual goals and objectives are set for each child based upon formal and informal assessments of their developmental level, special needs, and special problems or impairments. These are written into a formal plan called the IEP.*

● What does *individualization* mean in an early childhood intervention program?

Special education and therapeutic activities must be planned individually for each child. This is in direct contrast to regular early childhood programs, where learning activities generally are planned for a group of children on the basis of a preconceived notion about what children need. A quality early childhood intervention program for young handicapped children is tailored individually for the child; *the program must be appropriate for each child.* The child is not expected to be appropriate for an already defined program.

● What is an IEP?

An individualized education program (IEP) is a document required under PL 94-142 that must be prepared for each child and subsequently implemented to ensure that he or she receives an appropriate education based on identified needs. The law is specific about what the IEP document is to include:

1. A statement of the handicapped child's present levels of educational performance, including academic achievement, social adaptation, prevocational or vocational skills, psychomotor skills, and self-help skills.

2. A statement of annual goals describing the educational performance to be achieved by the end of the school year under the child's IEP.

3. A statement of short-term instructional objectives, which must be measurable, intermediate steps between the present level of educational performance and the annual goals.

4. A statement of the specific special education and related services to be provided to the child, including a description of:
   — the extent to which the child will participate in any regular education program. (Note: This may or may not be applicable to preschool handicapped children and would not apply to infants.)
   — any special instructional media and materials needed to implement the IEP.

5. The projected dates for initiation of services and the anticipated duration of services.

6. A justification for the type of educational placement that the child will have. (Note: This may not even be an issue in getting services to a handicapped child under school age.)

7. A list of the individuals responsible for implementation of the IEP.

8. Appropriate objective criteria and evaluation procedures (and schedules) for determining, at least on an annual basis, whether the short-term instructional objectives are being achieved.

● Who participates in preparing the IEP?

The following persons should be involved in planning and writing the IEP for a handicapped child:

1. The child's teacher or prospective teacher.

2. One or both of the child's parents, a surrogate parent, or guardian.

3. A representative of the local education agency who is qualified to provide or supervise the provision of special education-early childhood intervention services.

4. Other individual(s), at the discretion of the parent or the agency, who may be helpful to the IEP planning process (e.g., speech therapist, occupational or physical therapist, social worker, audiologist, medical personnel).

5. A member of the evaluation team who is knowledgeable about evaluation results on the child.

Why include so many participants? Each person increases the probability that the IEP will be appropriate for the child, that it indeed will be implemented, and that the necessary communication among key persons will occur. The administrator or representative of the local education agency is responsible for making the final placement, delivering and supervising services, following guidelines for the law, and maintaining accountability. The teacher and therapists are responsible for implementing programs to meet the IEP goals and objectives and for documenting a child's progress. The parent serves as advocate for the child and sometimes helps implement certain phases of the prescribed educational program. The evaluation team representative interprets assessment results and helps translate this information into appropriate services and instructional goals and objectives. Depending upon the specific case, additional individuals may be involved to provide information, assist in the problem-solving process, or give support to parents or staff.

- What planning procedures are used in writing the IEP?

Several meetings are required to achieve three different purposes: (a) initial development of the IEP, (b) review of the IEP and the child's progress, and (c) revision of the IEP. The initial IEP conference must be held within 30 days after a determination has been made that a child needs special education or related services. The IEP is written at that meeting, not before and not after. The IEP plan is a vehicle for then selecting the most appropriate placement for a child and for scheduling special services.

The law requires a second meeting to be held some time later for purposes of reviewing the IEP and determining whether it still represents an appropriate plan for that child. This meeting must be held at least once a year beginning with the anniversary date of the initial IEP conference. At this second meeting, the "annual update," a new IEP document is filled out and signed. The updated IEP may be similar to the previous one, simply reflecting the child's progress on annual goals and objectives. Sometimes the decision may be to terminate special education and to suggest a new placement. In other cases, it may be determined that a more extensive effort is needed, with additional services including new goals and objectives.

The third type of meeting can be held for purposes for revising the IEP. Although this can be done during the previously described annual update meeting, one important distinction here is that of timing. A revision meeting is held if changes in a child's IEP are needed *before* the annual review meeting would automatically be scheduled. All those involved in delivering services to a child, as well as the parent, are responsible for calling a meeting if major revisions are needed.

- What assessment strategies should be used to plan an individual program plan for each child?

Once a child has been identified as needing early intervention, further assessment is essential so the IEP can be written. This assessment must pinpoint the specific skills, deficits, and deviations to describe the child's current level of performance. Initial diagnostic evaluation may indicate that a child is cognitively delayed, hearing impaired, or has cerebral palsy but will not necessarily indicate exactly what the child can and cannot do. The assessment process for the IEP must yield precise and detailed information about the child's developmental functioning level in each key area or domain of development (e.g., social development, speech and language development, cognitive development, self-help development, motor development). This kind of *educational assessment,* described in chapter 7, is the type of evaluation that allows special educators and therapists to plan specific activities needed to to optimize a child's development and reduce the potential effects of his or her handicap.

- What skills and information should a teacher have to conduct an adequate educational assessment?

Assessment for educational program planning must interface with curriculum. The assessment of young children with moderate to severe handicaps therefore focuses on providing information on a child's *level* of development in each developmental domain, as well as on the *degree* and *type* of deviant development manifested. Four major aspects of teacher competency are related to educational program assessment.

First, the teacher must be able to choose appropriate instruments for educational assessment. To do this, the instrument should be analyzed in terms of the following factors:

Does it provide developmental descriptions of young children in each developmental domain, and is it based on a thorough analysis of developmental norms?

Does it provide a current picture of performance that can be translated directly into instructional goals and objectives?

Does it provide detailed sequences of behavior necessary for writing the training sequences that will lead toward the instructional objectives?

Is it appropriate or adaptable to the assessment of children whose handicapping conditions affect their test performance and thus require special consideration by the evaluator?

Second, the teacher must be able to administer the instruments appropriately to obtain accurate and complete information about the child. Skills related to administering educational assessment instruments are:

Familiarity with instructions for administering the test, including procedures for scoring each item.

The ability to adapt instruments to gain an accurate assessment of children whose handicap influences their ability to perform in a testing situation.

The ability to identify potential methods and training strategies based on the nature and type of responses the child makes during assessment.

Third, the teacher must be prepared to use informal assessments along with standardized and criterion-referenced instruments, including:

Conducting interviews with a child's former teachers, therapists, or parents to obtain useful information.

Reviewing and analyzing records on the child's past performance or developmental history for information that will be useful in conducting the educational assessment.

Planning and implementing observational methods for collecting data on a child's performance in various settings or with varied materials to get an accurate view of the child's capabilities and identify instructional methods that work with the child.

Finally, the teacher should be able to integrate the specialized assessment information related to particular handicapping conditions with the child's developmental profile, and then jointly plan goals and objectives with other members of an interdisciplinary team.

For example, the information obtained in a test of reflex development should be considered along with information about motor skills obtained on tests of developmental skills such as the Brigance Early Inventory of Skills or the Portage Guide to Early Education. Therefore, the teachers of young handicapped children should have:

A familiarity with the instruments and terminology used by other disciplines who provide therapeutic services to young handicapped children.

An ability to interpret results of specialized assessments and recognize their implications for program planning and instructional methodology.

● How are measurable annual goals and short-term objectives written?

Each child's program is written in statements that clearly specify the *intended outcome* of the program for the child. These *goals* are statements that indicate (a) areas in which the child will have programming, and (b) desired outcomes from the educational intervention. For example, an annual goal might read: "John will increase his developmental level on self-help skills by 6 months, as measured by the Brigance Inventory of Basic Skills, in the skill areas of dressing, toileting, and eating."

Objectives are more specific statements of (a) behaviors the child will acquire to show progress toward a goal for a particular developmental area, and (b) reductions to be made in the degree to which a disability interferes with a child's functional abilities. For example, an objective for a preacademic goal might read: "John will be able to name the color of pictures and objects for the colors of red, blue, green, yellow, white, orange, black, and brown with 100% accuracy on three consecutive occasions."

Goals and their subsequent objectives are written for each learning or developmental domain in which the child's educational assessment indicated that improvement is needed. They are stated as outcomes based on a reasonable estimate of the level (if sound educational and therapeutic procedures are applied) to which the child can progress in one year from where the educational assessment shows he or she is currently functioning. Figure 11.1 gives an example of annual goals and related short-term objectives in the IEP of a young handicapped child.

Suggested readings: Bender and Valletutti (1976a, 1976b); Cohen and Gross (1979); Fallen and Umansky (1985); Fiorentino (1981); Neisworth, Willoughby-Herb, Bagnato, Cartwright, and Laub (1980); Schafer and Moersch (1977); Ramey and Trohanis (1982); Torres (1977); H. Turnbull and A. Turnbull (1978); Turnbull (1986).

Individualized curriculum and learning activities

★ *Effective programming for handicapped and at-risk children requires that individual goals and objectives be translated into a specifically planned program of activities for each child in harmony with his or her developmental age and performance capabilities. This means that all children within a classroom will not necessarily be doing the same thing all together at the same time; several kinds of learning activities probably will be going on simultaneously.*

● If each child's program is individualized, does a curriculum or curricular focus for young handicapped children actually exist?

Figure 11.1

An Example of Annual Goals and Short-Term Objectives
in an IEP for a Young Handicapped Child

Ryan is age 3. He is classified as severely multiply handicapped. He is visually impaired and shows significant developmental delays across all areas. He uses a few words. He interacts with objects primarily by mouthing them. He will stand holding on to an object for support. He is not toilet trained. He must be fed but can grasp a spoon and use a cup, although he drops the cup when through drinking. He jabbers and says "mama, dada" with no consistent meaning.

GOAL: Ryan will demonstrate a 5-6 month gain in preambulatory motor development level by increasing his skills in the focus areas of standing, walking, and ball handling, as measured by the Brigance.

OBJECTIVES:
(Focus Areas)

Standing	1. Will pull to a standing position within 10 seconds for 3/3 times for 3 sessions.
	2. Will stand unsupported for 5 seconds for 10 consecutive trials for 3 sessions.
	3. Will lift his foot when his hand is held for a 3-second duration for 10 consecutive trials for 3 sessions.
Walking	4. Will walk with both hands held for a 1-minute duration for 3 consecutive sessions.
	5. Will walk sideways holding on to furniture for 1 minute duration for 3 consecutive sessions.
	6. Will walk with one hand held for 1 minute duration for 3 sessions.
Ball Handling	7. Will roll playground ball while in a sitting position 10 consecutive trials for 3 sessions.
	8. Will hurl playground ball while in a sitting position 10 consecutive trials for 3 sessions.

GOAL: Ryan will demonstrate a 6-month gain in social developmental level by increasing his skills in the focus areas of play and compliance, as measured by the Learning Accomplishment Profile.

OBJECTIVES:
(Focus Areas)

Play	1. Will play by another child, sharing manipulative toys, for 5 minutes for 3 sessions.
Compli-ance	Will put toys in container when told to "put in" after 5 consecutive sessions.

GOAL: Ryan will demonstrate a 4-6 month gain in speech and language development by increasing his skills in the focus areas of single-word utterances and direction following, as measured by the Sequenced Inventory of Communication Development (SICD) or the Learning Accomplishment Profile (LAP).

OBJECTIVES:
(Focus Areas)

Utterances	1. Will imitate sounds accurately for 10 consecutive trials for 3 sessions.
	2. Will say "mama" and "dada" with meaning.
	3. Will say "more" to request repetition of an action 2/3 times over 3 sessions.

Figure 11.1 (continued)

4. Will say "up" and "down" when he is in appropriate position with 90% accuracy for 3 sessions.
5. Will imitate words for 10 classroom objects with 80% accuracy for 3 sessions.
6. Will imitate words for the actions of 5 objects via tactile identification with 80% accuracy for 3 sessions.

Direction
Following
7. Will respond appropriately to directions "put in," "give," and "take" for 10 consecutive trials for 3 sessions.

GOAL: Ryan will increase his fine motor developmental level by increasing his skills in the focus area of small object manipulation, as measured by the Brigance.

OBJECTIVES:
(Focus Areas)

Manipulation
1. Will use a pincer grasp consistently when handling small objects for 10 sessions.
2. Will put small objects in a container for 10 consecutive trials for 3 sessions.
3. Will unwrap loosely wrapped objects for 5 consecutive trials in 2 minutes for 3 sessions.
4. Will place three graduated cups inside one another in 1 minute for 3 sessions.

GOAL: Ryan will demonstrate an 8-month gain in his cognitive-preacademic developmental level by increasing his skills in the focus areas of shape discrimination, knowledge of body parts, and use of objects, as measured by the Brigance.

OBJECTIVES:
(Focus Areas)

Shapes
1. Will complete a 3-piece form board (circle, square, and triangle) within 1 minute for 3 sessions.

Body Parts
2. Will point to 10 body parts when named with 100% accuracy for 3 sessions.

Objects
3. Will squeeze squeal toy, shake bell, and push button on appropriate toys with 80% accuracy for 3 sessions.

GOAL: Ryan will demonstrate a 6-month gain in his self-help developmental level by increasing his skills in the focus areas of toileting and self-feeding, as measured by the Brigance.

OBJECTIVES:
(Focus Areas)

Feeding
1. Will lift and return cup to the table after drinking for 5 consecutive sessions without spilling.
2. Will consistently use spoon to scoop food and take from plate to mouth with limited spilling for 5 consecutive sessions.

Toileting
3. Will imitate word "potty" when placed on potty-chair 3 times daily with 100% accuracy for 3 days.
4. Will eliminate in chair twice during classtime when placed there at regularly scheduled times with 90% accuracy over 10 occurrences.
5. Will wear training pants when previous objective is met, and will have no more than one accident per week.

Curriculum based on a preset notion about the similarities of young children and their shared needs for activities is not appropriate for young children with moderate to severe handicaps. Curriculum planning for handicapped children requires that the curriculum (a) accommodate all of the individualized program plans or IEPs written for the children enrolled in the program; (b) encompass learning experiences appropriate to the developmental age levels represented among the children, which can be highly varied; and (c) accommodate variations in the ability of each child to function independently, follow instructions, and work within a small or large group. The curriculum must be organized around training and therapy activities to increase each child's developmental functioning level in each of the developmental domains.

Although the developmental domains provide a framework for the curricular content of an early childhood special education program, the approach to training and therapy within each domain varies considerably from child to child. Goals may have to be written in each major domain for each child in the intervention program. If programs are truly individualized, to find that each child has the same objectives for each goal area would be most unlikely (in fact, unthinkable).

Consider the three children introduced at the beginning of this chapter and how their objectives might differ within the domain of fine and gross motor development.

Mary is unable to perform most basic preacademic skills. Although this may be related to her cognitive delay, it also could partially relate to inadequate fine motor skills. Down syndrome children often exhibit delays in this area, which are related to hypotonicity and primitive reflex development. Therefore, the objectives in this domain most likely will address her need for training in gross and fine motor skills and describe therapy and therapeutic outcomes in regard to increasing muscle tone, inhibiting immature reflexes, and promoting age-appropriate reflexive responses.

Pedro's motor development has not progressed beyond the stage of a very young infant and is both limited and deviant. Assessing his development on most typical developmental instruments (which are based on normal sequences of motor development for preschool-age children) is not possible. Specialized assessment of the degree of neurological impairment, range of motion and muscle strength and control therefore will form the basis for his objectives. Highly specialized therapeutic techniques and adaptive equipment will be required to implement his program in this domain.

Connie is well within, if not beyond, the developmental norms in motor skills. Her learning objectives in this domain would be similar to those for a normal 4-year-old. Emphasis likely would be placed upon providing age-appropriate experiences and training in motor development similar to those found in a preschool for nonhandicapped children.

Note how the motor development curriculum for each of these children differs. In Mary's case, the emphasis is on remedial training and therapeutic intervention. Emphasis in Pedro's case is on therapeutic and adaptive intervention. Finally, Connie's needs in this developmental area are similiar to those of normal peers, so the objectives for her would focus on age-appropriate activities and experiences.

In summary, a teacher of young handicapped children must be prepared to:

— provide curricular content organized around the major developmental domains.
— provide programming for the entire scope of skills related to the curricular domain.
— be cognizant of specialized techniques for diminishing the deviant aspect of development or the negative impact of the various handicapping conditions on development.

● How are IEPs turned into individualized daily activities?

Daily activities and experiences are planned to help each child move from his or her current functioning level to the levels projected in the IEP. Each child's goals and objectives are the basis for developing and implementing daily lesson plans. Questions such as "What types of activities should I plan for this child?" and "What do I want him or her to achieve?" therefore must be answered before doing any daily planning. Activities reflect already determined needs and intended outcomes for each child. Specifically identifying program outcomes increases the likelihood that a child will make progress. Selecting and following a roadmap is much easier if you know the destination before starting a trip.

Teaching activities and procedures generally are developed for *each* objective in a child's IEP. Considering the range of children needing early childhood intervention programs, the scope and complexity of learning activities they require can seem almost overwhelming. For example, activities to teach a blind youngster the concept of color have to be different from activities to teach colors to a sighted but cognitively delayed child. Different activities are needed to teach a child to tie shoes than to teach a child to button a coat.

Many teaching strategies work well with young children. Because of the limited scope of our discussion here, we will focus on a *general strategy for planning learning activities*. A teaching strategy based on an interventionist behavioral model is highly effective with young handicapped children. This strategy relies primarily on the concept of requiring children to respond in a specific manner and involves the following tactics by the teacher:

1. Writing objectives in terms of observable behaviors.
2. Breaking down learning tasks into small, sequential steps to enable the child to experience success and make continuous progress.
3. Planning cues, physical prompts, and corrections to assist the child until he or she can make a correct response independently.
4. Arranging contingencies to motivate the child to respond in a positive manner.
5. Making training procedures and activities for the child as functional as possible.

In using these four tactics, individual needs of each child must be taken into account. For example, the degree to which sequential tasks must be broken down into small steps varies depending on the functioning level and capability of each child. A child with severe impairments will require tasks that entail extremely small steps, whereas a child with mild disabilities will not need this. Figure 11.2 gives an example of a training sequence for a handwashing program that might be used with a young blind child. Notice the

Figure 11.2
Example of a Training Sequence

A learning sequence for teaching a blind preschooler to wash hands:

1. Step up on step-stool to sink.
2. Pull up on sink stopper.
3. Place hands on faucet handles.
4. Turn water on (faucets automatically turn off).
5. Place hands in water.
6. Find the soap.
7. Rub hands together with soap.
8. Put soap back on soap dish.
9. Rub hands together and over back and front.
10. Rinse hands in sink.
11. Push down stopper.
12. Ask for towel.
13. Dry hands on towel.
14. Give towel to trainer.
15. Step down off step-stool.

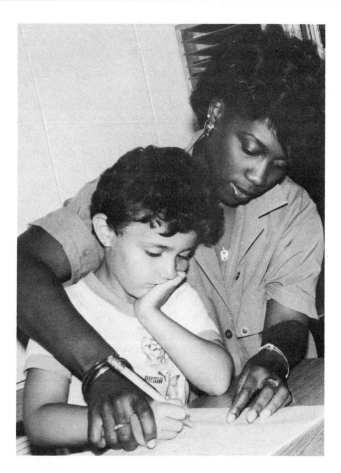

Special needs children often require learning tasks to be broken down into small steps as well as additional prompts, cues, and reinforcement to help them master a new skill. This is part of what an individualized program entails.

number of steps in the handwashing program and the sequential arrangement of those steps. The process of developing a training sequence by breaking down a task into small, sequential steps is called *task analysis*.

The type and number of cues, prompts, and corrections a teacher provides to facilitate each child will also have to be different. In speech and language training, a child with a hearing impairment will need many more visual cues and physical prompts related to tongue placement and lip position than will a child with normal hearing. A child with perceptual disorders will require more cues than other children to emphasize the relevant aspects of a stimulus. A child with a physical handicap will need more initial physical prompts or assistance in grasping required for a buttoning program than will a child who has no physical impairment.

Identifying what activities, interactions, objects, or edibles are reinforcing to a particular child is important. Children differ, as do adults, in regard to what is and is not rewarding to them. A child who may not respond to praise may respond to opportunities to play a favorite game or to eat a small piece of cheese. Once effective reinforcers have been identified for a child, these reinforcers should be dispensed contingent upon correct responses or appropriate behavior. Children also vary in the amount of reinforcement needed to facilitate adequate responding. Some children need very little reinforcement; others (handicapped children, in particular) need a great deal of initial extrinsic reinforcement.

In addition to using behavioral strategies for developing activities, a teacher should *make training procedures or activities for each child as functional as possible*. This means that whenever possible, training should:

— occur at a time and place similar to or in the actual setting in which the skill would be used naturally.
— occur in as normal or natural sequence as possible.
— utilize materials that are like actual materials the child would ordinarily use in daily living.

For example, self-feeding skills are best taught at actual mealtimes with real utensils. A handwashing program can be conducted each time the child uses the bathroom and prior to mealtimes. It should take place at a real sink with real soap, water, and towels as the training materials.

● How can teachers manage so many activities at the same time?

Because each child's goals and objectives are individualized, various activities will be happening at the same time. Consequently, the preliminary planning and scheduling required of staff will be more extensive and complex. Instead of planning one set of daily activities for the group, as takes place in many classrooms, a set of daily activities must be planned for *each* child.

Few programs have the necessary staff-student ratio to provide constant one-to-one instruction. Scheduling therefore should reflect logical groupings of children who share similar objectives or whose different objectives can be accomplished within a group setting. Learning activities will involve a variety of staff-student ratios including: (a) one-to-one instruction, (b) small-group instruction in which the group composition changes frequently, and (c) occasional large-group activities.

Planning a daily schedule for young handicapped children reverses the scheduling/ planning process typical of most preschools and kindergartens for nonhandicapped children. Schedules for the latter group generally are planned *before* knowing the specific children who will participate in the class. The schedule usually reflects the typical activities that all children are presumed to need. On the other hand, the schedule planned for a classroom serving young handicapped children must be planned to a large extent *after* the children's individual needs have been assessed and their individual program plans have been written.

When planning a daily schedule for an early childhood intervention program, four variables are important to consider. *First, the objectives of each child in the program should be reviewed to identify logical groupings of children.* In some cases, children may have nearly identical objectives, and in other cases the objectives may vary in difficulty level and complexity but can be taught at the same time by using flexible materials and activities. Consideration also should be given to whether particular children will profit from small- or large-group instruction.

The second variable to consider in planning a daily schedule concerns the transfer and generalization of skills. Whenever possible, training and therapy should be conducted in the environment where the behavior a child is learning should occur naturally. For example, speech and language training might take place in the classroom setting rather than in an isolated training setting. The child's daily activities and routines should reflect, to the fullest extent possible, those that the children are likely to encounter in a less restrictive environment. This is particularly critical for children with moderate handicaps who might be placed in a kindergarten setting on a part-time basis and for nonhandicapped children who will be moving on to regular education settings. Opportunities for both small- and large-group instruction and activities therefore are desirable for moderately handicapped, as well as nonhandicapped, children.

The third variable concerns the planning of variation in a child's schedule. Classroom schedules for young children should provide a balance between quiet and active times, structured and nonstructured periods, one-to-one training, and small- and large-group activities. More demanding learning activities that require a high level of attention should be scheduled early in the day. If these activities are left to the end of the day when children are tired, their ability to learn to perform well is decreased.

The fourth variable concerns the arrangement of schedules to provide consistency in a child's daily activities. The order of activities should be basically the same each day. This allows children to anticipate events and to be more independent in moving from one activity to another. Scheduling of classroom activities results in the development of two major documents: (a) an individual schedule for each child, and (b) a total master program schedule. The *individual schedule* should outline the activities in which a child will be involved each day and should match his or her objectives. The *master schedule* should outline what will be occurring on a daily basis for the total program and where staff members will be working. Individual child schedules and the master schedule must be planned simultaneously to create a balanced schedule that provides for functional grouping of children, individual training sessions, and efficient use of staff.

> Suggested readings: Bagnato and Neisworth (1981); Bender and Valletutti (1976a, 1976b); Cook and Armbruster (1983); Calhoun and Hawisher (1979); Cratty (1970); Fallen and Umansky (1985); Gaylord-Ross and Holvoet (1985); Garwood (1983); Garwood and Fewell (1983); Hare and Hare (1977); Snell (1978); Finnie (1975); Mori and Neisworth (1983); Fewell and Sandall (1983); Devenney (1983). Also see the entire issue of *Topics in Early Childhood Special Education*, 1983, 2(4).

Monitoring of each child's progress

★ *Effective programming necessitates the use of some type of performance monitoring system or ongoing data collection system whereby staff can continually monitor each child's developmental status and progress on goals and objectives defined in the IEP.*

● Why is monitoring the progress of handicapped children necessary?

As noted in chapter 7, once educational assessments have been conducted, keeping track of a child's progress is important. Without monitoring, daily training and therapeutic strategies for each child may be selected or continued inappropriately. Sensitive instructional and therapeutic decisions can be made for a child only if continual performance data are gathered.

Consider the likelihood of reaching your destination on a trip if you had selected a map and the roads you would take but failed to pay attention to highway and detour signs along the way! Similarly, by measuring and recording a child's daily performance on each activity relating to the goals and objectives in the IEP, we are more likely to know if our teaching methods are working. If the measurement shows that a child is making consistent progress toward the intended outcomes, we can assume that the types of activities and materials being used with that child are appropriate. If the monitoring data show little or no progress, we should assume that different activities and materials are needed. Or the child's goals and objectives may need revision.

● How do teachers keep track of children's progress?

Not only must planning take place to develop and schedule activities for each child, but planning should also include procedures for monitoring each child's performance on those activities. Specifically, the teacher must be able to:

— select the appropriate method of recording data that fits the type of behavior described in each short-term objective and that will measure the child's level and quality of performance and progress toward a specific criterion.
— apply some systematic procedure for reviewing and analyzing data so that decisions can be made as to whether revisions in teaching procedures are needed.

Figure 11.3
An Example of Data Collection on a Preschooler's Learning Task

Learning objective for Melissa:

Melissa will match 5 shapes by placing each in the correct bin (2 trials each, randomly presented) with 90% accuracy or better, 3 days in a row.

Method for Taking Data
to Monitor Melissa's Progress

A Graph Summarizing Melissa's Progress

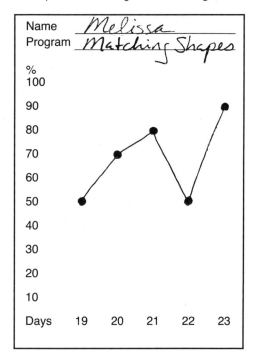

Name _Melissa_
Program _Matching Shapes_
Trainer _Clifford_
Week of _March 19_

Shapes	M	T	W	TH	F
Circle	+	+	+	+	+
Circle	−	+	+	−	+
Square	−	−	+	−	+
Square	−	+	−	−	+
Triangle	+	+	+	+	+
Triangle	+	+	+	+	+
Rectangle	−	−	+	−	+
Rectangle	−	+	+	−	+
Oval	+	+	−	+	−
Oval	+	−	+	+	+
% Correct	50	70	80	50	90

Name _Melissa_
Program _Matching Shapes_

Numerous methods can be used for recording and displaying data (see chapter 7). Figure 11.3 contains an example of a child's short-term objective and the recording sheet and graph used to monitor and document her progress. *Individual performance monitoring is closely related to program evaluation.* The degree to which objectives for all the children are successfully met is an indicator of overall program efficacy. Thus, summarizing individual child data on a regular basis and at the end of the year is one way a teacher can get a picture of the achievements of the children and the program.

Suggested readings: Bailey and Wolery (1984); Cohen and Gross (1979); Cross and Goin (1977); Paget and Bracken (1983); Coordinating Office for Regional Resource Centers (1976); Erickson (1976); White and Haring (1980); Young (1984).

Opportunities for interaction with appropriate peer models

★ *In the intervention setting for handicapped youngsters, opportunities should be present to interact, observe, and play with nonhandicapped peers who provide age-appropriate developmental models. This is especially important for children who are becoming socially aware and are functioning at a developmental level at which they are able to interact with peers in social and learning situations.*

● What types of classrooms or programs provide for integration of handicapped and nonhandicapped children?

Two classroom models that offer opportunities for young handicapped children to be with nonhandicapped peers were described in chapter 9. The *mainstreaming model* provides for placement of handicapped children in classrooms where the primary function is to serve nonhandicapped children. Mainstreaming might occur in kindergartens, community preschools, and Head Start programs. Handicapped children in these settings are in the minority, so the teachers must receive inservice training, and specialists might work with the handicapped children on an itinerant basis.

The second model, the *integrated classroom,* is sometimes referred to as mainstreaming-in-reverse. The primary function of these classrooms is to serve handicapped children, but nonhandicapped children are also enrolled to create a more normalizing environment. Nonhandicapped children are in the minority in these settings. The program staff usually includes specialists from several disciplines who are trained to work with young handicapped children and their normal peers.

Mildly handicapped children are served more typically in mainstreamed classroom settings. Moderately to severely handicapped children are more likely to be served in integrated classrooms where specialized services are available on a more intensive basis. Both program models, however, operate on the assumption that handicapped youngsters profit from exposure to nonhandicapped peers.

● How can teachers integrate handicapped and nonhandicapped children into the same activities?

Successful integration takes effort. If the full benefits of "normal" models are to be realized, specific teaching procedures must be used to assure that integration truly occurs. Research suggests that effective integration of handicapped and nonhandicapped peers is not a spontaneous outcome of enrolling both groups in the same classroom with the same teacher (Cavallaro & Porter, 1980; Guralnick, 1978; Peterson, 1982c; Peterson & Haralick, 1977). If strategies are implemented to ensure appropriate modeling and imitation, handicapped children are more likely to benefit from their interaction with nonhandicapped peers.

Opportunities for interaction are generated largely through thoughtful scheduling of individualized activities. Opportunities for interaction during instructional periods can be created by grouping children with similar objectives. If children's learning objectives are identical, group instruction is relatively easy to plan. If differences are present in regard to the level and complexity of children's learning objectives, flexible activities and materials are needed. In the latter cases each child can be directed to use a material or perform a task relative to her or his skill level. For example, the teacher may show the

Integration of handicapped and nonhandicapped children in early intervention settings offers handicapped youngsters an opportunity to observe, interact with, and imitate other children who can provide more developmentally appropriate and skilled models of behavior.

entire group a colored cube. He or she then might ask one child to find another cube that matches the color of the cube, and ask another child to name the color of the cube, and yet another to write the appropriate color word.

Specific opportunities for play and social interaction between handicapped and nonhandicapped children should be included in the daily schedule. To assume that shared instructional time with nonhandicapped children will allow an adequate amount of interaction opportunities for handicapped children is unwise. In fact, shared instructional time with nonhandicapped children may not be possible for some handicapped children. Interaction can be promoted during class activities that focus on play and social skills. Outdoor and indoor play periods are good examples. Lunch and snack time, as well as occasional large-group music activities, also can facilitate integration of both groups of children, especially if the activities are structured to enhance social interaction.

Training nonhandicapped children to function as peer models is important. Several procedures that promote the role of nonhandicapped children as models and elicit imitation in handicapped peers have been described in the literature (Cooke, Apolloni, & Cooke, 1977; Cooke, Cooke, & Apolloni, 1977; Strain & Kerr, 1981). These involve rehearsal periods for modeling, as well as training the peer model to actually function as a tutor or to use specific teaching procedures with a handicapped classmate.

A teacher should always encourage and prompt positive interactions between handicapped and nonhandicapped children (without forcing children to interact) whenever the opportunity presents itself. For instance, if a handicapped and a nonhandicapped child are playing in the block area, the teacher might suggest that they construct something together. Or the teacher might sit down and invite both children to join him or her and then gradually withdraw as they become involved in interactive play.

Suggested readings: Allen (1980); Guralnick (1978, 1980); Klein (1975); Meisels (1979); Peterson and Haralick (1977); O'Connell (1984); Peterson (1982c); Strain and Kerr (1981); Snyder, Apolloni, and Cooke (1977); Blancher-Dixon and Turnbull (1979).

An adaptive, supportive environment

★ *Quality early intervention programming means making adaptations both in the preschool environment and in instructional/play materials or equipment to assure maximum access for each handicapped child and to optimize learning in spite of a child's special problems.*

● What does adaptation of an early childhood classroom for handicapped children involve?

Both the needs of the teacher and the needs of the children affect how one designs and arranges the physical classroom environment: (a) the need to accommodate children with physical handicaps and special health problems; (b) the need to store and retrieve a wide range of specialized materials and equipment; (c) the need to accommodate several different activities and training sessions with children at the same time; and (d) the need to use the same space for various purposes. Furthermore, the classroom environment should be attractive, cheerful, and appropriately arranged for the age group being served. Attitudes of parents, staff, and children about a program are easily affected by the visual appeal of a classroom setting. Several guidelines are helpful in organizing the classroom environment:

1. Plan the arrangement of furniture and work centers so it is functional for the kinds of activities that will be conducted to achieve goals and objectives for individual children and for the overall group.
2. Arrange space flexibly so it can serve multipurpose needs.
3. Plan storage and placement of materials and equipment to maximize convenient retrieval for children, when appropriate, and for adults.
4. Anticipate which activities should occur simultaneously and plan space so that one activity will not disrupt the other.
5. Arrange space so that it accommodates the needs of physically handicapped children.
6. Utilize furniture and equipment, as well as visual cues and prompts, to designate areas for activities.
7. Think about traffic patterns you want and those that should be avoided, and arrange furniture to encourage those movement patterns.

● How are materials and equipment adapted for a handicapped child?

A good early childhood-handicapped program is built upon an appropriate selection of materials and equipment. This means that furniture, toys, and curriculum materials must be *cost-effective, safe, flexible,* and *appropriate* for the children. Commercially available materials and equipment often must be adapted for children who have either physical (motor or sensory) problems or special learning problems. When a child is failing with an instructional material or is unable to use a toy, one should analyze whether the mismatch is caused by physical problems (an inability to use the material) or by cognitive problems (an inability to understand the material). A teacher then can adapt, or modify, or possibly reconstruct from scratch, equipment and materials to make them appropriate for the child.

When a child is unable to use a material because of motor, sensory, or cognitive disabilities, several types of modifications may be necessary:

Enlarging materials for the visually or motorically handicapped child.

Cerebral palsied children may be able to play dominoes if the pieces are 6" long rather than 2". Redrawing a workbook page to fit an 11" x 18" piece of paper can give a child enough room to write answers legibly. Visually handicapped children may need enlarged print to see what is written on a printed page.

Stabilizing materials to enable better manipulation.

Rubber suction cups can secure plates to the table at mealtime to assist a child who has motor problems that affect feeding. Drawing paper can be taped to the table to enable a child with the use of only one hand to draw. Stabilizing materials also can be helpful for visually handicapped children; for example, a fine motor activity using a pegboard is easier for a blind child if the board is secured to the table.

Altering the child's mode of response.

Nonverbal children can respond to visual memory tasks by arranging pictures of objects they have seen, rather than naming them. A child whose physical handicaps prevent him or her from holding a crayon may be able to respond to reading readiness worksheets using a tape recorder. In the case of the first child, the response mode is adapted by changing from a verbal mode to a manual one. In the second case, the change is from a manual to a verbal response.

Adding cues to help a child respond appropriately to materials.

Some children simply need additional prompts to guide them as they work with materials or carry out some assigned task. The prompt may be a color cue or an arrow to show them where to start on a worksheet. Children sometimes have difficulty reproducing block design patterns with actual blocks unless they have extensive assistance. Giving the child a second card with a black outline of the design may help him or her perceive more clearly what block design is to be produced, and as skills improve, the outline can be removed.

Removing cues to reduce distractions.

Instructional items such as self-correcting materials sometimes have extraneous cues that diminish their effectiveness with a special child. Number puzzles may employ a shape discrimination cue as the self-correcting feature. A child who needs practice in counting may be more adept at shape discrimination so he or she can match the puzzles by the path of least resistance—shape discrimination. To give the child practice in counting, the teacher must modify the material, either by cutting off the shape discrimination cues or by remaking the number puzzles without the extraneous cues.

Making materials reusable to give extra practice.

Many materials do not provide sufficient practice for handicapped children, so additional opportunities for practice must be added. One way to do this is to teach children to use plastic overlays with workbook pages. The same page can be used repeatedly until the child achieves a criterion success rate. Without the overlay, the child gets only one chance on a worksheet regardless of whether he or she understands the concept.

Making materials more familiar or more personal for a child.

When teaching a young child to use a picture book correctly, beginning with a picture book of photographs of familiar items is helpful. Photos of the child's mother, pet, or favorite toy can create more interest than general drawings of the same concepts.

Learning by touch is how this 3½-year-old blind child will discover what a bottle is. This requires deliberate guidance by her teacher.

Adjusting materials or equipment to fit the age group (and size) of the children.

Chairs and tables should allow a child's feet to reach the floor. Dangling feet are particularly harmful to children with motor problems. If necessary, foot-stool adaptations should be build so that feet reach a flat, solid surface. Tables should meet children below the chest. Children should not have to raise their arms to adjust for a too-high table or to slump over a table that is too low. If proper furniture is not available, existing furniture should be modified to fit the size of the children in the classroom. Special consideration is necessary for children with physical handicaps who require additional support or posturing from furniture and equipment. Occupational and physical therapists can provide important information and assistance in adapting equipment and furniture for physically handicapped children.

When selecting new equipment and materials or adapting old ones, *room flexibility in any early childhood program is an important consideration. Flexible furniture and equipment are preferable to stationary or heavy items that must remain in one place.* Lightweight furniture and equipment with multiple uses are the best choices. An excellent example of furniture with multiple uses is a plastic cube chair that can be turned to offer seating for a toddler or turned in yet another way to become a small table.

Suggested readings: Bailey and Wolery (1984); Fallen and Umansky (1985); Horner, Voeltz, and Fredericks (1984); Johnson and Werner (1975); Leeper, Witherspoon, and Day (1984); Love and Wathall (1977); Robinault (1973); Thorum (1976).

A healthful and safe learning environment

★ *Special health and safety precautions are important in the early intervention setting, given the medical and physical problems of many handicapped children, to ensure that the environment is healthy and safe.*

● Why should special attention be given to health and safety factors in a classroom for young handicapped children?

Certainly *all* children should be served in healthy and safe settings! Young handicapped children, however, often require additional precautions. For example, children with epilepsy, cerebral palsy, or visual impairments are more likely to fall and injure themselves. Specific disabilities or lowered functioning levels of some handicapped children result in their working and playing on the floor more often, and hence they are more vulnerable to unsanitary conditions. Some handicapped children may drool or mouth toys excessively. These behaviors, plus the fact that many young handicapped children in early intervention programs are just learning toileting skills and some are still in diapers, increase the risk for spreading contagious diseases if precautions are not taken.

Furthermore, children with health impairments may be more susceptible to infection, prone to allergic reactions, and less likely to tolerate temperature changes. Many of the children require medications that must be readily available and routinely administered. The program staff should carefully consider the implications of each child's handicap in regard to health and safety precautions, develop procedures for handling health matters, and make appropriate environmental provisions.

● Are any general guidelines and procedures available to help ensure the good health and safety of young handicapped children?

Some suggested guidelines for classrooms with handicapped children are:

1. Floors should be carpeted or padded or cushioned linoleum to prevent injury.
2. Toys and materials should be examined for potential safety hazards.
3. Electrical outlets should be covered with protectors and checked for other potential safety hazards.
4. Cupboards for cleaning supplies should be *locked;* medicines and sharp objects should be placed out of reach of children.
5. Temperatures should be controlled to provide adequate heat or cooling.
6. Exits for emergency situations should be readily accessible (on same floor).
7. Escape procedures (e.g., for fire or tornado) should be planned, posted, and practiced regularly.
8. Toilets, bathroom areas, and tables should be scrubbed daily with soap and water.
9. Toys and other materials the children use should be sanitized with soap and water regularly.
10. Dishes should be washed in water hot enough to kill bacteria.
11. Disposable plastic gloves or plastic bags should be kept in bathroom area for use in handling diapers and in toilet training procedures.
12. Strong soap should be available for staff members to use before leaving a bathroom area.
13. A daily health check should be done as children arrive, to screen them for possible communicable diseases before they enter the classroom.
14. Standard immunizations should be required, and a record of each child's immunizations should be maintained in his or her file.
15. A list of each child's allergies or any other special health considerations should be kept in his or her file and posted in the classroom.
16. A list of any medication each child is taking and the medication's potential side effects should be maintained and continually updated.
17. A daily log of medication given during school time to any child should be maintained.
18. Emergency phone numbers should be posted near the telephone.
19. Each child's file should have numbers where parents and an alternative person can be reached in case of illness or emergency.
20. Staff should be trained and skilled in administering first aid.

Suggested readings: Decker and Decker (1976); Calhoun and Hawisher (1979); Coyner (1983); Green (1977); Linder (1983); Jones (1977); Marotz, Rush, and Cross (1985).

Interdisciplinary input, coordination, and teamwork

★ *Practitioners from a variety of related disciplines (such as special education*

Washing hands, toileting, and brushing teeth are an important part of self-help training for handicapped children in an early intervention program.

teachers, speech therapists, occupational therapists) should be involved and work together as a team to plan, implement, and coordinate their efforts in serving each child's comprehensive developmental and learning needs.

● What activities require that the teacher function as a team member?

Depending upon a child's particular disability and service needs, teachers frequently interact with professionals from other disciplines. Some argue that with these professionals available, a teacher need not be knowledgeable about the various disciplines and what they do. The case is not so simple. Realistically, these professionals are not and cannot be available throughout the school day because of typically heavy caseloads. Indisputably, the teacher remains the principal manager of the child's program. The teacher therefore can profit immensely by working with other professionals to learn how to do things such as transferring a child from wheelchair to toilet, positioning a child properly at a work table, and helping a child to develop the motor skills necessary for learning to self-feed. Specialists in other disciplines can provide invaluable consultation by helping teachers acquire specific skills to carry out these tasks with children.

Teachers as a group historically have not functioned as members of interdisciplinary teams. Early childhood-special education, however, is a field that to some extent redefines the role of teachers. If young handicapped children are to receive quality programs and services, the early childhood-special education teacher must function as a team member in activities such as:

— sharing assessment information with other disciplines in order to jointly identify a child's special needs and develop the individualized education plan.
— planning child and program schedules in coordination with other team members.
— sharing performance monitoring data on each child's progress in classroom instruction and in specialized therapy sessions in order to jointly determine the effectiveness of each child's individualized education program.
— consulting with other team members in regard to recommendations for matters such as:

handling physically handicapped children;
training procedures for physically and sensory handicapped children;
adapting materials and equipment for children with physical and sensory handicaps; and
reinforcing training strategies used by the other disciplines.

— applying some common record-keeping system across the team for information gathering and possibly for monitoring a child's development progress.

● What is the teacher's role in the interdisciplinary team process?

Early childhood-special education teachers or regular early childhood teachers who are mainstreaming young handicapped children play a pivotal role in any collaborative effort with professionals of other disciplines. The teacher usually is the one who carries primary responsibility for integrating the overall program. As the person who probably oversees a child's activities for the larger part of a day, the teacher is in a prime position on the interdisciplinary team to provide helpful information and feedback to clinicians who provide supportive services. The teacher can carry out complementary programs to help children generalize skills practiced in special therapy sessions into the classrooms. Often the teacher has the most frequent contact with parents and can best facilitate parent involvement in the early childhood program. Christoplos and Valletutti (1977) described the teacher as "the supreme generalist, deeply dependent upon information from other disciplines for greater understanding of the nature of clients and of subject matter, but independently responsible for applying information from other disciplines to the total learning environment" (p. 85).

The importance of the teacher's multifunction role is further explained by Scheuerman (1976). Although in theory a program can be designed by having each discipline provide services for a certain portion of the child's day, that approach could lead to a tragic situation—elimination of a stabilizer and coordinator or "orchestrator" of services. The teacher must ensure continuity within the interdisciplinary program. The teacher has the challenge of integrating language, motor, and cognitive skills into a viable and useful set of independent behaviors.

Teachers are in the best position to constantly monitor the well-being of children and to see where each child functions in each of the developmental skill areas. Through planning and selecting appropriate learning experiences for the child, a teacher becomes what Weiss and Morris (1978) called the "actualizer" in the interdisciplinary team. The teacher actualizes, by turning into everyday reality, the evaluations and intervention programs recommended by the team of professionals working with the child and the family. As actualizer, the teacher develops instructional procedures from the prescriptions made by the various disciplines and extends these daily instructional procedures to the home by counseling and instructional demonstrations. These interdisciplinary activities on the part of the teacher obviously call for close consultation with the various disciplines involved.

Suggested readings: Allen, Holm, and Schiefelbusch (1978); Beck (1976); Christoplos and Valletutti (1977).

Parent participation and input

★ *Quality early intervention programs involve children's parents in the intervention effort through participation in various types of activities: targeting of educational goals for their child, planning parts of the intervention program, and sharing some of the responsibilities for implementation of that program, at home or within the school environment.*

● What do teachers need to know to communicate with parents in positive, helpful ways?

Some basic elements of effective communication can be translated into guidelines for interacting with parents of young handicapped children:

1. Use clear terms and explanations, and avoid professional jargon.
2. Engage in active, attentive, empathic listening when parents are talking.
3. Use paraphrasing, as well as reflective and probing questions, to clarify communication.
4. Avoid defensive reactions.

● How can the staff encourage parents' involvement in their child's intervention program?

Chapter 10 pointed up the value of parent involvement, including the various roles parents can assume as they participate in their child's early intervention program. Parent involvement can be facilitated by providing information to encourage their involvement in meaningful ways. For example, parents must be aware of their own and their child's rights. They need to understand the nature and implications of their child's handicapping condition and its impact on development. They need to understand the rationale behind the therapy and training prescribed for their child. They must be familiar enough with the assessment practices, goals and objectives, and what teachers mean by the term "developmental domains" to be able to contribute to IEP planning. Inadequate or incomplete information limits parents' capacity to effectively participate in their children's educational program. Some information, materials, and activities that can aid parents in planning their children's IEPs are:

— developmental assessment instruments that are to be used to evaluate the child's development in each domain.
— a preliminary copy of goals and objectives the staff intends to recommend for the child, giving parents sufficient time to consider and react to these before the actual IEP meeting.

— a goals and objectives priority sheet for parents to bring to the conference, specifying their own training and therapy priorities for their child.

— planned opportunities for parents to present their reactions and considerations to each goal area throughout the meeting.

National, state, and local parent groups disseminate information useful to parents. Parent groups organized in conjunction with an intervention program can be particularly helpful. Parent training programs provide both information and skill training. Direct personal contacts by program staff or indirect communications via newsletters are other vehicles for informing parents. Information should be presented in a manner that parents can understand. Too frequently information relies heavily on specialized vocabulary, failing to accomplish the purpose for which the information is intended.

● What do early childhood-special education teachers need to know about parent rights?

PL 94-142 mandated certain procedures to ensure that parents participate in their child's educational program as informed and involved advocates. We already have addressed a number of procedures for involving parents in the IEP process that go beyond the letter of the law. The point is that teachers must be knowledgeable about parents' rights as specified in the law and make sure that parents receive information about their rights. Specifically, the rules and regulations mandate that procedures be followed regarding (a) the IEP, (b) due process procedures, (c) notification and informed consent, and (d) confidentiality and access to records.

The IEP

1. Parents must be contacted to set a mutually agreed-upon time and place for the conference.
2. Efforts to involve the parents through home visits, telephone calls, and letters (if they have not attended the IEP meeting) must be documented.
3. Efforts to use alternative methods to meet with parents in order to include them in the IEP planning should be made if they express a desire to be involved but cannot attend the meeting (e.g., a conference phone call may be an alternative).
4. Parental input at the IEP meeting should be encouraged. Parents are *not* to be presented with a pre-written IEP.
5. Parents have the right to bring other individuals to the meeting.
6. Parents must receive a written summary of the meeting and may request a copy of the IEP document.

Due process procedures

1. Parents may request a fair hearing in regard to any matter related to initiating or changing the identification, evaluation, or educational placement of their child, or the provision of an appropriate education for their child.
2. Parents should be informed of legal and other available services that are free or low cost.
3. Parents may be accompanied by counsel and advised during the hearing.
4. Parents or their counsel may give evidence, as well as cross-examine witnesses and compel the attendance of a witness.
5. Parents may prohibit the introduction of new evidence that has not been disclosed prior to 5 days before the hearing.

6. Parents may obtain verbatim records of the hearing.
7. Parents are to receive a copy of the written facts and decision within 45 days after the hearing.
8. Parents may appeal the decision of a hearing conducted by a local agency to the state education agency.
9. Parents may bring action if they disagree with the decision.

Notification and informed consent

1. All communications to parents are to be in the parents' native language and in clear, understandable wording.
2. Parents must be notified and asked to give their consent by signing approval for an evaluation to determine whether the child needs special education.
3. Parents are to be notified of *all* meetings dealing with identification, evaluation, and placement of their child for educational services in *advance* of the meeting.
4. Interpreters are to be present at the meetings if the parents' native language is not to be used.
5. Parents are to be notified of their right to have an outside evaluator, paid for by the local agency, if they disagree with the agency's evaluation.
6. Parents are to be notified of their rights in regard to the due process procedures.

Confidentiality and access to records

1. Parents must be informed of policies related to storage of records, disclosure to third parties, retention of records, and destruction of any information regarding their child.
2. Parents may inspect and review any record of the agency that is related to their child; no more than 45 days can pass before an agency responds to a parent's request to examine records.
3. Parents may request copies of the records. A reasonable fee can be charged.
4. Parents may request an explanation of the records.
5. Parents may select a representative to inspect their child's records.
6. Agencies must keep a record of third parties who obtain access to a child's records, which includes: (a) the person's name, (b) the date the records were inspected, and (c) the purpose for which authorization was given.
7. Parents may request a list of the types and locations of education records maintained by the agency.
8. Parental consent must be obtained before information is disclosed to anyone other than officials of the agency or if the information is to be used for purposes other than in regard to the child's education program (such as for research, etc.).
9. Transfer of the rights of privacy to children should take into consideration the age, type, and severity of the child's handicap.

Suggested readings: Brown and Moersch (1978); Crawford (1978); Fallen and Umansky (1985); Heward, Dardig, and Rossett (1979); Linder and Chitwood (1984); McAfee and Vergason (1979); Turnbull and Turnbull (1986); Shearer and Shearer (1977); Vergason and McAfee (1978).

Compliance with state early childhood or day-care regulations

★ *A quality early intervention program meets the regulations and standards for facilities, staff, and services set by the state that governs the licensing of early childhood centers.*

● How does one obtain information about the specific regulations and rules that govern the licensing of early childhood programs?

Most states have regulations for preschool and day-care centers. These usually are enforced by the state social service agency that defines the standards for licensing centers and issues licenses. To obtain a copy of the regulations and to determine if an early childhood-special education program must be licensed, contact should be made to the state agency or local social services or health departments. Usually, programs run by local school districts are not required to have a child-care license because public schools operate under a different set of regulations.

● What do state regulations require for a program to become licensed?

Regulations address a number of areas relating to program planning and implementation and therefore should be examined carefully early in the process of setting up a program. Most state licensing regulations include:

1. *Health and sanitation provisions:* (identified in the earlier discussion on provision of a healthy and safe environment).
2. *Nutritional requirements:* specify the type and quantity of food that must be provided for the children during a program day.
3. *Staff-pupil ratio:* generally is based on the age of the children but may also include guidelines for child-staff ratios for children based on the severity of their handicaps.
4. *Teacher and staff preparation:* typically requires that at least one staff member be trained in child development or early education and that all staff members have passed a basic course in first aid.
5. *Provisions for emergency situations:* require that emergency procedures be practiced, timed, and documented. For example, alternative emergency routes in case of fire must be preplanned. Fire drills must be conducted on a routine basis and documented in regard to both the date of occurrence and the amount of time taken to evacuate the building.
6. *Building and space requirements:* indicate the number of square feet needed per child, as well as equipment and structural requirements.

Health and safety policies generally are based on the following sources of information: (1) *Standards for Child Health Care* (3rd ed.), Evanston, IL: American Academy of Pediatrics, 1977; (2) *Report of the Committee on Infectious Diseases,* Evanston, IL: American Academy of Pediatrics, 1977; (3) *Standards for Day Care Centers for Infants and Children,* Evanston, IL: American Academy of Pediatrics, 1980; and (4) *DHEW Day Care Regulations,* Office of the Secretary of Education, Washington, DC (*Federal Register,* issued March 19, 1980).

• Do any other requirements exist?

Most communities have zoning laws, as well as fire and safety codes for public buildings. One should obtain this information from local city or county offices before selecting a building site for an early intervention program or planning and equipping a building.

> Suggested readings: Decker and Decker (1976); Leeper, Witherspoon, and Day (1984); Linder (1983); Marotz, Rush, and Cross (1985); Moore (1974); Weiser (1982).

Compliance with federal and state legislation

★ *Any early intervention program administered through local education agencies (LEAs) or those receiving federal or state funds must be in compliance with state and federal legislation concerning special education services.*

• What federal legislation addresses program requirements for young handicapped children?

Public Law 94-142 outlines certain practices or procedures for educators to follow in delivering special services to handicapped children. Passed and signed into law in 1975, the law's rules and regulations first appeared in the August 23, 1977, issue of the *Federal Register*. These regulations already have been covered in chapter 3 and earlier in this chapter. Anyone working with handicapped children should be well informed about this legislation and the procedures it mandates in regard to (a) assessment of handicapped children, (b) availability and delivery of appropriate services, (c) the content of IEPs, and (d) involvement of parents and protection of children's and parents' rights.

• What is the relationship between state legislation and PL 94-142 and program requirements for young handicapped children?

States cannot alter PL 94-142, the federal mandate, but they can make additions to this law to improve or enhance it. Therefore, one must be familiar with state guidelines. These can be obtained through the local education agency (LEA) or from the State Department of Education.

Frequently state regulations contain specific guidelines concerning early childhood-handicapped programs that are not addressed in PL 94-142. For example, pupil-teacher ratio is a major issue that arises in planning early intervention programs, and state guidelines often define what ratios programs must have. Although state guidelines vary on this issue, standards contained in the Kansas State Special Education Plan are shown here as an example in Table 11.1. Teacher-child ratios are based on the type of program model, the number of children served, and the severity of their handicaps. State plans usually specify other guidelines for acceptable early childhood-special education programs and require agencies serving this population to submit a written program plan. Obviously, then, as local early intervention programs are developed, careful attention should be given to the state plan.

Table 11.1
Example of Standards for Pupil-Teacher Ratios in Early Childhood-Special Education Classes

Minimum recommended staff for the various service delivery models and the additional staff necessary for including severely handicapped children and children under age 2½. A caseload must not exceed the program's ability to implement individualized education programs for the children enrolled.

	Number of Children	Approved Teacher EC or ECH*	Paraprofessionals	Additional Staff for Severe or Young Children**
Center-Based Group Model	**Special Classroom**			
	1-4 handicapped	1 ECH	0	1
	5-6 handicapped	1 ECH	1	1
	7-8 handicapped	1 ECH	1	2
	Integrated Classroom			
	12 (1-5 handicapped)	1 ECH	1	1
	12 (6-8 handicapped)	1 ECH	2	1
	18 (6-12 handicapped)	2 ECH	2	***
	Regular Classroom			
	18 (3 handicapped)	1 EC / 1 ECH Consultant	1	1
Home-Based Individual Model	8 handicapped	1 ECH	0	Not Applicable
	14 handicapped	1 ECH	1	
	20 handicapped	1 ECH	2	
	26 handicapped	1 ECH	3	

*EC = early childhood teacher certification; ECH = early childhood-handicapped teacher certification
**Children who are severely handicapped or under age 2½.
***This group size is not recommended for severely handicapped or very young children.

Source: *Early Education for the Handicapped in Kansas: A Planning Handbook,* 1982, Topeka: Kansas State Department of Education.

> Suggested readings: Torres (1977); H. Turnbull and A. Turnbull (1978); Weintraub and Ramirez (1985).

A final consideration: Competent and caring staff

Although we did not identify "competent and caring staff" as one of the 10 features of a quality early intervention program, effective staff members are critical to the success of a program. The role of each staff member is demanding and requires a broad range of competencies and a great deal of knowledge. Personal and professional efforts required of staff to deliver a quality program necessitate commitment to this field and genuine concern for young handicapped children. To be a part of a program that positively alters the developmental status of young handicapped children is important, and it can be very personally rewarding.

THE INTERDISCIPLINARY TEAM IN ACTION

Quality early intervention programs that encompass the features discussed in the previous section typically involve professionals from a variety of disciplines. If early education programs are to make a timely and lasting impact on the lives of young children with handicaps or at-risk conditions, teachers cannot work in isolation of other specialists. In fact, the diverse kinds of needs of these children create an urgency for cooperation among professionals and among the various agencies that seek to help them.

When persons from various disciplines come together as staff in an early intervention program, teamwork is a *must!* Programs cannot operate smoothly, nor can individualized programs be well integrated for each child, unless professionals are able to work together cooperatively. True teamwork means working together in a variety of ways: sharing information and skills, conducting joint assessments of children, planning instructional or therapeutic programs for each child, gathering information and preparing records, reviewing children's progress data, and coordinating their program schedules. Teamwork is crucial since no one professional has all the expertise or resources to address each child's every need. Given the complexity and interrelatedness of human development during the early years, any intervention that effectively addresses the special needs of young children must attend to their well-being in all areas of development, not just one or two. This can be accomplished only through the concerted, cooperative efforts of specialists from many disciplines working together.

Types of team approaches

The ways in which specialists from various disciplines work together are as diverse as the programs that serve young children. The team approach has no single format. Four approaches represent the general types of strategies typically used by teams in programs serving the handicapped: (a) the unidisciplinary or mini team, (b) the multidisciplinary team, (c) the interdisciplinary team, and (d) the transdisciplinary team. Table 11.2 summarizes the major features of these approaches.

The unidisciplinary approach   A team may consist of just two people in a profes-

Table 11.2
Summary of Various Disciplinary Approaches for Serving Handicapped/High-Risk Children

	DESCRIPTION	ADVANTAGES	DISADVANTAGES
Unidisciplinary Approach	A professional (or in some cases, more than one) from a single discipline serves the child. This is most typically found when one individual provides specialized therapy to a single client or a program is created that specializes in the type of children served or limits the type of treatment offered (e.g., a center offers only speech and language therapy and serves only speech impaired children).	• Appropriate when child presents a highly specific problem that does not require a comprehensive intervention approach. • May represent only option for getting some services to children when alternative would be no services at all. This approach is often used if programs have major funding limitations and are being set up in geographical areas where services are not mandated.	• Approach is seriously limited in capacity to meet needs of children with a variety of developmental disabilities and severity levels and who require a range of services. • Tremendous burden is placed on those who work with children presenting multiple developmental problems in view of the need for knowledge and expertise in all areas of development and all types of disability and for technical know-how to promote progress across multiple skill areas in the child. When handicapped or high-risk children obviously need comprehensive services, a mini-team approach is simply inadequate.
Multidisciplinary Approach	Professionals work independently evaluating and serving the client in their own domains. Each applies the expertise and techniques of his or her discipline in isolation of what professionals in other disciplines are doing concurrently with a child or parent. Little or no interaction or ongoing communication occurs among professionals who are dealing with the same client.	• Child is evaluated and given therapeutic intervention by several disciplines that provide more in-depth assessment and treatment than a single professional could provide. • May be more convenient for professionals involved in that no extra time demands are imposed for coordination and planning with members of other disciplines. Each is free to apply his or her own style of service delivery without compromise with others who may advocate other ways of dealing with the client.	• Does not facilitate an integrated, synthesized approach to assessment and early intervention programming. Practitioners do not gain benefits of feedback from other professionals; thus, the client does not get full advantage of the potential expertise that could be tapped if all professionals synchronized their efforts toward common goals. • Chances are increased that techniques used with the child by each discipline will be incompatible. The child is treated in pieces rather than holistically, promoting fragmentation of treatment and reduction of the power of intervention to impact upon child's total development.

Interdisciplinary Approach	Professionals from various disciplines work together cooperatively in both planning and delivering services to the child or parent. Emphasis is upon teamwork and interaction among team members, who help and rely upon each other to provide well coordinated, integrated services for the individual, although each discipline ultimately delivers the services in its own domain. Role definitions and modes of serving the client are relaxed in that staff does not necessarily work under its personal styles for implementing programs but, rather, adheres to a common system under which all team members agree to work.	• Services are planned and delivered with an orientation to the whole child and are better integrated to assure compatibility of treatment techniques across disciplines. • Provides a more enriching, stimulating context for professionals to work. The expertise and input of other disciplines offers a means for team members to discuss their perspectives, to learn and expand their own skills, to gain support in their work, and to have access to other sources that can aid them in treatment of the child.	• Requires experienced administrative, communication, and leadership skills among team members if they are to work effectively as a team. • Places heavy time demands on team members to participate in meetings for purposes of joint planning and coordination. Quality and quantity of teamwork can be restricted by heavy caseloads or simply in synchronizing schedules of team members. • Places a premium on personal qualities of professionals that make for good team effort and cooperation. Chances for staff conflict increase when individuals are protective of professional turf, lack respect for expertise of colleagues, or thwart common effort toward mutual goals.
Transdisciplinary Approach	Professionals from various disciplines work together cooperatively by educating one another in the skills and practice of their disciplines so that one team member can act as the single agent for carrying out services with a designated child or parent. This "role exchange" means that in working with a given child, a team member assumes the roles and responsibilities of other disciplines by delivering the treatment program based upon program prescriptions and instructions provided by joint planning of the total team.	• With one person working with a single client and synthesizing the treatment program, the burden for coordinating several separate therapy programs is lifted. Parents and child relate to only one person instead of many, making communication between client and interventionists less complicated. • Offers a means for delivering diverse services to children in rural areas or areas understaffed by various disciplines. Also a useful approach with severely-multiply handicapped populations in which training requires simultaneous attention to many handicapping conditions. • Enhances the professional skills of the classroom teacher, who is often the pivotal or focal point of this approach.	• Places considerable responsibility upon each team member to master the skills and methodologies of other disciplines sufficiently to deliver quality programming to the child or parent. May be viewed as an unnecessary investment of time, given the presence of already trained, skilled personnel on the team. • Requires considerable time for cross-sharing, planning, coordination, and training of the member designated to deliver the treatment program. Also necessitates a high level of cooperation and trust among disciplines. • Role release may be difficult to operationalize if professionals take a formal, legalistic view of their respective professional roles. State licensing may prohibit some aspects of role release.

sional-client relationship or "mini-team" (Valletutti & Christoplos, 1977). A major problem for a specialist in that situation, however, is the risk of professional "tunnel vision." Consider the example of the slow talker, as described by Holm & McCartin (1978):

> An ear-nose-throat specialist seeing such a child might emphasize that there are no medical problems; the audiologist might say that the hearing is normal. Neither might appreciate that something probably should be done about a child who is not talking at the usual age. A psychiatrist consulted about a child with delayed language development might get involved in a treatment program to improve mother-child relationships. A speech pathologist might develop a management program to enhance language development. Instead, maybe the child is one for whom placement in a special education preschool program designed to enhance all aspects of development in a retarded child would be most appropriate. Some of the specialists mentioned may not even be aware of the existence of remedial programs outside of their own professional field. (pp. 99-100)

Time can also be a problem in the single professional-client relationship, especially in the case of a multiply handicapped child or one with complex problems. Scheduling and accomplishing a complete examination by each professional working as an independent practitioner, could continue for as long as a year. Families can easily wear down, get lost in the clinical maze, or give up in discouragement or confusion. Others might become "clinic-hoppers," moving from one professional to another, seeking information they hope will help them to help their child. Under such protracted and fragmented service patterns, the child as an individual may be lost. "The needs of the individual are invariably separated into portions shaped to fit the organizational needs and biases of agencies" (Valletutti & Christoplos, 1977).

The multidisciplinary team approach   The multidisciplinary team approach usually involves a cluster of professionals, each of whom provides some type of service to children but who does not particularly interact with the others to plan or coordinate activities. This approach might be compared to "parallel play" in young children. At that stage, prior to emergence of cooperative play, they play side-by-side in independent activities but do not participate in interactive, mutually supportive play. Such is the behavior of professionals under a multidisciplinary approach. Often, members of a multidisciplinary team serve in the role of diagnostician by conducting initial evaluations and making subsequent recommendations. They may provide no direct services and may not see that as their responsibility. Some disciplines may provide specialized types of therapy, but apart from other services offered to a child.

The multidisciplinary team approach evolved from the medical model, in which a number of professional disciplines were called upon to conduct evaluations on a child and offer recommendations. Within special education this approach has been used primarily in obtaining initial diagnostic evaluations on exceptional students. Several individuals are called upon to evaluate the child, and the so-called team is thus constituted. Typically, results of each discipline's work are sent to one central person. Medical, audiological, psychological, social, and educational evaluation reports are prepared and sent to a person, such as the school nurse, a psychologist, or a teacher, who is managing the case. Team members may or may not talk with each other, although usually little discussion or interaction occurs. If it does, it often is between one discipline and the case manager. Under this approach, the chances for conflicting recommendations are great. If these are to be resolved, the individual case manager may or may not have the expertise to synthesize the disparate reports.

This approach leaves much to be desired. Major weaknesses that limit the potential benefits are:

1. Genuine problem solving among team members in behalf of the child is lacking. Each discipline typically performs its service in isolation of the other disciplines. The entire responsibility for interpreting information, resolving discrepancies and differences in opinion across disciplines, and perhaps translating the information into manageable service programs usually is left to the person who requested the information in the first place. This person may not be in a position to implement the recommendations.

2. Each discipline is forced to operate in isolation, viewing the child in just one behavioral or developmental domain and not necessarily gaining a picture of the total child.

3. Recommendations of each discipline often are made on the basis of ideals rather than on the basis of what is available, what is manageable, and what is realistic in view of the collective recommendations across all disciplines. Under this approach, actual implementation issues rarely are considered by the isolated disciplines and often are dismissed as not being the responsibility of the discipline. Again, implementation may fall back on the individual who initially asked for help, with an end result that is little more than formal verification from each of the consulting disciplines that the child indeed has a problem and something should be done.

The interdisciplinary team approach   Staff teams that are truly interdisciplinary are characterized by cooperative interactions. Team members work cooperatively to make role assignments according to the particular needs of a child or family. In an interdisciplinary team approach, team members independently evaluate a child. Everyone then shares and discusses the results. Group consensus—into which all members have input—is the vehicle used to act on recommendations and to prescribe services and intervention strategies for a given child. Responsibilities for actual delivery of the prescribed program are parceled out to each of the participating disciplines as needed. For example, the speech clinician usually handles speech objectives, with some possible carryover into the classroom. The occupational therapist is responsible for motor development, and the classroom teaching staff handles other objectives.

Cooperative planning and coordination of teaching strategies generally occurs among the disciplines to assure that activities carried out with the child by each of the disciplines are compatible and complementary. Members of interdisciplinary teams also work cooperatively to carry out roles that seem most expedient to successfully meet the needs of the child or family. In one case a nurse will take the social history. Another time a therapist and a social worker will do it together. In yet another instance a teacher will make a home visit to collect these data. The team might request that the teacher or an occupational therapist or a nutritionist explore a feeding problem. Or if the problem is complicated, they may do it together. At times the speech pathologist might ask the psychologist or the early childhood educator to assess whether psychological services are needed, and vice versa (Holm & McCartin, 1978). Interdisciplinary teams usually meet on a regular basis to review child progress and the degree of success of programs being conducted by each discipline.

Hart and Risley (1974) pointed out that in interdisciplinary approaches, as well as multidisciplinary approaches, the value of each team member's contribution depends upon several factors including the members' familiarity with the type of child being served and the capabilities of each team member for prescribing appropriate programs. With handicapped children, and in particular severely and profoundly disabled youngsters, not all team members may have sufficient expertise. Nor may all team members be convinced that the team should serve certain children. Some may even resist working with children who present extensive problems and disabilities. Several ingredients are essential for interdisciplinary teams to operate successfully:

1. A *team attitude or perspective* among all members is most important if an interdisciplinary approach is to be successful. Members must view themselves as part of a team rather than as independent service operations. No one discipline can view itself as superior or more necessary than another to the whole program. Each must see itself as a contributor to a total, comprehensive intervention program, of which each fulfills an important role but none is sufficient to stand alone.
2. Some type of *centralized management system* is necessary for coordinating team activities. That system must define procedures for team activities such as taking referrals, conducting evaluations, developing program prescriptions and IEPs for each child, assigning service responsibilities within the team, and monitoring child progress. If that system is not feasible, at least some set of compatible parallel systems used by each discipline must be present to avoid unnecessary duplication and confusion for the child or recipient of services.
3. Members of the team must develop *appreciation and respect* for the contributions of other members and must trust each other's capabilities to carry out intervention programs with the child. Members also must be able to recognize their own limitations and be ready to rely upon, build upon, and complement the skills of others within the team.
4. A means for keeping track of the child across disciplines and some kind of *accountability system* must be present to continually assess if programs are being implemented as planned and if prescribed procedures are bringing about desired results.
5. Team *members must be open and willing to let others know what they are doing* with the children they serve. In a sense, members must be able to exist in a "fish bowl," where their work is open to the observations or inquiries of others on the team. They must be willing to have others ask probing questions about intervention procedures, to give an accounting of progress, and to take suggestions. In other approaches, disciplines typically are not accountable to fellow professionals. Much of their work— be it successful or unsuccessful—is unseen and never questioned. Under the interdisciplinary approach, this privilege of secrecy or nonaccountability diminishes. It requires an openness, a willingness to be challenged and to defend or grow from the experience. It requires a willingness to explain the basis for one's work. Success of the team effort allows for no defensiveness on the part of any professional and no territorial or turf guarding.

The transdisciplinary team approach   In recent years the transdisciplinary approach has gained popularity, especially in programs serving severely/multiply handicapped children. Under this approach one member of the team is designated as the primary service "agent" who is to deal directly with a given child. Though the transdisciplinary approach does not differ from the multi- and interdisciplinary approaches in regard to the potential composition of a team, methods of implementing the child service programs do take a different form. Child evaluations and program planning are accomplished jointly by all members of the disciplinary team. Implementation of that plan, however, is not carried out by each of the disciplines in its own service domain but, rather, by only one team member in cooperation and consultation with the others. As a large number of children are served, each team member assumes some of the responsibilities traditionally held by other members. One team member represents the others in the delivery of services and carries out activities with a child based upon the prescriptions of all the disciplines (Hart, 1978).

The transdisciplinary approach was conceived in an attempt to reduce the compartmentalization and fragmentation of services that sometimes occur when many professionals are working simultaneously, yet separately, with a child. Hutchinson (1974), one of the primary advocates of this approach, stressed that this type of approach does not come off automatically. To be successful, it must be well planned. Hutchinson suggested several criteria for working effectively under a transdisciplinary team approach:

1. A team member must have depth and be particularly strong in his or her own discipline. Without this knowledge the member is in no position to make decisions or to pass on information in a form that another professional can implement.
2. Each team member's role must be continuously enriched by expanding his or her knowledge through training and supervision provided by other team members. For this to occur, the appropriate disciplinary representative must give "role release" and authorization of the designated team member to act as the direct service agent with a particular child in behalf of each discipline.
3. Team members must provide continuous consultative back-up to one another. Ongoing problem solving, information exchange, and feedback between the consulting discipline and the primary service agent of the team for a given child are critical. Procedures or new information may have to be tested by a disciplinary representative before being passed on to the overall team and prescribed as the treatment strategy for the primary service agent to use.
4. Throughout the transdisciplinary process each team member must remain accountable for the information and directives delivered to others. Each disciplinary representative also must remain accountable for how well the primary service agent learns the service delivery strategy for that discipline and carries it out with the child. Finally, every discipline involved must remain accountable for the child's progress under their own prescriptions.

Not all professionals involved in this type of collaborative activity are comfortable with the transdisciplinary approach and the concepts underlying it. Johnston (1977) noted some of the problems associated with that approach. The pediatrician, for example, is underused if called upon only to dispense medication; but equally inappropriate are attempts to incorporate the methods and skills of other disciplines into the pediatrician's own diagnostic and therapeutic repertoire. The transdisciplinary concept "disregards the clinical acumen and judgment that necessarily accompany a given discipline's practices and techniques that have evolved after years of training and experience" (Johnston, 1977). Holm and McCartin (1978), too, have voiced concern regarding the transdisciplinary label. They described the danger of solo practitioners, in whatever field, who have a smattering of skills from various child development areas. They did not deny that solo practice is helpful and legitimate, only that "the full array of knowledge and skills available in the child development field will never be offered by a single practitioner, however skilled."

Strategies for effective teamwork

Effective teamwork is a complex process. It can be challenging and rewarding for the various team members. At the same time it can be taxing and anxiety provoking. Professional roles may merge one into the other, specializations and hands-on treatment may be reduced for certain disciplines in some circumstances, and individuals may be asked to assume roles (such as team leader or case manager) that are foreign to them. The personal-social skills that the various team members need, in addition to their disciplinary expertise, comprises yet another dimension that the various professionals must address.

Defining and assigning roles   The recurring theme in the team processes discussed here is that the problems of young children with developmental disorders transcend the authority and expertise of any one discipline. Cooperative efforts of a wide range of professionals are needed to provide valid assessment, recommend treatment and establish treatment priorities, monitor progress, and carry through on long-term follow-up. Services to the child and the family require not only a collaborative interchange of expertise but also professional flexibility whereby team members of each discipline are willing to relinquish certain roles and teach their own specialized skills to others whenever possible (Allen, Holm, & Schiefelbusch, 1978; Fewell, 1983b; Harris & Tada, 1983).

Role exchange   The flexibility mentioned above results in a team process often referred to as role exchange. It is exemplified in the social worker who is comfortable having the nutritionist, psychologist, or early childhood educator make a home visit; in the physical therapist who teaches the teacher to position a child appropriately for various activities. The essence of this kind of exchange is professional competence and confidence. These attributes negate the need for defensiveness and allow for true sharing. Comfortable role exchange also requires that each professional make a conscious effort to learn about the professions of other team members and to develop an awareness of their operational strategies.

One way to acquire an understanding of other disciplines is to learn their specialized language—the basic vocabulary and conceptual constructs each discipline uses to communicate clearly and effectively. On the other hand, all disciplines should avoid excessive language specialization (jargon, medicinese, euphemisms, "alphabet soup") because verbal specialization can be an indirect and often unrecognized way of saying, "Stay out of my territory." Many professionals consider the lack of a common language or a common translation procedure as one of the most troublesome deterrents to effective role exchange within an interdisciplinary team. As professionals interact with each other, they must work toward the reduction of unnecessary jargon and overly specialized terminology.

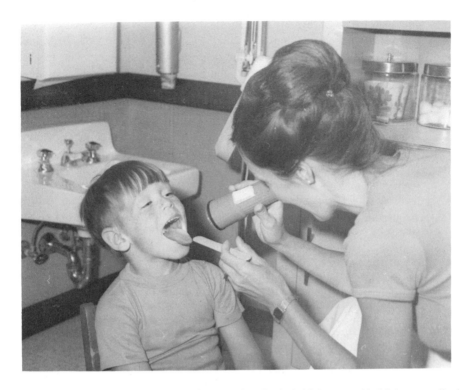

As early intervention programs serve younger (particularly birth to age 3) children, medical and health needs become an important part of the intervention and service programs. Coordination between health professionals and other early intervention personnel has become an even greater necessity.

Role exchange among professionals is facilitated by team members' realistic recognition of both the extent and the limitations of their own professional skills. Compiling case histories, making home visits, and managing parent conferences traditionally have been more likely assumed by certain disciplines than others; yet, almost every professional has the skills to perform such tasks. By the same token, professionals from each discipline must also recognize their own limitations; no professional is omniscient. No professional can be all things to all disabled children. Willingness to call upon others for consultation and assistance as needed is the benchmark of a truly competent disciplinary team.

Role assignments within the team   Each team must have a *team leader*. That team leadership should be accorded to the team member who has (a) the time to devote to the job so that the team can function efficiently and effectively, (b) the ability to get along with a variety of personalities and points of view, and (c) the necessary organizational and administrative talents. These qualifications are, for the most part, independent of disciplinary training and background.

Specifying one person to assume overall responsibility for each case, and to act as principal contact person for the family, also is of prime importance. Often, selection of case manager is based upon a child's most overriding problem. A nutritionist may be case manager for a severely malnourished child, while a speech pathologist may assume the role with a hearing impaired child. Or the preschool or day-care director may be perceived as the most functional case manager. In some instances the teacher may be the ideal case manager. The important point is that every team member, regardless of discipline, should be willing to assume the case manager role as the need arises.

The role of case manager is of key significance to success of the total disciplinary team. Without an effective case manager, a situation that Meier (1976) called the "Humpty Dumpty syndrome" can occur. A child's services will be broken up, fragmented, and intervention efforts irretrievably scattered. To forestall incoherent programming, the case manager oversees delivery of services to the client under his or her charge. This includes planning for the various assessments, synthesizing the findings, organizing and managing the case conference and parent conferences, and making certain that records and reports are up-to-date. It also includes arranging for follow-up and serving continuously as a source of contact, interpretation, and support for the family.

The processes of delivering interdisciplinary services   Delivery of disciplinary services to young impaired children is multidimensional and typically includes:

— assessing educational and treatment needs.
— prescribing and planning programs for children and parents.
— implementing integrated disciplinary services.
— coordinating team activities.
— keeping records and monitoring services across disciplines.

Specific procedures must be developed for managing and orchestrating these various dimensions of service delivery.

Developing a team perspective is an important prerequisite for effective interdisciplinary coordination because, "Piecemeal programming for a child can be inefficient, ineffective and even harmful" (Kenny & Clemmens, 1975). The current proliferation of knowledge about normal and dysfunctional development in each disciplinary area is so overwhelming that no one profession could possibly encompass all of the findings. This is another indicator that an interdisciplinary team, working harmoniously, is of prime importance in serving young handicapped children and their families.

Effective team effort requires good interaction skills and good communication skills. Rarely, however, is that training a formal part of professional preparation. Valletutti and Christoplos (1977) suggested that the development of awareness, understanding, and skill in group dynamics should be prerequisite to serving on a team, especially in settings where team members are expected to cooperate on numerous cases over time. They suggested further that "good will, a sense of humor, and freedom from status-bias among all members" are needed. Team members do not automatically possess these traits; in fact, they are often difficult to develop.

Honest differences of professional opinion must be honored if an interdisciplinary team is to work effectively. Certainly, no one correct way of diagnosing and intervening with developmentally deviant young children is possible. Yet, a team cannot function effectively if team members' philosophical or theoretical viewpoints are widely divergent. As Holm and McCartin (1978) pointed out, a professional who believes strongly in the efficacy of behavior modification probably will not be effective on a team oriented toward psychoanalytic practice and theory. Neither will a neurologist who is convinced that the course of cerebral palsy is unchangeable be of much benefit to a team that practices neurodevelopmental treatment of CP in young children. Thus, for the benefit of each other's professional effectiveness and integrity and the well-being of children and families whom they serve, a team must adopt one of two courses: (a) to arrive at a commonly agreed upon concept of child development based upon a particular theory (e.g., Piagetian, behavioral, psychodynamic), or (b) as suggested by Holm and McCartin (1978), to incorporate seemingly incongruent ideologies into an integrated *team philosophy:*

> New members bring in new ideas, experiences, and points of view to the team. These are explored, rejected or they are modified and eventually absorbed into the team philosophy. Such teams grow and develop, making participation in teamwork an exciting and dynamic process for the professionals involved. (p. 101)

Once a team philosophy and the basics of team give-and-take are established, the team is well situated to carry out its many functions.

SUMMARY

The job of teacher or therapist in a successful intervention program demands considerable experise and skill in the use of specialized training methods for handicapped infants and preschoolers. The staff must have a broad base of training and experience, since EC-SPED programs may serve a broad range of children—children from birth to age 5 or 6, those with all possible types of handicapping conditions and all levels of severity. Furthermore, any number of service delivery approaches, like those described in chapter 8, could be used. This can pose a tremendous challenge for any staff member, considering that teachers of school-aged students commonly specialize in just one handicapping area and one severity level (mild, moderate, or severe) and generally deal with students within a more narrow age-range.

To operationalize all the features that characterize quality early intervention programs is a task that no staff member can achieve alone. In fact, no single discipline has the expertise to meet all the special needs of young handicapped children. Neither does any one discipline have all the tools for putting into practice all the components that make up a comprehensive, well rounded early intervention program. Representatives of many disciplines can benefit by working together as team members to plan and implement quality programs.

Staff teams can work together in a variety of ways, but we recommend that the greatest attention be given to either the interdisciplinary or transdisciplinary approaches. The *interdisciplinary approach* involves specialists who work together in serving the same children by meeting, planning, coordinating services, and collaborating in the delivery of a common service plan. The *transdisciplinary approach* encompasses the interdisciplinary approach in planning and coordination but changes the delivery format. Team members engage in role exchange by assigning one team member as the primary agent to carry out the program prescribed by the team for an individual child. The approach has been applied most frequently with severely/multiply handicapped populations.

The following guidelines are suggested to help disciplinary teams function at their best:

1. Each disciplinary member must be committed to the team approach and perceive of himself or herself as an integral part of that team, not as a soloist.
2. Team members must trust the competence of the other members on the team and be willing to exchange or relinquish cherished roles, depending upon the needs of a particular child.
3. "Parallel play" has no place in a team operation; cooperation among members is necessary during every step of the process, from initial diagnosis to long-term follow-up.
4. A well articulated format for team management, decision making, and communication among members, both formal and informal, is essential.
5. Theoretical and philosophical compatibility is a necessity. Team members must agree on program goals, philosophy, team constituency (who will be included), and the manner in which services will be delivered.
6. Keeping track of all activities related to the many aspects of service delivery is of paramount importance. Thus, intake procedures, forms and records, planning systems, IEP development, assessment procedures, informing and reporting activities, and referral patterns must be orchestrated across all disciplines.
7. Parents and teachers must be kept in sharp focus as major change agents in all intervention procedures with young handicapped children.

12
Know Your
Professional Resources

If you had to do the following tasks, do you know what resources you could use to get the information you need?

- You are assigned to write a paper on the rationale for early intervention with handicapped infants. To do this, you must locate up-to-date research and professional literature on the topic, build a bibliography, and prepare your literature review, all in a very short time.

- Your local school board is considering a proposal to sponsor a preschool program for handicapped children in your community. The school board wants information on the effectiveness of other early intervention programs. As a member of the committee submitting the proposal, you are to assemble this information.

- You need information on screening and assessment instruments for use with handicapped infants and preschoolers. You want to know what is available and what instruments are most appropriate for children at these age levels.

- As a staff member in a special early childhood education program, you find yourself asking questions such as "What instructional materials can Mrs. Jones use to work with her hearing impaired son at home on his speech and language skills?" "What reading materials should we suggest for the mother of a child with cerebral palsy who needs information on how to feed and work with her child at home?" What resources are available to help you?

- You plan to start a potty training program with three handicapped preschoolers in your classroom. You want to know if any training programs already exist so you do not have to develop your own.

- As you develop a new early childhood-handicapped preschool program in your community, you want information about what service delivery approaches and curriculums are used in other similar programs across the country. You especially want to see program models developed under the Handicapped Children's Early Education Program (HCEEP), including the teaching strategies and materials they have used.

In each of the examples, the task requires three important professional skills. First, you must know *what resources are available* to help you deal with the problem or need. Second, you must know *how to gain access to those resources.* Third, you must know *how to use or work with each resource to make it functional* for your own purposes. A working knowledge of resources in your own field of expertise is an invaluable asset.

What exactly is a "resource?" In essence, *a resource is any source of information, services, materials, and other useful products that can be used by anyone to enable that person to work more skillfully and efficiently.* Agencies that provide special services or disseminate information are familiar types of resources. Aids for locating and retrieving information, such as a reference book, a computerized information research system, published abstracts of professional publications, or people whose expertise can be tapped to solve a problem are examples of other kinds of resources.

BENEFITS OF KNOWING YOUR RESOURCES

To be an effective user of the technology and resources of one's own professional field is an important professional competency. Good ideas and effective on-the-job problem solving do not occur in a vacuum. They require familiarity with fresh, new ideas, which comes through exposure to emerging practices, products, research, and the current professional literature. This means being tuned into the major "pipelines" of information in one's field. You must have a working knowledge of the major literature and information sources, key organizations and agencies, and other dissemination systems in your field.

Students who know their resources and can use them skillfully are better prepared to tackle assignments and meet the demands of their classes. Professionals who are knowledgeable and skillful users of resources are more valuable employees and can provide better leadership in the job roles they assume. This emphasizes one important principle:

★ *Individuals may not always have the answer to a problem at their fingertips or the information they need tucked away neatly in their heads. But if each of us knows* where *to find the information we need and* how *to retrieve it, our ability to perform efficiently and successfully in our jobs is enhanced tenfold.*

If you know the resources relevant to your professional field and use those resources, other practical benefits are:

— *continual learning in your profession.*   You can be linked up with ongoing information sources that help you keep current with what is happening in your field and stay informed about the newest research, theory, and information relevant to your discipline.
— *enhanced work efficiency.*   You likely will be more efficient and expert in doing your job because you have information and other helpful aids at your disposal that allow you to complete tasks more quickly, produce a better product, or make better decisions because you are well informed.
— *increased quality of service for others.*   You will be a better resource for colleagues, parents, or others who may seek you out to ask for information or specific kinds of help because they view you as knowledgeable. Because you will be able to retrieve information for yourself, you are in a better position to help them. Also, you are more alert to resources to which you can refer them so they can help themselves.
— *improved use of your own time and energy.*   You can save time and money if you can quickly locate and use existing materials/information/products that meet your requirements instead of attempting to develop them or gather information by yourself. This will streamline your own task, allow you to spend your time on other, more important tasks, and save valuable preparation time.
— *reduction of unnecessary duplication of effort.*   You can avoid "reinventing the wheel" by capitalizing upon the work of others or upon existing resources to provide information or materials. By locating products that others have already created, information that others have already assembled, or resources that exist to help in the very task you are tackling, you won't have to redo what others have already done.

TYPES OF RESOURCES

Early childhood-special educators should be familiar with five broad types of resources:

1. Resources for professional literature and information.
2. Resources for information search and retrieval.
3. Resource agencies for information dissemination and technical assistance.
4. Resources for professional affiliation and advocacy.
5. Resources for teacher and child-oriented instructional materials.

Frustrated? Sorting through piles of books and journals in search of information can be overwhelming. But if you know your literature resources and how to use computerized retrieval systems, you'll save time, reduce frustration, and be a more competent professional.

Resources for professional literature and information

Three particularly good resources for professional literature and information are: (a) professional journals and periodicals, (b) governmental documents and reports, and (c) professional reference materials that can be used to locate other materials and information sources.

Professional journals and periodicals   Literally hundreds of magazines and journals fill the shelves of university and public libraries. But how many times have you gone to the library and spent long, tiring hours hunting for what you need only to go home empty handed? Finding the materials you want can be accomplished without searching through hundreds of entries in card catalogs, computer screens, or dusty shelves. The point is: You have to be knowledgeable about the journals relevant to your field. Because the purpose of journals varies, their content also differs. To know what type of material is considered the major focus of each journal, then, is wise.

Some journals feature articles dealing with practical methods for assessing and instructing children with developmental disabilities. *Education and Training of the Mentally Retarded* and *Teaching Exceptional Children* are two examples. Some journals place greater priority upon theoretical and philosophical articles. *Focus on Exceptional Children* and *American Psychologist* are examples. Others, such as the *Journal of Applied Behavior Analysis* or *Child Development*, publish reports of empirical research. A few journals, such as *Review of Educational Research,* publish broad reviews of research literature to acquaint readers with research findings and recent trends in selected topic areas. The best way to become familiar with the content of major journals is simply to browse through them. A good strategy is to skim through the table of contents, read explanatory material on the front, inside, or back cover of the journal, and read an article or two.

Currently, two major publications focus specifically upon early education of young handicapped children: the *Journal of the Division for Early Childhood,* published since 1979 by the Council for Exceptional Children's Division on Early Childhood, and *Topics in Early Childhood Special Education,* published by Pro-Ed. Other relevant journals include:

— periodicals in the general areas of special education, child development, and early education. A listing of these journals is given in Table 12.1.
— periodicals that focus upon particular categorical disability areas within the field of special education. A listing of these journals is given in Table 12.2.
— periodicals focusing on relevant topical areas such as behavior analysis, assessment, mainstreaming, parenting of the handicapped child, instructional methodology, and so on. A selected listing of some of these journals is given in Table 12.3.
— periodicals from related service and professional disciplines outside education that are interested in handicapped individuals or in the growth and development of young children. Some of the major journals representing these disciplinary areas are listed in Table 12.4.

Government documents and reports   Governmental publications are available on every topic imaginable. An invaluable resource, these come in the form of technical bulletins, annual reports on programs, population data, investigative series, subject monographs, periodicals, handbooks, regulations relating to various federal programs and services, congressional reports, and copies of federal laws such as PL 94-142. A large amount of material has been published on topics such as child development, child care, special education and the handicapped, early intervention, child abuse, Head Start and other federally sponsored educational programs, parenting, and prenatal care. These publications can be purchased from the Superintendent of Documents in Washington, DC. Selected publications also are available through government bookstores located in regional government office buildings. They are relatively inexpensive and provide a rich source of information that often is not available through commercial publishers.

How does one find out what governmental publications are available and on what topics materials have been produced? One source is the *Monthly Catalog of.United States Government Publications,* a series of reference volumes containing indexed listings of available materials along with brief abstracts. A second source is the *Subject Bibliography Index,* also produced by the Government Printing Office.

The *Monthly Catalog of United States Government Publications* is composed of a series of catalogs, which are available in most university libraries and some large city libraries. The catalogs are published monthly and are compiled into both semiannual and yearly cumulative indexes. A series supplement, listing only periodical publications, is also available. To use these catalogs for locating governmental publications in one's interest area, information can be obtained through (a) the author index or (b) the subject

Table 12.1
Journals Relating to Special Education, Child Development,
and Early Education in General

General Special Education Journals
    Exceptional Child Quarterly
    Exceptional Children
    Exceptional Education Quarterly (now Remedial and Special Education)
    Focus on Exceptional Children
    Journal of Special Education
    Journal of Special Education Technology
    Journal for Special Educators
    Teacher Education and Special Education
    Teaching Exceptional Children

General Child Development/Early Education Journals
    Advances in Child Development and Behavior
    Child Care Quarterly
    Child Development
    Child Welfare
    Childhood Education
    Children (formerly Children Today)
    Day Care and Early Education Quarterly
    Developmental Psychology
    Directive Teacher
    Early Child Development and Care
    Early Years
    Education and Treatment of Children
    Infant Behavior Development
    Journal of Experimental Child Psychology
    Merrill Palmer Quarterly
    Monographs of Society for Research in Child Development
    Young Children

Table 12.2
Journals Relating to Categorical Areas Within Special Education

Early Childhood-Handicapped
    Journal of the Division of Early Childhood (DEC/CEC)
    Topics in Early Childhood Special Education

Mentally Retarded
    American Journal on Mental Deficiency
    Applied Research in Mental Retardation
    Education and Training of the Mentally Retarded
    Journal of Mental Deficiency
    Mental Retardation

Severely/Profoundly Handicapped
    Journal of the Association for Persons with Severe Handicaps
        (formerly the AAESPH Review)

Emotionally Disturbed/Behavior Disordered
    American Journal of Orthopsychiatry
    Behavior Therapy
    Child Behavior Therapy
    Child Psychiatry and Human Development
    Journal of Autism and Childhood Schizophrenia
    Journal of Child Psychology and Psychiatry

Speech and Hearing Impaired
    American Annals of the Deaf
    Deaf American
    Journal of Speech and Hearing Disorders
    Journal of Speech and Hearing Research
    Journal of Child Language
    Speech Monographs
    Teacher of the Deaf
    Volta Review

Blind and Visually Impaired
    Education of the Visually Handicapped
    Journal of Visual Impairment and Blindness
    New Outlook for the Blind (discontinued in 1976)

Orthopedically and Other Health Impaired
    Bulletin of Prosthetics Research
    Pediatrics

Learning Disabled
    Academic Therapy
    Journal of Learning Disabilities
    Learning Disability Quarterly
    Slow Learning Child
    Topics in Learning and Learning Disabilities

Gifted and Talented
    Gifted Child Quarterly
    Journal of Creative Behavior

Table 12.3
Journals Relating to Topic Areas in Education and Treatment of the Handicapped

---

Behavior Analysis
Behavior Modification Journal
Journal of Applied Behavior Analysis
Journal of the Experimental Analysis of Behavior

Assessment
Behavioral Assessment
Journal of Behavior Assessment
Journal of Psychoeducational Assessment

Legal and Legislative Topics and the Handicapped
Education for the Handicapped Law Report
Mental and Physical Disability Law Reporter

Mainstreaming
Education Unlimited (ceased publication in 1981)

Parents of and Parenting Handicapped Children
Exceptional Parent
Volta Review

Instructional Methodology and Curriculum
Directive Teacher
Education and Training of the Mentally Retarded
Learning
Teaching Exceptional Children

Other
Perceptual and Motor Skills

Table 12.4
Selected Journals of Other Related Disciplines

Psychology
Abnormal Psychology
American Journal of Psychology
American Psychologist
Applied Psychology
Comparative Psychology
Consulting and Clinical Psychology
Contemporary Educational Psychology
Contemporary Psychology
Counseling Psychology
Developmental Psychology
Educational Psychology
Journal of Abnormal and Social Psychology
Journal of Abnormal Child Psychology
Journal of Social Psychology
Personality
Psychological Bulletin
Psychological Review
Psychology Today

Social Work
American Sociological Review
Social Work

General Education
American Educational Research Journal
Educational Technology
Elementary School Journal
Harvard Education Review
Journal of Education
Review of Educational Research

Speech Pathology and Audiology
Child Language Teaching and Therapy
Journal of Child Language
Journal of Speech and Hearing Disorders
Journal of Speech and Hearing Research
Topics in Language Disorders

Occupational Therapy
American Journal of Occupational Therapy
Physical and Occupational Therapy in Pediatrics

Music Therapy
Journal of Music Therapy

Physical Therapy and Adaptive Physical Education
Physical Therapy Journal
Therapeutic Recreational Journal

Nutrition
Journal of American Dietetic Association

Medicine and Pediatrics
American Journal of Public Health
Journal of Pediatrics

Interdisciplinary
Analysis and Intervention in Developmental Disabilities
Learning Disabilities: A Multidisciplinary Journal

index at the back of each volume, or (c) the *Series Report Index* (if you have only the name or number of a government publication that has been published). By locating the government publication in one of the above indexes, a monthly catalog entry number can be obtained. This number enables one to find the correct monthly catalog volume containing an abstract describing the publication. Typically, the abstract includes: (a) the call number for locating the original document, (b) the author, (c) the title, (d) the publishing agency within the government, (e) price information, and (f) ordering information. Some libraries maintain collections of government publications, or publications can be ordered directly from the Government Printing Office in Washington, DC.

The *Subject Bibliography Index* is a particularly efficient means for quickly finding out what publications the government has produced on specific topics of interest. This resource consists of listings of materials printed by the federal government on single-subject areas. For example, bibliographies are produced regularly on topics such as child welfare, children, day care, and the handicapped. Publications in each topic area are listed in the *Subject Bibliography Index* in alphabetical order and include the federal call number and price of the document.

All of these indexes, bibliographies, and governmental publications can be obtained through the Superintendent of Documents, U.S. Government Printing Office, Washington, DC.

Reference materials and bibliographical listings   As a student in a university or as a practitioner in the field, you often need information on specific topics *quickly*. Suppose you were writing a literature review on mainstreaming of preschool handicapped children. Or suppose you wanted to get some articles on working with parents of young, handicapped children. What resources could you use to retrieve that information, and how would you go about finding it?

One strategy is to go directly to journals, such as those listed in Tables 12.1, 12.2, 12.3, and 12.4, and search through their tables of contents for relevant material. Direct contacts also can be made with experts in the field or with agencies and organizations that likely have access to the information. Depending upon the task, this strategy may be adequate—especially if the task is relatively small, if material is readily accessible, and if you already are familiar with sources where the information you need can be found.

Other excellent resources are available in the form of books and special publications. Although these are too numerous to be described here, a few examples will give you a glimpse. The volumes described provide major comprehensive summaries of literature relating to research and theory in education, education and development of the young child, and education of the handicapped.

Yearbook of Special Education. Initiated in 1975 and published yearly to summarize new developments in the field of special education, under 10 major headings. Covers the various handicapping conditions (e.g., mental retardation) and selected topics such as mainstreaming, rights and litigation, and teacher preparation. Information includes: bibliographies of educational materials, instructions for parent involvement, evaluation of model special education programs, national and state data on the handicapped and special education services, and guidelines for assessment of public school services. A *geographical index* lists information by states. The *Yearbook* is published by Marquis Academic Media, Marquis Who's Who, Inc., Chicago, IL, and is found in most reference sections of university/college libraries, as well as some public libraries.

Carmichael' Manual of Child Psychology (1983). Two large volumes edited by P.H. Mussen and published by John Wiley & Sons. The *Manual* provides a comprehensive summary of current philosophical and theoretical thinking and research in topics relating to the psychology of human development. The volumes not only compile current knowledge in selected topic areas but also provide critical analyses and evaluations of that literature. Major sections are devoted to topics such as: biological bases of development, infancy and early experience, cognitive development, and socialization in young children.

Review of Child Development.   A series of volumes published under the auspices of the Society for Research in Child Development, for the purpose of providing integrative reviews of literature in the field of child development. Provides excellent information resources for students, researchers, teachers, and other practitioners concerned with young children. A sampling of the literature reviews addresses: a history of child development (Vol. 5), development of deaf children (Vol. 5), child abuse (Vol. 5), effectiveness of environmental intervention programs (Vol.3), programs for disadvantaged parents (Vol. 3), psychological testing of children (Vol. 2), genetics and development of intelligence (Vol. 4). Volumes 1 and 2 of the *Review* were published by Russell Sage Foundation of New York; Volumes 3 to 6 were published by the University of Chicago Press.

International Review of Research in Mental Retardation.   Contains summaries of information on research and theory development in the field of mental retardation; international in scope. Beginning in 1966, several volumes edited by Norman Ellis have been published by Academic Press (New York). The volumes are primarily scholarly presentations of research and hence may be of less interest to practitioners seeking practical applications and less abstract material. Examples of chapters contained in this series of volumes include: measurement of intelligence (Vol. 4), cultural deprivation and cognitive competence (Vol. 6), research on mental deficiency during the last decade in France (Vol. 2), and physical and motor development of retarded persons (Vol. 7).

Current Topics in Early Childhood Education.   A growing series of volumes, initiated in 1977, produced under the auspices of the ERIC Clearinghouse on Early Childhood Education at the University of Illinois. Edited by Lilian G. Katz, the series is published to disseminate available material on early childhood education, in the form of integrative reviews, analyses and summaries of research, and information summaries on selected topics of interest. Examples of topics are: federal involvement in early education and a rationale for involving parents in the education of young handicapped children (Vol. 1); mainstreaming in the preschool, changing views of early experience, and what Head Start means to families (Vol. 2).

A second strategy for locating professional literature or other useful information about one's professional field is to build a bibliography or list of resources on a given topic by using reference guides that list published materials under alphabetized topical categories. This strategy works especially well when you do not know the primary sources where certain information might be located. It also is helpful when you want a representative sampling of literature on a specific topic. Under the first strategy discussed, the information retrieved may or may not be representative of the total body of literature on a topic. This second strategy provides a means for systematically working through indexed reference materials over a period of years to obtain a larger, more representative selection of publications. Reference guides you might use here are of three types:

— *bibliographical indexes* that list periodicals and other published literature under an alphabetized subject listing (occasionally author listings also are given).
— *bibliographical abstracts* in specific professional fields such as psychology or child development, which provide annotated references on publications within defined topic areas.
— *service directories* of agencies that can provide information or some type of special service.

The *bibliographical indexes* and *abstracts* typically are located in university/college libraries. Smaller collections sometimes can be found in community libraries. Table 12.5 lists some selected bibliographical reference materials that summarize available literature in areas such as special education, general education, child development and early education, psychology, and other related fields. Some of the most useful abstracted reference volumes for students or professionals interested in the young child, early education, and special education are: *Psychological Abstracts, Child Development Abstracts,* the ERIC abstracts *(Research Relating to Children* and *Current Index to Journals in Education),* and the *Social Sciences Citation Index.* To become familiar with the content and organization of these materials and learn how to use them efficiently, one should look through each of them.

Service directories typically list agencies within a defined geographical area that provide specialized services to children, families, or other service agencies. These directories are published by various state or federal agencies, and occasionally local community organizations. Locating these directories is sometimes difficult because they do not have wide distribution and are not always available in library collections. Often they can be found by inquiring at key state and federal agencies that handle services and funding resources for the handicapped, such as State Departments of Education, Regional Offices of Child Development, Regional Offices of Developmental Disabilities, and so on. The Educational Resources Information System (ERIC) also may provide a means of retrieving information about existing directories.

One of the most useful directory resources, produced by the U.S. Government Printing Office, is titled *Directory of National Information Sources on Handicapping Conditions and Related Services* (DHEW Publication No. (OHDS) 80-22007). This volume offers an extended listing of other national directories that give information on services and resources for the handicapped.

Other comprehensive directories providing extensive listings of agencies and service resources that may be useful to the special education early childhood-handicapped specialist are given in Table 12.6, including their addresses.

A third strategy for locating professional literature and information on a particular topic is to use one of the search and retrieval systems that have been established within the fields of education and psychology to gather information and make it accessible to potential consumers. Typically these information retrieval systems cover research literature, government and project reports, teaching materials and aids, and a variety of other media pertinent to the field they serve. Students and professionals alike can use these retrieval systems to great advantage. Information is retrieved from the computer banks on the basis of several descriptors specified by the person requesting the information. This approach is especially good when you are not sure where the desired information can be located. It also can be a considerable time saver. Computer-based information retrieval systems are described in the following sections.

Resources for information search and retrieval

Several information search and retrieval systems constitute particularly helpful resources. These search-retrieval systems are composed of large data bases of information collected from many different sources. The sources include journal articles, books, governmental documents, project reports, nonpublished reports and products, commercial materials, newsletters, and other forms of media. One can request a computer search within those

Table 12.5
Bibliographical Resources Relevant to Special Education and
Early Childhood Education

Bibliographical References (indexes only)
  Education Index
  Social Sciences Citation Index (SSCI)

Abstracted or Annotated Bibliographical Resources
  Child Development Abstracts and Bibliography
  Current Index to Journals in Education (CIJE)
  Dissertation Abstracts
  Dissertation Abstracts International
  DSH Abstracts (Deafness, Speech and Hearing)
  Education Abstracts
  Exceptional Child Education Resources
      (previously called Exceptional Child Education Abstracts)
  Psychological Abstracts
  PsychSCAN: LD/MR
      PsychINFO Retrospective: Mental Retardation—An Abstracted Bibliography
      PsychINFO Retrospective: Learning and Communication Disorders—
      An Abstracted Bibliography
  Research In Education (RIE)
  Research Relating to Children

---

data bases to locate information on specified topic areas. Six systems are of particular interest to those in professional fields concerned with education, the human sciences, and the handicapped:

- Educational Resources Information Center (ERIC)
- National Information Center for Educational Media (NICEM)
- CEC Information Services
- Psychological Abstracts Information Services (PAIS) and PsychSCAN: LD/MR
- SpecialNet Communication Network

Education Resources Information Center (ERIC)   ERIC is the most comprehensive access system available to educators. It was established in 1966 to gather all types of information relevant to every area within education. It includes both printed and audiovisual media. ERIC announces the availability of materials to potential consumers and makes them available to users such as administrators, teachers, policy makers, students, librarians, and the lay public.

ERIC operates through a network of 16 specialized clearinghouses, each of which is responsible for a particular subject area. Through the collective work of these clearinghouses, information is monitored, acquired, evaluated, abstracted, indexed, and finally listed in appropriate ERIC reference documents. To continuously scan the field for relevant materials, ERIC clearinghouses have established links with key professional associations, governmental and private agencies, and training institutions to assist in gathering materials that reflect new products and information in the field of education.

Table 12.6
Selected Directories for Agencies and Service Resources

A Training and Resource Directory for Teachers Serving Handicapped Students K Through 12 (1977)
Office of Civil Rights, HEW
Room 5146
330 Independence Ave., S.W.
Washington, DC 20201

Directory of Agencies Serving the Visually Handicapped in the United States (1978)
American Foundation for the Blind
15 W. 16th St.
New York, NY 10011

Directory of Directories
Information Enterprises
Distributed by Gale Research Co.
Book Tower
Detroit, MI 48226

Directory of Learning Resources for the Handicapped (1981)
(Edited by E. J. Buehler & D. Dugas)
Waterford, CT: Croft-Nei.

Directory of National Information Sources on Handicapping Conditions and Related Services (2nd ed.) (1980)
Clearinghouse on the Handicapped,
Office of Human Development Services
Office for Handicapped Individuals (2nd ed.).
U.S. Government Printing Office
Washington, DC

Directory for Exceptional Children: A listing of Educational and Training Facilities (8th ed.)(1978)
Porter Sargent Publishers
Boston, MA

Special Education Programs for Severely Handicapped Students: A Directory of State Education Agency Services
NASDE
1201-16th St., N.W.
Washington, DC 20036

International Directory of Mental Retardation Sources (1977)
(Edited by R. F. Dybwad)
President's Committee on Mental
Retardation
Washington, DC

Handicapped Funding Directory (1980-81)
(Edited by B. J. Eckstein)
Box 357
Oceanside, NY 11572

Directory of Services and Facilities for Handicapped Children
Council for Exceptional Children
1920 Association Dr.
Reston, VA 22091

Directory of Organizations Interested in the Handicapped (1980)
People-to-People Committee for the Handicapped
1522 K St., N.W.
Washington, DC 20005

Encyclopedia of Associations (1980)
Gale Research Co.
Book Tower
Detroit, MI 48226

Resource Directory of Rehabilitation Research and Training Centers (1980)
National Institute of Handicapped Research
Dept. of Health, Education, and Welfare
Washington, DC 20001

Youth-Serving Organizations Directory
Gale Research Co.
Book Tower
Detroit, MI 48226

Guide to Clinical Services in Speech-Language Pathology and Audiology
American Speech-Language-Hearing
Association
10801 Rockville Pike
Rockville, MD 20852

ERIC's clearinghouses span the entire field of education, covering specific subject areas such as counseling and personnel services, sciences and mathematics, and all levels of education (preschool, elementary and secondary education, and higher education). Of particular importance is the ERIC Clearinghouse on Handicapped and Gifted Children, operated by the Council for Exceptional Children in Reston, Virginia. Also of significance is the Clearinghouse on Elementary and Early Childhood Education, located at the University of Illinois, College of Education.

ERIC is an impressively large system for handling information, consisting of six interlinking components, which include (Chesley, 1979):

— a central processing facility that receives all documents to be entered into the ERIC system. Since ERIC's major responsibility is to gather materials, evaluate them, and build an indexed, computerized collection of the newest documents and journal articles germane to the field, over 2,000 documents are reviewed yearly.
— the 16 specialized clearinghouses located in various areas of the country, which are responsible for acquiring and handling materials in particular subject areas.
— an ERIC Document Reproduction Service (EDRS), which films documents and prepares microfiche on materials for sale to consumers.
— a publication called *Current Index to Journals in Education (CIJE),* which provides an extensive annotated bibliography of periodical literature. *CIJE* covers over 700 publications representing the major periodical literature in the field of education. Published monthly, this volume is a particularly useful resource to retrieve articles in education.
— a second reference volume, *Resources in Education (RIE),* published by the U.S. Government Printing Office, which provides a summary of the materials held by all of the 16 specialized ERIC clearinghouses. Prior to 1975, this volume was titled *Research in Education.* Literature or printed materials listed in *RIE* are available through ERIC in copy or, in many cases, microfiche.
— The central ERIC management team, located within the National Institute of Education, which sets ERIC policy and oversees the massive operations that comprise the ERIC system.

In addition to serving as a broker of information, ERIC offers what it calls its *user services.* For example:

● ERIC provides workshops at professional meetings to train professionals in the use of its resource system.
● ERIC prepares documents of current high interest, called *Computer Search Reprints.*
● ERIC conducts special computerized searches for users according to request. The *Directory of ERIC Computer Search Services* lists several hundred locations where educators can have computer searches run on topics for which they need information. Some institutions, universities, and colleges also subscribe to the ERIC computer tapes and have their own computer facilities so they can offer the ERIC resources to educators themselves.
● ERIC's Exceptional Children Clearinghouse (ERIC/EC) publishes information bulletins of ERIC *Fact Sheets,* which consist of one to two pages of questions and answers on certain topics with selected resources provided for the reader. ERIC/EC also has de-

veloped ERIC Short Bibliographies—single-topic, one-page annotated bibliographies and state-of-the-art papers entitled ERIC *Exceptional Child Education Reports*. Each report provides a summary of current knowledge on selected topics prepared by recognized authorities in the field.

Several publications provide more information on how to use the ERIC system. These include: *How to Use ERIC, Directory of ERIC Search Services, Directory of ERIC Microfiche Collections, and ERIC Information Analysis Products*. These can be obtained through the central ERIC processing and reference facility. University libraries usually have these publications as well.

National Information Center for Educational Media (NICEM)   Typically referred to by its acronym *NICEM*, this Center is another major resource for anyone in regular or special education. Of particular interest is a subdivision within NICEM called the National Information Center for Special Education Materials (NICSEM). *NICSEM* was established to develop a national bibliographical information retrieval system for educational materials specifically relating to the handicapped. It produces an indexed, computer-based listing of audiovisual educational materials such as films, filmstrips, audiotapes and videotapes, slide sets, and transparencies. The Center has accumulated a variety of other materials: materials directly usable by handicapped children, materials useful to state officials and school district personnel or early childhood center personnel for planning services, and materials applicable to the development of individualized education programs (IEPs) for children. The Center also has materials relevant for both parents and teachers to help in developing curriculum and individualizing instructional programs for handicapped children.

Access to the NICSEM materials can be gained by using the Center's catalogs and master indexes, through which material can be located in three different ways: by title, by subject, or by descriptor. The catalogs consist of:

Master Catalogue of the NIMIS/NICSEM Special Education Information System, which contains a total listing of all media and materials contained in the Center's data base. This catalog includes several indexes:

Index to Media and Materials for the Deaf, Hard of Hearing, Speech Impaired.
Index to Media and Materials for the Mentally Retarded, Specific Learning Disabled, Emotionally Disturbed.
Index to Media and Materials for the Visually Handicapped, Orthopedically Impaired, Other Health Impaired.
Index to Assessment Devices, Testing Instruments, and Parent Materials.
Index to Nonprint Special Education Materials.

These publications may be purchased from NICEM. Most State Departments of Education and university libraries also have these volumes. A NICSEM newsletter entitled *Frankly Speaking* provides information about programs, projects around the country, and products available in the field. It is free upon request.

CEC Information Services   This important resource has operated under federal support since 1966 by the Council for Exceptional Children. The computerized bank of information and materials covered by the CEC Information Services includes citations on literature from hundreds of journals, curriculum guides, teacher activity and instructional manuals, audio and visual media, project reports and products, assessment instruments and checklists, and other useful educational information. Materials not available through commercial sources also are included in this system. In addition, the CEC Information Services accesses information from the ERIC Information System described earlier. Literature for this system is collected continuously from colleges and universities, local, state, and federal agencies, funded projects, and private or special service agencies. Three types of assistance are available to users of the CEC Information Services:

- Custom computer searches can be run on specific topics by request. Searches are completed in 2-3 weeks and involve a fee. Requests for a custom search may be made in writing or by phone. Any request for information must be very clear; descriptors must be carefully selected to ensure that they reflect the exact type and content of material desired.
- Topical bibliographies are available, each containing up to 100 reference citations, with brief abstracts for each citation. These may provide enough information for users so that a custom computer search or further searching through abstract references is not necessary. The bibliographies are updated annually and are available upon request. Many bibliographies are available in topic areas relating to early identification and early childhood intervention.
- Exceptional Children Education Resources (ECER), described earlier as an annotated bibliographical reference volume, is available through CEC Information Services and usually through university libraries. This reference is particularly useful for gaining a general perspective of what materials are available before selecting specific items for retrieval. Formerly published as *Exceptional Child Education Abstracts,* this publication contains citations of current documents and literature references within the CEC Information Services data base on topics relating to the handicapped and gifted. It includes references to a variety of media materials intended for professional development and training, such as 16 mm films, videotapes and audiotapes, and filmstrips covering all areas of special education. Documents abstracted in the Exceptional Children Education Resources can be obtained from the CEC Information Center or through the ERIC Document Reproduction Service (described earlier).

Psychological Abstracts Information Services (PAIS)   PAIS is a computerized information source operated under the American Psychological Association. Its services help students, professionals, and other interested persons gain access to world literature in psychology and the related behavioral and social sciences. PAIS has five information components:

- *PAIS Data Base* contains summaries of literature in psychology and related disciplines published in *Psychological Abstracts* from 1967 to the current year. Abstracts of journal articles, book citations (often annotated), and book chapter citations are included.
- *Psychological Abstracts* is a monthly reference volume that gives brief summaries of articles covering major topic areas relating to psychology and human behavior. It contains specific topical sections of particular interest to those seeking literature on young handicapped children—for example, learning disorders and mental retardation,

speech and language disorders, special and remedial education, curriculum and pro-grams, and teaching methods. Several other sections pertain to the care and education of handicapped and nonhandicapped young children. A *Volume Index* is published twice yearly for *Psychological Abstracts,* to integrate all entries for the year by subject and author.

- *Three-year Cumulative Indexes* to *Psychological Abstracts* provide an additional sum-mary of all subject and author entries that have appeared over a 3-year period. The hours required to develop a bibliography for a topic can be reduced significantly by first using the *Three-Year Cumulative Index* rather than by working through each monthly or yearly index.

- *Thesaurus of Psychological Index Terms* provides a vocabulary of terminology and alternative topic descriptors. Locating relevant literature in a volume of abstracts is sometimes difficult simply because you may not use the same terminology that originally was applied to catalog the material. Consequently, literature that employs several alternative descriptor terms can be useful in locating the desired materials. This *Thesaurus* and others like it might help identify alternative terms to aid in your literature search.

- *Computerized Literature Search and Retrieval Services* under PAIS encompass several specialized systems. The service of most interest to a person in special education-early childhood or a related discipline is the *Psychological Abstracts Computer Search and Retrieval Service (PASAR).* Upon request, PASAR will conduct a literature search. Topic areas, or descriptors, serve as the basis for searching through the PAIS data base described earlier. This system is similar to the computer searches described under the CEC Information Services and the ERIC computer searches. These services carry a fee based on the computer time required to perform the search; costs are not related to the number of references ultimately retrieved.

In using any computerized literature retrieval system, one must remember that the computer output on a topic may or may not be totally representative of the available literature. Neither can it be assumed that after running a computer search, all literature relevant to a particular topic has been located. A computerized literature search is limited by the appropriateness and accuracy of the descriptors used to retrieve information. If the descriptors do not define and narrow a topic area, or if they do not fit those used to catalog the literature, a computer search may fail to retrieve the information you want. And, of course, a computerized literature search can be only as extensive as the original bank of materials in the computer.

PsychSCAN: LD/MR   In addition to the *Psychological Abstracts* and PAIS system, the American Psychological Association began publication of another system of quarterly abstract indexes in 1982, called PsychSCAN: LD/MR. It provides abstracts of documents on learning and communication disorders and on mental retardation. The abstracts are published in two volumes of bibliographies: (a) *PsychINFO Retrospective: Mental Retar-dation — An Abstracted Bibliography,* and (b) *PsychINFO Retrospective: Learning and Communication Disorders — An Abstracted Bibliography.* Each volume contains several thousand abstracts arranged by classified topics from the *Thesaurus of Psychological Index Terms* (within the PAIS system), including subject and author indexes.

SpecialNet communication network   SpecialNet has been designed to give professionals in the field of special education up-to-the-minute information regarding services and current happenings across national, state, and regional levels. Services of SpecialNet are obtained by subscribing to the SpecialNet Computer System, a large computer network operated by the National Association of State Directors of Special Education (NASDSE). In order to use SpecialNet, a potential user must have access to a computer terminal, microcomputer, or word processor. As a member of the SpecialNet System, a user can request information or technical assistance from a number of legal, technical, and content specialists in the field who are available to answer questions via SpecialNet. Users also can send confidential messages or general communications to other members on the system, and reports can be transferred electronically from agency to agency. A directory of SpecialNet users on the system is available.

Access to information on specific topics within SpecialNet is obtained by scanning the various topical "bulletin boards" on the computer system or by posting requests for information via one's computer terminal. The topical bulletin boards are updated daily. Information is sent back from the SpecialNet system to the user's own personal "mailbox." A bulletin board of particular interest is the one on early childhood, which gives its user access to the knowledge and expertise of individuals throughout the United States.

Resource agencies for information dissemination and technical assistance

A number of agencies or special service centers have been established across the nation to provide technical assistance and resource information to programs serving the handicapped. Although these agencies serve functions similar to those reviewed in the previous section, they are not designed as computerized clearinghouses and information systems. Their purpose is to give direct technical assistance to programs, disseminate selected types of information, and develop useful materials for practitioners in the field. Five of these agencies, listed below and described in the following pages, are:

— Regional Resource Centers (RRCs).
— Head Start Regional Resource Access Projects.
— BEH Technical Assistance Resource for Handicapped Children's Early Education Demonstration Projects/TADS—Technical Assistance Development System (Chapel Hill, NC).
— National Information Center for Handicapped Children and Youth (NICHCY).
— National Center for Special Technology Information Exchange.

Regional Resource Centers (RRCs)   Six Resource Centers are in operation around the nation. Their purpose is to assist states in meeting their responsibilities, as defined under PL 94-142, and to see that individualized education programs (IEPs) are developed for every handicapped child. The RRCs provide four basic kinds of services:

- Upon request, they conduct information searches and disseminate that information to help solve specific educational needs within a region.
- In cooperation with state and local education staff, they survey state and local needs. They then assist in planning and delivering inservice training programs, workshops, and the like.
- By request, they provide demonstrations of specific educational techniques and concepts such as workshops to present unique program models or inservice sessions on the use

of IEP planning strategies and assessment approaches.

- By request, they provide technical assistance to state and local agencies in the form of special consultations, development of particular educational products, statewide workshops, topical conferences, and so on.

Head Start Resource Access Projects (RAPs)   To help Head Start programs across the country serve young handicapped children, a network of 15 RAP centers was established by the Administration for Children, Youth, and Families. Each RAP center offers several important services such as: (a) identiftying and retrieving information about local, regional, and national resources that may be helpful to Head Start programs in their effort to serve young handicapped children,(b) assessing local Head Start needs and identifying local resources to help meet those needs, (c) coordinating the delivery of special services to Head Start centers, (d) providing technical assistance and training upon request, (e) facilitating cooperative activities between Head Start and other community and state agencies, and (f) providing resource materials to Head Start grantees.

RAP centers are especially useful for obtaining information on local or state resources for handicapped children. Some RAPs also have clearinghouses for materials relating to curriculum, parent participation and training, child identification, assessment, and instructional planning. These can be obtained on a loan basis. Local Head Start centers should be able to give you the location or address of the RAP center serving your regional area.

Technical Assistance Centers for Handicapped Children's Early Education Projects   The office for Special Education Programs in Washington, DC (formerly the Bureau of Education for the Handicapped) established technical assistance centers to help projects funded under the Handicapped Children's Early Education Program (HCEEP). The current one is *TADS (Technical Assistance Development System),* located within the Frank Porter Graham Child Development Center at the University of North Carolina, Chapel Hill. The TADS staff provides special assistance services to HCEEP demonstration projects and collects and disseminates information relating to early education of the handicapped. It assists in staff development and interagency coordination, helps in the evaluation of project efforts, and carries out any other forms of technical assistance and information retrieval that facilitate the HCEEP demonstration effort. TADS also publishes topical papers, bibliographies, monographs, planning and information guides, books, and a newsletter called *Emphasis* (Trohanis, 1983).

National Information Center for Handicapped Children and Youth   NICHCY is a free information service established as a part of Public Law 94-142 as amended by PL 98-199, to provide timely, accurate information for anyone in the country who requests it—parents, educators, administrators, university students, advocates, caregivers, and those interested in the lives of children and youth with handicaps. NICHCY answers questions and sends materials to those who mail their requests to the Center (Box 1492, Washington, DC 20013). It disseminates new information through fact sheets and newsletters, assembles information about other resources, gives advice to people working in groups such as task forces or committees, and connects individuals across the nation who are working on similar problems. The Center also develops new materials and collects existing information to fill information gaps, and it publishes a *News Digest* four times a year.

National Center for Special Education Technology Information Exchange

This national resource is operated by the Council for Exceptional Children, Reston, Virginia, in collaboration with LINC Resources, Columbus, Ohio, and JWK International, Annandale, Virginia. The Center's purpose is to serve as a clearinghouse of information about technological advances and applications to aid teachers, parents, administrators, and others in their development, selection, and use of technology with handicapped persons. The Center's staff collects, synthesizes, and disseminates information to individuals or organizations requesting help. For example, the Center maintains a specialized information base on articles and publications, practices, resources, vendors, technological products and technology oriented organizations, and hardware/software applicable to the handicapped. It also produces news releases, information memos, and journal articles.

The Center operates two electronic bulletin boards on SpecialNet, called TECH.LINE and TECH.TALK. TECH.LINE is a closed board that gives news about special education technology. TECH.TALK is an open board for the exchange of information among educators. One can contact the Center through its toll-free hotline (1-800-345-TECH) to ask questions, obtain consultation or referrals. (The hotline is open Monday through Friday, 1:00 p.m.-6:00 p.m. Eastern time).

Resources for professional affiliation and advocacy

Professional and parent organizations have played an important role in the history of special education and early childhood education. These organizations have been advocates for children and for the handicapped at local, state, and federal levels. In local communities with no special programs for the handicapped, parent groups often have been the catalysts to organize them. The Association for Retarded Citizens, for example, has been instrumental in starting preschool services for handicapped children in many communities. Parent organizations also have been a source of support and information for parents with handicapped children and have created opportunities for parents to interact with others who have similar interests and experiences.

Professional organizations, too, have parallel benefits for students and professionals in the field. These organizations act as a representative and advocate for a discipline. The larger, the more active, and the more vocal an organization is, the more influential it can be upon public or professional policy. Also, professional organizations provide an internal communication and dissemination network within their own discipline. New ideas and literature are disseminated through an organization's journals and newsletters. Local, state, and national meetings of the organization provide opportunities for members to meet and discuss pertinent issues and new developments in the field. Commercial producers of instructional materials and equipment exhibit their products at many of these conferences, giving members an excellent opportunity to examine new materials/equipment/published materials relating to the field. The exposure and stimulation from participating in conference sessions give one a broader perspective of the field. This broadened perspective transcends local concerns and problems and helps expand one's understanding of a field by examining problems and issues from state or national viewpoints.

Most professionals affiliate with at least one national organization relating to their field of work. Organizations encourage students to join and may offer reduced student membership rates. Students tend to regard themselves as outside of the profession until earning the college degree, but getting involved in the profession early, when one is still a student, is a good idea. Student divisions or chapters within an organization offer opportunities to make many long-lasting professional contacts, which can be an important part of one's professional training.

Organizations concerned with the care and education of children, including related areas in psychology and education, are abundant. The major ones relating to special education, early childhood, education, and psychology are described briefly in the next pages. Other relevant organizations are listed by interest area in Table 12.7.

Council for Exceptional Children (CEC)   CEC is the major professional organization in special education, with a national membership of over 41,000 (including some 12,000-13,000 student members). Its membership encompasses teachers, school administrators, directors of special education, university faculty and teacher trainers, and state/federal officials involved with the handicapped in some capacity. The organization is concerned with all areas of exceptionality including the gifted, and specific divisions have been created for particular areas of exceptionality. Divisions hold their own special meetings and publish their own division newsletters or journals.

Of particular note, of course, is the *Division for Early Childhood* (DEC), for persons interested in handicapped/at-risk infants, toddlers, and preschoolers. The Council for Exceptional Children plays a significant leadership role in the field of special education through its national, state, and local organizations. It is involved in professional training, materials and media production, legislative lobbying, and information retrieval and dissemination. The Council has its own computerized information services, described earlier, and it produces materials in response to particular informational and training needs in the field.

CEC publishes three major periodicals, and other specialized journals are available through individual CEC divisions. The major journals are: *Exceptional Children* (published eight times yearly), *Teaching Exceptional Children* (published quarterly), and the annotated bibliographical reference *Exceptional Child Education Resources* (produced by the ERIC Clearinghouse on Handicapped and Gifted Children, which is operated by CEC). This latter volume, described earlier as one for locating and retrieving references and materials within a particular topical area, is published quarterly.

National Committee for Very Young Children with Special Needs and Their Families (INTERACT).   Another organization that represents a particularly important resource, INTERACT is an organization with purposes similar to DEC.

National Association for the Education of Young Children (NAEYC)   NAEYC includes professionals in higher education and practitioners who are interested in child development and services for young children, such as day-care programs, nursery schools and preschools, compensatory education, and early intervention programs. The organization sponsors a national public campaign each year known as the "Week of the Young Child," publishes a journal entitled *Young Children,* and produces books, pamphlets, and

Table 12.7
Selected Parent and Professional Organizations Relating
to the Handicapped, Early Education, and General Education

Parent Organizations
    Association for Children with Learning Disabilities
    Children's Defense Fund
    International Parent's Organization (Deaf)
    Parents of Downs Syndrome Children
    United Cerebral Palsy Foundation

Organizations Relating to Specific Handicapping Conditions
    American Association of the Deaf
    American Association on Mental Deficiency
    American Speech, Language and Hearing Association
    Association for the Education of the Visually Handicapped
    National Society for Autistic Children
    Spina Bifida Association of America
    The Association for Persons with Severe Handicaps (TASH)

Organizations Relating to Early Childhood Education
    American Montessori Society
    Association for Childhood Education International
    Child Welfare League of America
    Day Care and Child Development Council of America
    National Association for the Education of Young Children

Organizations Relating to Other Associated Disciplines
    American Medical Association
    American Occupational Therapy Association
    American Physical Therapy Association
    Association for Care of Children's Health
    Association of University Affiliated Programs for the Developmentally Disabled
    National Association for Music Therapy
    National Association of Social Workers

Organizations Relating to General Education
    American Education Research Association
    National Education Association

other materials useful to individuals involved in the education and care of young children. National, state, and local divisions of NAEYC hold regular meetings and conduct activities in which both students and professionals in the field may participate.

This organization is particularly relevant for people interested in young handicapped children. It is the major organization for those who deal with early childhood service programs for nonhandicapped youngsters. Because the field of early education for the handicapped represents a blend of both special education and early childhood education, professionals will want to maintain contact with the professional organizations in both areas.

American Psychological Association (APA)   APA is the largest organization in the country relating to psychology and the social sciences. It is an important organization to students and professionals in special education because of its overall focus on human behavior and its numerous publications of relevance to special education. Many APA publications contain information and research relating to developmental disabilities, treatment of handicapped individuals, and theoretical or philosophical issues concerned with abnormal growth and development. The 33 divisions within the APA organization reflect the breadth of the field of psychology represented among its membership of over 45,000 professionals.

The American Psychological Association publishes a large number of journals. Those most pertinent to the special educator or the early childhood educator are: *Developmental Psychology, Journal of Educational Psychology,* and *Journal of Abnormal Psychology.* As discussed earlier, APA also publishes *Psychological Abstracts* and has its own computerized information search and retrieval systems—Psychological Abstracts Information System (PAIS) and PsychSCAN: LD/MR.

National Association for Retarded Citizens (NARC)   Primarily an organization of parents and professionals who have an interest in retarded persons, NARC has been particularly active in generating local services for the retarded. Its major activities include dissemination of public information at local and state levels, public advocacy, surveillance of the quality of special services for the handicapped, and advocacy for the rights and interests of the retarded. NARC publishes some pamphlets and small booklets that are particularly useful for local awareness campaigns and dissemination to lay and professional groups interested in the handicapped. NARC also publishes a bibliography series on various topics of interest such as the law and the handicapped. A bimonthly newsletter, *Mental Retardation News,* provides up-to-date information about legislative activities, special services, and general interest topics.

American Association on Mental Deficiency (AAMD)   A large, national organization, AAMD has a multidisciplinary membership of persons from medical, psychological, sociological, educational, and legal professions who are associated with service delivery and research relating to the mentally retarded. AAMD has played an important role in policy making, lobbying, and legislative efforts on behalf of retarded individuals. For example, AAMD established the standard, nationwide definition and classification system for mental retardation. AAMD also has been responsible for developing some assessment instruments for use with retarded preschool and school-age youngsters. A special AAMD committee on the prevention of mental retardation has been integrally involved in legislative efforts to protect the rights and educational needs of retarded children and adults. The Association publishes two major journals: *American Journal on Mental Deficiency* and *Mental Retardation.* Other manuals, books, and special topical monographs are produced intermittently.

Society for Research in Child Development (SRCD)   SRCD is important because of its significant involvement in research and its publication of some major literature in the field of child development. SRCD is a relatively small professional organization, but its membership is diverse, including pediatricians, anthropologists, dentists, educators, nutritionists, sociologists, psychologists, and statisticians. Although teachers and practitioners in the field may not be directly involved in this organization, those who have research interests will find it to be a particularly useful resource because of its publications. These include: *Child Development* (a journal published on a quarterly basis), *Review of Research in Child Development,* and *Monographs of the Society for Research in Child Development,* which are scholarly papers. The Society also publishes *Child Development Abstracts and Bibliography.*

American Educational Research Association (AERA)   AERA is a major national organization for professionals interested in the development and applications of research to the education of children and adults. Established in 1915 under the name of the National Association of Directors of Educational Research, its name was changed to the present one in 1930. The organization is composed of nine divisions. In addition, it sponsors over 25 interest groups to facilitate the formation of research specialties. One of these is an interest group on early education and child development. This special interest group focuses upon research relating to young children in topic areas such as child care, early education, teacher training, parent education, program development, and all areas of growth/development.

AERA is a key resource for major journals and other publications that summarize educational research. Three regular AERA publications that should be noted are: *Review of Educational Research, American Educational Research Journal,* and *Educational Researcher.* The *Review of Educational Research,* published quarterly, includes integrative reviews and interpretations of educational research literature. It also identifies and summarizes important studies in the field and publishes selected chapter bibliographies in various topic areas. The *American Educational Research Journal,* published quarterly, contains original research articles that are both empirical and theoretical in nature. Reviews of books and tests also are included.

Resources for teacher and child-oriented instructional materials

A final type of resource for practitioners working directly with handicapped young children is for use in the planning and delivery of individualized instructional programs. Where can teachers, clinicians, and others find information about instructional materials and special toys appropriate for young handicapped children? Where can teaching aids and curriculum programs be located to help prepare daily instructional lessons? Every practitioner knows the time, energy, and ingenuity required to create highly individualized educational programs. Because time is lacking to develop all instructional items by oneself, practitioners can and should draw upon materials developed by others. These instructional items can be used in their existing form; they can be adapted to fit a particular program's or child's special needs, or they can provide ideas for the development of other new materials. The task is to locate and gain access to instructional resources quickly when they are needed.

Many practitioners get into the habit of being continuously on the lookout for useful new teaching and child-oriented materials. These include many different types of items (Thorum, 1976):

- Educational or curriculum kits developed by commercial agencies or by federally funded research or demonstration programs. These kits generally are designed to teach children specific developmental or academic skills (e.g., Peabody Language Kits, Distar Programs).

- Entertainment toys and games, produced by commercial vendors, which can be adapted for use as educational devices.
- Instructional materials, toys, and games, developed by commercial vendors or by educational/demonstration and research programs, to enhance children's learning in one or several curriculum areas.
- Staff- or parent-developed materials created as part of an educational program in the field because of particular needs therein. These are often highly practical and informal and are not highly refined or field-tested. They nonetheless provide useful ideas and represent helpful teaching tools.

Producers and distributors of these types of materials number in the hundreds. New materials appear on the market so rapidly that keeping up with every new product is difficult. For our purposes here, this section presents a few of the major sources of information about curriculum and instructional materials currently available or where these items can be purchased or obtained on loan.

Agencies and clearinghouses of instructional materials   Some agencies have been created expressly for the purpose of making instructional materials more accessible to potential consumers. A few are described in the following paragraphs.

American Printing House for the Blind   This private agency, located in Louisville, Kentucky, is operated by funds appropriated by the U.S. Congress to produce and distribute materials for the visually impaired. Its materials, including both equipment and printed items, are distributed via *Regional Branch Libraries for the Visually Impaired and Blind*. By contacting your State Department of Education, Special Education Division, you can find out where these branch libraries are located, along with their addresses and phone numbers.

Through its branch libraries, The American Printing House offers the following resources to teachers and parents of blind and visually impaired children:

- An Instructional Materials Reference Center within the American Printing House serves as a clearinghouse for educational materials. The Center maintains a *Central Catalogue*—an inventory of all special print and braille books available for the visually impaired and blind. This catalog is available at several locations, such as in State Departments of Education and in the Regional Branch Libraries for the Visually Impaired and Blind. The Regional Libraries either can provide information on where these braille or special print books can be obtained or can actually acquire the books on a loan basis for the person requesting help. The Reference Center also responds to requests for information about specific materials and maintains a mailing list to give updates about new instructional items to educational personnel serving the blind.
- The Printing House offers for purchase a variety of educational aids to blind individuals and their teachers. These aids are itemized in a *Catalogue of Educational and Other Aids for the Blind and Visually Impaired,* published each year. It lists a variety of materials, such as special dark-lined paper for partially sighted persons, brailled items, and tactile materials (e.g., instructional stimulus materials, toys, and games).
- The Printing House has sponsored the development of a variety of special curriculum programs and instructional items for teachers to use in teaching visually impaired

children. Examples that are particularly applicable to very young children include a *Sensory Stimulation Program,* materials to teach braille reading readiness skills, such as a *Roughness Discrimination Kit* to teach tactile discrimination skills precursory to braille reading, and a series of *Readiness Workbooks.*

- The Printing House and its branch libraries have specialized equipment needed to produce items for use by the blind, visually impaired, or their teachers. For example, a Regional Branch Library may have a "thermoform press" that makes braille copies from braille books or from real objects such as coins and other small items that children learn to label or use for various instructional activities.

- The Printing House produces braille and large-type books, as well as recorded materials for all kinds of printed matter, including fiction and nonfiction books, textbooks, tests, magazines, and music. Additionally, the Printing House publishes a variety of helpful paperbound manuals for teachers to aid in their instructional planning. Two of these are: *The Visually Impaired Child—Growth, Learning, Development: Infancy to School Age* (Halliday, 1970) and *Aids for Teaching Basic Concepts for Sensory Development* (Barraga, Dorward, & Ford, 1973).

In describing resources for blind and visually impaired persons or people who work with them, two other useful agencies should be mentioned. The *Library of Congress, Division for the Blind and Physically Handicapped,* provides a free service for children and adults whose vision or other physical limitation prevents use of printed materials as a medium for learning. Through the Library of Congress a variety of books, magazines, special equipment, and accessories can be obtained on loan.

The Library also circulates music materials including braille and large-type music scores, recorded music books, and beginning instruction for certain instruments on cassette tapes. Of particular note are the *Talking Books* produced by the Library. As the name implies, these are recordings of books, as well as of magazines, and other printed materials. *Regional Cooperating Libraries* are designated as the distributors for *Talking Books.* Again, State Departments of Education have information on which libraries in a particular area serve this role. A *Catalogue of Talking Books* is available in both printed and recorded forms, summarizing the materials available. This includes listings of (a) *Talking Book discs*—small 8 rpm flexible records that must be played on a special talking book machine, and (b) *Talking Book cassette tapes.*

A second resource agency is the *American Foundation for the Blind.* It also produces materials (not including books) for the blind. These are itemized in a catalog, *Products for People with Vision Problems,* produced by its Consumer Products Department (15 W. 16th St., New York, NY 10011). Items include games, special canes, timers, clocks, watches, special toys, sports items, and other products.

Teachers of the blind have access to what is called *federal quota funds* for each legally blind child in their program. Each state receives an allocation from the federal government to assist in purchasing special materials for every legally blind child receiving educational services. This money can be used by the teacher or agency serving that child to purchase or rent materials that will help provide an appropriate educational program.

Other resource agencies for educational/instructional materials   Three other agencies (described earlier in the section on Information Search and Retrieval

Systems) should be noted here in regard to their role in providing instructional materials. *CEC Information Services* is a good source of information on instructional programs, learner materials, curriculums, and other educational items. An especially useful service for practitioners who need information quickly is the CEC Information Hot Line. A toll-free phone number provides quick access to a specialist who can direct the caller to appropriate resources. The Hot Line number is 800-336-3728 (for those in continental U.S. only); callers from Virginia should call collect using 703-620-3660.

The *ERIC Clearinghouses* and *Computer Information Retrieval Service* comprise a second excellent resource for teachers who want to locate information on education materials and curriculum. A major section in the ERIC data files deals with curriculum guides, instructional materials, and other "how to" publications.

A third resource is the *National Information Center for Educational Media (NICEM)*. As described previously, NICEM provides information on a wide range of media and materials for the handicapped, which are itemized in several comprehensive special education indexes. These include:

Special Education Index to Learner Materials
(ISBN 0-89320-024-7, LC# 79-84454)

Special Education Index to Parent Materials
(ISBN 0-89320-025-5, LC# 70-84458)

Special Education Index to Assessment Devices
(ISBN 0-89320-026-3, LC# 84457)

Special Education Index to Inservice Training Materials
(ISBN 0-89320-027-1, LC# 79-84458)

NICEM also holds a variety of "mini-indexes" to special education materials. These focus upon specific types of materials, such as materials for personal and social development of moderately and severely handicapped students, for independent living skills for moderately and severely handicapped students, and for functional communication skills.

Commercial publishers and distributors of educational materials

Many companies distribute child-oriented instructional materials as well as teacher-oriented materials appropriate for use with handicapped young children. These companies disseminate catalogs containing pictures of the items along with descriptive information, prices, and purchasing instructions. Not only do these catalogs provide useful information about the kinds of materials currently available for purchase, but they are also a wonderful source of ideas on items teachers can make on their own. Many good ideas can be gleaned by skimming through catalogs. Pictures of instructional materials in the catalogs can provide sufficient visual examples to construct homemade versions of similar kinds of materials.

If funds allow, however, an endless array of materials is available for purchase. Practitioners should keep a collection of catalogs from major companies on hand to keep up-to-date on new materials being produced. Catalogs can be obtained by writing directly to the companies. You might also ask them to put your name on their mailing list for future catalogs and promotional information on new materials. When writing to commercial publishers, one can weed out unneeded mailings by indicating the kinds of materials on which you want information. Also, national conferences for professional organizations such as the National Conference for the Council on Exceptional Children, the National Association for the Education of Young Children, and the American Association on Mental Deficiency offer opportunities to obtain catalogs from commercial vendors who are exhibiting their products there.

Where can you obtain information about the companies that produce or distribute educational materials appropriate for the very young or for the handicapped? A representative listing of commercial vendors would produce a lengthy manual. For our purposes, the sources listed below give information on commercial producers and distributors of materials in the U.S.

- *Instructional Materials for the Handicapped—Birth through Early Childhood,* by Arden R. Thorum (Salt Lake City: Olympus Publishing, 1976).
- *Directory of Special Education Materials/Producers* published in the journal *Early Years* (Vol. 7, May 1977). This directory identifies publishers and manufacturers whose products are used extensively in special education. Included are company names, addresses, and a brief description of the types of materials each offers.
- *NICSEM Source Directory,* which can be purchased from NICEM (National Information Center on Educational Media), described earlier. This comprehensive directory provides names and addresses of publishers, producers, and distributors of educational materials and equipment.

When purchasing instructional items available on the commercial market, one must be a wise and discriminating consumer. The quality and instructional value of commercial materials vary greatly, as do the prices. Although many instructional materials have been field-tested with children before being offered for purchase, many have not been tested or validated with the population of children for whom they are intended. Before purchasing major items such as instructional kits, curriculums, or workbooks, obtaining some preliminary information about them is recommended. One should try to find out how instructional objectives and content were determined and if instructional programs were field-tested. This can save considerable expense and ensure expenditures on items that will most likely produce the desired learning in young children.

Because educators have to be able to discriminate between quality instructional materials and mediocre or poor ones on the market today, every practitioner should be aware of an organization called the *Educational Products Information Exchange Institute*. Commonly known as EPIE, this nonprofit educators' "consumers union" is the only consumer advocacy group in the country operating to protect educators' interests by analyzing programs and products on the market. Its broad purpose is to provide useful consumer information to educators by helping identify items that are not of high quality or durability. EPIE alerts consumers to inferior and hazardous products and provides other useful information on instructional materials and equipment typically advertised in school catalogs. EPIE offers many additional consumer services; among them:

- Its staff conducts ongoing research on instructional materials and equipment.
- It regularly surveys the performance of instructional equipment most used in schools, including all types of audiovisual equipment.
- It conducts workshops for educators on how to select instructional materials.
- It disseminates unbiased analyses of materials and laboratory test findings on equipment through several publications:

EPIE Materials Reports—a selectors' and buyers' guide that provides summary information and analyses of instructional materials on the market.

EPIE Equipment Reports—a guide reporting research findings on equipment from EPIE's own testing laboratory, as well as from its surveys of schools throughout the country, on the operation of certain types of equipment produced by selected companies.

EPIEgram—a newsletter of which two versions are offered, one dealing with instrucional materials and one dealing with equipment. Each of these semimonthly newsletters provides up-to-date information on educational products and consumer concerns.

- It produces a variety of other reports for educators, to aid in their selection and use of educational items. Two reports of particular interest here are: EPIE Report #42—*How to Select and Evaluate Materials* (1972) and EPIE Report #68—*Early Childhood Education Materials (1975).*

Information on the EPIE reports can be obtained by contacting the Institute (P.O. Box 620, Stony Brook, NY 11790). Schools, agencies, and other institutions that use EPIE's services typically join the Institute, and as dues-paying members receive its regular reports, newsletters, and consultation services.

Materials produced under Handicapped Children's Demonstration/Research Projects

Special early childhood demonstration programs funded by the federal government represent another major source of materials for teachers and the children with whom they work. Earlier, the *Handicapped Children's Early Education Demonstration Projects* (HCEEP Programs) were discussed, as was the agency, TADS (Chapel Hill, North Carolina), whose purpose is to help disseminate products and information about these projects. The HCEEP projects have produced an impressive collection of materials including assessment tools, teacher manuals and instructional materials, curriculum guides, parent information and training packets, inservice teacher and paraprofessional training materials. Some of these materials have been field-tested and validated; others are still under development but are available as research editions; still others are informal products that provide good examples of teacher-made materials to meet individual child needs.

Many of these items are useful for other practitioners who operate similar programs. Information about them can be obtained in at least two ways:

- Direct contacts can be made with the projects themselves. Some items are provided free; others are available for a nominal fee. To learn about each of the individual HCEEP projects, a good resource is the *HCEEP Overview and Directory,* produced by the technical assistance agencies in cooperation with the Bureau of Education for the Handicapped (now the Office of Special Education Programs). It can be obtained from these agencies (such as TADS) or from ERIC. Included in the directory are short descriptions of each project, its target population, child program, staff development program, project address, and phone number.
- TADS holds listings of the products developed by the HCEEP programs. These listings

provide the necessary ordering information on each product. Information on these publications can be obtained from TADS.

Other published documents providing information/instructional materials

Since new items are being produced each year, the best way to find out about them is to make use of the ERIC Clearinghouses and Retrieval System, to browse through the reference sections of libraries, and to contact some of the agencies described earlier whose major purpose is to gather these materials to make their availability known to potential users. A few publications are briefly described here as samples of the type of resource materials available. This list is not comprehensive, nor is it intended to be representative of the best. Nonetheless, it represents good resource materials that provide information on other reference or resource materials:

Educator's Resource Guide to Special Education: Terms-Laws-Tests-Organizations (1970), by William E. Davis (Boston: Allyn & Bacon)

As the name implies, this book provides a well organized and quick reference on a variety of information needed by special educators. Addresses are provided on publishers of selected tests described in the manual, state divisions of special education within Departments of Education, and organizations concerned with exceptional people.

International Guide to Aids and Appliances for Blind and Visually Impaired Persons, 2nd ed. (1977) (New York: American Foundation for the Blind).

This manual provides descriptions of items for the blind and partially sighted and sources where they can be purchased. Included are descriptions of braille equipment, writing aids, and supplies; sound equipment; orientation and mobility aids, instructional materials; and special adaptive kinds of equipment for daily living.

Early Childhood Curriculum Materials—An Annotated Bibliography (1975), compiled by Gloria Harbin and Lee Cross (Chapel Hill, NC: Technical Assistance Development System).

Contained in this annotated bibliography are descriptions of curricular materials usable with young children or by their teachers for preparing instructional activities, and sources for purchasing the materials. Instructional materials are described for a number of areas including fine and gross motor development, perception, reasoning, language, social development, infants, and many other areas.

A Training and Resource Directory for Teachers Serving Handicapped Students: K-12 (1977) Department of Health, Education, and Welfare (obtainable from the Director of Technical Assistance Unit, Office of Program Review and Assistance, Office for Civil Rights, 330 Independence Ave., S.W., Washington, DC 20201)

National resources are described in this directory, along with addresses for each item or agency. Resources include national organizations and other national directories for materials and for organizations/clearinghouses serving the handicapped.

Books for Children: Bibliography, produced by the Association for Childhood Education International (3615 Wisconsin Ave., N.W., Washington, DC 20016)

This bibliography, which is revised regularly, provides a listing of books for children, ranging from picture and picture-story books for early childhood to books for older children. It contains a listing of materials particularly useful in teaching preschool or early primary classes. A directory of publishers is included.

GUIDELINES FOR USING RESOURCES EFFECTIVELY

Resources are useful only to the extent that you, as a potential user, are skillful in capitalizing upon them. Mere awareness of resources such as those described here is not enough. Knowing how to access and use these resources is essential. When a deadline is near and pressure is high to complete a task, scurrying about at the last minute to find appropriate resources is a fruitless activity. Similarly, if you have only a general knowledge about particular resources but have failed to spend time to become skillful in using them, they cannot be expected to jump to your aid and meet your immediate needs. The best policy is to *be prepared*. Here are a few suggestions:

1. *Continuously build and update your knowledge of resources that are potentially useful to you or those with whom you work.*

   Be on the alert for information about new resources. Take advantage of opportunities to learn about agencies, new materials and equipment, and published items by skimming through journals, attending special workshops or conferences, and writing to agencies for information. Most important, obtain enough information so that you actually can use a resource in an efficient, timely manner when the need arises.

2. *Keep a resource file and update it regularly to keep information current.*

   Resources relevant to the areas of general and special education, early childhood, the handicapped, and family-child services are far too numerous to allow you to remember detailed information about each of them. A solution is to collect and organize this information in a *resource file*. A file can be as comprehensive or as restricted in scope as your interests and job responsibilities dictate. A well developed resource file can include any one or a combination of:

   — collections of specific information on local/state agencies that provide services of interest.
   — notes on selected professionals whose expertise, research, or publications might be tapped.
   — catalogs from commercial suppliers of educational materials, equipment, media, and instructional supplies.
   — listings of and notes about professional journals, books, and other relevant professional materials.
   — information on various professional and parent organizations regarding services they provide, activities they sponsor, and publications they distribute.
   — topical collections of information in selected areas of interest, such as PL 94-142, IEPs, teaching strategies for working with visually handicapped children, screening and assessment tools for preschoolers, or finger plays for young children.

3. *Stay alert to work situations in which resources could be drawn upon to aid in doing your job more effectively or where you could refer others to helpful resources.*

   The motto is simple: Use your resources! It will expand your capabilities for dealing with problems, finding solutions, developing programs and new procedures for teaching young children, and assisting others. An important distinction should be made in regard to the professional and proper use of any resource, in that a skillful user must continue to assume responsibility for the task at hand and its completion rather than expecting some resource (such as an agency, a person, or an information retrieval system) to assume responsibility—unless responsibility is transferred by mutual agreement to a person or agency serving as a resource. Careless dumping of work or responsibility onto a person or agency that agrees to provide some assistance can become punishing for everyone concerned. Skillful resource users take care to determine when they actually should seek outside help or when the task represents work that they should do themselves. Agencies and individuals should not be expected to perform services beyond their own purposes and interests except by special arrangement and voluntary agreement of the people involved.

Good protocol dictates acknowledging the assistance given by resources we tap, giving due credit to the people, agencies, publishers, and writers whose input we utilize. And a thank-you note can go a long way with people who have spent their time helping you. These simple courtesies can help keep relationships positive and the doors open for future requests for help.

4. *Learn to be efficient in accessing resources by creating or following established procedures that allow you to make the best possible use of any given resource.*

Using a resource in a haphazard, disorganized way creates unnecessary confusion, and probably frustration if other people are involved. It even may result in loss of valuable time and generate more work than not using the resource at all. Because of these problems, people too often conclude, "I can do it better myself." Unfortunately, this usually is not the case; a better job could be done simply by being more skillful as a user of resources. Plan your strategy for approaching a task in which outside resources are to be used and how you will use those resources. A few important preparations can help to achieve this:

- Define clearly within your own mind what you are attempting to do, what you need from the resources to be used, and what final product or outcome is to be achieved.

- If the resource you need is provided by another person or agency, put sufficient forethought into the task so you can set forth your need clearly. It should be presented in writing or verbally, depending on which form your resource will respond to best. The clearer your requests, the easier it will be for you or the agencies/persons you approach to ascertain if they can serve your needs. And the clearer your request, the more likely you will be to actually get what you need.

- If you are gathering information or material, devise a way of organizing it as it accumulates. Keep a record of the source of information through which you have searched so that efforts will not be inadvertently duplicated or important sources missed accidentally. As in the case of collecting published materials, keep track of references and publication sources. From the very beginning, devise a system to note references.

- If you are working with an agency or with people as your resource, obtain a clear idea of what they will do and what you must do in turn. Define responsibilities as necessary, work out a joint plan, clarify questions initially, identify appropriate channels of communication, and follow through with any necessary documentation.

- Establish a timeline for your activities, and make it known to any agencies or resource persons whose input you need. This clarifies expectations and allows you to gauge when the task involved can be completed.

5. *Obtain the necessary closure once a task is complete and you have obtained what you want from your resources.*

What comprises adequate closure depends greatly upon the nature of the task and the resources you use. Whatever the case, appropriate closure is like clearing out the final details when the crowd is gone after a big convention, paying the piper, and reviewing what was accomplished. These final steps are easy to forget once our own needs have been met and the task has been completed, but they are too important to be neglected. As examples of good closure:

- Materials and information used in the activity should be organized and filed for future use. Borrowed items should be returned promptly to their owners.
- If agencies or individual persons provided services, appropriate reports or records or thank-you letters should be completed.
- If any items required payment of fees, these should be paid as promptly as possible.
- If new materials or products were created through your use of a resource, especially a major one, they should be shared with parties who helped you. These people likely will enjoy seeing the product and the results of their own efforts. To assure optimal use of your product, it should be stored or filed where it will be most accessible to you and the intended consumers.

A good resource is one you probably will want to use again and again. A key to good resource usage, then, is to build positive relationships with agencies and individuals who have provided helpful services and information to you. Maintaining these kinds of relationships depend, in part, upon your skill in following through with some of these final tasks. Follow-up courtesies are obvious and simple, yet all too frequently forgotten.

6. *Be a discerning consumer of resources—especially in regard to instructional materials, assessment tools, curriculum programs, toys, and other educational items.*

Just because instructional materials or equipment are available for purchase does not mean that they are of good quality. Materials on the market vary greatly in quality of construction and in their value as teaching tools. To be a discriminating consumer begins with a clear definition in your own mind of the educational goals and objectives you want to achieve with children. Materials should be selected on the basis of those goals and on the basis of the instructional approaches to be used. Random selection of materials, because they look interesting or because they simply address a relevant topic area, may result in collections of instructional items that are not used and that fail to meet your needs. Materials, particularly large curriculum packages or instructional programs, should be carefully examined before purchasing them. The various clearinghouses discussed earlier that lend materials to practitioners provide access to educational materials for this very purpose.

SUMMARY

Modern technology in the publishing industry, computers, and the mere availability of copy machines has revolutionized the dissemination of information today. Information and printed material available on any topic are proliferating at such an astounding rate that no student or professional can hope to read, let alone master, it all. Given such an abundance of information, the greatest challenge facing students and practitioners today is the task of locating pertinent information and making good use of it.

The secret to being a competent, knowledgeable professional (or student) in today's world thus begins with one simple rule: *Know your resources!* This entails three basic skills: (a) knowing what resources are available in one's various areas of interest, (b) knowing where these resources can be located or where help can be found to locate them, and (c) knowing how to access those resources in a timely, efficient way. Skillful use of resources can increase one's own work efficiency and provide a means for keeping up-to-date on new information in one's field. When resources are used effectively, time and money can be saved, and the quality of services for young children with special needs can be enhanced.

Resources exist in many forms. Only a few of these were described here. A resource is any source of information, services, published materials, or other useful products that can aid in our work. The five broad types of resources described here include: (a) literature and information sources such as journals, books, reference materials, and directories, (b) information search-and-retrieval systems such as computerized collections of published materials or dissemination centers, (c) agencies for information dissemination and technical assistance, (d) professional organizations and advocacy groups, and (e) resources for teacher- and child-oriented instructional materials.

Becoming an effective user of resources begins with a deliberate effort to become knowledgeable about the resources in one's professional field and skillful in actually using them. Any resource is of limited help if its user has to take a great deal of extra time accessing it and learning how to use it. Always ask yourself: Are there some resources I can use that will help me do my job better or more efficiently? The answer, of course, is yes, but the ultimate gain is in how well one is able to make use of the multitude of resources available.

References

Abelson, W. D., Zigler, E., & DeBlasi, C. L. (1974). Effects of a four-year Follow-Through program on economically disadvantaged children. *Journal of Educational Psychology, 66*(5), 756-771.

Achenbach, T. M., & Edelbrock, C. S. (1978). The classification of child psychopathology: A review and analysis of empirical efforts. *Psychological Bulletin, 85,* 1275-1301.

Ackerman, P. R., Jr., & Moore, M. G. (1976). Delivery of educational services to preschool handicapped children. In T. D. Tjossem (Ed.), *Intervention strategies for high risk infants and young children.* Baltimore: University Park Press.

Adelson, E., & Fraiberg, S. (1974). Gross motor development in infants blind from birth. *Child Development, 45,* 114-126.

Adelson, E., & Fraiberg, S. (1975). Gross motor development in infants blind from birth. In B. Z. Friedlander, G. M. Sterritt, & G. E. Kirk (Eds.), *Exceptional infant: Assessment and intervention* (Vol. 3). New York: Brunner/Mazel.

Aiello, B. (1976). Especially for special educators: A sense of our own history. In J. B. Jordan (Ed.), *Exceptional child education at the bicentennial: A parade of progress . . . .* Reston, VA: Council for Exceptional Children.

Aiken, L. R. (1985). *Psychological testing and measurement* (5th ed.). Boston: Allyn & Bacon.

Ainsworth, M. (1969). Object relations, dependency, and attachment: A theoretical review of the infant-mother relationship. *Child Development, 40,* 965-1025.

Ainsworth, M. (1973). The development of infant-mother attachment. In B. Caldwell & H. Ricciuti (Eds.), *Review of child development research* (Vol. 3). Chicago: University of Chicago Press.

Ainsworth, M. D. S. (1979). Attachment as related to mother-infant interaction. In J. S. Rosenblatt, R. A. Hinde, C. Beer, & M. C. Busnell (Eds.), *Advances in the study of behavior* (Vol. 9). New York: Academic Press.

Akers, M. (1972). Prologue: The why of early childhood education. In J. J. Gordon (Ed.), *Early childhood education.* Chicago: University of Chicago Press. (Reprinted from *Seventy-first yearbook of the National Society for the Study of Education*)

Alderman, M. (1972, January 14). Cerebral palsy: "My baby is slow . . . ." *Patient Care.*

Alford, C. A. (1977). Prenatal infections and psychosocial development in children born into lower socioeconomic settings. In P. Mittler (Ed.), *Research to practice in mental retardation: Biomedical aspects* (Vol. 3). Baltimore: University Park Press.

Alford, C. A., Stagno, S., & Reynolds, D. W. (1974). Congenital toxoplasmosis: Clinical, laboratory, and therapeutic consideration with special reference to subclinical disease. *Bulletin of the New York Academy of Medicine, 50,* 160.

Allen, K. E. (1980). *Mainstreaming in early education.* Albany, NY: Delmar.

Allen, K. E. (1984). Federal legislation and young handicapped children. *Topics in Early Childhood Special Education, 4*(1), 9-18.

Allen, K. E., Holm, V. A., & Schiefelbusch, R. L. (1978). *Early intervention—A team approach.* Baltimore: University Park Press.

Alonso, L., Moor, P. M., Raynor, S., Saaz von Hippel, C., & Baer, S. (1978). *Mainstreaming preschoolers: Children with visual handicaps—A guide for teachers, parents and others who work with visually impaired handicapped preschoolers* (DHEW Publication No. OHDS 79-31112). Washington, DC: Dept. of Health, Education, and Welfare.

Alper, A. E., & Horne, B. M. (1959). IQ changes of institutionalized mental defectives over two decades. *American Journal of Mental Deficiency, 64,* 472-475.

Alpern, G., Boll, T., & Shearer, M. (1980). *Developmental profile II.* Aspen, CO: Psychological Development Publications.

Als, H., Tronick, E., Adamson, L., & Brazelton, T. B. (1976). The behavior of the full-term yet underweight newborn infant. *Developmental Medicine & Child Neurology, 18,* 590.

Als, H., Tronick, E., Lester, B. M., & Brazelton, T. B. (1979). Specific neonatal measures: The Brazelton neonatal behavioral assessment scale. In J. D. Osofsky (Ed.), *Handbook of infant development.* New York: John Wiley & Sons.

American Foundation for the Blind. (1957). *Itinerant teaching services for blind children.* New York: American Foundation for the Blind.

American National Standards Institute. (1969). *Specifications for audiometers* (ANSI S3.6). New York: American National Standards Organization.

American Psychiatric Association. (1980). *Diagnostic and statistical manual of mental disorders—DSM III* (3rd ed.). Washington, DC: Author.

Amin-Zaki, L., Elhassani, S., Majeed, M. A., Clarkson, T. W., Doherty, R. A., & Greenwood, M. (1974). Intrauterine methylmercury poisoning in Iraq. *Pediatrics, 54,* 587.

Anastasiow, N. J. (1981). Early childhood education for the handicapped in the 1980's: Recommendations. *Exceptional Children, 47,* 276-284.

Anderson, B. J., Vietze, P., & Dokecki, P. S. (1977). Reciprocity in vocal interactions of mothers and infants. *Child Development, 48,* 1976-1981.

Antley, T. R., & DuBose, R. F. (1981). *A case for early intervention: Summary of program findings, longitudinal data, and cost-effectiveness.* Unpublished manuscript. (Available from University of Washington, Experimental Education Unit, Seattle)

Apgar, V. (1953). APGAR rating scale: A proposal for a new method of resolution of the newborn infant. *Current researchers in anesthesia and analgesia, 32,* 260-267.

Aram, D. M., Ekelman, B. L., & Nation, J. E. (1984). Preschoolers with language disorders: 10 years later. *Journal of Speech & Hearing Research, 27,* 232-244.

Aram, D. M., & Nation, J. E. (1975). Patterns of language behavior in children with developmental language disorders. *Journal of Speech & Hearing Research, 18,* 229-241.

Aram, D. M., & Nation, J. E. (1982). *Child language disorders.* St. Louis: C. V. Mosby.

Arend, R., Grove, F., & Sroufe, L. (1979). Continuity of individual adaptation from infancy to kindergarten: A predictive study of ego resiliency and curiosity in preschoolers. *Child Development, 50*(4), 950-959.

Arnold, L. E., Rowe, M., & Tolbert, H. A. (1978). Parent groups. In L. E. Arnold (Ed.), *Helping parents help their children*. New York: Brunner/Mazel.

Atomic Energy Commission. (1975). Radiation protection: Implementation of NCRP recommendations for lower radiation exposure levels for fertile women. *Federal Register, 40*(2), 779-780.

Ayers, J. (1972). *Southern California sensory integration tests*. Los Angeles: Western Psychological Services.

Badger, E., Burns, D., & DeBoer, M. (1982). An early demonstration of educational intervention beginning at birth. *Journal of the Division for Early Childhood, 5*, 19-30.

Bagnato, S. J. (1981). Developmental scales and developmental curricula: Forging a linkage for early intervention. *Topics in Early Childhood Special Education, 1*(2), 1-8.

Bagnato, S. J., & Neisworth, J. T. (1981). *Linking developmental assessment and curricula: Prescriptions for early intervention*. Rockville, MD: Aspen Systems Corp.

Bailey, D. B., Jr., & Simeonsson, R. J. (1984). Critical issues underlying research and intervention with families of young handicapped children. *Journal for Division of Early Childhood, 9*(1), 38-48.

Bailey, D. B., Jr., & Wolery, M (1984). *Teaching infants and preschoolers with handicaps*. Columbus, OH: Charles E. Merrill.

Bailey, E. J., & Bricker, D. (1984). The efficacy of early intervention for severely handicapped infants and young children. *Topics in Early Childhood Special Education, 4*(3), 30-51.

Bailey, P. W., & Trohanis, P. L. (Eds.). (1984). *Benefits of early intervention for special children* (TADS Series Paper #1). Chapel Hill, NC: Technical Assistance Development System.

Bakeman, R., & Brown, J. V. (1977). Early interaction: Consequences to the assessment of mother-infant interaction. *Child Development, 48*, 195-203.

Baker, B. L. (1984). Intervention with families with young, severely handicapped children. In J. Blacher (Ed.), *Severely handicapped young children and their families: Research in review*. New York: Academic Press.

Bakir, F., Damluji, S. F., Amin-Zaki, L., Murtadha, M., Khalidi, A., Al-Rawi, N. Y., Tikriti, S., Dhahir, H. I., Clarkson, T. W., Smith, J. C., & Doherty, R. A. (1973). Methylmercury poisoning in Iraq. *Science, 181*, 320.

Baltes, P. B., & Reese, H. W. (1984). The life-span perspective in developmental psychology. In M. H. Bornstein & M. E. Lamb (Eds.), *Developmental psychology: An advanced textbook*. Hillsdale, NJ: Lawrence Erlbaum.

Balthazar, E., & Stevens, H. (1975). *The emotionally disturbed mentally retarded*. Englewood Cliffs, NJ: Prentice-Hall.

Bandura, A. (1973). *Aggression: A social learning approach*. Englewood Cliffs, NJ: Prentice-Hall.

Bandura, A. (1977). *Social learning theory*. Englewood Cliffs, NJ: Prentice-Hall.

Bandura, A., & Harris, M. B. (1966). Modification of syntactic style. *Journal of Experimental Child Psychology, 4*, 341-351.

Barnes, A. C. (1968). *Intra-uterine development*. Philadelphia: Lea & Febiger.

Barnes, E. J. (1974). Cultural retardation or shortcomings of assessment techniques. In R. L. Jones & D. L. MacMillan (Eds.), *Special education in transition*. Boston: Allyn & Bacon.

Barraga, N. (1976). *Visual handicaps and learning*. Belmont, CA: Wadsworth.

Barraga, N., Dorward, B., & Ford, P. (1973). *Aids for teaching basic concepts for sensory development*. Louisville, KY: American Printing House for the Blind.

Barsch, R. H. (1969). The expectations of the parent. In R. H. Barsch (Ed.), *The parent-teacher partnership*. Reston, VA: Council for Exceptional Children.

Batshaw, M. L., & Perret, Y. M. (1981). *Children with handicaps: A medical primer*. Baltimore: Paul H. Brookes.

Battaglia, F. C., & Simmons, M. A. (1978). The low-birth-weight infant. In F. Falkner & J. M. Tanner (Eds.), *Human growth: Vol. 2. Postnatal growth*. New York: Plenum.

Bauer, M. L. (1972, July). *Health characteristics of low-income persons* (DHEW publication No. HSM 73-1500). Rockville, MD: National Center for Health Statistics.

Baum, D. (1975). Heart disease in children. In E. E. Bleck & D. A. Nagel (Eds.), *Physically handicapped children: A medical atlas for teachers*. New York: Grune & Stratton.

Baxter, B. L. (1966). Effect of visual deprivation during postnatal maturation on the electroencephalogram of the cat. *Experimental Neurology, 14*, 224-237.

Bayley, N. (1958). Value and limitations of infant testing. *Children, 5*, 129-133.

Bayley, N. (1969). Consistency and variability in the growth of intelligence from birth to eighteen years. *Journal of Genetic Psychology, 775*, 165-196.

Bayley, N. (1970). Development of mental abilities. In P. H. Mussen (Ed.), *Carmichael's manual of child psychology* (3rd ed.). New York: John Wiley & Sons.

Bayley, N. (1984). *Bayley scales of infant development*. New York: Psychological Corp.

Bayley, N., & Schaefer, E. S. (1964). Correlations of maternal and child behaviors with the development of mental abilities. Data from the Berkeley Growth Study. *Monographs of the Society for Research in Child Development, 29*(6), 80.

Beck, R. (1976). The need for adjunctive services in the management of severely and profoundly handicapped individuals: Part I—A view from primary care. In N. G. Haring & L. Brown (Eds.), *Teaching the severely handicapped* (Vol. 2). New York: Grune & Stratton.

Beckman, P. J., & Burke, P. J. (1984). Early childhood special education: State of the art. *Topics in Early Childhood Special Education, 4*(1), 19-32.

Beckman-Bell, P. (1981). Child-related stress in families of handicapped children. *Topics in Early Childhood Special Education, 1*(3), 45-54.

Bee, H. (1985). *The developing child* (4th ed.). New York: Harper & Row.

Beery, K., & Buktenica, N. (1967). *Developmental test of visual-motor integration*. Chicago: Follett Publishing Co.

Behrman, R. E., & Vaughan, V. C., III. (1983). *The Nelson textbook of pediatrics* (12th ed.). Philadelphia: W. B. Saunders.

Bell, R. Q. (1968). A reinterpretation of the direction of effects in studies of socialization. *Psychological Review, 75*(2), 81-95.

Bell, R. Q. (1974). Contributions of human infants to caregiving and social interaction. In M. Lewis & L. A. Rosenblum (Eds.), *The effect of the infant on its caregiver*. New York: John Wiley & Sons.

Bell, S. (1971). The development of the concept of object as related to infant-motor attachment. *Child Development, 41,* 291-311.

Beller, E. K. (1974). Impact of early education on disadvantaged children. In S. Ryan (Ed.), *Longitudinal evaluations: A report on longitudinal evaluations of preschool programs* (Vol. 1) (DHEW Publication No. OHD 714-24). Washington, DC: Office of Child Development. (ERIC Document Reproduction Service No. ED 093 500).

Bender, M., & Valletutti, P. J. (1976a). *Teaching the moderately and severely handicapped: Curriculum, objectives, strategies, and activities: Vol. 1. Behavior, self care, and motor skills*. Baltimore: University Park Press.

Bender, M., & Valletutti, P. J. (1976b). *Teaching the moderately and severely handicapped: Curriculum, objectives, strategies, and activities: Vol. 2. Communication, socialization, safety, and leisure time skills*. Baltimore: University Park Press.

Bennett, S. (1976). Infant-caretaker interaction. In E. Rexford, L. Sander, & T. Shapiro (Eds.), *Infant psychiatry*. New Haven, CT: Yale University Press.

Benson, H. A., & Turnbull, A. P. (1986). Approaching families from an individualized perspective. In R. H. Horner, L. H. Meyer, & H. D. Fredericks (Eds.), *Education of learners with severe handicaps: Exemplary service strategies*. Baltimore: Paul H. Brookes.

Bereiter, C., & Engelmann, S. (1966). *Teaching disadvantaged children in the preschool*. Englewood Cliffs, NJ: Prentice-Hall.

Bergner, S., & Susser, M. W. (1970). Low birthweight and prenatal nutrition: An interpretative review. *Pediatrics, 46,* 946-966.

Bernal, J. (1972). Crying during the first ten days of life and the maternal responses. *Developmental Medicine & Child Neurology, 14,* 362-372.

Berrueta-Clement, J. R., Schweinhart, L. J., Barnett, W. S., Epstein, A. S., & Weikart, D. P. (1984). *Changed lives, the effects of the Perry Preschool Program on youths through age 19*. Ypsilanti, MI: High/Scope Press.

Berry, H. K., Butcher, R. E., Brunner, R. L., Bray, N. W., Hunt, M. M., & Wharton, C. H. (1977). New approaches to treatment of phenylketonuria. In P. Mittler (Ed.), *Research to practice in mental retardation: Biomedical aspects* (Vol. 3). Baltimore: University Park Press.

Bettelheim, B. (1967). *The empty fortress*. New York: Free Press.

Birch, H. G. (1971, March). Functional effects of fetal malnutrition. *Hospital Practice*, pp. 134-139.

Birch, H. G., & Cravioto, J. (1968). Infection, nutrition, and environment in mental development. In H. F. Eichenwald (Ed.), *Prevention of mental retardation through control of infectious diseases* (PHS Publication No. 1692). Washington, DC: U.S. Government Printing Office.

Birch, H. G., & Gussow, J. D. (1970). *Disadvantaged children: Health, nutrition, and school failure*. New York: Grune & Stratton.

Birch, J. W., Tisdall, W. J., Peabody, R., & Sterrett, R. (1966). *School achievement and effect of type size on reading in visually handicapped children* (Cooperative Research Project No. 1766). Pittsburgh: University of Pittsburgh Press.

Bissell, J. S. (1971). *Implementation of planned variation in Head Start: I. Review of the Stanford Research Institute Intern Report*. Report to the Office of Child Development, U.S. Office of Education. Washington, DC: U.S. Government Printing Office.

Bissell, J. S. (1973). Planned variation in Head Start and Follow-Through. In J. C. Stanley (Ed.), *Compensatory education for children ages two to eight: Recent studies of educational intervention*. Baltimore: Johns Hopkins University Press.

Blacher, J. (1984). Sequential stages of parental adjustment to the birth of a child with handicaps: Fact or artifact? *Mental Retardation, 22,* 55-68.

Blacher, J., & Meyers, C. E. (1983). A review of attachment formation and disorders of handicapped children. *American Journal of Mental Deficiency, 87,* 359-371.

Black, P. D. (1980). Ocular defects in children with cerebral palsy. *British Medical Journal, 281,* 487.

Black, T. (1982). President's message. *DEC Communicator, 9,* 1-5.

Blackard, M. K., & Barsh, E. T. (1982). Parents' and professionals' perceptions of the handicapped child's impact on the family. *Journal of the Association for the Severely Handicapped, 7,* 62-70.

Blackman, J.A. (1984). *Medical aspects of developmental disabilities in children birth to three*. Rockville, MD: Aspen Systems Corp.

Blancher-Dixon, J., & Turnbull, A. P. (1979). Preschool mainstreaming: Definition, rationale, and implementation. *Education Unlimited, 1,* 6-8.

Blatman, S. (1974). Narcotic poisoning of children through accidental ingestion of methadone and in utero. *Pediatrics, 54,* 329-332.

Blatt, B., Bogdan, R., Biklen, D., & Taylor, S. (1977). From institution to community: A conversion model. In E. Sontag, J. Smith, & N. Certo (Eds.), *Educational programming for the severely and profoundly handicapped*. Reston, VA: Council for Exceptional Children.

Bleck, E. E. (1975a). Arthrogryposis. In E. E. Bleck & D. A. Nagel (Eds.), *Physically handicapped children: A medical atlas for teachers*. New York: Grune & Stratton.

Bleck, E. E. (1975b). Cerebral palsy. In E. E. Bleck & D. A. Nagel (Eds.), *Physically handicapped children: A medical atlas for teachers*. New York: Grune & Stratton.

Bleck, E. E. (1975c). Muscular dystrophy-duchenne type. In E. E. Bleck & D. A. Nagel (Eds.), *Physically handicapped children: A medical atlas for teachers*. New York: Grune & Stratton.

Bleck, E. E. (1979). Orthopaedic management of cerebral palsy. *Saunders Monographs in Clinical Orthopaedics* (Vol. 2). Philadelphia: W. B. Saunders.

Bleck, E. E., & Nagel, A. A. (Eds.). (1975). *Physically handicapped children: A medical atlas for teachers*. New York: Grune & Stratton.

Bloom, B. S. (1964). *Stability and change in human characteristics*. New York: John Wiley & Sons.

Bobath, B. (1965). *Abnormal postural reflex activity caused by brain lesions*. London: William Heinemann Medical Books.

Boles, G. (1959). Personality factors in mothers of cerebral palsied children. *Genetic Psychological Monographs, 59,* 159-218.

Boring, E. G. (1950). *A history of experimental psychology.* New York: Appleton-Century-Crofts.

Bowlby, J. (1969). *Attachment and loss: Attachment* (Vol. 1). New York: Basic Books.

Bowlby, J. (1973). *Attachment and loss: Separation* (Vol. 2). New York: Basic Books.

Bracken, B. (1984). *Bracken basic concept scale.* Columbus, OH: Charles E. Merrill.

Bradley, R. H., & Caldwell, B. M. (1976a). Early home environment and changes in mental test performance in children from 6 to 36 months. *Developmental Psychology, 2,* 93-97.

Bradley, R. H., & Caldwell, B. M. (1976b). The relation of infants' home environment to mental test performance at 54 months: A follow-up study. *Child Development, 47,* 1172-1174.

Brain, G. B. (1979). The early planners. In E. Zigler & J. Valentine (Eds.), *Project Head Start: A legacy of the war on poverty.* New York: Free Press.

Braine, M., Heimer, C., Wortis, H., & Freedman, A. (1966). Factors associated with impairment of the early development of prematures. *Monographs of the Society for Research in Child Development, 31*(4), 1-92.

Braun, S. J., & Edwards, E. P. (1972). *History and theory of early childhood education.* Worthington, OH: Charles A. Jones.

Bray, N. C., Coleman, J. M., & Brackmen, M. B. (1981). Critical events in parenting handicapped children. *Journal of the Division for Early Childhood, 3,* 26-33.

Brazelton, T. B. (1973). *Neonatal behavior assessment scale.* Philadelphia: J. B. Lippincott.

Brazelton, T. B., Koslowski, B., & Main, M. (1974). The origins of reciprocity: The early mother-infant interaction. In M. Lewis & L. Rosenblum (Eds.), *The effect of the infant on its caregiver.* New York: John Wiley & Sons.

Brazelton, T. B., & Robey, J. S. (1965). Observations of neonatal behavior. *Journal of the American Academy of Child Psychiatry, 4,* 613.

Breger, L. (1974). *From instinct to identity: The development of personality.* Englewood Cliffs, NJ: Prentice-Hall.

Bretherton, I., & Ainsworth, M. (1974). Responses of one-year-olds to strangers in a strange situation. In M. Lewis & L. Rosenblum (Eds.), *The origins of fear.* New York: John Wiley & Sons.

Bricker, D. D. (1978a). Early intervention: The criteria of success. *Allied Health & Behavioral Sciences Journal, 1,* 567-582.

Bricker, D. D. (1978b). A rationale for the integration of handicapped and non-handicapped preschool children. In M. J. Guralnick (Ed.), *Early intervention and the integration of handicapped and non-handicapped children.* Baltimore: University Park Press.

Bricker, D., & Casuso, V. (1979). Family involvement: A critical component of early intervention. *Exceptional Children, 46,* 108-115.

Bricker, D., & Gumerlock, S. (1985). A three-level strategy. In J. Danaher (Ed.), *Assessment of child progress* (TADS Monograph #2). Chapel Hill, NC: Technical Assistance Development System.

Bricker, D. D., & Iacino, R. (1977). Early intervention with

severely/profoundly handicapped children. In E. Sontag (Ed.), *Educational programming for the severely/profoundly handicapped* (pp. 166-176). Reston, VA: Council for Exceptional Children.

Bricker, D., & Littman, D. (1982). Intervention and evaluation: The inseparable mix. *Topics in Early Childhood Special Education, 1*(4), 23-33.

Bricker, D., & Sheehan, R. (1981). Effectiveness of an early intervention program as indexed by measures of child change. *Journal of the Division for Early Childhood, 4,* 11-27.

Brickman, L., & Weatherford, D. (Eds.). (1986). *Evaluating early intervention programs for severely handicapped children and their families.* Baltimore: University Park Press.

Brigance, A. H. (1978). *Brigance diagnostic inventory of early development.* North Billerica, MA: Curriculum Associates.

Bristol, M. M., & Gallagher, J. J. (1982). A family focus for intervention. In E. T. Ramey & P. L. Trohanis (Eds.), *Finding and educating high-risk and handicapped infants.* Baltimore: University Park Press.

Bristor, M. W. (1984). The birth of a handicapped child—a wholistic model for grieving. *Family Relations, 33,* 25-32.

Brockman, L. M., & Ricciuti, H. N. (1971). Severe protein-calorie malnutrition and cognitive development in infancy and early childhood. *Developmental Psychology, 4,* 312-319.

Bronfenbrenner, U. (1974). *A report on longitudinal evaluations of preschool programs, Volume II: Is early intervention effective?* (DHEW Publication No. OHD 7630025). Washington, DC: U.S. Government Printing Office.

Brooks-Gunn, J., & Lewis, M. (1981). Assessing young handicapped children: Issues and solutions. *Journal of the Division for Early Childhood, 2,* 84-95.

Brooks-Gunn, J., & Lewis, M. (1983). Screening and diagnosing handicapped infants. *Topics in Early Childhood Special Education, 3*(1), 14-28.

Brophy, J. E. (1977). Mothers as teachers of their own preschool children: The influence of socioeconomic status and task structure on teaching specificity. *Developmental Psychology, 13,* 242-248.

Broussard, E. G., & Hartner, M. S. (1971). Further considerations regarding maternal perceptions of the first born. In J. Hellmuth (Ed.), *Exceptional infant* (Vol. 2). New York: Brunner/Mazel.

Brown, S. L., & Moersch, M. S. (Eds.). (1978). *Parents on the team.* Ann Arbor: University of Michigan Press.

Bruininks, R., Woodcock, R., Weatherman, R., & Hill, B. (1984). *Scales of independent behavior (SIB).* Allen, TX: DLM Teaching Resources.

Buch, L., Collins, S., & Gelber, S. (1978). Language. In F. P. Conner, G. G. Williamson, & J. M. Siepp (Eds.), *Program guide for infants and toddlers with neuromotor and other developmental disabilities.* New York: Teachers College Press.

Buchanan, A., & Oliver, J. E. (1981). Abuse and neglect as a cause of mental retardation: A study of 140 children. *British Journal of Psychiatry, 131,* 458.

Buium, N., Rynders, J., & Turnure, J. (1974). Early maternal linguistic environment of normal and non-normal language learning children. *American Journal of Mental Deficiency, 79,* 52-58.

Burke, P. J. (1976). Personnel preparation: Historical perspective. *Exceptional Children, 43,* 144-147.

Butterfield, E. C., Wambold, C., & Belmont, J. M. (1973). On theory and practice of improving short-term memory. *American Journal of Mental Deficiency, 77,* 654-659.

Byrne, M. C., & Shervanian, C. C. (1977). *Introduction to communicative disorders.* New York: Harper & Row.

Bzock, K., & League, R. (1971). *Receptive-expressive emergent language scale (REEL).* Baltimore: University Park Press.

Caldwell, B. M. (1962). The usefulness of the critical period hypothesis in the study of filiative behavior. *Merrill-Palmer Quarterly, 8,* 229-237.

Caldwell, B. M. (1973). The importance of beginning early. In J. Jordan & R. F. Dailey (Eds.), *Not all little wagons are red.* Reston, VA: Council for Exceptional Children.

Caldwell, B. M. (1977). Evaluating program effectiveness. In B. M. Caldwell & D. J. Stedman (Eds.), *Infant education: A guide for helping handicapped children in the first three years.* New York: Walker.

Caldwell, B., & Bradley, R. (1978). *Home observation for measurement of the environment.* Little Rock: University of Arkansas, Center for Child Development & Education.

Calhoun, M. L., & Hawisher, M. (1979). *Teaching and learning strategies for physically handicapped students.* Baltimore: University Park Press.

Campbell, P. B. (1976). Adolescent intellectual decline. *Adolescence, 11*(44), 629-635.

Cansler, D. P., & Martin, G. H. (1974). *Working with families: A manual for developmental centers.* Reston, VA: Council for Exceptional Children.

Caplan, G. (1964). *Principles of preventive psychiatry.* New York: Basic Books.

Capute, A. J. (1975). Cerebral palsy and associated dysfunctions. In R. Haslam & P. J. Valletutti (Eds.), *Medical problems in the classroom.* Baltimore: University Park Press.

Capute, A. J., Accardo, P. J., Vining, E. P. G., Rubenstein, J. E., & Harryman, S. (1978). *Primitive reflex profile.* Baltimore: University Park Press.

Carey, W. B., & McDevitt, S. C. (1978). Ability and change in individual temperament diagnoses from infancy to early childhood. *Journal of Child Psychiatry, 17,* 331-337.

Carhart, R. (1970). Development and conservation of speech. In H. Davis & S. R. Silverman (Eds.), *Hearing and deafness.* New York: Holt, Rinehart & Winston.

Carney, I. H. (1983). Services for families of severely handicapped preschool students: Assumptions and implications. *Journal of the Division for Early Childhood, 7,* 78-85.

Carpenter, G. S. (1974). Visual regard of moving and stationary faces in early infancy. *Merrill-Palmer Quarterly, 20,* 181.

Carr, J. (1975). *Young children with Down's syndrome.* London: Butterworth.

Carr, S., Dabbs, J., & Carr, T. (1975). Mother-infant attachment: The importance of the mother's visual field. *Child Development, 46,* 331-338

Carta, J. J., & Greenwood, C. R. (1985). Eco-behavioral assessment: A method for expanding the evaluation of early intervention programs. *Topics in Early Childhood Special Education, 5*(2), 88-104.

Carter, C. H. (1978). *Medical aspects of mental retardation.* Springfield, IL: Charles C Thomas.

Cartwright, C. A. (1981). Effective programs for parents of young handicapped children. *Topics in Early Childhood Special Education, 3,* 1-9.

Casarett, L. J., & Doull, J. (Eds.). (1975). *Toxicology, the basic science of poisons.* New York: Macmillan.

Casler, L. (1968). Perceptual deprivation in institutional settings. In G. Newton & S. Levine (Eds.), *Early experience and behavior.* Springfield, IL: Charles C Thomas.

Cassel, J. (1973, May). *Planning for public health: The case for prevention.* Paper presented at the Conference on Education of Nurses for Public Health.

Caster, L. (1965). The effects of extra tactile stimulation on a group of institutionalized infants. *Genetic Psychology Monographs, 71,* 137.

Caster, L. (1971). Maternal deprivation: A critical review of the literature. *Monographs of the Society for Research in Child Development, 26* (2, Serial No. 80).

Casto, G., & Mastropieri, M. A. (1985). The efficacy of early intervention programs for handicapped children: A meta-analysis. Logan: Utah State University, Early Intervention Research Institute.

Casto, G., & White K. R. (1984). The efficacy of early intervention programs with environmentally at-risk infants. *Journal of Children in Contemporary Society, 17,* 37-48.

Casto, G., White, K., & Taylor, C. (1983). An early intervention research institute: Studies of the efficacy and cost effectiveness of early intervention at Utah State. *Journal of the Division for Early Childhood, 7,* 5-17.

Cavallaro, S. A., & Porter, R. H. (1980). Peer preferences of at-risk and normally developing children in a preschool mainstream classroom. *American Journal of Mental Deficiency, 84,* 357-367.

Cegelka, W. J., & Tyler, J. L. (1970). The efficacy of special class placement for the mentally retarded in proper perspective. *Training School Bulletin, 65,* 33-68.

Chase, H. C. (1977). Time trends in low birth weight in the United States, 1950-1974. In D. M. Reed & F. J. Stanley (Eds.), *The epidemiology of prematurity.* Baltimore: Urban & Schwarzenberg.

Chase, H. C. (1973). The effects of intrauterine and postnatal undernutrition on normal brain development. *Annals of the New York Academy of Sciences, 205,* 231-244.

Chase, H. P., & Crnic, L. S. (1977). Undernutrition and human brain development. In P. Mittler (Ed.), *Research to practice in mental retardation: Biomedical aspects* (Vol. 3). Baltimore: University Park Press.

Chase, J. B. (1975, October). Developmental assessment of handicapped infants and young children with special attention to the visually impaired. *New Outlook for the Blind,* pp. 341-348.

Cherian, E. J., & Associates, Inc. (1973). *A guide to Follow-Through* (Report for Contract OEC-0-72-0772 for Bureau of Elementary and Secondary Education, USOE). Washington, DC: Visual Communications.

Chesley, R. E. (1979). The educational resources information center. *Exceptional Children, 46,* 194-199.

Chess, S., & Hassibi, M. (1978). *Principles and practice of child psychiatry.* New York: Plenum.

Chinn, P. C., Winn, J., & Walters, R. H. (1978). *Two-way talking with parents of special children: A process of positive communication.* St. Louis: C. V. Mosby.

Christiansen, R. O. (1975). Juvenile diabetes mellitus. In E.

E. Bleck & D. A. Nagel (Eds.), *Physically handicapped children: A medical atlas for teachers*. New York: Grune & Stratton.

Christoplos, F., & Valletutti, P. J. (1977). Education. In P. J. Valletutti & F. Christoplos (Eds.), *Interdisciplinary approaches to human services*. Baltimore: University Park Press.

Churchill, J. A., Berendes, H. W., & Nemore, J. (1969). Neuropsychological deficits in children of diabetic mothers. *American Journal of Obstetrics & Gynecology, 105,* 257-268.

Cicchetti, D., & Scoufe, L. A. (1976). The relationship between affective and cognitive development in Down's syndrome infants. *Child Development, 47,* 920-929.

Ciminero, A. R., & Drabman, R. S. (1977). Current developments in the behavioral assessment of children. In B. B. Lahey & A. E. Kazdin (Eds.), *Advances in clinical child psychology* (Vol. 1). New York: Plenum.

Clarizio, H. F., & McCoy, G. F. (1976). *Behavior disorders in children* (2nd ed.). New York: Thomas Y. Crowell.

Clarke, A. M., & Clarke, A. D. B. (1974). *Mental deficiency: The changing outlook* (3rd ed.). London: Methuen.

Clarke, A. M., & Clarke, A. D. B. (1977). *Early experience: Myth and evidence*. New York: Free Press.

Clarke, R. S., Heron, W., Fetherstonaugh, M. L., Forgays, D. G., & Hebb, D. O. (1951). Individual differences in dogs: Preliminary reports on the effects of early experience. *Canadian Journal of Psychology, 5,* 150-156.

Clarke-Stewart, A., Friedman, S., & Koch, J. (1985). *Child development: A topical approach*. New York: John Wiley & Sons.

Clements, S. D. (1966). *Minimal brain dysfunction in children: Terminology and identification* (NINDB Monograph, No. 3). Washington, DC: U. S. Dept. of Health, Education, and Welfare.

Clifton, R. K., Graham, F. K., & Hatton, H. M. (1968). Newborn heart rate response and response habituation as a function of stimulus duration. *Journal of Experimental Child Psychology, 6,* 265-278.

Clunies-Ross, G. G. (1979). Accelerating the development of Down's syndrome infants and young children. *Journal of Special Education, 13*(2), 169-177.

Cohen, L. B., & Salapatek, P. (1975). *Infant perception: From sensation to cognition*. New York: Academic Press.

Cohen, L. B., & Strauss, M. S. (1979). Concept acquisition in the human infant. *Child Development, 50,* 419-424.

Cohen, M. A., & Gross, P. J. (1979). *The development resource: Behavioral sequences for assessment and program planning* (Vols. 1-2). New York: Grune & Stratton.

Cohen, M. M. (1968). The effect of LSD-25 on the chromosomes of children exposed in utero. *Pediatric Research, 2,* 486-492.

Cohen, S. (1973). Minimal brain dysfunction and practical matters such as teaching kids to read. In F. F. de la Cruz, B. H. Fox, & R. H. Roberts (Eds.), *Minimal brain dysfunction*. New York: New York Academy of Sciences.

Cohen, S., Semmes, M., & Guralnick, M. (1979). Public Law 94-142 and the education of preschool handicapped children. *Exceptional Children, 45,* 279-285.

Colarusso, R. P., Martin, H., & Hartung, J. (1975). Specific visual perceptual skills as long-term predictors of academic success. *Journal of Learning Disabilities, 8,* 651-655.

Cole, P. (1982). *Language disorders in preschool children*. Englewood Cliffs, NJ: Prentice-Hall.

Collmann, R. D., & Newlyn, D. (1958). Changes in Terman-Merrill IQ's of mentally retarded children. *American Journal of Mental Deficiency, 63,* 307-311.

Colvin, R. W., & Zaffiron, E. M. (Eds.). (1974). *Preschool education—A handbook for the training of early childhood educators*. New York: Springer.

Conner, F. P., Williamson, G. G., & Siepp, J. M. (1978). *Program guide for infants and toddlers with neuromotor and other developmental disabilities*. New York: Teachers College Press.

Cook, R. E., & Armbruster, V. B. (1983). *Adapting early childhood curricula: Suggestions for meeting special needs*. St. Louis: C. V. Mosby.

Cooke, S. A., Cooke, T. P., & Apolloni, T. (1977). Developing nonretarded toddlers as verbal models for retarded classmates. *Child Study Journal, 8,* 1-8.

Cooke, T. P., Apolloni, T. & Cooke, S. A. (1977). Normal preschool children as behavior models for retarded peers. *Exceptional Children, 43,* 531-532.

Coordinating Office for Regional Resource Center. (1976). *Preschool test matrix: Individual test descriptions*. Lexington, KY: University of Kentucky.

Cornblath, M. (1967). Neonatal hypoglycemia: A summons to action. *Hospital Practice, 2*(5), 56-60.

Cornwell, A. C., & Birch, H. G. (1969). Psychological and social development in homereared children with Down's syndrome. *American Journal of Mental Deficiency, 74,* 341.

Costello, J. M. (1984). *Speech disorders in children: Recent advances*. San Diego: College-Hill Press.

Coulson, J. M. (1972). *Effects of different Head Start program approaches on children of different characteristics: Report on analyses of data from 1966-67 and 1967-68 national evaluations* (Technical Memorandum TM4862001/00). Santa Monica, CA: Systems Development Corp. (ERIC Document Reproduction Service No. ED 072 859)

Cowart, V. (1983, September 9). First trimester prenatal diagnostic method becoming available in the U.S. *Medical News*.

Cowart, V. (1984, July 6). NIH considers large-scale study to evaluate chorionic villi sampling. *Medical News*.

Coyner, A. B. (1983). Meeting health needs of handicapped infants. In R. S. Zelle & A. B. Coyner (Eds.), *Developmentally disabled infants and toddlers: Assessment and intervention*. Philadelphia: F. A. Davis.

Crain, L. S. (1984). Prenatal causes of atypical development. In M. J. Hanson (Ed.), *Atypical infant development*. Baltimore: University Park Press.

Cratty, B. J. (1970). *Perceptual and motor development in infants and children*. New York: Macmillan.

Crawford, D. (1978). Parent involvement in instructional planning. *Focus on Exceptional Children, 10,* 1-5.

Cress, P., Spellman, C. R., & Benson, H. (1984). Vision care for the preschool child with handicaps. *Topics in Early Childhood Special Education, 3*(4), 41-51.

Crnic, K., Greenberg, M., Ragozin, A., Robinson, N., & Basham, R. (1983). Effects of stress and social support on mothers of premature and full term infants. *Child Development, 54,* 209-217.

Crome, L, & Stern, J. (1972). *The pathology of mental retardation*. Baltimore: Williams & Wilkins.

Cross, A. (1977). Diagnosis. In L. Cross & K. Goin (Eds.), *Identifying handicapped children: A guide to casefinding, screening, diagnosis, assessment, and evaluation* (First Chance Series). New York: Walker.

Cross, L. (1977). Casefinding. In L. Cross & K. Goin (Eds.), *Identifying handicapped children: A guide to casefinding, screening, diagnosis, assessment, and evaluation* (First Chance Series). New York: Walker.

Cross, L., & Goin, K. (Eds.). (1977). *Identifying handicapped children: A guide to casefinding, screening, diagnosis, assessment, and evaluation* (First Chance Series). New York: Walker.

Cross, L., & Johnston, S. (1977). A bibliography of instruments. In L. Cross & K. Goin (Eds.), *Identifying handicapped children: A guide to casefinding, screening, diagnosis, assessment, and evaluation* (First Chance Series). New York: Walker.

Crothers, B., & Paine, R. S. (1959). *The natural history of cerebral palsy*. Cambridge, MA: Harvard University Press.

Culley, W. J. (1978). Nutrition and mental retardation. In C. H. Carter (Ed.), *Medical aspects of mental retardation* (2nd ed.). Springfield, IL: Charles C Thomas.

Cummings, S. (1976). The impact of the child's deficiency on the father: A study of fathers of mentally retarded and chronically ill children. *American Journal of Orthopsychiatry, 46,* 246-255.

Cummings, S., Bayley, H., & Rie, H. (1966). Effects of the child's deficiency on the mother: A study of mothers of mentally retarded, chronically ill, and neurotic children. *American Journal of Orthopsychiatry, 36,* 595-608.

Daker, M. (1983). Chorionic tissue biopsy in the first trimester of pregnancy. *British Journal of Obstetrics & Gynaecology, 90,* 193-195.

Darley, F. L., Aronson, A. E., & Brown, J. R. (1975). *Motor disorders of speech*. Philadelphia: W. B. Saunders.

Datta, L. (1979). Another spring and other hopes: Some findings from national evaluations of Project Head Start. In E. Zigler & J. Valentine (Eds.), *Project Head Start: A legacy of the war on poverty*. New York: Free Press.

Davies, P., & Stewart, A. L. (1975). Low birth-weight infants: Neurological sequelae and later intelligence. *British Medical Bulletin, 31,* 85-91.

Davis, L. (1978). Prespeech. In F. P. Conner, G. G. Williamson, & J. M. Siepp (Eds.), *Program guide for infants and toddlers with neuromotor and other developmental disabilities* (Ch. 6). New York: Teachers College Press.

Day, B. D. (1980). Contemporary early childhood programs and related controversial issues. In D. G. Range, J. R. Layton, & D. L. Roubinek (Eds.), *Aspects of early childhood education: Theory to research to practice*. New York: Academic Press.

Day, M. C. (1977). A comparative analysis of center-based preschool programs. In M. C. Day & R. K. Parker (Eds.), *The preschool in action: Exploring early childhood programs* (2nd ed.). Boston: Allyn & Bacon.

Day, M. C., & Parker, R. K. (1977). *The preschool in action: Exploring early childhood programs* (2nd ed.). Boston: Allyn & Bacon.

Dearman, N. B., & Plisko, V. W. (1980). *The condition of education: 1980 statistical report* (National Center for Education Statistics). Washington, DC: U.S. Government Printing Office.

Decarie, T. G. (1969). A study of the mental and emotional development of the thalidomide child. In B. M. Foss (Ed.), *Determinants of infant behavior* (Vol. 4). London: Methuen.

Decker, C. A., & Decker, J. R. (1976). *Planning and administering early childhood programs*. Columbus, OH: Charles E. Merrill.

DeMyer, M. K. (1975). Research in infantile autism: A strategy and its results. *Biological Psychiatry, 10,* 433-452.

DeMyer, W. (1975). Congenital anomalies of the central nervous system. In D. B. Tower (Ed.), *The nervous system: The clinical neurosciences*. New York: Raven.

Denenberg, V. H. (1964). Critical periods, stimulus input, and emotional reactivity. *Psychological Review, 71,* 335-351.

Denhoff, E. (1967). *Cerebral palsy: The preschool years*. Springfield, IL: Charles C Thomas.

Denhoff, E. (1976). Cerebral palsy: Medical aspects. In W. M. Cruickshank (Ed.), *Cerebral palsy: A developmental disability*. New York: Syracuse University Press.

Denhoff, E., & Robinault, I. P. (1960). *Cerebral palsy and related disorders*. New York: McGraw-Hill.

Dennis, W. (1960). Causes of retardation among institutional children: Iran. *Journal of Genetic Psychology, 96,* 47-59.

Desmonts, G., & Couvreur, J. (1974). Congenital toxoplasmosis. *New England Journal of Medicine, 290,* 1110-1116.

Detterman, D. K. (1979). Memory in the mentally retarded. In N. R. Ellis (Ed.), *Handbook of mental deficiency* (2nd ed.). Hillsdale, NJ: Lawrence Erlbaum.

Deutch, M. (1965). The role of social class in language development and cognition. *American Journal of Orthopsychiatry, 35,* 78-88.

Devenney, S. (1983). Curriculum and effective instruction: Challenges for early childhood special educators. *Topics in Early Childhood Special Education, 2*(4), 67-83.

DeWeerd, J. (1977). Introduction. In J. B. Jordan, A. H. Hayden, M. B. Karnes, & M. M. Wood (Eds.), *Early childhood education for exceptional children: A handbook of ideas and exemplary practices*. Reston, VA: Council for Exceptional Children.

DeWeerd, J. (1981). Early education services for children with handicaps—Where have we been, where are we now, and where are we going? *Journal of the Division for Early Childhood, 2,* 15-24.

DeWeerd, J., & Cole, A. (1976). Handicapped children's early education program. *Exceptional Children, 43,* 155-157.

Dicks-Mireaux, M. J. (1972). Mental development of infants with Down's syndrome. *American Journal of Mental Deficiency, 77* 26-32.

Dirks, J., & Gibson, E. (1977). Infants' perception of similarity between live people and their photographs. *Child Development, 48,* 124-130.

Dobson, J. C., Kushida, E., Williamson, M., & Friedman, E. G. (1976). Intellectual performance of 36 phenylketonuria patients and their nonaffected siblings. *Pediatrics, 58,* 53-58.

Doll, E. (1966). *Preschool attainment record (PAR)*. Circle Pines, MN: American Guidance Service.

Doll, E. (1972). A historical survey of research and management of mental retardation in the United States. In E. P. Trapp & P. Himelstein (Eds.), *Readings on the exceptional child* (2nd ed.). New York: Appleton-Century-Crofts.

Doll E. (1985). *Vineland social maturity scale*. Circle Pines, MN: American Guidance Service.

Downs, M. P. (1977). Guidelines for hearing screening of the infant, preschool, and school-aged child. In M. J. Krajicek & A. I. Tearney (Eds.), *Detection of developmental problems in children*. Baltimore: University Park Press.

Downs, M. P., & Silver, H. K. (1972). The A.B.C.D.'s to H.E.A.R.: Early identification in nursery, office, and clinic of the infant who is deaf. *Clinic Pediatrics, 11,* 563-566.

Drage, J. S., Berendes, H. W., & Fisher, P. D. (1969). The APGAR score and four year psychological examination performance. *In Perinatal factors affecting human development* (Scientific Publication No. 185, pp. 222-226). New York: Pan American Health Organization.

Drillien, C. M. (1964). *The growth and development of the prematurely born infant*. Baltimore: Williams & Wilkins.

DuBose, R. F. (1979). Working with sensorily impaired children. In S. G. Garwood (Ed.), *Educating young handicapped children* (Parts 1 and 2). Rockville, MD: Aspen Systems Corp.

DuBose, R. F. (1981). Assessment of severely impaired young children: Problems and recommendations. *Topics in Early Childhood Special Education, 1*(2), 9-22.

Dudgeon, J. A. (1976). Infective causes of human malformations. *British Medical Journal, 32,* 77-84.

Dunlap, W. R., & Hollinsworth, J. S. (1977). How does a handicapped child affect the family? Implications for practitioners. *Family Coordinator, 26,* 286-293.

Dunn, L. M. (1968). Special education for the mildly retarded—Is much of it justifiable? *Exceptional Children, 35,* 5-24.

Dunn, L. M. (1973). *Exceptional children in the schools* (2nd ed.). New York: Holt, Rinehart & Winston.

Dunn, L. M. (1981). *Peabody picture vocabulary test—Revised edition*. Circle Pines, MN: American Guidance Service.

Dunst, C. J. (1981). *Infant learning: A cognitive-linguistic intervention strategy*. Hingham, MA: Teaching Resources.

Dunst, C. J. (1986). Overview of the efficacy of early intervention programs: Methodological and conceptual considerations. In L. Bickman & D. Weatherford (Eds.), *Evaluating early intervention programs for severely handicapped children and their families*. Baltimore: University Park Press.

Dunst, C. J., & Rheingrover, R. (1981a). An analysis of the efficacy of infant intervention programs with organically handicapped children. *Evaluation & Program Planning, 4,* 287-323.

Dunst, C. J., & Rheingrover, R. M. (1981b). Discontinuity and instability in early development: Implications for assessment. *Topics in Early Childhood Special Education, 1*(2), 49-60.

Dunteman, G. (1972, July). *A report on two national samples of Head Start classes: Some aspects of child development of participants in full year 1967-1968 and 1968-1969 programs* (Contract HEW 0570207). Research Triangle Park, NC: Research Triangle Institute.

Durham, G. H. (1979). What if you are the doctor? In T. Dougan, L. Isbell, & P. Vyas (Eds.), *We have been there*. Salt Lake City, UT: Dougan, Isbell & Vyas Associates.

Dweck, H. S., Saxon, S. A., Benton, J. W., & Cassady, G. (1973). Early development of the tiny premature infant. *American Journal of Diseases of Childhood, 126,* 28-34.

Eaves, L. C., Kendall, D. C., & Crichton, J. U. (1972). The early detection of minimal brain dysfunction. *Journal of Learning Disabilities, 5,* 454-462.

Egbert, R. L. (1973). *Planned variation in Follow-Through*. Unpublished manuscript. (Available from the author, University of Nebraska, Lincoln)

Egbert, R. L., & Brisch, M.E.G. (1979). The advantages of educational models. In *The High/Scope report*. Ypsilanti, MI: High Scope Press.

Egeland, B., & Sroufe, L. A. (1981). Attachment and early maltreatment. *Child Development, 52,* 44-52.

Eisenberg, R. B. (1965). Auditory behavior in the human neonate. *Journal of Auditory Research, 5,* 159-171.

Elardo, R., Bradley, R., & Caldwell, B. M. (1975). The relation of infants' home environment to mental test performance from six to thirty-six months: A longitudinal analysis. *Child Development, 46,* 71-76.

Elardo, R., Bradley, R., & Caldwell, B. M. (1977). A longitudinal study of the relation of infants' home environment to language development at age three. *Child Development, 48,* 595-603.

Ellis, N. E. (1977). Program alternatives. In N. E. Ellis & L. Cross (Eds.), *Planning programs for early education of the handicapped* (First Chance Series). New York: Walker.

Ellis, N. E., & Cross, L. (Eds.). (1977). *Planning programs for early education of the handicapped* (First Chance Series). New York: Walker.

Ellis, N. R. (Ed.). (1966-1974). *International review of research in mental retardation* (Vols. 1-7). New York: Academic Press.

Ellis, N. R. (1970). *Memory processes in retardates and normals*. In N. R. Ellis (Ed.), *International review of research in mental retardation* (Vol. 4). New York: Academic Press.

Elmer, E. (1977). A follow-up study of traumatized children. *Pediatrics, 59,* 273-279.

Elmer, E., & Gregg, C. D. (1967). Developmental characteristics of the abused child. *Pediatrics, 40,* 596-602.

Embry, L. H. (1980). Family support for handicapped preschool children at risk for abuse. *New Directions for Exceptional Children, 4,* 29-57.

Emmerich, W. (1971). *The structure and development of personal-social behaviors in preschool settings*. Princeton, NJ: Educational Testing Service. (ERIC Reproduction Service No. ED 063 971)

Emrick, J. A., Sorensen, P. H., & Stearns, M. S. (1973). *Interim evaluation of the national Follow-Through program, 1969-1971*. Menlo Park, CA: Stanford Research Institute.

Engen, T., Lipsitt, L. P., & Peck, M. B. (1974). Ability of newborn infants to discriminate sapid substances. *Developmental Psychology, 10,* 741-744.

Epstein, C. J., & Golbus, M. S. (1977). Prenatal diagnosis of genetic diseases. *American Scientist, 65,* 703-711.

Erickson, E. H. (1963). *Childhood and society* (2nd ed.). New York: W. W. Norton.

Erickson, M. L. (1976). *Assessment and management of developmental changes in children*. St. Louis: C. V. Mosby.

Erickson, M. T. (1968). The predictive validity of the Cattell Infant Intelligence Scale for young mentally retarded children. *American Journal of Mental Deficiency, 72,* 728-731.

Erickson, M. T. (1978). *Child psychopathology: Assessment, etiology, and treatment.* Englewood Cliffs, NJ: Prentice-Hall.

Evans, E. D. (1975). *Contemporary influence on early childhood education* (2nd ed.). New York: Holt, Rinehart & Winston.

Evans, I. M., & Nelson, R. O. (1977). Assessment of child behavior problems. In A. R. Ciminero, K. S. Calhoun, & H. E. Adams (Eds.), *Handbook of behavioral assessment.* New York: John Wiley & Sons.

Fagan, J. F. (1976). Infants' recognition of invariant features of faces. *Child Development, 47,* 627-638.

Falkner, F., & Tanner, J. M. (1978a). *Human growth: Principles and prenatal growth* (Vol. 1). New York: Plenum.

Falkner, F., & Tanner, J. M. (1978b). *Human growth: Prenatal growth* (Vol. 2). New York: Plenum.

Falkner, F., & Tanner, J. M. (1978c). *Human growth: Neurobiology and nutrition* (Vol. 3). New York: Plenum.

Fallen, N. H., & McGovern, J. E. (1978). *Young children with special needs.* Columbus, OH: Charles E. Merrill.

Fallen, N. H., & Umansky, W. (1985). *Young children with special needs* (2nd ed.). Columbus, OH: Charles E. Merrill.

Farber, B. (1959) Effects of a severely mentally retarded child on family integration. *Monographs of the Society for Research in Child Development, 24*(2).

Farber, B. (1968). *Mental retardation: Its social content and social consequences.* Boston: Houghton Mifflin.

Fechter, L. D., & Annaw, Z. (1977). Toxicity of mild prenatal carbon monoxide exposure. *Science, 197,* 680-682.

Federal Register (1977, August 23). *42*(163).

Federal Register (1977, Dec.), Part 3.

Feldman, F., & Scherz, F. (1967). *Family social welfare.* New York: Atherton.

Ferrier, P. E., Nicod, I., & Ferrier, S. (1973). Fetal alcohol syndrome. *Lancet, 2,* 1496.

Feshbach, S. (1970). Aggression. In P. H. Mussen (Ed.), *Carmichael's manual of child psychology* (Vol. 2). New York: John Wiley & Sons.

Fewell, R. R. (1983a). Assessing handicapped infants. In S. G. Garwood & R. R. Fewell (Eds.), *Educating handicapped infants: Issues in development and intervention.* Rockville, MD: Aspen Systems Corp.

Fewell, R. R. (1983b). The team approach to infant education. In S. G. Garwood & R. R. Fewell (Eds.), *Educating handicapped infants: Issues in development and intervention.* Rockville, MD: Aspen Systems Corp.

Fewell, R. R., & Sandall, S. R. (1983). Curricula adaptations for young children: Visually impaired, hearing impaired, and physically impaired. *Topics in Early Childhood Special Education, 2*(4), 51-66.

Findlay, D. C., & McGuire, C. (1957). Social status and abstract behavior. *Journal of Abnormal & Social Psychology, 54,* 135-137.

Finnie, N. R. (1975). *Handling the young cerebral palsied child at home* (2nd ed.). New York: E. P. Dutton.

Fiorentino, M. R. (1973). *Reflex testing methods for evaluating C.N.S. development.* Springfield, IL: Charles C Thomas.

Fiorentino, M.R. (1981). *A basis for sensorimotor development: Normal and abnormal.* Springfield, IL: Charles C Thomas.

Fisher, M. A., & Zeamon, D. (1973). An attention-retention theory of retardate discrimination learning. In H. R. Ellis

(Ed.), *The international review of research in mental retardation* (Vol. 6). New York: Academic Press.

Fishler, K., Graliker, B. V., & Koch, R. (1964). The predictability of intelligence with Gesell Developmental Scales in mentally retarded infants and young children. *American Journal of Mental Deficiency, 69,* 515-525.

Fitzgerald, I. M. (1983, May/June). The cost of community residential care for mentally retarded persons. *Programs for the Handicapped: Clearinghouse on the Handicapped Highlights, 3,* 10-14.

Flapan, D., & Neubauer, P. B. (1970). Issues in assessing development. *Journal of the American Academy of Child Psychiatry, 9,* 669-687.

Flavell, J. H. (1963). *The developmental psychology of Jean Piaget.* Princeton, NJ: Van Nostrand.

Fomon, S. J., & Anderson, T. A. (Eds.). (1972). *Practices of low income families in feeding infants and small children.* (DHEW Publication No. HSM 72-5605). Rockville, MD: Maternal & Child Health Service.

Ford, F. (1975). Normal motor development in infancy. In E. E. Bleck & D. A. Nagel (Eds.), *Physically handicapped children: A medical atlas for teachers.* New York: Grune & Stratton.

Foster, M., Berger, M., & McLean, M. (1981). Rethinking a good idea: A reassessment of parent involvement. *Topics in Early Childhood Special Education, 1*(3), 55-65.

Foster, R., Giddan, J., & Stark, J. (1973). *Assessment of children's language comprehension (ACLC).* Palo Alto, CA: Consulting Psychologists Press.

Fowler, W. (1975). A developmental learning approach to infant care in a group setting. In B. Z. Friedlander, G. M. Sterritt, & G. E. Kirk (Eds.), *Exceptional infant-assessment and intervention* (Vol. 3)(pp. 341-373). New York: Brunner/Mazel.

Fraiberg, S. (1974). Blind infants and their mothers: An examination of the sign system. In M. Lewis & L. A. Rosenblum, (Eds.), *The effect of the infant on its caregiver.* New York: John Wiley & Sons.

Fraiberg, S. (1977). *Insignts from the blind.* New York: Basic Books.

Fraiberg, S., Smith, M., & Adelson, M. A. (1969). An educational program for blind infants. *Journal of Special Education, 3,* 121-139.

Frankenburg, W., Dodds, J., & Fandal, A. (1973). *Denver developmental screening test manual/workbook for nursing and paramedical personnel.* Denver: Ladoca Publishing Foundation.

Frankenburg, W., Dodds, J., & Fandal, A. (1975). *Denver developmental screening test.* Denver: Ladoca Publishing Foundation.

Fredericks, B. (1985). Parents/families of persons with severe mental retardation. In D. Bricker & J. Filler (Eds.), *Severe mental retardation: From theory to practice.* Reston, VA: Council for Exceptional Children.

Fredericks, H. D., Baldwin, V., Grove, D., Moore, W., Riggs, C., & Lyons, B. (1978). Integrating the moderately and severely handicapped preschool child into a normal day care setting. In M. J. Guralnick (Ed.), *Early intervention and the integration of handicapped and nonhandicapped children.* Baltimore: University Park Press.

Freedman, D. G., & Boverman, H. (1966). The effects of

kinesthetic stimulation on certain aspects of development in premature infants. *American Journal of Orthopsychiatry, 36,* 223-224.

Freeman, H. E., Klein, R. E., Townsend, J. W., & Lechtig, A. (1980). Nutrition and cognitive development among rural Guatemalan children. *American Journal of Public Health, 70,* 1277-1285.

Freud, S. (1933). *New introductory lectures on psychoanalysis* (W. J. H. Sprott, Trans.). New York: W. W. Norton.

Friedman, R. M., Sandler, J., Hernandez, M., & Wolfe, D. A. (1981). Child abuse. In E. J. Mash & L. G. Terdal (Eds.), *Behavioral assessment of childhood disorders.* New York: Guilford.

Friedrich, M. P. H., & Boriskin, B. A. (1976). The role of the child in abuse: A review of the literature. *American Journal of Orthopsychiatry, 46,* 580-590.

Frodi, A. (1981). Contributions of infant characteristics to child abuse. *American Journal of Mental Deficiency, 85,* 341-349.

Frost, J. L., & Kissinger, J. B. (1976). *The young child and the educative process.* New York: Holt, Rinehart & Winston.

Fuller, J. L., & Clark, L. D. (1966). Effects of rearing with specific stimuli upon post isolation behavior in dogs. *Journal of Comparative Physiology & Psychology, 61,* 258-263.

Fuller, R., & Schuman, J. (1971). Treated phenylketonuria: Intelligence and blood phenylalanine levels. *American Journal of Mental Deficiency, 75,* 539-545.

Furey, E. M. (1982). The effects of alcohol on the fetus. *Exceptional Children, 49,* 30-34.

Furth, H. G. (1971). Linguistic deficiency and thinking: Research with deaf subjects, 1964-1969. *Psychological Bulletin, 96,* 58-72.

Furth, H. G. (1973). Further thoughts on thinking and language. *Psychological Bulletin, 79,* 215-216.

Furuno, S., O'Reilly, K., Hosaka, C., Inatsuka, T., Aleman, T., & Zeisloft, B. (1979). *Hawaii early learning profile (HELP).* Palo Alto, CA: VORT Corp.

Gabel, H., McDowell, J., & Cerreto, M.C. (1983). Family adaptation to the handicapped infant. In S. G. Garwood & R. R. Fewell (Eds.), *Educating handicapped infants: Issues in development and intervention.* Rockville, MD: Aspen Systems Corp.

Gabel, S., & Erickson, M. T. (Eds.). (1980). *Child development and developmental disabilities.* Boston: Little, Brown.

Gallagher, J. R., Beckman-Bell, P., & Cross, A. H. (1983). Families of handicapped children: Sources of stress and its amelioration. *Exceptional Children, 50,* 10-19.

Galler, J. R., Ramsey, F., Solimano, G., Lowell, W. E., & Mason, E. (1983a). The influence of early malnutrition on subsequent behavioral development. I: Degree of impairment in intellectual performance. *Journal of the American Academy of Child Psychiatry, 22*(1), 8.

Galler, J. R., Ramsey, F., Solimano, G., Lowell, W. E., & Mason, E. (1983b). The influence of early malnutrition on subsequent behavioral development. II: Classroom behavior. *Journal of the American Academy of Child Psychiatry, 22*(1), 16.

Garber, H., & Heber, R. F. (1977). The Milwaukee project: Indications of the effectiveness of early intervention in preventing mental retardation. In P. Mittler (Ed.), *Research to practice in mental retardation: Care and intervention* (Vol. 1). Baltimore: University Park Press.

Gardner, L. J. (1972, July). Deprivation dwarfism. *Scientific American, 7,* pp. 101-107.

Garland, C., Stone, N. W., Swanson, J., & Woodruff, G. (Eds.). (1981). *Early intervention for children with special needs and their families: Findings and recommendations* (Prepared by INTERACT: The National Committee for Services to Very Young Children with Special Needs and Their Families). Seattle: University of Washington, Western States Technical Assistance Resource (WESTAR).

Garwood, S. G. (1982). (Mis)use of developmental scales in program evaluation. *Topics in Early Childhood Special Education, 1*(4), 61-70.

Garwood, S. G. (1983). *Educating young handicapped children: A developmental approach* (2nd ed.). Rockville, MD: Aspen Systems Corp.

Garwood, S. G., & Fewell, R. R. (1983). *Educating handicapped infants: Issues in development and intervention.* Rockville, MD: Aspen Systems Corp.

Gasser, R. (1975). *Atlas of human embryos.* Hagerstown, MD: Harper & Row.

Gath, A. (1978). *Down's syndrome and the family.* London: Academic Press.

Gaylord-Ross, R. J., & Holvoet, J. F. (1985). *Strategies for educating students with severe handicaps.* Boston: Little, Brown.

Gesell, A. (1925). *The mental growth of the preschool child.* New York: Macmillan.

Gesell, A., & Amatruda, C. S. (1947). *Developmental diagnosis.* New York: Paul B. Holder.

Gesell, A., Ilg, F. L., & Bullis, G. E. (1949). *Vision: Its development in infant and child.* New York: Hoeber.

Gibson, E. J. (1969). *Principles of perceptual learning and development.* New York: Appleton-Century-Crofts.

Ginsburg, B. E., & Laughlin, W. (1971). Race and intelligence: What do we really know? In R. Cancro (Ed.), *Intelligence: Genetic and environmental influences* (pp. 77-87). New York: Grune & Stratton.

Ginsburg, H., & Oper, S. (1969). *Piaget's theory of intellectual development: An introduction.* Englewood Cliffs, NJ: Prentice-Hall.

Glick, P., & Norton, A. (1979). The future of the American family in current population reports (Special Studies Series P-23, No. 78). Washington, DC: U.S. Government Printing Office.

Goldberg, S. (1977). Social competence in infancy: A model of parent-infant interaction. *Merrill Palmer Quarterly, 23,* 163-177.

Goldfarb, W. (1945). Psychological deprivation in infancy and subsequent adjustment. *American Journal of Orthopsychiatry, 15,* 247-255.

Goldfarb, W. (1949). Rorschach test differences between family-reared, institution-reared, and schizophrenic children. *American Journal of Orthopsychiatry, 19,* 624-633.

Goldfarb, W. (1955). Emotional and intellectual consequences of psychologic deprivation in infancy: A re-evaluation. In P. H. Hoch & J. Zubin (Eds.), *Psychopathology of childhood.* New York: Grune & Stratton.

Goldfarb, W., Braunstein, P., & Lorgo, J. (1956). A study of speech patterns in a group of schizophrenic children. *American Journal of Orthopsychiatry, 26,* 544-555.

Goldhaber, D. (1979). Does the changing view of early experience imply a changing view of early development? In L. G. Katz (Ed.), *Current topics in early childhood education* (Vol. 2). Norwood, NJ: Ablex.

Goldman, R., Fristoe, M., & Woodcock, R. (1974). *Goldman-Fristoe-Woodcock test of auditory discrimination.* Circle Pines, MN: American Guidance Service.

Goldson, E. (1978). Child abuse: Its relationship to birthweight, Apgar score, and developmental testing. *American Journal of Diseases of Children, 132*(8), 790-793.

Goldstein, H. (1967). The efficacy of special classes and regular classes in the education of educable mentally retarded children. In J. Zubin & G. A. Jervis (Eds.), *Psychopathology of mental development.* New York: Grune & Stratton.

Goldstein, H., Arkell, C., Ashcroft, S. C., Hurley, O. L., & Lilly, M. S. (1975). Schools. In N. Hobbs (Ed.), *Issues in the classification of children* (Vol. 2.). San Francisco: Jossey-Bass.

Goldstein, L., & Murphy, D. P. (1929). Microcephalic idiocy following radium therapy for uterine cancer during pregnancy, *American Journal of Obstetrical Gynecology, 18,* 189.

Goodman, J. F., & Cameron, J. (1978). The meaning of IQ constancy in young retarded children. *Journal of Genetic Psychology, 132,* 109-119.

Goodman, L. V. (1976). A bill of rights for the handicapped. *American Education, 12*(6), 6-8.

Goodson, B. D., & Hess, R. D. (1975). *Parents as teachers of young children: An evaluative review of some contemporary concepts and programs.* Washington, DC: DHEW/OE, Bureau of Educational Personnel Development. (ERIC Document Reproduction Service No. ED 136 967)

Goodwin, W. L., & Driscoll, L. A. (1982). *Handbook for measurement and evaluation in early childhood education.* San Francisco: Jossey-Bass.

Gordon, J. J., & Breivogel, W. G. (Eds.). (1976). *Building effective home/school relationships.* Boston: Allyn & Bacon.

Gotoff, S. P., & Gotoff, M. L. (1978). Infectious diseases. In C. H. Carter (Ed.), *Medical aspects of mental retardation* (2nd ed.). Springfield, IL: Charles C Thomas.

Gottesman, J. J. (1968). Biogenetics of race and class. In M. Deutsch, J. Katz, & A. R. Jensen (Eds.), *Social class, race, and psychological development.* New York: Holt, Rinehart & Winston.

Gottesman, M. (1973). Conservation development in blind children. *Child Development, 44,* 824-827.

Gottesman, M. (1976). Stage development of blind children: A Piagetian view. *New Outlook for the Blind, 70,* 94-100.

Gottman, J., Gonso, J., & Schuler, P. (1976). Teaching social skills to isolated children. *Journal of Abnormal Child Psychology, 4,* 179-197.

Gotts, E. E. (1979). Early childhood assessment. In D. A. Sabatino & T. L. Miller (Eds.), *Describing learner characteristics of handicapped children and youth.* New York: Grune & Stratton.

Gradel, K., Thompson, M. S., & Sheehan, R. (1981). Parental and professional agreement in early childhood assessment. *Topics in Early Childhood Special Education, 1*(2), 31-39.

Graham, J. T., & Graham, L. W. (1971). Language behavior of the mentally retarded: Syntactic characteristics. *American Journal of Mental Deficiency, 74,* 623-629.

Green, J. A., Gustafson, G. E., & West, M. J. (1980). Effects of infant development on mother-infant interaction. *Child Development, 51,* 199-207.

Green, M. J. (1977). *A sign of relief: The first-aid handbook for childhood emergencies.* New York: Bantam Books.

Green, W. W. (1981). Hearing disorders. In A. E. Blackhurst & W. H. Berdine (Eds.), *An introduction to special education.* Boston: Little, Brown.

Greenberg, M. T., & Calderon, R. (1984). Early intervention: Outcomes and issues. *Topics in Early Childhood Special Education, 3*(4), 1-9.

Greenburg, P. (1969). *The devil wears slippery shoes: A biased bibliography of the child development group of Mississippi.* New York: Macmillan.

Gronlund, N. E. (1985). *Measurement and evaluation in teaching.* New York: Macmillan.

Grossman, H. J. (Ed.). (1983). *Classification in mental retardation* (rev. ed.). Washington, DC: American Association on Mental Deficiency.

Grotberg, E. (1969). Review of research: 1965-1969. Washington, DC: U.S. Office of Economic Opportunity, Project Head Start.

Gruenwald, P. (1975). *The placenta.* Baltimore: University Park Press.

Guralnick, M. J. (1976). The value of integrating handicapped and non-handicapped preschool children. *American Journal of Orthopsychiatry, 42,* 236-245.

Guralnick, M. J. (1978). *Early intervention and the integration of handicapped and nonhandicapped children.* Baltimore: University Park Press.

Guralnick, M. J. (1980). Social interactions among preschool children. *Exceptional Children, 46,* 248-253.

Guskin, S. L., & Spiker, H. H. (1968). Educational research in mental retardation. In N. R. Ellis (Ed.), *International review of research in mental retardation* (Vol. 3). New York: Academic Press.

Guthrie, J. T., & Goldberg, H. K. (1972). Visual sequential memory in reading disability. *Journal of Learning Disabilities, 5,* 41-46.

Hagberg, B. (1975). Pre-, peri- and postnatal prevention of major neuropediatric handicaps. *Neuropaediatric, 6,* 331-338.

Hallahan, D. P., & Kauffman, J. M. (1976). *Introduction to learning disabilities: A psycho-behavioral approach.* Englewood Cliffs, NJ: Prentice-Hall.

Halliday, C. (1970). *The visually impaired child—infancy to school age.* Louisville, KY: American Printing House for the Blind.

Halpern, R. (1984). Lack of effects for home-based early intervention—Some possible explanations. *American Journal of Orthopsychiatry, 54*(1), 33-42.

Hamilton, J. L., & Swan, W. W. (1981). Measurement references in the assessment of preschool handicapped children. *topics in Early Childhood Special Education, 1*(2), 4-48.

Hamilton, W. J., & Mossman, H. W. (1972). *Human embryology—Prenatal development in form and function* (4th ed.). Baltimore: Williams & Wilkins.

Haney, W. (1977). *The Follow-Through planned variation experiment: Vol. 5. The Follow-Through evaluation: A technical history* (Prepared for USOE, Office of Planning, Budgeting, and Evaluation, Contract No. OEC-0-74-0394). Cambridge, MA: Huron Institute.

Hansen, H. (1978). Decline of Down's syndrome after abortion reform in New York state. *American Journal of Mental Deficiency, 83,* 185-188.

Hanson, J. W., Jones, K. L., & Smith, D. W. (1976). Fetal alcohol syndrome: Experience with 41 patients. *Journal of the American Medical Association, 235*(14), 1458-1460.

Hanson, M. J. (1977). *Teaching your Down's syndrome infant: A guide for parents.* Baltimore: University Park Press.

Hanson, M. J. (1984a). Early intervention: Models and practices. In M. J. Hanson (Ed.), *Atypical infant development.* Baltimore: University Park Press.

Hanson, M. J. (1984b). Parent-infant interaction. In M. J. Hanson (Ed.), *Atypical infant development.* Baltimore: University Park Press.

Hanson, M. J. (1985a). Administration of private versus public early childhood special education programs. *Topics in Early Childhood Special Education, 5*(1), 25-38.

Hanson, M. J. (1985b). An analysis of the effects of early intervention services for infants and toddlers with moderate and severe handicaps. *Topics in Early Childhood Special Education, 5*(2), 36-51.

Hanson, M. J., & Hanline, M. F. (1984). Behavioral competencies and outcomes: The effects of disorders. In M. J. Hanson (Ed.), *Atypical infant development.* Baltimore: University Park Press.

Harbin, G. (1977). Educational assessment. In L. Cross & K. Goin (Eds.), *Identifying handicapped children: A guide to casefinding, screening, diagnosis, assessment, and evaluation.* New York: Walker.

Hardy, J. B., Drage, J. S., & Jackson, E. C. (1979). *The first year of life: The collaborative perinatal project of the National Institute of Neurological and Communicative Disorders and Stroke.* Baltimore: Johns Hopkins University Press.

Hardy, J. B., McCracken, G. H., Sr., Gilkeson, M. R., & Sever, J. L. (1969). Adverse fetal outcome following rubella after the first trimester of pregnancy. *Journal of the American Medical Association, 207,* 2414-2420.

Hardy, W. G. (1965). On language disorders in young children: A reorganization of thinking. *Journal of Speech & Hearing Disorders, 30,* 3-16.

Hare, B. A. & Hare, J. M. (1977). *Teaching young handicapped children: A guide for preschool and the primary grades.* New York: Grune & Stratton.

Harlow, H. F. (1958). The nature of love. *American Psychologist, 13,* 673-685.

Harlow, H. F. (1961). The development of affectional patterns in infant monkeys. In B. M. Foss (Ed.), *Determinants of infant behavior.* New York: John Wiley & Sons.

Harlow, H. F. (1965). Total social isolation: Effects on Macaque monkey behavior. *Science, 148,* 666.

Harlow, H. F., Harlow, M. K., & Hansen, E. W. (1963). The maternal affectional system of Rhesus monkeys. In H. Rheingold (Ed.), *Maternal behavior in mammals.* New York: John Wiley & Sons.

Harlow, H. F., & Mears, C. (1979). *The human model: Primate perspectives.* New York: John Wiley & Sons.

Harrington, M. (1962). *The other America: Poverty in the United States.* New York: Macmillan

Harris, J. C. (1982). Nonorganic failure-to-thrive syndromes:

Reactive attachment disorder of infancy and psychosocial dwarfism of early childhood. In P. J. Accardo (Ed.), *Failure to thrive in infancy and early childhood: A multidisciplinary team approach.* Baltimore: University Park Press.

Harris, R. J. (1979). Research in impulsive control and diagnostic and training implications for deaf children. In L. S. Liben (Ed.), *Theoretical and practical implications of the development of deaf children.* New York: Academic Press.

Harris, S. R., & Tada, W. L. (1983). Providing developmental therapy services. In S. G. Garwood & R. R. Fewell (Eds.), *Educating handicapped infants: Issues in development and intervention.* Rockville, MD: Aspen Systems Corp.

Hart, B. (1978). Organizing program implementation. In K. E. Allen, V. A. Holm, & R. L. Schiefelbusch (Eds.), *Early intervention—A team approach.* Baltimore: University Park Press.

Hart, B., & Risley, T. R. (1978). Promoting productive language through incidental teaching. *Education & Urban Society, 10,* 407-429.

Harvey, B. (1975). Cystic fibrosis. In E. E. Bleck & D. A. Nagel (Eds.), *Physically handicapped children: A medical atlas for teachers.* New York: Grune & Stratton.

Harvey, J. (1977). The enabling legislation: How did it all begin? In J. B. Jordan, A. H. Hayden, M. B. Karnes, & M. M. Wood (Eds.), *Early childhood education for exceptional children: A handbook of ideas and exemplary practices.* Reston, VA: Council for Exceptional Children.

Haslam, R., & Valletutti, P. J. (1975). *Medical problems in the classroom: The teacher's role in diagnosis and management.* Baltimore: University Park Press.

Havighurst, R. J. (1953). *Human development and education.* New York: Longman, Green.

Hayden, A. H. (1976). A center-based parent training model. In D. L. Lillie, P. L. Trohanis, & K. W. Goin (Eds.), *Teaching parents to teach.* New York: Walker.

Hayden, A. H., & Dmitriev, V. (1975). The multidisciplinary preschool program for Down's syndrome children at the University of Washington Model Preschool Center. In B. Z. Friedlander, G. M. Sterritt, & G. E. Kirk (Eds.), *Exceptional infant—Assessment and intervention* (Vol. 3). New York: Brunner/Mazel.

Hayden, A. H., & Edgar, E. B. (1977). Identification, screening, and assessment. In J. B. Jordan, A. H. Hayden, M. B. Karnes, & M. M. Wood (Eds.), *Early childhood education for exceptional children.* Reston, VA: Council for Exceptional Children.

Hayden, A. H., & Haring, N. G. (1976). Early intervention for high risk infants and young children: Programs for Down's syndrome children. In T. D. Tjossem (Ed.), *Intervention strategies for high risk infants and young children.* Baltimore: University Park Press.

Hayden, A. H., & Haring, N. G. (1977). The acceleration and maintenance of developmental gains in Down's syndrome school-age children. In P. Mittler (Ed.), *Research to practice in mental retardation: Care and intervention* (Vol. 1). Baltimore: University Park Press.

Hayden, A. H., & McGinness, G. D. (1977). Bases for early intervention. In E. Sontag (Ed.), *Educational programming for the severely and profoundly handicapped.* Reston, VA: Council for Exceptional Children.

Hayden, A. H., Morris, K., & Bailey, D. (1977). *Final report:*

Effectiveness of early education for handicapped children. Washington, DC: Bureau of Education of the Handicapped.

Hayden, A. H., & Pious, C. G. (1979). The case for early intervention. In R. L. York & E. Edgar (Eds.), *Teaching the severely handicapped* (Vol. 4). Columbus, OH: American Association for the Education of the Severely/Profoundly Handicapped.

Hazen, N. L., & Durett, M. E. (1982). Relationship of security of attachment to exploration and cognitive mapping abilities in two-year-olds. *Developmental Psychology, 18,* 751-759.

HCEEP Overview and Directory. (1979, 1984). Chapel Hill, NC: Western States Technical Assistance Resource (WESTAR) and Technical Assistance Development System (TADS).

Heber R. F. (1978). Sociocultural mental retardation: A longitudinal study. In D. G. Forgays (Ed.), *Primary prevention of psychopathology.* Hanover, NH: University Press of New England.

Heber R. F., & Dever, R. B. (1970). Research on education and habilitation of the mentally retarded. In H. C. Haywood (Ed.), *Social-cultural aspects of mental retardation.* Englewood Cliffs, NJ: Prentice-Hall.

Heber R., Dever, R., & Conry, T. (1968). The influence of environmental and genetic variables on intellectual development. *Behavioral Research in Mental Retardation.* Eugene: University of Oregon.

Heber R., & Garber, H. (1973). *Progress report II: An experiment in the prevention of cultural-familial retardation.* Proceedings, Third Congress, International Association for the Scientific Study of Mental Deficiency, The Hague, Netherlands.

Heber, R., & Garber, H. (1975). The Milwaukee Project: A study of the use of family intervention to prevent cultural-familial mental retardation. In B. Z. Friedlander, G. M. Sterritt, & G. E. Kirk (Eds.), *Exceptional infant: Assessment and intervention.* New York: Brunner/Mazel.

Heber R. F., Garber, H., Harrington, S., Hoffman, C., & Galender, C. (1972). *Rehabilitation of families at risk for mental retardation—Progress report.* Madison: University of Wisconsin Press.

Heinicke, C., & Westheimer, J. (1966). *Brief separations.* New York: International Universities Press.

Heinonen, O. P., Slone, D., & Shapiro, S. (1977). *Birth and drugs in pregnancy* (Data and report of the Collaborative Perinatal Project of the National Institute of Neurological and Communicative Disorders and Stroke). Littleton, MA: Publishing Sciences Group.

Hellman, L. M., & Pritchard, J. A. (1971). *Williams obstetrics* (14th ed.). New York: Appleton-Century-Crofts.

Helsel, E. (1978). In A. P. Turnbull & H. R. Turnbull (Eds.), *Parents speak out.* Columbus, OH: Charles E. Merrill.

Hershenson, M. (1964). Visual discrimination in the human newborn. *Journal of Comparative & Physiological Psychology, 58,* 270-276.

Hess, R. D. (1970). Social class and ethnic influences on socialization. In P. H. Mussen (Ed.), *Carmichael's manual of child psychology* (Vol. 2). New York: John Wiley & Sons.

Hess, R. D., & Croft, D. J. (1975). *Teachers of young children* (2nd ed.). Boston: Houghton Mifflin.

Hess, R., & Shipman, V. (1965). Early experience and the socialization of cognitive modes in children. *Child Develop-*

ment, 34(4), 869-886.

Heward, W. L., Dardig, J. C., & Rossett, A. (1979). *Working with parents of handicapped children.* Columbus, OH: Charles E. Merrill.

Hewett, F. M., & Forness, S. R. (1977). *Education of exceptional learners* (2nd ed.). Boston: Allyn & Bacon.

Hildebrand, V. (1985). *Guiding young children* (3rd ed.). New York: Macmillan.

Hingtgen, J. N., & Bryson, C. Q. (1972). Recent developments in the study of early childhood psychoses: Infantile autism, childhood schizophrenia and related disorders. *Schizophrenia Bulletin, 5,* 8-54.

Hirsch, J. (1971). Behavior-genetic analysis and its biosocial consequences. In R. Cancro (Ed.), *Intelligence: Genetic and environmental influences.* New York: Grune & Stratton.

Hirshoren, A., & Umansky, W. (1977). Certification for teachers of preschool handicapped children. *Exceptional Children, 44,* 191-193.

Hiskey, M. (1966). *Nebraska test of learning aptitude.* Lincoln, NE: Union College Press.

Hobbs, N. (Ed.). (1975). *Issues in the classification of children* (Vol. 2). San Francisco: Jossey-Bass.

Hockleiter, M. (1977). Vergleichende untersuchung von kindern mit zerebraler bewegungsstorang mit und ohne neurophysiologischer fruhtherapie. *Oesterreichichische Arzteztg, 321,* 18.

Hodges, W., Branden, A., Feldman, R., Follins, J., Love, J., Sheehan, R., Lumbley, J., Osborn, J., Rentfrow, R. K., Houston, J., & Lee, C. (1980). *Follow-Through: Forces for change in the primary schools.* Ypsilanti, MI: High/Scope Press.

Holden, R. H. (1972). Prediction of mental retardation in infancy. *Mental Retardation, 10*(1), 28-30.

Holland, A. (1984). *Language disorders in children.* San Diego: College-Hill Press.

Holm, V. A., & McCartin, R. E. (1978). Interdisciplinary child development team: Team issues and training in interdisciplinariness. In K. E. Allen, V. A. Holm, & R. L. Schiefelbusch (Eds.), *Early intervention—a team approach.* Baltimore: University Park Press.

Holtzman, N. A., Welcher, D. W., & Mellits, E. D. (1975). Termination of restricted diet in children with phenylketonuria: A randomized controlled study. *New England Journal of Medicine, 293,* 1121-1124.

Honzik, M. P. (1976). Value and limitations of infant tests: An overview. In M. L. Lewis (Ed.), *Origins of intelligence: Infancy and early childhood.* New York: Plenum.

Honzik, M. P., MacFarlane, J. W., & Allen, L. (1948). The stability of mental test performance between two and eighteen years. *Journal of Experimental Education, 17,* 309-324.

Hood, C. (1971). Social and cultural factors in health of children of immigrants. *Archives of Disease in Childhood, 46,* 371-375.

Horner, R., Voeltz, L. M., & Fredericks, B. (Eds.). (1984). *Education of learners with severe handicaps: Exemplary service strategies.* Baltimore: Paul H. Brookes.

Horowitz, F. D. (1980). Intervention and its effects on early development: What model of development is appropriate? In R. R. Turner & H. W. Reese (Eds.), *Life-span developmental psychology: Intervention.* New York: Academic Press.

Horowitz, F. D. (1982). Methods of assessment for high-risk

and handicapped infants. In C. T. Ramey & P. L. Trohanis (Eds.), *Finding and educating high-risk and handicapped infants*. Baltimore: University Park Press.

Horowitz, F. D., & Paden, L. Y. (1973). The effectiveness of environmental intervention programs. In B. M. Caldwell & H. N. Ricciuti (Eds.), *Review of child development research: Child development and social policy* (Vol. 3). Chicago: University of Chicago Press.

Horton, K. B. (1976). Early intervention for hearing impaired infants and young children. In T. D. Tjossem (Ed.), *Intervention strategies for high risk infants and young children*. Baltimore: University Park Press.

Howard, J. (1978). The influence of children's developmental dysfunctions on marital quality and family interaction. In R. M. Lerner & G. B. Spanier (Eds.), *Child influences on marital and family interaction: A life span perspective*. New York: Academic Press.

Hunt, J. M. (1961). *Intelligence and experience*. New York: Ronald Press.

Hunt, J. M. (1964). The psychological basis for using preschool enrichment as an antidote for cultural deprivation. *Merrill-Palmer Quarterly, 10,* 209-248.

Hurley, R. (1969). *Poverty and mental retardation: A causal relationship*. New York: Random House.

Hutchinson, D. A. (1974). *A model for transdisciplinary staff development. A nationally organized collaborative project to provide comprehensive services to atypical infants and their families* (Technical Report #8). New York: United Cerebral Palsy Association.

Hymes, H. L. (1972). The Kaiser answer: Child services centers. In S. J. Braun & E. P. Edwards (Eds.), *History and theory of early childhood education*. Worthington, OH: Charles A. Jones.

Iano, R. P. (1972). Shall we disband special classes? *Journal of Special Education, 6,* 167-177.

Ingleman-Sundberg, A. (1966). *A child is born: The drama of life before death*. New York: Dell.

Ireton, H., & Thwing, E. (1979). *Minnesota child development inventory*. Minneapolis: Behavior Systems.

Itard, J. M. G. (1962). *The wild boy of Aveyron*. New York: Appleton-Century-Crofts.

Jackson, R. N. (1968). Urban distribution of educable mental handicap. *Journal of Mental Deficiency Research, 12,* 312-316.

Jacob, T. (1975). Family interaction in disturbed and normal families: A methodological and substantive review. *Psychological Bulletin, 82,* 33-65.

Jacobson, M. (1978). *Developmental neurobiology* (2nd ed.). New York: Plenum.

Jeans, R. C., Smith, M. B., & Stearns, G. (1955). Incidence of prematurity in relation to maternal nutrition. *Journal of American Dietetics Association, 31,* 576.

Jensema, C., & Trybus, R. J. (1975). *Reported emotional/behavioral problems among hearing impaired children in special education programs: United States, 1972-73* (Series R, No. 1). Washington, DC: Office of Demographic Studies. (Abstract)

Jensen, A. (1966). Cumulative deficit compensatory education. *Journal of School Psychology, 4,* 137-147.

Jensen, A. (1968). Social class, race, and genetics: Implications for education. *American Educational Research Journal, 5,* 1-42.

Jensen, A. (1969). How much can we boost IQ and scholastic achievement? *Harvard Educational Review, 39,* 1-198.

Joffe, L. S., & Vaughn, B. E. (1982). Infant-mother attachment: Theory, assessment, and implications for development. In B. B. Wolman (Ed.), *Handbook of developmental psychology*. Englewood Cliffs, NJ: Prentice-Hall.

Johnson, B., & Morse, H. A. (1968). Injured children and their parents. *Children, 15,* 147-152.

Johnson, L. B. (1965). The economic report of the president—January 20, 1964. In *Public papers of the presidents of the United States* (pp. 164-165). Washington, DC: U. S. Government Printing Office.

Johnson, L. B. (1967, January 10). State of the Union message to U.S. Congress, 90th Congress, 1st session. *Congressional Record, 113*(1), 37. Quoted in R. Elmore (1977), *Follow-Through: Decision-making in a large scale social experiment* (pp. 111-112). Unpublished doctoral dissertation, Harvard University, Cambridge, MA.

Johnson, L. B. (1968, September 30). *Remarks: Signing of the Handicapped Children's Early Education Act, Lyndon B. Johnson* (Statements 8/21/68-12/4/68). Austin: Lyndon Baines Johnson Library.

Johnson, V. M., & Werner, R. A. (1975). *A step-by-step learning guide for retarded infants and children*. New York: Syracuse University Press.

Johnson-Martin, N. (1985). Sources of difficulty. In J. Danaher (Ed.), *Assessment of child progress* (TADS Monograph No. 2). Chapel Hill, NC: Technical Assistance Development System.

Johnston, R. B. (1977). Pediatrics. In P. J. Valletutti & F. Christoplos (Eds.), *Interdisciplinary approaches to human services*. Baltimore: University Park Press.

Joint Commission on Mental Health of Children. (1970). *Crisis of child mental health: Challenge of the 1970's*. New York: Harper & Row.

Jones, K. L., & Smith, D. W. (1975). The fetal alcohol syndrome. *Teratology, 12,* 1-10.

Jones, K. L., Smith, D. W., Streissguth, A., & Myrionthopoulos, N. (1974). Outcome in offspring of chronic alcoholic women. *Lancet, 1,* 1076-1078.

Jones, K. L., Smith, D. W., Ulleland, C. N., & Streissguth, A., (1973). Pattern of malformation in offspring of alcoholic women. *Lancet, 1,* 1267-1271.

Jones, M. H. (1977). Physical facilities and environments. In J. B. Jordan, A. H. Hayden, M. B. Karnes, & M. M. Wood (Eds.), *Early childhood education for exceptional children: A handbook of ideas and exemplary practices*. Reston, VA: Council for Exceptional Children.

Jordan, J. (1976). *Exceptional child education at the bicentennial: A parade of progress*. Reston, VA: Council for Exceptional Children.

Jordan, J. B., Hayden, A. H., Karnes, M. B., & Wood, M. M. (1977). *Early childhood education for exceptional children: A handbook of ideas and exemplary practices*. Reston, VA: Council for Exceptional Children.

Kagan, J. (1976). Resilience and continuity in psychological development. In A. M. Clarke & A. D. B. Clarke (Eds.),

Early experience: Myth and evidence. New York: Free Press.

Kagan, J., & Freeman, M. (1963). Relation of childhood intelligence, maternal behaviors, and social class to behavior during adolescence. *Child Development, 34,* 899-911.

Kagan, J., & Klein, R. E. (1973). Cross-cultural perspectives on early development. *American Psychologist, 28,* 947-962.

Kagan, J., Sontag, L. W., Baker, C. T., & Nelson, V. L. (1958). Personality and IQ change. *Journal of Abnormal & Social Psychology, 56,* 261-266.

Kanner, L. (1964). *A history of the care and study of the mentally retarded.* Springfield, IL: Charles C Thomas.

Kanner, L. (1965). Infantile autism and the schizophrenias. *Behavioral Science, 10,* 412-420.

Kansas State Department of Education. (1982). *Early education for the handicapped: A planning handbook.* Topeka: Special Education Administration Section.

Kaplan, A. R. (1971). In J. Wortis (Ed.), *Mental retardation and developmental disabilities* (Vol. 3). New York: Brunner/Mazel.

Karchmer, M. A., & Trybus, R. (1977). *Who are the deaf children in "mainstream" programs?* Washington, DC: Office of Demographic Studies. (Abstract)

Karnes, M. B. (1973). Evaluation and implications of research with young handicapped and low-income children. In J. C. Stanley (Ed.), *Compensatory education for children ages two to eight.* Baltimore: Johns Hopkins University Press.

Karnes, M. B., Kokotovic, A. M., & Shwedel, A. M. (1982). Transporting a model program for young handicapped children: Issues, problems, and efficacy. *Journal of the Division for Early Childhood, 6,* 42-51.

Karnes, M. B., & Lee, R. C. (1978). *Early childhood.* Reston, VA: Council for Exceptional Children.

Karnes, M. B., Schwedel, A. M., Lewis, G. F., & Esry, D. R. (1981). Impact of early programming for the handicapped: A follow-up study into the elementary school. *Journal of the Division for Early Childhood, 4,* 62-79.

Karnes, M. B., Studley, W. M., Wright, W. R., & Hodgins, A. S. (1968). An approach for working with mothers of disadvantaged preschool children. *Merrill-Palmer Quarterly, 14,* 174-184.

Karnes, M. B., & Zehrbach, R. R. (1975). Matching families and services. *Exceptional Children, 41,* 545-549.

Karnes, M. B., & Zehrbach, R. R. (1977a). Alternative models for delivering services to young handicapped children. In J. B. Jordan, A. H. Hayden, M. B. Karnes, & M. M. Wood (Eds.), *Early childhood education for exceptional children: A handbook of ideas and exemplary practices.* Reston, VA: Council for Exceptional Children.

Karnes, M. B., & Zehrbach, R. R. (1977b). Early education of the handicapped: Issues and alternatives. In B. Spodek & H. J. Walberg (Eds.), *Early childhood education.* Berkeley: McCutchan.

Katz, H. P. (1975). Important endocrine disorders of childhood. In R. Haslam & P. Valletutti (Eds.), *Medical problems in the classroom.* Baltimore: University Park Press.

Kauffman, J. M. (1981). *Characteristics of children's behavior disorders* (2nd ed.). Columbus, OH: Charles E. Merrill.

Kaufman, M. J., Gottlieb, J., Agard, J., & Kukic, M. (1975). Mainstreaming: Toward an explication of the construct. In E. L. Meyen, G. A. Vergason, & R. J. Whelan (Eds.), *Alternatives for teaching exceptional children.* Denver: Love

Publishing.

Kaufman, M. J., & Morra, L. G. (1978). The least restrictive environment: A major philosophical change. In E. L. Meyen (Ed.), *Exceptional children and youth: An introduction* (1st ed.). Denver: Love Publishing.

Kelly, J. F. (1982). Effects of intervention on caregiver-infant interaction when the infant is handicapped. *Journal of the Division for Early Childhood, 5,* 53-63.

Kempe, R., & Kempe, C. H. (1978). *Child abuse.* Cambridge, MA: Harvard University Press.

Kemper, M. B., & Frankenburg, W. K. (1979). Screening, diagnosis, and assessment: How do these types of measurement differ? In T. Black (Ed.), *Perspectives on measurement, a collection of readings for educators of young handicapped children* (pp. 11-19). Chapel Hill, NC: Technical Assistance Development System. (Proceedings document based on Measuring Child Progress Conference held by TADS in Nashville, TN)

Kennedy, C., Drage, J. S., & Schwartz, B. K. (1963). *Preliminary data with respect to the relationships between APGAR score at one and five minutes and fetal outcome.* Paper presented at spring scientific meeting of Collaborative Perinatal Project, National Institute of Neurological Diseases and Blindness, Washington, DC.

Kennell, J. H., Voos, D. K., & Klaus, M. H. (1979). Parent-infant bonding. In J. D. Osofsky (Ed.) *Handbook of infant development.* New York: John Wiley & Sons.

Kenny, T. J., & Clemmens, R. L. (1975). *Behavioral pediatrics and child development: A clinical handbook.* Baltimore: Williams & Wilkins.

Keogh, B., & Becker, L. (1973). Early detection of learning problems: Questions, cautions, and guidelines. *Exceptional Children, 40,* 5-11.

Keogh, B. K., & Sheehan, R. (1981). The use of developmental test data for documenting handicapped children's progress: Problems and recommendations. *Journal of the Division for Early Childhood, 3,* 42-47.

Kephart, J. C., Kephart, C., & Schwartz, G. (1974). A journey into the world of the blind child. *Exceptional Children, 40,* 421-429.

Kilpatrick, W. H. (1914). *The Montessori system examined.* New York: Houghton Mifflin.

King, R. R., Jones, C., & Lasky, E. (1982). In retrospect: A fifteen-year follow-up report of speech-language disordered children. *Language, Speech, & Hearing Services in the Schools, 13,* 24-32.

Kirk, S. A. (1958). *Early education of the mentally retarded: An experimental study.* Urbana: University of Illinois Press.

Kirk, S. A. (1973, July). The education of intelligence. *Slow Learning Child, 20.*

Kirk, S. A. (1977). General and historical rationale for early education of the handicapped. In N. E. Ellis & L. Cross (Eds.), *Planning programs for early education of the handicapped* (First Chance Series). New York: Walker.

Kirk, S. A., & Gallagher, J. J. (1979). *Educating exceptional children* (3rd ed.). Boston: Houghton Mifflin.

Kirk, S., McCarthy, J., & Kirk, W. (1978). *Illinois test of psycholinguistic abilities.* Baltimore: University Park Press.

Kirschner Associates. (1970, May). *A national survey of the impacts of Head Start centers on community institutions.* Albuquerque: Author. (ERIC Document Reproduction Service No. ED 046 416).

Klaus, M. H., Jerauld, R., Kreger, N. C., McAlpine, W., Steffa, M., & Kennell, J. H. (1972). Maternal attachment: Importance of the first post-partum days. *New England Journal of Medicine, 286,* 460-463.

Klaus, M. H., & Kennell, J. H. (1976). *Maternal infant bonding.* St. Louis: C. V. Mosby.

Klein, J. W. (1971). Planned variation in Head Start programs. *Children, 18*(1), 8-12.

Klein, J. W. (1975). Mainstreaming the preschooler. *Young Children, 30,* 316-328.

Kluppel, D. D. (1972). Educational management of speaking and listening. In J. V. Irwin & M. Marge (Eds.), *Principles of childhood language disabilities.* New York: Appleton-Century-Crofts.

Knobloch, H., & Pasamanick, B. (1960). Environmental factors affecting human development—before and after birth. *Pediatrics, 26,* 210-218.

Knobloch, H., & Pasamanick, B. (1967). Prediction from the assessment of neuromotor and intellectual status in infancy. In J. Zubin & G. A. Jervis (Eds.), *Psychopathology of mental development.* New York: Grune & Stratton.

Knobloch, H., Rider, R., Harper, B., & Pasamanick, B. (1956). Neuropsychiatric sequelae of prematurity: A longitudinal study. *Journal of the American Medical Association, 161,* 581.

Koch, R. (1963). A longitudinal study of 143 mentally retarded children (1955-1961). *Training School Bulletin, 1,* 4-11.

Koch, R., & de la Cruz, F. F. (Eds.). (1975). *Down's syndrome (monogolism).* New York: Brunner/Mazel.

Koehler, J. (1975). Spinal muscular atrophy of childhood. In E. E. Bleck & D. A. Nagel (Eds.), *Physically handicapped children: A medical atlas for teachers.* New York: Grune & Stratton.

Kogan, K. L., Tyler, N., & Turner, P. (1974). The process of interpersonal adaptation between mothers and their cerebral palsied children. *Developmental Medicine & Child Neurology, 16,* 518-527.

Kolstoe, O. P. (1972). Programs for the mildly retarded: A reply to the crisis. *Exceptional Children, 39,* 51-56.

Kopp, C. B., & Parmelee, A. H. (1979). Prenatal and perinatal influences on infant behavior. In J. D. Osofsky (Ed.), *Handbook of infant development.* New York: John Wiley & Sons.

Korner, A. F. (1974). The effect of the infant's state, level of arousal, sex, and ontogenetic stage of the caregiver. In M. Lewis & L. A. Rosenblum (Eds.), *The effect of the infant on its caregiver.* New York: John Wiley & Sons.

Korner, A., & Thoman, E. (1970). Visual alertness in neonates as evoked by maternal care. *Journal of Experimental Psychology, 10,* 67-68.

Korones, S. B. (1976). *High-risk newborn infants: The basis for intensive nursing care* (2nd ed.). St. Louis: C. V. Mosby.

Krajicek, M. J., & Tearney, A. I. (Eds.). (1977). *Detection of developmental problems in children.* Baltimore: University Park Press.

Kupfer, F. (1982). *Before and after Zachariah.* New York: Delcorte Press.

Lamb, M. E. (Ed.). (1976). *The role of the father in child development.* New York: John Wiley & Sons.

Lambie, D. Z., Bond, J. T., & Weikart, D. P. (1975).

Framework for infant education. In B. Z. Friedlander, G. M. Sterritt, & G. E. Kirk (Eds.), *Exceptional infant: Assessment and intervention* (Vol. 3). New York: Brunner/Mazel.

Landrigan, P. J., Gehlbach, S. H., Rosenblum, B. F., Schoults, J. M., Candelaria, R. M., Barthel, W. F., Liddle, J. A., Smrek, A. L., Staehling, N. W., & Sanders, J. (1975). Epidemic lead absorption near an ore smelter. *New England Journal of Medicine, 292,* 123.

Langley, M. B. (1979). Working with young physically-impaired children: Part B—Educational programming. In S. G. Garwood (Ed.), *Educating young handicapped children: A developmental approach.* Rockville, MD: Aspen Systems Corp.

Lansford, A. (1977). The high-risk infant. In M. J. Krajicek & A. I. Tearney (Eds.), *Detection of developmental problems in children.* Baltimore: University Park Press.

Lassman, F. M., Fisch, R. O., Vetter, D. K., & LaBenz, E. S. (1980). *Early correlates of speech, language and hearing.* Action, MA: Publishing Sciences Group.

LaVor, M. L. (1976). Federal legislation for exceptional persons: A history. In F. J. Weintraub, A. Abeson, J. Ballard, & M. LaVor (Eds.), *Public policy and the education of exceptional children.* Reston, VA: Council for Exceptional Children.

LaVor, M., & Krivit, D. (1969). Law review: The Handicapped Children's Early Assistance Act, Public Law 90-538. *Exceptional Children, 35,* 379-384.

Lazar, I. (1979, April). *Does prevention pay off?* Address delivered at the 57th Annual International Convention of the Council for Exceptional Children, Dallas, TX.

Lazar, I., & Darlington, R. (1979). *Summary report: Lasting effects after preschool.* (DHEW Publication No. OHDS 80-30179). Washington, DC: U.S. Government Printing Office.

Lazar, I., & Darlington, R. (Eds.). (1982). Lasting effects of early education: A report from the Consortium for Longitudinal Studies. *Monographs of the Society for Research in Child Development, 47*(2-3, Serial No. 195). (Summary report, DHEW Publication No. OHDS 80-30179)

Lazar, I., Hubbell, V. R., Murray, H., Rosche, M., & Royce, J. (1977). *The persistence of preschool effects: A long-term follow-up of fourteen infant and preschool experiments. Final Report* (Grant No. 18-76-07843, for Administration on Children, Youth, and Families, DHEW Publication No. OHDS 78-30130). Washington, DC: Dept. of Health, Education, and Welfare.

Leeper, S. H., Witherspoon, R. L., & Day, B. (1984). *Good schools for young children* (5th ed.). New York: Macmillan.

Leiter, P. (1948). *Leiter international performance scale.* Chicago: C. E. Stoelting.

LeMay, D., Griffin, P., & Sanford, A. (1981). *Learning accomplishment profile: Diagnostic edition* (revised). Winston-Salem, NC: Kaplan School Supply.

Lenneberg, E. H. (1967). *Biological foundations of language.* New York: John Wiley & Sons.

Lenneberg, E. H. (1972). Prerequisites for language acquisition by the deaf. In T. J. O'Rourke (Ed.), *Psycholinguistics and total communication: The state of the art.* Washington, DC: American Annals of the Deaf.

Lenz, W. (1962). Thalidomide and congenital abnormalities. *Lancet, 1,* 45-50.

Lerner, J. (1981). *Learning disabilities: Theories, diagnosis, and teaching strategies.* Boston: Houghton Mifflin.

Lerner, J. M., & Libby, W. J. (1976). *Heredity, evolution, and society.* San Francisco: W. H. Freeman.

Lerner, J., Mardell-Czudnowski, C., & Goldenberg, D. (1981). *Special education for the early childhood years.* New Jersey: Prentice-Hall.

Lester, B. M. (1975). The consequences of infantile malnutrition. In H. E. Fitzgerald & J. P. McKinney (Eds.), *Developmental psychology: Studies in human development.* Homewood, IL: Dorsey Press.

Lewis, M. (1972). State as an infant-environment interaction: An analysis of mother-infant behavior as a function of sex. *Merrill-Palmer Quarterly, 18,* 95-121.

Lewis, M. (1984). Developmental principles and their implications for at-risk and handicapped infants. In M. J. Hanson (Ed.), *Atypical infant development.* Baltimore: University Park Press.

Lewis, M., & McGurk, H. (1972). The evaluation of infant intelligence. *Science, 178,* 1174.

Lewis, M., & McGurk, H. (1973). Testing infant intelligence. *Science, 182,* 737.

Lewis, M., & Rosenblum, L. A. (Eds.). (1974). *The effect of the infant on its caregiver.* New York: John Wiley & Sons.

Lewis, M., & Wilson, C. D. (1972). Infant development in lower-class American families. *Human Development, 15,* 112-127.

Lidz, C. S. (1977). Issues in the psychological assessment of preschool children. *Journal of School Psychology, 15*(2), 129-135.

Lillie, D., & Harbin, G. (1975). *Carolina developmental profile.* Winston-Salem, NC: Kaplan Co.

Lillienfeld, A. M., & Pasamanick, B. (1956). The association of maternal and fetal factors with the development of mental deficiency: II. *American Journal of Mental Deficiency, 60,* 557-569.

Linder, T. W. (1983). *Early childhood-special education: Program development and administration.* Baltimore: Paul H. Brookes.

Linder, T. W., & Chitwood, D. G. (1984). The needs of fathers of young handicapped children. *Journal of the Division for Early Childhood, 9,* 133-139.

Ling, D. (1976). *Speech and the hearing impaired child.* Washington, DC: Bell Association for the Deaf.

Ling, D. (1984a). *Early intervention for hearing impaired children: Oral options.* San Diego: College-Hill Press.

Ling, D. (1984b). *Early intervention for hearing impaired children: Total communication options.* San Diego: College-Hill Press.

Lipton, M. A. (1976). Early experience and plasticity in the central nervous system. In T. D. Tjossem (Ed.), *Intervention strategies for high risk infants and young children.* Baltimore: University Park Press.

Loeffler, F. E. (1984). Prenatal diagnosis: Chorionic villus biopsy. *British Journal of Hospital Medicine, 31,* 418-420.

Loevinger, J. (1976). Ego development: Conceptions and theories. San Francisco: Jossey-Bass.

Londerville, S., & Main, M. (1981). Security of attachment, compliance, and maternal training methods in the second year of life. *Developmental Psychology, 17,* 289-299.

Lorenz, K. Z. (1937). The companion in the bird's world. *Auk, 54,* 245-273.

Lourie, R. (1971). The first three years of life: An overview of a new frontier in psychiatry. *American Journal of Psychiatry, 11,* 33-39.

Love, H. D. (1970). *Parental attitudes toward exceptional children.* Springfield, IL: Charles C Thomas.

Love, H. D. (1973). *The mentally retarded child and his family.* Springfield, IL: Charles C Thomas.

Love, H. E., & Wathall, J. E. (1977). *A handbook of medical, educational, and psychological information for teachers of physically handicapped children.* Springfield, IL: Charles C Thomas.

Lowenfeld, B. (1973). *The visually handicapped child in school.* New York: John Day Co.

Ludlow, B. L. (1981). Parent-infant interaction research: The argument for earlier intervention programs. *Journal of the Division for Early Childhood, 3,* 34-41.

Lueck, M., Orr, A. C., & O'Connell, M. (1982). *Trends in child care arrangements of working mothers* (U.S. Bureau of the Census Current Population Reports, Special Studies P-23, No. 117). Washington, DC: U.S. Government Printing Office.

MacCarthy, D. (1977). Deprivation dwarfism viewed as a form of child abuse. In A. W. Franklin (Ed.), *The challenge of child abuse.* New York: Grune & Stratton.

Maccoby, E. E., & Zellner, M. (1970). *Experiments in primary education: Aspects of Project Follow-Through.* New York: Harcourt Brace Jovanovich.

MacFarlane, J. W., Allen, L., & Honzik, M. P. (1954). *A developmental study of the behavior problems of normal children between twenty-one months and fourteen years.* Berkeley: University of California Press.

MacKeith, R. (1973). The feelings and behavior of parents of handicapped children. *Developmental Medicine & Child Neurology, 15,* 524-527.

MacMillan, D. L. (1971). Special education for the mildly retarded: Servant or savant? *Focus on Exceptional Children, 9,* 1-11.

MacMillan, D. L. (1982). *Mental retardation in school and society* (2nd ed.). Boston: Little, Brown.

MacTurk, R. H., & Neisworth, J. T. (1978). Norm referenced and criterion based measures with preschoolers. *Exceptional Children, 45,* 34-39.

Mahler, M., & Pine, F. (1975). *The psychological birth of the infant.* New York: Basic Books.

Main, M. (1973). *Exploration, play, and cognitive functioning as related to child-mother attachment.* Unpublished doctoral dissertation, Johns Hopkins University, Baltimore.

Mallory, B. L. (1981). The impact of public policies on families with young handicapped children. *Topics in Early Childhood Special Education, 1*(3), 77-86.

Mantle, J. A. (1982). *A comparison between teacher and primary caretaker ratings of handicapped and nonhandicapped preschoolers on two assessment tools.* Unpublished doctoral dissertation, University of Kansas, Lawrence.

Mardell-Czudnowski, C., & Goldenberg, D. (1983). *Developmental indicators for the assessment of learning—Revised (DIAL-R).* Edison, NJ: Childcraft Education Corp.

Marinelli, J. J. (1976). Financing the education of exceptional children. In F. J. Weintraub, A. Abeson, J. Ballard, & M. L. LaVor (Eds.), *Public policy and the education of excep-*

tional children. Reston, VA: Council for Exceptional Children.

Marotz, L., Rush, J., & Cross, M. (1985). *Health, safety, and nutrition for the young child.* New York: Delmar.

Martin, B. (1975). Parent-child relations. In F. D. Horowitz (Ed.), *Review of child development research* (Vol. 4). Chicago: University of Chicago Press.

Martin, E. W. (1970). A new outlook for education of handicapped children. *American Education, 6*(3), 7-10.

Martin, E. W., (1974). Breakthrough for the handicapped: Legislative history. In S. A. Kirk & F. E. Lord (Eds.), *Exceptional children: Educational resources and perspectives.* New York: Houghton Mifflin.

Martin, E. W. (1979). *A look at the 80's.* Speech to the Handicapped Children's Early Education Program Project Directors' Meeting, Washington, DC.

Martin, H. P. (1976). Which children get abused: High risk factors in the child. In H. P. Martin (Ed.), *The abused child: A multidisciplinary approach to developmental issues and treatment.* Cambridge, MA: Ballinger.

Mash, E. J., & Terdal, L. G. (Eds.). (1981). *Behavioral assessment of childhood disorders.* New York: Guilford Press.

Maslow, P., Frostig, M., Lefever, D., & Whittlesey, J. (1964). *Frostig developmental test of visual perception.* Palo Alto, CA: Consulting Psychologists Press.

Matas, L., Arend, R. A., & Sroufe, L. A. (1978). Continuity in the second year. The relationship between quality of attachment and later competence. *Child Development, 49,* 547-556.

Matsumoto, H. G., Goyo, L., & Takevchi, T. (1965). Fetal minamata disease: A neuropathological study of two cases of intrauterine intoxication by a methylmercury compound. *Journal of Neuropathology & Experimental Neurology, 24,* 563.

Mattsson, A. (1972). Long-term physical illness in childhood: A challenge to psychosocial adaptation. *Pediatrics, 50,* 801-811.

Maugh, T. H. (1973). LSD and the drug culture: New evidence of hazard. *Science, 179,* 1221-1222.

McAfee, J. K., & Vergason, G. A. (1979). Parent involvement in the process of special education: Establishing a new partnership. *Focus on Exceptional Children, 11*(2), 1-16.

McCaffrey, I., & Cumming, J. (1969). Persistence of emotional disturbances reported among second- and fourth-grade children. In H. Dupont (Ed.), *Educating emotionally disturbed children: Readings.* New York: Holt, Rinehart & Winston.

McCall, R. B. (1976). Toward an epigenetic conception of mental development in the first three years of life. In M. L. Lewis (Ed.), *Origins of intelligence: Infancy and early childhood.* New York: Plenum.

McCall, R. B., Appelbaum, M. I., & Hogarty, P. S. (1973). Developmental changes in mental performance. *Monographs of the Society for Research in Child Development, 38*(3).

McCall, R. B., Hogarty, P. S., & Hurlburt, N. (1972). Transitions in infant sensorimotor development and the prediction of childhood IQ. *American Psychologist, 27,* 728.

McCarthy, D. (1972). *McCarthy scales of children's abilities.* Atlanta: Psychological Corp.

McCormick, L., & Schiefelbusch, R. L. (1984). *Early language intervention.* Columbus, OH: Charles E. Merrill.

McDonald, E. T. (1980). Early identification and treatment of children at-risk for speech development. In R. L. Schiefel-

busch (Ed.), *Nonspeech language and communication: Analysis and intervention.* Baltimore: University Park Press.

McMichael, J. K. (1971). *Handicap: A study of physically handicapped children and their families.* London: Staples Press.

McNulty, B., Smith, D. B., & Soper, E. W. (1983). *Effectiveness of early special education for handicapped children.* Denver: Colorado Department of Education.

Meadow, K. P. (1984). Social adjustment of preschool children: Deaf and hearing, with and without other handicaps. *Topics in Early Childhood Special Education, 3*(4), 27-40.

Mealor, D. J., & Richmond, B. O. (1980). Adaptive behavior: Teachers and parents disagree. *Exceptional Children, 46,* 386-389.

Mecham, J. J. (1966). Appraisal of speech and hearing problems. In M. J. Mecham, F. G. Berko, & M. F. Palmer (Eds.), *Communication training in childhood brain damage.* Springfield, IL: Charles C Thomas.

Meier, J. H. (1976). *Developmental and learning disabilities.* Baltimore: University Park Press.

Meisels, S. J. (1979). *First steps in mainstreaming: Some questions and answers.* Boston: Massachusetts Department of Mental Health, Media Resource Center.

Meisels, S. J. (1985). The efficacy of early intervention: Why are we still asking this question? *Topics in Early Childhood Special Education, 5*(2), 1-11.

Meisels, S. J., Jones, S. N., & Stiefel, G. S. (1983). Neonatal intervention: Problems, purpose, and prospects. *Topics in Early Childhood Special Education, 3*(1), 1-13.

Melcher, J. (1976). Law, litigation, and handicapped children. *Exceptional Children, 43,* 126-130.

Melzack, R. (1962). Effects of early perceptual restriction on simple visual discrimination. *Science, 137,* 978-979.

Melzack, R., & Burns, S. K. (1965). Neurophysiological effects of early sensory restriction. *Experimental Neurology, 13,* 1-175.

Melzack, R., & Thompson, W. R. (1956). Effects of early experience on social behavior. *Canadian Journal of Psychology, 10,* 82-90.

Mendelson, A., & Atlas, R. (1977). Early childhood assessment: Paper and pencil for whom? *Readings in early childhood education* (pp. 269-271). Guilford, CT: Dushkin Publishing Group.

Menolascino, F. J. (1983). Developmental interactions of brain impairment and experience. In F. J. Menolascino, R. Neiman, & J. A. Stark (Eds.), *Curative aspects of mental retardation: Biomedical and behavioral advances.* Baltimore: Paul H. Brookes.

Menzel, E. W., Jr. (1964). Patterns of responsiveness in chimpanzees reared through infancy under conditions of environmental restrictions. *Psychologische Forschung, 27,* 337-365.

Menzel, E. W., Jr., Davenport, R. K., Jr., & Rogers, C. M. (1963). The effects of environmental restriction upon the chimpanzee's responsiveness to objects. *Journal of Comparative Physiological Psychology, 56,* 78-85.

Mercer, J. R. (1973). *Labeling the mentally retarded: Clinical and social system perspectives on mental retardation.* Berkeley: University of California Press.

MIDCO Educational Associates (1972). *Investigation of the effects of parent participation in Head Start* (Report to the Office of Child Development). Denver: MIDCO Education

Association. (ERIC Document Reproduction Service Nos. ED 080 215; ED 080 216; ED 080 218)

Miller, J. J., III. (1975). Juvenile rheumatoid arthritis. In E. E. Bleck & D. A. Nagel (Eds.), *Physically handicapped children: A medical atlas for teachers.* New York: Grune & Stratton.

Miller, L., Barrett, C., & Hampe, E. (1974). Phobias of childhood in a pre-scientific era. In A. Davids (Ed.), *Child personality and psychopathology.* New York: John Wiley & Sons.

Miller, W. A., & Erbe, R. (1978). Prenatal diagnosis of genetic disorders. *Southern Medical Journal, 71,* 201-207.

Milunsky, A. (1975). *The prevention of genetic disease and mental retardation.* Philadelphia: W. B. Saunders.

Monckeberg, F. (1975). The effect of malnutrition on physical growth and brain development. In J. W. Prescott, M. S. Read, & D. B. Coursin (Eds.), *Brain function and malnutrition: Neuropsychological methods of assessment.* New York: John Wiley & Sons.

Moore, C. (Ed.). (1974). *Preschool programs for handicapped children: A guidebook for the development and operation of programs.* Eugene: University of Oregon, Regional Resource Center for Handicapped Children.

Moore, K. L. (1977). *The developing human: Clinically oriented embryology* (2nd ed.). Philadelphia: W. B. Saunders.

Moore, M. G., Anderson, R. A., Fredericks, H. D., Baldwin, V. L., & Moore, W. G. (Eds.). (1979). *The longitudinal impact of preschool programs on trainable mentally retarded children.* Monmouth: Oregon State System of Higher Education, Exceptional Child Department, Training Research Division.

Moore, M. G., Fredericks, H. D., & Baldwin, V. L. (1981). The long-range effects of early childhood education on a trainable mentally retarded population. *Journal of the Division for Early Childhood, 4,* 94-110.

Moore, T. (1967). Language and intelligence: A longitudinal study of the first eight years. I: Patterns of development in boys and girls. *Human Development, 10,* 88-106.

Moores, D. F. (1973). *Research development and demonstration center in education of handicapped children, annual report (1972-1973).* Minneapolis: University of Minnesota Press.

Mori, A. A., & Neisworth, J. T. (1983). Curricula in early childhood education: Some generic and special considerations. *Topics in Early Childhood Special Education, 2(4),* 1-8.

Morley, M. E. (1967). *Cleft palate and speech* (6th ed.) Baltimore: Williams & Wilkins.

Morrison, G. S. (1978). *Parent involvement in the home, school, and community.* Columbus, OH: Charles E. Merrill.

Morse, C., Sahler, O., & Friedman, S. (1970). A three year follow-up study of abused and neglected children. *American Journal of Diseases of Children, 120,* 439-446.

Morton, K. (1978). Identifying the enemy—A parent's complaint. In A. P. Turnbull & H. R. Turnbull (Eds.), *Parents speak out.* Columbus, OH: Charles E. Merrill.

Moynihan, D. P. (1964, January). The President's task force on manpower conservation. In D. P. Moynihan (Ed.), *One-third of a nation: A report on young men found unqualified for military service.* Washington, DC: U.S. Government Printing Office.

Murphy, D. P., Shirlock, M. E., & Doll, E. A. (1942). Microcephaly following pelvic irradiation for the interruption of pregnancy. *American Journal of Roentgenology, 48,* 356.

Mussen, P. H., Conger, J. J., Kagan, J., & Huston, A. (1984). *Child development and personality* (6th ed.). New York: Harper & Row.

Myers, B. R. (1975). The child with a chronic illness. In R. Haslam & P. Valletutti (Eds.), *Medical problems in the classroom.* Baltimore: University Park Press.

Mysak, E. (1963). *Principles of a reflex therapy approach to cerebral palsy.* New York: Columbia University, Teachers College, Bureau of Publications.

Mysak, E. D. (1971). Cerebral palsy speech syndromes. In L. E. Travis (Ed.), *Handbook of speech pathology and audiology.* Englewood Cliffs, NJ: Prentice-Hall.

National Center on Child Abuse and Neglect. (1980, February). *Child abuse and developmental disabilities: Essays* (DHEW Publication No. OHDS 79-30226). Washington, DC: U.S. Dept. of Health, Education, and Welfare.

National Diffusion Network. (1975). *Highlight on BEH's validated projects—Handicapped Children's Early Education Project.* Washington, DC: Author.

National Institute of Health. (1981). *Cesarean childbirth.* Washington, DC: Author.

National Society for the Prevention of Blindness. (1966). *Manual on youth and the NSPB standard classification of causes of severe vision impairment. Vol. 2: Index of diagnostic terms pertaining to severe vision impairment and blindness.* New York: Author.

Neisworth, J. T., Willoughby-Herb, S. J., Bagnato, S. J., Cartwright, C. A., & Laub, K. W. (1980). *Individualized education for preschool exceptional children.* Rockville, MD: Aspen Systems Corp.

Nelson, K. (1973). Structure and strategy in learning to talk. *Monographs of the Society for Research in Child Development, 38* (1-2, Serial No. 149).

Nero and Associates. (1976). *Follow-Through: A description of sponsor implementation processes* (Research Report pursuant to Contract No. OEC-0-73-5256 with U.S. Office of Education). Portland, OR: Author.

Nero and Associates. (1976). *Follow-Through: A resource guide to sponsor models and materials* (Report to the U.S. Office of Education, Contract No. OEC-0-73-5256). Portland, OR: Author.

Newborg, J., Stock, J., Wnek, L., Guidubaldi, J., & Suinicki, J. (1984). *Battelle developmental inventory.* Allen, TX: DLM Teaching Resources.

Nirje, B. (1976). The normalization principle. In R. B. Kugel & A. Shearer (Eds.), *Changing patterns in residential services for the mentally retarded* (rev. ed.). Washington, DC: President's Committee on Mental Retardation.

Niswander, K. R., & Gordon, M. (1972). *The collaborative perinatal study of the National Institute of Neurological Diseases and Stroke: The women and their pregnancies* (Vol. 1). Philadelphia: W. B. Saunders.

Norris, A. S. (1978). Mental retardation associated with conditions due to trauma or physical agents in the prenatal period. In C. H. Carter (Ed.), *Medical aspects of mental retardation.* Springfield, IL: Charles C Thomas.

Norris, M., Spaulding, P. J., & Brodie, F. H. (1957). *Blindness in children*. Chicago: University of Chicago Press.

North, A. F., Jr. (1967). Project Head Start and the pediatrician. *Clinical Pediatrics, 6,* 191-194.

Northern, J. L., & Downs, M. P. (1974). *Hearing in children.* Baltimore: Williams & Wilkins.

Northern, J. L., & Lemme, M. (1982). Hearing and auditory disorders. In G. H. Shames & E. H. Wiig (Eds.), *Human communication disorders: An introduction.* Columbus, OH: Charles E. Merrill.

O'Connell, J. C. (1983). Education of handicapped preschoolers: A national survey of services and personnel requirements. *Exceptional Children, 49,* 538-540.

O'Connell, J. C. (1984). Preschool integration and its effects on the social interactions of handicapped and nonhandicapped children: A review. *Journal of the Division for Early Childhood, 8,* 38-48.

Odom, S. L. (1983). The development of social interchanges in infancy. In S. G. Garwood & R. R. Fewell (Eds.), *Educating handicapped infants.* Rockville, MD: Aspen Systems Corp.

Odom, S. L., & Fewell, R. R. (1983). Program evaluation in early childhood-special education: A meta-evaluation. *Educational Evaluation & Policy Analysis, 5,* 445-460.

Oelwein, P. L., Fewell, R. R., & Pruess, J. B. (1985). The efficacy of intervention at outreach sites of the program for children with Down's syndrome and other developmental delays. *Topics in Early Childhood Special Education, 5*(2), 78-87.

O'Keefe, R. A. (1979). What Head Start means to families. In L. G. Katz (Ed.), *Current topics in early childhood education* (Vol. 2). Norwood, NJ: Ablex.

Olshansky, S. (1970). Chronic sorrow: A response to having a mentally defective child. In R. Noland (Ed.), *Counseling parents of the mentally retarded.* Springfield, IL: Charles C Thomas.

Olweus, D. (1979). Stability of aggressive reaction patterns in males: A review. *Psychological Bulletin, 86,* 852-875.

O'Rahilly, R. (1973). *Developmental stages in human embryos.* Washington, DC: Carnegie Institution.

Orem, R. C. (1969). *Montessori and the special child.* New York: G. P. Putnam's Sons. (Reprinted by Capricorn Books, 1970)

Orlando, C. (1981). Multidisciplinary team approaches in the assessment of handicapped children. *Topics in Early Childhood Special Education, 1*(2), 23-30.

Ornitz, E. M. (1974). The modulation of sensory input and motor output in autistic children. *Journal of Autism & Childhood Schizophrenia, 4,* 197-214.

Ornitz, E. M. (1978). Biological homogeneity or heterogeneity? In M. Rutter & E. Schopler (Eds.), *Autism: A reappraisal of concepts and treatment.* New York: Plenum.

Ornitz, E. M., Guthrie, D., & Farley, A. H. (1977). The early development of autistic children. *Journal of Autism & Childhood Schizophrenia, 7,* 207-229.

Ornitz, E. M., & Ritvo, E. R. (1968). Neurophysiologic mechanisms underlying perceptual inconstancy in autistic and schizophrenic children. *Archives of General Psychiatry, 19,* 22-27.

Osborn, D. K. (1975). *Early childhood education in historical perspective.* Athens: University of Georgia, Education Associates.

Osofsky, J. D. (1979). *Handbook of infant development.* New York: John Wiley & Sons.

Ounsted, M., & Ounsted, C. (1973). On fetal growth rate. *Clinics in Developmental Medicine* (No. 46). London: Heinemann.

Page, D., & Garwood, S. G. (1979). Theoretical issues in social development. In S. G. Garwood (Ed.), *Educating young handicapped children.* Rockville, MD: Aspen Systems Corp.

Paget, K. D., & Bracken, B. A. (1983). *The psychoeducational assessment of preschool children.* New York: Grune & Stratton.

Palmer, F. H., & Andersen, L. W. (1979). Long term gains from early intervention: Findings from longitudinal studies. In E. Zigler & J. Valentine (Eds.), *Project Head Start: A legacy of the war on poverty.* New York: Free Press.

Palmer, F. H., & Siegel, R. J. (1977). Minimal intervention at ages two to three and subsequent intellectual changes. In C. Day & R. K. Parker (Eds.), *The preschool in action: Exploring early childhood programs.* Boston: Allyn & Bacon.

Palmer, J. O. (1970). *The psychological assessment of children.* New York: John Wiley & Sons.

Parker, M. C., & Day, R. K. (1977). *The preschool in action: Exploring early childhood programs* (2nd ed.). Boston: Allyn & Bacon.

Pasamanick, B., & Knobloch, H. (1966). Retrospective studies on the epidemiology of reproductive casualty: Old and new. *Merrill-Palmer Quarterly, 12,* 7-26.

Perske, R. (1973). *New directions for parents of persons who are retarded.* Nashville: Abingdon Press.

Peters, D. L., Neisworth, J. T., & Yawkey, T. D. (1985). *Early childhood education: From theory to practice.* Monterey, CA: Brooks/Cole.

Peterson, N. L. (1980). *Social interactions in mainstreamed classrooms.* Presentation at National Conference for the Council on Exceptional Children, Philadelphia, PA.

Peterson, N. L. (1982a). Early intervention with the handicapped. In E. L. Meyen (Ed.), *Exceptional children and youth: An introduction* (2nd ed.). Denver: Love Publishing.

Peterson, N. L. (1982b). Preschool education for the handicapped. In H. E. Mitzel (Ed.), *Encyclopedia of educational research* (5th ed.). Washington, DC: American Educational Research Association.

Peterson, N. L. (1982c). Social integration of handicapped and nonhandicapped preschoolers: A study of playmate preferences. *Topics in Early Childhood Special Education, 2*(2), 56-69.

Peterson, N. L., & Haralick, J. G. (1977). Integration of handicapped and nonhandicapped preschoolers: An analysis of play behavior and social interaction. *Education & Training of the Mentally Retarded, 12,* 235-245.

Peterson, N. L., & Mantle, J. A. (1983). Interagency collaboration: Applications of early intervention for the handicapped. In E. M. Goetz & K. E. Allen (Eds.), *Early childhood education: Special environmental, legal and policy considerations.* Rockville, MD: Aspen Systems Corp.

Phillips, L., Draguns, J. G., & Bartlett, D. P. (1975). Classification of behavior disorders. In N. Hobbs (Ed.), *Issues in the classification of children* (Vol. 1). San Francisco: Jossey-Bass.

Piaget, J. (1950). *The psychology of intelligence.* New York: Harcourt Brace Jovanovich.

Piaget, J. (1960). *The psychology of intelligence.* Paterson, NJ: Littlefield, Adams.

Piaget, J. (1963). *The origins of intelligence in children.* New York: W. W. Norton.

Piaget, J. (1970). Piaget's theory. In P. H. Mussen (Ed.), *Carmichael's manual of child psychology* (Vol. 1, 3rd ed.). New York: John Wiley & Sons.

Piaget, J., & Inhelder, B. (1969). *The psychology of the child.* New York: Basic Books.

Pinneau, S. R. (1955a). The infantile disorders of hospitalism and anaclitic depression. *Psychological Bulletin, 52,* 429-452.

Pinneau, S. R. (1955b). Reply to Dr. Spitz. *Psychological Bulletin, 52,* 459-462.

Plomin, R., DeFries, J., & McClearn, G. (1980). *Behavioral genetics: A primer.* San Francisco: W. H. Freeman.

Polani, P. E. (1974). Chromosomal and other genetic influences on birth weight variation. In *Size at birth* (CIBA Foundation Symposium 27, New series, pp. 127-164). Amsterdam, Netherlands: North-Holland.

Porter, J. H. (1977). Evolution of genetic counseling in America. In H. A. Lubs & F. de la Cruz (Eds.), *Genetic counseling: A monograph of the National Institute of Child Health and Human Development.* New York: Raven.

Potter, H. W. (1933). Schizophrenia in children. *American Journal of Psychiatry, 12,* 1253-1270.

Prather, E. M., Hedrick, D. L., & Kern, C. A. (1975). Articulation development in children aged two to four years. *Journal of Speech & Hearing Disorders, 40,* 179-191.

President's Panel on Mental Retardation (1963). *Report of the task force on prevention, clinical services and residential care.* Washington, DC: Public Health Service.

President's Task Force on Manpower Conservation. (1964). *One-third of a nation.* Washington, DC: U.S. Government Printing Office.

Price-Bonham, S., & Addison, S. (1978). Families and mentally retarded children: Emphasis on the father. *Family Coordinator, 27*(3), 221-230.

Prins, D. (1983). *Treatment of stuttering in early childhood: Methods and issues.* San Diego: College-Hill Press.

Prior, M., Perry, D., & Gajzago, C. (1975). Kanner's syndrome or early-onset psychosis: A taxonomic analysis of 142 cases. *Journal of Autism & Childhood Schizophrenia, 5,* 71-80.

Provence, S., & Lipton, R. C. (1962). *Infants in institutions.* New York: International Universities Press.

Purpura, D. (1975, May 9). In L. K. Altman, Fetal brain said to live at 28 weeks. *New York Times,* p. 30.

Quigley, M. E., Sheehan, K. L., Wilks, M. M., & Yen, S. S. C. (1979). Effects of maternal smoking on circulating catecholamine levels and fetal heart rates. *American Journal of Obstetrics & Gynecology, 133,* 685-690.

Radin, N., & Weikart, D. A. (1967). A home teaching program for disadvantaged preschool children. *Journal of Special Education, 1,* 183-190.

Ramey, C. T., & Baker-Ward, L. (1982). Psychosocial retardation and the early experience paradigm. In D. D. Bricker (Ed.), *Intervention with at-risk and handicapped infants:*

From research to application. Baltimore: University Park Press.

Ramey, C. T., Bell, P. B., & Gowen, J. W. (1980). Parents as educators during infancy: Implications from research for handicapped infants. In J. J. Gallagher (Ed.), *New directions for exceptional children.* San Francisco: Jossey-Bass.

Ramey, C. T., & Bryant, D. M. (1982). Evidence for prevention of developmental retardation during infancy. *Journal of the Division for Early Childhood, 5,* 73-78.

Ramey, C. T., Bryant, D., & Suarez, T. (1985). Preschool compensatory education and the modifiability of intelligence: A critical review. In D. Detterman (Ed.), *Current topics in human intelligence.* Norwood, NJ: Ablex.

Ramey, C. T., & Campbell, F. A. (1977). Prevention of developmental retardation in high risk children. In P. Mittler (Ed.), *Research to practice in mental retardation: Care and intervention* (Vol. 1). Baltimore: University Park Press.

Ramey, C. T., & Campbell, F. A. (1984). Preventive education for high risk children: Cognitive consequences of the Carolina Abecedarian Project. *American Journal of Mental Deficiency, 88,* 515-523.

Ramey, C. T., Campbell, F. A., & Wasik, B. H. (1982). Use of standardized tests to evaluate early childhood special education programs. *Topics in Early Childhood Special Education, 1*(4), 51-60.

Ramey, C. T., & Haskins, R. (1981). The modification of intelligence through early experience. *Intelligence, 5*(1), 5-19.

Ramey, C. T., & MacPhee, D. (1985). Developmental retardation among the poor: A systems theory perspective on risk and prevention. In D. C. Farran & J. D. McKinney (Eds.), *Risk in intellectual and psychosocial development.* New York: Academic Press.

Ramey, C. T., McGinness, G. D., Cross, L., Collier, A. M., & Barrie-Blackley, S. (1982). The Abecedarian approach to social competence: Cognitive and linguistic intervention for disadvantaged preschoolers. In K. Borman (Ed.), *The social life of children in a changing society.* Hillsdale, NJ: Lawrence Erlbaum.

Ramey, C. T., & Smith, B. J. (1977). Assessing the intellectual consequences of early intervention with high-risk infants. *American Journal of Mental Deficiency, 81,* 318-324.

Ramey, C. T., Starr, R. H., Whitten, C. F., Pallas, J., & Reed, V. (1975). Nutrition response contingent stimulation and the maternal deprivation syndrome: Results of an early intervention program. *Merrill-Palmer Quarterly, 21,* 45-54.

Ramey, C. T., Stedman, D. J., Borders-Patterson, A., & Mengal, W. (1978). Predicting school failure from information available at birth. *American Journal of Mental Deficiency, 82,* 524-534.

Ramey, C. T., & Trohanis, P. L. (Eds.). (1982). *Finding and educating high-risk and handicapped infants.* Baltimore: University Park Press.

Ramey, C. T., Yeates, K. O., & Short, E. J. (1984). The plasticity of intellectual development: Insights from preventive intervention. *Child Development, 55,* 1913-1925.

Rand Corporation. (1981) *Study of special education services. VI: Age, handicapping condition, and type of educational placement of the handicapped student population* (ED Contract No. 300-79-0733). Santa Monica, CA: Author.

Rapin, I. (1979). Effects of early blindness and deafness on cognition. In R. Katzman (Ed.), *Congenital and acquired cognitive disorders*. New York: Raven.

Reaves, J., & Burns, J. (1982, November). *An analysis of the impact of the handicapped children's early education program* (Final Report 2 for Special Education Programs, U.S. Dept. of Education, Contract No. 300-81-0661). Washington, DC: Roy Littlejohn Associates.

Reed, D. W., & Stanley, F. J. (1977). *The epidemiology of prematurity*. Baltimore-Munich: Urban & Schwarzenberg.

Report of the Ad Hoc Committee to Define Deaf and Hard of Hearing. (1975). *American Annals of the Deaf, 1120*, 510.

Report to Congress of the United States. (1979). *Early childhood and family development programs improve the quality of life for low income families*. Washington, DC: General Accounting Office.

Reynolds, M. C., & Birch, J. W. (1977). *Teaching exceptional children in all America's schools*. Reston, VA: Council for Exceptional Children.

Rheingold, H. L. (1969). The social and socializing infant. In D. A. Goslin (Ed.), *Handbook of socialization theory and research*. Chicago: Rand McNally.

Rhine, W. R. (Ed.). (1981). *Making schools more effective: New directions from Follow-Through*. New York: Academic Press.

Rhodes, W. C., & Paul, J. L. (1978). *Emotionally disturbed and deviant children: New views and approaches*. Englewood Cliffs, NJ: Prentice-Hall.

Rice, M. (1978). Identification of children with language disorders. In R. L. Schiefelbusch (Ed.), *Language intervention strategies*. Baltimore: University Park Press.

Richmond, J. B., Stipek, D. J., & Zigler, E. (1979). A decade of Head Start. In E. Zigler & J. Valentine (Eds.), *Project Head Start: A legacy of the war on poverty*. New York: Free Press.

Riesen, A. H. (1961). Stimulation as a requirement for growth and development. In D. W. Fiske & S. R. Maddi (Eds.), *Functions of varied experience*. Homewood, IL: Dorsey Press.

Riesen, A. H. (1965). Effects of early deprivation of phonetic stimulation. In S. F. Osley & R. E. Cooke (Eds.), *The biosocial basis of mental retardation*. Baltimore: Johns Hopkins University Press.

Riesen, A. H., & Aarons, L. (1959). Visual movement and intensity discrimination in cats after early deprivation of pattern vision. *Journal of Comparative Physiological Psychology, 52*, 142-149.

Rieser, J. J., Yonas, A., & Wikner, K. (1976). Radical localization of odors by human newborns. *Child Development, 47*, 856-859.

Rimland, B. (1964). *Infantile autism: The syndrome and its implications for a neural theory of behavior*. New York: Appleton-Century-Crofts.

Rimland, B. (1971). The differentiation of childhood psychoses: An analysis of checklists for 2,218 psychotic children. *Journal of Autism & Childhood Schizophrenia, 1*, 161-174.

Ritvo, S., & Solnit, A. (1958). Influences of early mother-child interaction on identification processes. *Psychoanalytic Study of the Child, 13*, 64-86.

Roberts, S. O., Crump, E. P., Dickerson, A. E., & Horton, C. P. (1965). *Longitudinal performance of Negro American children at 5 and 10 years on the Stanford-Binet*. Paper presented at the Annual Meeting of the American Psychological Association, Chicago.

Robertson, J., & Robertson, J. (1971). Young children in brief separation: A fresh look. *Psychoanalytic Study of the Child, 26*, 264-315.

Robinault, I. P. (Ed.). (1973). *Functional aids for the multiply handicapped*. New York: Harper & Row.

Robins, L. N. (1972). Follow-up studies of behavior disorders in children. In H. C. Quay & J. S. Werry (Eds.), *Psychopathological disorders of childhood*. New York: John Wiley & Sons.

Robinson, N. M., & Robinson, H. B. (1965, 1976). *The mentally retarded child* (1st ed. & 2nd ed.). New York: McGraw-Hill.

Robinson, R. O. (1973). The frequency of other handicaps in children with cerebral palsy. *Developmental Medicine & Child Neurology, 15*, 305.

Robson, E. B. (1978). The genetics of birth weight. In F. Falkner & J. M. Tanner (Eds.), *Human growth: Principles and prenatal growth*. New York: Plenum.

Robson, K. S., & Moss, H. A. (1970). Patterns and determinants of maternal attachment. *Journal of Pediatrics, 11*, 976-985.

Rogers, S. (1977). Characteristics of the cognitive development of profoundly retarded children. *Child Development, 48*, 837-843.

Rogers, S. J., & Puchalski, C. B. (1984). Social characteristics of visually impaired infants' play. *Topics in Early Childhood Special Education, 3*(4), 52-56.

Roos, P. (1975). Parents and families of the mentally retarded. In J. M. Kauffman & J. S. Payne (Eds.), *Mental retardation: Introduction and personal perspectives*. Columbus, OH: Charles E. Merrill.

Rosen, B. M., Bahn, A. K., & Kramer, M. (1964). Demographic and diagnostic characteristics of psychiatric clinic patients in the U.S.A.—1961. *American Journal of Orthopsychiatry, 34*, 455-468.

Rosen, J., Clark, G., & Kivitz, M. (Eds.). (1976). *The history of mental retardation* (Vols. 1-2). Baltimore: University Park Press.

Rosenbloom, L. (1975). The consequences of impaired movement: A hypothesis and review. In K. S. Holt (Ed.), *Movement and child development*. Philadelphia: J. B. Lippincott.

Rosenthal, R., & Jacobson, L. (1966). Teacher expectancies: Determinants of pupils' IQ gains. *Psychological Reports, 19*, 115-118.

Rosett, H. L., & Sander, L. W. (1979). Effects of maternal drinking on neonatal morphology and state regulation. In J. D. Osofsky (Ed.), *Handbook of infant development*. New York: John Wiley & Sons.

Ross, A. O. (1980). *Psychological disorders of children: A behavioral approach to theory, research and therapy*. New York: McGraw-Hill.

Ross, R. T., & Boroskin, A. (1972). Are IQ's below 30 meaningful? *Mental Retardation, 10*(4), 24.

Rothstein, P., & Gould, J. B. (1974). Born with a habit: Infants of drug-addicted mothers. *Pediatric Clinics of North America, 21*, 307-321.

Rotter, J. B. (1954). *Social learning and clinical psychology*. New York: Prentice-Hall.

Royster, J. (1977, June). *National survey of Head Start*

graduates and their peers. Cambridge, MA: Abt Associates.

Rubenstein, J. (1967). Maternal attentiveness and subsequent exploratory behavior. *Child Development, 38,* 1089-1100.

Rubin, R. A., Rosenblatt, C., & Barlow, B. (1973). Psychological and educational sequelae of prematurity. *Pediatrics, 52,* 352.

Russell, M. (1975). Incidence of conditions associated with the fetal alcohol syndrome in children born to women with a history of alcohol abuse. *American Journal of Epidemiology, 102*(5), 437.

Rutter, M. (1972). Childhood schizophrenia reconsidered. *Journal of Austism & Childhood Schizophrenia, 2,* 315-337.

Rutter, M. (1974). The development of infantile autism. *Psychological Medicine, 4,* 147-163.

Rutter, M., Birch, H. G., Thomas, A., & Chess, S. (1964). Temperamental characteristics in infancy and the later development of behavioral disorders. *British Journal of Psychiatry, 110,* 651-661.

Rutter, M., & Lockyer, L. A. (1967). A five to fifteen year follow-up study of infantile psychoses. II: Social and behavioral outcome. *British Journal of Psychiatry, 113,* 1183-1199.

Ryan, S. (1974). *A report on longitudinal evaluations of preschool programs: Longitudinal evaluations* (Vol. 1) (DHEW Publication No. OHD-7424). Washington, DC: U.S. Government Printing Office.

Sabatino, D. A., & Miller, T. L. (Eds.). (1979). *Describing learner characteristics of handicapped children and youth.* New York: Grune & Stratton.

Safford, P. L. (1978). *Teaching young children with special needs.* St. Louis: C. V. Mosby.

Salapatek, P. (1975). Pattern perception in early infancy. In L. B. Cohen & P. Salapatek (Eds.), *Infant perception: From sensation to cognition* (Vol. 1). New York: Academic Press.

Salvia, J., & Ysseldyke, J. E. (1981). *Assessment in special and remedial education* (2nd ed.). Boston: Houghton Mifflin.

Sameroff, A. J. (1975). Early influences on development. *Merrill-Palmer Quarterly, 21,* 267-294.

Sameroff, A. J., & Cavanaugh, P. J. (1979). Learning in infancy: A developmental perspective. In J. D. Osofsky (Ed.), *Handbook of infant development.* New York: John Wiley & Sons.

Sameroff, A. J., & Chandler, M. J. (1975). Reproductive risk and the continuum of caretaker casualty. In F. D. Horowitz, M. Hetherington, S. Scarr-Salapatek, & G. Siegel (Eds.), *Review of child development research* (Vol. 4). Chicago: University of Chicago Press.

Samuels, S. C. (1981). *Disturbed exceptional children: An integrated approach.* New York: Human Sciences Press.

Sandgrund, A., Gaines, R. W., & Green, A. H. (1974). Child abuse and mental retardation: A problem of cause and effect. *American Journal of Mental Deficiency, 79,* 327-330.

Sandler, A. (1963). Aspects of passivity and age development in the blind infant. *Psychoanalytic Study of the Child, 18,* 343-360.

Sanford, A. (1981). *Learning accomplishment profile for infants (Early LAP).* Winston-Salem, NC: Kaplan School Supply.

Scarr-Salapatek, S. (1975). Genetics and the development of intelligence. In F. D. Horowitz (Ed.), *Review of child development research* (Vol. 4). Chicago: University of Chicago

Press.

Scarr-Salapatek, S., & Williams, M. L. (1972). A stimulation program for low birth weight infants. *American Journal of Public Health, 62,* 662-667.

Scarr-Salapatek, S., & Williams, M. L. (1973). The effects of early stimulation on low-birth-weight infants. *Child Development, 44,* 94-101.

Schaefer, C. E. (1979). *Childhood encopresis and enuresis: Causes and therapy.* New York: Van Nostrand.

Schafer, D. S., & Moersch, M. S. (Eds.). (1977). *Developmental programming for infants and young children* (Vols. 1-3). Ann Arbor: University of Michigan Press.

Scheerenberger, R. C. (1983). *A history of mental retardation.* Baltimore: Paul H. Brookes.

Scheiner, A. P., Hanshaw, J. B., Simeonsson, R. J., & Scheiner, B. (1977). The study of children with congenital cytomegalovirus infection. In P. Mittler (Ed.), *Research to practice in mental retardation: Biomedical aspects* (Vol. 2). Baltimore: University Park Press.

Scheir, J. D., & Delk, M. T., Jr. (1974). *The deaf population of the United States.* Silver Spring, MD: National Association of the Deaf.

Schell, G. C. (1981). The young handicapped child: A family perspective. *Topics in Early Childhood Special Education, 1*(3), 21-28.

Scherzer, A. L., & Tscharnuter, I. (1982). *Early diagnosis and therapy in cerebral palsy.* New York: Marcel Dekker.

Scheuerman, N. A. (1976). Teachers' perspective. In M. A. Thomas (Ed.), *Hey, don't forget about me!* Reston, VA: Council for Exceptional Children.

Scholnick, E. K., Olser, S. F., & Katzenellenboger, R. (1968). Discrimination learning and concept identification in disadvantaged and middle-class children. *Child Development, 39,* 15-25.

Schopler, E. (1965). Early infantile autism and receptor processes. *Archives of General Psychiatry, 13,* 327-335.

Schwartz, S., & Johnson, J. H. (1981). *Psychopathology of childhood.* New York: Pergamon Press.

Schweinhart, L. J., Berrueta-Clement, J. R., Barnett, W. S., Epstein, A. S., & Weikart, D. P. (1985). Effects of the Perry Preschool Program on youths through age 19: A summary. *Topics in Early Childhood Special Education, 5*(2), 26-35.

Schweinhart, L. J., & Weikart, D. P. (1981). Effects of the Perry Preschool Program on youths through age 15. *Journal of the Division for Early Childhood, 4,* 29-39.

Scott, K. G., & Hogan, A. E. (1982). Methods for the identification of high-risk and handicapped infants. In C. T. Ramey & P. L. Trohanis (Eds.), *Finding and educating high-risk and handicapped infants.* Baltimore: University Park Press.

Sells, C. J., & Bennett, F. C. (1977). Prevention of mental retardation: The role of medicine. *American Journal of Mental Deficiency, 82,* 117-129.

Sever, J. L. (1970a). Infectious agents and fetal disease. In H. A. Waisman & G. R. Kerr (Eds.), *Fetal growth and development.* New York: McGraw-Hill.

Sever, J. L. (1970b). Rubella and cytomegalovirus. In F. C. Fraser, V. A. McKusick, & R. Robinson (Eds.), *Congenital malformations. Proceedings of Third International Conference.* New York: Excerta Medica Foundation.

Shah, C. P., & Wong, D. (1979). Failures in early detection of hearing impairment in preschool children. *Journal of the*

Division for Early Childhood, 1, 33-40.

Shanklin, D. R. (1978). Anatomy of the placenta. In F. Falkner & J. M. Tanner (Eds.), *Human growth: Principles and prenatal growth.* New York: Plenum.

Shearer, D. E., Billingsley, J. Froham, A., Hilliard, J., Johnson, F., & Shearer, M. (1976). *Portage guide to early education—Revised.* Portage, WI: Portage Project.

Shearer, M., & Shearer, D. E. (1972). The Portage report: A model for early childhood education. *Exceptional Children, 39,* 210-217.

Shearer, M., & Shearer, D. E. (1977). Parent involvement. In J. B. Jordan, A. H. Hayden, M. B. Karnes, & M. M. Wood (Eds.), *Early childhood education for exceptional children: A handbook of ideas and exemplary practices.* Reston, VA: Council for Exceptional Children.

Sheehan, R. (1979). Mildly to moderately handicapped preschoolers: How do you select program evaluation instruments? In T. Black (Ed.), *Perspectives on measurement, a collection of readings for educators of young handicapped children.* Chapel Hill, NC: Technical Assistance Development System.

Sheehan, R. (1982). Infant assessment: A review and identification of emergent trends. In D. D. Bricker (Ed.), *Intervention with at-risk and handicapped infants: From research to application.* Baltimore: University Park Press.

Sheehan, R., & Gallagher, R. J. (1983). Conducting evaluations of infant intervention programs. In S. G. Garwood & R. R. Fewell (Eds.), *Educating handicapped infants: Issues in development and intervention.* Rockville, MD: Aspen Systems Corp.

Sheehan, R., & Gallagher, R. J. (1984). Assessment of infants. In M. J. Hanson (Ed.), *Atypical infant development.* Baltimore: University Park Press.

Sheehan, R., & Keogh, B. (1981). Strategies for documenting progress of handicapped children in early education programs. *Educational Evaluation & Policy Analysis, 3,* 59-67.

Sheehan, R., & Keogh, B. (1982). Design and analysis in the evaluation of early childhood special education programs. *Topics in Early Childhood Special Education, 1*(4), 81-88.

Shertzer, B., & Linden, J. D. (1979). *Fundamentals of individual appraisal.* Boston: Houghton Mifflin.

Shipman, V. C. (1972a). *Disadvantaged children and their first school experiences: Demographic indexes of socioeconomic status and maternal behaviors and attitudes* (PR 7213). Princeton, NJ: Educational Testing Service.

Shipman, V. C. (1972b). *Disadvantaged children and their school experiences: ETS-Head Start longitudinal study. Structural stability and change in the test performance of urban preschool children.* Princeton, NJ: Educational Testing Service. (ERIC Document Reproduction Service No. ED 078 011)

Shonkoff, J. P. (1983). The limitations of normative assessments of high-risk infants. *Topics in Early Childhood Special Education, 3*(1), 29-43.

Siegel, L. E. (1972). Developmental theory and preschool education: Issues, problems, and implications. In L. J. Gordon (Ed.), *Early childhood education.* Chicago: University of Chicago Press.

Simeonsson, R. J., Cooper, D. H., & Scheiner, A. P. (1982). A review and analysis of the effectiveness of early intervention programs. *Pediatrics, 69,*635.

Simeonsson, R. J., Huntington, G. S., & Short, R. J. (1982).

Individual differences and goals: An approach to the evaluation of child progress. *Topics in Early Childhood Special Education, 1*(4), 71-80.

Simeonsson, R. J., & Wiegerink, R. (1975). Accountability: A dilemma in infant intervention. *Exceptional Children, 41,* 474-481.

Simmons-Martin, A. (1981). Efficacy report: Early education project. *Journal of the Division for Early Childhood, 4,* 5-10.

Singer, J. D., Fosburg, S., Goodson, B. D., & Smith, J. M. (1980). *Family day care in the United States: Final report of the National Day Care Home Study* (Vols. 1, 2, 3)(Prepared for Day Care Division of Administration for Children, Youth, and Families)(DHHS Publication No. OHDS 80-30283). Cambridge, MA: Abt Associates.

Sitko, M. C., & Semmel, M. I. (1973). Language and language behavior of the mentally retarded. In L. Mann & D. A. Sabatino (Eds.), *The first review of special education* (Vol. 1, pp. 203-259). Philadelphia: Journal of Special Education Press.

Skeels, H. M. (1966). Adult status of children with contrasting early life experiences. *Monographs of the Society for Research in Child Development, 31* (3, Serial No. 105).

Skeels, H. M., & Dye, H. B. (1939). A study of the effects of differential stimulation on mentally retarded children. *Proceedings and Addresses of the American Association on Mental Deficiency, 44,* 114-136.

Smith, A. C., Flick, G. L., Ferriss, G. S., & Sellman, A. H. (1972). Prediction of developmental outcome at seven years from prenatal, perinatal, and postnatal events. *Child Development, 43,* 495-507.

Smith, B. J. (1984). Expanding the federal role in serving young special-needs children. *Topics in Early Childhood Special Education, 4*(1), 33-42.

Smith, D. W., & Wilson, A. A. (1973). *The child with Down's syndrome.* Philadelphia: W. B. Saunders.

Smith, G. F., & Berg, J. M. (1976). *Down's anomaly* (2nd ed.). New York: Churchill Livingstone.

Smith, M. S. (1973, August). *Some short-term effects of Project Head Start: A preliminary report on the second year of planned variation, 1970-71.* Cambridge, MA: Huron Institute.

Smith, M. S., & Bissell, J. S. (1970). Report analysis: The impact of Head Start. *Harvard Educational Review, 40,* 51-104.

Snell, M. (Ed.). (1978). *Systematic instruction of the moderately and severely handicapped.* Columbus, OH: Charles E. Merrill.

Snow, C. (1977). The development of conversation between mothers and babies. *Journal of Child Language, 4,* 1-22.

Snyder, L. (1984). Communicative competence in children with delayed language development. In R. L. Schiefelbusch & J. Picker (Eds.), *The acquisition of communicative competence.* Baltimore: University Park Press.

Snyder, L., Appolloni, T., & Cooke, T. P. (1977). Integrated settings at the early childhood level: The role of nonretarded peers. *Exceptional Children, 43,* 262-266.

Snyder, R. D. (1971). Congenital mercury poisoning. *New England Journal of Medicine, 284,* 1014.

Snyder, R. T., & Freud, S. L. (1967). Reading readiness and its relation to maturational unreadiness as measured by the spiral after effect and other visual-perceptual techniques. *Perceptual & Motor Skills, 25,* 841-854.

Solkoff, N., Yaffe, S., Weintraub, D., & Blase, B. (1969).

Effects of handling on the subsequent development of premature infants. *Developmental Psychology, 1,* 765-768.

Solnit, A. J., & Stark, M. H. (1961). Mourning and the birth of a defective child. *Psychoanalytic Study of the Child, 16,* 523-537.

Sonksen, P. M. (1979). Sound and the visually handicapped baby. *Child: Care, Health & Development, 5,* 413-420.

Sontag, L. W., Baker, C. T., & Nelson, V. (1955). Personality as a determinant of performance. *American Journal of Orthopsychiatry, 25,* 555-562.

Sontag, L. W., Baker, C., & Nelson, V. (1958). Mental growth and personality: A longitudinal study. *Monographs of the Society for Research in Child Development, 23* (2, Serial No. 68).

Sparks, S. M. (1984). *Birth defects and speech/language disorders.* San Diego: College-Hill Press.

Speers, R. W., & Lansing, C. (1964). Some genetic-dynamic considerations in childhood psychosis. *Journal of the American Academy of Child Psychiatry, 1,* 328-344.

Spellman, C., & Cress, P. (1980). *Parsons visual acuity test.* South Bend, IN: Bernell Corp.

Spence, K., & Trohanis, P. (1985). Status in states of early childhood special education across twelve dimensions and state participation in five federal program networks. In *There ought to be a law? Ensuring statewide services for disabled and at risk infants and toddlers.* Washington, DC: National Center for Clinical Infant Programs. (Available from NCCIP, 733 - 15th St., N.W., Washington, DC 20005)

Spitz, R. A. (1945). Hospitalism: An inquiry into the genesis of psychiatric conditions in early childhood. *Psychoanalytic studies of the child* (Vol. 1). New York: International Universities Press.

Spitz, R. A. (1946). Anaclitic depression. *Psychoanalytic Study of the Child, 2,* 313-342.

Spitz, R. A. (1947). Hospitalism: A follow-up report. *Psychoanalytic Studies of the Child* (Vol. 2). New York: International Universities Press.

Spodek, B. (1973). *Early childhood education.* Englewood Cliffs, NJ: Prentice-Hall.

Spodek, B. (1978). *Teaching in the early years* (2nd ed.). Englewood Cliffs, NJ: Prentice-Hall.

Spradlin, J. E. (1968). Environmental factors and the language development of retarded children. In S. Rosenberg & J. H. Koplin (Eds.), *Developments in applied psycholinguistic research.* New York: Macmillan.

Spreen, O. (1965). Language functions in mental retardation: A review. *American Journal of Mental Deficiency, 70,* 351-362.

Spreen, O., Tupper, D., Risser, A., Tuokko, H., & Edgell, D. (1984). *Human developmental neuropsychology.* New York: Oxford University Press.

Sroufe, L. (1977). Wariness of strangers and the study of infant development. *Child Development, 48,* 731-746.

Sroufe, L. A. (1979). Socioemotional development. In J. D. Osofsky (Ed.), *Handbook of infant development.* New York: John Wiley & Sons.

Sroufe, L. A., & Waters, E. (1977). Attachment as an organizational construct. *Child Development, 48,* 1184-1199.

Stanford Research Institute. (1971a). *Implementation of planned variation in Head Start: Preliminary evaluation of planned variation in Head Start according to Follow-Through approaches (1969-1970).* Washington, DC: U.S. Dept. of Health, Education, and Welfare, Office of Child Development.

Stanford Research Institute. (1971b). *Implementation of planned variation in Head Start according to Follow-Through approaches (1969-1970)* (Publication OCD M 72-7). Washington, DC: U.S. Dept. of Health, Education, and Welfare, Office of Child Development.

Stanford Research Institute. (1971c). *Longitudinal evaluation of selected features of the national Follow-Through program.* Washington, DC: U.S. Dept. of Health, Education, and Welfare, Office of Education.

Stanford Research Institute. (1972). *Follow-Through program sponsors* (Report to USOE, Bureau of Elementary and Secondary Education, Contract No. OEC-0-8-522480-4633[100]). Menlo Park, CA: Stanford Research Institute.

Stark, R. E. (1977). Speech acquisition in deaf children. *Volta Review, 79,* 98-109.

Stebbins, L. B., St. Pierre, R. G., Proper, E. C., Anderson, R. B., & Cerva, T. R. (1977). *Education as experimentation: A planned variation model. Vol. 4-A: An evaluation of Follow-Through* (Final report to USOE, Office of Planning, Budgeting, and Evaluation, Contract No. 300-75-0134 and Report No. 76-196A). Cambridge, MA: Abt Associates.

Steele, B. F., & Pollock, C. B. (1974). A psychiatric study of parents who abuse infants and small children. In R. E. Helfer & C. H. Kempe (Eds.), *The battered child.* Chicago: University of Chicago Press.

Stein, Z. A., & Susser, M. (1977). Recent trends in Down's syndrome. In P. Mittler (Ed.), *Research to practice in mental retardation: Biomedical aspects* (Vol. 3). Baltimore: University Park Press.

Steinfels, M. O. (1973). *Who's minding the children? The history and politics of day care in America.* New York: Simon & Schuster.

Stephens, W. E. (1972). Equivalence formation by retarded and nonretarded children at different mental ages. *American Journal of Mental Deficiency, 77,* 311-313.

Stephens, W. E. (1973). Equivalence formation by retarded and nonretarded children in structured and unstructured tasks. *American Journal of Mental Deficiency, 77,* 445-450.

Stern, D. N. (1974). Mother and infant at play: The dyadic interaction involving facial, vocal, and gaze behaviors. In M. Level & L. A. Rosenblum (Eds.), *The effect of the infant on its caregiver.* New York: John Wiley & Sons.

Stevenson, J., & Richman, N. (1976). The prevalence of language delay in a population of three-year-old children and its association with general retardation. *Developmental Medicine & Childhood Neurology, 18,* 431-441.

Stile, S. W., Abernathy, S. M., Pettibone, T. J., & Wachtel, W. J. (1984). Training and certification for early childhood special education personnel: A six-year follow-up study. *Journal of the Division for Early Childhood, 8,* 69-73.

Stile, S. W., Cole, J. T., & Garner, A. Y. (1979). Maximizing parent involvement in programs for exceptional children: Strategies for education and related service personnel. *Journal of the Division for Early Childhood, 1*(1), 68-82.

Stillman, R. (1982). *Callier-Azuza scale.* Dallas: Callier Center for Communication Disorders.

Stoch, M. B., & Smythe, P. M. (1963). Does undernutrition during infancy inhibit brain growth and subsequent intellectual development? *Archives of Diseases of Childhood, 38,* 546-552.

Stock, J. R., Wnek, L. L., Newborg, J. A., Schenck, E. A., Gabel, J. R., Spurgeon, M. S., & Ray, H. W. (1976). *Evaluations of handicapped children's early education program (HCDEEP): Final report* (Contract No. OEC-0-74-0402). Columbus, OH: Battelle Center for Improved Education. (ERIC Document Reproduction Service No. ED 125 165)

Stone, N. (1979). Attachment in handicapped infant family systems. *Journal of the Division for Early Childhood, 1,* 28-32.

Stone, N., & Chesney, B. (1978). Attachment behaviors in handicapped infants. *Mental Retardation, 16,* 8-12.

Strain, P. S. (1984). Efficacy research with young handicapped children: A critique of the status quo. *Journal of the Division for Early Childhood, 9,* 4-10.

Strain, P. S., & Kerr, M. M. (1981). *Mainstreaming of children in schools: Research and programmatic issues.* New York: Academic Press.

Strauss, A. A., & Lehtinen, L. E. (1947). *Psychopathology and education of the brain-injured child.* New York: Grune & Stratton.

Strauss, M. E., Lessen-Firestone, J. K., Starr, R. H., & Ostrea, E. M. (1975). Behavior of narcotics addicted newborns. *Child Development, 46,* 877-893.

Streissguth, A. P. (1976). Psychologic handicaps in children with the fetal alcohol syndrome. *Annals of the New York Academy of Sciences, 273,* 140-145.

Suarez, T. M. (1982). Planning evaluation of programs for high-risk and handicapped infants. In C. T. Ramey & P. L. Trohanis (Eds.), *Finding and educating high-risk and handicapped infants.* Baltimore: University Park Press.

Suran, B. G., & Rizzo, J. V. (1979). *Special children: An integrative approach.* Glenview, IL: Scott, Foresman.

Swan, W. W. (1981). Efficacy studies in early childhood special education: An overview. *Journal of the Division for Early Childhood, 4,* 1-4.

Switzky, H., Rotatori, A., Miller, T., & Freagon, S. (1979). The developmental model and its implications for assessment and instruction for the severely/profoundly handicapped. *Mental Retardation, 17*(3), 167-170.

Tawney, J. W. (1981). A cautious view of mainstreaming in early education. *Topics in Early Childhood Special Education, 1*(1), 25-36.

Terman, L., & Merrill, M. (1972). *Stanford-Binet intelligence scale* (3rd ed.). Boston: Houghton Mifflin.

Tervoort, B. (1964). Development of language and the critical period. The young deaf child: Identification and management. *Acta Otolaryngol, 206* (Supplement), 247-251.

Tew, B. J., & Laurence, K. M. (1973). Mothers, brothers, and sisters of patients with spina bifida. *Developmental Medicine & Child Neurology, 15* (29, Supplement), 69-76.

The persistence of preschool effects. (1977). (HEW Publication No. OHDS 78-30130). Washington, DC: U.S. Government Printing Office.

Thoman, E. B. (1980). Disruption and asynchrony in early parent-infant interactions. In D. Sawin, R. Hawkins, L. Walker, & J. Penticuff (Eds.), *Exceptional infant* (Vol. 4). New York: Brunner/Mazel.

Thoman, E. B., Turner, A., Leiderman, P. H., & Barnett, C.

(1970). Neonate-mother interaction: Effects of parity on feeding behavior. *Child Development, 41,* 1103-1111.

Thomas, A., & Chess, S. (1977). *Temperament and development.* New York: Brunner/Mazel.

Thomas, A., & Chess, S. (1980). *The dynamics of psychological development.* New York: Brunner/Mazel.

Thomas, A., Chess, S., & Birch, H. G. (1968). *Temperament and behavior disorders in children.* New York: New York University Press.

Thomas, A., Chess, S., Birch, H. G., Hertzig, M. E., & Korn, S. (1963). *Behavioral individuality in early childhood.* New York: New York University Press.

Thompson, W. R., Melzack, R., & Scott, T. H. (1956). Whirling behavior in dogs as related to early experience. *Science, 123,* 939.

Thorum, A. R. (1976). *Instructional materials for the handicapped: Birth through early childhood.* Salt Lake City: Olympus.

Tjossem, T. D. (1976). Early intervention: Issues and approaches. In T. D. Tjossem (Ed.), *Intervention strategies for high risk infants and young children.* Baltimore: University Park Press.

Toronto, A., Leverman, C., Hanna, C., Rosengwies, P., and Maldonada, A. (1975). *Del Rio language screening test, English/Spanish.* Austin, TX: National Educational Laboratory Publishers.

Torres, S. (1977). *A primer on individualized education programs for handicapped children.* Reston, VA: Foundation for Exceptional Children.

Tracy, R. L., Lamb, M. E., & Ainsworth, M. D. S. (1976). Infant approach behavior as related to attachment. *Child Development, 47,* 571-578.

Trohanis, P. (1983). TADS and technical assistance. *Journal of the Division for Early Childhood, 7,* 41-53.

Trohanis, P., Cox, J. O., & Meyer, R. A. (1982). A report on selected demonstration programs for infant intervention. In C. T. Ramey & P. L. Trohanis (Eds.), *Finding and educating high-risk and handicapped infants.* Baltimore: University Park Press.

Trohanis, P., Meyer, R. A., & Prestridge, S. (1982). A report on selected screening programs for high-risk and handicapped infants. In C. T. Ramey & P. L. Trohanis (Eds.), *Finding and educating high-risk and handicapped infants.* Baltimore: University Park Press.

Tronick, E. (Ed.). (1982). *Social interchange in infancy.* Baltimore: University Park Press.

Trybus, R. J., & Karchmer, M. A. (1977). School achievement scores of hearing impaired children: National data on achievement status and growth patterns. *American Annals of the Deaf, 112,* 62-69.

Turnbull, A. P. (1982). Preschool mainstreaming: A policy and implementation analysis. *Educational Evaluation & Policy Analysis, 4*(3), 281-291.

Turnbull, A. P. (1983). Parent- professional interactions. In M. E. Snell (Ed.), *Systematic instruction of the moderately and severely handicapped* (2nd ed.). Columbus, OH: Charles E. Merrill.

Turnbull, A. P., Brotherson, M. J., & Summers, J. A. (1982, May). *The family's influence on the development of independence.* Paper presented at the Annual Meeting of the American Association on Mental Deficiency, Boston.

Turnbull, A. P., & Turnbull, H. R. (1978). *Parents speak out:*

Views from the other side of the two-way mirror. Columbus, OH: Charles E. Merrill.

Turnbull, A. P., & Turnbull, H. R. (1982). Parent involvement in the education of handicapped children: A critique. *Mental Retardation, 20*(3), 115-122.

Turnbull, A. P., & Turnbull, H. R. (1986). *Families and professionals: Creating an exceptional partnership.* Columbus, OH: Charles E. Merrill.

Turnbull, H. R. (1986). *Free appropriate public education: The law and children with disabilities.* Denver: Love Publishing.

Turnbull, H. R., & Turnbull, A. P. (1978). *Free appropriate public education: Law and implementation.* Denver: Love Publishing.

Turner, K., & Wade, G. C. (1982). Learning disabled, birth to three: Fact or artifact? *Journal of the Division for Early Childhood, 5,* 79-83.

U.S. Bureau of the Census. (1980). *American families and living arrangements.* Washington, DC: U.S. Government Printing Office.

U.S. Bureau of the Census. (1982). *Characteristics of American children and youth: 1980* (Current Population Reports, P-23, No. 114). Washington, DC: U.S. Government Printing Office.

U.S. Bureau of the Census. (1983). *Characteristics of the population below the poverty level: 1981* (Current Population Reports, P-60, No. 138). Washington, DC: U.S. Government Printing Office.

U.S. Department of Education. (1980). *Second annual report to Congress on the implementation of Public Law 94-142: The Education for All Handicapped Children Act.* Washington, DC: U.S. Government Printing Office.

U.S. Department of Education. (1984). *Sixth annual report to Congress on the implementation of the Education of the Handicapped Act: To assure the free appropriate education of all handicapped children.* Washington, DC: U.S. Government Printing Office.

U.S. Department of Education. (1985). *Seventh annual report to Congress on the implementation of the Education of the Handicapped Act: To assure the free appropriate education of all handicapped children.* Washington, DC: U.S. Government Printing Office.

U.S. Department of Health, Education, and Welfare. (1967). *Report of the Task Force on Child Development.* Washington, DC: U.S. Government Printing Office.

U.S. Department of Health, Education, and Welfare. (1979). *Report on preschool education.* Washington, DC: U.S. Government Printing Office.

Utley, B. L., Holvoet, J. F., & Barnes, K. (1977). Handling, positioning, and feeding the physically handicapped. In E. Sontag, J. Smith, & N. Certo (Eds.), *Educational programming for the severely and profoundly handicapped.* Reston, VA: Council for Exceptional Children.

Uzgiris, I., & Hunt, J. M. (1975). *Assessment in infancy: Ordinal scales of psychological development.* Urbana: University of Illinois Press.

Valentine, J. (1979). Program development in Head Start: A multifaceted approach to meeting the needs of families and children. In E. Zigler & J. Valentine (Eds.), *Project Head Start: A legacy of the war on poverty.* New York: Free Press.

Valentine, J., & Stark, E. (1979). The social context of parent involvement in Head Start. In E. Zigler & J. Valentine (Eds.), *Project Head Start: A legacy of the war on poverty.* New York: Free Press.

Valletutti, P. J., & Christoplos, F. (1977). *Interdisciplinary approaches to human services.* Baltimore: University Park Press.

Van Riper, C. (1978). *Speech correction principles and methods* (6th ed.). Englewood Cliffs, NJ: Prentice-Hall.

Van Riper, C. (1971). *The nature of stuttering.* Englewood Cliffs, NJ: Prentice-Hall.

Vane, J. R., & Motta, R. W. (1980). Test response inconsistency in young children. *Journal of School Psychology, 198*(1), 25-33.

Vaughan, V. C., McKay, R. J., Jr., Behrman, R. E., & Nelson, W. E. (1979). *The Nelson textbook of pediatrics* (11th ed.). Philadelphia: W. B. Saunders.

Vergason, G., & McAfee, J. K. (1978). A layman's guide to parents' rights under P.L. 94-142. *Exceptional Parent, 9*(5), i-iii.

Vernon, M. (1969a). *Multiply handicapped deaf children: A study of significant problems and causes of the problem.* (Council for Exceptional Children Research Monograph). Reston, VA: Council for Exceptional Children.

Vernon, M. (1969b). *Prenatal rubella and deafness* (Monograph of the National Association, March of Dimes). White Plains, NY: March of Dimes.

Vetter, D. K., Fay, W. H., & Winitz, H. (1980). Language. In F. M. Lassman, R. O. Fisch, D. K. Vetter, & E. S. LaBenz (Eds.), *Early correlates of speech, language, and hearing.* Littleton, MA: PSG Publishing.

Vietze, P., & Anderson, B. (1981). Styles of parent-child interaction. In M. Begab, H. C. Haywood, & H. Garber (Eds.), *Psychosocial influences in mental retardation* (Vol. 1). Baltimore: University Park Press.

Vorherr, H. (1975). Placental insufficiency in relation to postterm pregnancy and fetal postmaturity. *American Journal of Obstetrics & Gynecology, 123,* 67-103.

Wald, N. (1979). Radiation injury. In P. B. Beeson, M. D. McDermott, & J. B. Wyngaarden (Eds.), *Cecil textbook of medicine* (Vol. 1). Philadelphia: W. B. Saunders.

Waldrop, M., & Halverson, C. (1975). Intensive and extensive peer behavior: Longitudinal and cross sectional analysis. *Child Development, 46,* 19-26.

Walker, J. (1975). What the school health team should know about sickle cell anemia. *Journal of School Health, 45*(3), 149-153.

Walker, J. A. (1982). Social interaction of handicapped infants. In D. D. Bricker (Ed.), *Intervention with at-risk and handicapped infants: From research to practice.* Baltimore: University Park Press.

Wallace, G., & Larson, S. C. (1978). *Educational assessment of learning problems: Testing for teaching.* Boston: Allyn & Bacon.

Wallin, J. E. W. (1924). *The education of handicapped children.* Boston: Houghton Mifflin.

Wasserman, E., & Gromisch, D. (1981). *Survey of clinical pediatrics.* New York: McGraw-Hill.

Waters, E., Wippman, P., & Sroufe, L. A. (1978). *Attachment, positive affect, and competence in the peer group: Two studies in construct validation*. Unpublished manuscript.

Weber, C. U., Foster, P. W., & Weikart, D. P. (1978). An economic analysis of the Ypsilanti Perry Preschool Project. *Monographs of the High/Scope Educational Research Foundation No. 5*. Ypsilanti, MI: High/Scope Foundation.

Weber, E. (1969). *The kindergarten: Its encounter with educational thought in America*. New York: Teachers College Press.

Weber, E. (1970). *Early childhood education: Perspectives on change*. Worthington, OH: Charles A. Jones.

Wechsler, D. (1974). *Preschool and primary scales of intelligence* (WPPSI). Atlanta: Psychological Corp.

Wechsler, D. (1974). *Wechsler intelligence scale for children—revised* (WISC-R). Atlanta: Psychological Corp.

Weinraub, M., Brooks, J., & Lewis, M. (1977). The social network: A reconsideration of the concept of attachment. *Human Development, 20*, 31-47

Weintraub, F. J., Abeson, A., Ballard, J., & LaVor, M. L. (Eds.). (1976). *Public policy and the education of exceptional children*. Reston, VA: Council for Exceptional Children.

Weintraub, F. J., & Ramirez, B. A. (1985). *Progress in the education of the handicapped and analysis of P.L. 98-199: The Education of the Handicapped Act Amendments of 1983*. Reston, VA: Council for Exceptional Children.

Weisberg, H. I., & Haney, W. (1977). *Longitudinal evaluation of Head Start planned variation and Follow-Through*. Cambridge, MA: Huron Institute.

Weiser, M. G. (1982). *Group care and education of infants and toddlers*. St. Louis: C. V. Mosby.

Weiss, C. E., & Lillywhite, H. S. (1976). *A handbook for prevention and early intervention: Communicative disorders*. St. Louis: C. V. Mosby.

Weiss, J. A., & Morris, K. J. (1978). The teacher of young handicapped children. In K. E. Allen, V. A. Holm, & R. L. Schiefelbusch (Eds.), *Early intervention—A team approach*. Baltimore: University Park Press.

Welsh, M. M., & Odum, C. S. H. (1981). Parent involvement in the education of the handicapped child: A review of the literature. *Journal of the Division for Early Childhood, 3*, 15-23.

Werry, J. S. (1972). Childhood psychosis. In H. C. Quay & J. S. Werry (Eds.), *Psychopathological disorders of childhood*. New York: John Wiley & Sons.

Werry, J. S., Minde, K., Guzman, A., Weiss, G., Dogan, K., & Hoy, E. (1972). Studies on the hyperactive child. VII: Neurological status compared with neurotic and normal children. *American Journal of Orthopsychiatry, 42*, 441-451.

Westinghouse Learning Corp. (1969, June). *The impact of Head Start: An evaluation of the effects of Head Start on children's cognitive and affective development: Executive summary* (Report to the Office of Economic Opportunity). Athens: Ohio University. (ERIC Document Reproduction Service No. ED 036 321)

Whitbread, N. (1972). *The evolution of the nursery-infant school: A history of infant and nursery education in Brain, 1800-1972*. London: Routledge & Kegan Paul.

White, B. L. (1975). *The first three years of life*. Englewood Cliffs, NJ: Prentice-Hall.

White, K. R., Bush, D. W., & Casto, G. (1985). *Let the past be prologue: Learning from previous reviews of early intervention efficacy research* (Publication of the Early Intervention Research Institute). Logan: Utah State University.

White, K. R., & Casto, G. (1984). *An integrative review of early intervention efficacy studies with at-risk children: Implications for the handicapped* (Publication of the Early Intervention Research Institute). Logan: Utah State University.

White, K. R., Mastropieri, M., & Casto, G. (1984). An analysis of special education early childhood projects approved by the joint dissemination review panel. *Journal of the Division for Early Childhood, 9*, 11-26.

White, L. (1974). Organic factors and psychophysiology in childhood schizophrenia. *Psychological Bulletin, 81*, 238-255.

White, O., Edgar, E., Haring, N., Affleck, J., Hayden, A., & Bendersky, M. (1981). *Uniform performance assessment system (UPAS)*. Columbus, OH: Charles E. Merrill.

White, O., & Haring, N. (1980). *Exceptional teaching* (2nd ed.). Columbus, OH: Charles E. Merrill.

Wieck, C. A., & Bruininks, R. H. (1980). *The cost of public and community residential care for mentally retarded people in the United States*. Minneapolis: University of Minnesota, Department of Psychoeducational Studies.

Wiegerink, R., Hocutt, A., Psante-Loro, R., & Bristol, M. (1980). Parent involvement in early education programs for handicapped children. In J. J. Gallagher (Ed.), *New directions for exceptional children* (Vol. 1, pp. 67-86). San Francisco: Jossey-Bass.

Wiersma, W., & Jurs, S. G. (1985). *Educational measurement and testing*. Boston: Allyn & Bacon.

Willerman, L., Broman, S. H., & Fielder, M. (1970). Infant development, preschool IQ, and social class. *Child Development, 41*, 69-77.

Williamson, M. L, Koch, R., Azen, C., & Chang, C. (1981). Correlates of intelligence test results in treated phenylketonuric children. *Pediatrics, 68*, 161.

Willis, D. M. (1979). Early speech development in blind children. *Psychoanalytic Study of the Child, 34*, 83-117.

Wilson, J. G. (1973). *Environment and birth defects*. New York: Academic Press.

Wilson, J. G. (1974). Teratologic causation in man and its evaluation in nonhuman primates. In B. V. Beidel (Ed.), *Proceedings of the Fourth International Conference* (pp. 191-203). Dordrecht, Netherlands: Excerpta Medica.

Wilson, J. G. (1977). Environmental chemicals. In J. G. Wilson & F. C. Frazer (Eds.), *Handbook of Teratology* (Vol. 1). New York: Plenum.

Wilson, W. (1976). Behavioral assessment of auditory function in infants. In F. D. Minifie & L. L. Lloyd (Eds.), *Communicative and cognitive abilities: Early behavioral assessment*. Baltimore: University Park Press.

Wilton, K., & Barbour, A. (1978). Mother-child interaction in high-risk and contrast preschoolers of low socioeconomic status. *Child Development, 49*, 1136-1145.

Wing, J. K. (1966). Diagnosis, epidemiology, and etiology. In J. K. Wing (Ed.), *Early childhood autism: Clinical, educational, and social aspects*. New York: Pergamon Press.

Wing, L. (1969). The handicaps of autistic children: A comparative study. *Journal of Child Psychology & Psychiatry, 10*, 1-40.

Wing, L. (1976). *Early childhood autism* (2nd ed.). Elmsford, NY: Pergamon Press.

Winick, M. (1970a). Fetal malnutrition and growth processes. *Hospital Practice, 5,* 33-41.

Winick, M. (1970b). Nutrition and mental development. *Medical Clinic-North American, 54,* 1413.

Winick, M. (1970c). Nutrition and nerve cell growth. *Federal Proceedings, 29,* 1510-1515.

Winick, M. (1971). Cellular changes during placental and fetal growth. *American Journal of Obstetrical Gynecology, 109,* 166.

Winick, M. (1976). *Malnutrition and brain development.* New York: Oxford University Press.

Winick, M., & Rosso, P. (1969). The effect of severe early malnutrition on cellular growth of the human brain. *Pediatric Research, 3,* 181.

Winick, M., & Rosso, P. (1973). Effects of malnutrition on brain development. In G. E. Gaull (Ed.), *Biology of brain dysfunction* (Vol. 1, pp. 301-317). New York: Plenum.

Winick, M., & Rosso, P. (1975). Malnutrition and central nervous system development. In J. W. Prescott, M. S. Read, & D. B. Coursin (Eds.), *Brain function and malnutrition: Neuropsychological methods of assessment.* New York: John Wiley & Sons.

Witkin, H. A., Birnbaum, J., Lomonaco, S., Lehr, S., & Herman, J. L. (1968). Cognitive patterning in congenitally totally blind children. *Child Development, 39,* 767-786.

Witti, F. P. (1978, May). Alcohol and birth defects. *EDA Consumer.* Document No. HE 20.4010 12/4.

Wolery, M. (1983). Proportional change index: An alternative for comparing child change data. *Exceptional Children, 50,* 167-170.

Wolery, M., & Bailey, D. B. (1984). Alternatives to impact evaluations: Suggestions for program evaluation in early intervention. *Journal of the Division for Early Childhood, 9,* 11-26, 27-48.

Wolfensberger, W. (1967). Counseling the parents of the retarded. In A. A. Baumeister (Ed.), *Mental retardation.* Chicago: Aldine Press.

Wolfensberger, W. (1972). *The principle of normalization in human services.* Toronto: National Institute on Mental Retardation.

Wood, M. E. (1981). Costs of intervention programs. In C. Garland, N. Stone, J. Swanson, & G. Woodruff (Eds.), *Early intervention for children with special needs and their families: Findings and recommendations.* Seattle: University of Washington, Western States Technical Assistance Resource (WESTAR).

Wood, M. M., & Hurley, O. L. (1977). Curriculum and instruction. In J. B. Jordan, A. H. Hayden, M. B. Karnes, & M. M. Wood (Eds.), *Early childhood education for exceptional children: A handbook of ideas and exemplary practices.* Reston, VA: Council for Exceptional Children.

Wortis, J. (1980). *Mental retardation and developmental disabilities: An annual review* (Vol. 2). New York: Brunner/Mazel.

Wright, L., Schaefer, A., & Solomons, G. (1979). *Encyclopedia of Pediatric Psychology.* Baltimore: University Park Press.

Wynne, S., Ulfelder, L. S., & Dakof, G. (1975). *Mainstreaming and early childhood education for handicapped children: Review and implications of research: Final Report* (BEH Contract No. OEC-74-9056). Washington, DC: Wynne Associates.

Yarrow, L. J. (1963). Research in dimensions of early maternal care. *Merrill-Palmer Quarterly, 9*(2), 101-114.

Yarrow, L. J. (1965). Conceptual perspectives on the early environment. *Journal of American Academy of Child Psychiatry, 4*(2).

Yarrow, L. J. (1970). The etiology of mental retardation: The deprivation model. In J. Hellmuth (Ed.), *Cognitive studies* (Vol. 1). New York: Brunner/Mazel.

Yarrow, L. (1972). Attachment and dependency: A developmental perspective. In J. Gerwitz (Ed.), *Attachment and dependency.* Washington, DC: Winston.

Yarrow, L. J., Goodwin, M. S., Manheimer, H., & Milowe, I. D. (1973). Infancy experiences and personality development at ten years. In L. J. Stone, H. T. Smith, & L. B. Murphy (Eds.), *The competent infant.* New York: Basic Books.

Yawkey, T. D., & Bakawa-Evenson, L. (1975). The professional-parent-child: An emerging triad. *Child Care Quarterly, 4*(4), 172-179.

Young, E. C. (1984). A review of general language performance tests for preschool children. *Topics in Early Childhood Special Education, 4*(2), 100-111.

Zamenhof, S., VanMartens, E., & Margolis, F. L. (1968). DNA (cell number) and protein in neonatal brain: Alteration by maternal dietary protein restriction. *Science, 160,* 322-330.

Zamenhof, S., VanMartens, E., & Shimomaye, S. Y. (1976). The effects of early maternal protein deprivation on fetal development. *Federal Proceedings, 35,* 442.

Zausman, E., Peuschel, S., & Shea, A. (1972). A sensory-motor stimulation for the young child with Down's syndrome: Preliminary report. *MCH Exchange, 2,* 1-4.

Zeamon, D., & House, B. J. (1963). The role of attention in retardate discrimination learning. In N. R. Ellis (Ed.), *Handbook of mental deficiency.* New York: McGraw-Hill.

Zeibelson, J., & Borg, C. F. (1967). Concept development of blind children. *New Outlook for the Blind, 61*(7), 3-5.

Zeitlin, S. (1981). Learning through coping: An effective preschool program. *Journal of the Division for Early Childhood, 4,* 53-61.

Zigler, E. (1977). *The effectiveness of Head Start: Another look.* Paper presented at the annual meeting of the American Psychological Association, San Francisco.

Zigler, E. (1978). America's Head Start program: An agenda for its second decade. *Young Children, 333*(5), 411.

Zigler, E., & Anderson, K. (1979). An idea whose time has come: The intellectual and political climate. In E. Zigler & J. Valentine (Eds.), *Project Head Start: A legacy of the war on poverty.* New York: Free Press.

Zigler, E., & Balla, D. (1982). Selecting outcome variables in evaluations of early childhood special education programs. *Topics in Early Childhood Special Education, 1*(4), 11-22.

Zigler, E., & Berman, W. (1983). Discerning the future of early childhood interventions. *American Psychologist, 38,* 894-906.

Zigler, E., & Trickett, P. K. (1978). IQ, social competence, and evaluation of early childhood intervention programs. *American Psychologist, 33,* 789-798.

Zigler, E., & Valentine, J. (1979). *Project Head Start: A legacy of the war on poverty.* New York: Free Press.

Zigler, E., & Yale Research Group. (1976). *Summary of findings from longitudinal evaluations of intervention programs.* New Haven: Yale University Press.

Zimmerman, I., Steiner, V., & Pond, R. (1979). *Preschool language scale.* Columbus, OH: Charles E. Merrill.

Ziskin, L. Z. (1978). The story of Jennie. In A. P. Turnbull & H. R. Turnbull (Eds.), *Parents speak out.* Columbus, OH: Charles E. Merrill.

Name Index

Subject Index